P9-DDT-492

Second Edition

The Great Republic

A History of the American People

Volume I

Bernard Bailyn

HARVARD UNIVERSITY

David Brion Davis

YALE UNIVERSITY

David Herbert Donald

HARVARD UNIVERSITY

John L. Thomas

BROWN UNIVERSITY

Robert H. Wiebe

NORTHWESTERN UNIVERSITY

Gordon S. Wood

BROWN UNIVERSITY

D. C. HEATH AND COMPANY

Lexington, Massachusetts   Toronto

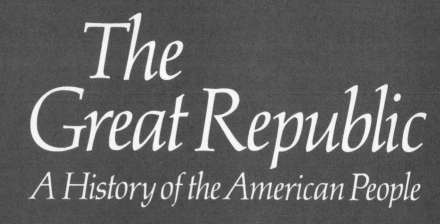

Second Edition

The Great Republic

A History of the American People

Volume I

Cover Illustration: "New York Ballance Drydock," 1877 by Jurgan Frederick Huge. (Collection of Mr. and Mrs. Jacob M. Kaplan. Photograph by Geoffrey Clements courtesy of Whitney Museum, New York)

Acquisitions Editor: Ann H. Knight

Developmental Editor: Louise M. Sullivan

Production Editor: Louise M. Sullivan

Photo Researcher: Sharon L. Donahue

Designer: Esther Agonis

Cover Designer: Herb Rogalski

Cartographer: Norman C. Adams

Copyright © 1981 by D. C. Heath and Company.
Previous edition copyright © 1977 by D. C. Heath and Company.

All rights reserved. No part of this publication may be reproduced or transmitted in any form or by any means, electronic or mechanical, including photocopy, recording, or any information storage or retrieval system, without permission in writing from the publisher.

Published simultaneously in Canada.

Printed in the United States of America.

International Standard Book Number: 0-669-02754-5

Library of Congress Catalog Card Number: 80-81431

Publisher's Foreword

Seldom has an introductory textbook inspired such keen interest and enthusiasm as *The Great Republic*. Certainly the reception of the first edition has made it clear that a great many historians share the authors' belief that a basic American history text should not be merely a narration of unrelated facts. It must attempt to explain and synthesize the whole complex history of our country.

Our goal in revising the book was clear: to maintain the book's quality, its fresh scholarship and bold interpretations, and at the same time make the book more accessible to today's undergraduates.

Our general approach to the Second Edition has been to reduce the number of pages; to put more material into concrete terms; to order the arguments, when possible, in a chronological fashion; to expand coverage of the important events of American history; and to add many more in-text subheadings to help students identify and organize what they read. In addition, the text is now organized so that Volume I of the paperback edition ends with a chapter on Reconstruction, and Volume II begins with the same chapter.

We hope you will agree that the new *Great Republic* is not only a rich and authoritative account of American history but also an extremely effective teaching tool.

Acknowledgments

We are gratified, as are the authors of *The Great Republic*, that so many historians offered their reactions, responded to questionnaires, and took time to discuss the book with our representatives and editors on campus and at professional meetings.

We especially wish to thank those who are listed below for their sensitive and informed comments and suggestions during the preparation of the Second Edition of *The Great Republic:* Thomas G. Alexander, Brigham Young University; Richard Amundson, Columbus College; Michael C. Batinski, Southern Illinois University at Carbondale; Nancy Bowen, Del Mar College; Richard J. Hopkins, The Ohio State University; Richard L. Hume, Washington State University; David Nasaw, The College of Staten Island of The City University of New York; John K. Nelson, The University of North Carolina at Chapel Hill; Mark A. Stoler, The University of Vermont; Sue Taishoff, University of South Florida; James C. Turner, University of Massachusetts, Boston; and Ken L. Weatherbie, Del Mar College.

Introduction

This book is a history of the American people, from the earliest settlements in the New World to the present. We call our book *The Great Republic*, adopting a phrase Winston Churchill used to describe the United States. No one can doubt the greatness of the American republic if it is measured in terms of the size of our national domain, the vastness of our economic productivity, or the stability of our government and basic institutions. Whether that greatness has been equaled in the realm of culture, in the uses of power, or in the distribution of social justice is more debatable; on these matters readers will make up their own minds. Our task has been to present the story of America as we understand it—a story of great achievement, of enormous material success, and of soaring idealism, but a story too of conflict, of tumultuous factionalism, of injustice, rootlessness, and grinding disorder.

Each of the six sections of the book contains its own thematic emphasis, set out in separate introductions. But there are two general themes that unify the book as a whole. The first theme is the development and constant testing of free political institutions in America. To understand the United States today, one must analyze the conditions of life in the colonial period that made popular self-government at first possible, then likely, in the end necessary. One must then see how the American Revolution expressed the longings of provincial Britons for a total reform of political culture and projected this idealism onto a nation of continental scale. One must discover how democratic institutions and practices expanded during the nineteenth century and received their crucial testing in the American Civil War. One must understand how urbanization and industrialization produced radical changes in American political life by the beginning of the twentieth century. And one must ask how free, democratic institutions have sustained themselves through recent decades of depression, international crises, and world wars, and what the legacy of this long, complex development has been to the present technological world. Only through understanding the origins and growth of popular self-government, from eighteenth-century republicanism to modern mass democracy, can sense be made of the history of the American people.

A second theme, which has persisted from the very earliest days, is the tension between divisive ambitions on the one hand and the good of the community at large on the other. From the beginning the New World provided a feast for individual aspirations. Its vast resources, open for exploitation by the talented, the shrewd, the enterprising, and the energetic, stimulated powerful ambitions that were often insensitive to the human costs of success and that helped produce a society constantly in danger of fragmentation. The huge geographical extent of the country nourished divisive interests of all kinds, and the admixture of peoples from every quarter of the world led to ethnic and cultural pluralism, at times so strong as to threaten the disintegration of the social fabric. At the same time, however, there have been, from the founding of the colonies to the present, forces that worked for social stability and agreement, and an ideology, bred in Judaeo-Christian and Enlightenment idealism, that generated concern for justice and civility, and respect for the dignity of man.

The Founding Fathers correctly recognized that the constant struggle between special interests and the general welfare posed a severe threat to the continuance of a self-governing democratic nation. They knew there would be no automatic harmonizing of regional, economic, and social ambitions, no easy reconciliation of competing needs and desires; they worried that minorities might become subject to the tyranny of majorities, and that the weak might be crushed by the strong. At the same time they feared a centralized government powerful enough to impose order on these conflicting and exploitative interests and to protect the weak against the forces of organized power. They hoped that public institutions sensitive to popular pressures would successfully reconcile these conflicts and somehow create a stable, nationwide agreement out of a tumult of clashing ambitions. And they hoped that reasonable people would find their own highest interest in the preservation of the rule of law.

Though the Founding Fathers did not wholly resolve this tension between the interest of the society as a whole and the special interests of its most ambitious and most powerful parts, the system they devised provided mechanisms for the mediation of the struggles and for the protection of human values. Often the balance has been precarious between the general welfare and the welfare of regions, states, and economic and social groups; between the power of majorities and the welfare of minorities. From time to time the balance has tipped, first in the one direction, then in the other, but only once, in the horrendous catastrophe of the Civil War, has it ever been completely upset. The nation's commitment both to social stability and to the rights of individuals remains intact—still effective after generations of complex adjustment.

The tracing of these two themes—the development of free political institutions in America and the struggle to protect the individual and the general welfare against powerful majorities and special interests—links together the six sections and gives an overarching unity to the book. The sections are further unified by the authors' shared view of the nature of history. We all believe that history is not simply the accumulation of information about the past. It is a mode of understanding. The historian is obliged not merely to describe what happened but to explain it, to make clear why things developed as they did. We share, too, an aversion to any deterministic interpretation of history. At certain junctures economic and demographic forces are dominant, but they are themselves shaped by cultural forces. Great political events are at times triggered by economic drives, but at other times they are responses to beliefs and to aspirations that are not a direct reflection of economic needs. Political decisions alter economic life, social organization, and even the way people think—yet economic, social, and intellectual forces change politics too.

History, we believe, falls into no predetermined pattern. The course of American history was not predestined; the nation did not have to develop as it did. Why it did, and hence what accounts for the condition of our national life now, must be explained historically, stage by stage. We have sought to provide that explanation in the pages that follow, as part of the narrative of American history. The book is therefore self-contained, in that it supplies the basic factual information and essential narrative that readers will need, and it presents that information within a framework of analysis and explanation.

We hope that *The Great Republic* will help readers understand why and how America developed as it did, and where, as a result of this historic evolution, we have arrived after more than three centuries of growth and two centuries of nationhood.

B.B.	J.L.T.
D.B.D.	R.H.W.
D.H.D.	G.S.W.

Contents

PART FOUR

Uniting the Republic, *1860–1877*

David Herbert Donald

CHAPTER 18

Stalemate, 1861–1862   468

CHAPTER 19

Experimentation, 1862–1865   493

CHAPTER 20

Reconstruction, 1865–1877   524

Maps and Charts

Second Edition

The
Great Republic

A History of the American People

Volume I

PART ONE

Bernard Bailyn

Shaping the Republic

to 1760

*T*he American Republic was created only in a legal sense in 1776. In a deeper and more general sense it was the product of a century and a half of development that preceded the establishment of American independence. The ultimate origins of this "Great Republic," as Winston Churchill called the American nation, lie far back in time—in desperate gambles of hard-pressed sixteenth- and seventeenth-century merchants involved in overseas trade; in the visions of Elizabethan dreamers who conceived of a western passage to the vast wealth of the Far East; in the courage and single-mindedness of religious refugees determined to carve a new life for themselves in the wilderness rather than compromise their beliefs; in the life-long labors of a quarter of a million Africans transported in bondage to the New World; and in the everyday struggles of five generations of transplanted Europeans and their descendants, farmers and tradesmen for the most part, who sensed, however vaguely, that theirs was a new world, more generous to human aspirations, freer, more supportive of human dignity, and richer—for those whose risks succeeded—than any land known before.

These multitudes in colonial North America did not seek to transform the world. Though adventurous, more often than not they were conservative by instinct or became conservative as they sought to establish familiar forms of life in an unfamiliar environment. But traditions could not be maintained in wilderness communities whose basic conditions were so different from those elsewhere, and a new pattern of life slowly evolved in the course of five generations. Gradually, without theory, as matters of fact and not of design, the character of community life as it had once been known—its demographic foundations, economic processes, social organizations, religion, and politics—all of this was transformed.

Yet not by desire or will—not in an effort to attain an ideal or realize a theory. Change, in the years before the Revolution, was suspect by some, resisted in part, and confined in its effects as the colonists sought to emulate the pattern of more traditional, cosmopolitan societies. Their own provincial world was seen not as a model but as a regression to a more primitive mode of life. Behavior had changed—had had to change—with the circumstances of everyday life, but habits of mind and the sense of the rightness of things lagged behind. Many felt that the changes that had taken place in the years before the Revolution were *away from*, not *toward*, something; that they represented deviance; that they lacked, in a word, legitimacy.

For most Americans this divergence between ideals, habits of mind, and belief on the one hand, and experience and patterns of behavior on the other, was ended at the Revolution. An upheaval that destroyed the traditional sources of public authority called forth the full range of advanced and enlightened

Overleaf: "A South Prospect of Ye Flourishing City of New York," 1717. Engraving by John Harris after William Burgis. *(New York Public Library)*

ideas. Long-settled attitudes were jolted and loosened. Suddenly it was seen that the slow erosion in patterns of social life that had taken place in the colonial period had been good and proper. In the context of Revolutionary beliefs, these changes were conceived of as steps in the direction of a new ideal—the ideal of a simpler, less encumbered existence, in which the individual would count for more and the state less; in which the weight of burdensome social institutions would be permanently lifted; in which the blight of privilege and of the misuse of power would forever be destroyed; in which corruption would be exposed before it could sap the nation's strength; and in which, as a result of all of this, the ordinary person's desire for personal fulfillment could at long last be satisfied.

Such at least were the ideals of the Revolution, formulated by a generation of brilliant political thinkers convinced that it was their great historic role to set the world on a new course. And in the context of these ideals—which, however modified, are still the highest aspirations of the American people—the changes of the colonial years took on a new meaning. The settlement of the colonies and their subsequent development, John Adams wrote, could now be seen as "the opening of a grand scene and design in providence for the illumination of the ignorant and the emancipation of the slavish part of mankind all over the earth." The glass was half-full, not half-empty; and to complete the work of fate and nature, further thought must be taken and changes accelerated rather than restrained.

Social change and social conflict took place during the Revolutionary years, but the beliefs and aspirations of the founders of the American nation, unlike those of the leaders of the French and Russian revolutions, did not require the destruction and remaking of society. The Revolution did not create new social and political forces; it released forces and intensified changes that had been developing from the day the first settlers set foot on Jamestown. Modern America—a massively developed, affluent, and tumultuous technological society of over 200 million people—is worlds away from the tiny farming hamlets and obscure port towns of the seventeenth century, huddled on the coastal fringe of an almost undeveloped continent. Yet there is a clear line of continuity in American history that links those quite primitive settlements to the sophisticated, dynamic world power of the late twentieth century. For modern America is not simply the product of modern forces—industrialism, political democracy, universal education, a consumer culture. It is the product too of the idealism of the eighteenth-century Enlightenment, reinforced and intensified by the openness and affluence of American life.

It is this powerful strain of idealism flowing from the very different world of the eighteenth century into all the complexities of modern America that is the most distinctive feature of the American Republic as it enters its third century of existence. How that ineradicable strain first entered American life, how it was nourished in the soil of a strangely altered society that grew from confused seventeenth-century origins, and how the characteristic American mixture of idealism and materialism was first compounded, reaching so soon, in the subtle figure of Benjamin Franklin, an apparently absolute and perfect form —how all this took place is the central theme of the colonial period of American history.

Far from being a quaint prologue to the main story, therefore, the history of the settlement and early development of American society is a critically important phase of our history. Without an understanding of the pre-Revolutionary era none of the rest of our history can be properly understood.

CHAPTER 1

The Background of English Colonization

*T*he United States evolved from the British settlements on the mainland of North America, first permanently established in 1607. But a century earlier a more powerful European power, Spain, had founded an empire in the Western Hemisphere that was in a high state of development when the British first entered the colonial world. The growth of the Spanish empire in the Western Hemisphere and of Spanish-American society forms a remarkable, and revealing, contrast to the evolution of the British empire and of Anglo-American society. In some ways, to be sure, Anglo-American society in British North America and Indo-Hispanic society in Central America and South America are so different as to be incomparable. But there is one area at least in which extremely illuminating contrasts may be drawn: the realm of government and politics.

By the early eighteenth century, politics in British North America was distinctive in its free competition and in the institutional and cultural conditions that made such open competition possible. Nothing quite like these unconfined, brawling struggles—faction against faction, groups against the state—existed in any other colonial region of the world. There was certainly nothing like this in Spanish America; yet at one stage, strangely enough, it seems that there might have been. It is worth attempting, therefore, at the very outset to explore the underlying reasons for the absence of a free competitive political system in Spanish America at the height of the colonial period, and in doing so to isolate by contrast forces and circumstances that would later shape the dynamic political society of British America as it existed on the eve of the Revolution.

Points of Contrast: Spain in America

There are important contrasts between Spanish and British America at every stage of development. The very origins of settlement were different. Whereas it took England half a century after its first contact with the Western Hemisphere to establish even a temporary colony there, Spain proceeded swiftly after

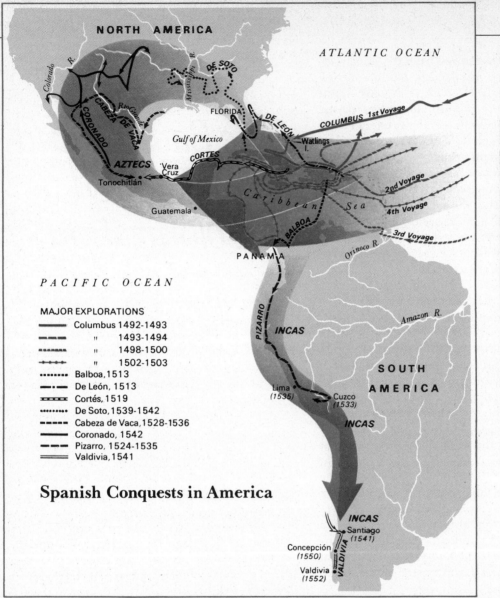

Spanish Conquests in America

MAJOR EXPLORATIONS

———	Columbus 1492-1493
– – –	" 1493-1494
—▪—▪—	" 1498-1500
—+—+—	" 1502-1503
·········	Balboa, 1513
—·—·—	De León, 1513
××××××	Cortés, 1519
••••••••	De Soto, 1539-1542
———	Cabeza de Vaca, 1528-1536
———	Coronado, 1542
– – –	Pizarro, 1524-1535
═══════	Valdivia, 1541

Columbus's world-transforming discovery of 1492 to exploit the territories it claimed. Led by the courageous, greedy, and often brutal *conquistadores*—adventurers for whom there are no equivalents in British experience—Spain's exploration of the Western Hemisphere, its conquest of the native peoples, and its establishment of a new civilization swept forward in three main waves.

The Spanish Conquests. Columbus himself explored much of the Caribbean on his four voyages (1492–1504), and within a generation of his death in 1506 Spanish adventurers seized possession of most of the coastal lands of Central America and South America. The conquest of the Caribbean basin climaxed in 1513 with Balboa's penetration of the Isthmus of Panama and his discovery of the Pacific, and near starvation, and attacks by natives to found Santiago, Concepción, and Valdivia before succumbing to native rebellion in 1553.

Radiating out from these three main lines of conquest (first, the subjugation of the Caribbean islands and coastal areas; then the reduction of Mexico and the exploration of southern North America; and finally the invasion of Peru, Chile, and northern Argentina), Spain's empire in America expanded in all directions. By 1607, when England established at Jamestown its first permanent settlement in America, Spain's American dominion extended nearly eight thousand miles, from southern California to the Strait of Magellan. Spain then possessed the largest empire the Western world had seen since the fall of Rome. Its only competitor in the Western Hemisphere had been Portugal, which had controlled the coastal areas of Brazil, until the union of the Spanish and Portuguese thrones (1580–1640) gave Spain legal ju-

risdiction even there. Spain's fabulous western empire was the result of sheer lust for adventure, greed, and a passion to convert the heathen people to Christianity; it was also the result of remarkable administrative skill.

The Spanish Empire.   Despite the vast distances involved and all the technical impediments to the coherent management of so vast a territory, Spain's American empire was well organized. The structure of government that had evolved during the sixteenth century was elaborate, ingeniously contrived, and, except for periods when royal authority collapsed in Spain itself, successful. And it was utterly different from the imperial system that Britain would devise a century later. It was most elaborately *bureaucratic*. Full-time salaried officials enforced detailed decrees and and laws governing the behavior of rulers and ruled— regulations that reached down into the daily life of

THE WORLD THE SPANIARDS FOUND
The Aztec priest's skull mask was meant to be worn with an elaborate feather headdress and rich robes. It must have had a terrifying effect on worshipers. The gold Mixtec chest plate represented the god of death. Opposite, Macchu Pichu, Peru, last refuge of the Incan emperors in their flight from the Spaniards. *(Opposite, Braniff International Photograph; below left, National Museum of Anthropology, Mexico City; right, Copyright The British Museum)*

the meanest peasants in the most remote corners of the empire, half a world away from the central administrative agencies in Spain. And the system was *patriarchal*. That is, it was hierarchical in structure, all authority ultimately centering in the patriarchal figure of the monarch of Castile, whose rule in his kingdom of America was conceived of as personal, an extension of his dynastic and domestic authority.

This projection of monarchical power into overseas territory by means of a complex bureaucracy had been initiated almost immediately upon the report of Columbus's discovery—a response that contrasts sharply with that of the British government a century later. By 1503, the first of the major imperial institutions, the *Casa de Contratación* (board of trade),

had been created. The *Casa*—in Seville—licensed all equipment and operations engaged in trade with America, enforced the commercial laws and regulations, collected customs duties and colonial crown revenues, and kept the commercial accounts for the entire empire. By virtue of its power over colonial commerce and the flow of treasure that poured into Spain from America, the *Casa* became in effect a major branch of the royal exchequer. From this original agency, Spain's imperial government, flung over half the globe yet bound by hundreds of rules and regulations enforced by an army of officials, developed within a single generation.

Yet in all of this the *Casa* was subordinate to the chief regulating agency in Spain, the Council of the Indies (created in 1524), which held the decisive control, in the king's name, of both the legislative and the executive governance of the colonies, and which constituted a branch of the royal court. All colonial laws and decrees, civil and religious, were issued by the Council; and the officials, clerical and secular, who enforced the regulations were appointed by the Council. It exercised a special responsibility for the spiritual and physical welfare of the Indians; it served as a court of last resort for the entire judiciary system of the colonies; it censored all publications in America; and it audited the accounts of the colonial treasurers.

The government agencies and officials in America were in one way or another subordinates of this supreme royal council. The chief governmental unit in America was the viceroyalty, of which two were created in the sixteenth century: New Spain (1535), which included all Spanish territory north of the Isthmus of Panama; and Peru (1542), covering all to the south except the coast of Venezuela. These massive jurisdictions were ruled by viceroys endowed with large and somewhat ambiguous portions of royal power and established in seats of glittering splendor.

The next level was that of the *audiencias*, of which there were seven by 1550; five more were added by 1661. Originally they were royal courts with direct access to the Council of the Indies and subject to its veto only; but the *audiencias* soon acquired administrative and political authority also, and they shared,

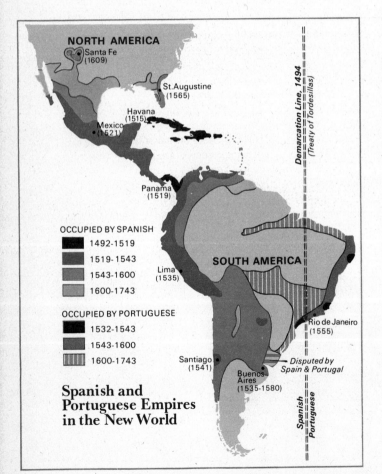

NORTH AMERICA
Santa Fe (1609)
St. Augustine (1565)
Havana (1515)
Mexico (1521)
Panama (1519)
Demarcation Line, 1494 (Treaty of Tordesillas)

OCCUPIED BY SPANISH
1492-1519
1519-1543
1543-1600
1600-1743

OCCUPIED BY PORTUGUESE
1532-1543
1543-1600
1600-1743

SOUTH AMERICA
Lima (1535)
Rio de Janeiro (1555)
Santiago (1541)
Disputed by Spain & Portugal
Buenos Aires (1535-1580)
Spanish
Portuguese

Spanish and Portuguese Empires in the New World

or contested, those powers with the viceroys. More clearly subordinate to the viceroyalties were lesser jurisdictions—*presidencias* and captaincies general—that were deliberately created as administrative subdivisions of the larger territorial governments.

These were the main jurisdictions. Below them lay a range of inferior units, whose chief officers were usually appointed by the viceroys or *audiencias,* with the approval of the Council of the Indies, and only occasionally by the crown itself. And below them, the lowest unit of civil government was the municipal corporation, or *cabildo.* Finally, in various lateral connections with the whole of this imperial hierarchy were various investigating and superintending officials appointed in Spain to strengthen the crown's authority throughout its American territories.

This elaborate structure of royal government was neither altogether rational in its construction, nor altogether efficient in its operation, nor altogether comprehensive in its reach. There were gaps and clumsy overlaps in authority. Subordinate jurisdictions, especially in the remote territories, found many ways of ignoring the superior authorities; and corruption was widespread, at least at the lower ranges of the hierarchy. Yet despite these weaknesses, the Spanish empire functioned for over three hundred years as a reasonably coherent state system, however inefficient its workings might appear to a modern analyst. And it was a system that was largely unchallenged. Of course there was resistance to this or that unpopular regulation and to the rule of any number of obnoxious officers sent out from Spain. But there was no openly organized political opposition to the state, only the passive refusal to comply with unacceptable or unenforceable crown orders, a pattern of action that was familiarly described by the formula, "I obey but I do not execute." Nor was there a body of ideas that would justify sustained opposition to the crown, nor political leaders experienced in challenging the authority of the state and motivated to do so. When in the end, more than three hundred years after its founding, Spain's empire in America succumbed to corruption, misgovernment, and rising democratic aspirations, there was no corps of native politicians capable of managing free governments and of creating respon-

sible and stable self-government. And the doctrines that shaped the Latin American independence movement of the early nineteenth century were largely alien ideas that expressed only clumsily the particular needs of the Spanish-American people.

Contrast to the British Empire.   In all of this, the contrast with British America could hardly be sharper or more significant. There was never an effective structure of imperial government in the Anglo-American empire. The authority of the British crown and of Parliament was scattered through half a dozen uncoordinated agencies of government, and it was never anything but superficial. It seldom penetrated much

Spain's Imperial Government in the New World, 1550

SEVILLE, FIRST CAPITAL OF THE SPANISH AMERICAN EMPIRE, BY ALONZO SANCHEZ COELLO
Linked by short river routes and canals to the Atlantic, Seville prospered enormously in
the sixteenth century. All shipping to and from America had to pass through the city. Its
Consulado, a gild of merchant houses, enjoyed a monopoly of Spanish trade with the New
World. In addition, the city was the seat of the *Casa de Contratación.   (Museo de América,
Madrid; Mas/Art Reference Bureau)*

beyond the docks or the customs houses, and its control of the American political system was weak. Yet, paradoxically, there was organized resistance to this weak and scattered authority from the start. By the middle of the eighteenth century, resistance had grown into a sophisticated process of competitive politics and had bred politicians long experienced in local self-government. The transition to independence and to responsible self-government in British America was consequently smooth, and, once the War of Independence was concluded, entirely bloodless.

This stark contrast between the Spanish-American and the British-American patterns becomes even more vivid, and paradoxical, if one considers the fact that in the early years of the Spanish-American empire there had existed institutions that could have developed into bases for just the kind of competitive

politics that developed in North America. But these institutions, instead of maturing into centers of open competition with the state, withered and disappeared. At the start, for example, the most powerful figures in Latin America were the *adelantados*, feudal lords granted extraordinary powers by the crown to subjugate the American frontiers—executive and judicial powers that were understood from the beginning to be essentially competitive with those of the crown. Yet few of the *adelantados* managed to transmit their authority to a second generation. Similarly, the *encomiendas*, which in the sixteenth century constituted another potential threat to the overall authority of the state, were eliminated as bases of political competition. Transferred as an institution from Spain to America in 1502, the *encomienda* was a grant of the labor of a specific number of native Indians—in effect a gift of slaves or serfs—and the land they occupied. The crown had intended to protect the natives by charging the grantees with responsibility for the Indians' spiritual and physical well-being, but the *encomiendas* quickly became the instrument of the most vicious oppression. The crown, determined to eliminate the institution, gradually succeeded in reducing the powers of the four thousand or so *encomenderos*, draining away their incomes and eliminating the heritability of the original grants. By the early eighteenth century the *encomienda* was no longer a political danger to the crown. In similar ways the threat of other, lesser competing political authorities—provincial assemblies and municipal corporations—was eliminated or reduced.

Why had all of these semi-independent agencies and institutions weakened or been absorbed into the state apparatus? Why had organized competitive politics died almost at birth in Spanish America while in British America it grew so quickly and so strongly? There is no simple explanation for this, but there were certain circumstances in Spanish America that form at least part of an explanation, and these circumstances contrast sharply with the conditions that shaped the development of the British American communities.

From the very start the crown—Ferdinand and Isabella in the first instance—actively and directly asserted its authority. Even before Columbus's discovery had been made, the monarchy had asserted its rule over lands conquered in its name, and not merely as commercial regulation but as territorial government in depth. The Spanish monarchs declared the whole of America to be a separate kingdom of the crown of Castile, its native peoples direct subjects of the crown, and its governmental jurisdictions subordinate agencies of the crown. This declaration was supported by the highest moral agency of the Western world, the papacy. Various papal bulls and encyclicals assigned the responsibility for the welfare of the natives, which meant primarily the task of converting them to Christianity, to the Castilian monarch. From that central Christian responsibility, jurists and theologians developed a massive body of legal, political, and theological commentary that strongly reinforced and justified the claims of the Spanish monarch to personal rule in America. And there were no competing intellectual centers from which contrary ideas could develop. The Catholic church, conservative in doctrine and royalist in politics, dominated the intellectual life of Latin America. Far from Spanish America proving to be a legitimate refuge for religious dissenters, as British America would become, it developed into a more tightly controlled bastion of Catholic orthodoxy than Spain itself. Dissenters and heretics of all kinds were barred by law from emigrating to America.

Yet declarations and political theory do not in themselves create political realities. There was something in the situation in Spanish America that guaranteed a welcome for the crown's supremacy and that helped stifle competitive institutions at their birth. If one turns from institutions to population characteristics and asks what groups had the capacity to maintain an active opposition to the crown and would have had an interest in organizing such opposition, the situation becomes clearer.

The Spanish-American Population. There were four principal social categories in the Spanish-American population, of which the most numerous by far was that of the native Indians. The Aztecs, the Incas, and the other native Americans whom the Spanish encountered were advanced people in certain ways; but to Europeans of the time they were primitive, particularly in technology and weaponry, and they were helpless before the onslaught of the Spanish conquerers. People in good social discipline, numerous, and stable in location, the native Americans quickly became a mass laboring population, and they were incapable of organizing their own political institutions to speak against the state.

At the other extreme from the native Indians were the major imperial officeholders—the viceroys, *audiencia* judges, high church officials, and governors—who might most readily have created areas of independent authority. But the crown's policies in recruiting and controlling these officers prevented them from moving in that direction. The great majority of the high officers of church and state who served in Spanish America in the three hundred years of the colonial period were Peninsular Spaniards—that is, men born in the Iberian Peninsula, unaffiliated with American interests, and committed to returning to Spain after

Guaina Potosi
or Jong Potosi

Tarapaia

TWO VIEWS OF THE FABULOUS SILVER MINE AT POTOSÍ
The external view appears in an atlas by Hermann
Moll, c. 1709–1720. The interior view (opposite) is an
imaginative depiction by De Bry which captures something of the degradation suffered by the Indian miners.
Thousands of these forced laborers perished in that
"mouth of hell" 16,000 feet above sea level. The wealth
produced at Potosí for over two centuries after the
mine's discovery in 1545 was stupendous, but the cost
in human suffering by whole populations of helpless
natives, slaving underground by dim candlelight for
days on end, was immeasurably greater. The city of
Potosí itself (in modern Bolivia) had a population of
120,000 by 1572 but remained a tumultuous mining
camp throughout the colonial period, swarming with
gamblers, prostitutes, and adventurers of all kinds.
*(Above, Harvard College Library; opposite, Rare Book Division,
New York Public Library)*

completing their tour of duty abroad. Further, controls were devised to limit any possible independence
these officials might have developed. Their tenure in
office was strictly limited; they were circulated within
the imperial system to prevent their acquiring too
strong an identification with any particular locality;
they were dependent on the crown treasury for their
salaries; and they were subjected to rigorous scru-
tinies of their conduct of office.

A third group was that of the Creoles, the American-born leaders of Spanish descent. Under favorable
conditions they might well have provided the initiative and organization for a vigorous political life,
for as opposed to the Indians they were politically
sophisticated, and as opposed to most high church
and state officers they were Americans, with American interests. And indeed, there were conflicts
between Creoles and Spanish officials, particularly
over officeholding and the enforcement of trade regulations. Further, late in the colonial period the sale
of public offices by the bankrupt Spanish state gave

Creoles increasing access to public authority. But in general the Creoles' small numbers and their social situation shaped a dependent political role. Of the total population of more than 9 million in Spanish America in the 1570s, only 118,000 or 1.25 percent were Creoles. In the entire first century of Spain's colonial period, approximately 240,000 Spaniards emigrated to America. The contrast with British America is startling. In the equivalent period (to 1700), approximately 400,000 emigrants had left the British Isles for America alone, a yearly average two-thirds greater than that of the Spanish. The occupational character of the Creole population followed directly from their numbers. A thin overlay on a very large population of natives, these Americans of European descent never constituted the mass base of the social structure. They filled the upper strata of the American communities; they were landowners, clerics, army officers, and merchants. Their identity as a ruling class, and consequently their well-being, derived not from their American birth but from their European

descent, which distinguished them racially from the mass of the population. As a consequence, despite their local interests, they continued to identify themselves with Spain, which was the source of their status, wealth, and power.

Finally, there were two other groups in the Spanish-American population: the blacks, who were imported as slaves and who never acquired an active political role; and, politically more important, the large segment of the population that was racially mixed. By the 1570s the racially mixed elements constituted appoximately 2.5 percent of the entire populace. By the end of the colonial period that figure had risen to over 30 percent (another striking contrast to British America, where the racially mixed population was numerically insignificant). There was a great variety of racial combinations, but the most important element by far was the *mestizos*, those of mixed European and Indian ancestry. Yet, though numerous, the *mestizos* in general were felt to be socially inferior to the dominant Spanish elements and constituted a lower middle class of small farmers and shopkeepers. In a society where status, wealth, and power were controlled by those of pure Spanish heritage, *mestizos* avoided asserting their identities through politics and tended to escape by fitting themselves as inconspicuously as possible into the situation as it existed. It would take a profound cultural change to release their suppressed aspirations and free them to assume effective political roles. When that took place, and only then, the colonial era of Spanish-American history was over.

These population characteristics, utterly different from the characteristics of the British-American world, go far toward explaining the failure of a free competitive political system to develop in colonial Spanish America despite the availability of institutions that originally could have supported such politics. The small elite of high state officials was bound to Spain in every way. The Creoles were a small self-conscious ruling class whose well-being, in the great sea of native Indians, blacks, and racially mixed, depended on a continuing identification with the sources of authority in Europe. Only the racially mixed were disposed to move toward political autonomy, but through most of three centuries they lacked the self-esteem, the numbers, and the experience to devise effective political weapons against the overwhelming Spanish establishment.

England's Overseas Expansion

England's entry into the Western Hemisphere was the very opposite of Spain's. Where Spain had been swift, England was slow; where Spain had been deliberate and decisive, England was muddled in purpose. For Spain, America almost immediately yielded immense wealth; for England, it created, at the start at least, more losses than profits. At no point were the differences more extreme and more consequential than at the very beginning of exploration and settlement.

PORTUGUESE CARRACKS OF THE EARLY SIXTEENTH CENTURY, PAINTING ATTRIBUTED TO CORNELIS ANTHONISZOON
These massive, high-built, unwieldy vessels designed for maximum freight capacity played a vital role in transoceanic shipping of the sixteenth century. The largest, over 1,800 tons, could carry 700 passengers and a cargo of 900 tons.   *(National Maritime Museum, Greenwich)*

For no less than fifty years, while Spain was conquering and exploiting vast areas of Central America and South America, England did nothing to develop its claim to North America. That claim had been established in 1497–98 when John Cabot, commissioned by Henry VII, had discovered and begun the exploration of Newfoundland, Labrador, and Nova Scotia. His son Sebastian had continued the exploration into the Hudson Bay region of Canada in 1508–09, but throughout the reign of Henry VIII (1509–47) neither the crown nor private enterprise showed any interest in developing these distant territories. The only English contact with America that remained through these years was the work of fishermen from the west country of England—Cornwall, Devonshire, Dorsetshire—who, together with fishermen from France, Spain, and Portugal, had begun to exploit the wealth of the Grand Banks off Newfoundland and the coastal waters around the mouth of the St. Lawrence River. They became familiar with the southern Canadian and northern New England coasts and built crude shacks for their immediate convenience during the fishing seasons, but they made no attempt to establish permanent settlements or otherwise assert England's claim to the land.

Then suddenly, in the early 1550s, the situation was transformed, and in this sudden reversal are to be found the beginnings of British colonization. This development was complex, and it is as important to understand what did not happen as it is to know what did happen. For there was no sudden eruption of interest in overseas settlement as such, and there was no sudden determination on the part of England to assert its claim to America. Instead there were two basic shifts in orientation, both of which would eventually involve colonization but neither of which was originally directed to that goal. The first shift was in England's economy, the second in its international relations.

Economic and Diplomatic Changes. England's prosperity in the first half of the sixteenth century had been based on the growing European demand for its raw wool and woolen cloth, marketed largely in Antwerp, in what is now Belgium. Through the reign of Henry VIII more and more capital and labor had become involved in this dominant commercial enterprise, more and more arable land had been turned to pasturing sheep, and England's financial stability had become increasingly dependent on Antwerp. Then in the late 1540s this elaborate commercial structure began to weaken. By 1550 the Antwerp market was saturated, and in 1551 it collapsed. Cloth exports fell off 35 percent within a year, and the financial world was thrown into turmoil. The merchants were forced to reconsider the whole of their activities. New markets would have to be found, new routes of trade devised, and capital risked in ways that a previous generation wold have thought wildly speculative.

Changes in England's international position helped channel these suddenly mobilized energies. Antagonism with France had dominated England's policies through the reign of Henry VIII, and in this rivalry Spain had been England's natural ally. As a result England had been willing to respect Spain's claim to the whole of the Western Hemisphere, which had been set out in papal bulls in 1493 and in the Spanish-Portuguese Treaty of Tordesillas (1494), assuring Spain of its title to all of the Western Hemisphere 370 leagues west of the Cape Verde Islands. England had found it diplomatically useful to support this claim, at least tacitly, and the support was confirmed by the marriage of England's Queen Mary (1553–58) to Philip II of Spain.

But the accession of Queen Elizabeth in 1558 began a reversal in international relations as England's Protestantism began to dominate its foreign policy. By the 1560s it was clear that Spain threatened England's independence as a Protestant nation and that England's long-range interests in Europe lay in the support of the rebellious Protestants in France and of the Protestant Netherlands struggling to free themselves from Spanish rule. From an ally of Spain, England had become an enemy, and while England felt too weak until the 1580s to engage in open warfare with the great imperial power, the country had every reason to want to harass and plunder Spanish territories in any way possible.

Thus, impelled by a sudden economic need to break out of the safe, conservative commerce of earlier years, and no longer hesitant to attack Spain's

ELIZABETH I BY M. GHEERAERTS THE YOUNGER
As shrewd in politics as she was cautious in finance, Elizabeth sponsored England's overseas adventures by subtle means until she was ready to challenge Spain directly in 1585. *(National Portrait Gallery, London)*

overseas territories, England entered a new phase in its history—but not by plunging directly and immediately into colonization. Its response to the economic and diplomatic shifts took several forms, and only eventually, and almost incidentally, did it involve overseas settlement. In response to the new economic pressures foreign merchants were expelled from the realm, and English merchants were favored in the conduct of trade. Land that had been converted to sheep grazing was forced back into tillage; textile production was limited; and entry into trade by newcomers was restrained. Above all, the commercial community poured capital into a search for new kinds of overseas commerce and for new, distant markets independent of European middlemen. In 1555 enterprising merchants formed the Guinea Company for trade to Africa and the Muscovy Company for trade with Russia. In 1579 the Eastland Company organized English trade to the Baltic. In 1581 the Levant Company was created to control England's commerce with the Middle East. Finally, a series of contacts with India and Southeast Asia led to the creation of the East India Company in 1600.

These were legitimate and official enterprises. During the same years, risk capital, some of it drawn secretly from royal sources, went into semipiratical raids on Spanish commerce and Spanish shipping. These enterprises began in 1562 when John Hawkins of Plymouth broke into the Spanish trade monopoly of the West Indies and the South American mainland with the first of a series of illegal but highly lucrative peddling voyages, the third of which, in 1567, led to open conflict with the Spanish. Francis Drake took up

the challenge at that point and began what proved to be twenty years of wildly adventurous raids on Spanish colonial properties, the culmination of which was his famous circumnavigation of the globe in 1577–80, a joint-stock enterprise which yielded, among other results, 4,600 percent profit to the shareholders.

By then English interest in the Western Hemisphere was rising—not primarily as a location for English colonies but as a route to Asian markets. The Cabots' explorations were recalled, and new information, commercial and geographical, flowed in to help justify the enthusiasm of a group of adventurers from the west of England. This group, led by Sir Humphrey Gilbert, determined to find a northwestern passage through the Western Hemisphere into the Far East. In 1565 the Privy Council heard a formal debate on possible new routes. The Muscovy merchants, naturally enough, urged endorsement of efforts to find an *eastern* passage, north of Siberia, and to exploit the Baltic hinterland. The westcountry gentry, long familiar with the North American coastal waters, urged

ESKIMO MAN, WOMAN, AND CHILD, BROUGHT BACK TO ENGLAND BY FROBISHER IN 1577

John White (see p. 20) accompanied Frobisher on his second voyage (1577) to Frobisher Bay, an inlet on the coast of Baffin Island, northeast of Hudson Bay, and probably sketched these three captured Eskimos on shipboard. The woman, whose child peeks out from within her hood, is tattooed in blue around the eyes. The Eskimos were sensations in Bristol, where they demonstrated the use of their kayak, but they died within a month of their arrival. Frobisher was convinced that the bay he found was the northwest passage leading to China and that ore picked up at the mouth of the bay contained gold. But his efforts to establish a mining settlement along the bay failed miserably even before it became clear that the ore contained no gold. (*Reproduced by courtesy of Trustees of the British Museum*) expeditions to the *west*, through the north of what is now Canada. Gilbert and the westerners were defeated in that debate, but with their support, in 1576–78, an enterprising mariner, Martin Frobisher, led three expeditions to the region northeast of Hudson Bay. He and his London backers, led by a merchant, Michael Lok, organized the short-lived Company of Cathay in response to the reports of gold—which later proved to be false—that were carried back. There were continuous frustrations for all of these western initiatives, but the search for the northwest passage went on, yielding in the end, after vain and desperate efforts to get through the ice and snow of the Canadian wilderness, a reasonably clear picture of that region of the globe.

First Attempts at Colonization. Gradually, within all of these overseas enterprises, the idea of colonization slowly developed. In his appearance before the Privy Council in 1565 Gilbert had suggested the value of colonies as way stations along the proposed routes to the Far East, and in 1578 he sought and received a crown charter for establishing a colony in America.

Gilbert's attempt in 1578 to establish a colony in New England or Nova Scotia—the first English effort to colonize in the Western Hemisphere—failed almost before it began. His small exploratory fleet was scattered by storms and diverted by the lure of privateering. Yet in the process of launching this first colonizing expedition, Gilbert acquired valuable experience in attempting to finance such ventures. He also engaged the enthusiasm of his gifted half-brother, Sir Walter Raleigh, in such ventures as these and drew into this realm of enterprise the two Richard Hakluyts, experts on overseas geography, who became important propagandists of colonization. The younger Hakluyt's *Discourse of Western Planting* (1584) shows the mingling of motives that existed in this advanced circle of enthusiasts. It was England's duty, Hakluyt argued, to Christianize the American pagans, especially since an American colony would provide a base for attacks on Spanish lands and Spanish treasure ships. More important would be the long-term economic gains from American colonies; they could supply England with exotic goods otherwise bought from Spain and create new markets for English consumer goods while at the

SIR WALTER RALEIGH AND HIS SON, 1602
Raleigh was an accomplished poet, soldier, courtier, and politician, and like many intellectuals of his time he was fascinated by geographical exploration and by the possibilities of overseas settlements—in Ireland as well as in America. He helped draw into the leadership of exploration and colonization the interrelated landed gentry of England's west country. The failure of his Roanoke settlement showed the impossibility of financing settlements in America by individual or family efforts. *(National Portrait Gallery, London)*

same time drawing off England's unemployed workers and turning their labor to advantage. New routes to Asia, new weapons against Spain, a new source of exotic supplies, and a new market for English goods as well as a new use for England's "surplus" population—all this would justify England's support for colonization.

Raleigh's and Hakluyt's ideas were not widely shared, and they did not become state policy. In 1584, after Gilbert had died on a voyage from Newfoundland, Queen Elizabeth transferred his patent to Raleigh, but she kept her government from directly supporting his plans for colonization. She made a minor contribution to financing a new expedition that he planned and gave his enterprise her personal blessing, but otherwise her government did nothing to help launch or sustain the famous "lost colony" that Raleigh established in America in 1585. This one English American settlement of the sixteenth century was thus of necessity almost entirely the *private* undertaking of a group of merchants and gentlemen from the west of England.

The history of this first English colony in the Western Hemisphere is quickly told. In three successive years separate groups of settlers were landed on Roanoke Island, a heavily wooded spot off the coast of North Carolina. The first group, 108 men, arrived there in 1585. They quickly fell out with the natives, ran through their food supplies as they explored the North Carolina coastal waters, and returned to England hurriedly the next year with Francis Drake when he unexpectedly appeared on his way home from a successful raid on the West Indies. Later that year—1586—the second group, 18 men, was left behind by a party sent out to relieve the original group, but this forlorn and helpless crew was soon slaughtered by the Indians. The island was therefore deserted when, the next summer, 1587, the third and main contingent, consisting of 117 men, women, and children, arrived under Governor John White. What happened to this largest and best-equipped group of Raleigh's settlers has never been discovered. White was obliged to return quickly to England to speed on more supplies, but the threat of open war with Spain and the attractions of privateering kept relief vessels from reaching the colony. It was only in 1590 that White finally managed to return, to find the settlers gone. Apparently they had moved off to Croatoan Island, to the south in the outer banks of Pamlico Sound, and White could not follow them there. Their disappearance marks the end of Raleigh's efforts at colonization.

A fumbling, failing, almost pathetic affair, all of this, next to the bold and hugely successful first thrusts of the Spanish in America. Yet Raleigh's Roanoke venture is as revealing of the basic conditions that would later, in the seventeenth century, shape the successful English settlements as it is of the limitations that defeated colonization in the reign of Elizabeth.

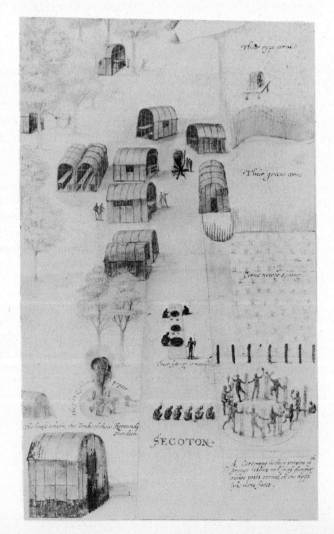

INDIAN VILLAGE OF SECOTON AND A CHIEF'S WIFE AND DAUGHTER

These watercolors are from a portifolio of accurate and superbly colored scenes of Indian life and the natural environment made by John White on his voyages to Raleigh's "Virginia" in 1585 and 1587. Note the three plantings of corn, and the child's doll in English dress. *(Reproduced by Courtesy of the Trustees of The British Museum)*

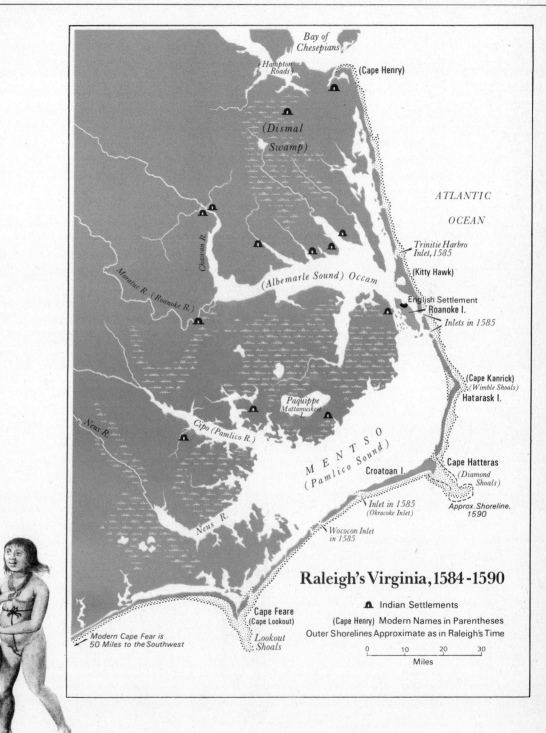

Bay of
Chesepians

(Hampton
Roads)

(Cape Henry)

(Dismal
Swamp)

ATLANTIC

OCEAN

Charran R.

Moratuc R. (Roanoke R.)

(Albemarle Sound) Occam

Trinitie Harbro
Inlet, 1585

(Kitty Hawk)

English Settlement
Roanoke I.

Inlets in 1585

(Cape Kanrick)
(Wimble Shoals)
Hatarask I.

Paquippe
Mattamuskeet

Neus R.

Cipo (Pamlico R.)

MENTSO
(Pamlico Sound)

Croatoan I.

Cape Hatteras
(Diamond
Shoals)

Inlet in 1585
(Okracoke Inlet)

Approx. Shoreline,
1590

Neus R.

Wococon Inlet
in 1585

Raleigh's Virginia, 1584-1590

⚲ Indian Settlements

(Cape Henry) Modern Names in Parentheses
Outer Shorelines Approximate as in Raleigh's Time

Cape Feare
(Cape Lookout)

Lookout
Shoals

Modern Cape Fear is
50 Miles to the Southwest

0   10   20   30
Miles

Personnel and the Role of the State

Several things of permanent importance had become clear during these earliest and least successful years of English colonization in America. In England, there was a leadership group available for colonization quite different from the Spanish *conquistadores*, "drunk with a heroic and brutal dream," as a Spanish poet later described them. Where the Spanish conquerors were the sons of impoverished farmers and townsmen, many of them illiterate, the leaders of English overseas enterprise—Gilbert, Raleigh, Grenville, Hawkins, Drake—were the well-educated younger sons of the westcountry gentry, bred in secure landed establishments, familiar with the sea from childhood, barred by the laws favoring eldest sons from inheriting family properties, and eager somehow to reestablish themselves on the land in the same genteel condition they had known before.

Second, it was clear that there was in England a mass of laborers available for emigration to overseas colonies. London was swollen with unemployed workers (its population rose from 60,000 in 1500 to 200,000 in 1600). The countryside was swarming with migrant farmhands called by contemporaries "sturdy beggars"; and in the centers of the wool industry—the west country and East Anglia (Essex, Suffolk, and Norfolk)—underemployment was already generating the discontent that would express itself forcefully in the religious protest of Puritanism. Elizabethans spoke of the "multitude of increase in our people." Responsible officials were convinced that England was overpopulated and its well-being threatened by an idle labor force that consumed more than it contributed to the general fund of wealth: "Our land hath not milk sufficient in the breast thereof to nourish all those children which it hath brought forth." For many, the most attractive remedy was colonization and emigration. But though the population of England and Wales rose from just over 3 million in 1550 to just over 4 million in 1600 to 5.2 million in 1695, and in the next twenty-five years increased by another 800,000, there was, in fact, no absolute "surplus" of people, as seventeenth-century English analysts came to realize. The sense of overpopulation was created by the widespread displacement of a mass population and an exceptionally high

THE CHEAPSIDE-CORNHILL DISTRICT OF LONDON, 1658

From this swarming urban concentration came hundreds of emigrants, joining a multitude of others from the countryside to settle England's first colonies in America. *(From William Faithorne and Richard Newcourt's* Exact Delineation of the Cities of London and Westminster . . . *)*

degree of geographical mobility that resulted from rapid economic growth, from inflation, and from the commercialization of agriculture. But however they were perceived, these developments—which made available for recruitment a mass of ordinary farm and town workers—would prove to be crucial to the early peopling of British North America.

Third, it became evident that there was capital available in sizable amounts for investment in overseas ventures, as well as entrepreneurial interest in mobilizing that capital and directing it to profitable uses in colonization. The costs of financing the Roanoke voyages and the first efforts at colonization had been borne almost entirely by the westcountry gentry, but their resources were clearly inadequate to support further, larger-scale efforts. In 1589 Raleigh transferred control of the Virginia enterprise to a London business syndicate headed by Sir Thomas Smith, one of the most powerful merchants of the age. The capital available to these merchants was far greater than that of the westcountry gentry, and it would be these men of business who would launch the first new wave of colonization in the early seventeenth century.

It had become clear, too, that when efforts at colonization would be resumed (as plans and probes in the later years of Elizabeth's reign indicated they would be), the role of the crown would continue to be minimal. The crown would legalize exploration and settlement, and it would exert some supervision of the plans that were made, but it would initiate nothing and organize nothing, nor would it sustain or reinforce any enterprise that was undertaken. More important, the English crown had no desire to extend its direct rule over distant territories conquered or settled by Englishmen. Some form of government would be provided, but it would not be crown government in depth. The burden of governing colonies, like the burden of financing them, would be borne not by the crown but by the enterpreneurs of settlement or by the settlers themselves. Colonial government, at the start at least, would therefore of necessity be self-government of some sort, and the imperial organization as it evolved would be a superstructure, an overlay imposed on semi-independent units of local government.

JAMES I, PORTRAIT ATTRIBUTED TO JAN DE CRITZ, C. 1620
(National Maritime Museum, Greenwich)

Financial Limitations and the "Starving Times"

Peace with Spain in 1604 released the powerful expansionist impulses that had been building up in England for half a century. The resulting lunge into overseas enterprise in the reigns of James I (1603–25) and his son Charles I (1625–49) was spectacular. The famous settlements at Jamestown, at Plymouth, and around the Massachusetts Bay were only fragments of a great mosaic of efforts that reached into many parts of the globe, that involved hundreds of thousands of Englishmen of all descriptions, and that cost millions of pounds sterling. In this great expansion,

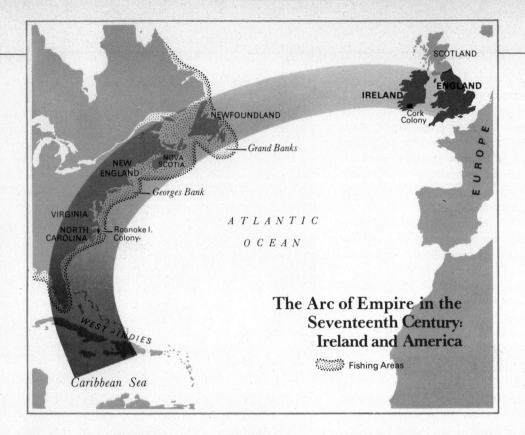

The Arc of Empire in the Seventeenth Century: Ireland and America

:::::: Fishing Areas

the chief center of colonization was not North America but Ireland, which had been the scene of England's first extensive and sustained efforts at overseas colonization. Henry VIII's failure to bind the Irish chiefs to him by feudal ties and gradually to infuse elements of English law and religion into his rebellious population had led, in 1566, to military conquest by the English. British communities were then transplanted to enclaves in southern Ireland which formed a "pale of settlement" against what were seen as utterly savage and ungovernable natives.

By 1604 Ireland and America were seen as equivalent centers of overseas expansion and they were linked geographically in Englishmen's minds. As they looked out at the world beyond England they saw a single arc of overseas territories suitable for colonization sweeping north and west from Britain, enclosing Ireland, Newfoundland, and the mainland coast of North America south to the Caribbean. It was therefore natural that nearby Ireland, which was described in a travel book of 1617 as "this famous island in the Virginia sea," would be the first and primary object of colonization in the explosion of

enterprise of the early seventeenth century. When in 1607 two of the most powerful Irish earls, resisting the authority of the English crown, fled from the British Isles, their vast properties, ultimately six of the nine counties of the northern province of Ulster, were confiscated. This immense territory was largely cleared of its native population and offered for sale to prospective "planters." London's city government and the largest gild corporations took up large grants. After the Irish rebellion of 1641 (which many linked to the Indian rebellion of 1622 in Virginia), 7 million more acres were cleared of their native inhabitants. Thousands of the native Irish were subjected to severe punishment for their involvement—proven or suspected—in the rebellion, and most of the Irish were driven beyond the English pale. Into these Irish plantations, in the same years that the North American settlements were being established, came a steady stream of English and Scottish emigrants. By 1642 an estimated 120,000 English and Scottish men, women, and children had settled in Ireland, a migration six times greater than the famous "Great Migration" that settled New England in the same period. Yet the Ulster plantation was only one, if the most extensive, of the colonization efforts of the time. Besides Ireland, and besides Virginia and Massachusetts, English settlements were established in Bermuda, in the Caribbean (Providence Island, Barbados, Saint Christopher, Nevis, Montserrat, Antigua), in Newfoundland, in Canada, in Nova Scotia, and on the mainland coast of South America. In addition, fragile contacts with India were developed first into flourishing trading "factories" and then into the beginning of the network of political control that would eventually cover much of the Indian subcontinent.

In this global context the first settlements on the mainland of North America were relatively small undertakings, and their early histories become understandable only in terms of the pattern of the greater whole. For while these American communities would ultimately acquire a unique historical importance, originally they shared characteristics common to the rest of these earliest seventeenth-century enterprises. And of these common characteristics none was more important than the way in which they were financed.

The Financing of the Colonies. Whatever their founders' ultimate dreams may have been, these earliest English colonies—whether in Newfoundland or Barbados, Ulster, Plymouth, or Virginia—were of necessity financed at the start by profit-seeking joint-stock companies. Eleven commercial companies bore the main financial burden of the settlements launched before 1640. They raised their capital (an estimated £13 million) by selling stock to a remarkably broad range of the English population. Thousands invested—landowners as well as merchants, people of ordinary means as well as those of wealth. And the management of the funds generated by these investments was, for the most part, in the hands of businessmen who worked not only within the usual constraints of business operations but also under two very special pressures; and these pressures explain much of the hardship and tragedy of life in the earliest American settlements.

First, the joint stocks—the initial capital funds —of these ventures were not expected to endure. Shareholders did not expect to leave their funds in

these companies and draw a steady income in dividends from them, but rather to benefit from the quick liquidation of the entire enterprise at the end of a single voyage or a set number of years, at which time the original capital plus whatever profits had accumulated would be distributed. Whether there would be any further investments beyond this initial one would depend on the business prospect when this complete division of the company's assets was made. The settlers, many of whom were in effect employees of these companies for a stated term of years, were consequently placed under great pressure to produce an immediate profit for the company. If they failed to ship back tangible proof of the financial value of the settlement, they would be cut off to fend for themselves as best they could. As a consequence, instead of searching carefully into the strange American environment, they spent time scrabbling for evidence of gold in every shallow stream, searching for routes to the Pacific Ocean around the bend of every broad river, and plunging almost suicidally into the backcountry to verify garbled Indian rumors of great cities or of vast sources of furs or precious metals.

The pressure on the settlers was further intensified by the technical fact that the legal liability of stockholders in these early joint-stock companies was unlimited. The backers of the settlements were personally liable, without limit, for any debts the settlement companies might incur, and they were therefore extremely sensitive to the possibility of failure. They had no choice but to abandon doubtful enterprises as quickly as possible.

The "Starving Times." The result was desperation and starvation, at times complete chaos, in these first colonies, and bankruptcy in the companies that first colonized mainland North America. For there were only three possible sources of quick profits: surface resources of great value in proportion to weight and bulk that might simply be lifted into boats and sent back to the investors; a docile native population that might be organized quickly into labor gangs to dig out less accessible resources; and the discovery of new routes to rich, exotic markets. None of these possibilities proved realistic on the coasts of North America, and as a consequence in the early years the life-sustaining supplies, after the first shipments, were withheld from the settlements, and one after another the companies failed. Sheer accident provided most of the profits that actually accrued at the start. In Bermuda, for example, ambergris, a secretion of whales used in making perfume and medicine, was found in large quantities; a shipment worth £10,000 saved the Bermuda Company, which later profited steadily from tobacco production. Similarly, the Providence Island Company had the good fortune to capture a Spanish treasure ship worth £50,000.

Such lucky accidents were rare, however. Almost every one of the companies that financed settlements in British North America failed, sooner or later, and as they did so the original investors sought desperately to find secondary sources of profit. Some of the stockholders, seeking to recover their losses, funded "magazines"—stores of goods to be sold at high prices to the desperate settlers. Some set up separately financed enterprises: glass and silk were favored in Virginia. Others attempted to develop "private plantations," that is, personal estates and jurisdictions in the new land given to them in place of the missing profits. The Virginia Company alone created fifty of these private domains. But few of these secondary enterprises succeeded. Perhaps the most successful subordinate joint stock created within the Virginia Company was the fund established to send over a hundred "maids" to Jamestown "to be made wives of." The investors in this venture realized 47 percent profit on their shares when they sold the women's work contracts to the colonists.

As the financial prospects dimmed, the investors withdrew altogether from the ventures. Often the colonists, cut off by their backers, found the transition to self-sustained community life desperately difficult. Even in the best of circumstances the first inhabitants of Jamestown or Bermuda or Plymouth would have had a shock in adjusting to the wilderness environment. Forced to search for sources of immediate profit while neglecting some of the most elemental provisions for survival, many found the struggle unendurable, and succumbed—to despair, to the ravages of disease, and to the harassment of hostile natives.

The narratives of the first settlements make painful reading. There was heroism, but there was murderous selfishness as well; there was industry, but also laziness and at times suicidal inertia. Death and misery were everywhere. It is perhaps not surprising that the best organized and most successful of the earliest communities were those dominated by passionate religious convictions. For only the transcendent goals, the fierce determination, and the inner certainty of the Pilgrim and Puritan leaders could withstand the disintegrating effects of the "starving times."

CHRONOLOGY

1492-1504	Columbus's four voyages to New World.
1494	Treaty of Tordesillas divides non-Christian world between Spain and Portugal.
1497-98	John Cabot explores Newfoundland, Labrador, and Nova Scotia, and establishes English claim to North America.
1503	Spain establishes board of trade, *Casa de Contratación.*
1508-9	Sebastian Cabot explores Hudson Bay region.
1509-47	Reign of Henry VIII.
1513	Balboa discovers Pacific Ocean after crossing Isthmus of Panama.
1513	Ponce de León discovers mainland of Florida.
1519-21	Cortés conquers Mexico.
1523	Verrazano explores coast of North America, establishing French claim.
1523-30	Spaniards conquer Honduras and Guatemala.
1524	Spain creates Council of the Indies.
1528-36	Cabeza de Vaca explores northern periphery of Gulf of Mexico, west to Gulf of California.
1532-35	Pizarro conquers Peru.

1534	Cartier's explorations establish French claim to St. Lawrence basin.
1535	Viceroyalty of New Spain created.
1535-39	Initial Spanish conquest of Ecuador, Chile, northern Argentina, and Bolivia.
1539-41	De Soto explores southeastern United States and discovers the Mississippi.
1540-42	Coronado seeks legendary cities of wealth in North American Southwest.
1540-53	Valdivia extends Spanish conquest of Chile.
1542	Viceroyalty of Peru established.
1551	Antwerp market for English woolen goods fails.
1553-58	Queen Mary reigns in England.
1558-1603	Elizabeth's reign in England.
1562-67	Hawkins trades and plunders in Spanish America.
1566	England begins conquest of Ireland.
1574	Gilbert leads expedition to Hudson Bay.
1577-80	Drake circumnavigates globe.
1578	Gilbert fails to establish colony in North America.
1584	Richard Hakluyt (the younger) publishes *A Discourse on Western Planting.*
1585-87	Raleigh fails to establish Roanoke Colony.
1585-98	England colonizes Ireland.
1603-25	Reign of James I.
1603-35	In eleven voyages, Samuel de Champlain establishes French colonies in Canada.
1606	Virginia Company chartered, includes two subcompanies.
1607	English colony established at Jamestown.

SUGGESTED READINGS

The discovery and conquest of Central and South America by Spain had been the subject of some of the greatest narrative histories written in the nineteenth century, notably William H. Prescott's *History of the Conquest of Mexico* (1843) and his *Conquest of Peru* (1847). This tradition of sweeping, dramatic narratives continues in our own time in the writings of Samuel E. Morison, particularly in his biography of Columbus, *Admiral of the Ocean Sea* (2 vol. and 1 vol. eds., 1942, condensed as *Christopher Columbus, Mariner,* 1956), and his *The European Discovery of America: The Southern Voyages, AD 1492–1616* (1974), a volume crowded with maps and photographs that was written after the author retraced the routes of the Spanish discoverers by ship and plane. John H. Parry has sketched the general development of European expansion, geographical discovery, and initial overseas settlements in two very readable books, *Europe and a Wider World, 1415–1715* (1949) and *The Age of Reconnaissance* (1963). And David B. Quinn has written a masterful summary of the first efforts of the Spanish, English and French to explore and settle North America in his *North America from Earliest Discovery to First Settlements* (1977).

There are several good introductory histories of Spanish America in the colonial period: Charles Gipson, *Spain in America* (1966); Hubert Herring, *A History of Latin America from the Beginnings to the Present* (3d ed., 1968), Parts I, II; Bailey W. Diffie, *Latin American Civilization: The Colonial Period* (1945); John H. Parry, *The Spanish Seaborne Empire* (1966); and Salvador de Madariaga, *Rise of the Spanish American Empire* (1947). An equivalent history of the Portuguese-American empire is C. R. Boxer, *The Portuguese Seaborne Empire, 1415–1825* (1969); on the French empire in America, see George M. Wrong, *The Rise and Fall of New France* (2 vols., 1928) and William J. Eccles, *Canada under Louis XIV* (1964) and *Canadian Frontier, 1534–1760* (1969). The best general account of the administrative and constitutional history of Spanish America is Clarence H. Haring, *The Spanish Empire in America* (1947). See also John L. Phelan, "Authority and Flexibility in the Spanish Imperial Bureaucracy," *Administrative Science Quarterly,* 5 (1960–61), 47–65; and for a theoretical analysis of the same subject in sociological terms, see Margali Sarfatti, *Spanish Bureaucratic-Patrimonialism in America* (1966). The underlying ideas of empire are described in John H. Parry, *The Spanish Theory of Empire in the Sixteenth Century* (1940).

On economic history, there are two classic works: Clarence H. Haring, *Trade and Navigation between Spain and the Indies . . .* (1918) and Earl J. Hamilton, *American Treasure* and the Price Revolution in Spain, 1501–1650 (1934). In addition, see Peter J. Bakewell, *Silver Mining and Society in Colonial Mexico . . .* (1971); Woodrow W. Borah, *New Spain's Century of Depression* (*Ibero-Americana, 35,* 1951); and relevant chapters in John Lynch, *Spain under the Hapsburgs* (2 vols., 1964–69).

There are several studies that concentrate on the particular topics emphasized in this chapter. On race relations and population characteristics: essays by Magnus Mörner, Woodrow Borah, and Peter Boyd-Bowman, in Fredi Chiapelli, ed., *First Images of America* (1976), Vol II; Charles Gipson, *The Aztecs under Spanish Rule* (1964); John H. Rowe, "The Incas under Spanish Colonial Institutions," *Hispanic American Historical Review,* 37 (1957), 156–91; Lesley B. Simpson, *The Encomienda in New Spain* (1929); C. E. Marshall, "The Birth of the Mestizo in New Spain," *Hispanic American Historical Review,* 19 (1939), 161–84; James Lockart, *Spanish Peru, 1532–1560, A Colonial Society* (1968) and his *Men of Cajamarca* (1972); Charles Gipson, "The Transformation of the Indian Community in New Spain, 1500–1800," *Journal of World History,* 2 (1955), 581–607; Lyle N. McAlister, "Social Structure and Social Change in New Spain," *Hispanic American Historical Review,* 43 (1963), 349–70; Lewis Hanke, *The Spanish Struggle for Justice in the Conquest of America* (1949); and Silvio Zavala, *New Viewpoints on the Spanish Colonialization of America* (1943). Nathan Wachtel, *The Vision of the Vanquished* (1977) is an attempt to portray the trauma of the Spanish conquest from the Indians' point of view. On the dominance of Peninsular Spaniards in high office and the slow rise of Creoles through purchase of public office, see M. H. Burkholder and D. S. Chandler, *From Impotence to Authority* (1977) and J. H. Parry, *The Sale of Public Office . . .* (1953). For an extended comparison of the Spanish American and the British North American colonial empires, see James Lang, *Conquest and Commerce: Spain and England in the Americas* (1975). The Brazilian comparison is also relevant, in Richard R. Beeman, "Labor Forces and Race Relations: A Comparative View of the Colonization of Brazil and Virginia," *Political Science Quarterly,* 86 (1971), 609–36. Comparisons of slavery in North and South America have been worked out in books by Frank Tannenbaum (*Slave and Citizen*), Carl N. Degler (*Neither Black nor White*), Herbert S. Klein (*Slavery in the Americas*), and most comprehensively by David B. Davis (*The Problem of Slavery in Western Culture*).

The essential writings on England's involvement in geographical discovery and overseas settlement in the sixteenth century are by David B. Quinn. His *Roanoke Voyages, 1584–1590* (2 vols., 1955) contains every document related to that enterprise, a subject he has summarized in an excellent brief account, *Raleigh and the British Empire* (London, 1947). In addition, Quinn has edited the documents of the colonizing efforts of Sir Humphrey Gilbert (2 vols., 1940), written a biography of Gilbert, edited Hakluyt's writings, and discovered the Pilgrims' original plans to settle on the islands in the gulf of the St. Lawrence. Most aspects of his writing are brought together in a volume of his essays, *England and the Discovery of America, 1481–1620* (1974) and summarized in his *North America,* cited above. Samuel E. Morison's *The European Discovery of America: The Northern Voyages, A.D. 500–1600* (1971), covers in the same vivid fashion as *The Southern Voyages* the Cabots' voyages and all of the Elizabethan explorations, and it contains in addition an excellent account of the Roanoke expeditions. A more traditional summary is John B. Brebner, *The Explorers of North America, 1492–1806* (1933). G. R. Elton, *England under the Tudors* (1955), chap. xii is a very brief but useful summary of Elizabethan exploration and expansionism; chap. ix contains a good sketch of the economic background. A. L. Rowse's *The Expansion of Elizabethan England* (1955) and his *Elizabethans and America* (1959) are good reading.

The important role of Ireland in the origins of Elizabethan colonization and the connections between Irish and American settlement are best described in David B. Quinn, *The Elizabethans and the Irish* (1966). Quinn has analyzed the development of English ideas of colonization in the Irish context, particularly the concept of "plantation," in "Sir Thomas Smith (1513–1577) and the Beginnings of English Colonial Theory," *Proceedings of the American Philosophical Society,* 89, no.4 (Dec., 1945), 543–60, and in "Ireland and Sixteenth Century European Expansion," T. D. Williams, ed., *Historical Studies: I . . .* (1958). See also James Muldoon, "The Indian as Irishman," *Essex Institute Historical Collections,* 111 (1975), 267–289; and Nicholas P. Canny, "The Ideology of English Colonization: from Ireland to America," *William and Mary Quarterly,* 3d ser.,* 30 (1973), 575–98.

The masterwork on the financial history of sixteenth- and seventeenth-century English exploration and colonization is W. R. Scott, *The Constitution and Finance of English, Scottish and Irish Joint Stock Companies to 1720* (3 vols., 1912). Theodore K. Rabb, *Enterprise and Empire . . . 1575–1630* (1967), demonstrates statistically the broad social basis of investment in colonization. For the financial background of England's parallel colonization of Ireland in the seventeenth century, see Karl S. Bottigheimer, *English Money and Irish Land* (1971).

*This journal will be referred to hereafter as *Wm. and Mary Q.*

CHAPTER 2

Transplantation

*I*n 1600 the eastern coastal region of mainland North America, some 362,000 square miles from Maine to Georgia and west to the Appalachian Mountains, was largely uncultivated, much of it covered by forests, but it was by no means an unbroken wilderness. A native Indian population grouped in well-organized tribes and sharing approximately the same culture lived fairly sedentary lives, many in semipermanent villages of up to one thousand persons. Concentrated in the fertile coastal plain and the broad river valleys, they communicated readily along an intricate network of riverways and forest trails. They subsisted on a generally nutritious diet of fish and farm crops, principally maize, as well as on game and wild foods, and they rarely suffered famines.

But the Indians' hold upon the land was light. Large areas of the Atlantic woodland region were completely uninhabited (the New England coastal population was decimated by smallpox just before the first English settlers arrived). The average population density for the entire region east of the Appalachians in the early days of European settlement has been estimated by anthropologists at thirty-four persons per hundred square miles. In the most populous region, New England and coastal New York, with an estimated population of 72,000 in 1610, the average density was between four and five persons per square mile; in coastal Virginia the density was roughly two persons per square mile. Nowhere was more than one percent of all the land available for cultivation actually being farmed, and nowhere was possession of land conceived of in European terms. The Indians did not view land as parcels of property owned by individuals, but rather as a common resource that was inherited from ancestors, held in trust by tribal chiefs for future generations, and used by everyone for their daily needs. Nor was warfare thought of in European terms. Deadly personal and intertribal struggles were common, and the treatment of enemies was brutal; but the Indians did not undertake war to annihilate their enemies, to create utter devastation, or to engage in wholesale massacre. Finally, only in one area of the entire Atlantic coastal region were the native inhabitants organized into a political structure effective beyond the tribal level. And even in that one famous and militarily important organization, the Iroquois Confederacy, control over the separate tribes was never secure.

By 1700 this vast coastal region had been transformed, and the foundations of British North American civilization established. The Indians had been eliminated from the seaboard lands—annihilated by the invading peoples in savage local wars and driven back beyond the western fringes of European settlement. The area now contained a quarter of a million transplanted Europeans and their children and grandchildren attempting to re-create the familiar pattern of European life in this undeveloped land. Recruited principally from two of the most dynamic and economically sophisticated nations of Europe, England and the Netherlands, they lived in communities that were parts of a commercial network spread across the entire Atlantic basin and that involved, directly or indirectly, all the nations of western Europe. Within this transplanted population, there were, mainly in Virginia and Maryland, over twenty thousand Africans bound in lifelong, heriditary, and debased servitude.

This transplanted population was organized into eleven provinces loosely controlled by an English government that was only beginning to understand the full importance of the colonial world it had acquired. A small proportion of the settlers, perhaps 8 percent, lived in the five main port towns (Boston, Newport, New York, Philadelphia, and Charleston) through which flowed most of the commerce and communications that linked this world to Europe. The rest lived in village communities numbering a few hundred souls, or on isolated family farms or "plan-

tations" modeled on European agricultural establishments but different from them in fundamental ways.

These tens of thousands of transplanted Europeans and Africans had arrived in no concentrated stream, under no centralized direction, and in no limited span of years. They had arrived, and in 1700 were continuing to arrive, irregularly, in various circumstances, their migration and settlement organized individually or by a variety of private organizations. The history of their migration and resettlement in America forms not one narrative but many. Yet these stories of colonization, for all their variety, follow a common pattern. They begin with high hopes and great plans—often utopian plans—designed by sponsoring individuals and groups whose imaginations

AN INDIAN SORCERER, 1585

Of this drawing by John White (see p. 20), Thomas Hariot, one of the Roanoke settlers of 1585, wrote: "They have sorcerers or jugglers who use strange gestures and whose enchantments often go against the laws of nature. For they are very familiar with devils, from whom they obtain knowledge about their enemies' movements." *(Reproduced by Courtesy of the Trustees of the British Museum)*

The map at far right is a composite reconstruction of all the trails known to have been used by the natives. It appears in Paul A. W. Wallace, *Indian Paths of Pennsylvania* (1965), which contains detailed descriptions of every path on the map.

were fired by the possibilities of starting the world anew, of creating new communities, and, usually, of profiting immensely by doing so. But contact with reality in an undeveloped land brought frustration, the failure of original high hopes, and disillusion. Thereafter, however, there was a creative adaptation by those who survived. This was the persistent pattern of English colonization in the seventeenth century: soaring expectations, disappointment, frustration, disaster or near disaster, and then a slow adjustment to the realities of life on the wilderness edge of the North American continent. Gradually, from this process, there emerged new forms of society made more complex by their superficial similarities to the familiar patterns of European life.

Virginia: Squalor, Struggle, and a New Way of Life

The settlement of Virginia is a classic case of high hopes shattered and a new world rescued from the ruins. It began in 1606 when the English crown chartered two Virginia Companies, one for Plymouth and one for London, incorporating the interests of the two main groups that had already been involved in western exploration and in the planning of American settlements: the gentry and merchants of the west country, and the London merchants to whom Raleigh had transferred his rights. The two groups were given separate though overlapping portions of the North American coast for settlement and instructed to ap-

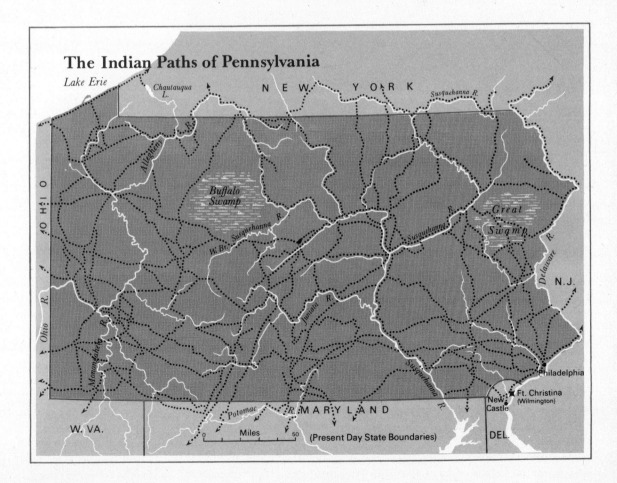

The Indian Paths of Pennsylvania

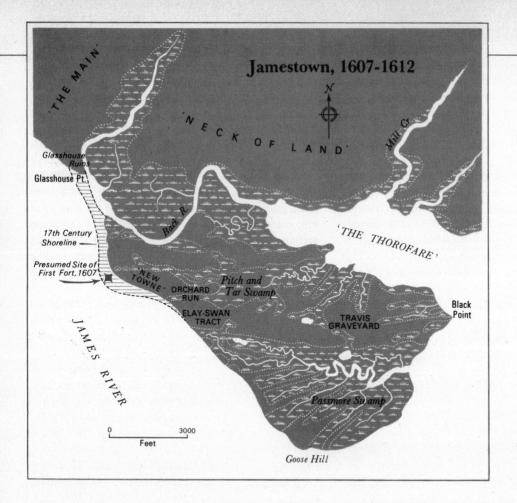

Jamestown, 1607-1612

'THE MAIN'

NECK OF LAND

Mill Cr.

Glasshouse Ruins

Glasshouse Pt.

17th Century Shoreline

Presumed Site of First Fort, 1607

Back R.

'THE THOROFARE'

NEW TOWNE

ORCHARD RUN

Pitch and Tar Swamp

ELAY-SWAN TRACT

TRAVIS GRAVEYARD

Black Point

JAMES RIVER

Passmore Swamp

Goose Hill

0   3000
Feet

point their own resident governments. In 1607 the Plymouth group, assigned the northern area between the Potomac River and the site of the present Bangor, Maine, attempted a settlement near the mouth of the Kennebec River (Sagadahoc, they called it), but everything went wrong. No sign of quick profits appeared, disease and Indian attacks decimated the small company huddled in the tiny fort, and within a year the effort was permanently abandoned.

Jamestown.   The London group, assigned the southern sector, was more ambitious and better financed. Its leaders, under Sir Thomas Smith, England's most powerful merchant, were extraordinarily energetic. In December 1606 they sent out three ships, the *Susan Constant,* the *Godspeed,* and the *Discovery*—tiny vessels scarcely able to hold the 144 people they carried, let alone survive a midwinter crossing of the Atlantic. It was April 1607 before they reached the Chesapeake,

and in May, on a low-lying island thirty miles upstream on the James River and close to the river bank, the 104 survivors of the voyage disembarked. On this spot, so permeated with stagnant water that no home site could be placed farther than 800 feet from malarial swamps, but safe from attack and believed to be close to passages through the continent to the Pacific, the Virginia Company of London established the first permanent British settlement in North America.

The colony survived, but only barely. During the eighteen years of the Virginia Company's existence (1606–24) Jamestown, the main settlement, was a disaster not only for those who lived there but for everyone in any way connected with it. Death was everywhere in the colony. Four out of five of the "planters" of the company years were victims of disease or of Indian attacks. That the company survived at all beyond its first two years was the result of the persistence of its leaders in pursuing delusive dreams of profits and of the financial support they were able to mobilize. Seldom has good money been thrown so extravagantly after bad; seldom have hard-headed businessmen been so mistaken in their expectations of success.

It quickly became clear that in Virginia there was neither easily extractable mineral wealth nor a discoverable passage through the continent, nor a useful native labor force. Hope came to rest on a new idea; that if the colony could be well populated and securely financed, it might produce more ordinary goods—grapes, sugar, tobacco, cotton, dye woods—which could be sold with substantial if not sensational profits in England. Once such a reliable foundation had been laid, the search for more dramatic and lucrative possibilities could then be resumed.

It was to establish the colony on this permanent basis that in 1609 the company in London obtained a revised charter and launched a new effort that gave the moribund colony hope for the future. Without the renewed effort of 1609, Jamestown would have followed Roanoke into oblivion—which it almost did in any case.

By the terms of the new charter, the company, hitherto financed by the contributions only of its incorporators and their personal acquaintances, was recast as a seven-year public joint-stock company. In February 1609 its books were opened for public subscriptions, and an elaborate publicity campaign was launched to stimulate the sale of these shares, especially in the form of pledges of personal service in the colony by prospective settlers. Such "adventurers of person" were given one or more shares of stock depending on their "quality" or special skills, each such share to be worth at least a hundred acres of land when in 1616 the company's total assets would be divided among the stockholders. At the same time, the stockholders were given more authority, and a new form of government was devised for the colony.

Under the first charter the resident government of the colony had consisted of an appointed council that elected its own president. The result had been wrangling among the leaders until Captain John Smith, a shrewd, hard-bitten, and commanding war veteran, seized power. It had been Smith—a romantic but intelligent adventurer—who by forceful leader-

ship had kept the forlorn band from starving to death. He had managed too, by a combination of cleverness and brutality, to keep the neighboring Indian tribes cordial or at least intimidated, and he had made important explorations of the Chesapeake region and surveyed its economic possibilities. The lesson of his leadership was not forgotten. Under the new regulations of 1609 all authority in the colony was to be exercised by an appointed governor who was to be advised, not controlled, by a council and whose authority was to be limited only by the "liberties, franchises, and immunities" due all Englishmen and by the instructions that would be issued to him by the company.

The publicity campaign of 1609 was sensational. Colonization was preached from the pulpits of London, and the price of the company's stock rose on the merchant exchanges. Support of the Virginia Company became, for the moment, a national cause. As a result, in June 1609 the company was able to send out to Virginia a fleet carrying 500 men and 100 women with large quantities of equipment and supplies. But the whole expedition seemed doomed. The vessel that carried among its passengers the newly appointed officers of the colony was blown off course and ended as a wreckage in Bermuda—an episode that is echoed in Shakespeare's *The Tempest*. The 400 leaderless settlers who arrived in Jamestown were exhausted by the long voyage and debilitated by the putrid shipboard food. Disease was already spreading among them when they landed. Too weak at first to work, then deeply discouraged by the sordid prospects before them, shaken out of their normal social discipline and confused by the disordered life around them, they fell into fierce factional struggles, lethargy, and despair, and they failed to plant the crops they would need for the coming year. In the midst of a rich land they starved and, unable to withstand disease, died in droves, miserably. When the fearful winter of 1609–10 was over only some 60 of the settlers were still alive. In May the leaders finally arrived from Bermuda and found a scene of utter desolation. Jamestown's palisades were in ruins, the houses burnt for firewood, the last scraps of food—including cattle and domestic animals—consumed; and people spoke secretly of cannibalism.

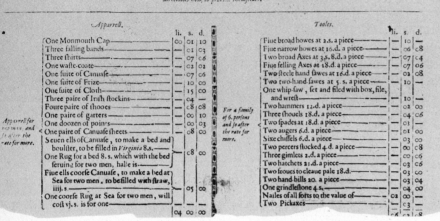

THE INCONVENIENCIES

THAT HAVE HAPPENED TO SOME PERSONS WHICH HAVE TRANSPORTED THEMSELVES

from *England* to *Virginia*, vvithout prouisions necessary to sustaine themselues, hath greatly hindred the Progresse of that noble Plantation: For preuention of the like disorders heereafter, that no man suffer, either through ignorance or misinformation; it is thought requisite to publish this short declaration: wherein is contained a particular of such necessaries, as either priuate families or single persons shall haue cause to furnish themselues with, for their better support at their first landing in Virginia; whereby also greater numbers may receiue in part, directions how to prouide themselues.

Apparrell.	li.	s.	d.
One Monmouth Cap	00	01	10
Three falling bands	—	01	03
Three shirts	—	07	06
One waste-coate	—	02	02
One suite of Canuase	—	07	06
One suite of Frize	—	10	00
One suite of Cloth	—	15	00
Three paire of Irish stockings	—	04	—
Foure paire of shooes	—	08	08
One paire of garters	—	00	10
One doozen of points	—	00	03
One paire of Canuase sheets	—	08	00
Seuen ells of Canuase, to make a bed and boulster, to be filled in Virginia 8.s.			
One Rug for a bed 8. s. which with the bed seruing for two men, halfe is	} 08	00	
Fiue ells coorse Canuase, to make a bed at Sea for two men, to be filled with straw, iiij.s.			
One coorse Rug at Sea for two men, will cost vj.s. is for one	} 05	00	
	04	00	00

Tooles.	li.	s.	d.
Fiue broad howes at 2.s. a piece	—	10	—
Fiue narrow howes at 16.d. a piece	—	06	08
Two broad Axes at 3.s. 8.d. a piece	—	07	04
Fiue felling Axes at 18.d. a piece	—	07	06
Two steele hand sawes at 16.d. a piece	—	02	08
Two two-hand sawes at 5. s. a piece	—	10	—
One whip-saw, set and filed with box, file, and wrest	—	10	—
Two hammers 12.d. a piece	—	02	00
Three shouels 18.d. a piece	—	04	06
Two spades at 18.d. a piece	—	03	—
Two augers 6.d. a piece	—	01	00
Sixe chissels 6.d. a piece	—	03	00
Two percers stocked 4. d. a piece	—	00	08
Three gimlets 2.d. a piece	—	00	06
Two hatchets 21.d. a piece	—	03	06
Two froues to cleaue pale 18.d.	—	03	00
Two hand-bills 20. a piece	—	03	04
One grindlestone 4.s.	—	04	00
Nailes of all sorts to the value of	02	00	—
Two Pickaxes	—	03	—

Apparrell for one man, and so after the rate for more.

For a family of 6. persons and so after the rate for more.

VIRGINIA COMPANY BROADSIDE, 1622
This detailed list of items which emigrants should take to Virginia was published by the company in 1622 in response to an appeal by John Smith that they send only "well provided" workmen in the future. The list, which with the cost of transportation added up to a cost of £20, is said to be "the usual proportion that the Virginia Company does bestow upon their tenants which they sent." The headright system of land grants is explained at the bottom of the sheet. *(Rare Book Division, The New York Public Library)*

The ravaged settlement, still lacking the supplies that had been paid for by the subscription of 1609, seemed hopeless. On June 7, 1610, it was abandoned. The settlers sailed down the James in four small vessels en route to Newfoundland and home.

The Settlement Restored. The colony was saved by a coincidence, which contemporaries attributed to the providence of God. For by chance the departing settlers were met near the mouth of the James by a longboat from a fleet just arrived that carried 300 men and the new governor, Lord De la Warr. The despairing and fearful settlers were ordered back, and De la Warr began the slow process of restoring discipline and confidence, creating a sound agriculture, and establishing profitable relations with the Indians. At home the company, with somewhat despairing vigor, continued its fund-raising and sent further reinforcements of over 600 men with hundreds of domestic animals and shiploads of equipment. Emphasis was thrown now exclusively on the development of Virginia's agricultural, industrial, and commercial possibilities. A satellite settlement was founded at Henrico on the upper James (the site of Richmond), and two others were located at the mouth of the James. Social discipline was imposed harshly by a new code of laws published in 1612 as *Lawes Divine, Morall, and Martiall*, which organized the community into a quasi-military corps committed to compulsory service on common projects and subject to severe penalties for failure to work or to share military obligations.

Thus reinforced and thus disciplined, the colony slowly and painfully became marginally self-sustaining. Humble products—furs, timbers, sassafras, some experimentally produced iron, and beginning in 1614 small quantities of tobacco—began to fill the holds of the returning vessels. But these cargoes, though encouraging, were not profitable enough to stimulate sizable new investments in a company whose expenses were escalating dangerously with the succession of lifesaving supply ships. More funds would have to be raised. Subscribers were dunned for further contributions, unredeemed pledges were pursued in the courts, a public lottery was authorized and launched, more pamphlets were written on Virginia's glowing promise, and once again sermons were preached on the moral obligation to support this *Nova Britannia*. But even all this could not generate the necessary support. To popularize the organization further and to broaden its base, the company obtained a third charter (1612) that again increased the voice of the ordinary shareholders in the company's management. Still, the company's finances remained weak, so weak that in 1616, when the seven-year terminus of the 1609 joint stock was reached, the company was too poor to provide the surveys necessary to make the promised distribution of one hundred acres per share. By then the colony's population, despite all the recent reinforcements, was a mere 350.

One last, great effort had to be made if the company was to be saved and any profit at all realized from the tens of thousands of pounds that had been invested. In 1618 a new group of leaders headed by Sir Edwin Sandys took over control of the company from Smith and initiated the final phase of its history.

The company under Sandys's influence drew up a uniform and generous policy of land inducements for the "ancient planters" and for prospective investors and settlers. The "headright" system was devised whereby anyone who transported a settler to Virginia, including himself, would receive the right to locate, survey, and patent fifty acres of land. More important to the immediate fortunes of the company, shareholders were allowed to pool their landholdings into jointly owned tracts within the Virginia patent, and these, together with certain other large personal estates, were granted minor governmental powers.

The creation of these "private plantations," or "hundreds"—seventy of them were authorized by 1663—began the uncontrolled expansion of settled territory. The lower James valley became dotted with self-contained subcolonies. At the same time, the rigid military discipline of the *Lawes* of 1612 was

MARTIN'S HUNDRED, ONE OF THE "PARTICULAR PLANTATIONS" ALONG THE JAMES RIVER

A modern artist's sketch, based on archaeological excavations. Founded in 1619 by a company of London investors, the plantation of 21,500 acres was located 10 miles east of Jamestown and originally housed over 200 settlers. By 1622 it was reduced by famine and disease to 20 inhabitants and then almost completely destroyed in the Indian massacre. Depicted here: in the foreground, the company's compound, consisting of a longhouse on the right joined to a stable and a storehouse; in the background, the fort to which the settlers fled when attacked. The excavations have unearthed grisly remains of the massacre, including a corpse whose skull had been broken in by a blow with a cleaver or tomahawk and then smashed to pieces by further blows when the body had fallen to the ground. *(By Richard Schlecht. © National Geographic Society)*

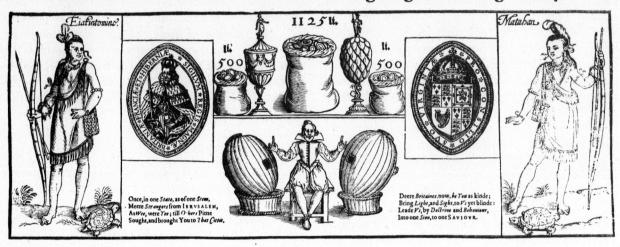

A Declaration for the certaine time of dravving the great standing Lottery.

(Copyright Society of Antiquaries of London)

withdrawn in favor of a more normal system of civil courts bound by rules of common law, and a representative assembly—the first in American history—was provided for. At its first meeting in 1619 the assembly, consisting of the governor and his council sitting together with representatives of each of four projected "boroughs" and of the private jurisdictions, made clear that it would not only express popular grievances, as Parliament had done time out of mind, but also protect Englishmen's fundamental rights as they were known "at home."

In addition to all of this, the company launched a new economic program. Some 4,500 additional settlers were sent out to Virginia and through them an intense effort was undertaken to establish staple crops and products. Expert craftsmen began the manufacture of pitch, tar, ships, and other timber products, as well as iron, salt, and glass; and experiments were made with growing tropical and semi-tropical crops and with producing a salable wine and marketable silk.

It was all a colossal gamble by the energetic entrepreneurs who had taken over the company—and it was hopeless. Simply launching these enterprises drained all of the company's cash, most of it produced by the lottery, which became such a public

nuisance that Parliament stopped it in 1621. Only a miraculous parlaying of small successes into basic security could rescue the company; and with no margin for error, a single disaster would mean the end.

Collapse and Legacy of the Virginia Company. In March 1622 the final disaster struck. The Indians, deprived of their lands, terrorized and brutalized in a hundred ways and fearful of the sudden growth of the English population, fell on the whole string of defenseless farms along the river and killed at least 347 of the inhabitants. Not only was the colony devastated physically, it was utterly demoralized. The settlers, fearful that the slaughter would be renewed and thirsting for vengeance, abandoned their fields at the start of the planting season and took up arms. The result was both a bloody reprisal and a crop failure in the fall that created a near famine. Hundreds who had escaped butchery by the Indians' arrows, knives, and clubs died of sickness in the winter. Two years later, in 1624, when the company's charter was finally annulled and the settlement became a dependency of the crown, there remained alive but 1,275 of the more than 8,500 souls who had ventured to settle in Virginia. In terms of its original purpose, the company was a complete failure.

Yet in a larger sense the Virginia Company had been successful. It had opened the North American mainland to British settlement; it had peopled a small portion of it—though at a fearful cost in wasted lives, both English and Indian. It had experimented with the economic possibilities of the Chesapeake region; and it had left behind a heritage of the rule of law, within the pale, and of the practice, however rudimentary, of colonial self-government. Above all, the company had set the pattern for Virginia's future development.

The general assembly, originally created by the company to rally support among the settlers, continued to exist when Virgina became a royal colony. Governor, council and representatives of the "burghs" (hence "burgesses") met together as a single group until, in the 1660s, the burgesses' interests became distinct enough from those of the council to justify their meeting as a separate body. This central government, plus county courts which were created in 1643, was the basic public authority that developed in this frontier community—a community whose everyday life was an unregulated response to the raw Chesapeake environment. By 1642, when Sir William Berkeley first arrived as governor—a position he would occupy for most of the next thirty-four years—the essential character of life in the first permanent British colony in America was clear.

This was no life of genteel ease on gracious "plantations," and there were no "cavalier" aristocrats. True, in the first years, when the settlement of Virginia was a sensational event promising all sorts of exotic rewards, the leadership of the colony had included intellectuals and sons of the nobility and of prominent churchmen and politicians. But by 1624 this early leadership had disappeared—casualties of the environment, victims of the Indians, disease, and discouragement. The new leaders established themselves by their sheer capacity to survive on rough, half-cleared tobacco farms and to produce material gains from the raw wilderness. Former servants, yeoman farmers, and adventurers of little social status or wealth, they lacked the attributes of social authority, but by brute labor and shrewd

manipulation they managed to prosper.

The leaders of Virginia in the generation after the company was dissolved were tough, unsentimental, quick-tempered, crudely ambitious men concerned with profits wrung from the soil and increased landholding, not the grace of life. They roared curses, drank exuberantly, and gambled extravagantly, sometimes betting their servants when other commodities were lacking. They asserted their interests fiercely. They wanted an aggressive expansion of settlement and trading enterprise and unrestricted access to land no matter what objections there might be from the Indians, and they sought from such governmental agencies as existed the legal endorsement of their hard-won acquisitions. They claimed large acreage; but it was cleared land that counted, and of that there was precious little for anyone. Because labor was in critically short supply, every effort was made to entice over from England workers whose labor could be counted on for periods specified in indentures (bonds of servitude). But though an average of 1,500 indentured servants arrived in the Chesapeake annually through most of the seventeenth century their terms of bonded service were short (normally four years) and most of them were quickly added to the general population of free tobacco farmers seeking to expand production and competing for hired labor.

Black "slave" labor (the meaning of the term was at first ambiguous) was known in Virginia as early as 1619. But black slaves were more expensive, in the short run at least, than white servants, and their absolute foreignness—in appearance, behavior, language, and skills—offended the English, who were indiscriminately suspicious of foreigners. A black labor force came into being only gradually. In 1640, only 150 blacks were reported in Virginia (not all of them slaves); in 1650, 300; in 1680, 3000; and in 1704, when the white population may have reached 75,600, there were roughly 10,000 blacks. And as the number of black laborers rose and as their importance to the developing economy became clear, a new status of bondage, "chattel slavery," took shape, something unknown hitherto in English law. As servitude for whites became progressively more limited in duration and less rigorous in demands, the laws began to specify that blacks would serve for life; that their offspring would automatically become the property of their masters; that conversion to Christianity would not lead to freedom; that nothing but discretion could limit the severity of penalties imposed upon them; that racially mixed marriages were forbidden; and finally that a "slave" was no longer, as heretofore, simply a servant of lowest condition but something absolutely different in the eyes of the law, a form of property to be bought and sold, a status applicable only and necessarily to blacks and to their descendants to the ultimate degree.

Such were the main provisions of the "slave codes" so devastating in their consequences for the whole of American history. The codes originated in the latter half of the seventeenth century in response to an acute need for labor, an elemental fear of foreignness, and an insensitivity to cruelty remarkable even for that callous age. But however peculiar the conditions that gave rise to these codes, once devised they became a fundamental part of the legal fabric of community life, and they intensified and perpetuated the racial fears and hostilities that had helped shape them. By 1700 it was becoming clear, to some at least, that chattel slavery, rising like some terrible germ-laden cloud, was poisoning the very soil and roots of human relations.

The Pilgrims' "Sweet Communion"

It is difficult, perhaps impossible, for twentieth-century Americans fully to recapture the state of mind of those who led the settlement of New England. The Puritans and Pilgrims are too easily caricatured: the former as God-intoxicated demons of self-righteousness or as intellectual gymnasts cogitating day and night on exquisite subtleties of theology; the Pilgrims as altogether simple Christians spotless in their uncompromising Biblicism. But as with most caricatures there is truth behind the obvious distortions. Both groups were products of the attempted reformation of the Elizabethan Church of England and of the desire for a more direct experience of God

than the church allowed. But otherwise they were very different. Their aims, their styles, their accomplishments were different, and their contributions to American life lie in altogether different spheres.

The Pilgrims were one of a series of radical "separatist" groups that first appeared in England in the 1570s. Loyal to the English state, they were determined to break altogether with the too ritualistic, too highly institutionalized, still too Catholic, Church of England. They formed their own pure and primitive churches—mere cells, conventicles, stripped bare of all ritual, unaffiliated with each other except for shared aspirations, and composed exclusively of true believers gathered voluntarily into covenanted brotherhoods. Defiant of persecution and without hope of forcing their views upon the world at large, yet never questioning the authority of the civil state, these fugitive groups of religious radicals were naturally drawn to the physical margins of the English world, where in isolation they might find peace to worship as they chose and yet still enjoy the protection of the English state.

The Separatists. One such conventicle of pious, humble, and stubborn believers, gathered in the village of Scrooby in Nottinghamshire, became famous as the Pilgrim Fathers. They had no desire to settle in America. To escape the corrupting English world, they fled first to Amsterdam, then to Leyden. But there was no escape, even in that tolerant Dutch university town. Their children, not steeled as they themselves had been in the fires of persecution, were attracted by the town's temptations, and would be lost to the true faith, the Pilgrims feared, if nothing were done. They would have to move again, to a less comfortable, more remote site, better suited to the establishment of a pure church of Christ. They considered various alternatives—elsewhere in the Netherlands, on the north coast of South America, on the islands in the gulf of the St. Lawrence River, which they had already investigated. Finally they settled on Virginia, with whose managers they had several contacts and which was then offering to groups such as theirs the semiautonomy of private plantations. By 1619 they had obtained approval from the Vir-

LEYDEN, IN THE NETHERLANDS,
TO WHICH THE PILGRIMS FLED
IN 1609
"A fair and beautiful city,"
Bradford wrote, where the
Pilgrims "grew in knowledge
and other gifts and graces of
the spirit of God" but where
their children were "drawn
away by evil examples into
extravagant and dangerous
courses ... so that they saw
their posterity would be in
danger to degenerate and be
corrupted." (Rare Book Division, The New York Public
Library)

ginia Company to settle within its jurisdiction, a promise from the crown not to molest them in America, and financial help from an English investment group headed by one Thomas Weston. After many hesitations the Separatists willing to go to America sold their property to purchase shares in the joint undertaking with Weston, each planter's labor being reckoned as a single share of stock.

In July 1620, 35 of the 238 members of the Leyden congregation took leave of their brethren in a scene so poignant, so prayerful and tearful, that even casual Dutch onlookers wept. They sailed to Southampton on their own small vessel, the *Speedwell,* to join an English contingent of Separatists and the 180-ton *Mayflower,* which had been rented for them by the merchants. After two false starts that led them to abandon the unseaworthy *Speedwell* and that discouraged many from completing the voyage, the remaining Pilgrims and the laborers hired by the merchants crowded into the *Mayflower,* packed high with furniture, equipment, food, and animals, and on September 16 they set sail for Virginia.

There were 101 passengers in all, perhaps 87 of them Separatists or members of Separatist families. Outwardly they fared well on the overcrowded vessel: only one passenger died on the voyage, and two children were born on board. But the voyage lasted over nine weeks, and by the time Cape Cod was sighted (November 9) and they debarked at Provincetown at the tip of the cape (November 11), the entire party, crew and passengers, was ridden with disease, primarily scurvy, and so weakened by malnutrition that they were incapable of withstanding attacks of ordinary illnesses in the months that followed. The weather during this first winter in Plymouth, 1620–21, was quite mild for New England, but it proved to be one of the worst "starving times" recorded anywhere in British America. When spring at last arrived, half of those who had crossed on the *Mayflower* were dead.

They had settled, of course, in New England, though they carried with them a title to land in Virginia. But when they finally landed at Provincetown and "fell upon their knees and blessed the God of Heaven who had brought them over the vast and furious ocean and delivered them from all the perils and miseries thereof," they were determined to voyage no more and to ignore the legal problems that might arise. An exploring party found Plymouth Harbor on December 11, and there on a slope rising westward from the shore, probably the site of an abandoned Indian cornfield, they built the simple village of their desires.

Plymouth Plantation. Plymouth's history up to 1691, when it was absorbed into the more powerful Massachusetts Bay Colony, is a tale of modest triumphs—and a tale too of the defeat of human aspirations by the ravages of time, growth, and decay. All of it—the trials, the triumphs, and defeats—is recorded in Governor William Bradford's magnificent history, *Of Plymouth Plantation,* which he began in 1630 with a review of the earlier years and continued as a documentary journal and commentary covering the next sixteen years. It is one of the most moving and eloquent documents in the entire literature of American history. Its vivid Elizabethan imagery and its biblical cadences blend perfectly to express Bradford's hopes and struggles and finally his sense of tragedy and defeat.

Of the blessings he recorded, one was always paramount. At long last the Pilgrims were free, Bradford wrote, "to see, and with much comfort to enjoy, the blessed fruits of their sweet communion." The church was theirs, unfettered, unintimidated, and responsive to their ultimate desires. But there were troubles from the start. The first and most pressing was financial. For several years they failed as businessmen, and the merchants at home, bickering among themselves and fearful of mounting costs if they continued to resupply the settlers, sold out or simply abandoned their investments. By 1626 the company was bankrupt, but the Pilgrims, more honest than shrewd, continued to honor their original obligations. They struggled for years to squeeze enough profit from fur trading, fishing, and the sale of lumber, Indian corn, and wampum to pay off the original debts. By the time they succeeded, in 1648, many of the founders were dead.

More threatening than debts were the scattering

THE PLYMOUTH PLANTATION
Leyden Street, Plymouth, as it appears in the modern restoration. "The houses," a visitor wrote in 1628, "are constructed of clapboards, with gardens also enclosed behind and at the sides with clapboards, so that the houses and courtyards are arranged in very good order." *(Plimoth Plantation)*

of settlement and the dissipation of purpose which grew with the passage of years. A series of vessels had followed the *Mayflower* to Plymouth, and the population had risen steadily. By 1657, the year of Bradford's death, there were over 1,360 inhabitants. Plymouth no longer a single covenanted community but a colony of eleven towns that could not be enclosed within a single purpose, infused with a single spirit. Even if the gentle leaders had sought to impose discipline and control, they would have lacked the legal means to do so. Their original patent from the Virginia Company was worthless in New England, and a patent they received in 1621 from the Council for New England (which had taken over the legal rights of the old Virginia Company of Plymouth) was simply a vague land grant and an equally vague license to establish a local government. The government evolved slowly and uncertainly and was never sanctioned by charter or the approval of the crown.

The starting point was the Mayflower Compact, a document devised to control the restless noncommunicants while the Pilgrims were still at sea. It was simply an agreement—signed, on November 21, 1620, by 41 Pilgrims, hired laborers, and sailors—to obey whatever laws and officers the community would create. The signing of the Mayflower Compact in the cabin of the rocking vessel was a dramatic event. But the document was no constitution. The unsanctioned government that developed in Plymouth was primitive in organization. The freemen simply came together annually to choose a governor (Bradford was elected thirty times) and a group of assistants to support him; otherwise these electors met only on extraordinary occasions when called together by the governor.

So feeble was the colony's political structure, so weak the second and third generations' loyalty to Plymouth, that when the whole region was included within the boundaries of Massachusetts in the Bay Colony's second charter of 1691, the Pilgrims' colony slipped without a ripple into the larger jurisdiction. By then the erosion in the original purposes and piety was such that those who had inherited the leadership from Bradford could only rejoice that the government would at least continue to be in the hands of saints,

EDWARD WINSLOW, 1651

Winslow, the only Pilgrim of whom a portrait is known, was one of the better educated and more worldly wise of the group. His career illustrates the cosmopolitanism of the first generation of settlers in British America (see p. 113). His long years of service as Plymouth's chief business agent, Indian negotiator, and propagandist brought him often to England where in 1654 Cromwell engaged him on a diplomatic mission and then appointed him to head the expedition that seized Jamaica from the Spanish. Governor of Plymouth for three years, governor's assistant for over 20 years, he was largely responsible for setting up Plymouth's successful Indian trade and for exploring the adjacent territories. *(Courtesy, Plimoth Plantation)*

even if they were not saints of the Separatists' own persuasion.

But the essential destruction of the founders' utopia had taken place years before. Bradford's "sweet communion" in its fullest form had rested on deeply shared aspirations and on isolation from the corruptions of the changing world. When town begat town and the churches multiplied, and when the ordinary world was created within Plymouth itself by strangers and by children who failed to recapture their parents' piety, the Pilgrims' hopes were shattered.

Lacking all instinct for power, rejecting the world rather than seeking to reform it, and tolerant of the errors of others in their humble pursuit of personal piety, the Pilgrims were incapable of perpetuating the community they built, and their impact on American life was confined to the realm of ideals. For always, in the years that have followed the founding of their fragile utopia in Plymouth, the example of their selfless pursuit of an unattainable ideal and their rejection of the satisfactions of wealth, power, comfort, and self-glory in favor of deeper, spiritual rewards have been part of America's collective memory and part of its essential culture. But this model of life, though emulated in various ways at every stage of American history, has never been dominant. Far more vital in American culture has been the very different legacy of the Puritans.

The Puritans: Power in the Service of God

The Puritans shared with the Pilgrims a desire for a direct experience of religion free from the encumbrances of an elaborate church. They shared also certain theological views as well as a stubborn moral dignity.* But the Puritans, in America as in England, were proud and driving, and as demanding of themselves as they were of the world about them. They sought power—not for its own sake, to be sure, but for Christian purposes; and they sought it relentlessly, intolerantly, and successfully.

The decisions that led to this formative development in American history were made in stages within a hectic three-year period. In 1628 a group of around ninety active nonconformists, deeply troubled by the repressive tendencies of both church and state in England and well aware of the value of overseas settlements as refuges for people of their persuasion, came

*On Puritanism as a religious movement, see Chapter 3, pages 87–91.

together as the New England Company to obtain a land patent enclosing most of the present-day Massachusetts and New Hampshire. They sent out an advance party to rebuild a settlement on Cape Ann, north of Boston, that had recently been abandoned by a Puritan fishing company, but their anxieties continued to mount. Increasingly concerned about the future of nonconformity, they sought and obtained in 1629 a crown charter that created the Massachusetts Bay Company. This elaborate document, empowering them not only to trade and settle within the boundaries of their earlier land patent but "to govern and rule all His Majesty's subjects that reside within the limits of our plantation," was a legal bulwark behind which a powerful social movement could organize and develop.

The new corporation's efficiency was quickly demonstrated. Within weeks of its creation it sent off five vessels bearing more than two hundred settlers to join the earlier group then living in thatched cottages on the shores of Cape Ann. But far greater enterprises were stirring beneath the surface of the Massachusetts Bay Company. In the spring and summer of 1629 political and ecclesiastical conditions in England continued to worsen for critics of the Church of England, and in addition the Puritans learned of the defeat of Protestantism throughout Europe in the international war then raging. Moreover, the king dissolved Parliament, and with it went the hope of political remedies. On top of all of this, an economic depression created great distress in just the districts most prone to religious dissent.

The Great Migration. It was in this atmosphere of social, political, and economic panic in the spring and summer of 1629 that men of experience, ability, and established position turned their thoughts not merely to creating a refuge for people of their persuasion but to their own personal escape from England to some world apart, some fresh, uncorrupted realm. Within six months of the creation of the Massachusetts Bay Company a coalition of merchants, landed gentlemen, lawyers, and minor officials alienated from their own society, turned to the new Massachusetts Bay corporation and found in it a means of escape and of serving their own, and Puritanism's, higher purpose.

Only some of this gathering group of substantial Englishmen had been directly involved in the company before. Chief among the newcomers was John Winthrop, an intensely pious, well-connected forty-one-year-old Puritan landowner and attorney recently dismissed from his government position. Faced suddenly with unemployment and with the prospect of continuing harassment, and convinced that England was being overwhelmed by corruption, he came to see a providential significance in the work of the Massachusetts Bay Company. He was no mild and passive Pilgrim. Winthrop and the other leaders of the Massachusetts Bay Company were men of affairs, self-confident, energetic, and used to exercising authority. But their love of action in the ordinary world was disciplined by an equally powerful religious commitment. They loved the everyday world, but they loved it, as they liked to say, "with weaned affection." *In* the world but not *of* the world, they sought not to abandon the Church of England but to seize it, purge it of its corruptions, and reconstruct it in the image of a pure and unadorned Christianity, if not in England then in New England. And far from withdrawing from society, they sought to seize that too and transform it—to create, by persuasion if possible, by force if force were necessary and available to them, a society likely to gain God's approval. They were separatists only with respect to the English state, and this they made clear in the conclusion they reached at a momentous meeting in Cambridge late in August of 1629.

The twelve leaders who assembled secretly in Cambridge pledged themselves "ready in our persons" to join the migration to New England, taking with them their families and whatever provisions they could gather, and "to inhabit and continue in New England" —*provided* that the company officially transfer itself, its charter and government, to the colony. Three days later the corporation concurred, in effect voting itself out of business as a commercial organization and transforming itself into a rudimentary civil government. In October Winthrop was elected governor, and five months later, in March 1630, the great Puritan migration began. Before the year was out a fleet of seventeen ships had borne well over 1,000 settlers to Massachusetts. In all, during the years of the Puritan exodus, 1630–43, some two hundred

GOVERNOR JOHN WINTHROP
The leader of Puritan New England in its heroic age, a devout, able, and strong-willed leader, Winthrop directed his energies and talents to creating a pure version of the Church of England and a society directed to God's will. The set jaw, full but tightly drawn lips, and raised brows suggest intense self-discipline and resolution. *(American Antiquarian Society)*

vessels transported over 20,000 Englishmen to the Bay Colony.

No one community could contain them all. The original settlement, Salem on Cape Ann, became a staging area for groups moving south along the coast. First Charlestown, then Boston became the central settlement. From Boston groups moved on quickly to settle a ring of satellite towns immediately around the bay. Subsequently others founded a secondary ring of communities—Haverhill, Concord, Sudbury—some twenty or thirty miles inland. Finally, beginning in 1636, the migrating subgroups of the Puritan exodus broke contact altogether with the central settlement in Boston by establishing an independent cluster of towns—Hartford, Wethersfield, Windsor—on the Connecticut River over one hundred miles from Boston

Bay. By banding together politically, these towns became the colony of Connecticut, which formed its own government in 1639 and was chartered by the crown in 1662.

Church and Community. The dispersal of the Puritans into towns all over New England was remarkable for its speed; it was remarkable even more for the degree to which it carried forward the purposes of the Puritans. The dispersal of the colonists was no random scattering of people but a well-organized multiplication of church societies that became political bodies and land corporations as soon as they were founded. Groups that wished to establish towns sought the approval of the colony's legislature, the General Court. When the court's franchise was granted, it carried with it not only the legal right to create a limited governmental jurisdiction—a town—and to send representatives to the General Court; it also carried authority over a large parcel of land—a township—to be divided among the original heads of households in proportion to wealth or status. These town founders consequently not only owned their own individual shares of land but also, collectively, controlled the undistributed land as well. The same men, since they were the founding members of their covenanted church, controlled too the vital area of religion, and they constituted also the initial voting membership of the town's political meeting that regulated the mundane affairs of village life. Since all of these powers fell to the founders and not automatically to others who later joined the villages, these town fathers and their direct heirs controlled full participation in all the main spheres of life.

Their control was not resented, in the early years at least. Later there would be opposition and factionalism as newcomers found their way into these small farming villages and as the Puritans' fierce passion to reform the world faded into mere repressive austerity. But while the fires of the original faith still burned brightly and Puritanism was still a way of embracing the world, not of rejecting it, these oligarchic yet democratic villages remained cohesive bodies, closely bound into the larger Bible commonwealth.

The unity of the Massachusetts colony as a whole is remarkable when one considers the rapid and wide dispersal of the settlers. It reflects not only a widespread commitment to a particular way of life and to certain beliefs but also the founders' gift for self-government and their refusal to tolerate dissent.

The Massachusetts charter, being the articles of incorporation of a commercial organization, contained, of course, no provision for an independent civil government. It did, however, create the equivalent of a self-governing corporate borough, and the government that developed in Massachusetts emerged along the lines of that model. In John Winthrop the company, now the colony, had a duly elected governor; in the seven or eight available members of the company's board of directors there was a rudimentary council of magistrates, or governor's assistants; and in the adult male heads of households there were the "freemen," or voters, necessary to complete the membership of the transformed General Court. Soon the perpetuation of this government was provided for and basic rules laid down. In 1632 the freemen were given the power to choose not only the assistants but the governor and deputy governor as well. In 1634 it was agreed that taxes could be levied on the towns only by vote of the entire General Court and that in the future the entire body of freemen need not assembly in person for General Court meetings but could select representatives instead. These representatives, two or three from each town, were empowered to make laws, grant land, levy taxes, and transact whatever other business might come before the General Court.

Thus a civil government evolved from the organization of a commercial corporation. It was quickly completed. Since the representatives, or deputies, as they were commonly called, met together with the assistants or magistrates, they could conclude no business without the magistrates' agreement and hence had no distinct voice of their own and no impulse to develop their own rules and procedures. In 1644 this problem was overcome. In a sensational court case that pitted popular emotions against strict legality, the views of the more numerous representatives were vetoed by the minority votes of the mag-

THE OATH OF A FREE-MAN

I A.B. being by Gods Providence an Inhabitant and FREEMAN within the Iurisdiction of this Commonwealth; doe freely acknowledge myselfe to be subject to the Government thereof.

AND therefore doe here sweare by the Great and Dreadful NAME of the Everliving GOD, that I will be true and faithfull to the same, and will accordingly yield assistance & support thereunto with my person and estate as in equity I am bound; and will also truly endeavour to maintaine & preserve all the liberties & priviledges thereof, submitting myselfe to the wholesome Lawes & Orders made and established by the same. *** AND further that I will not Plot or practise any evill against it, or consent to any that shall so doe: but will timely discover and reveal the same to lawfull authority now here established, for the speedy preventing thereof.

MOREOVER I doe solemnly bind myselfe in the sight of GOD, that when I shall be called to give my voyce touching any such matter of this State in which FREEMEN are to deale *** I will give my vote and suffrage as I shall judge in mine own conscience may best conduce and tend to the publicke weale of the body without respect of person or favour of any man.
So help me GOD in the LORD IESVS CHRIST.

Printed at Cambridge in New England:
by Order of the Generall Courte:
Moneth the First - 1639

(American Antiquarian Society)

istrates. In the furor that resulted the two groups drew apart, permanently as it proved, into two separate houses, each capable of expressing itself independently of the other, though the agreement of both was still needed for legislative enactments. The lower house thereupon organized itself separately, electing a Speaker and working out parliamentary rules, a committee system, and other procedures modeled on those of the English House of Commons.

During the same years a court system was devised, largely copied from the local court system of England, and a code of laws agreed on. *The Lawes and Libertyes* of 1647 expressed not only the English common law in terms appropriate for life in the wilderness but also the Puritans' devotion to precepts of the Bible.

Puritan Control and Dissent. For despite all the involvements in such secular pursuits as clearing the wilderness and organizing towns, courts, and a general government, and despite the swift development of coastal and transatlantic commerce that also took place in these years, Massachusetts remained a Bible commonwealth. The legal device that secured the Puritan domination was not the clergy's control of government, for the clergy did not hold public office, but the restriction of the colony's electorate to the members of the church, a step that was taken in 1631. As a result of this measure, no matter how the population within the towns might change, or how the sources of immigration might shift, or how the people at large might drift away from the church, the central government of the colony would continue to represent primarily those loyal to the original Puritan purposes.

This arrangement was not challenged, for it expressed a broad consensus in the founding generation. The opposition to the Puritan establishment that did arise in these early years challenged not the basic religious character of the Puritan colony but specific points of doctrine; it flowed not from a deficiency of religious commitment but from an excess. Such opponents of the Puritan regime as Anne Hutchinson and Roger Williams were even more fanatical in their pursuit of religious truth, more relentless in their theology, more single-minded in their beliefs than the Puritan leaders themselves. In one way or another they went to extremes on issues the leaders felt obliged to keep in delicate balance.

Anne Hutchinson—passionate and inflexible in her convictions, brilliant in argument—was convinced that "justification," that is, the infusion of divine grace, the mysterious transfiguration by which sinful man becomes elect of God, was all that essentially mattered; "sanctification," that is, moral conduct, Christian behavior, piety, even prayer, was for her the mere husk of religion. And so, rejecting "works," rejecting in the end all ordinary worldly discipline and responsibility, and standing only for the ravishment of the soul by God, she gathered around her a band of followers, a church within a church, and thereby challenged the Puritan establishment to de-

RICHARD MATHER

Founder of a virtual dynasty of New England preachers and intellectuals, Mather is shown here in a woodcut by John Foster (c. 1670), which is probably the first print made in British America. Mather preached an austere Calvinism in Massachusetts for 34 years. (*American Antiquarian Society.*) In the background, notes taken on sermons heard in Boston by a spiritually tormented merchant, Robert Keayne. Convicted of overcharging and hence of greed and unchristian behavior, Keayne fell into an agony of protest and self-recrimination, which he expressed in an extraordinary fifty-thousand-word will. (*Massachusetts Historical Society*) stroy her or destroy itself by tolerating her. But she could not be disposed of easily. In 1637 when the General Court tried her, it brought in a battery of ministers to assist in the prosecution, but in the dramatic trial that resulted, Anne Hutchinson held them off with astonishing skill, defending herself learnedly and wittily. But at last, in exhaustion and perhaps also in exaltation, she blurted out defiantly that her knowledge of God was "an immediate revelation," free of all institutions, independent of all earthly authority. This was the ultimate heresy, condemned as "antinomianism," an arrogance of such cosmic dimensions that the court could safely and in good conscience banish her from the colony and silence her followers thereafter.

Roger Williams was more learned than Anne Hutchinson and more respectable, but he was at least as "divinely mad" as she and as passionate in his beliefs. He could never accommodate himself to the halfway reforms of the nonseparating Puritan churches and to the colony's peculiar constitutional foundation. Not only did he denounce the validity of the colony's charter, but from his Salem pulpit he challenged the mingling of church and state that was the essence of the Bible commonwealth. Civil officers, he insisted, should have power only over the civil affairs of men, over their outward state and behavior, not over matters of conscience and religion. While it would only be in later years in England and in banishment in Rhode Island that Roger Williams would develop the doctrine of religious toleration for which he would become famous, he was clearly heading in that direction, and the mere approach to such a position was intolerable to the rulers of the colony. Beyond all of that, he condemned the colony's churches for their refusal to break altogether with the polluted Church of England. Church *reform* was not enough he insisted; purification was not enough. *Perfection* was the goal—a church of absolute purity, more "primitive" even than the church of the Separatists in Plymouth. Such a church was not to be had in Massachusetts. The colony's leaders regretfully—for Williams was a fine intellect and even to the Puritans a true Christian in his way—attempted to correct this wayward saint, then banished him too from the colony.

Later there would be other deviants from the Puritan way, other challengers, who were either silenced or ejected from the colony. Some of these dissidents moved south to Narragansett Bay where Roger Williams, certain followers of Anne Hutchinson, a few Quakers, and others unacceptable to Massachusetts were attempting to form communities in which they would be completely free to pursue their own special version of truth. But the scattered Narragansett villages were torn by discord; they splintered and regrouped repeatedly, until finally by the late 1640s four or five fairly stable communities emerged. Although the prosperous merchants who founded and dominated the island town of Newport were the most worldly of the Rhode Islanders, it was Roger Williams, the founder of Providence at the head of the bay, who recognized that only confederation of the towns and legal authorization from England would preserve the freedom of these

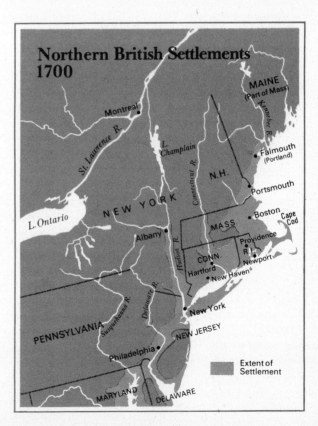

Northern British Settlements 1700

tiny refugee settlements. And it was he who secured the refugee towns' independence by extracting from the English government first, in 1644, a patent creating "The Incorporation of Providence Plantations," and then, in 1663, a crown charter that legalized the permanent existence of the colony of Rhode Island.

Connecticut and Rhode Island were both products of the Massachusetts Bay Colony—the one a reproduction of the Puritans' culture, the other a rejection of it. Together, the central Puritan colony and its satellites to the west, south, and in scatterings north, formed the most vigorous transplanation of English life anywhere in the Western Hemisphere. At the heart of Puritan New England lay the determination to wipe out the corruptions of an old and oppressive world and create a new Jerusalem, in which power would not be rejected or despised but mobilized, and devoted to the service of the Lord.

A Catholic Refuge on the Chesapeake

How pervasive religion was in the establishment of British overseas settlements and how greatly America profited by England's willingness to allow its empire to develop as a refuge for religious minorities can be seen with special clarity in the founding of Maryland.

The refugee community in this case was not radical Protestant but Roman Catholic, more obnoxious to the Church of England than Protestant extremists. The dynamic force was a single family, the Calverts, ennobled in 1625 as the Lords Baltimore. This family, well connected with the rulers of England and only recently converted to Catholicism, had long been involved in overseas enterprises. In 1628–29 the first Lord Baltimore had traveled to the Chesapeake to investigate a possible asylum for refugee Catholics. Upon his return to England he had set in motion the elaborate process of obtaining a separate royal charter for a colony that would be safe for his co-religionists, and although he died just as the charter was being approved, his project was carried through, and his ambitions fulfilled, by his twenty-six-year-old son, Cecilius Calvert, the second Lord Baltimore.

The key to much of what happened subsequently lies in the terms of the remarkable charter that was issued to the young Lord Baltimore in 1632 and in the use that the Calvert family made of the powers it bestowed. The charter granted Lord Baltimore the entire territory from the Potomac River north to the latitude of Philadelphia and west hundreds of miles to the Appalachian sources of the Potomac. The charter also gave Baltimore extensive governmental powers: the government was his to shape as he chose, and he was empowered to create a system of feudal relationships through land grants if that archaic practice appealed to him.

Significantly, it did. For in this case as in so many others the barrenness of America, its openness, challenged men's imagination and led them to project their desires and their fantasies in plans for new communities.

Toleration and Proprietary Plans. Success came quickly at first. The young Lord Baltimore, who was the proprietor of Maryland until his death in 1675, sent his brother Leonard to the colony as governor with detailed instructions on the management of the colony. Maryland, the proprietor made clear, was to be a Catholic refuge, but Catholics, Baltimore knew, could survive in the English world only as a tolerated minority, and they were therefore in no position to impose their will on others. Furthermore, he knew that the success of the colony would depend on the flow of immigrants into the area, and most of these prospective settlers would necessarily be Protestants. At the very start, therefore, Baltimore prohibited discrimination of any sort against Protestants. He also forbade Catholics from engaging in public controversies on religion, and ordered them to make every effort to live at peace not only with the colony's neighbors in Virginia but with the Puritans and Dutch to the north.

This much was necessary and realistic. Fantasy entered Lord Baltimore's thinking only as he contemplated his personal proprietorship of the land

and his extensive powers of government. How was one to use this princely domain and these extensive powers? What model could there be for such a vast personal estate and such extraordinary private authority? Feudalism, and its economic foundations in manorialism, provided a model of sorts for the Calverts to follow. Their provisions for land distribution, courts, and governance were the result of an effort to create some rough semblance of a feudal-manorial system. They designed proprietary manors of 6,000 acres complete with private courts, which were reserved to the blood relations of the Lord Proprietor, and ordinary manors limited to 3,000 acres. It was expected that all of these manors would be populated by tenants, whose labor would produce the rents and dues necessary to support the lords. The rest of the population would be landowning farmers and their dependents in various statuses, all appropriately submissive to the domination of the provincial nobility. It was a rational but hopelessly unrealistic design. Yet though the reality proved to be quite different from the blueprint, these original plans helped shape the community that in fact developed in Maryland.

In 1632 the Calverts set up a recruiting office for settlers on the outskirts of London, advertised their colony (though not their religion) widely, and were able to induce over two hundred settlers to join the first expedition. The prospective settlers arrived in the Chesapeake in March 1634, in good time for the year's planting and well equipped to survive the inevitable rigors of the first winter in a new colony. The Calverts located their main settlement, which they called St. Mary's, on a creek just north of the Potomac River. There they constructed a palisaded fort similar to that of early Jamestown. After the first winter in the fort, when it became clear that the colony would have supplies sufficient for its survival and that the neighboring Indians were friendly, the distribution of land began and the inevitable dispersal of population got under way.

Distribution of Land.   As planned, the proprietor's relatives were given title to 6,000-acre tracts, and lesser manors were distributed to others, together with rights to private courts and other quasi-feudal

CECILIUS CALVERT, 2D LORD BALTIMORE (1605–1675)
Baltimore, who devoted his life to developing the colony that his father had planned, was never able to visit Maryland himself, governing instead through deputies. He is pictured here with his grandson, who had been born in Maryland and died at the age of 14, holding a "new map of Maryland" ("Nova Terrae-Mariae Tabula") dated 1635 and attended by a handsomely dressed black servant. The boy's father, Charles, governor since 1661, succeeded as proprietor and 3rd Lord Baltimore upon Cecilius' death in 1675. *(Enoch Pratt Free Library. Photograph from the Maryland Historical Society)*

privileges. The manorial lords, in turn, as well as the proprietor himself, began selling parcels of land to those who could afford to pay for them and renting property to others. They reserved farms for their own use—"demesne" farms— and all the undivided property. But none of the manorial arrangements survived. The settlement of the countryside was in fact shaped by forces that were almost indistinguishable from those that had determined the development of Virginia.

As in Virginia, the primary cash crop in Maryland was tobacco, and the central difficulty in expanding production was similarly the shortage of labor. Every effort was made to stimulate the importation of laborers for the farms that spread out from several centers on the mainland and on the eastern shore of Chesapeake Bay. A series of laws required prospective manor lords to import at first five workers, then ten, then twenty. Virginia's headright system was introduced in Maryland in 1640, and independent householders who settled in the colony were given special land grants for themselves and the members of their families. The population rose rapidly, partly because migration continued and partly because the availability of fresh tidewater land attracted farmers from Virginia and other neighboring areas. By 1660 the population had probably reached 8,000 and was beginning to grow by natural increase. By 1670 it had grown to over 13,000, and a contemporary map identified 823 cultivated farms in the colony, scattered through a strip of settled territory along the lower shores of Cheaspeake Bay and the banks of the major rivers.

By then, forty years after the initial settlement, it was clear that the Calverts had created something quite different from a feudal–manorial regime. Maryland was dominated by a landholding oligarchy with an almost monopolistic control of public offices, set off from the bulk of the population by religion as well as by wealth and power.

In the earliest years the grants of large estates had meant little since the labor shortage allowed only small segments of these properties to be cultivated. As a result the terms of servitude were generous and freed servants acquired land and estab-

lished themselves as independent farmers with ease. But property values rose as the more fertile and accessible land came under cultivation and as a growing population competed more intensely for the best of the undistributed land. Freed servants found it more difficult to establish themselves in independent households and tended increasingly to serve, for a time at least, as tenants, their labor further increasing the value of the land they worked, to the ultimate advantage of the landlords. In this situation the original "manorial" grants became increasingly valuable simply as land, quite aside from the legal privileges that were supposed to accompany them. The original grantees and their heirs—especially those closely related to the Calverts—found themselves not manorial lords but well-to-do landowners in a world of tobacco farms, with control over properties valuable both for the rents they could produce and for the sale price they could ultimately command in a rising market.

The same men controlled the central offices in the government of the colony, which except for the years 1655–58 remained in the power of the proprietor, Lord Baltimore. He filled them with members of his family and their close associates, most of whom were Catholic. As in Virginia, the governor's council quickly became the central governing body. But in Maryland membership on the council was less the result of achieved prominence than of personal appointment by the lord proprietor. As a result the earliest political struggles in Maryland were not, as in Virginia, between the governor and the councillors but between the governor and the council on the one hand and the local representatives on the other. Fiercely competitive politics was part of the life of Maryland almost from the first years of settlement.

Leonard Calvert's instructions obliged him to call an assembly of freemen and to submit all laws to that body for approval. But he retained the right to summon, adjourn, and dismiss the assembly, and the exclusive right too of initiating all legislation, while the proprietor in England retained the power to veto any actions taken by the assembly. The first full meeting of the assembly (1638) was, like the first assemblies of Massachusetts and Virginia, a confused affair. Any freemen who chose to appear were seated. To free themselves from the dictatorial influence of the proprietary group, the representatives insisted that the assembly arrange itself like the House of Commons, take the power of convening and adjourning into its own hands, and adopt parliamentary rules. Gradually they won these demands, though the proprietor never relinquished the theoretical rights granted him in the charter. When the Long Parliament in England and the Civil War (1640–49) threw all Anglo-American relations into confusion, the assembly seized the power of initiating legislation, and the representatives forced the proprietor to allow them to meet independently of the council. Thereafter the representatives formed a separate lower house of the assembly.

By 1650 the structure of forces that would persist in seventeenth-century Maryland was fully evolved. The colony was governed by an absentee proprietor, his resident governor, and his appointed council, almost all of whom were Catholic. Together they monopolized the important public offices and the profits of office, and they were at the same time the major landlords. But the majority of the population, largely Protestant, had a legitimate voice in government through the lower house. They maintained a continuing battle, in the assembly and out, to force the proprietor and his followers to relinquish their special privileges. In no other colony, by the middle of the seventeenth century, was politics so sophisticated and so bitter as it was in the colony that had first been conceived as an oasis of manorial harmony.

The Failure of the Dutch

The founding of what would become New York differed radically from the pattern of the other British colonies. It was the Dutch, not the English, who founded this colony, which was not originally conceived of as a community at all. Its population from the start was culturally diverse. No legal system was effectively established and no government evolved comparable to the assemblies of Virginia and Maryland and to the General Court of Massachusetts Bay.

New Netherland, as the colony was called until its conquest by England in 1664, was an almost accidental creation of the Dutch West India Company, a trading organization centered in Amsterdam, that was founded in 1621. The colony was never the chief concern of this complex commercial company whose enterprises included trading forts on the Amazon River and establishments in West Africa and Brazil as well as in North America. The company set out, not to create a colony at all, but simply to exploit the fine fur supply and other resources of the middle Atlantic region that had been revealed by the explorations of Henry Hudson in 1609 and thereafter by voyages of a short-lived Dutch fur-trading company.

New Amsterdam. In 1624 the Dutch West India Company sent over thirty Dutch and Walloon (French-speaking Belgian) families to open settlements at Fort Orange and Esopus on the upper Hudson and at several points on the Delaware. Supplies, equipment, and a total of perhaps two hundred people followed in 1625. In that year too a blockhouse was built at the tip of Manhattan Island, which lies at the mouth of the Hudson River, to protect Dutch shipping and to serve as a convenient transfer point for shipments to and from the Hudson and Delaware river posts. The next year, 1626, the beginning of a regular village was constructed around the blockhouse on Manhattan Island—windmills for sawing wood and grinding corn and some thirty log houses spaced along the west side of the island. At the same time an energetic company officer, Peter Minuit, purchased the whole of the island from the native Manhates Indians and began to consolidate in this central village, called Fort Amsterdam or New Amsterdam, the main force of the scattered Dutch settlers. He withdrew some of the settlers from the distant and exposed posts on the upper Hudson and the Delaware, leaving only skeleton forces there to channel furs to New Amsterdam and to defend the Dutch claims. The population in New Amsterdam grew slowly, reaching only 450 in 1646 and perhaps 1,500 in 1664.

By midcentury the village of New Amsterdam consisted of the original blockhouse and windmills

and a number of houses, all enclosed within a palisade, or wall (which became Wall Street), the whole compound surrounded by a canal. Scattered in the open area beyond the wall and canal were about fifty small farms (bouweries). In 1650 the village of New Amsterdam was a frontier community in which people of all sorts mingled, traded, and brawled. Men and women from half-a-dozen nations—Dutch, Walloons, French, English, Portuguese, Swedes, Finns, and Brazilian blacks—speaking, it was reported, eighteen different languages and professing every religious persuasion from Catholicism to Anabaptism, flocked to the settlement seeking to turn a profit on exchanges of furs, goods, produce, and land. It was as quarrelsome and disorderly a village as could be found in North America, torn by hostilities and constant disruption, constrained by no common purpose, disrespectful of the regulations that the company's loutish, blustering agents attempted to enforce, and above all neglected by the company that had sponsored the settlement and that remained legally responsible for its welfare.

For the company never doubted that whatever profits it was likely to make in North America would result from the fur cargoes that came in from the posts on the Hudson, Delaware, and Connecticut rivers, and from nothing else. The directors had no intention of throwing good money after bad, as the Virginia Company had done, in the vain hope of establishing a populous and prosperous agricultural and industrial community. They made no serious efforts to populate the colony, nor did they have available for that purpose as mobile a population as the English colonizers had had. To the company's directors, settlers meant private competition for their corporate control of the fur trade. They made every effort to monopolize that commerce, to impose heavy import and export duties on the colonists, and to lay taxes and fees in an effort to squeeze a profit from the settlements. Yet the profits that were made from the Dutch colony were made not by the company, which never recovered its initial investment, and not by the ordinary settlers, who lived little above the subsistence level in these early years, but by a few

This view appeared as a miniature inset in a large map of New Netherland issued by Nicholas Visscher. *Legend:* *A:* Fort; *B:* Church of St. Nicholas; *C:* Jail; *D:* Governor's House; *E:* Gallows; *G:* West India Company's Stores; *H:* Tavern.

troonships," large estates that would be financed by groups of investors who would share in the profits but not in the management of these plantations, which would be controlled by the "patroons" alone.

Ten such investment groups were created, but only one patroonship, Rensselaerswyck, on both sides of the Hudson surrounding Fort Orange, developed in the form provided for in the charter and survived through the seventeenth century. To this huge estate Van Rensselaer, the patroon, sent a flow of goods, cattle, and equipment of all sorts, and he dispatched also at his own expense farmers and miscellaneous workers to populate the grant. By 1655 he had leased sixteen farms on the estate and had developed his personal manor efficiently despite all the confusions and difficulties of managing such property through deputies. And although it is doubtful that in the end Van Rensselaer recovered his heavy investment in the estate, he did establish on the upper Hudson a prosperous agricultural community.

The province of New Netherland as a whole, however, remained, as a contemporary wrote, "a wild country"—ill-organized, ill-managed, and contentious. The continuing disorder was partly the result of the uncontrolled multiplication of thinly populated villages, poorly organized and incapable of defending themselves. They appeared on all sides: on upper Manhattan (New Haarlem); in Westchester, across the Harlem River; on Staten Island; in New Jersey (Bergen); and especially on Long Island, where five Dutch towns appeared by the 1640s. The confusion in these border towns was compounded by the agitations of the neighboring English who moved in to New Netherland from the surrounding colonies. Attracted by the company's offer of freedom of worship, local self-government, and free land that would remain tax exempt for ten years, these migrants, while they helped populate the company's lands,

Dutch middlemen in New Amsterdam. These enterprising merchants and artisans fell in with the resident company officials to manipulate for their own benefit the monopolized sale of goods and supplies and the prices offered for furs and surplus farm products.

Contention and Indian Wars. At least one of the company's directors in the Netherlands, however, had a broader vision of the colony's future, and his strenuous efforts made a difference. Kiliaen Van Rensselaer, a wealthy Amsterdam jeweler, argued for the creation of large-scale private agricultural estates, like the proprietary manors in Maryland. These farming establishments, he claimed, would not only help stabilize the colony but would provide provisions, cattle, and other necessary supplies for the Dutch ships heading for the West Indies and elsewhere in the Western Hemisphere. His efforts resulted in the Charter of Freedoms and Exemptions issued by the company and confirmed by the Dutch government in 1629. The charter authorized the creation of "pa-

PETER STUYVESANT, c. 1660

Director-general of New Amsterdam for 17 years, this storming, peg-legged war veteran swore he would die before surrendering New Amsterdam to the English, but in fact he gave up the fort quietly in 1664 and retired peacefully to his farm in New York City. It had become his home, and there he died in 1672. *(Courtesy of The New-York Historical Society, New York City)*

South, on the Delaware River, Maryland challenged the Dutch openly. In the years preceding the English conquest of New Netherland the English settlers in the border areas had moved to open revolt.

None of these difficulties were eased by skillful management on the part of the Dutch officials or by the effectiveness of the colony's political institutions. Of the directors-general (governors) sent over by the company, only Peter Minuit (1626–31) was reasonably efficient and judicious. His two immediate successors were hopelessly inefficient, made more enemies than friends in the colony, and were finally removed from office in response to repeated charges that they were ruining the colony by their arrogance, corruption, indolence, and constant drunkenness. The second of them, Willem Kiefft (1638-47), personally set on foot a savage war against the neighboring Indians.

It began in 1642, after a number of Indian raids on outlying farms, with the slaughter of 110 unsuspecting and peaceful Indians encamped near New Amsterdam. This butchery was carried out with a barbarism that appalled even contemporary observers ("some came running to us from the country having their hands cut off; some lost both arms and legs; some were supporting their entrails with their hands, while others were mangled in other horrid ways, too horrid to be conceived"). All of this set the terms of a conflict that devastated New Netherland until, after three years, the Dutch hired the veteran English Indian fighter Captain John Underhill, who led 150 men in a midnight raid on an Indian village. Some 500 Indians were shot or burned alive in the conflagration that completed Underhill's victory. The peace that was concluded in 1646 was a peace not of reconciliation but of mutual exhaustion and fear of annihilation. When in 1647 the next, and last, director-general, Peter Stuyvesant, arrived, the colony was badly reduced in size, hard pressed by its competitive neighbors, and virtually abandoned by the failing company.

Stuyvesant, an autocratic ex-governor of the Dutch island of Curaçao, commissioned to oversee all Dutch interests in the Caribbean as well as to rule New Netherland, plunged into a hopeless tangle of conten-

created difficult administrative problems for the Dutch officials. In addition, these alien and discontented groups began agitating against the Dutch rule, advocating English conquest of the border areas if not of the whole colony. So acute were these border conflicts with the English that a formal treaty was drawn up between New Netherland and the confederation of New England colonies that had been created in 1643. The Treaty of Hartford (1650) set the Dutch-Connecticut boundary ten miles east of the Hudson River and eliminated Dutch claims beyond that line. But the New Englanders on Long Island continued to resist the Dutch authorities, and in the tion. Given to fits of rage, savage in his efforts to wipe out all dissent from the colony's official Reformed Calvinism, and endowed with almost dictatorial executive powers, he made little headway in solving the colony's multiplying problems. By 1654 when the Dutch West India Company finally went bankrupt, all that remained to bear witness to the company's original hopes were a few wharves and bridges, a neglected fort, and a nondescript town hall and market area. In 1655 the Indians, in delayed vengeance, launched a new reign of terror on the faltering and battered settlements, and the colony's feeble resources were still further drained in the effort to survive. At the same time, the English in Connecticut laid plans to seize the colony and began more resolute encroachments on Dutch-claimed territory. By 1664, when an English fleet captured New Amsterdam, the colony as a whole was helpless, and in its desolation could only look to the new English authorities with hopes that had never been stirred by the Dutch West India Company or by such storming, hard-drinking martinets as William Kiefft and Peter Stuyvesant.

Royal Rewards: Carolina and the Jerseys

Thus by the 1640s—within a single generation of the chartering of the Virginia Company—large-scale, permanent colonies with a total population of over fifty thousand had been established along the Chesapeake Bay and the rivers of northern Virginia, at the mouth and along the banks of the Hudson River, and in central and southern New England. But no claim had yet been made to two great territories that adjoined these earliest European settlements: the mid-Atlantic region, between New Netherland and Maryland, and the land south of Virginia to the Spanish settlement at Saint Augustine, Florida. The settlement of these two major coastal regions—from one of which would be carved the Jerseys and Pennsylvania, and from the other the Carolinas and Georgia—took place in very different circumstances from those of the earlier settlements. Yet the earlier pattern of high hopes and imaginative designs followed by failure, disillusion,

CHARLES II
His return from exile and restoration to the throne (1660) marked a new phase in England's overseas expansion. He chartered the Carolinas, the Jerseys, and Pennsylvania, and his government enacted legislation that turned a collection of scattered settlements into a mercantile empire (Chapter 4). *(National Portrait Gallery, London)*

and then a slow emergence of communities in unexpected forms emerged in these later colonies as well.

Before these territories were settled, however, the greater world had been transformed. In the two decades after 1640 England was convulsed by civil war, by the execution of Charles I and the exile of Charles II, and by the creation of Oliver Cromwell's republican regime, which in the end became an autocratic "protectorate." In the midst of these domestic convulsions England engaged in two international wars: one with the Dutch, largely fought at sea (1652–54), and the other with Spain (1656–59), mainly in the Caribbean. By 1658, when Cromwell died, to be succeeded briefly as lord protector by his son, England was exhausted by the turmoil and eager for stability and reconciliation. When Charles II, now supported by disillusioned defectors from the conflict-torn Commonwealth, declared amnesty for all, liberty of conscience, and an endorsement of existing land titles, he was welcomed by a special parliamentary convention. He returned to England and to a restored monarchy in May 1660.

The Carolina Charter.   The main flow of colonization had been interrupted during these two tumultuous decades, but it was quickly resumed in the enterprising reign of Charles II (1660–85). While still in exile in France he and his followers, deprived of all

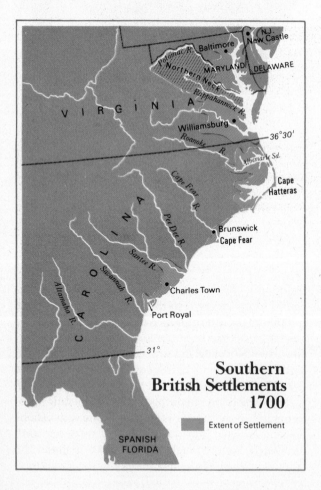

Southern British Settlements 1700

Extent of Settlement

other properties and prospects, had eyed the colonies as a rich field for exploitation. In 1649 the king had rewarded the loyalty of seven of his close followers with the proprietorship of the Northern Neck of Virginia, a domain of 5 million acres between the Potomac and the Rappahannock rivers. Once the court was reestablished in England, it turned its attention more fully to the colonies. In the competitive, exuberant atmosphere of Charles II's court, a syndicate of the most powerful courtiers was formed to promote the colonizing designs of an exceptionally enterprising plantation owner of the island of Barbados, Sir John Colleton.

Colleton, a well-connected royalist recently returned to London, knew that Barbados, the most profitable of England's West Indian islands, was producing a surplus population of land-hungry farmers displaced by the growth of slave plantations, and he knew too that Virginians and a few New Englanders were already attempting small experimental settlements in the lands just south of Virginia. He proposed to facilitate the settlement of this region, and quickly drew into his enterprise some of the most powerful figures of the realm. Among them were his kinsman the Duke of Albemarle, who had managed Charles' return to the throne; the Earl of Clarendon, Charles II's chief minister; Lord Berkeley, brother of the governor of Virginia, Sir William Berkeley; and above all, Sir Anthony Ashley Cooper, who as the Earl of Shaftsbury would become an important political power. For these imaginative and enterprising men Colleton's proposal was irresistible. No funds, time, or effort seemed to be required of them. Since settlement was already proceeding by spillovers from the older colonies, the proprietors had merely to design a system of government and land distribution, open a land office, appoint officials, and collect the rents.

The charter of Carolina that was issued to the eight partners in 1663 (extended in 1665) granted them title to all of the land lying between Virginia and Northern Florida and across the continent from sea to sea, and it gave them full rights of governance over this vast domain. The direct management of this immense territory did not interest them; they were not territorial imperialists. They had their eyes on the commercial possibilities of three tiny spots on the coastal fringe: first, a northern settlement safe behind the long spits of land that formed Albemarle Sound; second, a middle settlement at the mouth of the Cape Fear River where a cluster of New Englanders had already gathered; and third, a community at Port Royal, in the deeper south, close to what would later become the colony of Georgia. From these bustling nuclei would proliferate—the proprietors hoped—three well-populated, land-buying, rent-paying communities. They therefore divided the grant into three huge counties centered on these projected settlements. Then in "A Declaration and Proposals to All That Will Plant in Carolina" they designed governments patterned after the older British colonies, with veto powers retained by the proprietors. Freedom of religion was assured, as was a system of land distribution based on headrights of various dimensions, and large proprietary estates were reserved in every settlement.

It was a typical projection of enthusiastic colonial entrepreneurs, and it was typically unrealistic. The few Virginians in Albemarle were happy enough to organize an assembly to protest the terms of land allotment, but their settlement, from which would eventually develop the colony of North Carolina, was isolated from transoceanic commerce by coastal sand dunes and yielded not a penny of profit. And nothing, it seemed, could induce settlers in any numbers to remain on the swampy, sandy coastal land of Cape Fear, the proposed middle settlement, which was surrounded by hostile Indians. By 1669 the entire enterprise of Carolina was on the point of extinction, when it was suddenly taken over by Ashley, who rescued it from failure—though not in the way he planned.

With the assistance of the philosopher John Locke, who was his secretary, physician, and general counsel, Ashley reorganized the undertaking. He decided that funds would have to be raised from the sponsors themselves; that settlers would be sent out directly from England; and that the target would be the third, most southerly location, Port Royal, the site most favored by the Barbadians. With new capital raised from

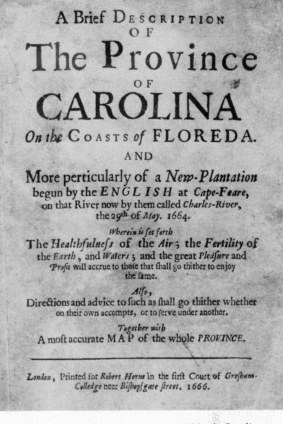

(North Carolina Collection, University of North Carolina Library)

the original proprietors, Ashley was able to send out from England three vessels with about a hundred colonists and a large supply of equipment. The fleet was instructed to refit in Barbados and to recruit more settlers there, but misfortunes of every kind befell the expedition. Only a handful of settlers survived to establish a settlement, which they located not where one had been planned but much farther inland, out of reach of the Spanish. In 1670 that community, isolated from principal transportation routes, was still only a palisaded garrison surrounded by a few small subsistence farms. More vessels followed, however, especially from Barbados, and the leaders undertook a search for town sites suitable for the grand design of land distribution that had been set out by the proprietors. One of the promising sites they discovered, never contemplated by the proprietors, was Oyster Point, where the Ashley and Cooper rivers flow together, some sixty miles north of the original Port Royal. Gradually the superior attractions of this location, safe from coastal raids yet open to ocean commerce and at the hub of a network of river routes into the interior, overcame the proprietors' original plans for concentrated settlements. Family groups and individual farmers from the older mainland settlements and from Barbados began to move to this unplanned center of the colony and to establish claims to what quickly became valuable land along the banks of the rivers. By 1683 Oyster Point had been renamed Charles Town (a century later it would be called Charleston), and with a population of a thousand had become the center of a quickly growing colony. It was altogether different from the community at Albemarle, three hundred miles to the north, and altogether different too from anything that had been contemplated by the Carolina proprietors.

"Fundamental Constitutions." Of Ashley's and Locke's hopes and plans for Carolina after the reorganization of 1669 there is an extremely detailed picture in one of the most remarkable documents of the age, "The Fundamental Constitutions of Carolina," which they wrote in collaboration. It presented an elaborate blueprint for a hierarchical manorial world dominated by three orders of nobility—proprietors, "landgraves," and "caciques"—in which the association of landed property and public roles was designed to create stability. Utopian, intricately contrived, a mixture of nostalgic romanticism and hardheaded realism, the system that was detailed in the "Fundamental Constitutions," involving a legislative Council of Nobles and a system of manorial courts, was a dream that could never be put into effect. The government that in fact emerged in the first decades soon came to resemble that of the other proprietary colonies. In the eighteenth century, when the original Carolina charter was annulled, the colony's public institutions easily fell into the standard pattern of royal governments. Yet though the romantic notions that Ashley and Locke wrote into

their "Constitutions" died stillborn, a number of the document's provisions, which conformed to patterns of life that were otherwise developing in America, did become effective and did help shape the emerging community.

Religious toleration, provided for in the original Carolina charter, was reinforced and elaborated in the Ashley-Locke "Constitutions," and it contributed significantly to the development of the Carolinas. In addition, full naturalization of aliens was made extremely simple. Further, the "Constitutions" required that two-fifths of all the land of each county be granted in large estates to the nobility, and the way was thereby paved not so much for the creation of a landed nobility as for land speculation on a grand scale. Finally, the "Constitutions" established the rule of English law and outlined a structure of local administration similar to that of England—provisions that would remain fundamental to the exotic variant of British society that was developing at the end of the century in the southern part of the Carolina grant.

Carolina: Society and Economy. For what would become South Carolina *was* exotic, even in relation to the unusual communities that were elsewhere developing in mainland British America. Its quickly growing population, still a mere five to seven thousand by the end of the century, was peculiarly complex. It included not only New Yorkers, Puritan New Englanders, and Virginians, but also over five hundred English Presbyterians and Baptists and also a group of Presbyterian Scots. Recruitment of French Huguenots from their refuge in the Netherlands began in the earliest years and increased greatly after 1685 when these Protestant refugees lost all hope of returning to France; by 1700 at least five hundred Frenchmen were settled in the colony. But the dominant element from the start was the West Indians: several thousand tough, experienced frontier farmers displaced by the growth of the plantation economy in the sugar-producing islands and determined to establish themselves and prosper in this hot, fertile, unexplored land.

Experienced in the production of semitropical crops, experimental in their approach to agriculture, and familiar with slavery as a labor system, the West Indians, through the typical "starving times" of the early years, led the colony in the search for a staple crop. The first marketable products were familiarly British and held no great promise: timber, cattle, and foodstuffs, all of which had to be exchanged for sugar in the West Indies and in that form redeemed in the British markets. But gradually more exotic and more lucrative possibilities became clear. The first was the trade in furs, which remained a crucial element in the economic and social life of South Carolina for half a century. As early as the 1680s pack horses could be seen hauling into Charles Town and the other coastal villages animal skins bought through a series of exchanges from Indian hunters ranging deep in the wilderness south and west of the Savannah and Altamaha rivers. The Carolina fur traders, the least squeamish of men, working at the remote fringes of Western civilization, did not limit themselves to tracking down animals; they brought back humans as well. They led into Charles Town and the other villages troops of Indians captured from hostile tribes, and sold them into slavery at home and abroad.

Slavery—African, West Indian, American Indian—was a basic fact of life from the earliest days of South Carolina. There is evidence that in the early years of hardship, when survival was at stake, whites and blacks, freemen and slaves, worked together—"slaved" together—in conditions of relative equality. But that did not last. By the 1690s when the first successful experiments were made in the production of rice—the crop that, with indigo and the fur trade, would ultimately secure the colony's economy and require an ever-increasing work force of slaves—the condition of the blacks was reduced to absolute degradation. As early as 1708 blacks outnumbered whites in South Carolina, and by then the colony's black code, based on the savage slave laws of Barbados, was fully elaborated and rigorously enforced.

Such were the results of the enterprise of the Restoration courtiers who had been granted the great gift of Carolina in 1663. By the turn of the century South Carolina's survival was assured. The colony would prosper and grow—not as the utopia of balanced social orders that Locke and Ashley had dreamed of, but as a competitive world of rice plantations, savage race relations, land speculation, and commerce. Its most prominent families, as their fortunes rose, were increasingly eager for gentility, leisure, and the grace of life; but even more than the leaders of other colonies they were directly exposed to the wildness of the frontier and the barbarism of chattel slavery.

Settlement of the Jerseys. Of the Jerseys, founded at the same time as the Carolinas and under similar circumstances, less need be said. For there the proprietors' powers and claims almost immediately dissolved into an unchartable maze of divisions and subdivisions that left the territory open to largely unregulated settlement. There were, of course, high hopes at the start on the part of the two proprietors who in 1664 were granted the tract of approximately 5 million acres between the Delaware and Hudson rivers by the Duke of York, overlord of the territory conquered from the Dutch. But though these first proprietors of New Jersey, Lord John Berkeley and Sir George Carteret, both of whom were already proprietors of the Carolinas, issued grandiose plans modeled on the first Carolina designs, they had even less interest in managing this province than they had in governing the Carolinas.

In 1674 Berkeley sold his rights to a group of Quakers, setting in motion a bewildering exchange of shares, in the course of which, in 1676, the province was formally divided into two provinces, East Jersey and West Jersey. In the eastern sector heirs of Carteret attempted vainly to organize a coherent government out of the scattered settlements that had been founded by squatters. The new Quaker proprietors of the western portion attempted, amid paralyzing legal complications, to establish a refuge for their persecuted community. Harassed alike by the duke's governor in New York and the government at home, the Quaker leaders, among them William Penn, issued in 1677 an extraordinarily liberal and humane document "The Concessions and Agreements of the Proprietors, Freeholders and Inhabitants of ... West New Jersey in America," which guaranteed a democratically elected popular assembly, individual rights including absolute freedom of conscience, and adult male participation in local and provincial government. The first West Jersey assemblies of the early 1680s attempted, with uneven success, to enact all of this into law. But though groups of settlers appeared and began the cultivation of West Jersey, the Quakers' interests in colonization soon shifted to Pennsylvania, and West Jersey followed East Jersey into the hands of land speculators interested principally in the financial value of the proprietary claims. Scottish entrepreneurs led a Scots Presbyterian migration into East Jersey where they further compounded the mixture of peoples. Gradually, as farms and towns were built in both districts, a familiarly English pattern of local government emerged, in relation to which the proprietors were quite marginal. Yet title to the undistributed land remained in the proprietors' hands, even when the

crown took temporary control of the two governments (1688–92) and after the two colonies were finally and permanently rejoined into the single crown colony of New Jersey (1702).

By then the territory that the Duke of York had so casually bestowed on his two followers contained a population of approximatley fourteen thousand, almost all of whom lived on one-family farms of from 50 to 150 acres. The ethnic and religious diversity was extraordinary, even for a British North American colony. Only New York was demographically more complex, but there a single group, the Dutch, predominated. In New Jersey no one group predominated. There were Africans, West Indians, Dutch, Germans, Huguenots, English, Scots, and Irish, worshiping as Congregationalists, Baptists, Quakers, Anglicans, Presbyterians, and Dutch and German Reformed. The colony had no particular

(Rare Book Division, The New York Public Library, Astor, Lenox and Tilden Foundations)

ADVERTISEMENT,

To all Tradef-men, Husbandmen, Servants and others who are willing to Transport themselves unto the Province of New-East-Jersy in America, a great part of which belongs to Scots-men, Proprietors thereof.

WHereas several Noblemen, Gentlemen, and others, who (by undoubted Rights derived from His Majesty, and His Royal Highness) are Interested and concerned in the Province of *New-East-Jersie*, lying in the midst of the *English* Plantations in *America*, do intend (God-willing) to send several Ships thither, in *May, June,* and *July* ensuing, 1684. from *Leith, Montrofs, Aberdeen* and *Glafgow.* These are to give notice to all Tradef-men, Husbandmen and others, who are willing and desirous to go there, and are able to Transport themselves and Families thither , upon their own Cost and Charges, to a pleasant and profitable Countrey, where they may live in great Plenty and Pleafure, upon far lefs Stock, and with much lefs labour and trouble then in *Scotland,* that as foon as they arrive there, they shall have confiderable quantities of Land, fet out Heretably to themselves and their Heirs for ever, for which they shall pay nothing for the first four or five years, and afterwards pay only a fmall Rent yearly to the Owners and Proprietors thereof, according as they can agree. And all Tradef-men, Servants, and others, fuch as, Wrights, Coupers, Mafons, Millers, Shoe-makers, &c. who are willing to go there, and are not able to Transport themselves, that they shall be carried over free, and well maintained in Meat and Clothes the first four years, only for their Service, and thereafter they shall have confiderable quantities of Land, fet out to themselves and their Heirs for ever , upon which they may live at the rate of Gentlemen all their lives, and their Children after them: Their ordinary Service will be cutting down of Wood with Axes, and other eafie Husband-Work, there being plenty of Oxen and Horfes for Plowing and Harrowing, &c. Let therefore all Tradef-men, Husband-men, Servants, and others who incline to go thither, and defire further Information herein, repair themselves to any of the Persons underwritten, who will fully inform them anent the Countrey , and every other thing neceffary , and will anfwer and fatisfie their Scruples and Objections, and give them all other Incouragements according to their feveral abilities and capacities; *viz.*

At *Edinburgh* let them apply themselves to the Lord Thefaurer-Deput, the Lord Register, Sir *John Gordon,* Mr. *Patrick Lyon.* Mr. *George Alexander,* Advocates, *George Drummond* of *Blair, John Swintoun, John Drummond, Thomas Gordon, David Falconer, Andrew Hamilton,* Merchants; at *Brant-Ifland* to *William Robifon,* Doctor of Medecine; at *Montrofs,* to *John Gordon* Doctor of Medecine, *John Futherton* of *Kinaber,* and *Robert* and *Thomas Fulertons* his Brothers; in the Shire of the *Mearns,* to *Robert Barclay* of *Urie,* and *John Barclay* his Brother ; at *Aberdeen,* to *Gilbert Molefon, Andrew Galloway, John* and *Robert Sandilands, William Gerard* Merchants ; in the Shire of *Aberdeen,* to *Robert Gordon* of *Clunie,* and *Robert Burnet* of *Lethanty*; in the Shire of *Pearth* to *David Tifbach* of *Monyvard* and Captain *Patrick Macgreiger*; In *Merfi* Shire, to *James Johnston* of *Spotefwood*; At *Kefo,* to *Charlesormiston* Merchant ; In the *Lewis,* to *Kenith Mackinzie* younger of *Kildin :* And if any Gentleman or others be defireous to buy or purchafe any fmall shares or portions of Land in the faid Province, they may repair to any of the forefaid Perfons, who will direct them how they shall be ferved, providing they do it timoufly, becaufe many more Perfons are dayly offering to buy, then can be gotten well accommodated.

cultural character or social organization, and its mixed farming economy was in no way distinctive in the agricultural world of the northern colonies.

Pennsylvania: A Godly Experiment and a Worldly Success

Of all the colonies, it is perhaps Pennsylvania that shows most vividly the contrast between soaring aspirations and mundane accomplishments. In part the vividness of the contrast was a consequence of the speed with which everything happened in Pennsylvania; in part too it was a reflection of the fame of the original plans and the force of the original hopes; and in part also it reflected the incongruous mixture of elements in William Penn's personality.

Quaker Immigrants. The founding of Pennsylvania was the accomplishment of one of the most radical religious sects of the seventeenth century. The Quakers, as religious extremists, had suffered severe persecution during their thirty years of existence as a group before the founding of Pennsylvania. Devoting themselves to finding the divine "inner light" within each soul, they practiced a religion free of all the encumbrances of church, clergy, and ritual. They were proud, courageous, and defiant of secular authority to the point of refusing to take ordinary oaths of loyalty. They advocated absolute freedom of conscience, were pacifists and political reformers.

By 1680 there were some fifty thousand members of this famous radical sect in Britain, largely among the poorest people, and there were smaller numbers scattered through continental Europe and North America. After the hysteria of the Popish Plot (1678), when it was alleged that England was being taken over by a French Catholic conspiracy led by the royal family, and after the Exclusion Crisis (1679–81), in which efforts were made to exclude the Catholic Duke of York from the succession to the throne, the English government launched savage attacks on all dissidents, especially such extremists as the Quakers. Some 1400 of these gentle but radical nonconformists were thrown in jail, and they were fined heavily both

for attending Quaker meetings and for failing to attend services of the Church of England. In default of payment (and most Quakers could not pay the fines) their goods—including their means of livelihood—were seized and destroyed or carted away. Victims of such persecution were crippled not only economically but spiritually as well, for Quakers regarded work as a divine calling, and the incapacity to pursue their vocations was a further inhibition of their religious life.

William Penn, though a well-educated son of one of England's most influential naval officers and a familiar and respected figure at the court of Charles II, shared in these disabilities as he did in all the fortunes of the Quakers whom he had joined as a young man. But his outlook was curiously complex. Convinced of the truth of the Quakers' tenets, he brought to the movement great energy, high-level contacts, a lawyer's shrewdness in polemics and court proceedings, and a businesslike approach to the endless controversies in which the group was embroiled. He was a radical—certainly in religion but also in politics—in that he sought every means of protecting the individual from the arbitrary power of the state and believed that government existed to improve the welfare of the masses. But he remained an aristocrat all his life. A political reformer and extremist in religion, he was nevertheless a monarchist. He continued to believe that the well educated and highly placed should have the decisive voices in public affairs, and though he suffered for his Quaker views, he managed to keep contact with the sources of his patronage at the court of Charles II.

Why Charles II granted this outspoken dissident a princely domain as a personal gift has never been fully explained. No doubt a long-standing crown debt to Penn's father was a factor, and the king may have thought he could get rid of the Quakers in this convenient way. But Penn's personal relations with the royal family were probably decisive, and of that very little is known. In any case, Charles II bestowed on Penn personally in 1681 the last unassigned portion of the North American coast. The grant encompassed the entire area between New York and Maryland, stretching west almost 300 miles from the New

Jersey border at the Delaware River—a total of 29 million acres, almost the size of England.

Penn was the outright owner of this territory, and he received also the authority to form a government, make most appointments to public office, and promulgate laws subject only to the approval of an assembly of freemen and the crown's right of veto. The charter established the supremacy of England's commercial regulations, but otherwise Penn was free to govern as he wished. He immediately set forth a Frame of Government—the first of a series, as it turned out. It is a strange document: in part a code of moral principles, including absolute freedom of worship and conscience; in part an intricate formulation of traditional arrangements for civil administration, reformed to satisfy Quaker ideals; and in part a blueprint for a remarkably *un*democratic government. A governor and a large council were to initiate and execute all laws, which the assembly, elected only by property owners, might accept or reject but not amend. Thus, amid striking statements of private and public morality and appeals to humanity and decency, Penn gave power not to the people at large but to their "natural" governors, though unlike the Calverts in Maryland he never thought of himself as a feudal overlord. From this fusing of benevolence and paternalism Penn expected a community of brotherly love to emerge, tolerant, free, secure, and above all peaceful. With those hopes in mind he turned with passion and skill to making his dreams come true.

In the end he was deeply disillusioned. Simply maintaining the legal title to his colony was an endless struggle, and his relations with the settlers were profoundly embittering. His colonizing efforts, however, were extraordinarily successful, especially at the start.

Growth of the Colony. Circulation of recruitment pamphlets through Britain and in translation in western Europe made Pennsylvania the best advertised

WILLIAM PENN'S MAP OF PHILADELPHIA, c. 1681
(Courtesy, Library Company of Philadelphia)

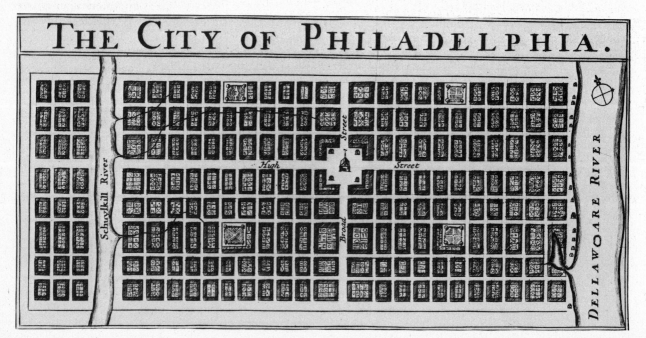

of all American colonies. A central "city of brotherly love," Philadelphia, was founded at an excellent site one hundred miles up the Delaware River where it meets the Schuylkill, and a well-designed street plan was laid out. A generous system of land distribution was set up. Land along the Delaware south of Philadelphia (the "lower counties") was added to Pennsylvania by the Duke of York to assure the colony's access to the sea. Quaker merchants invested heavily in the colony's expenses, and an assembly met within a year and composed a "Great Law" to serve as a temporary code of legislative and administrative principles and procedures. Above all, settlers arrived in large numbers.

By 1682, when Penn visited the province, the population was already 4,000—a remarkable swarming of people within a few months. There were Dutch, Swedes, and Finns from earlier settlements on the Delaware; West New Jerseyites; a large and influential influx of Welsh Quakers; Germans from the Rhineland who settled Germantown near Philadelphia; and above all English Quakers who flocked to the refuge Penn had provided for them. Fifty vessels brought 3,000 more settlers in 1683. By 1700 the colony's population was a remarkable 21,000. But by then Penn knew all the difficulties that his proprietorship entailed.

He was thoroughly embroiled with Lord Baltimore over the southern boundary of the province (a dispute that would be finally settled only with the drawing of the Mason-Dixon line on the eve of the Revolution). He was faced with stiff resistance to his authority by the settlers in the newly acquired "lower counties," a district that would ultimately form the state of Delaware; he was forced to allow them their own assembly in 1701. He was unfortunate in his choice of deputy governors and suffered from their clumsiness. Above all, he was faced with fierce opposition to his concept of government, an opposition that was led by some of the most deeply committed Quakers among the settlers.

From the beginning the colonial leaders insisted that the representative assembly, and not Penn or his deputy governors, have the determining voice in government. The house seized the power of initiating

legislation, and in 1696 forced Penn to concede that right. It insisted, against Penn's will, on amending bills presented to it by him, and it challenged his title to the undivided land. Pressure was maintained year after year in the 1690s until finally, after bitter disputes, and several revisions of the original Frame of Government, Penn agreed to an altogether new Frame. Written in 1701 by a joint committee of the council and the house, this charter of liberties, which would serve as the constitution of Pennsylvania until the Revolution, marked the final defeat of Penn's political ideals. It eliminated the council altogether from the legislative process, thus constituting the only unicameral government in British America. The king's veto of laws was retained but not Penn's, and the inhabitants were explicitly freed from any special allegiance to Penn or his descendants. What remained beyond dispute to the founder and his heirs was title to the undistributed land and the authority to appoint the resident governors. All the other chartered powers were either eliminated or challenged, and not by a democratic, populist majority of the population but by an oligarchy of Quaker politicians and representatives elected on a limited franchise, a quarrelsome, opinionated, ambitious clique that would dominate the colony's politics for the next half-century.

Penn had lost control of the province. But though Pennsylvania had failed to develop into the utopia of its founder's dreams, it was a fabulous worldly success. Contentious in politics but populous and prosperous from the start, open and attractive equally to penniless refugees and ambitious merchants, perfectly located and peopled for maximum economic growth, the distribution center for a mass population of laborers and yet a center too of provincial high culture, Pennsylvania became within a single generation the dynamic heart of the British North American world. It was with a sure instinct in 1723 that the ambitious seventeen-year-old Benjamin Franklin left Boston to seek his fortune in Philadelphia. William Penn was only five years dead, but his City of Brotherly Love had become a vigorous, prosperous community of ten thousand souls, a vital part of a colonial world that was evolving in unexpected ways.

CHRONOLOGY

1607	Virginia Company of London establishes settlement at Jamestown.	1634	First settlements in Maryland.
1609	Pilgrims flee to Holland to avoid religious persecution.	1635	Roger Williams banished from Bay Colony.
1609	Second charter of Virginia Company.	1636	Harvard College founded. First permanent English settlements in Connecticut and Rhode Island.
1612	Third charter of Virginia Company.		
1619	First Africans arrive in Virginia. First North American representative assembly meets in Virginia.	1638	Anne Hutchinson convicted of heresy in Massachusetts; flees to Rhode Island.
1620	Mayflower Compact signed; Pilgrims establish Plymouth Colony.	1639	Fundamental Orders adopted in Connecticut.
		1642	Basic literacy law passed in Massachusetts Bay.
1621	Dutch West India Company chartered.	1642–48	Civil war in England.
1622	Indian rebellion in Virginia.	1643	Confederation of New England colonies.
1624	Virginia Company charter annulled; English crown takes control of Virginia. First settlements in New Netherlands.	1644	Rhode Island receives patent.
		1647	Law requiring towns to maintain schools passed in Massachusetts Bay Colony.
1625–49	Reign of Charles I.	1649	Northern neck of Virginia granted to courtiers in exile.
1626	Dutch settle Manhattan.		
1629	Massachusetts Bay Company chartered.	1663	Carolina charter granted to eight proprietors; Rhode Island granted charter.
1630	Puritan emigration from England begins; continues until 1643.	1664	English conquest of New Netherland; grant of New Jersey to two proprietors.
1632	Cecilius Calvert, Lord Baltimore, receives charter for Maryland colony.	1681	Charles II issues Pennsylvania charter to William Penn.

SUGGESTED READINGS

There have been two recent efforts to summarize the English background of seventeenth-century colonization: Wallace Notestein, *The English People on the Eve of Colonization, 1603–1630* (1954) and Carl Bridenbaugh, *Vexed and Troubled Englishmen, 1590–1642* (1968). But more revealing than either of these general descriptions, which are based largely on literary sources, are studies that have nothing to do with colonization directly but make clear the disarray, mobility, and vitality of English society which underlay the extraordinary exodus of English men and women overseas: Peter Laslett, *The World We Have Lost* (1965); Peter Clark and Paul Slack, eds., *Crisis and Order in English Towns 1500–1700* (1972); John Patten, *English Towns, 1500–1700* (1978); Peter Spufford, "Population Mobility in Pre-Industrial England" (three essays in *Genealogists Magazine*, 1973–74); and the writings of W.G. Hoskins on English local history, most of which are listed in his *Local History in England* (1959). The best introduction to the economic history of pre-industrial England is Charles Wilson, *England's Apprenticeship, 1603–1763* (1965), two-thirds of which is on the seventeenth century; chaps. i–iii are particularly relevant.

The most comprehensive survey of the native North American population is the massive volume 15 (1978) of the Smithsonian Institution's new series, *Handbook of North American Indians*. This volume, subtitled *The Northeast*, summarizes all the available information—historical, anthropological, and archaeological—concerning all the native tribes from Maine to North Carolina and west to the Great Lakes. T. J. Brasser's chapter on early Indian-European contacts, Christian Feest's on the Chesapeake and North Carolina tribes, and Elizabeth Tooker's on the League of the Iroquois are particularly valuable. Writings on the extremely difficult subject of the size, distribution, and structure of the Indian population are listed in H. F. Dobyns, *Native American Historical Demography* (1976) to which should be added S. F. Cook, *The Indian Population of New England in the Seventeenth Century* (1976) and several of the contributions to the *Handbook*, cited above. For a useful sketch of the seaboard Indians on the eve of European colonization see T. J. Brasser, "The Coastal Algonkians: People of the First Frontiers," in Eleanor B. Leacock and Nancy O. Lurie, eds., *North American Indians in Historical Perspective*, 1971. There are detailed accounts of the conflicts of races for only a few of the seventeenth-century colonies: Allen W. Trelease, *Indian Affairs in Colonial New York: The Seventeenth Century* (1960); Alden W. Vaughan, *New England Frontier: Puritans and Indians, 1620–1675* (1975); Douglas E. Leach, *Flintlock and Tomahawk: New England in King Philip's War* (1958); Nancy O. Lurie, "Indian Cultural Adjustment to European Civilization," in James M. Smith, ed., *Seventeenth-Century America* (1959); and Francis Jennings, *The Invasion of America* (1975). Jennings' book is a bitter outcry against the wrongs done the North American Indians by the Puritans (and in this, a criticism of Vaughan's more even-handed treatment) and a boiling polemic against historians' characterization of the Indians as sparse in numbers, hostile to Europeans, savage, heathen, and unsophisticated in agriculture, trade, and politics. What the Indians were, aside from the victims of Puritans and mythologizing historians, does not emerge. Jennings' bibliography is excellent. For a survey of the wars between the European settlers and the Indians in the seventeenth century, see Wilcomb Washburn's chapter in the *Handbook*.

The most detailed and comprehensive single narrative of the English settlements in the seventeenth century is Charles M. Andrews, *The Colonial Period of American History* (vols. I–III, 1934–37), which concentrates on constitutional history and the development of public institutions. A more up-to-date and broad-ranging account of the planting and early growth of the southern colonies is Wesley F. Craven, *The Southern Colonies in the Seventeenth Century, 1607–1689* (1949). The settlement stories are retold in briefer scope in John E. Pomfret, *Founding the American Colonies, 1583–1660*

(1970) and Wesley F. Craven, *The Colonies in Transition, 1660–1713* (1968), both of which contain extensive bibliographies. There are excellent essays on local government in the colonies in Bruce C. Daniels, ed., *Town and County* (1978).

On the founding of Virginia, there are, besides the relevant chapters of Andrews *Colonial Period*, vol. I, and Craven's *Southern Colonies*, a detailed narrative of public events in Richard L. Morton, *Colonial Virginia* (2 vols., 1960); an excellent short summary in Alden T. Vaughan, *American Genesis* (1975); a revealing account of the high culture of the initiators of settlement, in Richard B. Davis, *George Sandys* (1955); biographies of Pocahontas and John Smith by Philip L. Barbour; and two excellent collections of documents: L. G. Tyler, ed., *Narratives of Early Virginia, 1606–1625* (1907) and Warren M. Billings, ed., *The Old Dominion in the Seventeenth Century . . .* (1975). Sigmund Diamond's provocative essay, "From Organization to Society: Virginia in the Seventeenth Century," *American Journal of Sociology*, 63 (1958), 457–75,[1] interprets the founding as the transformation of a quasi-military organization into a fully formed society of multiple relationships. Bernard Bailyn, "Politics and Social Structure in Virginia," in Smith, ed., *Seventeenth-Century America*, pp. 90–115,* considers the development of politics in its relation to the evolving social structure. Edmund Morgan considers the human cost of the colony's success in terms of the exploitation of labor in "The First American Boom: Virginia 1618–1630," *Wm. and Mary Q.*, 18 (1971), 169–98,* a topic discussed in a broader context in his *American Slavery, American Freedom* (1975).

The labor problem in Virginia involves the difficult question of the origins of chattel slavery. The modern debate on that question was initiated and framed by a brilliant article by Oscar and Mary F. Handlin, "Origins of the Southern Labor System," *Wm. and Mary Q.*, 7 (1950), 199–222,* reprinted as chap. i of Handlin's *Race and Nationality in American Life* (1957). Handlin's view is that chattel slavery in British America was a unique institution, different from slavery in any other form or place; that the concept of "slavery" in its American meaning was created in the seventeenth-century Chesapeake; and that it arose as a legal condition, in response not so much to race prejudice

---

[1]This essay and several mentioned in the references that follow have been reprinted in an excellent collection, *Colonial America: Essays in Politics and Social Development* (Stanley N. Katz, ed., 2d ed., Boston, 1976). Essays and selections from books that appear in this volume are indicated by an asterisk(*).

as to an effort to attract voluntary white labor by debasing the condition of involuntary black labor. For differing views, emphasizing race prejudice, the fear of foreignness, and religious differences, see Winthrop Jordan, *White over Black* (1968), Part I*, and Carl N. Degler, "Slavery and the Genesis of American Race Prejudice," *Comparative Studies in History and Society,* 2 (1959), 49–66. For a listing of recent writings on the subject, see Vaughan, *American Genesis,* p. 198.

On the Pilgrims and Plymouth, see George D. Langdon, Jr.'s general account, *Pilgrim Colony* (1966) and John Demos's social analysis, *A Little Commonwealth* (1970). George F. Willison's *Saints and Strangers* (1945) is a breezy, amusing interpretation. Bradford's great history, *Of Plymouth Plantation,* is available in a modern edition prepared by Samuel E. Morison (1952).

On the founding and early development of the Puritan colonies in New England, see, besides Andrews' chapters in *The Colonial Period,* Edmund S. Morgan's short biography of John Winthrop, *Puritan Dilemma* (1958); Darrett Rutman's *Winthrop's Boston* (1965); Samuel E. Morison's *Builders of the Bay Colony* (1930); Raymond P. Stearns, *The Strenuous Puritan: Hugh Peter* (1954); and above all, Winthrop's own *Journal . . . 1630–1649* (J. K. Hosmer, ed., 2 vols., 1908). For a theatrical and psychological account of Anne Hutchinson's career, see Emery Battis, *Saints and Sectaries* (1962), and on Roger Williams there are books by S. H. Brockunier, Perry Miller, and Edmund S. Morgan. On seventeenth-century Connect-icut, besides Andrews, see Isabel M. Calder, *The New Haven Colony* (1934) and Mary J. A. Jones, *Congregational Commonwealth* (1968). On Rhode Island, see Sydney V. James, *Colonial Rhode Island* (1975), and on Maine and New Hampshire, Charles E. Clark, *The Eastern Frontier* (1970), Part I.

Maryland is well covered in Andrews' and Craven's general books, but in the case of New York the general accounts should be supplemented by Thomas J. Condon, *New York Beginnings* (1968); Van Cleaf Bachman, *Peltries or Plantations* (1969); and the early chapters of Michael Kammen, *Colonial New York* (1975). M. Eugene Sirmans, *Colonial South Carolina* (1966) and Peter H. Wood, *Black Majority* (1974) are essential on South Carolina. Hugh T. Lefler and Albert R. Newsome, *North Carolina* (1954) is a good summary of that colony's early history. Wesley F. Craven, *New Jersey and the English Colonization of North America* (1964) is the best short book on that colony, though there are a number of more detailed studies by John E. Pomfret. The most recent history of the founding of Pennsylvania is Edwin B. Bronner's *William Penn's "Holy Experiment"* (1962); on the colony's early political history, see Gary B. Nash, *Quakers and Politics . . . 1681–1726* (1968). Catherine O. Peare, *William Penn* (1957) narrates the essential facts of the founder's life in a somewhat exclamatory fashion; Mary M. Dunn, *William Penn, Politics and Conscience* (1967) is an excellent study of Penn's ideas and religious beliefs.

Thus, through these many agencies—commercial companies, religious organizations, individual entrepreneurs, syndicates of courtiers —communities of Europeans were established on mainland North America. By 1700 these colonies formed an almost continuous line of seaboard settlements from New Hampshire to South Carolina and westward irregularly a hundred miles or so to the first falls of the coastal rivers. The total population of some 250,000 Europeans and Africans and their descendants, most of them English-speaking, were by no means spread evenly through this broad area. They clustered along river valleys to take advantage of the fertile soil and easy lines of communication, and they left behind large pockets of unsettled land. Even in the oldest communities of Massachusetts and Virginia this was still a frontier world, fundamentally shaped by its continuing encounter with the wilderness. Yet there were areas populated by native-born children of native-born parents—a third generation in America. For them, home was the colony, however much they might acknowledge a greater "home" abroad. Though they did not think of themselves as peculiarly "American," they lived settled lives in communities familiar to them from birth, and these were communities whose distinctive characteristics were becoming clear.

Newcomers to the colonies in 1700 (and immigration continued in all areas, though least in New England) were no longer faced with the bewildering disarray that earlier settlers had known. But neither did they find themselves in communities quite like any seen before. By 1700 the British colonies had acquired distinctive characteristics. There were great variations region by region and settlement by settlement, but despite the differences, common elements of a re-ordering of European life could be found in these communities.

This re-ordering of social life was not the result of design, or planning, or intent. Planning, as we have seen—elaborate designs and soaring dreams —there had been in abundance. But none of these original plans had been fulfilled; all had been quickly destroyed or slowly dissolved upon contact with the harsh reality. The deviations from European life

CHAPTER 3

Europe in the Wilderness
American Society in the Seventeenth Century

that had developed by 1700 were products of the impact of circumstance upon the culture of essentially conservative immigrants, most of whom sought personal satisfactions, personal freedoms, and security within familiar patterns of life. For many, the changes that took place were felt to be regressions rather than advances. Change was more often resisted than pursued. Only later would the alterations in community life be seen as advances toward an ideal—the ideal, expressed in the Enlightenment goals of the Revolution, of a freer, more fulfilling way of life.

Population Growth and Structure

American society in the seventeenth century was shaped in large part by demographic characteristics. Because the first American population was an immigrant population and because life in the colonies was harsh and was known to be harsh, the society that resulted was no evenly balanced re-creation of the social structure of Europe. The upper strata of traditional society were absent from the start. Of Europe's ruling nobility, there were no representatives at all. There were few even of what might loosely be called the aristocracy or of the upper gentry, few even of professional upper middle class, if one may use these modern terms. For then, as now, society's leaders and those who were well established did not easily tear up their roots, migrate, and struggle to secure themselves in an undeveloped land.

The Free Population. Most of the free population in mainland North America was recruited from the lower working population of England and the Netherlands—not for the most part the lowest, not destitute vagrants and outcasts, but farm workers, industrial workmen, tradesmen, and artisans. In the immigrant lists of the time, the two occupations most commonly entered were "yeoman," or "husbandman" (a farm worker, usually with some degree of independence) and artisan, or tradesman. Outside of New England, between one-half and two-thirds of all white immigrants were indentured ser-

vants. They were bound, for four years or more, to serve some master faithfully in exchange for their transatlantic passage, care and protection, and "freedom dues," which often included a small parcel of land. Averaging approximately 1,500 arrivals a year between 1630 and 1700, these immigrants to the Chesapeake, originally bound in various conditions of servitude, totaled more than 100,000 by 1700.

Further, the free population as it emerged from the seventeenth century was peculiarly mobile. The population was originally recruited, and continued to be recruited, from groups already dislodged from secure roots. Often for these people resettlement in America was not a unique transplantation but a second or third uprooting. And outside of New England, institutional or legal restraints on mobility, so vital a part of life in traditional European societies, scarcely existed at all. People were free to move where they would. The large majority of the indentured servants in the Chesapeake region survived servitude to enter the community free of involvement, commitment, or obligation, free to follow the attractions of security, profit, or congeniality wherever they might be found.

More important still, the free population of the northern colonies in the seventeenth century, and of the southern colonies too by the early eighteenth century, was unusual in the speed of its growth. The information that historians have recently gathered on the demographic characteristics of early New England reveals a society that was remarkably fertile. In an era in which most of European society was scarcely reproducing itself, the most prolific of the settled communities in America may have reached the extraordinary growth rate of 5 to 6 percent a year. Until the 1650s, it is true, Virginia and Maryland seem to have remained a death trap of disease. A random list of ninety-nine adult deponents before one Virginia county court shows an average age at death of only 48 in the years between 1637 and 1664. These were mostly men; the life expectancy of women aged 20 in the same region was only 40. In Maryland the population began to reproduce itself only in the 1680s; before then only the constant flow of immigrants, highly vulnerable to the diseases common to the Chesapeake region, accounted for population growth. But the death rate in the Chesapeake colonies fell rapidly in the later seventeenth century as the proportion of native-born in the population, who developed immunities to the prevalent diseases early in life, increased. The population of Virginia, supplemented by constant immigration, rose rapidly: it stood at 8,000 in 1644, quadrupled to 32,000 in the next thirty years, and then more than doubled once again in the next thirty years, reaching an estimated 75,600 in 1704.

In New England, once the initial immigration was completed, the population grew during the seventeenth century at an average rate of 2.6 or 2.7 percent a year, which meant that the settled population, quite aside from further immigration, was doubling approximately every twenty-seven years. And whatever else may be said about such a phenomenon as this, it meant that all other social changes were intensified by sheer demographic pressure.

How can this extraordinary growth rate be explained? Not, apparently, by an unusual birthrate. The birthrates available for selected American communities are similar to birthrates in French and English villages of this period. The root of the difference apparently lies in the lower death rate in the American colonies, once the original "starving times" were over and once the deadly "seasoning" times in the southern colonies came to an end. In Plymouth, Massachusetts, the life expectancy of men who survived to the age of 21 was 69.2 years, and in Andover, Massachusetts, the average age at death of the first settlers was 71.8 years; for their sons the average was 65.2. In that same village community, life expectancy at birth for males in the seventeenth century was longer by 12.6 years than it would be for men in England two hundred years later.

This rapidly growing population was unusual too in its age structure, which is associated with population growth. The American population was youthful. Most of the tens of thousands of indentured servants were between 18 and 24 years of age when they arrived. In Bristol, Rhode Island, 54 percent of the population were children; in seventeenth-century England the equivalent figure is 42.6 percent.

ALICE MASON, 1670

This forthright, unpretentious portrait by an unknown artist illustrates not only the appearance of children in the seventeenth century but attitudes toward children and childhood. This is not a child but a miniature adult, an individual who happens to be short and deficient in certain important ways, especially in the capacity to enjoy full religious experience, but for the most part fully endowed and responsible for her actions. The modern concept of childhood was a later development. *(U.S. Department of the Interior, National Park Service. Adams National Historic Site, Quincy, Massachusetts)*

The American population, being youthful, was less vulnerable to the ravages of disease than a more evenly age-distributed population would have been. The survival rate reflects too a higher proportion of women who were in the years of fertility, 15–45, and in addition a younger average age at marriage, at least in the northern colonies, especially for women.

In England, where 15 percent of the population were servants constrained from marrying young and where socioeconomic circumstances made establishing new households difficult for those without inheritances, it appears that the average age at first marriage was 28 for men and 24 for women. For one Massachusetts community that has been closely studied (Dedham), the equivalent figures are 25.5 and 22.5. In Plymouth the average age at first marriage for women at the end of the seventeenth century was 22.3; in Bristol, R.I., before 1750, the average age for women's first marriages was 20.5. As a result of these younger marriages women commonly bore children from their very early twenties until they were in their mid-forties. Younger marriages also assured a higher survival rate of children since the offspring of such marriages in preindustrial societies seem to have been more resistant to disease.

Finally, of the population characteristics that distinguish the emerging American communities from the parent communities abroad, there was an altered sex ratio. In England through these years, as in most settled societies, there were more women than men. The figures for England in the period 1574–1821 are 91.3 men to every 100 women. In the early years of settlement in America the figures are wildly inverted. In Virginia in 1625, over 75 percent of the settlers were men, and by midcentury the proportion was still approximately 6 to 1. Even in New England, where immigration by family was more common, there were 3 men for every 2 women in the middle of the century (a ratio reached in Virginia only in 1700), and while the proportion tended to level out as the century progressed, the traditional preponderance of women was by no means reached by 1700.

The Black Population.   All of this pertains to the free white population. No such precise figures can be given for the growing black population. We know only that of the 250,000 inhabitants of British North America in 1700, perhaps 10 percent were blacks, almost all of them slaves. Most had arrived from Barbados or elsewhere in the West Indies. It was only in 1674 that the Royal African Company brought the first shipment direct from Africa. Thereafter,

as the flow of white indentured servants from Britain slackened due to changes in the English labor market and to the growing attractions of the nonplantation colonies, shipments of slaves from Africa increased steadily. The decisive turning point—a landmark in American history—was the mid-1680s when black slaves for the first time outnumbered white servants in the southern labor force. When in 1698 the Royal African Company lost its monopoly, a flock of small operators entered the grim but profitable trade in human lives, and the floodgates were open: 10,000 slaves arrived in the Chesapeake colonies in the years 1698–1709.

In the seventeenth century, however, the number of blacks was still small, and partly because of that they lived lives of extreme degradation on the southern plantations. Family life—any kind of dignified existence—was impossible in a population of slaves, predominantly male, torn from their homes and brutalized in an utterly alien world where disease devastated infants and childbearing women, and where plantations were so small, isolated, and primitive that there were no tasks except the most degrading kinds of field labor. Often slaves lived not even in small huts or sheds in which a semblance of family life or familiar culture might be constructed, but in laborers' barracks. A measure of relief would come only a generation later, when an American-born black population was settled long enough to develop a more balanced sex ratio; when plantation life had evolved to the point where the need for artisanship and household help would allow escape for some of the slaves from the worst kind of field drudgery; and when stable communities of blacks were large enough to nourish a distinctive subculture, mingling African and American traditions—a subculture that would persist and flourish and in the end help shape the national culture of the American people.

Economic Instability

As American society emerged in the early eighteenth century, economic life, social organization, and the practice of religion varied greatly from region to region and from colony to colony. But running through all these major areas of life was a common characteristic, namely, the glaring difference between the colonists' assumptions, ideals, and expectations on the one hand, and on the other hand the actualities of life as it was experienced in America. In considering each of these three areas, one may most profitably start by isolating the colonists' assumptions and expectations, the ideal by which the reality would instinctively be measured. Against this background the departures of American life stand out most clearly, and their impact on the inner experiences of settlers seeking to re-create a familiar and controllable world may most clearly be assessed.

Assumptions and Expectations.   The dominant view of the economy that the colonists brought with them was that of a stable system through which a more or less constant supply of goods and services flowed for the benefit of a population of relatively unchanging needs and desires. The object of individual effort in such a system was to secure oneself within it and to help preserve its organization. Difficulties, when they arose, were assumed to be disturbances in the established relations among the producing, distributing, and consuming elements, and remedies were sought that would bring the elements back into their established and proper proportions. The object of primary concern was the consumer not the producer, and a consumer of fixed, not growing, wants. Controls were assumed to be necessary to keep the economy in proper working order, especially to prevent greed or accidents from disturbing the system. And controls were not assumed to be solely those of the state. Lesser bodies, such as gilds and municipal governments, which stood between the individual and the state, were assumed to be proper agencies of economic regulation.

Such were the ordinary assumptions and the ideal expectations of colonists still close to late medieval culture, still far from the modern world of dynamic economic systems in which an ever-rising production and the manipulation of consumption are essential keys to success. How well did the developing colonial economies conform to these traditional assumptions? The economies that developed north and south violated these expectations on every point, and in doing so created a sense of jarring disarray until, ultimately, the American economic system became established and familiar, and Americans learned to accommodate themselves to the high instability that lay at the heart of this new system.

New England's Economy.   In New England there had originally been little desire to create a commercial system that would link the Bay Colony's small port towns to an intricate network of Atlantic commerce and involve the Puritans in the greater world they had left behind. The original goal was economic self-sufficiency, the condition most likely to preserve the Bible commonwealth free of corruption and contamination. But by the late 1650s circumstances had led the Puritans to create the peculiarly complex economic system, closely involved with Atlantic commerce, that would continue basically unchanged until the Revolution.

The failing effort to perpetuate the Bay Colony's economic independence, once the capital of the original settlers had been exhausted, took two main forms. First, Puritan entrepreneurs, with the active support of the colony's government, sought to produce locally the supplies needed by the settlers, which meant establishing manufactures of iron goods and cloth. An elaborate scheme set on foot by John Winthrop, Jr., the governor's son, resulted in the establishment in Saugus, Massachusetts, of a complete ironworks. It was the product of prodigious efforts by a few devoted entrepreneurs, of the investment of over £12,000 by English businessmen, and of gifts from the General Court of land, tax exemption, and a monopoly of the local markets. But the Saugus Works flourished only briefly and then collapsed into bankruptcy, the victim of a destructive squeeze between inescapably high costs and low profits.

Similarly ineffective was the colony's effort to establish a local cloth industry. A Massachusetts law of 1656 hopefully but quite unrealistically ordered all idle hands in the Bay Colony to busy themselves with spinning and weaving and assessed every family an amount of cloth proportionate to the number of avail-

SAUGUS IRONWORKS
In this restoration of the works as they existed in 1650, the forge is at the left, the rolling
and slitting mill at the right. *(Richard Merrill, photographer)*

able "spinners" in the household. But there were no "idle hands" in this labor-short society. Every available "hand" could find more than enough employment in the fields of the newly opened towns. There was no effective response to the government's demands and exhortations.

But if neither of the two basic manufactures—iron goods and cloth—could be locally produced, self-sufficiency of a sort might yet be created by discovering a small, lightweight, and highly valuable commodity which might be exchanged directly in England for the needed goods. For a few years in the early economic history of New England it seemed as though this would be the ultimate solution. The settlers found a rich supply of fur-bearing animals in the coastal region and just beyond, and they began

a quick exploitation of this highly profitable resource. The easily available beavers, otters, and raccoons were taken by the hundreds and their pelts shipped home in direct exchange for manufactures. But furs proved to be a limited resource. The animals reproduced themselves far more slowly than they were killed, and by the 1650s the supply in the immediate coastal region was exhausted. The New Englanders then pressed west against the Dutch on the Hudson who blocked them from contact with the sources of furs in northern New York and the Great Lakes region. Some furs continued to flow into Boston from trading posts on the Maine coast and the upper Connecticut River, but furs as a basis for the economy, after a decade of wonderful promise, faded from the economy of New England.

Failing to create economic independence or a direct exchange with England, a generation of small merchants in the Bay Colony worked out a system of exchanges throughout the Atlantic world that would produce the needed imports of finished goods. Increasingly, as the population grew, foodstuffs, fish, and timber products became available and the commercial possibilities they created became clear. These products could be sold not in England, which also produced them, but in Catholic Europe (France, Spain, and the Wine Islands of Madeira, the Azores, and the Canaries). These markets could use all the fish that could be sent, and the West Indies could absorb not only fish and other food supplies needed to feed the labor force but also timber for buildings and horses to help work the sugar mills. From the West Indies in turn sugar products could be obtained for sale elsewhere in America and in the English markets; and from Madeira, the Azores, and the Canary Islands wine could be procured for sale in the Atlantic ports. And other contacts could be made. Tobacco could be picked up in the Chesapeake, fish in Newfoundland, and various agricultural products in New York and later in Pennsylvania. An intricate circuit of exhanges could be created—horses and fish for sugar, sugar for bills of exchange, wine, tobacco or locally produced goods.

The purpose of these series of exchanges, which might go on for months or even years before being concluded, was the eventual establishment of credits in the ledgers of some merchant in London or Bristol. The credits would finance the purchase of manufactures to be imported to the colony for profitable sale. These profits would in turn make possible bigger shipments in the next cycle and perhaps investment in shipbuilding as well.

So the commercial system evolved in New England, to be re-created with variations in all the northern colonies. Each colony's system was distinctive, but all were interlocked and had common characteristics. These were no stable, easily controllable commercial flows. They were highly unstable, driven by uncertainty and inescapable risks. Everything conspired to make this commercial world dynamic and erratic.

COD FISHING ON THE GRAND BANKS AND THE NORTH AMERICAN SHORE

This French print of 1705 shows all stages of the fishing industry, from catching the fish (*C*) to gutting and scaling (*F,G*) and drying and packing (*V,Q*). Fish at the upper left are being carted away for salting, and the press at lower left (*R*) is extracting oil from the cod livers, the waste draining into the tub (*S*), the oil into the barrel (*T*). *(Library of Congress)*

For, to begin with, the local production of salable commodities was unreliable and irregular. Not only were there ordinary crop failures but the hinterland farmlands were still being opened and their location and volume of production were still experimental. Even less reliable were the West Indian and Atlantic island markets, which might easily be glutted by a few shipments and from whom it was impossible to obtain reliable market information before cargoes were sent. Further, this commerce was managed not by a few big

SHIPPING MANIFEST, 1687

(Massachusetts Historical Society)

firms whose decisions and agreements might stabilize the system, but by many small and highly competitive merchants. Finally, specialization for any of these small merchant entrepreneurs was virtually impossible if only because a chronic money shortage led to the necessity for payment in goods, with the result that every merchant had to be prepared to sell—or barter—almost any commodity at any time in any market he could find.

As a result of all these conditions, it was nearly impossible to match available goods to available markets. Between the initial shipment of goods and their arrival at an ultimate destination, the entire commercial picture could change. The merchants ventured largely into the dark and were victims of sudden gluts and unpredictable famines and of vicious price fluctuations. There was no fixed geometry of trade. There was no rigid "triangular" trade, in the seventeenth century or after. There were only constantly shifting polygons, forming and reforming as merchants undertook what were in effect peddling voyages up and down the North American coast and in the Caribbean and Atlantic commercial lanes.

Overseas trade proved to be a highly competitive, risky business, in which success was the result of speculative venturing, intelligent risk-taking, and driving entrepreneurship. The principle of success was not the completion of safe, carefully planned exchanges but the almost limitless accumulation of exchanges of all sorts of commodities in a great variety of markets. It was a dynamic system, impelled by powerfully expansive forces.

For over a century this commercial system provided the northern colonies with the goods they needed and helped produce the material basis for a flourishing provincial culture. And from this system important social consequences flowed. In such a commercial world there could be no hard and clear definition of a merchant "class." The situation encouraged the participation of newcomers, starting with very little, who would have been rejected as interlopers in English commercial towns. There were no effective institutional boundaries that might confine the group. Neither gilds nor municipal corporations developed to limit the merchant community or to regulate its activities. Anyone's contribution to the struggling commercial economy was valuable, and the purpose of government intervention could only be to stimulate innovation, not limit it. A dynamic, unstable, unpredictable yet successful commercial system had produced a fluid merchant group, constantly recruiting newcomers from among successful tradesmen and farmers and seeking security and wealth in a system whose essence was risk.

The Southern Economy. No less risky, competitive, and unstable was the economic system that developed in the Chesapeake region around the production and marketing of the staple crop of tobacco. The details are of course altogether different from those of the northern commercial system, but here too success would come not from sharing in regular production and a stable process of distribution but from involvement in runaway cycles of production and a lurching, unpredictable distribution system. And in the South as in the North, a dynamic economy produced uncontrollable social consequences.

Originally there had been little enthusiasm for producing tobacco, which was considered harmful to health and was associated with general immorality. In the reign of James I (who himself wrote *A Counterblaste to Tobacco* in 1604), tobacco pipes were used as doorsigns of brothels. But then as now, however harmful it was to health, tobacco sold, and it sold extremely well in England, originally as an expensive luxury item imported from Spain. Once Americans began to sell tobacco in England they worked diligently to exploit the market, and quickly flooded it. By the late 1630s the price of tobacco in England had dropped precipitously, to a point less than the cost of production. There was a mild recovery of prices in the early 1640s and then further collapses in the 1660s as production rose still further in the Chesapeake colonies. By the end of the century, prices were still low, and a pattern of recoveries and collapses had emerged that would persist throughout the colonial period.

The low prices and the uncontrollable cycles were symptoms of profound problems in the tobacco economy. The primary problem was overproduction. By the end of the 1630s, little more than a decade after the first marketable crop had reached England, the Chesapeake colonies were producing 1.5 million pounds of tobacco a year. By 1700 the figure had risen to about 38 million pounds annually. In addition, the Chesapeake industry suffered from serious competition. Spain continued to send the best-quality crop, which commanded the highest prices, and sizable shipments also arrived from the Caribbean Islands. England too was a competitor, since tobacco was a well-established crop in Gloucestershire. To compound the troubles further, as production rose, American tobacco deteriorated in quality, and the middlemen assumed that it would fetch the lowest prices. Perhaps even more important were the technical difficulties of marketing this product of the scattered Chesapeake farms.

The tobacco specialists who appeared quickly within the London merchant community worked out a marketing procedure that survived for a century. In this "consignment" system the English merchants were primarily selling agents. The planters sent their crops to these merchants, usually on the merchants' vessels, for sale through them in the English and European markets. The English merchants advanced funds for all the necessary charges—freight, fees, taxes, storage, and so on—and repaid themselves, with profit, when the crop was eventually sold. In addition, they advanced goods to the planters charged against the eventual tobacco sales, and so they became the planters' bankers and creditors as well as merchandisers. There was a rough efficiency in this system, but it victimized the planters by involving them in endless debt cycles. Any given crop was in effect mortgaged long before it was sold. Further, the planters had no control whatever over the sale of their crops; they had no choice but to rely entirely on the merchants' goodwill. Finally, it was impossible, by this system, ever to adjust production to demand. Often two years would go by between shipment and and news of eventual sale, by which time several new crops would have been produced and disposed of. The net result of this system was constant debts and an unmanageable rigidity in the economic process that governed the planters' lives.

As if overproduction, keen competition, deteriorating quality, and a rigid marketing system were not burdens enough, there was the decisive problem of breaking into the markets of continental Europe. England could absorb relatively little of the enormous Chesapeake production. Of the approximately 38 million pounds of tobacco exported to England in 1700, 25 million pounds were reexported to the continent. Thus these ultimate markets were crucial to the prosperity of the American tobacco farmers.

At first the continental countries banned American tobacco altogether; then they imposed high duties; and finally they established "farms," that is, state-controlled or state-owned and state-operated monopolies of imports, which determined how much tobacco would be imported, what grades would be allowed in, and what prices would be charged. And as this mechanism matured and the political complexities of tobacco marketing in Europe multiplied, Dutch middlemen became increasingly important in transmitting the commodity to the ultimate markets. And so still another burden was added to the already heavily encumbered trade.

Such was the array of problems that developed in the seventeenth century as the southern economy took shape. Throughout the century strenuous efforts were made to overcome these problems, with only partial success. The English government taxed Spanish tobacco out of the English markets and rooted out tobacco planting in Gloucestershire; at the same time, the West Indian producers withdrew from this increasingly competitive industry. But Dutch shippers were shrewd competitors, and until the force of the Navigation Acts was felt toward the end of the century, they remained effective participants in the shipping trade. And neither the English nor the colonial governments could force the individual American tobacco growers to limit their production. Quite the contrary. Most planters were ever more convinced that the more they produced the greater would be their income; and as a consequence the system was propelled forward as if by a powerful internal accelerator. Production continued to expand, and so too did the area of land under cultivation.

The social consequences of this risky and unstable economy were profound. The constant expansion of the area of settlement went forward without regard for the Indians, who were driven back behind ever-expanding frontiers. As the planters pressed deeper into the interior in search of fresh lands, they forced even the friendly Indians into hostility. There were frontier skirmishes long before the full-scale race war broke out that touched off Bacon's Rebellion (1676).*

Further, the tobacco economy generated a desperate need for a large labor force. Hired or indentured servants were never available in sufficient numbers, and as a result the tobacco farms remained relatively small (an average of 250 acres). Slavery was an obvious solution to the labor problem even if its capital costs were greater than those of a free labor system. By the end of the century it was clear that the demands of the tobacco economy were inexorably enlarging the slave labor force and thereby compounding one of the greatest evils of American life.

The peculiar economy of tobacco, finally, eliminated the possibility that an urban society would develop to the south of Pennsylvania. The organization of the tobacco trade prevented local merchants from developing into independent entrepreneurs since the commercial processes were provided for in England. As a consequence the secondary activities that ordinarily develop around "entrepreneurial headquarters" (shipbuilding, service trades, brokerage, and shopkeeping) were frustrated from the start. On the eve of the Revolution, Williamsburg had a total population of but two thousand, and even that small population was largely the result of the government's residence in the town. Baltimore and Norfolk, with populations of six thousand each, developed not in the heart of the tobacco country but at the borders of more diversified economies.

Social Instability

No aspect of community life came under more intense pressure than social organization. The genera-

*On Bacon's Rebellion, see pp. 109–10.

tion that settled in America in the years before 1660 was still close to the Elizabethans, who in a period of rapid social change had spelled out clearly the traditional assumptions of an ideal community structure. The Elizabethans, and their colonizing descendants, assumed that society was not a miscellaneous collection of people pursuing their separate goals and relating to each other haphazardly. For them, society was a disciplined organism, a fabric closely "knit together," as they liked to say, whose overall character was more meaningful than any of the separate parts that composed it. Specifically, they assumed that society would display at least three essential characteristics.

They expected, first, that the parts of a community would complement each other and fit together harmoniously to compose the commonwealth as a whole. They expected, too, that the structure of society would be essentially hierarchical, organized into distinct levels of inferiority and superiority, levels not of "class" but of status and dignity, characteristics related to occupation and wealth but not defined by them. And they assumed, third, that the hierarchy of society was a unitary structure in which people of superior status in one aspect of life would be superior in all others. Thus the rich would be politically powerful, educated, and dignified; leadership in public and private affairs would fall to the highborn, the firstborn, the natural leaders, equipped to rule by all the attributes of social superiority.

These were characteristics of all coherent societies, the Elizabethans believed, and those among them who voyaged to America had no intention of recasting or rejecting such fundamental notions. But in fact the world that emerged in mainland North America did not conform to these ideals. To be sure, there was no total breakdown, once the horrors of the "starving times" were overcome; there was no instant transformation into a different mode of life. But from the first years of settlement there were acute stresses and strains that made social life in the colonies tense, strange, and difficult.

The sources of some of these problems were obvious. The colonists were well aware that the political and economic leadership of the communities was being assumed by people who, though capable of dealing with the raw environment, lacked the traditional social attributes of command—a sense of natural superiority, habitual dignity, personal authority. The respect due to the leading figures was not, as a result, automatically forthcoming. Political and economic leaders were vulnerable to criticism and challenged in ways their social superiors would not have been.

Puritanism and Social Order. In New England this general problem was peculiarly compounded. Within the Puritans' distinctive status system purity of religion, piety, and rectitude were decisive in establishing distinction. At the same time, every effort was made to perpetuate a traditional social structure. Allotments of land in the newly opened townships, for example, were by common agreement made larger for persons of wealth, position, and professional training. Even so vague a distinction as "ability" was materially rewarded. But the conflict with religious values could not be avoided.

The problem was at least clearly understood. One of the Puritans' most influential English leaders, Lord Say and Sele, considered joining the Great Migration in 1636, but then paused. Was it not true, he wrote the Reverend John Cotton in Boston, that men could attain the franchise in Massachusetts simply by being accepted into the church, no matter what their social condition might be? If so, what certainty was there that people like himself would be able to play their proper roles? Cotton tried to reassure him. Everyone knew that "monarchy and aristocracy are both of them clearly approved and directed in scripture" and that God never ordained democracy to be "a fit government either for church or commonwealth." So His Lordship need have no fear of finding in New England a world turned upside down. Still, Cotton had to admit, the Puritans *were* committed to the service of the Lord: religious considerations in the end would prevail and *should* prevail. For is it not better, he asked, "that the commonwealth be fashioned to the setting forth of God's house, which is his church, than to accommodate the church frame to the civil state?" The noble lord read the message correctly and stayed home. The Bay Colony's tumults in the founding years continued to reflect the

NEW ENGLAND HOUSES OF THE SEVENTEENTH CENTURY

Below, the Ironmaster's House, Saugus, built in the 1630s and enlarged 20 years later, is an exceptionally imposing residence for the period. The ordinary workers at Saugus lived in thatch-roofed cottages even simpler than the houses in Plymouth (p. 40). *Left,* the Paul Revere house in Boston, 1680. The overhanging second story and heavily leaded casement windows are typical of the substantial artisans' houses of the time. *(Below, Mark Flannery, photographer)*

strange confusion and intermixture of religious and social distinctions.

Social Structure and Family Life. Everywhere in the colonies there were difficulties and confusions in maintaining a traditional social order in the raw wilderness world. On the farms, whether in New England, New York, the Chesapeake colonies, or Carolina, it was physically impossible to maintain the expected differences in styles of life—differences not merely between masters and servants who labored side by side, but between field workers on the one hand and preachers, teachers, and doctors on the other. Laboring side by side day after day, masters and servants found their life-styles approaching each other until the differences rested only on a legal statement, a scrap of paper establishing the servants' dependency, a formality whose force, deprived of material sanction, grew weaker with time. There were few luxuries anywhere, and nowhere was there the material basis for leisure. The few people of professional training lived far more primitive lives than their education and occupational roles would traditionally have assured them.

In the towns the problems of maintaining traditional status differentiation were especially dramatic. The standard refrain through the century was that the free workers—the handicraftsmen, shipwrights, carpenters, shoemakers, tailors—had lost all respect for traditional roles and social distinctions. The wages they claimed were astronomical, it was commonly said; their social pretensions insufferable. They flaunted their prosperity outrageously, and aped their superiors in ways that offended all sense of decency and social order. Every effort was made to contain the social disorder that they created by eliminating the causes of this alleged misbehavior or by limiting its effects. Occasionally when the problem became acute, the assemblies sought to limit wages in order to restrict the workers' ambitions and protect the public against their apparent greed. But such laws could not be enforced. The workers' services were indispensable; people would pay almost anything they demanded. And the workers' arguments were convincing too: prices, they said, were rising;

they had expenses to meet. Let prices be fixed if wages were. But price fixing was as futile as wage fixing, and what a later generation would call "escalator clauses" were tried with only temporary effect on the demands and behavior of the free, self-employed workers.

By 1660 the effort to eliminate the source of the workers' extravagance had clearly failed, and it was left for the assemblies to try to discipline behavior itself, to try to confine dress and social intercourse to appropriate forms of decency. Sumptuary legislation restricted the wearing of finery, limited display, and lectured an apparently disordered population on the confusion of the times. The Massachusetts Bay Colony's sumptuary law of 1651 is perhaps the most eloquent testimony of the age to the founders' pervasive sense of disarray. The General Court declared its

utter detestation and dislike, that men or women of mean condition should take upon them the garb of gentlemen, by wearing gold or silver lace, or buttons, or points at their knees, or to walk in great boots, or women of the same rank to wear silk or tiffany hoods or scarves which, though allowable to persons of greater estates or more liberal education, yet we cannot but judge it intolerable in persons of such like condition.

The times were deeply disordered, the court said, and it therefore ordered

that no person within this jurisdiction, ... whose visible estates shall not exceed the true and indifferent value of £200 shall wear any gold or silver lace, or gold and silver buttons, or any bone lace above 2 shillings per yard, or silk hoods or scarves, upon the penalty of 10 shillings for every such offense.

And then, in a devilishly clever provision, the court decreed that if the town selectmen found anyone they judged "to exceed their ranks and abilities in the costliness or fashion of their apparel," they were to increase the offender's tax rate to the level of wealth he or she pretended to—all of this *provided*, the General Court added in an afterthought that illuminates the unstable social landscape like a flare, that the law *not* apply to any of the colony's magistrates or their families, to any regular military officers or soldiers

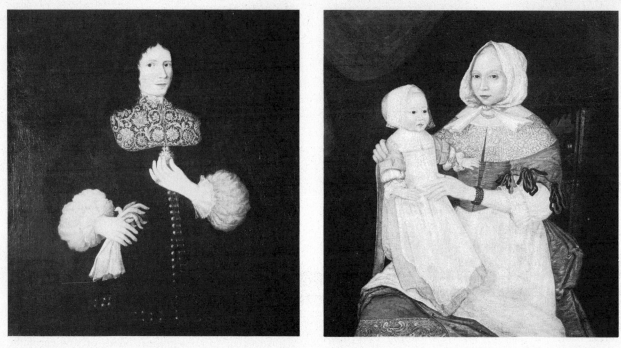

JOHN FREAKE AND HIS WIFE ELIZABETH AND CHILD, 1674
Freake was one of the successful merchants who arrived in Boston well after the original Puritan migration and brought with him a "corrupting" luxuriance of style. His buttons are silver, his collar fine lace, his sleeves puffed muslin, and his gold brooch studded with precious stones. His wife's embroidered petticoat is carefully revealed. *(Worcester Art Museum)*

on active duty, or to anyone else *"whose education and employment have been above the ordinary degree, or whose estates have been considerable, though now decayed."*

"Though now decayed"—the phrase echoes a profound sense of disordered change, of a decline of standards. And in no aspect of life was this sense more acute than in the realm of the family. Here, it was felt, the erosion went deepest, the disorder was most manifest. The Puritan magistrates repeatedly denounced the loosening of family ties and the defiance of authority in this most intimate and fundamental of all social units. Repeatedly they commanded parents to do their duty to their children and to themselves, and ordered children to respect and obey their parents and to fulfill their family obligations. The laws grew more stringent as the years passed. In New Hampshire, Massachusetts, and Connecticut, in conformity with the biblical injunction, death was de-

creed for children who struck or cursed their parents (the law was invoked at least once, though never enforced). In Massachusetts, tithingmen were made responsible for the good order of groups of ten families, and the church synod of 1679, blaming the evils of the time on "defects of family government," commanded the tithingmen to redouble their efforts to reinforce the failing discipline of weak-willed parents.

In fact, of course, the family was not being destroyed. On the surface, at least, the institution was little weaker at the end of the century than it had been at the start. But something *had* happened. There *were* problems, and those problems, if properly understood, help explain the outcries, the sense of disarray, and the efforts to remedy what was felt by many to be a disastrous decline in the traditional good order of family life.

To understand these problems, it is necessary to

note that families in the seventeenth century were considered the archetype of all social order. In this micro-community, it was believed, all order began, all patterns of inferiority and superiority took shape. The political commonwealth was but an enlargement of the family. Rulers were conceived of as patriarchs whose dominance as heads of commonwealths was justified by God the father of all. All of this was a cliché of the age, but a cliché that, like most commonplaces that pass unchallenged, was essentially realistic. For most Englishmen experienced a larger, more highly structured, more complex, and more disciplined family unit than now exists in the Western world, but not because the nuclear family (parents and children) was significantly larger than it is now. Most completed families in seventeenth-century England contained only two or three children, though many more were born and died young. The sense of complexity, structure, and discipline grew from the fact that family meant or implied the household--all those who lived together under one roof—and almost all Englishmen at some time in their lives had experienced the household-family as a complex and disciplined institution. For servants were traditionally part of this artificially extended family, and servitude was remarkably widespread. Something like a third of all English families had servants; at any one time, between 10 and 15 percent of the entire English population was serving in another's household—and serving not merely as day workers exchanging limited services for wages but as family members committed to total employment in exchange for maintenance, protection, and to some extent education. In addition, free children of other families circulated as guests, often for long periods, in more affluent households or even in households of equivalent social position. As a result, at least 45 percent of all English people lived in households of six or more members. Consequently most people, at least in their youth, experienced families as complex, to some extent even partriarchal, units.

In traditional settings, material circumstances reinforced and helped perpetuate these household-families. Young people found it difficult to break away and establish new independent households. For eco-nomic independence was largely made possible in this predominantly agricultural world by the purchase, or the long-term lease, of plots of arable land, and it was extremely difficult to make such transactions in the absence of available public land. As a result, many servants found themselves obliged to remain dependent beyond the time of their contractual obligations; marriages were delayed, since married couples were expected to live in their own establishments and not within other households; and family discipline developed naturally and remained a familiar, accepted fact of life.

In the colonies of seventeenth-century America these material reinforcements of traditional family life were either greatly weakened or eliminated. Where land was far more freely available than in England, the establishment of independent households, though difficult physically, became a relatively easy matter economically. What is remarkable in these circumstances is not that the average age at first marriage fell, but that it did not fall even further and faster than it did, and that there was not more pressure against traditional family organization than there was.

But the availability of land was only one of the alterations in reinforcement of traditional family life in the colonies. The acute and continuing labor shortage, which shifted the dependency relations within the family and household, meant that parents and masters depended on their children and servants as never before. They needed them, sometimes desperately, to provide critically necessary labor. In this sense, the parents became dependents—but not only in this sense. The young learned to cope with the environment more rapidly than their seniors; they adapted to change more easily; and in the end they inevitably became lifelines to the world for their elders. They became, in effect, their parents' teachers, despite the unquestioned and continuing assumption of parental superiority.

In the Chesapeake region through most of the seventeenth century the common disorder of family life was greatly increased by the fearful death rate. Where only half the people born would live to age 20, and where two out of every three marriages were broken by the death of one of the partners (more often the husband), family and household life was chaotic.

Widows, left with several children in a rough frontier society where there were many more men than women, remarried quickly, if only for survival. Often their husbands brought children from earlier marriages, and the households, in which wives acquired greater importance and authority than was normal for the age, were crowded with half-siblings and stepchildren. And there were orphan children everywhere.

The consequences of the tensions and widespread disarray ran deep. Gradually the law responded to these altered circumstances. Primogeniture—the legal requirement that real property descend only to the eldest son so that the family estate would remain intact—was commonly ignored where land was plentiful. The common practice was to divide property among the members of a family, perhaps with double portions for the wife and eldest son. Orphan courts appeared in the South to protect the interests of children otherwise uncared for. And the law became more responsive to the interests of women. In Massachusetts laws were passed that prohibited husbands from striking their wives—"unless it be in his own defense." Women, north and south, acquired new rights to own, administer, and legally protect property; to conduct business; and to represent themselves in court. And they were treated more equitably by the courts in divorce proceedings. In general, women enjoyed a higher social status in seventeenth-century America than they did in England, where the traditionally severe subordination of females, inherited from the medieval past, continued largely unchanged.

The legal position of bonded servants also improved. In some places the severity of punishment was limited by law; in others, working conditions were improved; and in all the colonies every effort was made to use the law to keep servants at work despite the liberating forces that surrounded them. A case is recorded in which a servant ran away after being punished for attempting to rape his master's ten-year-old daughter—the suit being filed not to punish the culprit but to get him back and to force him to complete his term of service! Everywhere the conditions of contractual obligations grew lighter as the ease of transition to personal independence was recognized.

Social order was not destroyed in the seventeenth-century colonies, nor was the world transformed. But on this western frontier of European civilization, society had acquired new instabilities, along with new freedoms for traditionally subordinated elements in the nonslave population. In calmer years and in more settled circumstances, some of these changes would recede into more traditional forms, but most would become part of a permanently altered way of life.

Religion

Religion was inevitably involved in the larger social changes, for the colonists' culture was still profoundly Christian and churches were still the preeminent cultural institutions as well as vital social agencies. The seventeenth century was an age of intense religious controversy; men and nations struggled savagely over differences in religious opinion. Yet a few nearly universal presumptions were shared by almost all religious groups—presumptions that illuminate the history of religion in early America particularly well.

Christians, save for the most extreme radicals, generally assumed that there was a universally true religion and that a plurality of beliefs should not be encouraged. However much most seventeenth-century Christians differed on what doctrines were orthodox, they assumed that *some* doctrines were absolutely right and others wrong and that the effort to eradicate, or at least to heavily constrain, heresy and to extend orthodoxy was altogether legitimate. Equally axiomatic was the belief that religion was not simply a spiritual matter nor of concern only to the church. The agencies of the state were understood to have a major responsibility to supervise religion and to enforce orthodoxy. Finally, as overseas emigration became a prominent part of the life of western Europe, it was assumed that church institutions established in the colonies would follow familiar organizational patterns and fit somehow into some larger pattern of religious institutions. No one expected that churches established in the frontier borderlands would become institutions with special characteristics.

The history of religion in the first two or three generations can be seen as the story of the violation of these presumptions and the struggle to retain them in the face of adversity. Christianity in more or less familiar outward form of course survived, but it survived with significant alterations that were forced into being, not by will or doctrine, but by intractable circumstances. Not for another century would these changes be fully accepted and incorporated into the deliberate design of religious organization and practice. But the seeds of what would later evolve into America's distinctive denominational organization of religion were planted and nourished in the complex social history of the seventeenth century.

The Anglican Church in Virginia. The most revealing example of the way in which environment shaped the development of Christianity in America lies in the history of the Church of England in Virginia. Here the sense of orthodoxy was strong and free from pressures of reform and from doctrinal conflicts; here the fullest re-creation of traditional forms was attempted; and here the failure of expectation was particularly severe.

The Virginia Company and the government that followed it assumed that the Church of England in its established form would simply be reproduced in the settlements along the James River, and that these local branches of the church would be easily incorporated into the national church. But there were severe problems from the start, most of which flowed from the difficulty of devising a workable economic basis for the newly founded church institutions. In England churches were usually supported by land endowments, gifts of income-producing property donated by patrons. In Virginia the company, and subsequently the crown, took over the role of patron to the newly founded parishes. In 1618 the company set aside as church land 100 acres (later increased by the crown to 200 acres) in each of the still vague "boroughs." The income from this land, to be produced by the labor of tenants, was to support a minister and the upkeep of the church. But tenants were not easily obtainable in Virginia, and the land was worthless until some kind of labor could be provided. This left two alternatives for the support of the church. First, the clergy could become almost full-time farmworkers and produce

ST. LUKE'S CHURCH, ISLE OF WIGHT COUNTY, VIRGINIA (LATE SEVENTEENTH CENTURY)
A typical Anglican parish church, with its bell tower, arched windows, and buttresses. *(Courtesy, Virginia State Travel Service)*

the expected income, a prospect that in itself discouraged the recruitment of well-trained clergymen. Alternatively, a new kind of support would have to be forthcoming. This new form—taxation—was anticipated by the company when it ordered parishioners to supplement the income of the church land until its yield equaled £200 a year. Such supplements quickly became common, then universal. It soon became standard practice for the parishioners' governing body, the vestry, to vote funds for the church as an annual tax rate.

Once taxation became the financial basis of the church, the size of the parish became a critical problem. If the parish were to be defined by the number of people, with the standard set by the population of the usual English parish, the resulting territory would spread so widely along the colony's creeks and rivers that proper ministrations would be impossible. On the other hand, if the geographical size of the parish were kept small so that the parishioners could gather easily

COLLEGE OF WILLIAM AND MARY, PICTURED IN THE 1730s
Founded in large part to educate Virginians for the Anglican ministry, it was built to the
plans of Christopher Wren. The central building was erected by the end of the century
but had to be rebuilt after a fire of 1705.   *(Library of Congress)*

and ministers could be in constant communication with flocks, the per capita cost of support would be extremely high. The inevitable result, in the underdeveloped and struggling economy, was a pattern of unworkably large parishes and, because of variations in population density and wealth, great variations in the support of the clergy.

By the end of the first generation, the dilemma facing the church was officially recognized. In 1662 the assembly tried to make all church salaries uniform at £80 a year. But this figure had to be translated into set amounts of tobacco, which was the medium of exchange, and when the real value of tobacco fell, so too did the real worth of the ministers' salaries. In any case, being paid in tobacco, the clergy were at the mercy of local variations in quality and were dependent too on the goodwill of their parishioners for the selection of tobacco that was made.

From this simple and fundamental economic problem flowed profoundly important consequences in the lives of the clergy and in the life of religion in general. By English standards the ministers were almost everywhere grossly underpaid, and they were faced with next-to-impossible conditions of work. Further, they were stripped of economic independence because of their reliance on annual gifts of the parish. Nor did they acquire security of tenure. In England the patrons (or their heirs) who endowed the churches nominated ministers for lifetime appointment as rectors, and the bishops confirmed them in office. In Virginia, the patrons, given the tax base of the ministers' salaries,

proved to be the vestries, the self-perpetuating bodies of lay leaders of the church in each parish. The vestries were instructed by the church officers in England to present their nominees to the governors for formal induction into office. But in most cases they refused (only 10 percent of the Virginia clergy in the seventeenth century were ever formally inducted into their offices), claiming that the available candidates were so inferior in quality that they did not deserve permanency of tenure.

It was a self-intensifying problem. The vestries refused to present candidates for formal induction to permanent tenure because the quality of the clergy was too low to justify such confidence and respect; but their refusal was an important reason why well-qualified candidates refused to settle in Virginia. The declining spiral fell lower and lower. Many well-qualified and able young clergymen were present in Virginia in the early years, but by the end of the century their numbers had declined to insignificance. Recruitment seemed to come from the dregs of the ecclesiastical barrel. Efforts of church missionaries and later of the Church's Society for the Propagation of the Gospel in Foreign Parts (founded in 1701) led to a series of proposals to remedy the situation. One of the early proposals resulted in the chartering of the College of William and Mary in 1693 to provide a means of educating Virginians locally for the ministry. But it was extremely difficult to improve the situation. By 1724 the reputation of the clergy in Virginia had become so scandalous that the following almost farcical proposals were included in a comprehensive plan of reform submitted to the Bishop of London, whose jurisdiction included the American colonies.

And to prevent the scandals of bad life in the clergy, let it be enacted that whatsoever minister shall be found guilty of fornication, adultery, blasphemy, ridiculing of the Holy Scriptures, or maintaining . . . any doctrine contrary to the 39 Articles shall . . . lose his living [income] and be suspended from all exercise of the ministerial function for three years. . . . And because drunkenness is one of the most common crimes and yet hardest to be proved . . . let it be enacted that the following proof shall be taken for a sufficient proof of drunkenness, viz., first, let the signs of drunkenness be proved such as sitting an hour or longer in the company where they were a drinking strong drink and in the meantime drinking of healths or otherwise taking his cups as they came around like the rest of the company; striking, challenging, threatening to fight, or laying aside any of his garments for that purpose; staggering, reeling, vomiting, incoherent, impertinent, obscene, or rude talking. Let the proof of these signs proceed so far till the judges conclude that the minister's behavior at such a time was scandalous, indecent, and unbecoming the gravity of a minister.

The debasement of the clergy was one aspect of the general transformation of the Church of England in Virginia. Another development, in the long run equally important, was the destruction of the hierarchical structure of the church. This came about as a result of the distance from higher controls in England and by the local vestries' assumption of absolute power in church affairs. Control fell to the parish level, and the result was in effect a congregational institution, despite the official affiliation with the Church of England, which was governed by bishops and archbishops. Further, the practice of religion was simplified, even secularized to some extent. Since most ministers could not reach all areas of their parishes, lay readers were appointed to fulfill certain ministerial functions. The general simplicity of life and the lack of funds for embellishments meant that the sacraments were administered without the proper vestments or ornaments of church ritual. The dead were buried in private cemeteries more often than in parish burial grounds; the holy days were neglected; and marriage was performed in private residences under lay auspices. Further, the church as a judicial body declined into insignif-

icance, for the members of the vestries and of the local civil courts were often the same people. It was more reasonable, in view of the weakness of the church, for cases of moral offenses to be brought before the civil courts than before the church courts. And it was the civil courts rather than the weak parish institutions that became the repositories for vital statistics.

No one, of course, doubted that the Church of England had been established in Virginia, but it was a strange establishment indeed. Conditions had led the church as an institution toward what might be called nonseparating Congregationalism—institutionally the position adopted in New England—not as a matter of doctrine but as a matter of social and institutional fact.

Toleration in Catholic Maryland. Maryland shared the same environmental conditions, and its religious institutions would have conformed to the same pattern except for two basic facts: first, the government of the colony was in the hands of a Catholic proprietor who conceived of the colony as a Catholic refuge; and second, the great majority of those available for settlement in the colony were Protestants, and the success of the colony depended on the success of recruitment. The proprietor's Catholic interests would have to be handled with the greatest care.

At the start, the Calverts issued to their governors instructions they thought would satisfy the conflicting demands. They ordered the Maryland officials to give no offense to Protestants because of their religion; to see to it that Catholicism was practiced as privately as possible; and to leave those who professed Christianity in any form free to worship as they chose. It was a vague, pragmatically liberal position, and it was promptly attacked both by the Jesuits who had accompanied the settlers, demanding that Catholicism be established far more substantially than this, and by the Protestants in the colony, whose opposition to Catholic rule erupted into open rebellion in the early years of the English Civil War. It was to stabilize the situation in the face of these cross pressures and to protect Maryland's charter that the Calverts issued in 1649 their famous Act Concerning Religion.

This document, though remarkable for its era, is not an act for full freedom of religion. It begins, in fact, by ordering the death penalty for any non-trinitarian Christians who insisted on professing their religion in Maryland. But it goes on to say that, in order to assure public tranquility—and for that reason alone—all trinitarian Christians were guaranteed the right to profess and practice their religion. Nothing in this document, which remained in effect through the century, challenged the prevailing idea of orthodoxy. It contained no hint of the principles of the separation of church and state, or of freedom of conscience and worship as good in themselves—no hint of any of the soaring ideals of liberty of thought and conscience that would later find expression in Jefferson's great Statute of Religious Freedom. The Calverts' act specified toleration on the narrowest possible ground—for just those groups whom it was expedient to tolerate: Catholics, Anglicans, and moderate Protestant dissenters. Yet it was a significant departure, if limited and pragmatic, and it fitted perfectly the decentralization of religion that was otherwise developing in the colony. For in Maryland as in Virginia the necessary tax base of church support meant full control by local authorities, in most places by the vestries. This, together with the official toleration of most differing groups, meant the emergence in this colony of a multi-denominational Christianity whose institutional form was essentially congregational.

The Dutch Church in New York. The same result in even more extreme form emerged in New York. The Dutch, like the English, assumed at the start that their national church, Dutch Reformed Calvinist, would be re-created in America, and that it would be controlled by that church's ruling body, the Classis of Amsterdam. But from the earliest years, New Netherland was complex in its religious character, and there were no effective controls from the home country. Besides Dutch Calvinists, Jews, and a broad range of sectarian radicals that included Anabaptists and Quakers, there were Lutherans, whose insistence on the right to public worship led to their suppression and persecution by Stuyvesant. The Dutch West India Company's policy was to permit *private* wor-

ship of any kind, so long as the Dutch church was officially recognized and supported by universal taxation. The Lutherans, however, insisted on the right to public worship. The question remained unsettled, the source of fierce animosities, until after the English conquest. Then, in 1665, the freeholders of each community in New York were ordered to vote for some one Protestant church, which would then be locally established. Once chosen, the denomination would be supported by general taxation, though private worship was allowed to continue.

The Dutch church remained dominant, of course, since most of the colonists were Dutch, and in this situation of local option it sought to perpetuate its heritage and mode of worship. But here as in the Chesapeake colonies settlements were scattered, the recruitment of properly qualified ministers was extremely difficult, and proper ministrations proved impossible to perform. Here too lay readers presided when ordained ministers were unobtainable, and there was a radical decline in the outward quality of religious life. Worse still, after the English conquest the Dutch church became a branch of an alien national church. How could this American branch relate to the home body? If the Dutch settlers in New York acknowledged the supremacy of the Dutch church fully, they would in effect be challenging the supremacy of the English crown; if they did not make that challenge, implicitly at least they would not be faithful to their own religious profession. It was

SYMBOLISM ON PURITAN GRAVESTONES

Folk art (see color section) was never absent from the colonies. In Puritan New England it took particularly imaginative form in the portrayal of death, sin, and salvation in gravestone carvings. *Far right,* the John Foster stone, Dorchester, Massachusetts, 1681, depicts Time holding back the hand of Death from extinguishing the flame of life atop the globe. The allegory was copied from an illustration in *Hieroglyphiques of the Life of Man* (1638) by Francis Quarles, a popular English poet. *Right,* panel of a stone of 1692 in which a naked imp of the underworld carries both Time's hour glass and Death's dart. *(Both photographs, Allan Ludwig)* a dilemma that could not be resolved but might be endured if the issue was never pressed.

New England Puritanism.   In the context of these unexpected developments elsewhere in the colonies, the outward form of religion that became established in New England is perhaps not so unique. Everywhere the hierarchy of church organization had failed to develop, ritual had become simplified, sacramental functions of the church were reduced, and laymen shared pulpits with ordained ministers. None of this, however, had been the consequence of doctrine or belief or intent. All of it had developed in response to the circumstances of life in the new American colonies. In New England the same developments were small parts of a general plan of religious reform that was pursued almost fanatically and fortified by a theological position whose refinement was the work of men of subtle mind and great intellectual energy. But Puritanism was not only an intellectual system and it did not satisfy only the needs of theologians. It was a social movement as well as an intellectual movement, and it performed, in New England

as in Old England, a notable social function.

The central character of New England Puritanism emerges most clearly if one defines it precisely; and its social role becomes apparent if one concentrates on the question of why its force continued once the original settlements were stabilized.

New England Puritanism was one specific expression within a broad protest movement against the religious conservatism of the Church of England as it existed under Elizabeth. Those who would later be known as Puritans felt that England's break with the Roman Catholic Church under Henry VIII had not gone far enough. The differences between the Puritan reformers and the conservative churchmen did not lie in central theological points. Both groups were predestinarian: both believed that human salvation was ultimately determined by decisions of a mysterious God. The differences lay in two questions concerning the nature and function of the church as an institution.

The first was the question of how effective the church could be in assisting people in their search for salvation. The Anglican churchmen, like Cath-

olics, believed that the church could be instrumental in bridging the world of ordinary, physical humanity and that of men in a state of God's grace. The difference between physical existence and true sanctity was not, the church insisted, total and absolute, bridgeable only by God's gift of spiritual rebirth; qualified priests and the procedures and rituals of the church could assist in the great search for salvation. With this, the Puritans disagreed. The gap between nature and grace was for them absolute and total, and could be mediated only by God in direct contact with an open and willing soul and by the Bible, which contained God's recorded words. The church's institutions and its ritual—all such outward "works"—merely interfered with the essential experience of religion, which for the Puritans was the experience of man struggling to make contact with an inscrutable God.

The second question that came to define Puritanism concerned the visibility of God's church. Orthodox Anglicans felt that it was impossible ever truly to tell who had achieved a state of grace and who had not. This was the ultimate mystery, and therefore the church existed for everyone, in the hope that its good offices would help some to achieve a better life and would be a natural home for those who were already members of God's elect. For Anglicans the membership of the "visible" church (that is, the worldly institution of the church) should include the whole of society; people should be born into the church as a fact of their mortal existence. The Puritans disagreed vehemently with this position. They felt that it was possible though difficult to distinguish the elect from ordinary mortals. Tests could be devised and signs detected that would dis-

FIRST PARISH MEETING HOUSE, HINGHAM, MASS. 1681
This famous building, whose exterior is largely the work of the eighteenth century, retains much of the original seventeenth-century interior. Lacking models for the spacious but austere building they had in mind and spurning all architectural embellishments, the ship carpenters hired for the occasion simply built a ship's keel in reverse to form the interior roof. (*Photos by Arthur B. Mazmanian from his* The Structure of Praise © *The Beacon Press*)

tinguish these "saints" from unredeemed humanity and make it possible to confine full church membership to those visibly sanctified people. Church membership should not include everyone in society, the Puritans felt; it should be a gathering of saints. The visible church, they said, and God's church of the elect should, as far as possible, be one.

These two key issues defined the protest movement of the late sixteenth century which in the broadest sense was Puritanism. But Puritanism in this broadest sense includes a wide range of positions on the question of the church's relation to society, only one of which was established in the Bay Colony. The Massachusetts Puritans believed that church membership should be limited to the elect of God, but they also continued to believe that the church, even so reduced, should control society as a whole and be responsible for creating conditions favorable to the search for salvation. For them there could be no denial of responsibility for the everyday world as it existed. The condition of all people was the responsibility of the saints, and the church, though only of the saints, must somehow be active in the affairs of the unredeemed.

How such a program could be effected was a matter of endless discussion and writing both in England and in America. But in England the Congregational Puritans' energies had been absorbed in the struggle for survival against an authoritarian church determined to eliminate active dissent. In Massachusetts and Connecticut, however, the Puritans, protected from interference by the charters, could work out fully the implications of their "nonseparating," Congregationalist position.

Because profoundly committed Puritans were in full charge of the community in Massachusetts and Connecticut, and because their beliefs hinged on the identification of the visible and invisible churches, the passage into full church membership took on a significance it had nowhere else. For in England, where the Congregationalist Puritans were a persecuted minority, there was no scramble on the part of ordinarily religious but unsanctified people to gain membership in these congregations. Only the fully committed and utterly sincere would have wished to join a group so embattled politically and so demanding in its practices. In New England the situation was altogether different. Here the Congregational Church leaders held all the powers; they *were* the government, and the resources and power available in the community were at their disposal. Where the Congregational Church was fully established and where social rewards were attached to membership in the church, the passage into full church affiliation became a critical issue for the society as a whole. Quickly, therefore, procedures were devised that opened access to the population at large but allowed in only those who objectively demonstrated superiority in spiritual gifts.

Candidates were obliged to make a public "profession"—to give an open account of the act of saving grace that had brought them to the condition of redemption that justified membership in the church. This was followed by a public interrogation by church officials and experienced laymen, an inquisition, often exceedingly subtle in its demands, in which these public professions could be challenged for their authenticity and defenses made to these challenges. Finally, if this exhibit and defense had been successful, a formal ritual of acceptance was devised by which membership was officially conferred.

This was no casual procedure. Gaining entrance to the church was the central event in religious life of the Puritan communities. The subsequent history of the church in New England would be shaped by the fate of these procedures.*

Defining the process of entering into the church was one side of the central problem of the Bible commonwealth. The other side was how to justify the rule of the saints to those who were not church members, those excluded from the social rewards the church could bestow. The *intellectual* justification of the rule of the elect was never in doubt. A central idea of the Puritans was the doctrine of the covenant, which asserted the obligation of the saved to do whatever mortals could do to pave the way for the unregenerate to attain salvation. According to the covenant, the elect were obliged to expose ordinary men to truth, to remove impediments to their redemption, and to urge them to seek an ultimate salvation.

*See Chapter 5, pp. 135–36.

But theories do not answer people's urges and longings, their fears and aspirations. A mass population will not accept an elite rule obnoxious to them merely because a theory urges them to. No one can be argued into a willing subservience. There is every reason to believe that the mass of the settlers accepted, indeed welcomed, the rule of the saints. We do not know exactly how many New Englanders in the first two generations reached full membership in the church. One informed estimate is 47 percent, though that is probably too high. We do know that of the twenty thousand or so immigrants of the Great Migration, few returned to England, and there were no rebellions against the religious zeal of the Puritan leaders. Such protests as there were mainly took the form of differing opinions on specific points of doctrine, and most often were led by individuals— Roger Williams, Anne Hutchinson—even more zeal-

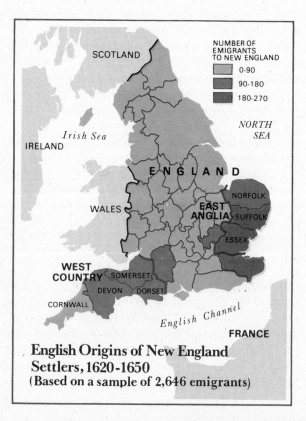

English Origins of New England Settlers, 1620-1650
(Based on a sample of 2,646 emigrants)

ous in religion than the Winthrops.

The explanation for the Puritans' success, in psychological and sociological terms, is related to the sources of the Great Migration. The mass of the settlers were husbandmen and artisans drawn primarily from East Anglia and the west country of England, which were not merely the chief centers of Puritanism but the centers too of economic distress in the 1620s and 30s. Crop failures and an extended depression in the cloth industry, whose two main centers were in these regions, created a mass of discontent and severe social dislocation. Puritanism fed on these disturbed conditions. Its teachings offered an explanation in moral terms of what was happening in the lives of this apprehensive and unrooted population. For the Puritans' social views were medieval rather than modern. They were suspicious of the life of trade, feared the effects of greed on the flow of necessary goods, and urged the necessity of subordinating the individual to the welfare of the community. Though the personality traits that Puritanism fostered—diligence, accountability, self-denial, and the scrupulous use of every God-given moment of time—would later serve to stimulate the development of an unqualified capitalism, its social doctrines confined these characteristics to goals set by the good of the whole. Puritanism stimulated acquisitiveness but at the same time preached the control of greed and self-satisfaction, and it sought to create a society in which social controls in behalf of the community good would predominate.

The thousands of unregenerate found in Puritanism not tyranny but a source of security for which they longed. Uprooted and buffeted by economic upheaval and social dislocation, they found in New England a society that officially restrained economic appetites and translated the incomprehensible workings of the marketplace into familiar moral language. More than that, they found in close-knit village communities a system of group controls that would effectively eliminate the threat of arbitrary economic fluctuations and create the security that was one of the main goals of their existences.

By the end of the century this vital function of Puritanism was losing its power as the third generation, born secure, lost contact with the original aims of the Great Migration. But for a moment in history—two lifetimes, more or less—Puritanism had been a comfort and not an affliction, a source of security otherwise unattainable by ordinary victims of social change.

No more in religion than in social organization or economic life was this a world transformed. But everywhere, in these small and obscure but swiftly growing communities, there were instabilities, uncertainties, and changes that had not yet settled into permanent new forms.

SUGGESTED READINGS

There is no single comprehensive and detailed history of American society in the seventeenth century. The subject has only recently been conceived of in the terms discussed in this chapter, and the student must draw for details on a scattering of publications. This is especially true of the first topic discussed in this chapter: population. There has recently been an extraordinary burst of interest in the field of historical demography, especially for the seventeenth century, in large part stimulated by innovating studies of the French and English populations of the same period. Their influence on early American history is summarized in Philip J. Greven, Jr., "Historical Demography and Colonial America," *Wm. and Mary Q.*, 24 (1967), 438–54. Of the older publications, two are still useful: the compilation of contemporary population estimates in Evarts B. Greene and Virginia D. Harrington, *American Population before the Federal Census of 1790* (1932) and Abbot E. Smith, *Colonists in Bondage* (1947), a study of immigrant convicts and indentured servants. The new writings, based on statistical analysis of small communities, originally concentrated on New England; the most recent and most elaborate of these studies relate to the Chesapeake region. A summary of New England's extraordinary growth rate appears in Daniel S. Smith, "The Demographic History of Colonial New England," *Journal of Ecomonic History*, 32 (1972), 165–83. Other important writings on population growth are Philip J. Greven, Jr., *Four Generations . . . Andover, Massachusetts* (1970); John Demos, "Notes on Life in Plymouth Colony," *Wm. and Mary Q.*, 22 (1965), 264–86;* and the same author's *A Little Commonwealth* (1970). The contrasting high death rate in the earliest years in Virginia and the eventual recovery and rapid growth of population there too are discussed in Edmund S. Morgan, *American Slavery, American Freedom* (1975). Most of these studies reveal the distorted age structure and sex ratio in the settlement years, but there is important additional information on both in John Demos, "Families in Colonial Bristol,

R.I. . . . ," *Wm. and Mary Q.*, 25 (1968), 40–57; in Irene W. D. Hecht, "The Virginia Muster of 1624/5," *ibid.*, 30 (1973), 65–92; and in Herbert Moller's occasionally fanciful "Sex Composition and Correlated Culture Patterns of Colonial America," *ibid.*, 2 (1945), 113–53. On migration to early New England, see T. H. Breen and Stephen Foster, "Moving to the New World . . . ," *ibid.*, 36 (1973), 189–223, and Charles Banks, *Planters of the Commonwealth* (1930); on the spread of population, see Lois K. Mathews, *The Expansion of New England* (1909), chaps. ii–iii. On the peopling of the Chesapeake area, the most notable writings are found in two collections of essays: A. C. Land, L. G. Carr, and E. C. Papenfuse, eds., *Law, Society, and Politics in Early Maryland* (1977); and T. W. Tate and D. L. Ammerman, eds., *The Chesapeake in the Seventeenth Century* (1979). Essays in J. M. Smith, ed., *Seventeenth-Century America* (1959) and Wesley F. Craven, *White, Red, and Black* (1971) are also useful.

There are two valuable sketches of the overall development of the early American economy: Stuart Bruchey, *Roots of American Economic Growth, 1607–1861* (1965) and George R. Taylor, "American Economic Growth before 1840," *Journal of Economic History*, 24 (1964), 427–44. The world context of American commercial development is well presented in Ralph Davis, *Rise of the Atlantic Economies* (1973).

The growth of the commercial economy in early New England is traced in Bernard Bailyn, *The New England Merchants in the Seventeenth Century* (1955) and in Bernard and Lotte Bailyn, *Massachusetts Shipping, 1697–1714* (1959). The psychological turmoils of a Puritan merchant, caught between entrepreneurial and pietistic impulses, emerge in Bailyn, ed., *The Apologia of Robert Keayne* (1965). Curtis P. Nettels, *The Money Supply of the American Colonies before 1720* (1934) covers various aspects of American and Atlantic commerce as well as monetary history. For a social description of the emerging port towns, see Carl Bridenbaugh, *Cities in the Wilderness* (1938).

Many aspects of the southern economy are described in Lewis C. Gray, *History of Agriculture in the Southern United States to 1860* (2 vols., 1933), and there is still value in Philip A. Bruce's *Economic History of Virginia in the Seventeenth Century* (2 vols., 1896). The master historian of the tobacco economy, however, is Jacob M. Price; it is from his writing particularly that one learns of the worldwide commercial network that shaped the lives of the Chesapeake farmers. In his *The Tobacco Adventure to Russia . . . 1676–1722* (*Transactions of the American Philosphical Society*, 1961), Price traces the failure of the London tobacco merchants to market Chesapeake tobacco in Russia, an effort which, if it had succeeded, would have transformed the economy and society of the American South. Price also discusses the French-American tobacco trade in *France and the Chesapeake* (2 vols., 1973).

Traditional ideals of social organization are depicted in E. M. W. Tillyard, *Elizabethan World Picture* (1943) and in Gordon J. Schochet, *Patriarchalism in Political Thought* (1975); the latter has an excellent chapter on the ideals and actuality of the family in seventeenth-century England, a subject discussed at length by Peter Laslett in *The World We Have Lost* (1965) and in his introduction to *Household and Family in Past Time* (1972). Many of the new community-demographic studies cited above, particularly those of Greven and Demos, make clear the difficulty of maintaining traditional forms in the wilderness setting. See also Sumner C. Powell, *Puritan Village* (1963) and Edmund S. Morgan, *Puritan Family* (1944). Kenneth A. Lockridge, *New England Town: Dedham . . .* (1970) locates the disarray only at the end of the seventeenth century. On social mobility there are several important writings: William A. Reavis, "The Maryland Gentry and Social Mobility, 1637–1676," *Wm. and Mary Q.*, 14 (1957), 418–28; Russell R. Menard, "From Servant to Freeholder," *ibid.*, 30 (1973), 37–64; Linda A. Bissell, "From One Generation to Another," *ibid.*, 31 (1974), 79–110; and Menard *et al.*, "Opportunity and Inequality," *Maryland Historical Magazine*, 69 (1974), 169–84. The political consequences of social mobility and conflict are depicted in Bernard Bailyn, "Politics and Social Structure in Virginia,"* James M. Smith, ed., *Seventeenth-Century America* (1959). On the altered role of women in seventeenth-century America, see Roger Thompson, *Women in Stuart England and America* (1974); on children and childhood, see R. W. Beales, Jr., "In Search of the Historical Child," *American Quarterly*, 27 (1975), 379–98. Philip Greven has sketched the history of child-rearing in early America in terms of shifting patterns of family life, religious experience, and self-identity in *The Protes-*

tant Temperament (1977).

On religion, Sydney E. Ahlstrom, *Religious History of the American People* (1972), surveys generally the European background as well as the transplantation of European institutions, ideas, and beliefs to the North American continent. For a particularly thoughtful overall interpretation, stressing the colonial period, see Sidney E. Mead, *The Lively Experiment* (1963). For the seventeenth century, the subject has been dominated by the prolific scholarship on Puritanism. The master scholar in that subject has been Perry Miller. His two-volume *New England Mind* (*The Seventeenth Century*, 1939; *From Colony to Province*, 1953); his many essays, collected in *Errand into the Wilderness* (1956) and *Nature's Nation* (1967); and his and Thomas H. Johnson's anthology of sources, *The Puritans* (1938) have made New England Puritanism one of the most absorbing subjects of modern historiography. Miller's books set in motion a flood of writing on Puritanism, which is surveyed in Michael McGiffert, "American Puritan Studies in the 1960's," *Wm. and Mary Q.*, 27 (1970), 36–67. The closest approach to a new general interpretation of Puritan thought since Miller's *New England Mind* is David D. Hall, *The Faithful Shepherd: A History of the New England Ministry in the Seventeenth Century* (1972). Among the many other important writings on Puritanism are Alan Simpson, *Puritanism in Old and New England* (1955); Edmund S. Morgan, *Visible Saints* (1963); James F. MacLear, "The Heart of New England Rent," *Mississippi Valley Historical Review*, 42 (1956), 621–52; Emil Oberholzer, Jr., *Delinquent Saints* (1955); and Timothy H. Breen, *The Character of the Good Ruler* (1970). Darrett B. Rutman, *American Puritanism* (1970) is an interesting essay of interpretation. Most recently Sacvan Bercovitch, *The Puritan Origins of the American Self* (1975) has shown the enduring impact of Puritan ideals on American self-imagery and culture.

No other religious community of the seventeenth century has received even remotely comparable study. On Anglicanism, in general, see George M. Brydon, *Virginia's Mother Church* (1947) and Elizabeth H. Davidson, *Establishment of the English Church in the Continental American Colonies* (1936); on the efforts to reform the Anglican Church in the late seventeenth and early eighteenth centuries, see Parke Rouse, Jr., *James Blair of Virginia* (1971). On the Catholics, see John T. Ellis, *Catholics in Colonial America* (1965); on the Dutch Reformed, Frederick J. Zwierlein, *Religion in New Netherland* (1910); and on the Baptists, William G. McLoughlin, *New England Dissent, 1630–1833* (2 vols., 1971).

*See footnote on page 65.

Thus, the founding of British America is the story of the efforts of private groups and individuals to profit in some way from the exploitation of the North American continent. The leading organizers had various motives. For some, the predominant goals were economic, for others, religious. For most, however, there was a mingling of religious, economic, and patriotic interests stimulated by discontent at home, lure of adventure, and the hope that in an open land, free of inherited encumbrances, their fortunes would improve. This scattering of private enterprises, some of them protected in their independence by crown charters, had developed without overall plan or general organization. By 1660 there was little sense on either side of the Atlantic that these settlements together formed an effective empire.

In the two generations that followed the restoration of the Stuarts to the throne of England (1660), efforts were made to draw these unrelated settlements into an overall governmental organization, to impose regulation and control of some sort over this miscellaneous collection of towns, villages, and farms. The way this was done, and the way in which these efforts at regulation interacted with the natural growth and maturing of the American communities, had a permanent effect on the character of American life.

Empire

Three interest groups, dominant at the Restoration court of Charles II (1660–85), account for the extension of the authority of the British government to America. The first were courtiers, the most active of them the Carolina proprietors, who had assisted in restoring Charles II to the throne and had remained his key advisers. Their stake in America deepened as the possibilities of extracting profit from the settlements became more realistic. And to advance their interests in the colonies most of these courtiers were willing to share in the work of devising appropriate administrative machinery and to serve as members of the agencies that were created.

A second and ultimately more influential group was composed of the merchants and their allies in government who marketed American products and sold

CHAPTER 4

Elements of Change
1660–1720

JAMES II AT THE TIME OF HIS ACCESSION
James's stubborn insistence on imposing a Catholic regime on a Protestant nation and his autocratic disregard of political realities led to his downfall in the Glorious Revolution (1688) and to a great advance in British liberalism. *(National Portrait Gallery, London)*

royal family itself, particularly those of the king's brother, James, Duke of York, and his private entourage. As proprietor of New York, an expert on naval affairs, and an unusually energetic administrator, James made clear soon after the Restoration that he would be a leading figure in designing an empire from among the scattered American settlements.

It was the combination of these three groups—courtiers, merchants, and the royal family, particularly James—all with stakes in the colonies, that accounts for the organization of the British empire at the end of the seventeenth century. Their goals were not identical, and there was no coordinated planning, but their interests converged in efforts at three levels.

Administration. Together they created, first, through a fumbling, pragmatic process of evolution, a network of administrative controls. Immediately after the Restoration, the king's Privy Council began appointing committees of its own members, occasionally supplemented by others, to deal with colonial problems as they arose. The volume and importance of the business that came before these committees soon justified the appointment of a standing committee, called the Lords of Trade (1675), composed only of members of the Privy Council. This committee, irregular in its efforts and lacking reliable staff, was a bridge to the permanent supervisory body, the Board of Trade and Plantations, which was created in 1696.

As an independent agency the Board of Trade, consisting of eight high state officials and eight paid members, remained the central pivot of the British imperial administration throughout the eighteenth century. But as a "Council of the Indies," it had notable weaknesses. First, the range of its duties was unrealistically broad. It was expected effectively to supervise all the trade of Britain, its fisheries, and the care of the poor throughout Britain, as well as all colonial matters. In dealing with the colonies it was expected to have a special responsibility for reviewing all crown appointments in America and all the legislation that emerged from the colonies. Yet despite these responsibilities, the board's actual power proved to be severely limited. Other, better-established branches of government took over some measure of the control of colonial af-

manufactured goods to the colonists. These merchants were aware that a significant part of the English economy would become involved in the colonies, and they became leaders in the growing movement to assert British control over the American settlements—not for the sake of power, glory, and "empire" in some abstract sense, but for the sake of trade and England's economic growth.

Finally, there were the personal interests of the

fairs, and the board's power failed to mature.

The essential conflict lay between the board and the secretary of state for the Southern Department, in whose geographical jurisdiction the Western Hemisphere fell. This secretary of state was one of the chief executive officers of the government, with particular responsibility for international relations. The center of his concerns was not the struggling settlements on the coast of North America but the glittering court of Louis XIV in Paris. Nevertheless, by 1704 the secretary of state for the Southern Department successfully challenged the Board of Trade for executive authority over the colonies, and the result was a fundamental weakness at the heart of the British overseas administration. The Board of Trade remained an information-gathering body, in effect the colonial office of that era, in charge of a substantial flow of information to and from the colonies; but it lacked the power to enforce regulations, make appointments, or otherwise direct the course of events. It could advise, counsel, admonish; but orders came from the secretary of state's office which might or might not have available to it the board's voluminous files and which tended to view colonial affairs in the context of western European diplomacy.

That significant division of authority was not the only source of administrative confusion as the empire took shape. Almost every major branch of the central government discovered some interest in the colonies and managed to secure some corner of control. The Treasury took responsibility for the colonial customs administration. The Admiralty successfully claimed jurisdiction over naval stores and other colonial products vital to the British navy, and took responsibility for patrolling the coastal waters to enforce the growing body of commercial regulations. Further, the War Office took charge of army operations on the North American mainland during the many years when European international conflicts involved overseas territories. The army's contracting, like that of the navy, had a powerful influence on the economic development of the colonies, and its strategic planning involved American manpower as well. Weaving through all of these ill-assorted jurisdictions was the authority legitimately exercised by England's attorney general, solic-

itor general, and several auditors and collectors of the king's revenues.

By the early eighteenth century an imperial administration had taken shape in the British world. But it was a very different structure from the Spanish American empire. There was no central authority equivalent to the Spanish Council of the Indies, which had at its disposal both information and executive authority and drew together all the other agencies of government that had a finger in colonial matters. The various British agencies conflicted with each other. There were overlaps in jurisdiction, and also significant gaps in authority. As a result, there was a minimum of effective central control.

Yet for Britain this administrative inefficiency was not acutely distressing. For the guiding principles behind the organization of the British empire did not require tight administrative efficiency in the years before 1760, and it did not require territorial government in depth. The colonies could largely be left alone so long as certain minimal expectations were met, and these expectations centered almost entirely on the regulation of commerce.

Mercantilism and Commercial Regulation. Britain's was a mercantilist empire. It came together as an extension of England's commercial growth. Its guiding principles were derived from mercantilism, the ancient doctrine that the state must intervene to regulate economic activity for the public welfare. In the heated commercial rivalries of the seventeenth century, mercantilists made two assumptions that framed the regulations of Britain's American empire: first, that the economic universe was composed of competing national states; and second, that there was a fixed amount of wealth ultimately available. According to mercantilist theory, the purpose of commercial regulation for each nation-state was to secure economic self-sufficiency and, by maintaining a favorable balance of trade, to avoid falling into dependence on rival states. In this competition among nations, the colonies were fundamentally important. If they did not provide Britain with needed colonial products, these commodities would have to be purchased from other nations and hence wealth would be drained by the rival states. It followed that every effort would have to be made to direct the flow of valuable colonial products to Britain alone. Further, the colonies, as markets for the sale of manufactured goods, were to be monopolized by Britain, for every purchase of goods from a rival state meant some small drainage in the national treasure.

It was to put these ideas into effect that the famous navigation acts were passed by Parliament in three main groups beginning soon after the Restoration. The first of these enactments (1660) restricted the shipping and marketing of all colonial goods to British subjects. England alone, it was decreed, would enjoy the profits of shipping and reexporting colonial goods. Further, a special list was prepared of "enumerated" commodities that could be shipped only to England or other British ports. The basic list included all the goods that England would otherwise have had to buy from other imperial powers: sugar, tobacco, cotton, indigo, ginger, certain dyes, and special wood products. Later other commodities were added to the original list: rice and molasses in 1704; naval stores in 1705 and 1729; copper and furs in 1721.

The act of 1660 was the basic law governing colonial trade. Two others completed the pattern of mercantilist regulation. The so-called Staple Act of 1663 gave England a monopoly of the sale of European manufactures to the American colonies. European goods, the law stated, could not be shipped directly to America from Europe, even if the ships that carried them were British. These goods would have to be sent first to England, unloaded there, and reshipped to the colonies. Thus valuable customs duties would be produced for the English Treasury and at the same time foreign merchants would be put at a disadvantage. Certain exceptions were made, either because, like salt, they were necessary for American industry, or because like servants, horses, and provisions from Scotland and Ireland, or wines from Madeira or the Azores, they involved no competition with English production. A supplementary law, that of 1673, quite technical and the source of endless confusion, sought to plug gaps created by the wording of the earlier legislation.

Thus, out of the convergent interests of courtiers, merchants, and the royal family had come the beginning of an imperial system operating at three levels: as an administrative unit; as a doctrine (mercantilism);

and as a set of commercial regulations. It was, by 1700, an empire of world importance; but its government was decidedly limited in effectiveness. It was limited administratively because of the ill-coordinated jumble of agencies that governed it. It was limited in theory by the mercantilist doctrines that prevailed—doctrines that demanded not territorial governance in depth but only regulation of external commerce. And it was limited also by the intricacy of the governing legislation and the great difficulty of enforcing these laws three thousand miles from home. By the early eighteenth century no one could doubt that the American colonies were part of an empire; but neither could anyone conceive of the ill-managed, superficial administration as a centralized dominion. The passion for territorial rule was not there, nor the drive of dynastic ambition.

James II and the Dominion of New England.   The limits of the British imperial system become particularly clear when one considers the efforts that were made later in the seventeenth century to turn the empire into something more powerful than this—something more effective than it ever in fact became. For there was one person at the center of the English government who did have ambitions akin to those of continental monarchs, and who also had the instincts of an efficient administrator and a personal entourage capable of managing an efficient system.

The instincts that led the Duke of York, subsequently James II (1685–88) to seek to expand and deepen the controls of empire can be traced back to his childhood training as a military leader in the autocratic court of France; to his desire, as a royal refugee, to exercise the power that had been denied him; and to the fortunate position he found himself in when his brother, Charles II, returned to the throne. As Lord High Admiral with a loyal following of war-seasoned officers, James took command of garrisons all over England and appointed as governors those hungry veterans who had merged their fortunes with his. For him the colonial world was but an extension of the realm. Soon his captains turned up as governors and other high officers in the Caribbean and North American governments. His base on the mainland was New York, which he ruled as proprietor from the time it was captured from the Dutch. Slowly he expanded this center into a larger imperial dominion, his efforts coinciding with the more general efforts the English government was then making to restrict the private jurisdictions that had been created in the early years of colonization.

For in the later seventeenth century and continuing into the early years of the eighteenth century, the British government, as part of its elaboration of empire, undertook to cut back the chartered powers of the private jurisdictions in America. Progress was slow, erratic, and in the end incomplete. Virginia, when the company failed in 1624, and New York, when James II acceded to the throne in 1685, both automatically became crown colonies. Also, it was not difficult to separate New Hampshire from Massachusetts (1680) and assign it a royal governor. But for the rest, the charters created serious problems, and they had to be attacked directly. Between 1684 and 1691 the charters of Massachusetts, Connecticut, Rhode Island, New Jersey, Pennsylvania, Maryland, and Carolina were confiscated.

It was in the early years of this campaign against these partly independent jurisdictions that James's grand and ill-fated design unfolded. As king, his ultimate ambition, it seems, was to create two centralized viceroyalties in America which would be ruled by crown-appointed governors and councils. The Delaware River at 40 degrees latitude (the division between the two original Virginia companies) was apparently seen as the boundary between the two great domains. During his short and tumultuous reign James focused his attention on the northern section, which became known as the Dominion of New England.

In a legal sense, the Dominion came together easily after 1685. To the core colony of New York were added New Hamphire, Massachusetts, Connecticut, Rhode Island, and New Jersey as each of their charters was annulled or suspended. To rule the Dominion, in place of the existing officials, James sent over one of his closest allies and former comrades in arms, Edmund Andros, who had served him well in several other positions, particularly as governor of New York (1674–81). To assist Andros at his headquarters in Boston, James appointed a royal council which included a majority of recently arrived merchants who had struggled against the Puritan establishment, hitherto with little effect. Together, royal governor and royal council moved to work out the implications of direct and full territorial government similar to that of the Spanish crown in the Southern Hemisphere.

To the horror of the Puritans throughout New England, Andros declared toleration for all groups, and confiscated Boston's Old South Church for the use of Church of England services. Equally offensive was his disregard of the ancient principles of English self-government. He continued by mere executive declaration taxes that had originally been levied in Massachusetts by the representative General Court. Worse still was Andros's land policy. He commanded that all town lands be regranted in the name of the king and be subject to the payment of annual quitrents to the crown, and that the towns' undistributed common lands be placed at the council's disposal. Finally, to complete the destruction of the local jurisdictions, he limited the activities of the town meetings to electing officials who would help collect taxes.

Andros's efforts never reached beyond Massachusetts, indeed scarcely beyond Boston and the coastal towns. But their implications were widely known and they stimulated ferocious opposition. His tax policy provoked an open rebellion in the town of Ipswich, led by the Reverend John Wise, and to the imprisonment of that outspoken preacher and four of his followers. Resistance grew among the Puritan leaders and the landholders throughout New England. By the time Andros's royal master was deposed in the Glorious Revolution in England, the royalist regime in Boston was so universally hated and so isolated that the rebellion that rose against it and that imprisoned the governor and his closest allies took place, in April 1689, almost without a struggle.

All of James's colonial plans disappeared with his fall from power. When this high tide of imperial ambition fell back, the more permanent forms of Anglo-American relations emerged as the charters were restored, though with qualifications, and the slow, partial elimination of private jurisdictions continued. The two Jerseys were reunited into a single royal colony in 1702. In the Carolinas a popular rebellion against the proprietors (1719) and constant pressure against them in England led in 1729 to the formal separation of the two districts into two royal colonies. The one residue of the Carolinas' proprietary origins was the retention of one of the eight original shares by the diplomat and politican the Earl Granville, heir of Sir George Carteret. When consolidated in 1745, his inheritance, the so-called Granville District, constituted title to the undistributed land of fully half of North Carolina on which lived perhaps two-thirds of the colony's population. The charters of Pennsylvania and Maryland were restored to the Penn and Calvert families; but in both cases the selection of the governor had thereafter to be approved by the crown, and all legislation was subject to review by the crown's legal officers.

The British American Empire.   The results of these developments after the collapse of James's Dominion was a return to the limited and superficial empire that had existed long before 1685, modified by the reduction of chartered privileges in several colonies. In its decentralization and inefficency, Britain's empire was far different from Spain's, but it was still a visible, extensive empire. Its visibility, by the early eighteenth century, appeared most dramatically to most Americans not so much in law enforcement or in recast institutions as in the increasing number of officials sent to America to manage the new system. In most port towns there were customs collectors appointed by the Treasury who brought with them small teams of assistants. There were auditors and surveyors of the king's revenues. And there were officers of the vice admiralty courts created by the law of 1696—subordinate arms of the admiralty court system that held jurisdiction over maritime law in Britain. The judges and clerks of these "prerogative" courts (operating without juries and by rules different from those of the common law courts) were part of the imperial presence, as were, indirectly and for the limited purpose of enforcing the navigation laws, the governors and lieutenant governors of all of the royal colonies.

The importance of these officials, most of whom were newcomers to America at the end of the century, cannot be exaggerated. They represented—indeed embodied—the empire. The way they approached their work, the attitudes they brought to Anglo-American relations, and the ways in which they related to the local communities became matters of importance in the life of the American people. They affected not only the actuality of government but the image of government and of political authority more generally.

These officials were not efficient imperial bureaucrats, and they were seldom committed to promoting the strength of the empire. Their offices were minor parts of the patronage system of the English government, and hence were seen as a kind of private property parceled out by political leaders to their deserving followers. Appointees were expected to profit by their positions through fees, gifts, and perquisites, as well as through salaries. Appointments were made almost randomly with respect to administrative ability or interest in public affairs. What counted were connections and the applicant's capacity to force his patron to reward loyalty and previous service.

At times the appointments were bizarre, even those at the highest level. The governor of New York from 1701 to 1708 was a rapacious transvestite, Lord Cornbury, a member of the Clarendon family, who traipsed around the colony in women's clothes and squeezed profit from anything he could lay his hands on. The governor of Virginia from 1705 to 1737 was the Earl of Orkney, who never had the slightest intention of setting foot in America, and never did. He had been a war companion of William III and was the Duke of Marlborough's leading infantry commander. His appointment was a reward too, however, for somewhat less heroic service. He had made what may have been a supreme sacrifice by marrying William III's mistress, Elizabeth Villiers.

Orkney's career as absentee governor of Virginia is revealing in many ways. The stated salary of the position was £2,000 a year. Orkney in effect sold the office for £1,200 to a series of lieutenant governors who served in his place, with the understanding that they were entitled to make as much out of the job as they could. He selected, as it happens, some able men: Robert Hunter, 1706 (who, because of accidents at sea and his wife's connections, ended up governor not of Virginia but of New York, a post he filled with distinction); Alexander Spotswood, in 1709; and William Gooch, in 1727. These three had only one thing in common: they had all fought as officers under Orkney and Marlborough. No less than nine veterans of the battle of Blenheim received colonial governorships for their service.

Under these conditions, what is surprising is not that colonial offices were occasionally filled by avaricious deviants like Cornbury or by psychological cripples like Sir Danvers Osborn, who hanged himself in a fit of melancholy a week after his arrival as New York's governor, nor that lesser posts were frequently held by altogether unqualified hacks. What is remarkable is that some appointees were in fact conscientious and honest, and sought dutifully to serve the imperial interest as well as the local population.

Still, it is the randomness of these appointments, the disregard of the incumbents' ability and experience, and hence in the end the arbitrariness of the system, that had the deepest effect on American life. The consequences were profound.

First, these appointments to offices in the colonies served to increase the existing superficiality of the British imperial system. Officeholders, always insecure in tenure, knew that the same arbitrary movement of the patronage system that put them in office could easily eject them. Sooner or later, they knew, quite without regard to the quality of their work, they would be replaced by someone closer to the levers of power. Consequently they were highly susceptible to compromises and vulnerable to local pressures. If the situation required speed in making a profit from office, they would be quick about it, at the expense, if need be, of the strict execution of their duties.

Further, British officialdom, as it emerged from these formative years, inculcated in Americans a sense that government, far from being a seamless web uniting high and low through a series of responsible links, was essentially a structure composed of two distinct and antagonistic levels, a level of local,

LORD CORNBURY, GOVERNOR OF NEW YORK, IN FEMALE DRESS
Of Lord Cornbury, a cousin of Queen Anne, an eighteenth-century historian wrote that he used "to dress himself in a woman's habit and then to patrol the fort in which he resided. Such freaks of low humor exposed him to the universal contempt of the people." His avarice led the Assembly to assert its control over tax revenues, and his zealous Anglicanism resulted in broader religious toleration. *(New-York Historical Society, New York City)*

internal government that expressed the dominant interests of the local community, and a superior, external authority which was in its nature hostile to local interests. Often the external power became identified with executive authority and the local and benevolent authority with legislative power. Such a sharp distinction between these functions of government was extraordinary for the time and was destined to have a continuing importance in American history.

Even more general still, among the consequences of British officialdom, was the growth on the part of politically active Americans of a kind of cynicism to all government, an attitude of anti-authoritarianism stimulated by the character and behavior of these officials. These officeholders represented a nation that was revered by most of the colonists; but in themselves these officers were often incompetent, poor, and supercilious, a bad enough combination made worse by their easy corruptibility. Americans could only wonder whether the power such people represented deserved automatic compliance.

Beyond all of this lay the sense, as the imperial officialdom developed, that the social and political worlds were far from unified, that social and political leadership at the highest level was dissociated. The native social leaders of the colonies did not represent the state. In fact, when local leaders competed with strangers for high office in their own colony, they did so often on unequal terms, and their failures were embittering. Thus William Byrd II, a second-generation American who spent fifteen years being educated and making contacts in England before taking over the family property in Virginia, failed in his bid to buy the lieutenant governorship of his native colony from Orkney and spent years struggling with his successful rival, Spotswood, who had no original stake in the colony and no knowledge of it when he arrived on the scene. Byrd finally acquired a seat on the colony's council, but only after ten years of diligent effort.

What made all of these consequences of the growth of officialdom especially important was the fact that they coincided with the natural emergence of local elites in the mainland colonies. The dominance of these local leaders within the maturing communities could not be doubted, and their demands for recognition—in politics as in other spheres of life—could not easily be ignored.

Anglo-American Aristocracy

The rise of a provincial aristocracy toward the end of the seventeenth century and in the early eighteenth century was the result of the exploitation, by skillful, energetic, and ambitious men, of opportunities that suddenly became available. These opportunities were created by basic developments in social and economic life.

Land as the Basis of Aristocracy.　The material basis for most social distinctions in the colonies, as in England, was the ownership or control of land. The thirty years that bridged the turn of the century, 1690–1720, saw a significant shift in this basic relationship. Between these two dates the land area under active cultivation remained approximately the same, because of Indian wars and the difficulty of overcoming natural barriers in the way of westward expansion. But during these same years the population more than doubled: it rose from approximately 210,000 to 460,000. Land was still far easier to acquire in the colonies than it was in England, but the increasing population pressure created significant changes in social relations, and in itself accounts for the emergence of new social elites.

In New England the emergence of a landowning aristocracy in the long-settled towns was marked by dramatic conflicts almost everywhere. In its original form the New England town had been a kind of democracy of male heads of households, all of whom were full church members, freemen in the town meeting, and landowners with shares in the undivided common land. As time passed and migration among towns grew while immigration into the colonies continued, questions arose about how newcomers would share in these original privileges. Certain answers came quickly. Access to membership in the church was controlled by a procedure calculated to make the entry of newcomers possible but still highly selective. Access to participation in the town meeting was less easily determined but in the end was opened to all respectable male inhabitants. But there was no easy resolution of the question of control of the undivided land. The heirs of the original grantees had no desire to share their inheritances with newcomers, and they closed ranks against the claimants.

Without originally intending to do so, these second- and third-generation colonists began to form exclusive companies of landholders. Challenged in the town meeting by those excluded from sharing in the common property, they drew apart and met separately, only to have their rights to the undivided land challenged at law. In certain towns they sought compromises by allocating plots—often dismissed as bribes—to conspicuous opponents or to those with special claims. Most often, however, confrontation could not be evaded. The challenges went up to the General Court, whose decisions, after a period of uncertainty, favored the heirs of the original grantees.

As a result, not only did the fortunate heirs continue to enjoy the increasingly valuable property, but they shared control of the still undivided common land. With this inherited capital, they were in the best possible position to build fortunes out of real estate. Those shrewd or enterprising enough to take full advantage of the opportunities that lay at hand broadened out their operations from small local transactions to large-scale land speculation. Some moved into trade through successes in commercial farming; the most enterprising did both. In Connecticut the most successful became known as River Gods because of their valuable properties along the colony's main waterway. Everywhere in New England land claims proved a rich ore available for refinement into gold, prestige, and power.

The same was true in the South; but there, as tobacco cultivation spread westward, profits from the land were intimately tied up with the problem of labor, and that increasingly meant slavery. It was in the later seventeenth century that the critical importance of slavery first emerged in southern society. A great revolution in social relations as well as in the economy was created by the spread of slavery and the growth of the black population. Slavery accounted not only for the introduction of a major component of the American population but also for a basic source of social stratification within the white population. The logic of this development quickly became clear.

With profits from tobacco production small and at times nonexistent, the *extensiveness* of planting seemed increasingly important. Land was available for expansion, but labor was not. The immigration of white indentured servants from England declined sharply after 1660 because of a slackening in England's population growth and an improved English labor market, especially in the London area. Slaves alone, it seemed, provided an answer to the labor problem, and they were increasingly available as the British slave trade entered a period of expansion and

increasing efficiency. Slaves *in the long run* were cheap. Their upkeep, averaged over a lifetime of labor, was perhaps £1 per year, as opposed to a servant's annual maintenance cost of £2–£4. But if slaves were cheaper than servants in the long run, they were more costly in the short run because they required a higher initial investment. And cost were rising constantly. Average slave prices doubled between 1660 and 1750, and by the Revolution they had tripled. In 1700 a newly imported "prime field hand" cost £20 in Virginia; in 1750, £30. Nevertheless their numbers continued to rise as their importance in the spreading tobacco culture became clearly understood. An estimated 20,000 slaves were brought to British North America in the two decades after 1700; 50,000 arrived in the subsequent two decades. In 1715 blacks formed a quarter of Virginia's total population, by the 1730s 40 percent. In South Carolina blacks outnumbered whites by 1708; by 1720 the ratio was almost 2 to 1, and the black population was growing at a faster rate than the white.

The growth of the slave labor force, which made possible a significant increase in tobacco cultivation and eventually in rice and indigo production, created a deepening social distinction within the white population. Capital was the critical determinant. Since profits depended on the extent of cultivation and since that in turn depended on slave labor which required high capital outlays, the line between those who had capital available and those who did not, or between those who could acquire it and those who could not, became crucial. Those with greater assets formed a new class of "great planters" in a society that as late as 1700 consisted almost entirely of farm operations of small and medium size. In Lancaster County in northern Virginia in 1716, a majority of taxpayers owned slaves, but few had more than 2 or 3; only four owned over 20; one, however—Robert Carter—had 126. At his death in 1732 Robert "King" Carter—planter and above all land agent and speculator, son of a settler of 1649 who had brought capital with him and had accumulated the land claims of no less than five wives—was said to possess 300,000 acres and £10,000 in cash. Capital and inherited land claims, in a world of steeply rising land values, deter-

INDIGO CULTURE IN SOUTH CAROLINA
The plants of the blue dyestuff are being carried to fermenting vats, and the resulting
liquid flows down the sluice at left into containers.   *(Charleston Library Society)*

mined who would succeed and who would not, who would control the land and who would not, and who would live like princes on the land—bourgeois, enterprising princes, to be sure, desperately concerned with markets, prices, and the humblest details of farming—but princes nevertheless.

Trade as the Basis of Aristocracy.   In the main commercial centers the merchant community as a whole remained open, free of the formal limitations of gilds and other artificial barriers to entrance. But toward the end of the seventeenth century, and increasingly in the early eighteenth century, significant differences within the merchant group appeared nevertheless, and a mercantile aristocracy of sorts began to make its appearance.

As the commercial system settled into its com-

plex pattern of oceanic routes covering the North Atlantic basin, certain portions of the network proved crucial and dominated the others. Entrance into this primary route became more and more difficult to achieve, and the colonial merchants who controlled it became dominant figures. For as the magnitude of imports from England increased and as the marshaling of colonial products in ever larger quantities made greater and greater demands on colonial entrepreneurs, the English specialists in North American trade began to concentrate their shipments to a few ports and to a relatively few merchants. They sought commercial correspondents who could be relied on to send payments quickly in good bills of exchange or salable commodities. Once involved in these primary circuits of trade, through which flowed the all-important "dry goods" (iron products and textiles, primarily) a merchant had a cumulative advantage over others. The main profits of the commercial system tended to center in these major importers, while the smaller merchants, confined to local routes, fell more and more clearly into subordinate roles.

In the large port towns the dominant entrepreneurs who were in direct contact with the English merchants and in control of the critical goods formed an aristocracy of sorts. It was an aristocracy that was still limited in affluence, fluid in membership, and insecure, but it was a visible elite nevertheless, and its fortunes rested on the primary flows of commerce.

Political Influence as the Basis of Aristocracy. Thus economic developments—in the ownership of land in New England, in the expansion of the tobacco economy in the Chesapeake, and in the maturing of commerce in the main centers in the North—underlay the development of native elites. But the forces behind this development were not only economic. They were political as well. As the colonial governments took firm shape in the middle and later years of the century, the value of political patronage and the yields of the public office became unmistakably clear. The possibilities were seen first in Virginia, where what might be called the first "court house gang" took form during the long governorship of Sir William Berkeley (1641–52, 1659–77).

The appointments that Berkeley could make gave him power over many aspects of the colony's life. In addition to appointing justices of the peace, sheriffs, and tax collectors, he could nominate members of the council, who not only enjoyed considerable prestige but benefited materially from the privileges available to them. Over the twenty-nine years of his administration Berkeley, through his appointments, formed a clique of officials loyal to himself to whom he channeled these benefits. A similar little oligarchy developed simultaneously around the proprietary interest in Maryland.

It was not in Virginia or in Maryland, however, but in New York that these possibilities were most dramatically revealed. There in the 1690s a new landowning elite was created almost overnight, largely by a single governor attempting to make his own fortune and the fortunes of his followers as quickly

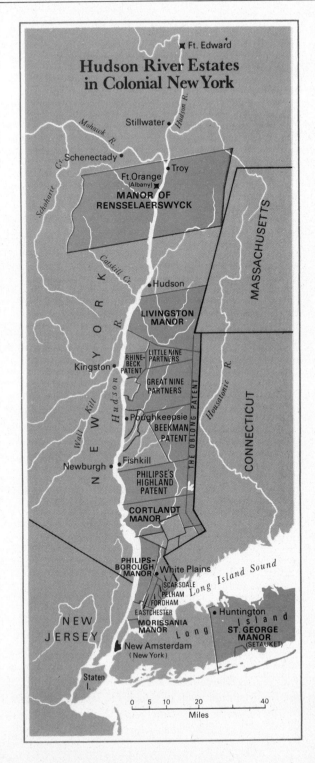

Hudson River Estates in Colonial New York

as possible. In New York's tumultuous and competitive politics at the end of the century, the ruthless partisanship of Governor Benjamin Fletcher (1692–97) was extraordinarily effective. Personally rapacious, surrounded by a mercenary gang of petty plunderers whom he had brought with him, Fletcher—and Cornbury after him—proceeded to buy the loyalty of the dominant group of local powers by bestowing on them enormous grants of land and confirming others previously made.

He did not invent the procedure. One patroonship had survived in flourishing shape from the Dutch period—Rensselaerswyck, a manor of close to a million acres on both sides of the Hudson—and several other great estates had been granted subsequently. Of these, the most important was Livingston Manor, a grant of 160,000 acres that had been extracted from the Dominion government by a particularly supple Scottish-Anglo-Dutch politician, Robert Livingston—a man Fletcher said, who began as "a little bookkeeper" but who "screwed himself into one of the most considerable estates in the province, . . . never disbursing sixpence but with the expectation of twelve." It was just such sharp-eyed opportunists and hustling politicians, scrambling in the bonanza land grab of late seventeenth-century New York, whose appetites Fletcher fed. The estates he parceled out in Dutchess and Westchester counties varied in size and in legal and political privileges, but almost all exceeded 100,000 acres. Some grants were literally open-ended: sixteen miles, commonly, along a river bank running back indefinitely into the unsurveyed countryside.

Profits from the French and Indian Wars. The results of political influence were not limited to landholding. Politics also affected the development of trade and the establishment of the merchant leadership, for at the end of the century government contracting, political in its essence, became a prime source of economic advancement, especially during war years. The colonies became involved in both of the international wars in which England fought during these years: the inconclusive War of the League of Augsburg (1689–97), in which England led a coali-

tion against France's effort to dominate central Europe, and the more consequential War of the Spanish Succession (1702–13) in which England and Holland joined to block Louis XIV's claim to the crown of Spain. Both of these wars, whose main operations spread over large areas of Europe, led to hostilities between the English colonies and the French in southern Canada. The slow-growing colony of New France had been settled at the same time as the English colonies; but, limited in its development by religious restrictions on immigration, rigid systems of land distribution and of social relations, and a tightly controlled colonial bureaucracy, it had achieved a population of only 6,000 by 1660 and perhaps 15,000 by 1700. Nevertheless, the French had been aggressive fur traders, trappers, and fishermen from the beginning, and for years there had been minor clashes between them and the English settlers, especially in Nova Scotia. Those clashes escalated into savage border warfare and extended struggles for inland territories during the two international wars that spanned the years 1689–1713. Both of these wars involved the English colonists as much economically as militarily.

In the first, known as King William's War in the colonies, the French, with Indian support, fought the English for control of Hudson Bay, and in 1690 fell on the exposed northern borders of English settlement with devastating raids on an arc of towns from Portland, Maine, to Schenectady, New York. The Anglo-American efforts concentrated on capturing Port Royal in Nova Scotia, which was taken but then lost by Massachusetts troops in 1690–91, and on an elaborate attack on the center of French Canada, which failed miserably.

The same pattern was repeated in the second of these wars, known in the colonies as Queen Anne's War. Once again the Maine settlements were raided; and Deerfield, Massachusetts, was destroyed. In retaliation the colonists razed Nova Scotian villages and attacked Port Royal twice before finally taking that fortress. And far to the south during the same war, a force of Carolinians and Indians burned St. Augustine and destroyed the string of Spanish missions that linked the Spanish coastal settlements to French Louisiana. By the Treaty of Utrecht (1713),

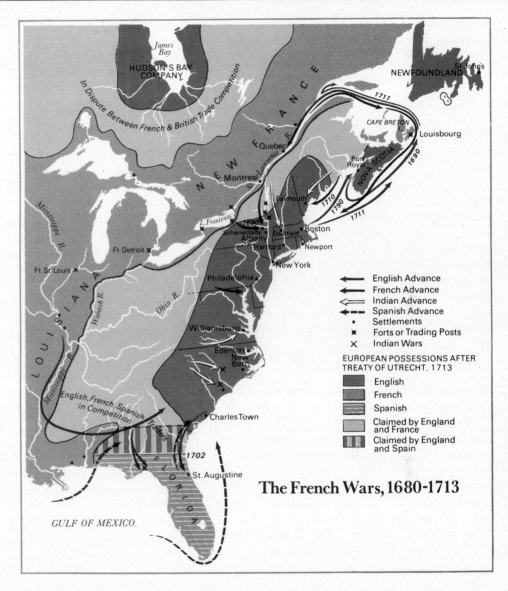

The French Wars, 1680-1713

whose main provisions marked a significant British victory in Europe, Britain secured permanent title to Newfoundland, Acadia (Nova Scotia), and Hudson Bay, though not all the boundaries were clear, and won a thirty-year contract to supply Spanish America with 4,800 slaves and a cargo of goods annually.

All of the American efforts in these wars of the European powers made great demands on the fragile colonial economies and accounted for significant inflows of funds. Troops had to be mobilized, housed, transported, and fed; ships had to be built, equipped, and manned; and native sources of naval supplies had to be exploited. The management of these efforts during these two decades of war fell into the eager hands of a few colonial merchants. Some were experienced. Andrew Belcher, once a Cambridge innkeeper, had made his first successes in trade as

PETER FANEUIL (1700–43)
Nephew and heir of the Huguenot refugee Andrew
Faneuil, who made a fortune in trade in Boston in the
early 18th century, Peter devoted himself to commerce
and public affairs. In 1740 he gave the city its famous
Faneuil Hall, which became a cockpit of Revolutionary
activity. *(Massachusetts Historical Society)*

a supplier to the Massachusetts government during
its brief and bloody war against the local Indians,
King Philip's War (1675–76). In the international
conflicts that followed, Belcher became the colony's
principal contractor. By his profits he established
a family that would rise to the governorship and to
other important offices and would enjoy grand tours
of Europe and the acquaintance of monarchs. The
Faneuil family, Huguenot refugees from France, also
established itself partly through wartime contracting.
In New York another Huguenot, Stephanus De-
Lancey, and the Schuyler brothers in Albany, all
active in many enterprises, used government con-

tracting as a major source of profits. Through that
business, political in its origins, these contractors
established families as important in New York as
the Belchers and Faneuils were in Massachusetts.

The Limits of Social Distinction.   So in these many
ways the situation made possible, toward the end
of the century, the growth of local elites. Enterprising
merchants like Belcher and Faneuil, landowning
squires like the Connecticut River Gods, planters
like the Fitzhughs, the Carters, and the Byrds, and
manorial "lords" like the Livingstons of New York
formed an aristocracy of sorts, a leadership group
distinguished by wealth or substantial claims to
wealth, political influence, and a superior style of
life. But if this was an aristocracy, it was a limited
aristocracy indeed. The limitations of their distinctions, the essential weakness of their positions, and
the instability of the membership of these groups
were as important as the eminence that they had
achieved.

They formed, to begin with, no "class"—that is,
no body of corporate interests, known and acknowledged, that dominated individual or family interests.
The concerns of these striving merchants, hustling
land speculators, and hard-pressed planters were
personal, local, and immediate. They identified their
interests not with the stable concerns of a particular
stratum of society that had existed before them and
would persist after them and that defined each member's particular welfare. Their interests were their
own, only occasionally and erratically merging with
the concerns of others in similar situations to form
common commitments and a common program of
public action.

Further, these emerging elites were distinguished
from most of their contemporaries by wealth alone,
and wealth of a particularly fragile kind. In education, in race, in ancestry, in cultural disposition, in
speech and personal style, they were largely indistinguishable from hundreds of others who competed with them openly. They had achieved, simply,
a degree of wealth, and wealth, in the colonial situation, was remarkably insecure. There was almost
no way to invest a fortune securely. "Urban" properties provided perhaps the steadiest yields but were

limited in scale and availability. Most capital was tied up in daily trading or planting operations or in land bought on speculation, and momentary upsets could prove to be disasters. Bankruptcies were common occurrences. Repeatedly names rose from obscurity only to disappear back into the population at large.

Even when wealth was maintained, however, it could provide no institutional protection for distinctions once they were achieved. There were no legal barriers or institutional forms that could protect these fragile aristocracies—no system equivalent to ennoblement, no institution like a House of Lords, no estate of nobles, no organization of any kind, secured in law, by which membership once created could be fixed and transmitted across the generations. The colonial councils were political bodies, and while membership in them expressed an enviable status, seats were not legally heritable and membership remained open not merely to local competition by every striving merchant, planter, and landowner, but to officials sent from abroad.

Of all the limitations in the distinctions of new elites, however, the most striking was the lack of visible distance between them and the bulk of the population from which they had emerged. They had not traveled very far; in so short a time they had not been able to create a world set far apart. They built manor houses, town houses, and plantation "seats" that had some style, and they shared in other efforts to establish the outward forms of a superior way of life. But the scale, the magnitudes, of all their efforts was yet modest—lavish, perhaps, by the standards of frontier tobacco farmers and petty shopkeeper-merchants, but incomparable to the establishments of aristocracies abroad. The Van Cortlandt's manor house on their estate on the Hudson was a modest one-and-one-half story wooden building—a pleasant summer house, a farmhouse more or less, improved for middle-class comfort but hardly suitable for an affluent country gentleman in England. "Westover," the Byrds' estate in Virginia, was more elegant and

VAN CORTLANDT MANOR HOUSE, CROTON-ON-HUDSON, NEW YORK

The manor, granted to Stephanus Van Cortlandt in 1697, originally included 86,123 acres. The restored manor house, shown here, was built around an even simpler structure by Stephanus's grandson, Pierre, over a period of years beginning in 1749. *(Courtesy, Sleepy Hollow Restorations, Tarrytown, New York)*

WILLIAM BYRD II, HIS WIFE
MARIA, AND HIS ESTATE,
WESTOVER
Son of a successful Virginia
trader and planter, Byrd spent
about 20 years in England
before settling down to his
inheritance. The present
house was the third erected
on that site, and became one
of the showpieces of colonial
Virginia. *(Top, The Library of
Congress; left, The Virginia Historical Society; right, The Metropolitan Museum of Art, Fletcher
Fund, 1925)*

more substantial, with pretentions to a higher, more sophisticated style in its carved interior woodwork and up-to-date exterior brick façades. But much of its ultimate beauty was acquired gradually, in successive additions and refinements. In its original form it was a square abode of eight main rooms and like so many of the other proud houses of the time it was solidly middle class. So too the most elegant and famous house in Boston in this period, built by the merchant John Foster between 1689 and 1692 and destined to descend in the Hutchinson family, seemed an immense achievement by the standard of the place and time, but it would have been indistinguishable from the ordinary town houses of prosperous tradesmen in any of the major cities of Europe. There was nothing anywhere in America to compare with the great urban residences and palatial country houses of the truly rich, or even the middling rich, of Europe—nothing to compare with the more modest "seats" of the lesser aristocracy which were then being built with fine taste in England.

The heights achieved by the Van Cortlandts, the Hutchinsons, the Belchers, and the Byrds were within the reach of many and never free from competition. Conversely, the surrounding ordinary world enjoyed a remarkably high level of general well-being. There was, to be sure, poverty in early eighteenth-century America. There was indigence and misery as there has been in every society that has ever existed; but among the ordinary free population there was a degree of affluence that was unique for the time. Land remained available, even if it was increasingly difficult for freed servants to rise to full independence and public influence; and entrance to wholesale trade, though narrower than before, remained open to competition. If there were a few great landlords, there were a great many independent farmers. If there were a few suddenly rich merchant "princes," there was a large number of others who had some share in the profits of trade. In the years of Queen Anne's War, one-third of the entire adult male population of Boston (544 individuals) were part owners of some seagoing vessel. And no fewer than 207 of these investors—12 percent of the adult male population of the town—called themselves "merchants."

Rebellion: The Measure of Social Strain

It was the sudden emergence of these new elites—proud but still striving and well within the range of rivals close behind—that explains the intensity of the rash of rebellions that occurred in the American colonies in the later 1600s. These are very small events in the scale of Western history, but seen within the context of the rapid maturing of Anglo-American society, they are extremely revealing. They show the inner seams, the strains and tensions, of communities whose social structure was still forming and in which no group's dominance and no individual's eminence were safe from effective competition.

There were five outbreaks, and their dates are significant:

Virginia	Bacon's Rebellion	
Carolina	Culpeper's Rebellion	1677
Massachusetts	Rebellion against Andros and the Dominion of New England	1689
New York	Leisler's Rebellion	1689
Maryland	The Protestant Association	

The origins of three of these rebellions—those in Massachusetts, New York, and Maryland—coincided with the arrival of news of the Glorious Revolution in England. In all three cases the insurgents explicitly associated themselves with that rebellion in England, which forced James II into exile and destroyed the threat of his autocratic rule. But the parallels, while not altogether fanciful, are superficial. None of the basic accomplishments of the Glorious Revolution were duplicated in the colonies. In England a king was deposed and sovereignty was shown to lie not in anointed monarchs and not in popular mobs, but in Parliament and the consensus of political and social leaders. Further, in England the supremacy of law—statute law and common law—had been established above any action of executive and crown, and judges had been made independent of "the pleasure of the prince." The legislature, finally, had declared the independence of its existence; its elections and its convenings were fixed in regular schedules and altogether disengaged from dictates of the crown. The American rebellions duplicated none of this. Sovereignty was in no way an issue in these provincial upheavals; the American executives retained the arbitrary powers that were eliminated in England; judges remained subordinate to "the pleasure of the prince"; and the existence and convening of the representative assemblies remained subject to executive decree.

The colonial insurrections were events of a different order. They differed greatly in their immediate causes. But whatever the original incitements may have been, once in process they expressed the social strains of communities in which social controls and political dominance were subjects of controversy, objects of challenge and continuous struggle.

Bacon's Rebellion. Thus Bacon's Rebellion began, in a period of economic distress, as an unauthorized war against the Indians on Virginia's northwestern frontier. Governor Berkeley's policy had been to stabilize the boundaries between Indians and whites and to protect the natives from land-hungry settlers. Although it was a sincere attempt to deal with a difficult problem, it was also a conservative policy, favoring the well-established planters and especially Berkeley's supporters and beneficiaries. As such, it was offensive to newcomers like Nathaniel Bacon, who had quarreled with the governor and had been denied the monopoly of the Indian trade he sought, and to Bacon's chief ally, Giles Bland, who had arrived in the colony in 1671 as customs collector but had been fined by the governor for "barbarous and insolent behaviors," then arrested, and finally dismissed from his post.

Around Bacon and Bland an opposition group formed. Victims of Berkeley's new establishment and increasingly resentful of the benefits that clique had acquired, they demanded land, without regard to the rights or needs of the border Indians squeezed between the double pressure of rival tribes behind them and white settlers before them. A violent conflict between Indians and the settlers in the border area that Bacon sought to control provided an excuse to launch a full-scale war, which became a civil war in 1676

when Berkeley repudiated Bacon and his allies and sought to bring them to justice. The rebels, having suppressed the border Indians in bloody battles, turned back upon the colony, seized the government, defeated and scattered Berkeley's forces, and burned Jamestown to the ground. But they could not sustain the insurrection. Bacon died of exposure and exhaustion in the midst of a confused military campaign. Deprived of his leadership, the rebellion faded out, and Bacon's chief allies were soon hanged for treason.

In all this turmoil the Baconites' voice rose loud and clear. Who are these men "in authority and favor," they demanded to know in their "Manifesto," to whose hands the dispensation of the country's wealth has been committed? Note, they cried, "the sudden rise of their estates compared with the mean quality in which they had first entered the country,"

. . . and let us see whether their extractions and education have not been vile, and by what pretense of learning and virtue they could [enter] so soon into employments of so great trust and consequence; let us . . . see what sponges have sucked up the public treasure and whether it hath not been privately contrived away by unworthy favorites and juggling parasites whose tottering fortunes have been repaired and supported at the public charge.

But these challengers were themselves challenged. For another element in the upheaval, expressed in the laws of "Bacon's Assembly" of 1676, was the discontent among the ordinary settlers at the *local* privileges of some of the same newly risen county magnates—the Baconites—who assailed the privileges of Governor Berkeley's inner clique. At both levels, local and central, the rebellion challenged the stability of newly secured authority.

The wave of rebellion in Virginia, which broke suddenly and spread quickly, soon subsided. By the end of the century the most difficult period of adjustment had passed and the colonists generally accepted the fact that certain families were indeed distinguished from others in riches, in dignity, and in access to political authority, and were likely to remain so. There had never been a challenge to British supremacy or to the idea that some people would inevitably be "high and eminent in power and dignity; others mean and in subjection." Protests and upheaval had resulted from the discomforts of discovering who was, in fact, which, and what the particular consequences of "power and dignity" were.

Culpeper's Rebellion.   More confused than Bacon's Rebellion was the almost comic-opera insurrection that took place in 1677 in Albemarle, the northern sector of Carolina. There some three thousand farmers struggled to survive in the swampy, sandy coastal lands and to profit from smuggling tobacco with the help of a few enterprising New England merchants. When the proprietor's group, no less hard-drinking, ill-tempered, and profiteering than their opponents, attempted to collect customs, they were set upon by a gang of rivals led by a belligerent malcontent named John Culpeper who accused them of malfeasance and treason, jailed them, seized the government, and sent charges against them to England. After endless confusion and an almost farcical series of attacks and counterattacks between the two groups, the Carolina proprietors finally managed to restore order. But the rebellion died slowly, partly because the legal proceedings in England were protracted but in greater part because of the continuing uncertainty of legitimate leadership in the rough, tumultuous backwoods community.

Leisler's Rebellion.   In New York the struggle between an emerging establishment and a resentful opposition was clearer than it was in the South, but also more bitter and more permanently consequential in politics.

When word of the Glorious Revolution arrived in New York, the lieutenant governor, Francis Nicholson, decided to strengthen Manhattan's garrison with militia troops. One of the captains of the militia was a well-to-do, cantankerous merchant, Jacob Leisler. Relations between the militia and Nicholson's regular troops grew difficult, then explosive, especially since Nicholson's legal status was unclear once James II had been deposed. In June 1689 the militia, led by Leisler, seized the fort in the name of the new English monarchs, William and Mary, and Nicholson sailed for England. In December William III's message to the chief officer of government arrived, instructing him to

retain his post, and Leisler interpreted this directive as addressed officially to himself as the colony's acting governor. He drew around him what was at first a large group of supporters, who proceeded to parcel out the colony's offices and run the government, including its feeble war effort. In 1691 when the next royal governor, the well-named Henry Sloughter, arrived and demanded that Leisler surrender the city and the government, Leisler, whose support had steadily eroded in two years of erratic rule and who by then scarcely controlled any of the colony outside the city walls, refused. Sloughter's superior power prevailed, Leisler and his followers surrendered, and after a quick and legally dubious trial he and his chief assistant, his son-in-law Jacob Milbourne, were hanged for treason and their property confiscated.

But these savage sentences, which Parliament legally annulled in 1695, hardly ended the struggle. By the time Leisler's regime had ended, the political leadership of the colony was broken into two violently antagonistic parties, the Leislerians and the anti-Leislerians, who thereafter alternated in power with successive governors, each party attempting literally to annihilate the other when the opportunity arose, or failing that to crush them politically so that they would never regain power. Again, the social background is crucial. Behind this see-sawing political conflict lay a latent struggle that had been in progress since the English conquest. During those years an Anglo-Dutch leadership group had taken form under governors sent out by the Duke of York. The colony's official patronage had come to center on this small group of families, whose ultimate rewards would come in the land grants of Benjamin Fletcher. Gradually this Anglo-Dutch cabal—the Bayards, Van Cortlandts, Philipses, Livingstons, and Schuylers—had made arrangements that satisfied their interests: a flour milling and exporting monopoly for New York City, which in effect gave them control of that vital industry; a New York City monopoly for shipping on the Hudson; and an Albany monopoly of the colony's Indian trade.

The offices had been theirs, and so too was the colony's economy, to the increasing resentment of those excluded. Gradually a combination of alienated factions had taken shape. Led by the merchants, especially those of Dutch origins, who were denied access to these privileges, it had included the city artisans, who were indirect victims of the junto's monopolies, and the Long Island townsmen, most of whom had migrated from Connecticut. Increasingly, the focus of this rising discontent had centered on Leisler, who had fought the Anglo-Dutch leaders on several issues, had been jailed in a religious controversy in Albany, had thereafter refused to pay customs, and had defied all efforts to bring him into court. His associates had had similar careers.

It had been this group of alienated, resentful, and enterprising outsiders, many of whom, under the Dutch, had been in positions of authority, who had sparked the opposition to Nicholson and turned it into a rebellion against the new Anglo-Dutch establishment. In principle, Leisler and his followers were no more "democrats" than were the Baconites in Virginia, but they found in the language of the Glorious Revolution a "Protestant" program—against monopolies, against autocracy, in favor of open access and a broad sharing of benefits—that served their interests well.

The Protestant Association. In Maryland, resentment, long-smoldering against the Calverts' Catholic ascendency, had erupted as early as 1676 in an obscure rebellion in Calvert County. When news of the Glorious Revolution arrived, the same small group of insurgents, further antagonized by a particularly obnoxious proprietary governor, led two hundred and fifty of the settlers to seize the colony's government. Calling themselves the Protestant Association, they issued a declaration condemning the proprietary party for excessive fee-taking, for resisting royal authority, and for arbitrary taxation; they identified telltale signs of an incipient papal plot; and they petitioned the crown to take over the government from the Calverts, which was promptly done.

It was only in 1715 that the Calverts' control of Maryland was returned to them, but by then the family had turned Protestant and the government had been drawn into the general pattern of colonial governance which required crown approval of executive appointments and of the colony's legislation. The rebellion

PETER SCHUYLER, MAYOR OF ALBANY, 1686–94 BY NEHEMIAH PARTRIDGE
Also for many years chief English negotiator with the Indians, Schuyler is pictured here in 1718, eight years after he took four Iroquois chiefs to London where they were received with honor by Queen Anne. *(Collection City of Albany, New York)*

had sprung out of the jostling instability of late seventeenth-century animosities, and while the proprietary group thereafter still dominated the executive government, it could no longer block the advance of the planter aristocracy or ignore a legislative body whose influence was built into the structure of government.

The Downfall of Andros. Though in Massachusetts there were special, local peculiarities in the rebellion that took place, there was also a similar underlying conflict. The continuing dominance of the Puritan regime, protected by the original charter, delayed the characteristic struggle of social groups. But after the confiscation of the charter in 1684 and the establishment of the Dominion, the pattern seen elsewhere quickly developed. Almost immediately, the favors of patronage and power began to flow to a small group of speculators and merchant insiders, some of them in Andros's entourage, some of them adventurous natives who gravitated to the new establishment. For four years this newly dominant group enjoyed a feast of privilege and in the process generated resentments among others that found expression in an uprising made especially bitter by the Puritan animosities that fueled it.

These rebellions are obscure events, and they are confused events, especially the last three in which the rebels claimed association with the successful revolutionaries in England. Everywhere the insurgents sought to identify themselves with the struggle for English liberty and against various forms of tyranny. None, however, questioned the basis of public authority; all submitted to legitimate crown power when it appeared; none fought for the full range of liberties that would be set out in the English Bill of Rights (1689) and the Act of Settlement (1701), which concluded the revolution in England. They did not question the nature of government but its control; not its structure and essential character, but its personnel; not what and how, but who. Enclosed in their provincial world, they sought, above all, equity in the actions of government that properly reflected the balance of society as it had emerged through a period of rapid growth and change.

Provincial Culture

These insurrections of the late seventeenth century were not only obscure events in the scale of Western history; they were also—significantly—provincial events. And as such they were characteristic of Anglo-American culture generally as it emerged in the early 1700s. For that culture had greatly changed in its relations to the parent culture from which it had developed. In the early years the settlements, however small, distant, and isolated, had been part of a vital movement in the forefront of western European life. The key figures were products of the European world. They were isolated physically in America but not psychologically or intellectually or spiritually. They never lost the sense that they were engaged in a momentous enterprise, something that mattered in an important way to the world they had left behind. They felt they could easily return, and when they did, they found themselves enhanced, not diminished, by their sojourn in the exotic frontier west. Thus the poet, traveler, and scholar George Sandys, son of the Archbishop of York, slipped back easily into Lord Falkland's literary circle after his stay in Virginia, having made good progress on his translation of Ovid's *Metamorphoses*. So Roger Williams returned to Cromwell's council of state, and Winthrop's nephew George Downing, sent off to Harvard College to improve his morals and manners, became Cromwell's chief intelligence officer, was knighted, and ended as England's ambassador to Holland. The settlements had been relevant and vital to the most forward-looking minds of the time.

By 1700 none of this was true. As the colonies grew, they grew apart, into a separate world of their own—connected with the greater world beyond, but still fundamentally removed. The success or failure of the colonists' daily affairs no longer mattered as they once had. The settlers no longer made news; they listened for it, intently, from abroad, and imitated what they could of styles of thought, of ways of living and patterns of behavior. They knew themselves to be provincials in the sense that their culture was not self-contained; its sources and superior expressions were to be found elsewhere than in their

JOHN WINTHROP, JR., BY AN UNKNOWN 17TH CENTURY PAINTER

Sophisticated, learned, and enterprising, the younger Winthrop was more versatile and more genial than his austere father and less passionately committed to the Puritans' spiritual quest. The features of the two Winthrops' faces are strikingly similar (see p. 43), but their expressions are entirely different, reflecting quite different life experiences and outlooks. *(Courtesy, Harvard University Portrait Collection)*

own land. They must seek it from afar; it must be acquired, and once acquired, be maintained according to standards externally imposed, in the creation of which they had not shared. The most cultivated of the colonists read much, purposefully, determined to retain contact with the greater world at home. The diary of William Byrd II with its record of daily stints of study is a stolid testimonial to the virtues of regularity and effort in maintaining standards of civilization set abroad.

This basic transformation can be seen particularly well in the later career of the gifted and learned son of the patriarch John Winthrop. John, Jr., was educated at Trinity College, Dublin, and in London at the lawyers' Inner Temple. As a young man he had helped manage an English overseas military expedition, and had traveled in the Mediterranean and the Middle East. A physician, amateur scientist, and imaginative entrepreneur who served as governor of Connecticut for eighteen years, he struggled to maintain contact with the Royal Society in London of which he was the first American member. There was "a current of loneliness, almost pathos," the younger Winthrop's latest biographer writes, "in his anxiety to stay in touch." He wrote letter after letter to the society's secretary; he sent over scientific specimens—rattlesnake skins, birds' nests, plants, crabs, strange pigs; he studied the society's *Transactions* so as not to fall too far behind; and to those concerned with the propagation of the gospel he dispatched John Eliot's Algonquian translation of the Bible and two essays written in Latin by Indian students at Harvard. But these were failing efforts. In the end loneliness and isolation overcame him. He died in 1676, venerated in the villages along the Connecticut River—themselves changing like autumn leaves from vital, experimental religious communities to sere, old-fashioned backwoods towns—but forgotten in the greater world at home. His sons, however, provincial land speculators and petty politicians, had no such memories as their father had had, and no such aspirations; they suffered therefore, no such disappointments. They were native to the land, and their cultural horizons had narrowed to its practical demands.

This was a silent drama—of a high culture, temporarily transferred, becoming permanently provincial; and it was a drama played out most vividly in the field of education. For education, in its broadest sense, serves more than any other social process to liberate people from local, parochial environments and bring them into contact with larger worlds and broader horizons. Education is perhaps the most sensitive index to the changing character of American life as it developed in these transition years. It is also one of the most difficult subjects to interpret. For there were great accomplishments, but there were also great defeats; soaring ambitions, but serious neglect.

Education.   Certain things, however, are clear. In New England the founding generation made a remarkable effort not only to perpetuate education as it was then known but to improve it—to spread it more widely and more effectively through the entire population than it was even in England, where formal education was extraordinarily widespread for the time. The Puritans' efforts in education stemmed primarily from their religious convictions, specifically their insistence that every person, saint or sinner, have personal access to the Holy Scriptures, which meant the capacity to read. That was a mere beginning, however, for to the Puritans the truly religious person was a student not only of the Bible but also of commentaries on the Bible, including those intricate oral commentaries preached at prodigious length from every pulpit in the land. To perpetuate this biblical culture in the population at large would require schooling that went beyond the normal Elizabethan assumption that the goal of formal education was training in vocational roles. For the Puritans, there was only one essential vocation, and that was spiritual. Though true salvation was in the end a God-given grace, the preparation for grace—the opening of the mind and soul to such a possibility—was a matter of education, knowledge, and will.

It was not this central religious commitment alone, however, that led the Puritans to their remarkable efforts in education. Partly too they were driven by a sense that in their wilderness condition the family, which traditionally had borne so much of the burden of transmitting the elements of culture across the generations, had weakened and was failing in its duty and capacity. This fear bore heavily on the minds of the founding elders.* They looked ahead to the future and noted that if extraordinary precautions were not made in time they would leave behind not a Bible commonwealth but a tribe of rustic barbarians. If family discipline were loose, if parents were slack

*For pressures on family life in the seventeenth century, see pp. 79–82.

in their responsibilities, the public—the government, the magistrates—would have to provide for the future.

Ambitious, therefore, not merely to perpetuate education but to extend it, the Puritans turned instinctively to the willingness of people voluntarily to establish and support formal institutions of education. For they knew that the recent wave of educational foundations in England had been accomplished by private philanthropy; by gifts from institutions (gilds, universities) and even more from individual donors, usually in the form of land endowments. And in the first fifteen years, the records of six towns show that a number of relatively rich inhabitants *did* attempt to establish schools with the traditional endowment base. But the land was wild, tenants were scarce, and endowments were worth nothing if they produced no rents. Other forms of financing would have to be found. In place of pleas to the rich, there must be commands. The towns ordered the wealthy to volunteer, then took to group action, assigning some of the towns' common land to schools. But the hoped-for income failed for lack of reliable tenants. In the end, there was only one resource: taxation. It began as a supplement to private gifts and ended as almost the sole and universal basis of elementary education.

So for a decade and more the Puritans struggled with the problem of education, experimented, and came to fear that their whole endeavor would fail unless some uniform provisions were made, some universal standards set, and facilities provided that would guarantee the survival of their hopes into the future. In the 1640s they made their great departure in two famous laws. By a law of 1642, the Massachusetts General Court charged all parents and ministers with the responsibility for the "calling and employment of their children, especially of their ability to read and understand the principles of religion and the capital laws of this country." Five years later, in 1647, the legislative provisions were completed: the General Court ruled that all towns of 50 families must provide for the maintenance of elementary schools, and all towns of 100 families must support Latin grammar schools. These laws became models for the rest of Puritan New England. Connecticut followed with similar provisions in 1650, and Plymouth in two stages, 1658 and 1677. Wherever these enactments remained on the books they were innovative and creative. But they are easily misunderstood.

For these laws do *not* provide for public education as it has been known since the nineteenth century. The concept of a strict distinction between "private" and "public" did not exist in the seventeenth century. Neither of these laws of the 1640s specified "public" moneys as the financial basis of the community's schools; neither made formal schooling obligatory at any level. What they *did* do was, first, to establish a minimum level of educational accomplishment (not schooling) by specifying masters' and parents' obligations and reinforcing these obligations with sanctions of fines and the threat of removing children to other households. Second, the laws required that schooling, at both elementary and secondary (Latin grammar) levels, be made universally *available* for those who wished to take advantage of it. Third, these laws established a community-wide obligation to support formal institutions of education without reference to the benefits any individual or family derived from these schools. Finally, the laws made clear that the government's role in the whole area of education would not be merely supplementary or supportive or supervisory, but positive and compelling.

All of this, written into these innovating American laws on education, was highly creative. But these famous laws are the beginning, not the end, of the historical development. The question is not merely what was hoped for and what was provided for, but what happened to these hopes and these provisions in later years. What effect did these remarkable provisions have on the lives of the people?

By the end of the seventeenth century it was clear that the hopes of the Puritans were not being evenly and satisfactorily fulfilled. Fines against delinquent towns were common. Subsequent revisions and codifications of the laws cite continuing neglect on the part of masters, parents, and towns. The old fears not only continued but seemed to grow more intense. In Massachusetts in 1671 the fines on towns that neglected to maintain grammar instruction were

doubled. In 1689 Cotton Mather, third generation scion of a great clerical dynasty and self-appointed guardian of the ancestral hopes, bemoaned his people's fate. He doubted, he declared in a sermon of that year, if New England suffered "under an iller symptom than the too general want of education in the rising generation." If not overcome, this neglect, he said, would "gradually and speedily dispose us to that sort of Creolean degeneracy observed to deprave the children of the most noble and worthy Europeans when transplanted into America."

But even Mather's magisterial voice could not halt the movement of change. In 1718 the General Court, again increasing the delinquency fines, condemned the "many towns that not only are obliged by law but are very able to support a grammar school, yet choose rather to incur and pay the fine and penalty than maintain a grammar school." As settlements spread throughout the countryside, as contact with the centers of high culture grew thin, and as the original fires of Puritanism cooled, the instinct somehow to modify the law or adjust it to the realities of everyday life grew bolder, stronger, and more effective, though the laws remained on the books and magistrates sought to enforce them. Sometimes there was outright evasion. A town would obey by hiring a teacher who knew no Latin to teach that subject "as far as he was able." More commonly, a new institution was used, the "moving school," which satisfied the law by providing for a schoolmaster and his equipment but distributed his services on a circuit that moved through the town's lands in proportion to the spread of population. Thus Gloucester, Massachusetts, had a Latin grammar school, but the teacher and his books moved about in a cycle of three years, settling in seven places in the following monthly proportions: 9, 7, 5½, 5½, 4½, 3, 1½. Thus even the most remote corner of the township had contact with the "moving school," but it was available for children in that most isolated area only one and a half months every three years.

Finally, by the mid-eighteenth century the towns found a permanent solution: the district school. The towns were now formally divided into school districts, each district drawing its proportionate share of the available funds and using it as its own local school committee decided. Schools thus existed in almost every town; but the variations were great. For the management of the schools was now entirely in the hands of the localities, some of them limited, isolated localities, incapable of and uninterested in transcending their narrow environments. Some schools were excellent, some poor, some dismal. Often the Latin grammar school proved to be a common school in which children of all ages were taught at their own levels. Uniformity was lost, but the "Creolean degeneracy" that Mather had feared had failed to take hold. New England emerged in the eighteenth century still a literate culture, still open to a high level of cultural attainment.

All of this was a flame, sparked by the original creators of the Bible commonwealth, that burned fitfully at times but never failed. How remarkable an accomplishment it was may be seen by the contrast with the slow and irregular development of education elsewhere in the colonies, where the churches and a few generous individuals sought to provide for schooling. In 1671 Governor Berkeley of Virginia wrote about his colony, "I thank God there are no free schools nor printing," these being sources, he declared, of "disobedience and heresy and sects." By 1689 there were still only six schools of various kinds in Virginia. In the same year Maryland had one school. New York, mainly through the efforts of the Dutch church, may have had eleven.

The Colleges. That education at the elementary and secondary levels developed as it did in New England was in part the result of the reinforcement it received from higher education, established in the same years, which too became closely bound to the immediate needs of these provincial communities.

There can be little doubt about the Puritans' primary reason for founding in 1636 the institution that became Harvard College. They dreaded, they said, "to leave an illiterate ministry to the churches when our present ministers shall lie in the dust." There were other motives too, especially the hopes

LT. GOV. WILLIAM STOUGHTON OF MASSACHUSETTS
In the background is the building that this dour, wealthy, old-fashioned Puritan gave to his alma mater, Harvard, in 1699. It was the first American college building donated by an alumnus. *(Courtesy of the Harvard University Portrait Collection, Gift–John Cooper, 1810)*

of those who sought an instrument for propagating the gospel to the native Indians through preachers trained at the college who would go out to deliver the word. But though the gospel mission failed miserably amid the general failure of civilized relations between Indians and whites, the effort to maintain a college primarily for training preachers and secondarily for educating gentlemen in the liberal arts

COLONIAL COLLEGES

College	Colony	Founded
Harvard College	Massachusetts	1636
College of William and Mary	Virginia	1693
Yale College	Connecticut	1701
College of New Jersey (Princeton University)	New Jersey	1746
College of Philadelphia (University of Pennsylvania)	Pennsylvania	1754
King's College (Columbia University)	New York	1754
College of Rhode Island (Brown University)	Rhode Island	1764
Queen's College (Rutgers University)	New Jersey	1766
Dartmouth College	New Hampshire	1769

took root and flourished. By the time the College of William and Mary, the second English colonial college, was chartered in 1693 as part of the effort to improve the condition of the Anglican clergy in Virginia, Harvard College, named after its first private benefactor, John Harvard, was a stable institution. Its influence, through its graduates, was great and its continued existence, written into the terms of the colony's second charter of 1691, was firmly guaranteed.

Yet like so much else in American life, this college, and those that would follow it, grew apart from the models on which they were based and became something different. The Puritan founders intended to create a familiar university-college, a residential institution whose ownership and direction would lie in the hands of the teachers—the resident tutors and professors. But the colonial colleges did not develop in that way. Instead, by an intricate process of evolution, ownership of the property and the ultimate government of the colleges came to rest not in the teachers but in boards of trustees external to the educational process, who hired the teachers and supervised the work of the colleges on behalf of the founding community. For the central impulse in creating these colleges was the community's desire to perpetuate a learned clergy and to advance learning in the wilderness setting. Later in American history the nature of the founding community

would shift—to denominations serving their particular concerns and to states reconizing the need for experts in technical fields and seeking to provide for the public's general education. But from the establishment of the first college in 1636 onward, the initiating impulse and the resources have come from groups outside the profession of teaching and learning, and the governance of higher education has reflected the groups' insistence on seeing that the institutions fulfill these community mandates. In this sense all the American colleges and universities have been community schools—products not so much of the world of education and learning as of desires and decisions of the community at large. Control has therefore rested with the founding communities, and as, in the colonial period, the horizons of the communities narrowed, the mandates of the colleges narrowed too. A learned clergy was indeed perpetuated, and higher education made generally available, not only in Massachusetts, Virginia, and Connecticut, but in New Jersey, Pennsylvania, New York, Rhode Island, and New Hampshire. Through these institutions the pursuit of learning and the cultivation of the arts were advanced and transmitted across the generations. But at the root of their foundations lay not so much a love of learning for its own sake as the parochial concerns of communities of limited horizons, determined to sustain their founders' commitments to serving local, provincial needs.

CHRONOLOGY

1660 Restoration of Stuart monarchy (Charles II, 1660–85).
Basic navigation law, monopolizing colonial trade and shipping for Britain, passed by Parliament; includes "enumeration" clause.

1662 Massachusetts Bay ministers sanction halfway convenant.
Colony of Connecticut chartered by crown.

1663 New royal charter issued to Rhode Island.
New navigation act (Staple Act) passed, channeling colonies' importation of European goods through England.
Charter of Carolina given to eight courtiers.

1664 England conquers New Netherland, which becomes proprietary colony of Duke of York.
New Jersey charter issued to two courtiers.

1665 Duke's Laws for New York promulgated.

1669 Fundamental Constitutions of Carolina issued.

1673 New navigation act imposes "plantation duties."

1675 Lords of Trade appointed as committee of Privy Council.

1675–76 King Philip's War in New England.

1676 Bacon's Rebellion in Virginia.
New Jersey divided into East and West Jersey.

1677 West New Jersey's Concessions and Agreements issued.
Culpeper's Rebellion in Carolina.

1680 New Hampshire given royal charter.

1681 Pennsylvania charter granted to William Penn; first settlements in 1682.

1684 Massachusetts Bay charter annulled by crown (charters of Connecticut, Rhode Island, New Jersey, Pennsylvania, Maryland, and Carolina abrogated in following years, to 1691).

1685–88 Duke of York becomes James II; his accession royalizes New York.

1686 Dominion of New England established.

1688 Glorious Revolution in England drives out James II in favor of William and Mary.

1689 Successful rebellion in Boston against Dominion of New England.
The Protestant Association in Maryland rebels.

1689–91 Leisler's Rebellion in New York.

1689–97 King William's War (colonial phase of Europe's War of the League of Augsburg).

1691 Massachusetts Bay Colony gets new charter.

1692 Witchcraft hysteria in Salem, Massachusetts; twenty "witches" executed.

1693 College of William and Mary founded.

1696 English government establishes Board of Trade and Plantations.
Passage of comprehensive navigation act, extending admiralty court system to America.

1699 Woolen Act passed by Parliament.

1701 Yale College founded.
New and permanent Frame of Government adopted in Pennsylvania.

1702–13 Queen Anne's War (colonial phase of Europe's War of the Spanish Succession), concluded in Treaty of Utrecht.

1702 West and East New Jersey formed into single royal colony.

1702–14 Reign of Queen Anne.

1708 Saybrook Platform adopted in Connecticut.

1714–27 Reign of George I, beginning Hanoverian dynasty.

1719 Rebellion against proprietors in Carolina.

SUGGESTED READINGS

The fullest account of the origins of the British imperial system, in both theory and institutions, is Charles M. Andrews, *The Colonial Period of American History,* IV (1938). On the theory of empire, see in addition Richard Koebner, *Empire* (1961) chap. iii; on the all-important customs administration in the colonies, Thomas C. Barrow, *Trade & Empire* (1967); and on the difficulty in the late seventeenth century of imposing regulations on the scattered settlements, see Michael G. Hall, *Edward Randolph and the American Colonies* (1969). On the influence of the Duke of York (James II) and his entourage on the evolution of empire and the importance of his and his lieutenants' military background, see Stephen S. Webb, "... The Household of James Stuart in the Evolution of English Imperialism," *Perspectives in American History,* 8 (1974), 55–80. On the patronage sources of colonial appointments and other aspects of the politics of the early empire, see Webb's "Strange Career of Francis Nicholson" and "William Blathwayt, Imperial Fixer," *Wm. and Mary Q.,* 23 (1966), 513–48; 26 (1969), 373–415—a subject presented in full in Webb's *The Governors-General* (1979). On James II's ill-fated effort to organize a territorial government, see Viola F. Barnes, *The Dominion of New England* (1923).

The emergence of a native Anglo-American aristocracy is traced generally, in the case of Virginia, in Bernard Bailyn, "Politics and Social Structure in Virginia,"* James M. Smith, ed., *Seventeenth-Century America* (1959) and Louis B. Wright, *First Gentlemen of Virginia* (1940); in the case of commercial New England, in Bernard Bailyn, *New England Merchants in the Seventeenth Century* (1955); in the case of New York, in Thomas Archdeacon, *New York City, 1664–1710* (1976); and in the five main port towns, in Carl Bridenbaugh, *Cities in the Wilderness* (1938). The origins of rural aristocracies in New England, rooted in the shifting relations between population and land, are described in Roy H. Akagi, *The Town Proprietors of the New England Colonies* (1924) and probed analytically in Richard L. Bushman's thoughtful *From Puritan to Yankee* (1967) and in the individual community studies listed in the references to chapter III. For the reflection of this development in government, see Kenneth A. Lockridge and Alan Kreider, "Evolution of Massachusetts Town Government, 1640–1740," *Wm. and Mary Q.,* 23 (1966), 549–74. For case studies of the emergence of the southern aristocracy, see the essays on social mobility in the Chesapeake area cited for the previous chapter; Louis B. Wright's edition of Byrd's diaries and literary writings; and Richard B. Davis, ed.,

William Fitzhugh and His Chesapeake World, 1676–1701 (1963). The political aspects of a rising aristocracy are analyzed in the case of New York in Patricia U. Bonomi, *A Factious People* (1971), chaps. ii, iii; in Archdeacon's *New York City;* and in Lawrence H. Leder, *Robert Livingston* (1961).

The late seventeenth-century wars (the subject of Francis Parkman's dramatic classics, *Count Frontenac and New France under Louis XIV,* 1877; and *A Half-Century of Conflict,* 1892) are sketched briefly in Howard H. Peckham, *The Colonial Wars, 1689–1762* (1964), but their deeper significance for the development of Anglo-American politics, trade, and society is suggested in G. M. Waller, *Samuel Vetch, Colonial Enterpriser* (1960).

The colonial rebellions of the late seventeenth century are described, insofar as they relate to the English rebellion against James II, in David S. Lovejoy, *The Glorious Revolution in America* (1972); there is a documentary collection related to these events in a book of the same title edited by Michael G. Hall, Lawrence H. Leder, and Michael G. Kammen. But as social events these uprisings are to be associated with Bacon's Rebellion, which is described generally in Wilcomb E. Washburn, *The Governor and the Rebel* (1957) and analyzed in social terms in Bailyn, "Politics and Social Structure"*; in Wesley F. Craven, *Southern Colonies in the Seventeenth Century* (1949); and in Edmund Morgan, *American Slavery, American Freedom* (1975). For the social background of Leisler's Rebellion, see Archdeacon's book cited above (excerpted into essay form as "... The Age of Leisler in New York City,"*) and Jerome R. Reich, *Leisler's Rebellion* (1953), which exaggerates the "democratic" impulses of the rebels. On Boston's rebellion, see Barnes, *Dominion of New England.* The most exhaustive study of the social background of any of these rebellions, however, is Lois G. Carr and David W. Jordan, *Maryland's Revolution of Government 1689–1692* (1974).

The deepening provincialism of American culture in the late seventeenth century emerges in the colonists' writings, analyzed with subtlety in the opening chapter of Kenneth S. Lynn, *Mark Twain and Southwestern Humor* (1959); in the careers of third-generation Anglo-Americans such as the Winthrops (Richard S. Dunn, *Puritans and Yankees: The Winthrop Dynasty of New England, 1630–1717,* 1962, Bk. III) and the Mathers (Robert Middlekauff, *The Mathers: Three Generations of Puritan Intellectuals, 1596–1728,* 1971, Bk. III); in the missionary efforts of the Anglicans (Parke Rouse, Jr., *James Blair of Virginia,* 1971; Leonard W. Cowie, *Henry Newman: An American in London, 1708–43*, 1956); in travelers' accounts (Jasper Danckaerts [1679–80], pub. 1867; the Frenchman Durand [1687], pub. 1923; Sarah Knight [1704], latest pub. 1972); and above all in education.

For a comprehensive, detailed, and broadly conceived account of early American education, see Lawrence A. Cremin, *American Education: The Colonial Experience, 1607–1783* (1970), Parts I–III; for a general interpretation of the social role of colonial education, see Bernard Bailyn, *Education in the Forming of American Society* (1960); and for the deepening localization of standards, described in the text, Harlan Updegraff, *Origin of the Moving School in Massachusetts* (1907). Robert Middlekauff has traced the persistence of the classical tradition in the face of provincial difficulties in *Ancients and Axioms* (1963). James Axtell, *The School upon a Hill* (1974) shows through education in the broadest sense, how New England's culture was transmitted across the generations.

On the origins of higher education, see Samuel E. Morison's magisterial works, *The Founding of Harvard College* (1935) and *Harvard College in the Seventeeth Century* (2 vols., 1936), both summarized in his *Three Centuries of Harvard: 1636–1936* (1936). Though these learned and highly readable books remain fundamental, Morison's general interpretation has been challenged: by Winthrop S. Hudson, "The Morison Myth Concerning the Founding of Harvard College," *Church History*, 8 (1939), 148–59; and by Jurgen Herbst, "The First Three American Colleges: Schools of the Reformation," *Perspectives in American History*, 8 (1974), 7–52, in which parallels are drawn between Harvard, Yale, and William and Mary on the one hand and the *"gymnasia illustria,* academies, or *Gelehrtenschulen* on the Continent" on the other. Yale's origins have recently been detailed with great care by Richard Warch in *School of the Prophets: Yale College, 1701–1740* (1973) and William and Mary's in Rouse, *Blair*. All aspects of education and artistic expression are discussed in Richard B. Davis, *Intellectual Life in the Colonial South, 1585–1763* (3 vols., 1978).

*See footnote on page 65.

CHAPTER 5

American Society in the Eighteenth Century

The end of the War of the Spanish Succession in 1713 and the creation of a stable political regime in England under Sir Robert Walpole, prime minister from 1721 to 1742, introduced a period of great expansion in all spheres of Anglo-American life. In the two generations that followed the war, despite minor involvements in other international conflicts and repeated cycles of commercial recession, the American colonies grew so rapidly and matured so fully that they came to constitute an important element not only in British life but in the life of the Atlantic world generally. Developing on scattered seventeenth-century foundations, becoming more and more distinctive though outwardly seeking to conform to the normal patterns of European life, and drawn more and more elaborately into the ill-organized structure of empire, the colonies acquired characteristics that would remain permanent in American life.

The New Population: Sources and Impact

Fundamental to all aspects of eighteenth-century American history was the phenomenal growth of the population. In 1700 the population was approximately 250,000; by 1775 it had grown tenfold, to 2.5 million, which was fully a third of the size of the population of England and Wales (6.7 million). A fifth of the American people were black, almost all of them slaves, nine-tenths of whom lived south of Pennsylvania. They constituted two-fifths of the population of Virginia and almost two-thirds of the population of South Carolina.

Bu the 1760s the settlements formed an almost unbroken line along the seaboard, from Maine to Florida, and they reached deep into the interior. In New England, groups moving up the Connecticut River and the coastal streams penetrated into New Hampshire and Vermont. In New York, settlements spread through the rich Hudson, Mohawk, and Schoharie valleys, and in Pennsylvania and the Carolinas extended back to the Appalachians. In a few places, especially southwestern Pennsylvania, the Appala-

chian mountain barrier had been breached by frontiersmen who were actively opening fresh lands to
cultivation in Indian territories.

The population was almost entirely rural. Of the
towns, the most populous was Philadelphia, with approximately 35,000 inhabitants. The five largest communities (Philadelphia, New York, Boston, Charleston, and Newport, Rhode Island) had a combined
population of 90,000, or 3.6 percent of the total. Fifteen smaller towns, ranging from New Haven, Connecticut, with 8,000 to Savannah, Georgia, with 3,200,
account for another 77,500; but very few of the total
town population of approximately 167,500 lived in
circumstances that can be called "urban" in a modern
sense.

The rapid increase in the size of the population
—it almost doubled every twenty-five years—was in
large part the result of natural growth. But it was
the result too of new flows of immigration. While the
basic recruitment from England continued, though
at a reduced rate, and while between 250,000 and
300,000 Africans were imported directly or indirectly from their homelands, new groups began to
make important contributions. Religious persecution in France led to the immigration of several thousand Huguenots (French Protestants, forced to flee
after 1685 when the tolerant Edict of Nantes was
revoked); and from Scotland came groups of Jacobites
(those faithful to the exiled James II and his son)
after their military defeat by the English in 1715. But
the main new flows came from two quite different
sources, which together supplied approximately 20
percent of the total American population when the
first national census was taken in 1790.

The Irish. The first new source was Ireland—not
Catholic Ireland but Protestant northern Ireland,
which had been the first overseas colony of the English people. The efforts of the English in the early
seventeenth century to colonize a great "plantation"
in Ulster, the six northern counties of Ireland, had
attracted to that region a large migration from Scotland, where social and religious conditions throughout the seventeenth century were unsettled. By 1715
perhaps 150,000 Scots had crossed the Irish Sea to

settle on Irish estates where rents were originally
low. From this heartland of "Scotch-Irish" Presby-
terianism a large migration to America took place
in the eighteenth century. How many were involved
we do not know exactly, but the best estimate is a
yearly average of 4,000 through most of the century,
totaling nearly a quarter of a million. It was said by
W. E. H. Lecky, Ireland's greatest historian, that the
loss of so great a number of Irish Protestants to America in the eighteenth century ended forever the hope
of balancing the religious communities in that tormented island.

The Germans. The other new source of the American population was the upper Rhine valley, in southwestern Germany. This area, especially the district
west of the Rhine, which formed the Rhenish Palatinate, had been badly ravaged in the religious wars
of the seventeenth century and then, in 1688–89,
devastated by French armies. In addition, Catholic
princes, particularly the Palatinate's ruling Elector,
had begun to persecute the increasingly numerous
Protestant sects. When, further, crop disasters in
1708 and 1709 reduced much of the same population
to beggary and a new English naturalization law
made British territory an attractive refuge, a movement of peoples began that ended in furnishing a
major component of the American population. William Penn had begun recruiting settlers in the Rhineland as early as the 1680s, and it was to his colony
eventually that the greatest number of German-
speaking people came. These "Pennsylvania Dutch"
(from *Deutsch:* that is, Germans, not Hollanders) comprised one-third of that colony's population by 1775.
The census of 1790 showed almost as many German-
born or German-descended Americans (9 percent of
the population) as there were Scotch-Irish, and their
influence was at least as important in the development of American society.

For in the end it is not only the numbers involved that account for the importance of migrations
like these. More important are the attitudes, apti-
tudes, and ambitions of the immigrants and their
influence on the development of the community's
life. In the case of these two groups, the impact was

GERMAN PIETIST EMIGRANTS

The man carries in one hand the orthodox Lutheran "Augsburg Confession" and in the other Johann Arndt's classic of pietistic devotion, *Vom Wahren Christentum* (1605; republished in Philadelphia in 1751). His pack bears the motto, "God is with us in need," hers, "God has done great things for us"; and between the two in the original print was the caption "Nothing but the gospel drives us into exile. Though we leave the fatherland, we remain in God's hand." In the background is a German servant's indenture dated 1736, a year in which a large number of Salzburg emigrants, such as the two depicted here, were fleeing religious persecution. *(Foreground: Library of Congress. Background: Photo by Pennsylvania Historical and Museum Commission, Harrisburg, Pa.)*

profound. Both were alienated groups—alienated from authority both civil and ecclesiastical. Both groups were hostile to all establishments, stubborn in defense of their rights, and ambitious for economic security. Both contributed powerfully to the shaping of American social and political life.

Attitudes of the New Immigrants. For the Scotch-Irish, resentment if not hatred of the English establishment had long been a way of life. Britain had excluded Irish products from sale elsewhere in British territory and thereby blighted Ireland's economic growth. Further, the Anglo-Irish landlords, mainly absentees, had increased rents whenever leases fell due, and in addition the Scotch-Irish, being Presbyterian nonconformists, were victimized by the Anglican religious establishment, which they were obliged to support by special taxes. In 1704 a sacramental test excluded Presbyterians from all public offices, and marriages solemnized in their churches were declared invalid. As a result of all of this, the first wave of Scotch-Irish immigrants, arriving in Boston and the Delaware ports between 1717 and 1720, carried with it a burning resentment of the English establishment in all its forms. Those who followed, attracted by enthusiastic letters promising "liberty and ease as the reward of . . . honest industry," freedom from escalating rents, and access to public office, shared these attitudes in varying degrees and carried these resentments through the length and breadth of the colonies.

The Germans, legally aliens, had no natural affinity with the British establishment and no political contacts to help protect them in this exploitative world. Further, their legal position was weak. Before 1740, they could become British subjects only by specific deeds of "denization" or by naturalization granted by the colonial governments. Both were generous in the rights they bestowed, but both were revocable; neither bound the *British* government (hence locally naturalized Germans could not qual-

ify as "British" subjects under the Navigation Acts); and neither was automatically accepted in any colony but the original. Many of these problems were eliminated by Parliament's general Naturalization Law of 1740, which permitted aliens who had resided continuously for seven years in any of the British colonies to become naturalized subjects of all colonies. But naturalization by this process was time consuming; excluded Catholics; involved an oath offensive to Jews, Quakers, and certain other Protestants; and did not carry over fully to England itself, where naturalized colonists were not automatically entitled to own land or hold crown office.

Alienated from, if not actively hostile to, the British government, these Scotch-Irish and German

German Settlements in 18th-Century America

Palatinate Homelands

- Rhenish Palatinate
- Other "Palatinate" Districts

newcomers had little reason to feel close to the colonial governments either, or to the groups that dominated these governments. As settlers they were often physically remote from the capitals, taking up land in backcountry areas far distant from the seats of power. At times they did not even know which governmental jurisdiction they belonged to as they moved through the backcountry. Often their arrival preceded that of the local government, whose agents therefore appeared as exploiters. And in addition, the immigrants were often deliberately exploited, not merely by land speculators and managers of the infamous trade in German "redemptioners" (those who had to sell their labor for a term of years in order to cover the costs of transportation) but almost officially by the colonial governments.

The Blacks and Slavery. If these two major new elements in the American population, the Scotch-Irish and the Germans, were in various ways alienated from the Anglo-American establishment, they at least had access to the processes of law and ultimately of politics by which to express their grievances. But for the black population there were no such possibilities of relief and assimilation. Their separateness was rigidly fixed by the alienation of race and by the debasement of slavery.

How this large population of black people accommodated themselves to North American life, the fearful human cost of that accommodation, and the character of their resistance to the brutal system that dominated their lives we do not fully know, and probably never will know. There are no documents that record directly the blacks' feelings and the intimate details of their personal lives. But from the indirect evidence that has been assembled, one catches glimpses not only of degradation but of bewildering ambiguities and paralyzing tensions in human relations, as well as heroic efforts to maintain some measure of human dignity.

Slavery as it developed in the eighteenth century had many shadings, many variations. Only 10 percent of the slave population lived north of Maryland, constituting 4 to 5 percent of the population of that region. Spread thinly through the northern

colonies, their highest concentration was in New York City, where they may have formed as much as 17 percent of the population. Working side by side with white field servants in the countryside and as laborers in the towns, they mingled with the poorest elements among the whites, formed stable families, and even managed to accumulate small sums on the side when they were "hired out" by their masters to work for others. These northern blacks—field hands, town laborers, and factory workers—were native-born Americans for the most part, and they formed part, though a severely deprived part, of the general Anglo-American world.

The opposite was true of the tens of thousands of transplanted Africans (a third of all the North American blacks) who lived in the Carolinas and Georgia. The worst conditions were those on the fearful rice and indigo plantations of South Carolina. There, in tropical heat, laboring half the year knee-deep in the muck of the rice fields, the slaves lived unspeakably wretched lives, utterly isolated from the dominant society and alienated from the roots of their own culture. In the face of the appalling mortality in the disease-ridden environment, they grew in numbers only by the continuous addition of new importations—thousands upon thousands of newly enslaved Africans who had survived the 20 percent death rate on the transatlantic voyage and had been sold like animals in the great Charleston slave market. On these isolated plantations in the Deep South, the blacks' culture remained closer to that of West Africa than it did anywhere else in British North America.

The Chesapeake tobacco plantations, on which over half the black population lived, were quite different. By the 1760s some of the plantations had become large enough to support slave quarters that constituted well organized communities. Family life was relatively stable, and the population grew by natural increase. Further, the need for house servants and artisans of all kinds relieved a sizable percentage of the black population from the worst kind of field work. Here, in this long-established tobacco world, where black kinship groups of second- and third-generation American natives spread across

(American Antiquarian Society)

groups of plantations, a stable Afro-American culture, distinctive in religion, folk art, and social patterns, developed most fully. But the civility of the slaves' lives, where it existed at all, was extremely superficial. However assimilated they may have been in the North, and however involved they may have been in kinship networks in Virginia and Maryland, slaves everywhere were debased by the bondage that confined them. Humane masters might create plantations akin to biblical patriarchies, and wise masters might discover the economic value of allowing blacks to enjoy a modicum of leisure, a degree of independent activity, and the dignity of family

life; but everywhere brutality was never far below the surface. And everywhere there was resistance of some sort.

On the plantations in the South, untrained slaves fresh from Africa were most often sent off to outlying plots of land where they lived out their lives in unending field work. Still bearing, often, the ritual face scars of their earlier tribal life, where they had learned companionship and cooperation and where they had thought of time not in terms of hourly routines but of seasonal cycles, they found it extremely difficult, at times impossible, to adjust to the grueling labor. Some ran off, seeking to return to Africa or to set up villages to re-create the life they had known. A few, in the early years, found refuge in "maroon" (fugitive) encampments in the Carolina swamps and deep in frontier forests, but most of the fugitives were returned exhausted, half-starved, and in rags after long exposure in the woods and swamps, to continue their inescapable "seasoning." In time, however, these field hands found effective means of resistance, not in hopeless efforts to escape but in malingering, wasting equipment, damaging crops, and silently disobeying. Their rebelliousness, directed at the plantation and only occasionally at their overseers or masters, could have no long-term results, but at least it gave immediate relief to their feelings.

More complex and more self-damaging was the resistance of the American-born slaves employed as personal servants in and around the planters' houses. Enclosed within households of patriarchal discipline, they were forced into continuous close contact with masters who were made tense and insecure by the blacks' constant presence and whose domestic lives were poisoned by the helpless availability of slaves of both sexes. Commonly the slaves perfected techniques of petty harassment that increased their masters' insecurity. Convenient personality disguises (the seemingly obedient "Sambo") minimized the likelihood of clashes with masters whose tensions could be released in sadistic rages.

The most openly rebellious of the eighteenth-century slaves were the most thoroughly assimilated, the highly skilled artisans, whose talents gave them a measure of independence and who could deal with the environment as effectively as the whites. They were the most likely to survive as fugitives, and the most capable of easing their everyday burdens by shrewd manipulation. Closest to the white-man's world, these skilled workmen understood the full meaning of their bondage, and while they lived somewhat more comfortably, they may have even suffered more. Everywhere slavery meant profound degradation and constant fear—for the whites as well as for the blacks.

A Maturing Economy and a Society in Flux

The single most distinctive fact of the American economy as a whole in the eighteenth century was the broad spread of freehold tenure—the outright ownership of land—throughout the free population. In contrast, all of the land of England in the mid-eighteenth century was owned only by one-tenth of all heads of households; 400 great landlords, representing a mere 3/100 of 1 percent of all families, held between 20 percent and 25 percent of all the land of the realm. Over 80 percent of the land was worked by tenants, whose rent constituted the income upon which the owners of the land lived. The social experience of the great majority of the English people was based on tenancy; it shaped the structure of English society and the organization of politics, for both rested on the existence of a leisured aristocracy supported by the income that others produced from the land. And the unspoken assumption that the more land one owned the greater one's income would be—an assumption based on the scarcity of arable land relative to the available labor—was the force behind all agrarian enterprise.

The situation in the American colonies was entirely different. From the beginning the great attraction had been the availability of free land, and that attraction had not proved false. Though there were important regional variations, the large majority of nonslave farmworkers owned the land they worked, even if only at the end of their working lives and

even if not in the form and quantities they desired. This dominant fact of eighteenth-century American life created conditions altogether different from those that existed elsewhere. How unusual the resulting situation was may perhaps best be seen by examining the apparent *exceptions*—situations, that is, where a re-creation of the traditional life of landlords would appear to have taken place.

The Great Landowners. Thus the population growth and the resulting increase in land values led those who had proprietary claims to large tracts of land derived from the seventeenth-century charters to cash in on them if at all possible. Four such claims were particularly imposing: those of the Penn family to the undistributed land of Pennsylvania; those of the Calvert family to Maryland's residual land; those of Earl Granville, the heir of Sir George Carteret, to one share of the original Carolina grant, a claim that was calculated to cover most of the northern half of the present state of North Carolina; and those of Lord Fairfax, as the heir to the Northern Neck of Virginia, the 5 million acres between the Potomac and the Rappahanock rivers that had originally been granted by Charles II in 1649. By the mid-eighteenth century these colossal properties were no longer wild land but territories being opened to cultivation, and they were suddenly becoming valuable to their owners. But with the exception of Fairfax, who lived in Virginia after 1753, none of these great landowners were resident landlords and none were personally engaged in managing and developing landed estates worked by permanent tenants in the familiar European pattern. Their greatest profits came less from steady rents than from sales in rising land markets.

The operations of these great proprietary landowners were not essentially different from those of lesser land speculators throughout the colonies. Since the land was originally wild, the owner had the choice either of making a high capital investment to clear the land, improve it, and otherwise make it rentable at a profit, or of letting it out at low or no rent, and benefiting from the increase in value created by the labor of the tenants as they cleared and worked the land. The former was clearly uneconomic. Investments in many other forms of enterprise were more profitable than preparing wild land for lucrative rentals. The best strategy was to rent the land at low fees to tenants who would break it open to cultivation and who looked forward themselves to becoming the ultimate purchasers. Profits from such land sales, based on the initial labor of tenants, could be huge, and also continuous, since the purchasers often bought the farms on loans from the original landowners secured by mortgages on the land itself.

In a few places in the colonies, however, there were landowners, who *did* seek to establish themselves as landlords in a traditional sense, and they encountered sharp and at times even violent opposition. On a few estates along the Hudson, and in New Jersey to a lesser extent, many of the traditional forms of landlordism were re-created: high perpetual rents, incidental taxes and fees, and insecurity of tenure. These burdens could be enforced because of the landlords' political influence; because of a recording system that carefully protected their land claims; and because of the landlords' control of the courts through which the tenants would normally have sought relief. But the result was not in the end the re-creation of a traditional landlord system. It was trouble—more trouble than could be easily handled. Many of the tenants simply refused to accept the burdens. They protested continually, and resorted to all sorts of devices to destroy the landlords' control. They commonly acquired dubious titles to the land they worked from Indians or from New England land speculators and sought to validate these claims legally.

By the 1750s the situation on the tenanted estates in eastern New York and in New Jersey was explosive. The tenants refused to pay rents and duties, and when the courts tried to extract the payments due, the tenants formed an armed insurrection. The climax came in 1766 in a wave of rioting. Tenants simply renounced their leases and refused to get off the land when ordered to do so. In Westchester County in New York, rebellious farmers, declared to be "levellers" by the landlords, formed mobs, opened the jails, and stormed the landlords' houses. It took a regiment of regular troops with militia auxiliaries to put down the insurrection. Yet even then

tenancy could not be uniformly enforced. Many of the farmers simply moved off to the nearest vacant land, particularly in Vermont, which as a result of this exodus from the Hudson River estates and of a parallel migration of discontented New Englanders was opened to settlement for the first time.

Plantations in the South. To the extent, then, that landlordism on the Hudson River estates was an exception to the general American pattern, it was one that could be sustained only with great difficulty. A more glaring exception to the rule of freehold tenure was in the South, where plantations worked by slave labor would seem, in some measure at least, to have created the economic basis of a landed aristocracy. But the southern aristocracy of the eighteenth century lived in a completely different world from that of the English gentry and aristocracy whom they sought to emulate. There were large estates in the South (though not a great many: in Maryland only 3.6 percent of all estates were worth over £1,000), and they did support an aristocracy of sorts. But the plantation estates in the South were far different from the tenanted estates of the English aristocracy, quite aside from the obvious fact that the labor force was composed of slaves rather than of legally free tenants.

An English estate was not a single unit of production: it was a combination of many separate producing farms managed by individual tenants. A plantation in the eighteenth-century American South, on the other hand, was a single unit of production—a unified agricultural organization of considerable size under a single management. The whole enterprise was operated as a unit in managing labor and in planning production. From these basic conditions flowed the central characteristics of the life of the southern gentry.

No more in the eighteenth century than in the seventeenth were the southern planters leisured landowners living comfortably on profits produced by others. They were actively drawn into the process of crop management, land use, and labor direction, and they thus became active producers of their own income. Even if overseers were the immediate super-

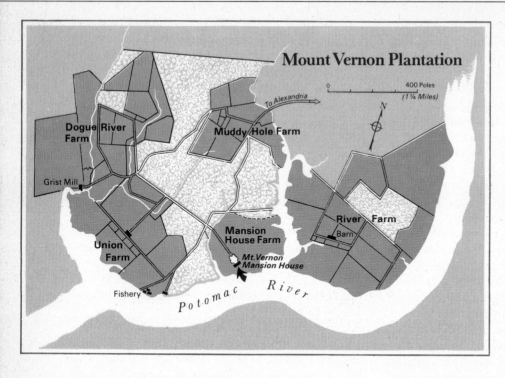

Mount Vernon Plantation

Dogue River Farm

Muddy Hole Farm

Grist Mill

To Alexandria

0   400 Poles
(1¼ Miles)

N

River Farm

Barn

Mansion House Farm

Union Farm

Mt. Vernon Mansion House

Fishery

P o t o m a c   R i v e r

MOUNT VERNON PLANTATION, ABOUT 1787

The plantation, which occupied about 10,000 acres, consisted of four working farms and the mansion house property. It was a largely self-sufficient community, containing, besides the slave quarters and agricultural buildings on the farms, a coach house and stables, a smoke house, a spinning house, a spring house, a wash house, carpenter's, tailor's, shoemaker's, and blacksmith's shops, and vegetable gardens.

visors of work on the plantations, the planters discovered at their cost that the managerial responsibility was theirs. A glance at such vivid documents as Landon Carter's diaries shows, not what Edmund Burke correctly called the prime requisite of a true aristocracy, "uncontending ease, the unbought grace of life," but the worried concerns of hard-pressed agrarian businessmen, absorbed in ledgers, profit margins, and the endless difficulties of farm production and labor management. Though the plantation owners attained a certain graciousness in style of living, that elegance was a light veneer over a rough-grained life of land dealing, ministering to the physical needs and managing the disciplinary problems of a partially dehumanized and latently rebellious slave labor force, and attempting to steer a profitable course through a commercial world that was largely insensitive to the pressures the planters might bring to bear.

Plantations in the South differed from European estates in that the increase in the size of the unit of ownership did not increase the income available to the owner. The larger the plantation, the more ex-

posed the owner was to economic dangers and the more precarious the profits he might secure. For the larger the estate, the larger the fixed charges of maintaining slaves and equipment. These expenses remained constant or grew in size no matter what the marketing situation might be, and in bad years debts could rise drastically. Indeed, once started, a marketing depression tended to deepen rapidly and uncontrollably as unsold goods carried over from one season to the next, enlarging the glut to catastrophic size.

In such periods of reversal, planters, far from enjoying the "unbought grace of life," struggled desperately to cut overhead costs or otherwise compensate for the marketing losses. Some concentrated on attaining self-sufficiency in the production of food and clothing so that indebtedness would not mean actual penury. Others turned to crop diversification. Starting on the eastern shore of the Chesapeake in the 1720s and continuing west rapidly, planters began converting to the production of grains and livestock, though the preponderance of tobacco production was never eliminated. And still others took what benefit they could from a new form of marketing introduced by Scottish entrepreneurs, whose investments in the southern American economy in the eighteenth century were a significant new development.

The Scottish merchants and bankers, principally in Glasgow, concentrated on developing the interior of the Chesapeake region. In the backcountry the units of tobacco production tended to be smaller than they were in the East, there was very little capital to start with, and there was no direct contact with ocean shipping. The old consignment system of marketing tobacco was therefore inappropriate for the development of this region. In an effort to reduce freight charges and to increase efficiency, the Scottish firms established stores in the backcountry that were managed by "factors." These agents bought tobacco crops outright, stored them, and in the end shipped them to central distribution points where vessels sent from Scotland could take up cargoes as fast as they could load.

From the merchants' point of view, this system had the advantage of eliminating the waiting time that vessels otherwise would have in collecting a cargo, and hence meant a material reduction in shipping costs. For the planters, it offered somewhat greater control, since they were in a position to oversee the actual sale of their crops without having to account for the complexities of the European tobacco markets. Like the tidewater planters, these inland tobacco growers also accumulated debts to the merchants, but their debts were less for consumption than for production: they took the form of loans for the purchase of slaves, equipment, and the other costs of initiating production. In organizing this trade and in making these investments the Scots became the financiers of the development of the western tobacco lands. It was estimated that in 1765 Glasgow firms had £500,000 of credits outstanding in the Chesapeake. And by then their "factors" had become prominent figures—usually unpopular figures—in the region's society.

In none of this was there a reproduction of the economic basis of a traditional landlord class. In all areas and in every subcategory of the agricultural economy, something new had evolved, and what appeared to be traditional was not. The few princely properties of the heirs of the original proprietary families were not so much tenanted estates as the capital of personal land companies whose greatest profits came from the sale of the land. The southern planters did not form a leisured aristocracy but were active, hard-pressed farm and labor managers whose profits were as likely to be threatened as to be enhanced by an increase in their holdings. In this world of widespread freehold tenure, attempted recreations of traditional landlord systems led not to reliable incomes and a life of agrarian gentility but

ISAAC ROYALL, JR., AND HIS FAMILY, BY ROBERT FEKE (1741)
This painting, one of the earliest by the self-taught American painter Feke and one of the earliest group portraits painted in America, shows (right to left) Royall, his wife and child, his sister-in-law, and his sister. Royall, then 22 years old, had inherited a fortune from his father, an Antiguan sugar planter who moved to Massachusetts in 1732 and settled his family on a handsome estate in Medford. The younger Royall, who served on the Massachusetts Council for over 20 years, was a loyalist during the Revolution; his estate was confiscated, and he died in England in 1781. *(Harvard University Law School Collection)*

to controversy, even violent conflict. There were peaceable tenants, it is true, in many areas; but tenancy, far from being the normal pattern of life for those who worked the land, was an exceptional and often transitory condition and its economic function was ordinarily different from what it traditionally had been. Above all, land speculation—the use of land as a salable commodity rather than as an income-bearing property—was an almost universal occupation.

The World of Commerce.   The commercial sector of the economy was equally distinctive. Its focus lay in the larger port towns, comparable in size to the second and third rank English provincial cities. All of them but Boston (whose population was stable at around 16,000) continued to grow quickly. Though visitors often noted their outward resemblance to such cities as Edinburgh and Bristol, they noted too some of the differences, which resulted from the fact that they were products of a frontier economy. There was of course, in all of these towns, a laboring population, but most of the urban workers were self-employed artisans or workmen in small-scale, often family-sized, businesses. There was a small though growing number of casual laborers—dock hands, laborers in shipbuilding enterprises, and others—who picked up what employment they could in menial tasks around the towns. They formed a volatile element in these communities, and they suffered in times of depression. But there is no evidence of mass destitution. The number of those who received charity, while it increased, never approached the figures of the dependent poor in Europe. In England at times one-third of the population was impoverished, and in the cities, where beggars crowded the cellars and attics, massed in back alleys, and overwhelmed the charitable institutions, another third was poor enough to be rendered destitute by the repeated economic crises. But Philadelphia did not even build an almshouse until 1732; New York built one only in 1736. Rarely before 1760 were more than one hundred people supported by poor relief in Philadelphia. At no time during those years did as much as 1 percent of the population of New York and Philadelphia receive charity in any form.

A series of close statistical studies of the British mainland North American colonies in the 1700s re-

SEA CAPTAINS CAROUSING IN SURINAM, BY JOHN GREENWOOD (1758)

Surinam (Dutch Guiana) on the northern coast of South America was a favorite port of call for American merchants who exchanged horses and tobacco there for sugar products. Greenwood, a Bostonian who lived in Surinam, painted in the faces of several well-known Rhode Island merchants. *(The St. Louis Art Museum)*

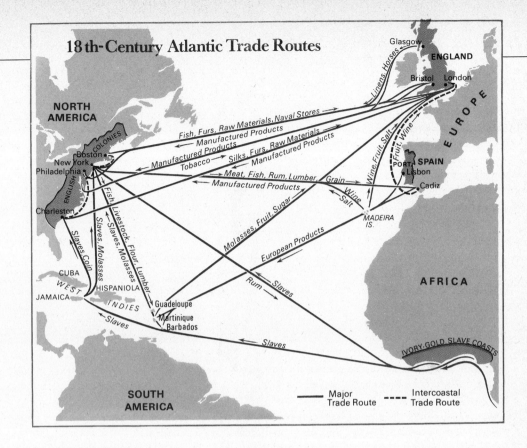

18th-Century Atlantic Trade Routes

veals a level of living that "was probably the highest achieved for the great bulk of the population in any country up to that time," and that was as true in the towns as in the countryside. Though a relatively small part of the urban population controlled an increasing proportion of the total wealth, and though the gulf between rich and poor deepened, "the fact remains that not only were the rich getting richer but the poor were too, albeit at a slower rate." There was poverty in the pre-Revolutionary towns, but no mass starvation; there were riots, but no "bread riots"; and the "mobs" that became highly visible were not spearheads of a desperate proletariat inflamed by utopian aspirations and seeking to transform the structure of society. They were crowds of young apprentices, dock workers, and seamen temporarily idle between voyages, usually led by lesser merchants or independent craftsmen.

It would have been surprising had it not been so, for the society of the commercial towns retained the characteristics of a pioneer world. Labor remained relatively scarce, which meant that wages remained high

enough to make small savings possible. Day laborers in Boston were paid twice as much as their equivalents in London. Furthermore, in the typical small-scale enterprise the distance between employer and employee remained narrow, both objectively (in terms of life-style and function) and subjectively (in terms of feelings of superiority or alienation). The typical artisan worked closely with his employer, and their activities were not unbridgeably different. Labor troubles took a quite different form from those in modern society. Strikes were protests not by urban workers against conditions or wages but by master workers, employers, and independent artisans against price levels set by the community for the sale of their products, or efforts to stop widespread infiltration by outsiders into licensed trades. Town workers were periodically distressed by the movements of the economy, which lurched through repeated phases of bust and boom, but there was no permanently alienated "proletariat."

The urban communities were dominated by the merchants, who in this period became figures of importance throughout the Atlantic world. The merchant

BALTIMORE IN 1752

Aquatint by William Strickland, done in 1817 after a sketch made by John Mole, Esq., in 1752. *(I. N. Phelps Stokes Collection, The New York Public Library)*

group as a whole developed between two quite opposite sets of pressures, two conflicting tendencies. During the early and middle years of the eighteenth century there were forces that tended to limit and stabilize the mercantile leadership—to make of these leading figures an elite merchant aristocracy. But at the same time there were other forces tending to upset the dominance of all would-be merchant elites, and these forces were related to the deepest elements of the developing economy.

A significant degree of stability was created in the merchant group of the early eighteenth century in part by political stability in England. The secure arrangement of politics, patronage, and influence devised by the prime minister Robert Walpole in the 1720s helped stabilize the organization of Atlantic commerce, involved as it was with politics and government contracting. At the same time, specialization within the English mercantile establishment increased through the period, and the specialist wholesalers who controlled shipments to the colonies restricted their trade to selected American correspondents. And there were technical improvements in trade and finance, particularly the development of marine insurance, that helped make possible growing concen-

tration of commercial capital and entrepreneurial control.

All of these developments, plus the general fact that large operators could effect economies of scale, meant that the commercial community was acquiring elitist characteristics. Yet despite this emergence of dominant groups, the merchant community as a whole, and commerce as a whole, remained highly competitive and fluid in membership. For, first, as raw frontier areas matured into settled agricultural producing regions, successful farmers branched out into marketing, became inland traders, and ultimately merchants. Prosperous market farmers, particularly those located at transfer points on the rivers or inland trade routes, parlayed their advantages in goods and location into trading operations and drifted into commercial pursuits, combined often with land speculation.

But it was not only a matter of old settled areas producing surpluses from which market farmers could build careers in commerce. Wholly new hinterlands developed almost overnight, and from them emerged new men who proved effective competitors indeed.

In 1720 the chief agricultural producing areas were located northeast of the Hudson and in the Chesapeake region. Thereafter the preponderance shifted to the middle colonies, the area between the Hudson and Chesapeake Bay. Surplus goods, chiefly grain, flowed to the swiftly growing port of Philadelphia from the Pennsylvania backcountry, from New Jersey, and from parts of Maryland; and this flow enriched a new mercantile aristocracy, particularly of Quakers, in Philadelphia. By the 1760s the value of their trade with England exceeded that of all of New England. Similar developments took place in other regions. Within a space of only ten years in the 1740s and 1750s Baltimore rose from a wilderness village to a thriving urban center serving the marketing needs of a new hinterland area, and within a single generation Baltimore's merchants became important figures in the commercial world.

The result of all these movements in agriculture and trade was a highly dynamic mercantile world. Although conditions made possible the stabilization of a merchant leadership group, the rapid development of the economy in long-settled areas and the constant opening of new areas of agricultural production created a continuous recruitment of new merchants and a continuous tension of competition between established figures and newcomers. There was a widespread sense that certain merchant families, established by the 1760s for two, three, or even four generations, were forming into an oligarchy; but at the same time there were always new faces, new families, capable of taking the same successful risks that had once served to establish the older families.

Religion: The Sources of American Denominationalism

The tensions within the commercial world were moderate next to those that developed in religion. Since American culture in the mid-eighteenth century was still largely religious in its orientation, these tensions lay at the heart of the social world everywhere in the colonies, north and south, seaboard and inland.

The central event in the history of religion in America in the eighteenth century was the Great Awakening, the revivalist eruptions of the late 1730s and the 1740s, which roared through the colonies like a sheet of flame and left behind a world transformed. In part this wave of passionate evangelicalism was a typical expression of a general movement that swept through much of the Western world. The Great Awakening coincided with an outpouring of Anglican evangelicalism—which would become Methodism—in England and Wales and with a wave of Pietism in the German-speaking world. There were direct connections between the American revivalists and their European counterparts, but there was something unique too in the American evangelical movement, and it produced quite distinctive results.

Religion and Society in New England.   In New England the background and sources of the Awakening came closest to the European pattern of such evangelical waves. By the early eighteenth century the Congregational churches had experienced the draining away of inner fervor and of emotional commitment that is typical of all long-established churches and that characteristically gives rise to evangelical searchings and outbursts. It is paradoxical that this should have been so since Puritan Congregationalism had itself originally been a protest against a formal church establishment, the Church of England, and it had contained two essential characteristics that had distinguished it from any established church. First, membership in the Congregational churches had not been an automatic consequence of physical birth but had resulted from individual acts of deliberate association based on an inner experience; and second, church institutions had been decentralized into Congregational units.

These original characteristics of New England Puritanism did not survive unchanged into the eighteenth century. By the mid-seventeenth century the New England churches had faced a crisis that arose from the failure of the second and third generations to duplicate the spiritual experiences of the founders and to come forward into membership through an act of saving grace. The founders' children had been baptized in the church on the basis of their parents' profession and the likelihood of their own ultimate conversion; but full membership awaited the childrens' own personal "calling." In fact, many were never converted. Should, then, the children of these baptized but unconverted members of the church also be baptized?

This was the agonizing problem that had faced the Puritans in the mid-seventeenth century. If the answer had been Yes, then the church as a body of converted Christians would have been destroyed. But if the answer had been No, then, as conversions became fewer and fewer, the church would have grown apart from the society as a whole; it would have become a mere sect, without the basis for social control that was so fundamental a part of Puritan life. The solution came in a convention of ministers that met in 1657 whose decision was confirmed by a synod of 1662. By the arrangement devised then, which became known as the "halfway covenant," unregenerate members *could* transmit membership in the church automatically to their children, but only a *halfway* membership: such children would be baptized, but they would not be offered the sacrament of communion, nor would they be entitled to vote as members of the church. As halfway members, they would be required to make a public pledge to obey the rulings of the church and to bring up their children as proper Christians. Still, they were members, if only partial, and the distinction between them and the full members who sat with them in church week after week was thin, and grew thinner and more technical as the years passed.

The "halfway covenant" was an unstable compromise that deeply eroded the Puritans' original concept of the church as a body of proven saints. Conservatives and liberals alike found the halfway distinction illogical and unmanageable, turned to baptizing all, and sought to bring everyone to communion who was willing to accept it.

It was partly in an effort to control such permissive innovations that the more orthodox Puritan churches moved toward institutional centralization and away from congregational autonomy. In Massachusetts regional ministerial associations were formed which sought to impose certification and disciplinary powers over the clergy and over the general management of church affairs. Though in 1705 the effort to create such an organization in civil law was defeated, informal communication among the churches was

strengthened. In Connecticut a parallel effort succeeded completely. There, the so-called Saybrook Platform of 1708 became a public law, creating county "consociations" of the Congregational churches with disciplinary powers, regional associations of ministers, and a colony-wide general association of delegates of the ministers.

By all of these developments—a slackening in religious fervor, a growing identity of church and society, and the spread of general controls over originally independent congregational bodies—the Puritan churches increasingly approached the condition of a formalized establishment. The process had obvious limits. In the eyes of British law, Congregational churches were nonconformist and therefore their advantages as an established group in British territory could never have the full sanction of law behind them. The Church of England, paradoxically a dissenting body in New England, led all opposition groups in claiming the privileges accorded nonconformists in England. And in this they were successful. In the 1720s Anglicans, Quakers, and Baptists gained full rights of worship in Congregational New England and of using their church taxes for their own support. They were free, too, to hold office and to attend all institutions of learning. But they still remained *tolerated* groups, obliged to register with the authorities. No one was free of the obligation to support religion, and no group but these three was allowed the privileges of dissent.

New England Congregationalism was thus a loose establishment, but it was an establishment nevertheless, and one in which religion as an inner experience had tended to fade and in which formal observance and institutional ritual had grown increasingly important. Less and less did the churches satisfy people's inner yearnings; more and more were these churches vulnerable to the charge of excessive formalism and of a deadening complacency.

Religion and Society South of New England. Even less were the churches in the other colonies capable of satisfying the deeper needs of a still generally religious society. In Virginia the long-standing inability of the Church of England to serve the needs of the com-

Prospect of the City of New-York

1 Fort George	6 The Prison.	11 Old Dutch Church	16 Quaker's Meeting
2 Trinity Church	7 New Brick Meeting	12 Jew's Synagogue	17 Calvinist Church
3 Presbyter. Meeting	8 King's College	13 Lutherian Church	18 Anabaptist Meeting
4 North D. Church	9 St. Paul's Church	14 The French Church	19 Moravian Meeting
5 St. George's Chapel	10 N. Dutch Cal. Church	15 New Scot's Meeting	20 N. Lutheran Church

(Department of Rare Books and Special Collections, Princeton University Library)

munity was now compounded by its ambiguous relationship to the new settlers, almost all non-Anglicans, who moved into the backcountry in the 1720s and 1730s. Maryland too, after 1702, had an established Anglican church, but the Anglican community in that colony was numerically small, and its hold on the population at large was even looser than that of the Church of England in Virginia.

Elsewhere the institutional character of religious life was so chaotic and so volatile that it eludes clear description. In the Carolinas and Georgia (the latter settled in 1732 by Anglican philanthropists as a refuge for England's paupers and as a buffer against Spanish Florida), there were Anglican establishments of sorts. Nonconformists were welcomed, however, and little effort was made to regulate religious life as a whole, which in many areas was overwhelmingly non-Anglican. Pennsylvania, Rhode Island, and New Jersey had no established churches at all. In Pennsylvania and Rhode Island the very idea ran against the principles of the influential Quakers, and in New Jersey the religious diversity was so extreme and the Anglican community so small that no agreement on a privileged religion could be reached. And in New York, where dissenters outnumbered Anglicans by at least 15 to 1, the only flourishing Anglican institution was New York City's Trinity Church, which Governor Fletcher had endowed with an independent source of income.

The overwhelming fact, amid the institutional confusion of religion in eighteenth-century America, was that the dominant churches, no matter what their definition, were failing to minister effectively to the needs of a people for whom religion continued to be a primary emotional and cultural experience. It is significant that the most vigorous branch of the Church of England in eighteenth-century America was its missionary arm, the Society for the Propagation of the Gospel in Foreign Parts. Originally formed to bring the Christian gospel to the Indians, it had instead devoted itself to guaranteeing the survival of the Anglican Church in America and strengthening it in every possible way. Under its first leader, the Reverend Thomas Bray (1656–1730), the SPG, as it was called, launched missionary expeditions to likely points throughout the colonies, helped maintain existing parishes and organize new ones in the great desert of American nonconformity, and in its activities created the church's only effective organization above the parish level.

The Great Awakening. It was into this ill-served, parched, and questing religious world that the evangelicalism of the Great Awakening fell like a blazing torch. The revival did not begin all at once. There were early stirrings in the Connecticut River valley, touched off by the remarkable young minister of Northampton, Massachusetts, Jonathan Edwards.

He was heir to a famous ecclesiastical tradition.

JONATHAN EDWARDS, BY JOSEPH BADGER
Painted a few years before Edwards was expelled from
his Northampton pulpit for insisting on conversion as a
basis for church membership and for attempting to
discipline children of leading families. After seven years
as a missionary to the Indians, Edwards was chosen
president of the College of New Jersey (Princeton) but
died after a few months in office, at the age of 55. *(Yale
University Art Gallery. Bequest of Eugene Phelps Edwards)*

Grandson of the powerful "Pope" Solomon Stoddard of Northampton, whom he eventually succeeded,
Edwards, from the time of his graduation from Yale
at the age of seventeen, devoted himself to the central philosophical and theological problems of the
age. While preaching and fulfilling his other pastoral duties, he worked out a body of thought so
subtle and so original that it has established him
as one of the powerful thinkers of the eighteenth
century. His chief professional task, however, was
more ordinary: it was to bring sinful men to a knowledge of God and to the experience of spiritual rebirth. Stoddard had stirred local revivals in the 1720s;

and in 1734 and 1735 Edwards, to his own great surprise and gratification, suddenly found his own people responding overwhelmingly to his closely rea-
soned sermons on justification by faith. Northampton
was overcome with religious enthusiasm. Dozens
of once complacent parishioners went through tumultuous passions of regeneration.

Word of a providential revival spread swiftly
through the farming hamlets of the Connecticut
River valley and then eastward along Long Island
Sound, touching off similar outbreaks as it went.
By the time Edwards published an account of his
local revival, his *Faithful Narrative of the Surprising Work
of God* (1737), the wave had passed, but it had become famous throughout the colonies and in Great
Britain as well. It had stirred ministers everywhere to
new exertions in bringing sinful people to an experience of God's grace, and it had created a brimming
expectancy that some vast outpouring of religious
zeal, if not the actual establishment of God's kingdom on earth, was about to take place. By 1740, when
George Whitefield, the brilliant English preacher
who had already stirred successful revivals on two
tours through the middle and southern colonies, appeared in New England, anticipation was spilling
over into fulfillment. It was Whitefield, following
in the wake of Edwards's revival, who finally threw
open the floodgates and let loose an outpouring of
soul-shaking evangelicalism that flooded New England for four tumultuous years.

Whitefield's tour of New England was spectacular. In Boston, preaching first to hundreds who
jammed the churches until they could hold no more,
then to thousands in open-air meetings, the young
impassioned orator transfixed listeners used to hearing scholarly sermons read to them from carefully
prepared texts. He was equally successful in a series
of meetings in northern New England, and then in
the West. In Northampton his preaching was so affecting that Jonathan Edwards, Whitefield reported,
"wept during the whole time of exercise." After stops
south along the valley towns that had already experienced the revival, Whitefield ended his tour in
New York.

His preaching, he correctly reported, had made
a great difference in the North. So too did that of the

second great leader of the Awakening, Gilbert Tennent. This second-generation Scotch-Irish minister for a decade had led the "New Light" (evangelical) party within the growing Presbyterian communities of New Jersey and New York. He had been educated in his father's "Log College" in Neshaminy, Pennsylvania, devoted to propagating the principles of

GEORGE WHITEFIELD PREACHING, BY JOHN WOLLASTON. (1741, WHEN WHITEFIELD WAS 27)

He appeared, a Connecticut farmer recalled, "almost angelical; a young, slim, slender youth before thousands of people with a bold, undaunted countenance, . . . he looked as if he was clothed with authority from the Great God, . . . and my hearing him preach gave me a heart wound." "What a spell he casts over an audience," Jonathan Edwards' wife wrote, "by proclaiming the simplest truths of the Bible. I have seen upwards of a thousand people hang on his words with breathless silence, broken only by an occasional half-suppressed sob." *(National Portrait Gallery, London)*

"experimental" religion—that is, deeply experienced rather than intellectual and doctrine-bound religion. Tennent's tour through southern New England lasted three months in the fall and winter of 1740–41. They were tumultuous months of mass excitement, profound emotional upheaval, and inner transformation.

Elsewhere too the revival continued its blazing progress. It tore through the Presbyterian and Dutch Reformed communities of the middle colonies, splitting them into conservative and evangelical wings. The "New Side" evangelical Presbyterians of Pennsylvania and New Jersey formed their own synod in 1741 and sent out their own itinerant preachers to invade districts dominated by the "Old Side." It was these revivalist Presbyterians moving southward from Pennsylvania who had the greatest impact in Virginia. Their most effective preacher, Samuel Davies, sustained in Hanover County the most important of the southern revivals, and in the process spurred the Anglican authorities to take repressive measures against nonconformity by fining unlicensed preachers. Even more influential in the southern colonies were the evangelical Baptists. They reached out more effectively than any other church or sect to the unchurched common people of the backcountry, and most successfully proselyted among the new settlers on the southern frontier. And at the end of the colonial period, evanglicals of the Church of England led by the Reverend Devereux Jarratt, who would soon organize as the Methodist Church, also began to share in the work of extending the Awakening to the settlers on the expanding frontier.

Effects of the Great Awakening. Such was the greatest event in the history of religion in eighteenth-century America. Its effects were more revolutionary by far than those of the parallel movements in Europe—Pietism in Germany and Methodism in England and Wales. The differences are revealing. The revivals in America were not, as elsewhere, distinctively lower class affairs that gave new voice to the aspirations of the socially deprived. Nor were they limited to any particular geographical group: they were as successful in the large towns as in the countryside. Their impact could not be confined. At least four areas of American social life were irreversibly affected by the great revivalist wave.

First, the authority and status of the clergy were permanently weakened. The revivalists cared little for offices, formal status, education, learning, or even, within reasonable limits, outward behavior. For them, qualification for religious leadership was gained only by force of inner experience and by the ability to unlock parishioners' spiritual aspirations. It followed naturally that they would challenge the authority of established educational institutions like Yale and Harvard whose training for the ministry seemed to them to be intellectual and formalistic. When Connecticut barred from the ministry anyone not trained at Yale, Harvard, or a foreign Protestant university, the Presbyterian New Lights not only formed a new synod devoted to evangelical preaching but in 1746 created a new college, the College of New Jersey (later Princeton) which would emphasize religion of the emotions, of the spirit, as well as of the mind. Rutgers, Brown, and Dartmouth also were founded in response to the revival movement, for the Awakening, which challenged all preachers to justify their authority by their own spiritual gifts and by their power to reach into other souls, could not tolerate merely formal qualifications of any kind.

Second, the Awakening tended to destroy the identification of churches with specific territorial boundaries. The revivalists believed their call extended not to the few people who happened to have employed them as preachers but to anyone anywhere who would heed their word, and especially to all those whose ministers were unconverted. They therefore naturally became "itinerants," invading established parishes. If welcomed, they preached officially as visiting ministers: if not, they set up in barns or open fields and preached to anyone who came. The establishment vehemently objected to such invasions, and "itineracy" became one of the central controversies of the revival. But it could not be stopped, and where it occurred it tended to free the churches from specific territorial foundations, released them into a universe of competing groups.

Related to this was a third effect of the Awakening, nothing less than the near destruction of institutional religion as the organizing framework of small-group society. For in all the new settlements, and continuously on the disorganized frontiers, the church had provided a vital center for society itself. When the Awakening hit the more vulnerable communities, a series of splits most often occurred. A split-off of a New Light faction from a stubborn Old Light majority could severely rupture a community; and even if the splinter group eventually returned, it did so more or less free of general control. Often there was no point at which the disintegration could be stopped. Whole units simply disappeared in the course of successive splinterings, ending in a mere cluster of family-sized factions, free of all constraints of church organization.

Finally, the Awakening put unsupportable pressures on what remained of church-state relations, not in doctrine but in practice. The revivalists did not believe themselves to be unorthodox. Quite the contrary. They claimed that they alone represented the true orthodoxy in Protestant Christianity and denounced the establishments for their deviations. In so doing they created new grounds for challenging the practical right of any church to claim a privileged place in the eyes of the law. They thereby moved closer to the conclusion that the very notion of an establishment of religion was false and that the only safe and correct course was to deny any and all privileges of the state to any religious group.

Denominationalism.   From all of the developments in religion that had been in motion from the time of the first English settlements in North America—developments now greatly intensified and compounded by the Great Awakening—religion in America acquired a new character. It became essentially voluntaristic—an activity one was free to join or not to join—even for the high church groups whose official doctrines assumed an inescapable identification of church and society enforced by the state. Organized religion had also developed an emphasis on persuasion as its essential activity. The churches, lacking the sanction of the state to guarantee membership, lacking, too, secure institutional structures and effective group discipline, swung their efforts toward

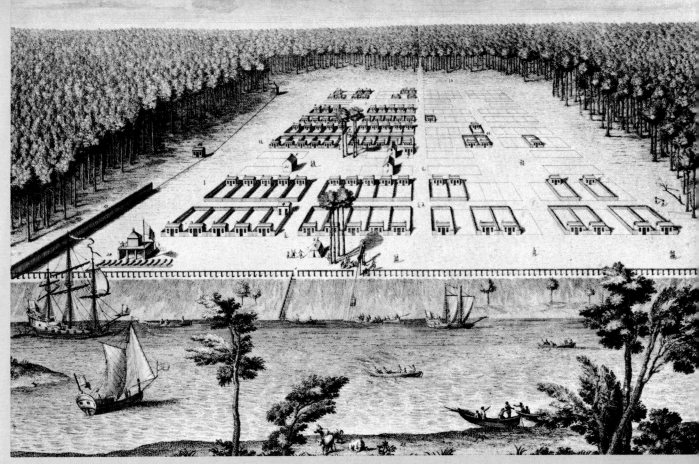

View of Savannah, 1734. *The I. N. Phelps Stokes Collection, The New York Public Library*

Embellishing the Wilderness

T he European settlement of North America was an intrusion into the wilderness, a struggle to impose the familiar forms of an advanced civilization into an environment that was almost totally unredeemed from its natural, uncultivated state. The awareness of this struggle was as vivid to those who settled the last British colony, Georgia, and who pictured Savannah in 1734 as a tiny clearing at the edge of a vast forest as it had been to the settlers of Virginia a century and a quarter earlier. The struggle took its toll. Not only were there significant modifications in the conduct of everyday life —regressions and simplifications, it seemed—but at the margins there were complete surrenders to the wilderness. There were always frontiersmen who spent months drifting from one isolated primitive encampment to another, and emerging from time to time to buy with animal skins what they needed for survival and to tell remarkable tales of worlds beyond the mountains and the swamps. But these wandering semi-primitives were rare in British America—much rarer than they were in French Canada, where half-savage trappers and woodsmen (the famous *coureurs de bois* who roamed the wilderness for years at a time) formed a significant part of the population.

British America from the beginning was a bourgeois society. The wilderness exerted no fatal seduction; it proved to be a challenge to the arts of cultivation, to the nesting instinct, to the impulse to domesticate and to embellish. Beauty, in European terms, was sought from the start, transferred at first from "home" and then imitated, however crudely, by local craftsmen. The artifacts of daily living had to be made from materials that lay at hand, by men whose task it was to provide the necessities of life, not the refinements. But though the products were often rough, they were rarely primitive. Occasionally, even in the earliest years, some striking embellishment, some special grace of line, balance, or proportion, some flash of vivid and

(*Above*) Massachusetts press cupboard, late seventeenth century. *Courtesy, Museum of Fine Arts, Boston. Gift of Mr. and Mrs. William R. Robinson*

(*Left*) Spindled chair, 1640–1660. *Courtesy, Museum of Fine Arts, Boston. Photo by Richard Cheek*

(*Opposite*) Queen Anne chair from Philadelphia.

harmonious color, emerged to mark the point at which craft turned to art.

So furniture was crafted in the seventeenth century from local woods, its bare, hard surfaces as uncomfortable as they were serviceable and durable; but sometimes even in the earliest years the furniture was embellished too, with a conscious style, decorated and beautified. Spindled oak pieces like the Ipswich, Massachusetts, press cupboard were stained with vegetable dyes to give them tone, and their ornaments painted black to simulate ebony; the result was a complex, dappled black-brown surface. Later such embellishments grew more sophisticated as the Queen Anne chair reveals; and by the early 1700s japanned highboys

(Above) Crewel petticoat border, mid-eighteenth century. *Courtesy, Museum of Fine Arts, Boston. Gift of Mrs. J. R. Churchill*

(Right) Japanned chest, early eighteenth century. *Courtesy, Metropolitan Museum of Art, Purchase 1940, Joseph Pulitzer Bequest*

were being produced with structural designs in classical modes and oriental scenes in brilliant color. Quite independently the Dutch in New York and the Germans in Pennsylvania developed from their own folk traditions a distinctive pattern of decoration. And everywhere craftsmen learned to produce not only beautifully designed wooden furniture in contemporary styles but upholstered pieces that were colorful as well as solid and comfortable.

Textile embellishments took many forms, from embroidered chair seats and petticoat borders to crewel bed hangings and draperies. And the skill of the silversmiths developed quickly too. By the end of the seventeenth century intricately designed and handsomely worked silver bowls, tankards, coffee pots, and sugar boxes were seen on tables in the South as in the North. Craftsmen like John Coney were creating objects in silver that would delight their users and viewers for generations to come.

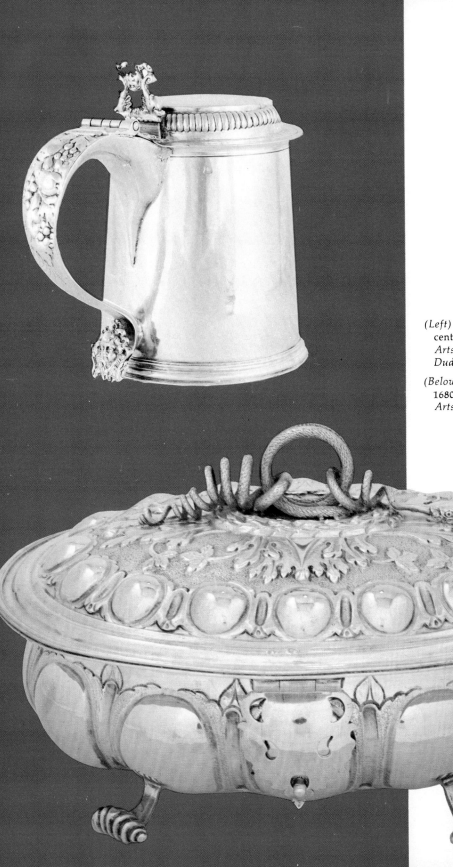

(*Left*) Silver tankard, late seventeenth century. *Courtesy, Museum of Fine Arts, Boston. Gift of Mr. and Mrs. Dudley Pickman*

(*Below*) Sugar box, by John Coney, 1680–1690. *Courtesy, Museum of Fine Arts, Boston, Elliot Fund*

Everyday life was visibly enhanced—not transformed into a wonder world of aristocratic ostentation but simply embellished, decorated, elevated above mere practicality. Clock faces and inlaid rifle stocks became minor works of art, the clock cases and gun grips beautifully worked wood. Door frames were improved by conscious imitation of metropolitan models. Glassware evolved in unexpected forms, and metal workers produced weathervanes that had the animated beauty of modern mobiles.

(Opposite) Bed hangings, c. 1745. *Old Goal Museum, York, Maine*

(Above) Glass sugar bowl, late eighteenth century. *Courtesy, The Henry Francis du Pont Winterthur Museum*

(Right) Doorway of Fowler Tavern, mid-eighteenth century, Westfield, Massachusetts. *Courtesy of the Metropolitan Museum of Art, Rogers Fund, 1916*

Raleigh Tavern, Williamsburg, Virginia. *Colonial Williamsburg Foundation*

Siteman/Stock, Boston

The wilderness remained—a threat to European civilization and a constructive challenge to creativity in a people conscious both of the simplicity of their lives and of the richness of their cultural heritage. Young men like Jefferson grew up in a borderland world, looking out from Queen Anne rooms of spare elegance onto a wild, uncultivated land.

promotion and outward activity and away from the purification of doctrine and the maintenance of internal order. Finally, the role of individual decision shifted. Where in traditional situations involvement with a dominant religion was automatic, the momentous decision was to break with the association into which one was born. As a consequence, religious indifference could go hand in hand with extensive church membership. In the colonies the opposite was true: to do nothing was likely to mean to have no affiliation at all, and the momentous decision involved joining, not severing, a religious association. As a result, broad waves of religious enthusiasm could go hand in hand with low church membership.

By the end of the colonial period these characteristics were taking on a patterned and stable form, which would later be called Denominationalism. Products of the intractable realities of the colonial situation, these characteristics would find expression in theory, law, and formal doctrine during the Revolution and in the years that followed.

The Origins of American Politics

The key to much in pre-Revolutionary America was the gap that developed between expectation and reality. This discordant pattern was more extreme and more consequential in politics and government than in any other area of life. For not only did the discrepancy between theory and expectation on the one hand and actuality on the other shape the character of American public life, but it laid the basis for the transformation of the relations between Britain and the colonies.

The Structure of British Politics. All formal notions of public life in the British world rested on the belief that the British political system of the mid-eighteenth century was the freest and best that existed, and that the colonial governments and political systems were more or less imperfect replicas of that world-famous model. In theory, balance was the key to the British constitution. From classical antiquity had come the notion, reaffirmed in the Renaissance

and in seventeenth-century England, that there were three pure forms of government. Any one of these if properly maintained could serve the people properly but all tended to degenerate into evil forms that created oppression. Monarchy, the rule by one, degenerated into tyranny; aristocracy, the rule of a few, became oligarchy; and democracy, the rule of the whole political population, declined into the rule of the mob. The challenge to political thinkers had long been the problem of devising a balance among these forms that would stabilize government and bring the degenerative processes to a halt. The British constitution, it was generally agreed, had achieved precisely such a stable balance of pure forms, its balance embodied in the competition among the crown, representing monarchy; the House of Lords, representing the nobility or aristocracy; and the House of Commons, representing the democracy.

Such was the theoretical explanation of the working of the British constitution in the mid-eighteenth century, a theory that was almost universally believed to explain the stability and freedom that had been achieved in Britain. Yet, as a description of the actual working of the British government, it was misleading. The balance of these elements was more apparent than real. The supposed preserves of the elements of the constitution were thoroughly infiltrated by the others, and their functioning was different from the idealized description. In fact the source of the political stability of mid-eighteenth century Britain lay not in the supposed balance of these socioconstitutional orders, which Americans sought to emulate, but in two sets of special conditions, both highly relevant to an understanding of the peculiar form of politics that developed in eighteenth-century America.

The main underlying condition that made Britain's stability possible was the fact that the great constitutional issues of the seventeenth century had been settled in the Glorious Revolution of 1688: the problem of the extent of crown authority and the problem of the relation of church and state. As to the first, the terms of settlement of the Glorious Revolution stipulated that the monarch would not create courts without statute or dismiss judges without formal impeachment; would not impose taxes without grant of Parliament; and would not maintain a standing army in peacetime or engage in wars for foreign territory without Parliament's consent. The crown had been forced to agree further not to limit unduly or extend the existence of a Parliament or interfere with its regular meetings—elections and convenings being placed on a regular calendar schedule. In addition, it was understood, at least after 1707, that the king would not veto acts of Parliament.

As to the religious settlement after the Glorious Revolution, the established Church of England continued to enjoy the privileges and benefits of the state, and all who did not explicitly reject it were considered to be members of its community. But the desire for an enforced uniformity was abandoned. Dissent was tolerated, though penalized. The great majority of nonconformists were permitted to worship as they pleased; they enjoyed almost full civil rights, and in the course of the century attained most political rights as well.

These underlying conditions made stability possible. That stability was actually achieved was the result of the informal accommodation that was worked out between the crown and the House of Commons. A working relationship between the two was achieved by a set of operating conventions so fundamental as to comprise in effect a private, informal constitution. The ministry, acting for the crown, disciplined and manipulated the House, in part by managing elections into the House through its control or outright ownership of "rotten boroughs" or other easily dominated constituencies, and in part by distributing crown patronage to Members so as to assure safe majorities on controversial issues. In the mid-eighteenth century about 200 of the 558 Members of the House of Commons held crown appointments or gifts of one sort or another, and another 30 or 40 were more loosely tied to government by awards of profitable contracts. A fluctuating num-

THE HOUSE OF COMMONS IN THE MID-EIGHTEENTH CENTURY

The facing benches, separated only by the speaker's table and the few feet of open floor space, encouraged direct debate. Like so much of British political life, this seating arrangement was widely imitated in the colonies (see p. 145).

ber of other Members was bound to the administration less directly, particularly by the gift or promise of one or more of the 8,000 excise offices available.

It was this use of "influence" in managing elections and in controlling votes in the two Houses that, together with the settlement of the main policy questions, explains the stability of English political life in the mid-eighteenth century. There were certain technical requirements for such stabilizing control: an abundance of patronage available for disposal by the ministry; a small electorate, for the larger the voting population the greater the difficulty of control; and a system of representation that was not related to the shift and growth of the population or closely bound to the wishes of a broad electorate.

Differences in the Colonies.   All of these conditions existed in eighteenth-century Britain, but none of them existed in anything like the same measure in the mainland colonies of British North America. Yet the similarity between the British government and the separate colonial governments was an axiom of political thought in eighteenth-century America. As bicameral legislatures developed in the colonies during the seventeenth century, with the lower houses more and more clearly standing for local, popular interests and the Councils appearing to approximate the classical houses of the aristocracy, the assumption grew that the colonial governments were miniatures of the British government. Dr. William Douglass of Boston explained in his *Summary, Historical and Political . . . of the British Settlements in North America* (1749–51) that, by the governor,

representing the King, the colonies are monarchical; by the Council, they are aristocratical; by a House of Representatives or delegates from the people, they are democratical: these three are distinct and independent of one another . . . the several negatives being checks upon one another. The concurrence of these three forms of government seem to be the highest perfection that human civil government can attain to in times of peace.

Such irregularities and exceptions as there were in the American replicas, Douglass said, "doubtless in time will be rectified."

But while in England the mixed and balanced constitution produced a high degree of political harmony, similar institutions in the colonies produced the opposite. Conflict, so intense at times that it could lead to a total paralysis of government, was common in American politics. There was conflict, first, between the branches of government—between the executive on the one hand and the legislatures on the other. But it was not only a matter of conflict between branches of government. There was, besides this, factionalism that transcended institutional boundaries and at times reduced the politics of certain colonies to an almost unchartable chaos of competing groups. Some were personal groups, small clusters of relatives and friends that rose suddenly at particular junctures and faded quickly, merging into other equally unstable configurations. Others were economic, regional, and more generally social interest groups, some quickly rising and quickly falling, some durable, persisting through a generation or more, though never highly organized and only intermittently active, and continually shifting in personnel. Still others (though these were fewer) were groups formed to defend and advance programs that transcended immediate personal and group interests. Most were vocal and difficult to control; and while in certain colonies at certain times political life attained the hoped-for balance and tranquility, most governors in the eighteenth century at one time or another echoed the weary question and the anguished plea of William Penn to the political leaders of the City of Brotherly Love soon after it was founded: "Cannot more friendly and private courses be taken to set matters right in an infant province? . . . For the love of God, me, and the poor country, be not so *governmentish!*"

But Pennsylvania remained, in Penn's words, "noisy and open in [its] dissatisfactions," and so did most of the other colonies during the three generations that preceded the Revolution. For beneath the apparent similarities in the formal constitutions of government in England and America, there were basic differences in the informal structure of politics. The similarities in government were superficial, the differences in politics so profound as to seem almost an inversion of the universally admired British model.

WEATHERVANE, BY SHEM DROWNE
(MID-EIGHTEENTH CENTURY)
Swivelling atop the cupola of the Massachusetts Province
House with its glass eyes flashing in the sun, this 4½-
foot gilded weathervane was the work of an untutored
craftsman. The visual and symbolic effect of the almost
life-sized American archer swinging vigilantly year after
year over the residence of the royal governors, always
aiming an arrow to fly with the wind, was striking. It
"bedazzled the eyes of those who looked upward,"
Nathaniel Hawthorne wrote in a story inspired by
Drowne, "like an angel of the sun." (*Massachusetts
Historical Society*)

The settlement of the Glorious Revolution had
not extended to the colonies. The governors in all
but the chartered colonies of Rhode Island and Connecticut had the executive authority to veto legislation, which could also be disallowed by the Privy
Council or the proprietors in England. The royal

governors, in addition, had the authority to delay
sittings of the lower houses of the assemblies or dissolve them at will, and they quickly became accustomed to using those powers. As a result, the lower
houses were as dependent on executive will for their
existences as the House of Commons had been under
the Tudor and Stuart monarchs. Nor was the judiciary
in the colonies protected as it was in England. Judges
at all levels, from justices of the peace to the chief
justices of the supreme courts, were appointed on
nomination of the governors and dismissible by the
executives' will. Similarly, the governors in all but
the three charter governments could create courts
without note of the legislature, and did so repeatedly,
especially chancery courts, which sat without juries
and were concerned with such unpopular matters as
collecting arrears of quitrents. Associated with these
"prerogative courts" in the colonists' minds were the
vice admiralty courts, which operated over maritime
matters, also without juries, with a jurisdiction
broader than that exercised by equivalent courts in
England.

Lesser powers that had been eliminated in England were also accorded the executive in America:
power over the election of the Speakers of the House;
power over church appointments; power over fees.
But it was in the more consequential areas primarily—
the vetoing of colonial legislation, dismissing and
dissolving legislative bodies, and firing judges and
creating courts—that the legal power of the executive
was felt to be the most threatening and a source of
danger to liberty and to the free constitution.

But what distinguished the American colonial
governments from the British even more than the
exaggeration of executive authority was an array of
other circumstances that radically reduced, sometimes eliminated, the force of that "influence" by
which the executive in England disciplined dissent
and conflict in the political community and maintained its supremacy in government.

To begin with, the colonial executives lacked the
flexibility they needed for successful engagement in
politics. The royal governors arrived in the colonies
not merely with commissions that outlined their
duties, but with instructions that filled in the details

so minutely and with such finality that in some of the most controversial and sensitive public issues the executive was politically immobilized. Further, the armory of political weapons so essential to the successful operation of the government of Walpole was reduced in the colonies to a mere quiverful of frail and flawed arrows. Very little political patronage—gifts of public office, contracts, honors, or other benefits of government—was available to the colonial governors by which to buy off opposition and maintain their dominance over the legislatures. Further, the highly irregular, inequitable, and hence easily manipulated electoral system was absent in America.

There were no rotten boroughs in the colonies. No assembly seats were owned outright by the government, and there were no defunct constituencies easily manipulated by the administration, for there had been no gradual accumulation of "liberties" bestowed in ancient times in recognition of once active but long since extinct political forces. While in England the House of Commons was frozen in composition throughout the eighteenth century, most of the colonial assemblies had been created at a stroke on general principles—so many delegates per unit of local government—and were continually expanding. So normal had the expectation of expansion become by midcentury that when governors, fearing the total eclipse of their influence in the legislatures because of the increasing numbers of representatives, tried to stop the multiplication of constituencies and seats they found themselves involved in serious political struggles. What is important is not that by enlightened twentieth-century standards apportionment was here and there inequitable in the colonial legislatures, but that by normal eighteenth-century standards it was so well-adjusted to the growth and spread of population and so insensitive, as a consequence, to pressure from embattled executives.

Other practices created additional problems for the governors. From the earliest years it had been common in Massachusetts for towns to instruct their representatives on how to vote in the General Court in regard to controversial issues, and this practice continued irregularly into the eighteenth century, used when the localities were committed to particular views they wished to have represented no matter what influence was brought to bear against them. Elsewhere, too, representatives were instructed on delicate issues, and often when delegates were not instructed they themselves postponed acting until—as in New York in 1734—"they had taken the sentiments of their constituents." Further, delegates were often required to be residents of the communities they represented at the time of their incumbency. The result, the eighteenth-century historian William Smith wrote, was that the assemblies seemed to be composed "of plain, illiterate husbandmen, whose views seldom extended farther than to the regulation

THE VIRGINIA HOUSE OF BURGESSES

As in the British House of Commons (p. 142), the speaker's chair (rear, under the center window) and table separate the facing benches. The room is small, and the arrangements encouraged intimate discussion. *(The Colonial Williamsburg Foundation)*

of highways, the destruction of wolves, wildcats, and foxes, and the advancement of the other little interests of the particular counties which they were chosen to represent." Residential requirements were not universal in the eighteenth-century colonies, but they were common enough to contribute measurably to the enfeeblement of "influence."

But of all the underlying characteristics that distinguished politics in America from the English model, the sheer number of those who could vote was perhaps the most dramatic. A broad franchise had not originally been planned or desired. Most colonies sought to do no more than re-create, or adapt with minor variations, the forty-shilling freehold qualification (the ownership that is, of real estate worth 40s. a year in rents), which had prevailed in the county constituencies of England for three hundred years. But if ownership of land worth 40s. a year was a restrictive qualification in England, it was permissive in the colonies where freehold tenure was widespread among the white population. So ineffective was this traditional franchise definition that most colonies went on to specify the restriction more elaborately. But everywhere the effect was to broaden the franchise, rather than to restrict it. Some colonies defined the requirements for voting in terms of acreage: in Virginia 100 acres unsettled, or 25 acres settled; in North Carolina and Georgia, 50 acres whether settled or unsettled. In other colonies permanent or even lifetime leases were declared to be as valid for the franchise as freehold property, and in some, personal property of any description was allowed to serve as qualification. Inflation of local currency values further eased the restrictions of franchise qualification. In Rhode Island a £400 property "restriction," measured in local paper money, opened the franchise to 75 percent of the colony's adult males. To the disgusted Governor Thomas Hutchinson in Massachusetts, it seemed that "anything with the appearance of a man" was allowed to vote.

Generalizing across the variety of statutory provisions and practices of the various colonies, one can safely say that 50 to 75 percent of the adult male white population was entitled to vote—far more than could do so in Britain, and far more too, it appears, than wished to do so in the colonies themselves.

Apathy in elections was common. Yet however neglected, the broad franchise was potentially a powerful weapon, certain to work against the ability of the executives to control elections and voting in the assemblies for the interest of the state.

The Pattern of Colonial Politics.   The overall configuration of early American politics was a patchwork of contradictions. There was a firmly rooted belief that the colonial constitutions corresponded in their essentials to the English model of mixed government. That assumption was violated, however, first, by what were believed to be excessive powers in the hands of the executive, and second, by the absence in the colonies of the devices by which in Britain the executive maintained discipline, control, and stability in politics. Swollen claims and shrunken powers, especially when they occur together, are always sources of trouble, and the political trouble that resulted from this combination can be traced through the history of eighteenth-century politics.

But the structure of American politics in the eighteenth century is not wholly revealed in this. The nature of leadership too was a source of controversy. Americans, like all Britons—indeed, like all Europeans of the eighteenth century—assumed that political leadership was only one of a number of expressions of leadership within society, and that in the nature of things those who enjoyed superiority in one sphere would enjoy and exercise it in another. In a society of stratified "dignities" (if not classes), political leadership was expected to rest with the natural social leaders of the community, whose identity, it was assumed, would be steadily and incontestably visible. And so indeed it was in America—in *some* of the colonies, in *certain* respects, at *certain* times.

In Virginia in the three generations that followed Bacon's Rebellion, a hierarchy of the plantation gentry emerged in stable form, dominated by social and economic leaders whose roots could be traced back to the 1650s and whose dominance in politics was largely uncontested. So too in Connecticut, a landed gentry of "ancient" families consolidated its control in the early eighteenth century and came to dominate the political life of the colony. But even in these extreme examples there were premonitions of disturbances to

War of Jenkins' Ear.   During the years after 1713, Britain engaged in three wars with European powers, and the colonies were involved in varying degrees in all of them. The first, the so-called War of Jenkins' Ear (1739–42) was fought with Spain over trading rights in the Caribbean and Central America. In the peace treaty of 1713 that ended the War of the Spanish Succession Britain had been granted the privilege of selling a limited number of slaves and a specified quantity of goods in the Spanish West Indies. The legitimate presence of British trading vessels in these otherwise closed markets had encouraged smuggling, which was countered by mutual rights of search. Spain's brutal handling of these shipboard searches had been no more improper or illegal than the British smuggling, but it had outraged British public opinion. When a certain Captain Robert Jenkins presented to a parliamentary committee one of his ears, which he said had been cut off by the Spanish seven years earlier as a punishment for smuggling, Parliament demanded a war of revenge for such atrocities, which the head of the government, Robert Walpole, who wished to avoid war, could not refuse.

The war, which ranged widely, was fought at first in the Western Hemisphere. A makeshift army of South Carolina and Georgia troops invaded Florida but failed to capture St. Augustine or to relieve the pressure on the southern frontier, and the action turned to the Caribbean. There the main effort was an assault on the Spanish town of Cartagena, on the Colombian coast, for which an American regiment of 3,500 men was recruited, to serve under British commanders. That campaign, in 1740, was a ghastly failure. A hopelessly slow and ill-mounted attack on the fort led to the butchery of the American troops, which was succeeded by an epidemic of yellow fever and a loss of supplies. After further failures in Cuba, the remains of the expedition, which had been largely financed as well as manned by the colonies, staggered home. The losses were shocking. Only 600 Americans survived, and they brought back with them a bitter resentment of the callousness, incompetence, and superciliousness of the British military commanders. Years later Americans still recalled the agonies their countrymen had endured on this senseless campaign and the appalling waste of lives and goods.

King George's War.   In 1740 the Spanish war had broadened into a general European conflict when Prussia seized the Austrian province of Silesia. Britain went to Austria's aid, and France joined Spain. Thereupon Britain, ever fearful of a single continental power controlling Europe, concluded peace with Spain (1742), and in 1744 declared war on France. This complicated series of struggles, which had begun with the Prussian invasion of Silesia, was known in Europe as the War of the Austrian Succession (1740–48) and in America as King George's War (1744–48). While its conclusion in the Treaty of Aix-la-Chapelle was no more than a truce to allow for recuperation, that arrangement left yet another source of resentment between Britain and the colonies in Britain's abandonment of an important American victory.

The focus of conflict in the Western Hemisphere during King George's War was the French naval station at Louisbourg, a massive fortification on Cape Breton Island just north of Nova Scotia, which guarded the entrance to the St. Lawrence River, sheltered French privateers, and controlled the rich fishing waters between mainland North America and Newfoundland. When Governor William Shirley of Massachusetts heard that its garrison was undermanned and dispirited and its fortifications in disrepair, he rallied support from the Massachusetts merchant community and persuaded the General Court to finance an expedition to capture the citadel. Equipment and troops were gathered from all over New England and from colonies as far south as Pennsylvania, arrangements were made for British naval support under a New Yorker, Commodore Peter Warren, and the troop command was given to a popular Maine merchant and militia colonel, William Pepperrell.

As the transports, warships, supplies, and men gathered in Boston, the campaign, in the aftermath of the Great Awakening, took on the air of a festive crusade. The clergy preached fire and destruction to the French "papists" and their pagan Indian allies. In April 1745 four thousand New England troops

SIR WILLIAM PEPPERRELL, 1747, BY JOHN SMIBERT
Pepperrell is posed on a hill overlooking Louisbourg, to which he points and into which two cannon balls are gracefully falling. An engraving of this painting of the popular hero was promptly made for wide distribution. *(Courtesy, Essex Institute, Salem, Mass.)*

landed safely near the fortress of Louisbourg, turned the cannons of a captured defense battery against the central fortification, and attacked, not by sea, as the French had expected, but by weakly defended land approaches. The French held off the attackers through all of April and May while the New Englanders—who were not soldiers but undisciplined farmers, fisherman, and town workers—bumbled and stumbled their way to control of the harbor islands. Just as Warren was preparing to land an untrained

amphibious force to take the partly demolished fortress, the French, hopelessly outnumbered and lacking food supplies and naval support, surrendered. On June 17 the "Gibraltar of the New World" was handed over to Pepperrell.

For New England, indeed for all of America, it was a glorious victory. Warren, who made a fortune from his capture of French merchant ships, was promoted to admiral; Pepperrell was knighted. But the war was far from over. Disease decimated the troops occupying Louisbourg, and the frontiers from Maine to New York were set aflame in savage raids. Border garrisons in Vermont, western Massachusetts, and New York were attacked, captured, retaken, and attacked again. Massachusetts, promised repayment by Parliament for its expenses in capturing Louisbourg, planned a massive assault on Quebec but then abandoned it when news arrived of a large French expedition moving to recover Louisbourg. And though that French fleet, scattered by storms and swept by disease, never made contact with the fortress, and though another French fleet on the same mission was captured by Warren, the border raids continued and spilled over into Nova Scotia. The war disintegrated into miscellaneous violence. Isolated towns and farmhouses were burned and their inhabitants slaughtered, though the butchery could make no possible difference to the outcome. Prisoners were taken, then exchanged. Grand campaigns were hatched with Indian allies then dissolved before any action could be taken and for reasons that could not be clearly explained. Spain's raids on several forts along the southern British coast were equally inconclusive and equally ill-designed to affect the outcome of the war.

Nothing substantial had been accomplished when in December 1748 news arrived that peace had been concluded in Europe. It brought relief from bloodshed, but in exchange for the return of Madras in India, which France had taken, England returned Louisbourg, the symbol of American military pride, to the French. Five hundred Americans had died in action to accomplish nothing, and twice that many had been killed by disease, exposure, and accidents. The return of Louisbourg would be recalled along with bitter memories of the Cartagena expedition—and with the memories of another famous episode of King George's War.

In 1747 Commodore Knowles's naval press gangs had attempted, in the fashion of the time, to shanghai likely recruits for the royal navy on the streets of Boston. But Boston, he discovered, was not London. To his amazement, his men were fought off by an incensed mob in one of the most violent town riots of the pre-Revolutionary years. The townsmen's rampage against this flagrant though traditional invasion of civilian rights lasted for four days, and it remained a living memory for a generation to come.

The French and Indian War. The third and last of these pre-Revolutionary wars followed in part the pattern of the others. This time, however, America was the central theater of war, not a marginal one; and this time the outcome was conclusive, and the resentment generated between Britain and the colonies was of a different order of magnitude.

The immediate cause of the Seven Years' War (1756–63), known in the colonies as the French and Indian War, was a series of clashes between French army units on the one hand and Virginians on the other. The French units were trying to secure the Ohio River valley for France by establishing a string of forts there. The Virginians had claims to this territory that went back to the original charter, and these were now being advanced by a powerful group of land speculators. The French repulsed the Virginians' efforts to found a British fort at the strategic junction of the Ohio, Allegheny, and Monongahela rivers and early in 1754 established their own Fort Duquesne there instead. A small force under the twenty-two-year-old Major George Washington failed to dislodge them and was itself then defeated at a stockaded encampment called Fort Necessity.

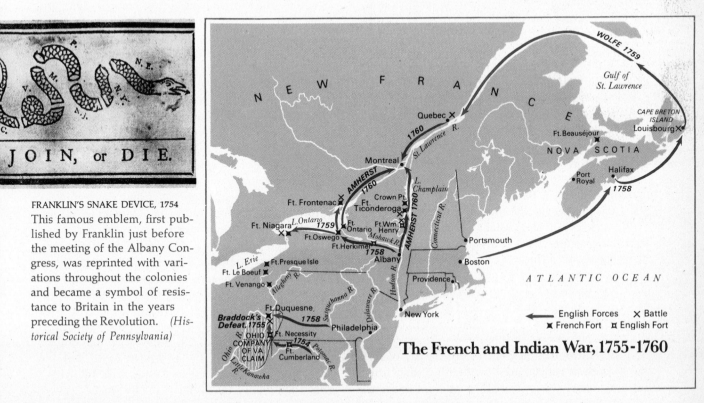

FRANKLIN'S SNAKE DEVICE, 1754
This famous emblem, first published by Franklin just before the meeting of the Albany Congress, was reprinted with variations throughout the colonies and became a symbol of resistance to Britain in the years preceding the Revolution. *(Historical Society of Pennsylvania)*

The French and Indian War, 1755-1760

Shortly after this engagement, representatives of seven colonies, anticipating a larger conflict than any of the previous wars, met at Albany in a fruitless effort to coordinate defense plans among themselves and with their Indian allies. Though they adopted in principle Benjamin Franklin's proposal for a political and military union of the colonies, they could not convince a single colonial assembly to ratify the plan for a general government that was drawn up. Meanwhile the British government moved ahead with a design for a large-scale war that involved dispatching a sizable army to America, enlisting colonial troops, and collecting in America quantities of provisions and equipment. Early in 1755, Major General Edward Braddock, an arrogant disciplinarian with little sympathy for difficult colonials and no sense of how to handle them, arrived with the advance regiments. He undertook, in the wilderness of western Pennsylvania, the first engagement in a war that was not formally declared until May 1756 but that, once declared, spread quickly to all points of contact among the major European powers—not only in Europe, America, and the Caribbean but in Africa, India, and the Philippines as well.

For two years the British suffered defeat after defeat. Braddock's army, moving west to eliminate Fort Duquesne, fell into confusion at the first, accidental contact with the enemy and was almost annihilated by a small French and Indian force hidden along the sides of the road. There were 1,000 casualties in an army of 1,400; only 23 of 86 officers survived. Washington, who helped lead the pell-mell retreat, buried Braddock in the road to keep his grave from being discovered. To the north, Nova Scotia, whose boundaries were disputed and whose native Acadians were either pro-French or unreliably neutral, had to be retaken by the British; 6,000 of the Acadians were rounded up and deported south to the thirteen colonies. But though this action isolated Cape Breton and its fortress of Louisbourg, the effort by the new commander in chief, Lord Loudoun, to capture that citadel in 1757 failed. So too did Governor Shirley's ambitious effort to force the French from the arc of forts that formed the northwest boundaries of the British colonies. Instead of the British taking the two French forts—Frontenac and Niagara—on Lake Ontario, the French under the adroit commander Montcalm took the British fort, Oswego, on the eastern side of that lake. Then, secure in Crown Point on Lake Champlain, the French moved deeper into New York by establishing Fort Ticonderoga ten miles to the south on Champlain. Finally, in August 1757 they seized Fort William Henry even farther to the south, on Lake George, and captured with it 2,000 British troops. But even this was not the end of the disasters. While in Europe, where Austria and Prussia had reversed sides, French and Austrian armies overran Britain's client state Hannover and threatened Prussia, the French on the western American frontier penetrated to Fort Herkimer on the Mohawk River, murdering noncombatant German farmers along the way. The whole of central New York and western New England was exposed; Albany seemed doomed.

It was at this absolute low point in British fortunes that the planning of that strange, brilliant, imaginative, and neurotic war minister, William Pitt, began to have its effect. Appointed secretary of state in 1757 and possessing a vision of imperial greatness that was unique for the time, Pitt conceived of something akin to a total war. He demanded huge government expenditures, heavy subsidies for the European allies to neutralize the continental zone, and large commitments by the colonies, to be financed by Parliament. He conceived of an American army of 24,000 British regulars and 25,000 colonial troops—a very large force for the time.

Passing over established but ineffective generals in favor of younger and more energetic commanders, he launched a series of efforts to break the French arc of forts north and west of the mainland colonies. The first of his plans—an attack on Ticonderoga in July 1758—failed miserably. But that was his only failure. Later the same month, a force of 9,000 regular army troops and 500 colonials under the young General Jeffrey Amherst and the thin, sickly, but tigerish Brigadier James Wolfe, only thirty-one years old, took Louisbourg. A month later, in a swift raid, the British swept over the critical supply depot of Fort Frontenac, the link between the St. Lawrence River and the French posts to the farther west and south, and with it seized control of Lake Ontario. In November a mixed force led by three excellent commanders including

Colonel Washington finally redeemed Braddock's defeat by forcing the French from Fort Duquesne, thereby seizing for Britain the entire upper Ohio Valley.

By early 1759, the year of Britain's greatest victories, the iron ring around the northern British colonies had been broken at three critical points: on the east (Louisbourg and Nova Scotia), the west (Frontenac and Lake Ontario), and the south (Duquesne). And there were successes not only in America but in India and Africa and at sea. Then Pitt, riding the crest of great popularity at home, planned the kill. Canada was to be sealed off in the far west by the capture of Fort Niagara; General Amherst was to invade Canada by way of Lake Champlain and the St. Lawrence Valley; and Wolfe was to take Quebec in an amphibious expedition moving west up the St. Lawrence River. For all of this, a fortune in supplies, transports, and firearms, in addition to three large armies with substantial naval support, was required.

Somehow, these great demands were met. In July 1759 Fort Niagara, which linked New France to the far west, was captured. At the same time, the French withdrew from Ticonderoga and Crown Point, leaving them to Amherst. By the time his troops had rebuilt these forts it was too late for him to proceed with the planned thrust into Canada from the south. But Wolfe, in one of the best-organized, most daring, and luckiest exploits in British military history, succeeded in his assigned task in Pitt's strategy.

Moving almost 10,000 men in over 200 warships and transports through the St. Lawrence to Quebec without serious loss, Wolfe fumbled for over seven weeks seeking a way to penetrate the heavily fortified city built atop the 150-foot cliffs that form the north shore of the St. Lawrence at that point. Finally, on the night of September 12, 1759, he led 4,500 men up the cliff along a diagonal roadway he discovered and into battle formation on the Plains of Abraham, just west of the city. When the French, without waiting for reinforcements, charged the carefully disposed British army rather wildly, they were met with a dis-

A VIEW OF THE TAKING OF QUEBEC, SEPTEMBER 13, 1759
This detail of a print of 1760 telescopes the debarking of the troops, their dislodging of the French defenders of the cliffside trail, and the final battle on the Plains of Abraham. *(Royal Ontario Museum, Toronto)*

ciplined and efficient barrage that broke their ranks, and they were driven from the field defeated. Among the relatively few British casualties (60 dead, 600 wounded) was Wolfe; among the French, Montcalm. On September 17, Quebec surrendered.

A year later Amherst's army, moving north and east from the lakes, converged on Montreal and with contingents from Quebec forced the French governor to surrender the whole of New France. In the final peace treaty of 1763, Britain gained undisputed possession of all of North America east of the Mississippi save for New Orleans, including all of Nova Scotia and all of Canada. Furthermore, Spain, which had entered the war only in 1762, was forced to concede Florida to Britain in exchange for the return of Cuba, which a British expedition had captured in 1762. Spain's compensations were New Orleans and the land west of the Mississippi, which France had rashly pledged to Spain as a reward for its entry into the war.

It was a great triumph of British arms, and it was matched by other British successes all over the world. But there were serious hidden costs. The most obvious was the huge debt that England acquired in prosecuting the war, which set in motion a reaction against grand and costly overseas adventures and would lead the government of George III to consider new forms of taxation. Less obvious was the immediate effect of the war on Anglo-American relations. While Americans rejoiced in the victory and for the first time in their history were relieved of the threat of French and Spanish stimulation of Indian attacks on the frontiers, they learned to fear the presence of large professional armies and to insist that militias alone were forces compatible with liberty. They learned, too, to an extent they had not before, that, though they were British, they were somehow a separate people, yet not an inferior people as the army commanders under whom they fought so often seemed to assume. For through all these wars—from the catastrophe before Cartagena to the triumph on the Plains of Abraham—they experienced the arrogance, indifference, and often the stupidity of an officer class that was a traditional part of European life but was alien, abrasive, and in the end intolerable in America.

Beyond all of that there were resentments at the imperial regulations—some of them newly devised, some newly enforced during the French and Indian War. As part of his program for a total national effort, Pitt sought to eliminate all violations of the navigation acts, all smuggling, indeed all commercial contact with the enemy that might bolster his economy or help supply his troops. It was not an altogether new effort. As early as 1756, the Privy Council had ordered the colonial governors to enforce the strict letter of the law and to eliminate the trade with the enemy that was well known to be taking place in neutral ports. In pursuit of these goals and in support of the efforts of the customs officials, the highest colonial courts had issued writs of assistance to customs officials. These general warrants, authorizing customs officers to command the assistance of court officials in searching for smuggled goods, were granted by the high court of Massachusetts in 1755, 1758, 1759, and 1760, and were valid throughout the lifetime of the reigning sovereign. They served their purpose well, but they were deeply resented by the merchant community, which was determined to seek relief when the opportunity arose.

Pitt's insistence on enforcing the letter of the law elevated all of these efforts to a new level. In the course of his brief but powerful ministry (he was forced to resign in 1761), he issued stringent orders that closed loopholes in the regulations, brought the complex rules together into an integrated whole, and fixed responsibility for negligence. Governors were drawn directly into the business of imperial law enforcement, and the navy became a more effective police arm than it had been before. Conflict was implicit in all of this. Well before 1763 certain colonial merchants and politicians who were antagonistic to the imperial establishment were beginning to question the value of a connection of which they suddenly seemed to be victims.

Yet all of this was but the tip of an iceberg. Attempts to enforce the mercantilist system during the last colonial war brought to the surface of public controversy other conflicts in imperial relations that had hitherto been submerged.

The Alienation of the State

Long before Pitt became involved in public affairs, three problems had arisen in Anglo-American relations that had not been solved but merely put off, patched up with makeshift solutions, and then ignored. They could be ignored because they had developed largely as a consequence of the mercantilist system, and as long as that system was not rigidly enforced the pressure of these problems was slight. The problems remained, nevertheless, and there was a price to be paid for evasion and neglect. Even in their moderated form they created a distance, an alienation, between Britain and America, and that alienation was as much a part of the Anglo-American world in 1760 as the universal welcome accorded the young monarch, George III.

Smuggling and the Balance of Payment. The first of these problems arose from the fact that the rapidly increasing American population created a growing market for British goods which was not matched by an equivalent growth of a market within Britain itself for the products that the colonies could sell. By the 1730s American consumption of British goods rose well beyond the colonists capacity to pay for them through direct exchanges with Britain. By the late 1760s the colonists were running a trade deficit with Britain of £1,800,000 a year, over 90 percent of it incurred by the northern and middle colonies.

The deficit had been largely made up by invisible earnings such as shipping services and by the profits of trade with southern Europe and the West Indies. The West Indies trade was particularly important in maintaining the colonies' solvency, and exchanges with the *foreign* West Indies—especially with the French sugar islands of Guadeloupe, Martinique, and Santo Domingo—had become a vital part of that trade. Dealings with the French islands, where the American merchants could buy cheaply and sell at unusually high rates, were particularly important in making up the deficits in payments to Britain and thus in keeping the commercial colonies solvent. But that trade was increasingly resented by the British West Indian

SUGAR CANE AND THE ART OF MAKING SUGAR, FROM A PRINT OF 1749
(Library of Congress)

planters and their merchant associates in England. They recognized that the more successful this foreign trade was, the higher the cost of provisions would be on their own plantations and the lower the price they could obtain for their own products.

The issue became embattled as early as 1730. The British planters and merchants moved to protect themselves against French competition by seeking to establish high duties on foreign sugar products imported into the mainland colonies. The American merchants and the colonial agents in London rose in opposition, claiming that such duties were more than the trade could bear and that they would wreck the Anglo-American commercial system and bankrupt the northern colonies. A fierce debate raged in the newspapers and pamphlets and in the House of Commons, but the result, given the power of the West Indian lobby in London, was foreordained. In 1733 Parliament passed the so-called Molasses Act, which imposed prohibitive import duties on foreign sugar products.

This established the terms of the problem as it existed in 1760. For the Molasses Act set in motion the development of a network of illegal importations. Customs officers in the North American ports were systematically bribed, and became accustomed to ignoring the strict letter of the law and settling for a certain percentage of the legal duties. Techniques for smuggling were perfected, and gradually a large part of the northern commercial economy developed a stake in the systematic corruption of the law—law that seemed arbitrary, the product of a distant, alien, and hostile government.

Conflict Over Manufactures. Something of the same sense developed from a second problem in Anglo-American economic relations that arose during the same years. The mercantile system was based on the assumption that colonial areas were producers of exotic goods and raw materials and that they were consumers, not producers, of finished goods. Large-scale manufacturing, it was assumed, was an activity reserved to the home country, and the law reflected that assumption by prohibiting the manufacture of certain basic goods in the colonies. English statutes from the end of the seventeenth century forbade the export from England of machines or tools used in the clothing industry. The Woolen Act (1699) prohibited the export of American wool or woolen products from any one colony to another. A law of 1718 forbade the free emigration of skilled artisans from Britain, and the Hat Act (1732) barred the exportation of American-made hats from the colony where they were manufactured.

Yet increasingly, as the American economy developed, investments in manufactures seemed attractive and proved to be lucrative as small accumulations of capital appeared in various areas. The sums were not large by English standards, but what surplus capital was available in the colonies was peculiarly disposed to such investments. For other outlets were limited. Some profits could be plowed back into expansion of commercial enterprise. Surpluses could be invested too in urban properties, in financing land speculation, in English government bonds, in personal loans or in equipment for business. But most such investments were limited to face-to-face transactions; there were no investment institutions that could broaden the range and magnitude of the money market. In a society not prone to extravagant consumption, those who controlled the slowly growing surplus turned more and more to manufactures. There were adverse conditions that restricted what could be done: a continuing labor shortage, a poor overland transportation system, and limited markets. But wherever these disabilities were to some degree overcome, the results were impressive.

In shipbuilding the problems of both transportation and markets were eliminated, since England's need for merchant vessels was continuous and heavy. By the late colonial period almost 40 percent of all British-owned merchant vessels were built in the thirteen colonies. About 100 vessels were sold to Britain annually, worth at least £140,000. Iron production presented greater difficulties which were only partly overcome by dispersal into small producing units and the use of slave labor. Nevertheless iron production too rose remarkably, not only in the large Principio works in Maryland and the Hasenclever plants in New Jersey but in dozens of smaller establishments scattered through the colonies. At the end of the colonial period there were 82 blast furnaces and 175 forges in the colonies (more than existed in England and Wales), and they produced 30,000 tons of crude iron a year. This product was less than half of Britain's, but it was an imposing achievement nevertheless.

Of the products manufactured in the colonies, only ships and rum were produced in such quantities that the colonists' needs were filled. But the manufacture of other goods was increasing steadily, and British authorities recognized the danger this posed to the principles of mercantilism. Britain's restrictive legislation grew more elaborate. The manufacture or export from the colonies of specific textiles was outlawed in 1750. And in that year too the most famous restrictive enactment, the Iron Act, was passed. Though it removed duties on the importation of pig and bar iron into Britain, this act prohibited the erection of finishing plants for iron goods in all the colonies.

The effect of these laws in economic terms is difficult to gauge. Surplus wealth available for investment in manufactures was never large, and there were other factors, quite aside from restrictive legislation, that tended to impede industrial growth. But in the less measurable area of attitudes to the authority responsible for such legislation, the impact of restrictive legislation was significant. It further heightened the colonists' awareness of hostile interests in the government "at home" and deepened their feelings of hostility and alienation.

Currency and Banking. The same effect resulted from the handling of the money problem, which remained an acute issue through most of the mid-eighteenth century. The problem was created by the virtual absence of specie, or coin, as a medium of exchange. The coinage of money, being a sovereign prerogative, was prohibited in the colonies after the confiscation of the charter of Massachusetts, under whose jurisdiction the "pine tree shilling" had been minted in the seventeenth century. The colonists made every effort thereafter to attract Spanish coin to the British colonies, but the negative balance of trade made their efforts unsuccessful. The solution was paper money—unusual in the eighteenth-century—which entered into the economy in two forms.

The first form was bills of credit that were issued by the colonial governments to repay debts the governments owed to merchant contractors. Massachusetts began this practice in 1690, and in the years that followed before 1760 almost every other colony did the same. These bills, which were in effect IOUs to be redeemed eventually by the governments, were declared legally valid as payment for taxes. As a consequence, they entered into general circulation, their value maintained by the expectation of eventual redemption. But these bills were not generally made full legal tender (that is, valid for payment of all debts, public and private), and they continued to be thought of as wartime expedients. The quantity available depended less on the needs of the economy than on the occasional demands for public expenditure.

The second form of paper money was that issued by land banks, which were in effect public loan agencies. They were created to issue money to individuals at 5 percent interest, repayable gradually and secured against default by mortgages on land or other real property. The success of these banks, which by 1750 were in existence in every colony but Virginia, was striking. They injected a badly needed flow of currency; they reduced taxation (through the income produced from the interest on the loans); they created a source of low-interest credit needed for agricultural development; and they built up purchasing power that may have helped soften the effects of depressions. Further, as opposed to bills of credit, the land banks put funds at low interest directly into the hands of the farmers; bills of credit went first to the merchants, who translated them into credit for the farmers on less generous terms. Both, however, provided a needed medium of exchange and, despite their experimental character, were on the whole successful. Bills of credit were especially sound in the middle colonies where both merchants and officials backed the issues and limited them carefully.

In parts of New England and the South, however, there was overissuance and serious depreciation. In these areas creditors feared they would be repaid in paper money that had lost value since the debts had been incurred. Even more apprehensive were the English merchants, who feared severe losses if their credit were in any way affected by the cheapening of currency. Together, creditors in the colonies and in England pressured the British government to send strict orders to the colonial governors not to allow bills to be issued as full legal tender and to insist that the currency laws state the times of redemption clearly, and that these specifications be honored to the letter.

But such strict controls were difficult to enforce, and a crisis arose in New England in the 1730s. Rhode Island's bills flooded the region (that colony issued £100,000 worth of paper bills in 1733 alone), and the Boston merchants refused to honor them. The pressure for more issues continued, however, and in 1739 a group of Massachusetts merchants formed a *private* land bank, which was authorized by the General Court to issue £150,000 worth of bills at 3 percent interest. Many members of the business community were greatly alarmed at this, especially since repayment was allowed in commodities of uncertain value, and they formed in opposition to the land bank what was called a silver bank, which would issue notes redeemable in silver, not commodities. The two groups fought bitterly, and in the end the governor and council declared the land bank's bills invalid, although £50,000 had already been placed in circulation. The leading land bankers organized public protests, which became riotous. There were arrests and jailings, and in the end the British government adopted repressive measures. In 1741 the so-called Bubble Act was extended to the colonies, which outlawed all joint-stock companies not authorized by Parliament (in effect outlawing all private banks). Years of litigation followed in Massachusetts as creditors who had already accepted payment in the

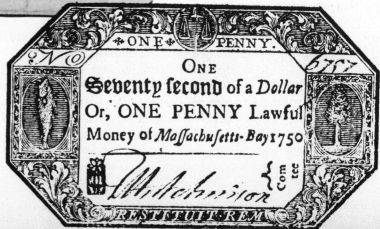

COLONIAL PAPER MONEY
The Massachusetts paper penny bears the signature of Thomas Hutchinson, the future loyalist governor, then a member of a committee in charge of issuing bills of credit. The issue of 1750 was a victory for Hutchinson's hard money policy. Based on £180,000 of silver that Parliament sent in repayment of wartime expenses, it replaced all of the colony's inflated currency in circulation. *(American Antiquarian Society)*

bank's bills demanded repayment in valid money. It was the worst upheaval in the Bay Colony between the establishment of the Dominion of New England in the 1680s and the early years of the Revolution. Samuel Adams's father was one of the local officials removed from office for continuing to support the land bank.

But the more traditional *public* land banks continued to exist, and the value of their issues continued to fluctuate. In Massachusetts, paper was discounted from par at a ratio of 9 to 1. In Rhode Island, nine issues of paper were in circulation in 1750, representing a par value of £465,000, and in addition there was £60,000 worth of bills of credit legally available. But by then more comprehensive legislation was being drafted. In 1751 Parliament passed the Currency Act, directed to the New England colonies alone. By its terms, no new land banks could be created in New England; no paper money could

thereafter be made full legal tender; all bills were to be retired on the strict schedule of the original legislation; and bills could be issued to pay for government expenses only if provision were made for their redemption by taxes within two years.

Though the Currency Act applied only to New England, it constituted a warning and threat to all the colonial governments against allowing any looseness in the management of paper money. Orders went out from London severely restricting the use of this currency in all the colonies, though it had become an essential part of the American economy and though those responsible for the paper issues were by no means wildcat inflationists. Every knowledgeable merchant knew the value of sound paper money, and many, like Franklin, correctly saw that its controlled expansion could be a stimulus to the entire economy. In this case also, as in the prohibitive taxation of the trade with the foreign West Indies and in the restriction of American manufactures, the action of the British government was seen to be not merely unfairly competitive but hostile. The action seemed arbitrary and unreasonable—an imposition that called into question the grounds of loyalty. To obey such laws as these was a form of humiliation exacted by a government that seemed distant, alienated from the people it governed and unresponsive to their needs.

The American

The antagonisms between Britain and the colonies that resulted from their uneasy collaboration in wartime and the resentments created by Britain's seemingly arbitrary and hostile legislation were problems largely of policy and management. Potentially, at least, they were within the realm of political control. A deeper and less manageable source of distance and alienation between Britain and America lay in the area of cultural perceptions—the sense Americans had of who they were in relation to the other peoples of the world, of what their life was like, and who, in contrast, the British were within the same set of considerations. These attitudes and perceptions are

facts which in the end are as important as battles and laws and political campaigns, although they are more difficult to establish, to measure, and to describe.

Through the two generations of growth and expansion that preceded the accession of George III, Americans had gradually acquired a sense of themselves as a separate people—separate not in law or politics or constitution, but in character and culture. It was a complex image, composed of many strands, and it could be seen as positive or negative depending on the context or point of view. It was an image of a simple, rustic, innocent, uncorrupted, and unsophisticated people, an appropriate self-image for a colonial people, perhaps, but no simple reflection of reality. For it was, first, a compound of several intellectual traditions and influences; it was, in addition, a reflection of the ideas and attitudes of Europe's enlightened thinkers; and it was, finally, a product of certain specific political ideas of great potential power.

In its origins this image can be traced back to the ambiguous picture that Europeans formed of the American Indians soon after their first contact with the Western Hemisphere, a picture compounding simplicity and savagery, vigor and barbarism, innocence and paganism. By the eighteenth century this mingled image in the case of British North America came to be applied as much to the Creoles—that is, natives of European descent—as to the Indians, whom the English had long since come to think of as unredeemably savage, if not satanic. This transfer of traits from the natives to the European colonists was facilitated by the common belief that the colonists had deliberately copied certain practices and skills from the Indians and as a result had acquired from them certain peculiar characteristics. Infants strapped to boards, for example, were thought to develop like Indians whatever their race or culture; American women, like Indians, were believed to be taller than European women and to suffer fewer miscarriages. This notion was reinforced by the "scientific" arguments of the environmentalists, an influential group of continental European thinkers who believed that life in all its forms was determined by the material conditions in which it was lived. It seemed reasonable to believe, from this point of view, that what

had long been true of the Indians in the great American laboratory of nature would eventually, if it did not already, apply to the colonists too.

But more practical and immediate influences were also at work detailing the Americans' simplicity, innocence, and rusticity. The image of the American colonists—their own view of themselves as well as the view that others had of them—was shaped too by the recruiting propaganda that had circulated throughout Europe and America for over a century. All of these publications, from the advertisements of the Virginia Company to the publications of the German "newlanders" operating along the Rhine and the pamphlets distributed in Ireland by American land speculators, stressed the idyllic wonders of a simple, loosely institutionalized, benign society where land was free, where government scarcely existed, and where religion was practiced in absolutely uncontested freedom.

Perhaps the greatest influence of all in propagating the image of British America as a land of simple, innocent, independent, and virtuous folk was the widespread knowledge of the kinds of people who had in fact gone there—self-respecting servants, ambitious artisans, sturdy yeoman, Puritans—and above all, and most sensationally, Quakers. The symbolic importance of the Quakers to the world at large was overwhelming. In the seventeenth century they had been thought of principally as exotic radicals. They were famous throughout Britain and France for their fanatical independence of mind and their absolute refusal to respect mere earthly authorities (hence their practice of addressing people of all ranks with the familiar "thee" and "thou"). In the more tolerant atmosphere of the early eighteenth century their reputation had shifted from that of defiant and fanatical seekers of religious freedom to that of genial advocates of pacifism, toleration, simplicity in religion, and ordinary human rights in the face of aristocratic and authoritarian power. It was this cluster of traits that attracted Voltaire to them during his stay in England (1726–29) and that led him to praise them extravagantly again and again. For this powerful figure of the European Enlightenment, the Quakers as a group were the embodiments of civic virtue; and the essence of their virtues, he believed,

28 LETTERS *concerning*

different perfuasion, embrac'd him tenderly. *William* made a fruitlefs exhortation to his father not to receive the facrament, but to die a Quaker; and the good old man intreated his fon *William* to wear buttons on his fleeves, and a crape hatband in his beaver, but all to no purpofe.

WILLIAM PEN inherited very large poffeffions, part of which confifted in crown-debts due to the vice-admiral for fums he had advanc'd for the fea-fervice. No monies were at that time more fecure than thofe owing from the king. *Pen* was oblig'd to go more than once, and *Thee* and *Thou* king *Charles* and his minifters, in order to recover the debt; and at laft inftead of fpecie, the government invefted him with the right and fovereignty of a province of *America*, to the fouth of *Maryland*. Thus was a Quaker rais'd to fovereign power. *Pen* fet fail for his new dominions with two fhips freighted with Quakers, who follow'd his fortune. The country was then call'd *Penfilvania* from *William Pen*, who there founded *Philadelphia*, now

the ENGLISH NATION. 29

now the moft flourifhing city in that country. The firft ftep he took was to enter into an alliance with his *American* neighbours; and this is the only treaty between thofe people and the Chriftians that was not ratified by an oath, and was never infring'd. The new fovereign was at the fame time the legiflator of *Penfilvania*, and enacted very wife and prudent laws, none of which have ever been chang'd fince his time. The firft is, to injure no perfon upon a religious account, and to confider as brethren all thofe who believe in one God.

HE had no fooner fettled his government, but feveral *American* merchants came and peopled this colony. The natives of the country inftead of flying into the woods, cultivated by infenfible degrees a friendfhip with the peaceable Quakers. They lov'd thefe foreigners as much as they detefted the other Chriftians who had conquer'd and laid wafte *America*. In a little time, a great number of thefe favages (falfely fo call'd) charm'd with the mild and gentle difpofition

30 LETTERS *concerning*

pofition of their neighbours, came in crowds to *William Pen*, and befought him to admit them into the number of his vaffals. 'Twas very rare and uncommon for a fovereign to be *Thee'd* and *Thou'd* by the meaneft of his fubjects, who never took their hats off when they came into his prefence; and as fingular for a government to be without one prieft in it, and for a people to be without arms, either offenfive or defenfive; for a body of citizens to be abfolutely undiftinguifh'd but by the public employments, and for neighbours not to entertain the leaft jealoufy one againft the other.

WILLIAM PEN might glory in having brought down upon earth the fo much boafted golden age, which in all probability never exifted but in *Penfilvania*. He return'd to *England* to fettle fome affairs relating to his new dominions. After the death of king *Charles* the fecond, king *James*, who had lov'd the father, indulg'd the fame affection to the fon, and no longer confider'd him as an obfcure Sectary, but as a very great man,

THE EUROPEAN IMAGE OF AMERICA: VOLTAIRE ON PENNSYLVANIA AND THE QUAKERS.
Voltaire's account of Anglo-American life, which first appeared in English translation in 1733, was published in France in 1734 as *Lettres Philosophiques* and promptly condemned to be burnt by the hangman as "likely to inspire a license of thought most dangerous to religion and civil order." The book nevertheless circulated widely. This passage on Penn as a great lawgiver, on Pennsylvania as a utopia, and on the Quakers as humble people of civic virtue and peace was taken over almost verbatim into the great French *Encyclopédie* (1751–1780), the massive summary of European liberal thought, and hence entered the mainstream of the Enlightenment. *(Reproduced by permission of Houghton Library, Harvard University)*

could be seen in Pennsylvania, where all their dreams and the dreams of all mankind, he thought, had reached fulfillment. Here, Voltaire wrote, an enlightened republican lawgiver had created a human paradise. Philadelphia, he wrote in one of his *Philosphical Letters* (1734), was so prosperous that people flocked to it from all over the continent; Penn's laws were so wise that no one of them had ever been changed; the Indians had been won over to friendship; there was equality and religious freedom without priests; and there was peace everywhere. "William Penn might glory," he wrote, "in having brought down upon the earth the so much boasted golden age, which in all probability never existed but in Pennsylvania."

The world, it seemed, agreed. Montesquieu, perhaps the most widely respected and influential political analyst of the age, called Penn the greatest lawgiver since classical antiquity. The monumental French *Encyclopédie* of enlightened ideas included Penn among the cultural heroes of Europe. And in addition to all of this, every informed person in the Western world knew something about Pennsylvania, and about America in general, through the extraordinary figure of Benjamin Franklin.

BENJAMIN FRANKLIN, BY ROBERT FEKE, AND
"POOR RICHARD'S ALMANAC"
The portrait was painted about the time of
Franklin's retirement from business. Thirty
years later Franklin's image was completely
transformed (see p. 166). *(Left, Fogg Art
Museum, Harvard University; below, The His-
torical Society of Pennsylvania)*

Poor Richard, 1733.

AN

Almanack

For the Year of Chrift

1733,

eing the First after LEAP YEAR:

And makes fince the Creation   Years
By the Account of the Eaftern *Greeks*   7241
By the Latin Church, when ☉ ent. ♈   6932
By the Computation of *W. W.*   5742
By the *Roman* Chronology   5682
By the *Jewifh* Rabbies   5494

Wherein is contained

The Lunations, Eclipfes, Judgment of
the Weather, Spring Tides, Planets Motions &
mutual Afpects, Sun and Moon's Rifing and Setting, Length of Days, Time of High Water,
Fairs, Courts, and obfervable Days.
itted to the Latitude of Forty Degrees,
and a Meridian of Five Hours Weft from *London*,
but may without fenfible Error, ferve all the adjacent Places, even from *Newfoundland* to *South-
Carolina.*

By *RICHARD SAUNDERS,* Philom.

PHILADELPHIA:
inted and fold by *B. FRANKLIN*, at the New
Printing-Office near the Market.

The Third Impreffion.

Franklin and the Image of America. Franklin, the most famous American of the eighteenth century and one of the most famous and influential Americans who has ever lived, was born in Boston in 1706, the son of a candle and soap maker. At the age of seventeen he ran away to Philadelphia, where he eventually prospered as a printer and an organizer of printing establishments in several colonies. At the age of forty-two he retired from business to devote himself to public causes, to writing, and to scientific experimentation. He corresponded with English scientists and intellectuals, particularly Peter Collinson, a Quaker merchant and a member of the Royal Society, on the problems of electricity, and it was in the form of letters to Collinson that he published the results of his studies, *Experiments and Observations on Electricity* (1751). This book was one of the great sensations of the eighteenth century. It went through five editions in English, three in French, one in Italian, and one in German before 1800, and it elevated Franklin to the highest ranks of Western thinkers. Buffon, the greatest French naturalist of the age, himself arranged for the French edition; the encyclopedist Diderot declared Franklin to be the very model of the modern experimental scientist.

And who was Franklin? A simple, unsophisticated product of the primitive society of British North America—yet he had outdone the most sophisticated intellectuals of Europe in their own field of endeavor. The implications were sensational. In the context of the great wave of reform thinking that is called the Enlightenment, Franklin's mere existence as a successful intellectual conveyed a powerful message. It reinforced the arguments of reformers everywhere and demonstrated conclusively the validity of their challenge to the establishment.

Though Enlightenment thought was complicated in its details, in its essence it was clear and simple. At its heart lay discontent with the condition of life as it was known and a general approach to improvement. All enlightened thinkers in one way or another pictured human nature as good, or if not good, then at least capable of great improvement and of far greater happiness than was commonly experienced.

The evils of the world that reduced people to misery were seen mainly as artifacts—constructions of men and women themselves. To Voltaire, the chief evils were the great public institutions, especially the church and a corrupt and dogmatic priesthood. To the physiocrats, the French economic reformers who believed that agriculture alone produced wealth, the great evil was the irrational constraints on agricultural production and marketing; to Locke, it was the arbitrary, authoritarian state; to Rousseau, it was civilization itself. For all, the cruelties and miseries of life were products of constructions that people themselves had made, and the solution was the reform of these structures so that human nature would be released to attain the happiness of which it was capable.

But there were powerful counter-arguments. These great imposing institutions—the state, the church, the regulated economy, and the social structures that gave power to a hereditary aristocracy—were, after all, the guardians of social order and stability; they were also the carriers of high culture and the sponsors of the finest human achievements. To eliminate them or change them radically might create not freedom but anarchy, not a higher civilization but barbarism. What was needed by all the enlightened thinkers was an example, not of thuggish primitivism but of civilized simplicity—a Christian society free from the encumbrances of rigid and powerful institutions, a society in which reason had been used in fashioning public institutions and in which, despite the simplicity of life, high culture was maintained and advanced. In British North America generally, in Pennsylvania more specifically, and above all in the figure of Franklin—apparently an untutored genius, a simple and unaffected but accomplished virtuoso of science, letters, and statecraft—they had the example they wanted. If Franklin had never existed it would have been necessary for the philosophers of the Enlightenment to invent him—a fact which Franklin understood perfectly, which he shrewdly played upon, and which he expressed most clearly in the *Autobiography* that he wrote in the later years of his life.

FRANKLIN, THE ENLIGHTENMENT'S PHILOSOPHER

Top, a painting by John Trumbull. It expresses perfectly the image Franklin had projected to the enlightened world ever since the publication of his experiments. *Bottom,* the popularization of Franklin's image. A box cover, probably of the 19th century, showing the great triumvirate of the Enlightenment—"The Light of the Universe" —Voltaire, Rousseau, and Franklin. *(Top, Yale University Art Gallery; bottom, The Metropolitan Museum of Art, Gift of William H. Huntington, 1883)*

To much of the Western world, Franklin *was* America; he was the American incarnate. Caught up in the imagery of simplicity and natural gifts demanded by Enlightenment aspirations, he demonstrated the meaning of the New World to the Old, and thereby helped shape Americans' self-awareness as well as Europe's perception of the provincial society beyond the sea.

America and the Grounds of Political Freedom. Inevitably Franklin played on the theme of the social and moral grounds of political freedom, for it was in this area that American self-imagery came into its sharpest focus and acquired its greatest relevance for the affairs of the everyday world. It was universally believed that in the end the success of Britain's celebrated constitution, or of any constitution that protected the people's liberties, depended on the virtue of the political population. To maintain the balance of forces in government that prevented the misuse of power required eternal vigilance. Freedom from oppression rested on the ability of the people to resist the encroachments of a priviliged and arrogant aristocracy and on the capacity of the aristocracy to resist the corruptions of profit and power and to continue to use its privileges for the good of the whole. If the people's will to protect their own liberties weakened, or if Britain's aristocracy succumbed to sloth and self-indulgence as had the aristocracies of continental Europe, freedom would be destroyed by the predictable encroachments of arbitrary power.

The signs, for Americans of the late provincial period, were worrisome. Repeatedly they found reason to question the moral qualities of English society, to doubt the independence of "the democracy" in Britain and the impartiality and responsibility of the British aristocracy. American visitors to England sent back disturbing reports. John Dickinson of Pennsylvania, in England in the election year 1754, wrote home that he was "filled with awe and reverence" by his contact with scenes of ancient greatness and by the sophistication and variety of life in London. But he was shocked too by the corruption of English politics. Over £1 million, he reported to his father, was spent in efforts to manipulate the election.

WATCH PAPERS ENGRAVED BY NATHANIEL HURD, 1762
These circular portraits were designed to fit inside the cover of a pocket watch. *(American Antiquarian Society)*

If a man cannot be brought to vote as he is desired, he is made dead drunk and kept in that state, never heard of by his family or friends till all is over and he can do no harm. The oath of their not being bribed is as strict and solemn as language can form it, but is so little regarded that few people can refrain from laughing while they take it. . . . Bribery is so common that it is thought there is not a borough in England where it is not practiced. . . . We hear every day in Westminster Hall leave moved to file information for bribery, but it is ridiculous and absurd to pretend to curb the effects of luxury and corruption in one instance or in one spot without a general reformation of manners, which everyone sees is absolutely necessary for the welfare of the kingdom. Yet Heaven knows how it can be effected. It is grown a vice here to be virtuous.

This was not simply provincial prudery. English writers too decried the loss of virtue, warning of its implications for politics, and their voices were clearly heard in America. James Burgh's *Britain's Remembrancer* (1746) denounced "our degenerate times and corrupt nation"; the British people, he said, were wallowing in "luxury and irreligion . . . venality, perjury, faction, opposition to legal authority, idleness, gluttony, drunkenness, lewdness, excessive gaming, robberies . . . a legion of furies sufficient to rend any state or empire . . . to pieces." Burgh's pamphlet was reprinted first by Franklin in 1747, then by another Philadelphia printer in 1748, and again in Boston in 1759. So too Dr. John Brown's blistering attack on English corruption, *An Estimate of the Manners and Principles of the Times* (1757), found an eager audience in America—an audience convinced of the superiority and virtue of its own uncorrupted manners and of its own moral capacity to satisfy the demands of freedom if freedom were ever challenged.

So the American people entered the age of George III. Their prospects were excellent despite the troubles that lay beneath the surface of Anglo-American life and the doubts they had of the moral quality of the British people and the responsibility of the British leaders. Conscious of their characteristics as a colonial people—provincial but vigorous, unsophisticated but uncorrupted, contentious but free, undeveloped in all the main institutions of society but more prosperous than any large population in the Western world—they saw themselves growing powerful and mature as part of an enriching imperial connection.

CHRONOLOGY

1727–60 Reign of George II.

1729 Separate royal colonies, North and South Carolina, created.

1732 Georgia established to furnish buffer against Spanish and as philanthropic effort to relocate England's paupers.

1733 Molasses Act restricts colonial importation of sugar goods from French West Indies.

1734–35 Jonathan Edwards touches off evangelical revival in Northampton, Massachusetts, and throughout Connecticut River valley.

1735 New York jury acquits John Peter Zenger of charge of seditious libel on ground that printing truth can be no libel.

1739–40 George Whitefield tours America and ignites major phase of Great Awakening.

1739–42 War of Jenkins' Ear, fought with Spain principally in Caribbean and Central America.

1740–41 Private land bank created in Massachusetts; outlawed by Parliament.

1744–48 King George's War (colonial phase of Europe's War of the Austrian Succession, 1740–48); concluded in Treaty of Aix-la-Chapelle.

1745 New England troops take fortress of Louisbourg on Cape Breton Island (returned to France at end of war).

1750 Iron Act, limiting production of finished iron goods in colonies, passed by Parliament.

1751 Currency Act, restricting issuance and currency of paper money in New England colonies, passed by Parliament.
Publication of Franklin's *Experiments and Observations on Electricity.*

1754 Albany Congress and Plan of Union.

1754–63 French and Indian War (colonial phase of Europe's Seven Years' War, 1756–63.)

1759 Quebec falls to British army.

1760 George III accedes to throne.

SUGGESTED READINGS

The eighteenth-century colonial wars were the subject of Francis Parkman's most dramatic narratives—still immensely readable—in his nine-volume series, *France and England in North America.* His *Half-Century of Conflict* (2 vols., 1892) covers King George's War, and his *Montcalm and Wolfe* (2 vols., 1884) the French and Indian War. A modern, technical, scholarly work covering the same ground in greater detail but lacking Parkman's narrative style is Lawrence H. Gipson's *British Empire before the American Revolution*, vols. VI-VIII (1946–53). Excellent also among the general works on the pre-Revolutionary military events are Stanley Pargellis, *Lord Loudoun in North*

America (1933) and John Shy, *Toward Lexington* (1965), chaps. i–iii. Howard H. Peckham, *The Colonial Wars, 1689–1762* (1964) provides a brief introduction to the whole subject.

On the three problems of Anglo-American relations discussed in the second section of the chapter, the balance of payments and commerce with the West Indies are discussed in James F. Shepherd and Gary M. Walton, *Shipping, Maritime Trade, and the Economic Development of Colonial North America* (1972), esp. App. IV; Richard B. Sheridan, "The Molasses Act and the Market Strategy of the British Sugar Planters," *Journal of Economic History*, 17 (1957), 62–83 and *Sugar and Slavery* (1974); Richard Pares, *Yankees and Creoles* (1956) and *War and Trade in the West Indies, 1739–1763* (1936); and Thomas C. Barrow, *Trade and Empire* (1967). On manufactures: Victor S. Clark, *History of Manufactures in the United States* (3 vols., 1929); Eleanor L. Lord, *Industrial Experiments in the British Colonies . . .* (1898); Curtis P. Nettels, "The Menace of Colonial Manufacturing, 1690–1720," *New England Quarterly*, 4 (1931), 230–69; Arthur C. Bining, *British Regulation of the Colonial Iron Industry* (1933); Shepherd and Walton, *Shipping* (cited above), esp. App. VI. And on the money supply and banks, see E. James Ferguson, "Currency Finance . . . ," *Wm. and Mary Q.*, 10 (1953), 153–80; Theodore G. Thayer, "The Land Bank System in the American Colonies," *Journal of Economic History*, 13 (1953), 145–59; Andrew M. Davis, *Currency and Banking in . . . Massachusetts Bay* (2 vols., 1901); Richard A. Lester, *Monetary Experiments . . .* (1939); and George A. Billias, *Massachusetts Land Bankers of 1740* (1959). For a general assessment of the importance of the colonies' trade and manufactures to Britain's economy, see Jacob M. Price, "Colonial Trade and British Economic Development, 1660–1775," *Lex et Scientia*, 14 (1978), 106–26.

On cultural relations between the colonies and Europe, see, besides the Boorstin and Savelle books cited for chapter 5, Michael Kraus, *The Atlantic Civilization: Eighteenth-Century Origins* (1949); Sacvan Berkovitch, *The Puritan Origins of the American Self* (1975); Durand Echeverria, *Mirage in the West . . . the French Image of American Society to 1815* (1957); Gilbert Chinard, "Eighteenth Century Themes on America as a Human Habitat," *Proceedings of the American Philosophical Society*, 91 (1947), 25–57; Howard M. Jones, *O Strange New World* (1964); and Bernard Bailyn, *Ideological Origins of the American Revolution* (1967), chaps. ii–iii. On Franklin's extraordinary role in cultural relations between Europe and America, see Alfred O. Aldridge, *Franklin and His French Contemporaries* (1957); Antonio Pace, *Franklin and Italy* (1958); I. Bernard Cohen's edition, *Benjamin Franklin's Experiments* (1941) and his *Franklin and Newton* (1956); and Charles C. Sellers, *Benjamin Franklin in Portraiture* (1962). The full standard biography is Carl Van Doren, *Benjamin Franklin* (1938); a shorter but well-rounded account is Verner W. Crane, *Benjamin Franklin and a Rising People* (1954).

PART TWO

Gordon S. Wood

Framing the Republic

1760–1820

The American Revolution is the single most important event in American history. Not only did it create the United States, but it defined most of the persistent values and aspirations of the American people. The noblest ideals of Americans—the commitments to freedom, equality, constitutionalism, and the well-being of ordinary people—were first defined in the Revolutionary era. The Revolution gave Americans the belief that they were a people with a special destiny to lead the world toward liberty. The Revolution, in short, gave birth to whatever ideology Americans have had. The United States was the first nation in the modern world to make political and social principles the foundation of its existence. A society composed of so many different races and peoples from so many different places could not be a nation in any traditional sense of the term. It was the Revolutionary experience and the ideals and beliefs flowing from it that have held Americans together and made them think of themselves as a single people.

The origins of such a momentous event necessarily lay deep in America's past. A century and a half of dynamic developments in the British continental colonies of the New World had fundamentally transformed inherited European institutions and customary patterns of life and had created the basis for a new society. Suddenly in the 1760s Great Britain thrust its imperial power into this changing world with a thoroughness that had not been felt in a century, and precipitated a crisis within the loosely organized empire. American resistance turned into rebellion; but as the colonists groped to make sense of the peculiarities of their society this rebellion became a justification and idealization of American life as it had gradually and unintentionally developed over the previous century and a half. In this sense, as John Adams later said, "The Revolution was effected before the war commenced." It was a change "in the minds and hearts of the people."

But this change was not the whole American Revolution. The Revolution was also part of the great transforming process that carried America into modernity. Despite the corrosive and disruptive effects of the wilderness that by 1760 had fundamentally altered the institutions and lives of the American colonists, mid-eighteenth-century society still retained, along with powdered

Overleaf: "Globe Village" by Francis Alexander c. 1882. *(Courtesy of the Jacob Edwards Library, Southbridge, Massachusetts)*

wigs and knee breeches, many traditional habits of behavior and social relationships that separated it from the more fluid, bustling, individualistic world of the early nineteenth century. Although by 1760 much had changed, more remained to be changed.

The Revolution released and intensified forces that, by the early years of the nineteenth century, helped create in America a society unlike any that had existed before, a society almost as different from America in 1760 as colonial America had been from eighteenth-century England. This complicated Revolution developed through several phases. Although its origins went back to the seventeenth-century settlements and its consequences are with Americans still, the Revolution can be essentially encompassed between 1760 and 1820. Some Americans thought the Revolution was over in 1776 with the Declaration of Independence and the creation of new state governments. Others, however, believed the Revolution ended only with the reconstruction of the national government in 1787; and still others thought it was not finished until the new central government was infused with strength and energy in the 1790s. Yet many other Americans saw these later centralizing developments as a repudiation of the original Revolution and thus sought to recover the spirit of 1776. For them the election of Thomas Jefferson as president of the United States in 1800 was the real fulfillment of the Revolution, a fulfillment that required ratification by another war against Great Britain in 1812.

By the end of that second war against Britain, the central impulses of the Revolution had run their course. At last the future and stability of the Republic seemed secure. Democracy and equality were no longer issues to be debated; they had become articles of faith to be fulfilled. The ideological antagonisms that the Revolution had aroused had finally petered out. In place of a collection of little more than 2 million monarchial subjects huddled along the Atlantic coast, America by 1820 had become a huge, expansive nation of nearly 10 million republican citizens, active, energetic, and filled with the sense of great possibilities that lay before them.

CHAPTER 7

Sources of the Revolution

In 1763 Great Britain straddled the world with the greatest and the richest empire since the fall of Rome. From India to the Mississippi its arms had been victorious. The Peace of Paris that concluded the Seven Years' War gave Britain unrivaled dominance over the northern and eastern half of North America. From the defeated powers, France and Spain, Britain acquired huge chunks of territory in the New World—all of Canada, East and West Florida, and millions of fertile acres between the Appalachians and the Mississippi. Since Spain received the territory of Louisiana from France in compensation for losing the Floridas, France, Britain's most fearsome enemy, was removed altogether from the North American continent.

Yet at the moment of Britain's ascendancy there were powerful forces at work that would soon, almost overnight, change everything. In the aftermath of the Seven Years' War British officials found themselves having to make long-postponed decisions concerning the colonies that set in motion a train of events that ultimately shattered the empire.

The Changing Empire

Since the formation of the empire in the late seventeenth century, there always had been some royal officials and bureaucrats interested in reforming the awkwardly imposed imperial structure and in expanding royal authority over the colonists. But most of their schemes had been thwarted by English ministries more concerned with the patronage of English politics than with colonial reform. These ministers were anxious to keep disruptive colonial issues out of Parliament, where they might be readily exploited by opposition politicians. Under such circumstances, the empire had been allowed to grow haphazardly without much control from London. People from all countries had been encouraged to settle in the colonies, and land had been freely dispensed.

Although few imperial officials had ever doubted that the empire was supposed to be a hierarchical structure and that the colonies were inferior to and dependent upon the mother country, in fact it had

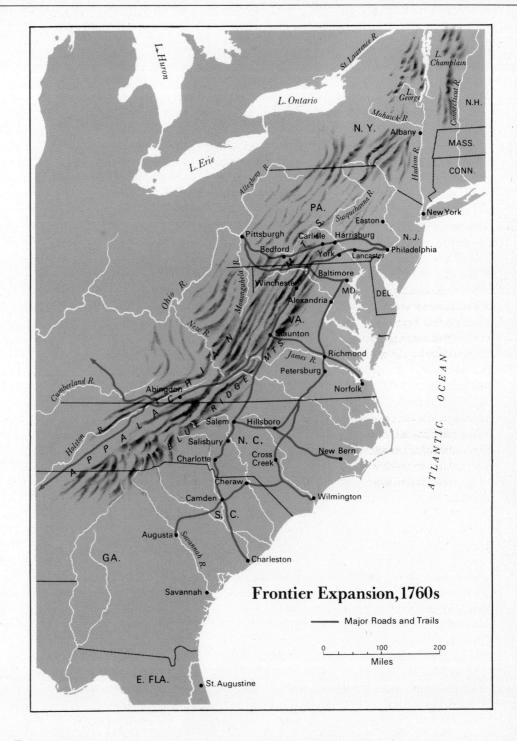

Frontier Expansion, 1760s

——— Major Roads and Trails

0   100   200

Miles

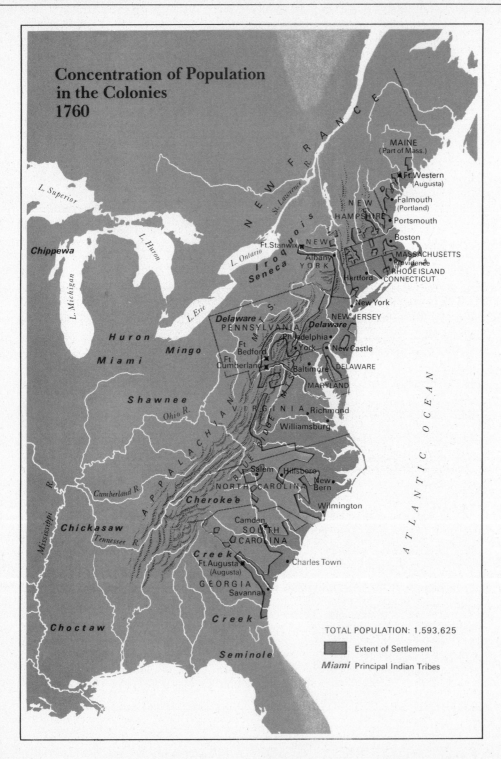

**Concentration of Population
in the Colonies
1760**

L. Superior

NEW FRANCE

St. Lawrence R.

MAINE
(Part of Mass.)

Ft. Western
(Augusta)

Falmouth
(Portland)

NEW
HAMPSHIRE

Portsmouth

Chippewa

L. Huron

L. Ontario

Ft. Stanwix

Iroquois

Seneca

Albany

NEW
YORK

Boston

MASSACHUSETTS

Providence

RHODE ISLAND

Hertford

CONNECTICUT

L. Michigan

L. Erie

Huron

Mingo

New York

Miami

Delaware

PENNSYLVANIA

Delaware

NEW JERSEY

Philadelphia

Ft
Bedford

York

New Castle

Ft
Cumberland

Baltimore

DELAWARE

Shawnee

Ohio R.

MARYLAND

VIRGINIA

Richmond

APPALACHIAN MTS.

Williamsburg

BLUE RIDGE MTS.

Cumberland R.

Salem

Hillsboro

New
Bern

Mississippi R.

Chickasaw

Tennessee R.

Cherokee

NORTH CAROLINA

Wilmington

Camden

SOUTH
CAROLINA

Creek

Ft. Augusta
(Augusta)

Charles Town

GEORGIA

Savannah

Choctaw

Creek

ATLANTIC OCEAN

Seminole

TOTAL POPULATION: 1,593,625

Extent of Settlement

Miami Principal Indian Tribes

opening up paths westward through the Appalachians. Settlers, mostly small farmers, soon followed. Some moved southward to the valley of the Holston and the headwaters of the Cumberland and Tennessee rivers, and others spread northwest into the Ohio Valley and Kentucky basin. Some drifted down the Ohio and Mississippi rivers to join overland migrants from the southern colonies in the new province of West Florida, and thus completed a huge encirclement of the new western territory.

During the decade and a half before Independence, New England throbbed with movement. New towns were created by the founding of new settlements and the division of existing ones. By the early 1760s the number of transients drifting from town to town throughout the region multiplied dramatically, in some counties doubling and more than tripling the numbers of the previous decade. Many farmers gave up searching for opportunities within established communities and set out for distant places on the very edges of the expanded empire. Massachusetts and Connecticut colonists not only trekked to northern New England and Nova Scotia but traveled to areas as far away as the Susquehanna in Pennsylvania and the lower Mississippi. Indeed, the largest single addition to the population of West Florida came from the settlement of four hundred families from Connecticut in 1773–74. In the late 1760s the migration to the Wyoming Valley in Pennsylvania of people from Connecticut was so massive that in 1774 Connecticut annexed these Pennsylvania settlements and made them part of one of its counties. Between 1760 and 1776 some twenty thousand people from southern New England moved up the Connecticut River into New Hampshire and what would later become Vermont. In that same period migrants from Massachusetts streamed into Maine and founded 94 towns. In all, during the years between 1760 and 1776, 264 new towns were established in northern New England.

So momentous was this explosion of peoples in search of land that British and colonial authorities could scarcely comprehend what was happening. The colonists, one astonished official observed, were moving "as their avidity and restlessness incite them. They acquire no attachment to place: but wandering about seems engrafted in their nature; and it is a weakness incident to it that they should forever imagine the lands further off are still better than those upon which they are already settled." Land fever infected all levels of the society. While someone like Ezra Stiles, minister at Newport, Rhode Island, and later president of Yale, bought and sold small shares in places all over New England and in Pennsylvania and New York, more influential figures like Benjamin Franklin were concocting gargantuan speculative schemes in the vast unsettled terrain of the West.

All of this movement had far-reaching effects on American society and its place in the British empire. The fragmentation of households, churches, and communities increased, and the colonial governments lost control of mushrooming new settlements. In the backcountry, lawlessness and vagrancy became more common, and disputes over land claims and colonial boundaries increased sharply. But the most immediate effect of this rapid spread of people, and the most obvious to imperial officials in the 1760s, was the pressure the migrations placed on the Indians.

Indians.   At the beginning of the Seven Years' War the problems of the Indians in the West compelled the British crown for the first time to assume direct control of Indian affairs from the colonies. Two British Indian superintendents, one each for the northern and southern regions, now had the task of pacifying tribes of Indians who were, as one superintendent said, "the most formidable of any uncivilized body of people in the world." New England had few Indians left, but New York had 2,000 warriors, mostly fierce Senecas, remaining from the once powerful Six Nations of the Iroquois. In the Susquehanna and Ohio valleys were a variety of tribes, mostly Delawares, Shawnees, Mingos, and Hurons, who claimed about 12,000 fighting men. On the southern frontiers the Indian presence was even more forbidding. From the Carolinas to the Yazoo River were some 14,000 warriors, mainly Cherokees, Creeks, Choctaws, and Chickasaws. Altogether this native population formed an imposing barrier to British western expansion.

After French authority had been eliminated from

INDIANS

The story of Indian-white relations in North America is a tragic one. Already by the middle of the eighteenth century many of the Indian tribes had become dependent on the white man's goods, including tools, weapons, and liquor. Thus not only were the Indians losing their lands to the whites but they were inadvertently collaborating in the corruption and destruction of their culture. *Top*: "Cherokee Indians brought to London, 1730" by Alexander Cuming; *center*, Choctaw burials, (*both, Smithsonian Institution, National Anthropological Archives*); *right*, "Outewas Indian, 1759," by George Townshend (*National Portrait Gallery, London*)

Canada and Spanish authority from Florida, the Indians were no longer able to play one European power off against the other. Britain now had sole responsibility for regulating the lucrative fur trade and for maintaining peace between whites and Indians. The problems were awesome: not only were many whites prepared to use brandy and rum to achieve their aims, but they had conflicting interests. Traders competed among themselves: some favored regulation of the fur trade; most did not. But all traders wanted Indian reservations established in the West which settlers could not invade, and they drew upon the support of humanitarian groups concerned with the fate of the Indians. Land speculators, however, wanted to push back the Indians and open the West to settlement. Confused, lied to, and cheated of their land and their furs by greedy white traders and land-hungry migrants, the Indians retaliated with atrocities and raids. Some tribes attempted to form coalitions and wage full-scale war.

Thus the end of the Seven Years' War did not end violence on the frontier. From the devastating Cherokee War in 1759–61 in South Carolina to the assault on the Shawnees in 1774 by Lord Dunmore, the royal governor of Virginia, British officials repeatedly had to resort to troops to put down the Indians' resentment at white encroachments on their lands and the deceitful practices of the traders. The biggest Indian uprising of the period occurred in 1763 following the British takeover of the former French forts in the West. In just a few weeks Indians from several tribes under the leadership of an Ottawa chief named Pontiac surprised and destroyed all but three of the British posts west of the Appalachians. Before they were defeated by British troops, the angry warriors had penetrated eastward into the backcountry of Pennsylvania, Maryland, and Virginia and had killed more than two thousand colonists. No wonder then that many royal authorities in the 1760s concluded that only the presence of regular troops of the British army could maintain peace in the American borderlands of the empire.

Backcountry Disorder. The rapid growth and spread of peoples in the mid-eighteenth century affected more than white-Indian relations on the frontier.

Thousands of migrants flowed into the backcountry beyond the reach of the colonial governments. So removed from authority were the settlers that sometimes only vigilante groups were able to impose order. In South Carolina in the 1760s, backcountry people organized vigilante "Regulators" to put down roving gangs of thieves, but these illegal posses often turned raiders themselves. By the early 1770s the Green Mountain Boys of Vermont under the leadership of Ethan Allen and his brother were terrorizing all who submitted to New York's jurisdiction, and Connecticut Yankees were fighting Pennsylvanians for control of the settlements along the Susquehanna River. Sometimes out of necessity frontiersmen in these trans-Appalachian areas joined to form compacts of government for their raw societies, which often consisted of little more than "stations" or primitive palisaded forts surrounded by huts.

Everywhere in the backcountries the rapid influx of people weakened the legitimacy of existing authority. In the rapidly growing interiors of both Pennsylvania and North Carolina, settlers in the 1760s rose in arms against what they believed was exploitation by remote eastern governments. In western Pennsylvania, Scotch-Irish settlers led by the Paxton Boys rebelled against their underrepresentation in the pacifist, Quaker-dominated legislature. In 1763–64, they killed Indians who were under the government's protection, and then marched on Philadelphia. Only the diplomacy of Benjamin Franklin and the promise of a greater voice in the colonial assembly turned the rebels back. In North Carolina not only was the backcountry underrepresented in the provincial legislature but its local government was under the corrupt management of carpetbagging officials and lawyers from the east. In 1767 a group of western vigilantes, assuming the familiar title of "Regulators," erupted in violence, took over the county courts, and petitioned the North Carolina government for more equitable representation, lower taxes, and local control of their affairs. Although at the so-called battle of the Alamance in 1771 two thousand of these "Regulators" were dispersed by the North Carolina governor and his force of eastern militia, the deeply rooted fears among many Americans of the dangers of inequitable representation and remotely wielded political power

ACONOSTOTA (CUNNE SHOTE) (?–1785)
Cherokee Indian chief who repaid white treachery in
South Carolina with his own. In 1760 he led Cherokee
warriors against Carolina frontier settlements and massacred the defenders of Fort Loudoun. During the Revolution he fought for the British.   (The Thomas Gilcrease
Institute of American History & Art, Tulsa, Oklahoma)

JOSEPH BRANT (1742–1807)
This chief of the Mohawks was educated by English
Indian Superintendent Sir William Johnson, sent to
London, and presented to the Court. He fought effec-
tively on the British side during the Revolution. As an
Anglican convert he translated the New Testament and
the Prayer Book into his native tongue.

could not be so easily dispelled by royal officials.
Indeed, these Westerners were only voicing toward
their own colonial governments the same attitudes
Americans in general had about British power.

Economic Expansion.   All of these consequences
flowing from the increased numbers and movement
of people in North America were bound to heighten
Britain's interest in its colonies. But not merely demographic forces were at work reshaping British attitudes toward the colonies and transforming American
society. Equally important was the related expansion
of the Anglo-American economy that took place in
the middle decades of the eighteenth century.

By 1750 the immediate origins of what would
soon become the Industrial Revolution were already
visible in Britain. British imports, exports, and industrial production of various sorts—all the major indi-
cators of economic growth—were rapidly rising. Americans were deeply involved in this sudden economic
expansion of the mother country, and by the 1760s
were feeling its reverberating effects everywhere.

In the years after 1745 colonial trade with Great
Britain grew dramatically and became an increasingly
important segment of the English and Scottish economies. Nearly half of all English shipping was engaged in American commerce. The North American
mainland alone was absorbing 25 percent of England's

exports, and Scottish commercial involvement with the colonies was growing even faster. From 1747 to 1765 the value of colonial exports to Britain doubled, from about £700,000 to £1,500,000, while the value of colonial imports from Britain rose even faster, from about £900,000 to over £2 million. For the first time in the eighteenth century Britain's own production of foodstuffs could not meet the needs of its suddenly rising population; by 1760 Britain was importing more grain than it exported.

This increasing demand for foodstuffs—not only in Great Britain but in southern Europe and the West Indies as well—meant soaring prices for American exports. Between the 1740s and the 1760s the price of American wheat sent to the Caribbean increased nearly 60 percent, flour 54 percent, pork 48 percent. Even tobacco prices went up 34 percent in the same period. This heightened demand and rising prices for American exports enticed more and more ordinary farmers into producing for distant markets. By the 1760s remote trading centers in the hinterland such as Staunton, Virginia, and Salisbury, North Carolina, were shipping large quantities of tobacco and grain eastward along networks of roads and towns to the sea. Port cities like Baltimore, Norfolk, and Alexandria grew up almost overnight to handle this swelling traffic.

These soaring prices for agricultural exports meant rising standards of living for more and more Americans. It was not just the great planters of the South and the big merchants of the cities who were getting richer, but ordinary Americans too were now buying luxury items—what were increasingly called "conveniences" that had traditionally been purchased only by the gentry—from Irish linen and lace to matched sets of Wedgwood dishes.

Although nineteen out of twenty Americans were still engaged in agriculture, the rising levels of taste and consumption drew more colonists into manufacturing, at first mostly crude textiles and shoes. Transportation and communications rapidly improved as roads were built and regular schedules were established for stage coaches and packet boats. In the 1750s the post office under the leadership of Benjamin Franklin, the British deputy postmaster general, cre-

ated weekly mails between Philadelphia and Boston and cut the delivery time in half, from six to three weeks. The growing population, better roads, more reliable information about markets, and the greater variety of towns, all encouraged domestic manufacturing for regional and intercolonial markets. By 1768 colonial manufacturers were supplying Pennsylvania with eight thousand pairs of shoes a year. Areas of eastern Massachusetts were becoming more involved in manufacturing: in 1767 the town of Haverhill, with fewer than three hundred residents, had forty-four workshops and nineteen mills. By this date many colonial artisans and would-be manufacturers were more than eager to support associations to boycott English imports.

But most colonists still preferred British goods. Since by the mid-1760s Americans were importing from Britain about £500,000 worth of goods more than they were exporting to the mother country, the trade deficit with Britain that had existed earlier in the century continued to vex the colonists. Part of this deficit in the colonists' balance of payments with Britain was made up by the profits of shipping, by British wartime expenditures, and by increased sales to Europe and the West Indies. But a large part was also made up by liberal extensions to the colonists of English and Scottish credit. By 1760 colonial debts to Britain amounted to £2 million; by 1772 they had jumped to over £4 million. After 1750 a growing proportion of this debt was owed by colonists who earlier had been excluded from direct dealings with British merchants. Small tobacco farmers in the Chesapeake gained immediate access to British credit and markets through the spread of Scottish factors or stores in the hinterlands of Virginia and Maryland. By 1760 it was not unusual for as many as 150 petty traders in a single port to be doing business with a London merchant house.

These demographic and economic forces had a corrosive effect on the traditional structure of colonial society. The ties of kinship and patronage that held people together, never strong in America to begin with, were now further weakened. Even in Virginia, one of the most stable of the colonies, the leading gentry planters found their authority challenged by

"ATTEMPT TO LAND A BISHOP IN AMERICA"

By 1768 proposals for establishing an Anglican bishop in America had become identified with British efforts to deprive the colonists of their liberties.

small farmers cut loose from older dependent economic relationships. During the middle decades of the eighteenth century, ordinary people of Virginia left the established Church of England in growing numbers and formed new evangelical religious communities that rejected the high style and luxury of the dominant Anglican gentry. Within a few years,

succeeding waves of enthusiastic New Light Presbyterians, Separate Baptists, and finally Methodists swept up new converts from among the common farmers of the Chesapeake. Between 1769 and 1774 the number of Baptist churches in Virginia increased from seven to fifty-four.

The Virginia gentry blamed this growth of religious dissent on the long-existing laxity of the Anglican clergy, who in turn accused the lay vestries of Anglican planters of not supporting them. Amid these mutual recriminations, the Virginia House of Burgesses passed acts in 1755 and 1758 that fixed the standard of value of tobacco used to meet debts and public obligations at two pence a pound. Since tobacco prices were rising rapidly, this legislation, known as the "Two Penny Acts," penalized creditors and those public officials like the clergy who were used to being paid in tobacco. British merchants and the Virginia clerical establishment protested and were able to get the king's Privy Council to invalidate the act of 1758 passed by the House of Burgesses. In 1763 in one of the Virginia clergy's legal suits for recovery of wages lost by the Two Penny Act, known as the Parsons' Cause, a rising young lawyer, Patrick Henry, first made his reputation. Henry argued that, because he had disallowed the act, the king "from being the father of his people [has] degenerated into a Tyrant, and forfeits all rights to his subjects' obedience." In similar ways in all the colonies authority, both local and imperial, was being placed under increased pressure.

It is doubtful whether anyone anywhere in the mid-eighteenth century knew how to control these powerful social and economic forces at work in the Anglo-American world. Certainly the flimsy administrative arrangement that governed the British empire was unable to manage this dynamic world. By mid-century many British officials realized that some sort of overhaul of this increasingly important empire was needed. But few understood the explosive energy and the sensitive nature of the people they were tampering with. The empire, Benjamin Franklin warned, was like a fragile Chinese vase that required delicate handling indeed.

The Reorganization of the Empire

After 1748 imperial reforms of one sort or another were in the air. The eye-opening experience of fighting the Seven Years' War amid colonial evasion and corruption of the navigation laws had provoked Pitt and other royal officials into strenuous but piecemeal reforms of the imperial system. But these beginnings might have been stifled, as others had been, if it had not been for the enormous problems created by the Peace of Paris in 1763.

The most immediate of these problems was the disposition of the new territory acquired from France and Spain. New governments had to be organized; the Indian trade had to be regulated; land claims had to be sorted out; and something had to be done to keep the conflicts between land-hungry white settlers and the restless Indians from exploding into open warfare.

Even more unsettling was the huge expense confronting the British government. By 1763 the war debt totaled £137 million; its annual interest alone was £5 million, a huge figure when compared with an ordinary yearly British peacetime budget of only £8 million. There was, moreover, little prospect of military costs declining. Since the new acquisitions were virtually uninhabited by Englishmen, the government could not rely on its traditional system of local defense and police. Lord Jeffrey Amherst, commander in chief in North America, estimated that he would need ten thousand troops to maintain order among the French and Indians and to deal with squatters, smugglers, and bandits. Thus at the outset of the 1760s the British government made a crucial decision—a decision that no subsequent administration ever abandoned—to maintain a standing army in America. This peacetime army was more than double the size of the army that had existed in the colonies before the Seven Years' War, and the costs of maintaining it quickly climbed to well over £400,000 a year.

Where was the money to come from? The landed gentry in England felt pressed to the wall by taxes; a new English cider tax of 1763 actually required troops to enforce it. Under the circumstances—with the tales of American prosperity brought back by returning British troops, with the benefits of the new land and the peace apparently accruing to the colonists—it seemed reasonable to the British government to seek new sources of revenue in the colonies and to make the navigation system more efficient in ways that royal officials had long advocated. A half century of "salutary neglect" had to come to an end.

George III and British Politics. Disruptions within the delicate balance of the empire were therefore inevitable. But the accession in 1760 of a new monarch, the young and impetuous George III, aggravated the changing Anglo-American relations. George III was only twenty-two, shy and inexperienced in politics, but he was stubbornly determined to rule personally in a manner distinctly different from that of the earlier Hanoverian monarchs. Influenced by his inept Scottish tutor and "dearest friend," Lord Bute, George aimed to purify English public life of its corruptions and factionalism and to substitute duty to crown and country for party intrigue. The results of George's good intentions were the greatest and most bewildering fluctuations suffered by English politics in a half-century—all at the very moment the long-postponed reforms of the empire were to take place.

Historians no longer depict George III as a "tyrant" seeking to undermine the English constitution by choosing his own ministers against the wishes of Parliament. But there can be little doubt that men of the time felt that George III, whether he intended to or not, was violating the political conventions of the day. When he chose Lord Bute, his Scottish favorite who had little political strength in Parliament, to head his government and excluded such Whig ministers as William Pitt and the Duke of Newcastle, who did command political support in Parliament, the new king may not have been acting unconstitutionally, but he certainly was acting against customary political realities. Bute's retirement in 1763 did little to ease the opposition's apprehensions that the king was seeking the advice of Tory favorites "behind

GEORGE III (1783–1820)
George III had one of the longest reigns in English history. He was sincere but slow-witted, and suffered from a hereditary disease that eventually caused him spells of madness. The artist, Benjamin West, was an American who became in 1772 historical painter to the king and later president of the Royal Academy. (*The Cleveland Museum of Art, Gift of Mr. and Mrs. Lawrence S. Robbins.*)

NORTH (1732–1792)
North was the first political leader George III found who could organize a stable government. He had the political skills to manage the House of Commons but he had no knowledge of waging war. Despite his repeated talk of resigning, he lasted as prime minister from 1770 to 1782. (*Library of Congress.*)

the curtain" and attempting to impose decisions upon the leading political groups in Parliament rather than governing through them. By diligently attempting to shoulder his constitutional responsibility for governing in his own stubborn, peculiar way, George III helped to increase the political confusion of the 1760s.

A decade of short-lived ministries in the 1760s contrasted sharply with the stable and long-lasting Whig governments of the previous generation. It almost seemed as if the headstrong king trusted no one who had the support of Parliament. After Pitt and Newcastle had been dismissed, and Bute had failed, the king in 1763 turned to George Grenville, Bute's protégé, because he could find no one else acceptable to him to be his chief minister. Although Grenville was responsible for the first wave of colonial reforms, his resignation in 1765 resulted from a personal quarrel with the king and had nothing to do with colonial policy. Next, the Whigs connected with the Marquess of Rockingham, for whom Edmund Burke was spokesman, formed a government; but this Whig coalition never had the confidence of the king, and lasted scarcely a year. In 1766 George at last called upon the aging Pitt, now Lord Chatham, to head the government, but Chatham's illness (gout in the head, critics said) and the bewildering parliamentary factionalism of the late 1760s turned the ministry into a hodgepodge, which Chatham scarcely ruled at all.

By 1767 no one seemed to be in charge. Ministers shuffled in and out of offices, exchanging positions and following their own inclinations even against the wishes of their colleagues. Amid this confusion only Charles Townsend as chancellor of the exchequer gave any direction to colonial policy, and he died in 1767. Not until the appointment of Lord North as prime minister in 1770 did George find a politician whom he trusted and who also had the support of Parliament.

Thus in 1763 the British government was faced with the need to overhaul its empire and gain revenue from its colonies at the very time when the English political situation was more chaotic and confused than it had been since the early decades of the eighteenth century. No wonder it took only a bit more than a decade for the whole shaky imperial structure to come crashing down.

The Proclamation of 1763 and the West.   The government began its reform of the newly enlarged empire by issuing the Proclamation of 1763. This crown Proclamation created three new royal governments—East and West Florida and Quebec—and enlarged the province of Nova Scotia. It turned the vast trans-Appalachian area into an Indian reservation, and prohibited all private individuals from purchasing Indian lands. The aim was to maintain peace in the West and to channel the migration of peoples northward and southward into the new colonies. There, it was felt, the settlers would be in closer touch with both the mother country and the mercantile system and more useful as buffers against the Spanish and the remaining French.

But circumstances undid these royal blueprints. Not only were there bewildering shifts of the ministers in charge of the new policy, but news of Pontiac's Indian rebellion in the Ohio Valley in 1763 forced the government to rush its program into effect. The demarcation line along the Appalachians that closed the West to white settlers was hastily and crudely drawn, and some colonists suddenly found themselves living in the Indian reservation. The new trading regulations and sites were widely ignored and created more chaos in the Indian trade than had existed earlier. So confusing was the situation in the West that the British government could never convince the various contending interests that the Proclamation was anything more than, in George Washington's words, "a temporary expedient to quiet the minds of the Indians." The unsteady British governments, beset by hosts of speculators and lobbyists, were compelled to negotiate a series of Indian treaties shifting the line of settlement westward. But each modification only whetted the appetites of the land speculators and led to some of the most grandiose land schemes in modern history. The climax of this speculative frenzy was reached in 1769 when a huge conglomerate, the Grand Ohio Company, whose membership involved prominent figures on both sides of the Atlantic, petitioned the crown for the rights to millions of acres in the Ohio Valley.

The British government finally tried to steady its dizzy western policy with parliamentary help in the Quebec Act of 1774. This act transferred the land and the control of the Indian trade in the huge area between the Ohio and Mississippi rivers to the province of Quebec and allowed its French inhabitants French law and Roman Catholicism. As enlightened as this act was toward the French Canadians, it managed to anger all American interests—speculators, settlers, and traders alike. This arbitrary alteration of provincial boundaries threatened the security of all colonial boundaries and frightened American Protestants into believing that the British government was trying to erect a hostile popish province in the North and West.

The Sugar and Stamp Acts.   The new colonial trade policies were more coherent than Britain's western policy, but no less provocative. The Plantation Act, or Sugar Act, of 1764 was clearly a major successor to the great navigation acts of the late seventeenth century. It prescribed a series of regulations designed to tighten the navigation system and in particular to curb the colonists' smuggling and corruption. Absentee customs officials were ordered to their posts and given greater authority and protection. The jurisdiction of the vice-admiralty courts in customs cases was broadened. The navy was granted greater power in inspecting American ships. The use of writs of assistance (or search warrants) was enlarged. To the earlier list of enumerated colonial products like tobacco and sugar that had to be exported directly to Britain were added skins, iron, timber, and others.

A TEST IMPRESSION OF ONE OF THE STAMPS THE BRITISH GOVERNMENT PLANNED TO USE IN THE COLONIES IN 1765.

These British reforms, which threatened to upset the delicately poised patterns of trade built up in the previous generations, could be regarded as part of Britain's traditional authority over colonial commerce. But the next step in Britain's new imperial program could not. Grenville's ministry, convinced that the customs reforms could not bring in the needed revenue, was determined to try a decidedly different method of getting at American wealth. In March 1765 Parliament by an overwhelming majority passed the Stamp Act, which levied a tax (to be paid, like all duties, in British sterling, not in colonial paper money) on legal documents, almanacs, newspapers, and nearly every form of paper used in the colonies. Although stamp duties had been used in England since 1694 and by several colonies in the 1750s, such a parliamentary tax, directly touching the everyday affairs of Americans, exposed the nature of political authority within the empire in a way no other issue in the eighteenth century ever had.

American Resistance

The atmosphere in the colonies could not have been less receptive to these initial efforts by the British government to reorganize the empire. In the early 1760s, with the curtailing of wartime spending, the commercial boom collapsed. Between 1760 and 1764 American markets were glutted with unsold goods at the same time that bumper tobacco crops (the result, in part, of new independent producers) drove tobacco prices down by 75 percent. Such developments threatened the entire credit structure, from London and Scottish merchant houses to small farmers and shopkeepers in the colonies. As a result, business failures and bankruptcies proliferated. By the middle 1760s the colonial market economy was in confusion, beset by an adverse balance of trade, severe restrictions on credit, low prices, and a shortage of currency. Aggravating the collapse was the large number of small merchants who had been enticed into participating in the market during the previous decade or so.

And finally the requirements of American shippers for posting bonds and obtaining certificates of clearance were so greatly increased that nearly all colonial merchants, even those involved only in the coastwise trade, found themselves enmeshed in a bureaucratic web of bonds, certificates, and regulations.

To these frustrating rigidities now built into the navigation system were added new customs duties, which raised the expenses of American importers in order to increase British revenue. The Sugar Act imposed duties on foreign cloth, sugar, indigo, coffee, and wine imported into the colonies and eliminated the refunds of duties hitherto made in England on foreign goods reexported to America. Most important, the Sugar Act reduced the supposedly prohibitory duty of sixpence a gallon on foreign molasses, set by the Molasses Act of 1733, to threepence a gallon; in 1766 the duty was further reduced to one penny a gallon on all molasses. The government assumed that with the smaller duty it would be cheaper for American merchants to import molasses legally than to resort to smuggling and bribery. The lower duty would therefore earn money for the crown.

It is not surprising that the victims of the collapse sought to blame their shifting fortunes on the distant government in England. In fact the British government's response to the financial crisis could not have been more clumsy and provocative. In 1764 Parliament passed a new Currency Act, which extended to all the colonies the 1751 prohibition against New England's issuing of paper money as legal tender. This sweeping and simple-minded resolution of a complicated problem was only one of the many ways in which British power in these years brought to the surface the latent antagonisms between the colonies and the mother country.

The Sugar Act, coinciding with this postwar depression, created particularly severe problems for all those who depended on trade with the French and Spanish West Indies. Paying the duty on foreign molasses, the colonists feared, would make it too expensive to import. Yet without foreign sugar products the northern rum industry would be ruined, the export trade in fish and foodstuffs to the Caribbean would be curtailed, and America's ability to pay indirectly for English imports would be endangered. These fears, together with hostility to all the new trade regulations accompanying the Sugar Act, stirred up opposition and boycotts by merchants in the northern ports and provoked the first deliberately organized intercolonial protest. The assemblies of eight colonies drew up and endorsed formal petitions pleading economic injury from the Sugar Act and sent them to royal authorities in England.

Britain's next step, however, Grenville's stamp tax of 1765, excited not a protest, but a firestorm that swept through the colonies with a force that amazed everyone. This parliamentary tax, however fiscally justifiable it may have been, posed such a distinct threat to the jurisdictions of the colonial legislatures and the liberties of the colonists that Americans could no longer contain their opposition within the traditional channels of remonstrance and lobbying.

When word reached America that Parliament had passed the Stamp Act without even considering any colonial petitions against it, the colonists reacted angrily. Merchants in the principal ports formed protest associations and pledged to stop importing British goods in order to bring economic pressure on the British government. Newspapers and pamphlets, the number and like of which had never appeared in America before, carried articles that seethed with resentment against what one New Yorker called "these designing parricides" who had "invited despotism to cross the ocean, and fix her abode in this once happy land." At hastily convened meetings of towns, counties, and legislative assemblies, the colonists' anger boiled over in fiery declarations.

This torrent of angry words could not help but bring the constitutional relationship between Britain and her colonies into question.* In the spring of 1765 the Virginia House of Burgesses adopted a series of resolves denouncing parliamentary taxation and asserting the colonists' right to be taxed only by their elected representatives. These resolves were introduced by Patrick Henry, who at age twenty-nine had just been elected to the legislature. Henry had already made a name for himself in a county court house two years earlier during the Parsons' Cause. Now in the more august setting of the House of Burgesses Henry dared to repeat his earlier challenge to crown authority by declaring that, as Caesar had his Brutus, and Charles I his Cromwell, so some American would undoubtedly stand up for his country. He was stopped by the Speaker for suggesting treason, and some of his resolves, including one proclaiming the right of Virginians to disobey any law not enacted by the Virginia assembly, were too inflammatory to be accepted by the legislature. Nevertheless, colonial newspapers printed them all as though they had been endorsed by the Virginia assembly and convinced many that Virginians had virtually asserted their legislative independence from Great Britain.

Such boldness was contagious. The Rhode Island assembly declared the Stamp Act "unconstitutional" and authorized the colony's officials to ignore it. In

*For a full discussion of the constitutional issues, see Chapter 8, pp. 203–11.

PATRICK HENRY (1736–1799)
Unlike most of the other Revolutionary leaders, Henry left almost no writings. What he did leave were vivid memories of his impassioned oratory. He introduced to the political world of the Virginia gentry the fervor and style of an evangelical preacher. (*Library of Congress*)

October 1765 thirty-seven delegates from nine colonies met in New York in the Stamp Act Congress and drew up a set of formal declarations and petitions denying Parliament's right to tax them. But remarkable as this display of colonial unity was, the Stamp Act Congress, with its opening acknowledgment of "all due Subordination to that August Body the Parliament of Great Britain," could not fully express American hostility.

Ultimately it was the eruption of violence designed to prevent the stamps from being distributed that nullified the Stamp Act in America. On August 14, 1765, a crowd destroyed the office and attacked the home of Andrew Oliver, the stamp distributor for Massachusetts. The next day Oliver promised not to enforce the Stamp Act. Twelve days later a mob gutted the home of the person who seemed to be responsible for defending the Stamp Act in Massachusetts, Oliver's brother-in-law, Lieutenant Gover-

nor Thomas Hutchinson. As news of the rioting spread to other colonies, similar violence and threats of violence spread with it. From Newport, Rhode Island, to Charleston, South Carolina, local groups organized for resistance. In many places fire and artillery companies, artisan associations, and other fraternal bodies formed the basis for these emerging local organizations, which commonly called themselves "Sons of Liberty." Led mostly by members of the middling ranks—shopkeepers, printers, master mechanics, small merchants—these Sons of Liberty burned effigies of royal officials, forced stamp agents to resign, compelled businessmen and judges to carry on without stamps, developed an intercolonial network of correspondence, and generally enforced nonimportation and managed antistamp activities throughout the colonies.

British Reactions.   In England, with the Rockingham Whigs now in charge of the ministry, the British government was prepared to retreat. Not only were the Whigs eager to disavow Grenville's policies, but they had close connections with British merchants hurt by American economic boycotts. In February 1766 Parliament repealed the Stamp Act. Yet British anger over the rioting in America and the constitutional issue raised by colonial protests forced the Rockingham Whigs to couple the repeal with a Declaratory Act stating that Parliament had the right to legislate for the colonies "in all cases whatsoever."

Despite the British government's attempt to offset its repeal of the Stamp Act by this declaration of parliamentary supremacy, after 1765 the imperial relationship and American respect for British authority—indeed, for all authority—would never again be the same. The crisis over the Stamp Act aroused and unified Americans as no previous political event ever had. It stimulated bold political and constitutional writings throughout the colonies, deepened political consciousness and participation, and produced new forms of organized popular resistance. By compelling the resignation of stamp agents and obedience to popular measures, the people, through "their riotous meetings," as Governor Horatio Sharpe of Maryland observed in 1765, "begin to think they

OPPOSITION TO THE STAMP ACT

In Philadelphia, newspaper publisher William Bradford announced the suspension of publication of his *Pennsylvania Journal,* while in Massachusetts a local stamp agent was hung in effigy to protest the new tax. (*Historical Society of Pennsylvania; The Metropolitan Museum of Art, Bequest of Charles Allen Munn, 1924*)

can by the same way of proceeding accomplish anything their leaders may tell them they ought to do."

The British government could not satisfy with mere declarations its continuing need for more revenue. Since the colonists evidently would not stomach "direct" and "internal" taxes like the stamp tax, British officials concluded that the government would have to gather revenue through the more traditional "indirect" and "external" customs duties. After all, the colonists as a result of the Sugar Act were already paying duties on molasses, wine, and several other inported products. Consequently, in 1767 Parliament led by Chancellor of the Exchequer Charles Townshend imposed new levies on glass, paint, paper, and tea imported into the colonies. Although all the new customs duties, particularly the lowered molasses

duty of 1766, began bringing in an average yearly revenue of £45,000—in contrast to only £2,000 a year collected before 1764—the yearly sums raised were scarcely a tenth of the annual cost of maintaining the army in America.

Convinced that something more drastic had to be done, the British government reorganized the executive authority of the empire. In 1767–68 the government created an American Board of Customs, located in Boston and reporting directly to the Treasury, and erected three new superior vice-admiralty courts at Boston, Philadelphia, and Charleston, besides the one already at Halifax. To cap the entire structure, in belated recognition of the importance of the colonies, it established a new secretaryship of state exclusively responsible for American affairs. At the same time, for the sake of economy, the government decided to pull back much of the army from its costly deployment in the West and to close many of the remote posts. The army was now to be stationed in the coastal cities, where, according to the new parliamentary Quartering Act of 1765, the colonists would be responsible for its housing and supply. Not only did this withdrawal of the troops eastward away from the French and Indians contribute to the chaos in the western territory, but concentrating a standing army in peacetime amid a civilian population blurred the original mission of the army in America and heightened the colonists' fears of British intentions.

By 1768 there was a new determination among royal officials to put down the unruly forces that seemed to be loose. Amid the ministerial squabbling of the late 1760s some officials were suggesting that British troops be used against American rioters. Revenue from the Townshend duties was earmarked for the salaries of royal officials in the colonies so that they would be independent of the colonial legislatures. The colonial governors were instructed to maintain tighter control of the assemblies and not to agree to acts that increased popular representation in the assemblies or the length of time the legislatures sat. Some royal officials toyed with more elaborate plans for remodeling the colonial governments, proposing that the Massachusetts charter be revoked and that the royal councils be strengthened. Some even suggested introducing a titled nobility into America to sit in the colonial upper houses.

The Townshend Crisis in America. In the atmosphere of the late 1760s, these measures and proposals were not simply provocative; they were explosive. After the Stamp Act crisis, American sensitivities to all forms of English taxation were thoroughly aroused. With the passage of the Townshend duties, the earlier pattern of resistance reappeared and expanded. Pam-

TRADE BETWEEN THE COLONIES AND BRITAIN, 1763–1776

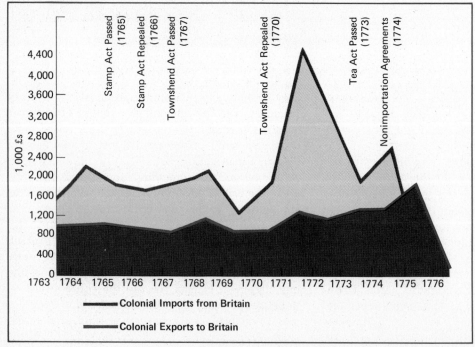

phleteers and newspaper writers again leapt to the defense of American liberties. The cultivated Philadelphia lawyer John Dickinson, in his *Letters from a Farmer in Pennsylvania*, the most popular pamphlet of the 1760s, disavowed all parliamentary taxation, whether "internal" or "external," and called for reviving the nonimportation agreements that had been so effective in the resistance to the Stamp Act. Following Boston's lead in March 1768, merchants in the colonial ports again formed associations to boycott British goods. Despite much jostling among different groups of merchants and jealousy between the ports, by 1769–70 these nonimportation agreements had cut British sales to the northern colonies by nearly two-thirds. The wearing of homespun cloth was encouraged, and in New England villages "Daughters of Liberty" held spinning bees. By now more Americans than ever were involved in the resistance movement. Extralegal groups and committees, usually but not always restrained by popular leaders, emerged to inspect tobacco in Maryland, punish importers in Philadelphia, mob a publisher in Boston, or harass customs officials in New York.

Nowhere were events more spectacular than in Massachusetts. There the situation was so inflammatory that every move triggered a string of explosions that widened the gap between the colonists and royal authority. Forty-six-year-old Samuel Adams, with his puritanical zeal, organizational skill, and abiding hatred of crown authority, soon became a dominant political figure. It was later said that 1768 was the year Adams decided on independence for America. Given the events in Massachusetts during that year, it is easy to see why.

In February 1768 the Massachusetts House of Representatives issued a "Circular Letter" to the other colonial legislatures denouncing the Townshend duties as unconstitutional violations of the principle of no taxation without representation. Lord Hillsborough, the secretary of state of the newly created American Department and a hardliner on controlling the colonies, ordered the Massachusetts House to rescind its Circular Letter. When the House defied this order by a majority of 92 to 17 (thereby enshrining the number "92" in patriot rituals), Gov-

SAMUEL ADAMS, BY JOHN SINGLETON COPLEY
Of all the American leaders, Sam Adams came closest to being a professional revolutionary, selflessly devoted to the cause. As "one of Plutarch's men," Adams took seriously the spartan severity of classical republicanism. (*Courtesy, Museum of Fine Arts, Boston*)

ernor Francis Bernard dissolved the Massachusetts assembly. With this legal means for redressing grievances silenced, mobs and other unauthorized groups in the colony erupted. Boston, which was rapidly becoming a symbol of colonial resistance, ordered its inhabitants to arm and called for an extralegal convention of town delegates. Beset by mobs, customs officials in Boston found it impossible to enforce the navigation regulations, and they pleaded for military help. When a British warship arrived at Boston in June 1768, customs officials promptly seized John Hancock's ship *Liberty* for violating the trade

"THE BOSTON MASSACRE" ENGRAVED BY PAUL REVERE

This print was scarcely an accurate depiction of the "Massacre." It aimed for rhetorical and emotional effect and became perhaps the most famous piece of antimilitary propaganda in American history. (*Library of Congress*)

acts. Since Hancock and his great wealth were prominently associated with the resistance movement, the seizure was intended to be an object lesson in royal authority. Its effect, however, was to set off one of the fiercest riots in Boston's history.

Hillsborough, believing virtual anarchy existed in Massachusetts, dispatched two regiments of troops from Ireland. They began arriving in Boston on October 1, 1768, and their appearance marked a crucial turning point in the escalating controversy: for the first time the British government had sent a substantial number of soldiers to enforce British authority in the colonies. By 1769 there were nearly four thousand armed redcoats in the crowded seaport of fifteen thousand inhabitants. Since the colonists shared traditional English fears of standing armies, relations between townspeople and soldiers deteriorated. On March 5, 1770, British troops fired upon a threatening crowd and killed five civilians. The "Boston Massacre," especially as it was depicted in Paul Revere's engraving, aroused American passions and inspired some of the most sensational rhetoric heard in the Revolutionary era.

This resort to troops to quell disorder was the ultimate symptom of the ineffectiveness of the British government's authority, and many Britishers knew it. Such coercion, it was argued in Parliament and in the administration itself, only destroyed the goodwill on which the colonists' relation to the mother country must ultimately rest. Indeed, throughout the escalation of events in the 1760s many of the ministers remained confused and uncertain. "There is the most urgent reason to do what is right, and immediately," wrote Lord Barrington, secretary at war, to Governor Bernard in 1767, "but what is that right and who is to do it?" English officials advanced and retreated, cajoled and threatened in ever-more desperate efforts to enforce British authority without aggravating the colonists' hostility. In the winter of 1767–68 the British responded to the disorder in Massachusetts with a series of parliamentary resolutions and addresses to the king, condemning Massachusetts' denial of parliamentary supremacy and threatening to bring the colonial offenders to England for trial. Yet strong minority opposition in the House of Commons and the ministry's unwillingness to precipitate further crises made these resolutions empty gestures. The government was content now to wage only what one Englishman called "a paper war with the colonies."

By the end of the 1760s British plans for reorganizing the empire were in shambles. Colonial legislatures and royal governors were at loggerheads; Britain's authority was denounced daily in print; and mobs were becoming increasingly common in the countryside as well as in city streets. Customs officials under continuous intimidation quarreled with merchants, naval officers, and royal governors.

The customs officials' entanglement in local politics made efficient or even-handed enforcement of the trade acts impossible. What enforcement there was thus appeared arbitrary and discriminatory, and drove many merchants, like the wealthy South Carolinian Henry Laurens, who had earlier been contemptuous of the Sons of Liberty, into bitter opposition.

The financial returns to the British government from the customs reforms seemed in no way commensurate with the costs. By 1770 less than £21,000 had been collected from the Townshend duties, while the loss to British business from American nonimportation movements during the previous year was put at £700,000. It was therefore not surprising that the British government now abandoned the hope of securing revenue from the duties and labeled the Townshend program, in Lord Hillsborough's words, "contrary to the true principles of commerce." In 1770, after years of ministerial chaos, reorganization of the king's government under Lord North prepared the way for repeal of the Townshend duties. Only the duty on tea was retained, in Lord North's words, "as a mark of the supremacy of Parliament, and an efficient declaration of their right to govern the colonies."

Yet the stabilization of English politics with the formation of North's ministry and the repeal of the Townshend duties could scarcely undo what had already been done. Whatever ties of affection had earlier existed between the colonists and Great Britain were fast being destroyed by irritation and suspicion. Many Americans were coming to believe that their interests and their hopes, their rights and their liberties, were threatened by British power. Although politicians on both sides of the Atlantic were by the early 1770s calling for a return to the situation before 1763, going back was clearly no longer possible.

For two years there was a superficial tranquility. Then the struggle began again. In 1772 Rhode Islanders, angry at the imperious enforcement of the navigation acts, boarded the British naval schooner *Gaspée*, sank it in Narragansett Bay, and wounded its captain. A royal commission, empowered to send all suspects to England for trial, was dispatched from England to inquire into the sinking. This authority seemed to fulfill earlier British threats to bypass regular judicial procedures, and it provoked Virginia into calling for the creation of legislative committees of correspondence, to which five assemblies responded.

Massachusetts towns, under Boston's and particularly Samuel Adams's leadership, had already begun organizing committees of correspondence. In the fall of 1772 the town of Boston published an inflammatory document, *The Votes and Proceedings* of its town meeting, which listed all the British violations of American rights. These included taxing and legislating for the colonists without their consent; introducing standing armies in peacetime; extending the powers of vice-admiralty courts, which used no jury trials; restricting colonial manufacturing; and threatening to create an Anglican episcopate in America. The publication was sent to the 260 towns of Massachusetts, and more than half responded positively in the greatest outpouring of common local opinion the resistance movement had yet seen. By the end of 1773 independence was being discussed freely in colonial newspapers. Since the North government was determined to uphold the sovereignty of Parliament, an eventual confrontation seemed unavoidable.

The Climax: The Tea Act and Coercive Acts.

Parliament provided the occasion in 1773 by granting the East India Company the exclusive privilege of selling tea in America. Although the North government intended this Tea Act only to be a means of saving the East India Company from bankruptcy, it set off the final series of explosions. Not only did the act allow colonial radicals to draw attention once again to the unconstitutionality of the existing tax on tea, but it also permitted the company to grant monopolies of selling tea to particular merchants in the colonies, thus angering those traders who were excluded. An alarm was spread throughout the colonies. In several ports ships were prevented from landing the company's tea. In Boston, when that

happened, Governor Thomas Hutchinson, whose mercantile family was one of those consigned a right to sell tea, refused to allow the ships carrying tea to leave without unloading their cargo. In response, on December 16, 1773, a group of patriots disguised as Indians dumped about £10,000 worth of tea into Boston harbor. "This is the most magnificent movement of all, " exulted John Adams, an aspiring young lawyer from Braintree, Massachusetts. "This destruction of the tea is so bold, so daring, so firm, intrepid and inflexible, and it must have so important consequences, and so lasting, that I can't but consider it an epocha in history."

Adams was right. To the British the Boston Tea Party was the ultimate outrage. Angry officials and much of the political nation of Great Britain clamored for a retribution that would squarely confront America with the issue of Parliament's right to legislate for the colonies. "We are now to establish our authority," Lord North told the House of Commons, "or give it up entirely." In 1774 Parliament passed a succession of laws that came to be known as the Coercive Acts. The first closed the port of Boston until the destroyed tea was paid for. The second altered the Massachusetts charter and reorganized the government: the Council was made appointive, town meetings were restricted, and the governor's power of appointing judges and sheriffs was strengthened. The third allowed royal officials charged with capital offenses in the colonies to be tried in England or another colony to avoid a hostile jury. The fourth gave the governor power to requisition private buildings instead of using barracks for the quartering of troops. At the same time, Thomas Gage, commander in chief of the British army in America, was made governor of the colony of Massachusetts.

The First Continental Congress.

The Coercive Acts provoked open rebellion in America. Whatever royal authority was left in the colonies dissolved. In many areas local communities, with a freedom they had not had since the seventeenth century, attempted to put together new popular governments from the bottom up. Mass meetings that sometimes attracted thousands of aroused colonists endorsed resolutions and called for new political organizations. Committees of different names and sizes—committees of safety, of inspection, of merchants, of mechanics, of Fifty-One, of Nineteen, of Forty-Three—vied with each other for political control. In the various colonies royal government was displaced in different ways, depending on how extensive and personal previous royal authority had been. In Massachusetts, where royal authority had reached into the villages and towns through appointments of justices of the peace, the displacement was greater than in Virginia, where royal influence had scarcely touched the planters' oligarchic control of the counties. But everywhere there was a fundamental transfer of authority that opened new opportunities for new men to assert themselves.

By the end of 1774 in many of the colonies local associations were controlling and regulating various aspects of American life. Committees overawed voters, directed appointments, organized the militia, managed trade, intervened between creditors and debtors, levied taxes, issued licenses, and supervised the courts or closed them. Royal governors stood by in helpless amazement as new informal governments gradually grew up around them. These new governments ranged from town and county committees and newly created provincial congresses (which often duplicated but sometimes greatly enlarged the former assemblies) to a general congress of the colonies—the First Continental Congress—which convened in Philadelphia in September 1774.

In all, fifty-five delegates from twelve colonies (all except Georgia) participated in the First Continental Congress. Some colonists, and even some royal officials, hoped that this Congress might work to reestablish imperial authority. Those who were eager to break the bond with Great Britain, however, won the first round. Led by the cousins Samuel and John Adams from Massachusetts, and by Patrick Henry and Richard Henry Lee from Virginia, the Congress endorsed the inflammatory Resolves of Suffolk County, Massachusetts, which recommended outright resistance to the Coercive Acts. But Congress was not yet ready for independence. It came very close—failing by the vote of a single colony—to considering further and perhaps adopting a plan of union between Britain and the colonies proposed by Joseph Galloway, leader of the Pennsylvania assembly and spokesman for the conservative congressional delegates from the middle colonies. Galloway's plan was radical enough as it was; it envisioned a grand colonial council along the lines earlier proposed by the Albany Congress of 1754. Enactments by either the American grand council or the British Parliament were to be subject to mutual review and approval.

By 1774, however, too many colonists had determined that Parliament had no more right to make laws for them than it did to tax them. The Congress in its Declaration and Resolves of October 14, 1774, said as much, conceding that the colonists were willing to abide by parliamentary regulation of their external trade, but only "from the necessity of the case." By this date it was unlikely, even if the Congress had adopted Galloway's plan, that it could have reversed the transfer of authority that was taking place in the colonies. In the end, the Continental Congress simply recognized the new local authorities in American politics and gave them its blessing by adopting the Continental Association. This continentwide organization put into effect the nonimportation, nonconsumption, and nonexportation of British goods that the Congress had agreed on. Committees in all the counties, cities, and towns were now ordered by the Congress "attentively to observe the conduct of all persons," to condemn publicly all violators as "enemies of American liberty," and to "break off all dealings" with them.

With the new sanction of the Congress expressed in this Association, the local committees, speaking in the name of "the body of the people," proceeded with the political transformation taking place. Groups of men, from a few dozen to several thousand, marched through villages and city streets searching out enemies of the people. Such suspected enemies were often forced to recant unfriendly words or designs against the public, to sign confessions of guilt and penitence, and to swear new oaths of friendship to the people. In all the colonies there were signs of an emerging new political order.

WOODEN FIGURE OF "VIRTUE"
CARVED BY SIMEON SKILLIN (C. 1790)

With the creation of the United States, republican Americans replaced the image of the Indian maiden with a classical goddess, often depicted bearing a liberty cap, which since antiquity had been a symbol of men newly freed from slavery. (*Yale University Art Gallery. The Mabel Brady Garvan Collection*)

The Popularization of Politics

These remarkable political changes were not simply the product of the colonists' resistance to British imperial reform. Britain's attempts to reorganize its empire took place not in a vacuum but in complicated, highly charged situations existing in each colony. In some cases these local political conditions had as much to do with the escalation of the controversy between the colonies and the mother country as did the steps taken by the British government three thousand miles away. Everywhere in the 1760s there were colonial gentry eager to exploit popular resentment against the British reforms for local political advantage with little or no appreciation of the ultimate consequence of their actions.

Thus in New York, for example, political factions led by the well-to-do families of Livingstons and DeLanceys vied with each other in whipping up opposition to the imperial legislation, in seeking the support of extralegal popular groups like the Sons of Liberty, and in generally expanding the rights and the participation of the people in politics. They did this not with the aim of furthering electoral democracy but only for the tactical purpose of gaining control of the elective assemblies. While this sort of unplanned popularization of politics had gone on in the past, particularly in urban areas, the inflamed atmosphere that the imperial crisis generated gave it a new cutting edge with new and unpredictable implications.

In colony after colony local quarrels, often of long standing, became so entangled with imperial antagonisms that they reinforced one another in a spiraling momentum that brought into question all governmental authority. Even those authorities not directly exercised by Great Britain, such as the proprietary governments of Pennsylvania and Maryland, were victimized by the imperial crisis. Thus in Maryland in 1770, a proclamation by the proprietary governor setting the fees paid to government officials seemed to violate the principle of no taxation without representation made so vivid by the imperial debate. This executive proclamation provoked a bitter local struggle that forced Daniel Dulany, wealthy councillor and former opponent of the Stamp Act, into defending the governor. In the end the controversy destroyed the governor's capacity to rule and made Dulany a loyalist to the British cause.

By the 1770s, all these developments, without anyone's clearly intending it, were revealing a new kind of politics in America. The rhetoric of liberty now quickened long-existing popular political tendencies. Various craftsmen and religious minorities were no longer willing to have wealthy gentlemen speak for them and were demanding explicit representation of their members in political organizations. Politicians in some colonies called for a widened suffrage, the use of the ballot, legislatures opened to the public, printed legislative minutes, and recorded legislative divisions—all in an effort to enlarge the political arena and limit the power of those who clung to the traditional ways of private arrangements and personal influence. Everywhere in the colonies "incendiaries," as royal officials called them, were taking advantage of the people's resentments against the British regulations to compete for political leadership. More and more "new men" were using electioneering to short-circuit the narrow and controlled channels of politics.

Changes in Public Rhetoric. As more Americans became literate, political consciousness broadened and deepened. This development could be seen and heard in the public rhetoric. Throughout the eighteenth century and at the outset of the imperial controversy, most newspaper essays and pamphlets were written by gentlemen, and most speeches in legislative and other public bodies were spoken by gentlemen for restricted audiences of educated men like themselves. Their speeches and writings were often stylized by rhetorical rules and were usually embellished with Latin quotations and references to the literature of Western culture. The gentry's speeches and writings did not have to influence directly and simultaneously all the people but only the leaders, who in turn would bring the rest of the people with

them. By the time of the Revolution, however, this world was beginning to change.

The astonishing popularity of Patrick Henry's oratory and Thomas Paine's writing epitomized this change. Both these Revolutionary agitators emerged from obscurity in these years. Henry, although the son of a locally important planter of Hanover County, Virginia, was a failure as a planter and storekeeper. At age twenty-three he taught himself law and in the 1760s became the gentleman-spokesman for poor and middling farmers and religious dissenters of southwestern Virginia. Paine, a onetime English corsetmaker and schoolmaster and a twice-dismissed excise officer, only arrived in the colonies at the end of 1774, thirty-seven years old and filled with rage at the establishment that had pressed him down. Within little more than a year he had written *Common Sense*, the most incendiary and popular pamphlet of the entire Revolutionary era; it went through twenty-five editions in 1776 alone.

As agitators, both Henry and Paine sought to reach out to wider audiences. Like the evangelical preachers he listened to as a youth, Henry was a master of the oral culture in which most ordinary people still exclusively lived. Paine, for his part, looked for readers everywhere, but especially in the artisan- and tavern-centered worlds of the cities. Believing that existing conventions of speech and writing would not allow them to express to ordinary people new feelings of revulsion and aspiration, both men deliberately rejected the traditional methods of persuasion and thus aroused the awe and consternation of the gentlemanly elite. Both lacked formal schooling, both were accused of using ungrammatical language and coarse imagery, and both relied on their audiences knowing only one literary source, the Bible. Both Henry and Paine aimed to break through the usual niceties and forms of rhetoric; and in their public expression, they meant to declare— in the words of one contemporary, speaking of Henry —that "it was enough to feel." Fancy words, Latin quotations, and learned citations no longer mattered as much as honesty and sincerity and the natural revelation of feelings. With this change in values, new sorts of men who held at once deep animosities and high hopes for bettering the world released their passions and enthusiasms into public life.

Men who, like Thomas Hutchinson, had been reared in the old ways and benefited from them stood bewildered and helpless in the face of these popularizing developments. They possessed neither the psychological capacity nor the political sensitivity to understand, let alone to deal with, this kind of popular politics and the moral outrage and fiery zeal that lay behind it. They intrigued and schemed, and tried to manipulate those whom they thought were the important people in the opposition (in 1768, for example, offering John Adams the office of advocate-general in the Massachusetts admiralty court). And they accused those individuals of demagoguery or ridiculed them as upstarts. Frightened by the increased violence, they struck out furiously at the kinds of popular politics they believed were eroding authority and causing the violence. Such traditional and prudent men could not accept a new and different world, and after the Declaration of Independence they either fell silent or became "loyalists," determined to remain faithful to the king and support the society that had bred them.

CHRONOLOGY

1760   George III accedes to throne.

1763   Treaty of Paris ends Seven Years' War between Great Britain, and France and Spain.
Pontiac's rebellion, uprising of Indians in Ohio Valley.
Proclamation line drawn along Appalachians by British forbids settlement in West by whites.
Parsons' Cause, resulting from efforts by Anglican clergy in Virginia to recover salaries lost from Two Penny Acts.
Paxton uprising by Scotch-Irish settlers in western Pennsylvania.

1764   Sugar Act passed by Parliament, reducing duty on foreign molasses.
Currency Act prohibits issues of legal-tender currency in the colonies.
Brown University founded.

1765   Stamp Act passed.
Stamp Act Congress meets in New York.

1766   Stamp Act repealed by Parliament, which adopts Declaratory Act asserting its authority to bind the colonies "in all cases whatsoever."
Antirent riots by tenant-farmers in New York.

1767   Townshend duties passed.
American Board of Customs established.
John Dickinson's *Letters from a Farmer in Pennsylvania.*
Organization of the Regulators in backcountry of South Carolina.

1768   Secretary of State for the Colonies established in England—first executive department with exclusively colonial concerns.
Circular Letter of Massachusetts House of Representatives.
John Hancock's ship *Liberty* seized.
British troops sent to Boston.

1769   American Philosophical Society reorganized, with Benjamin Franklin as president.

1770   Lord North's ministry formed.
Townshend duties repealed, except for duty on tea.
Boston Massacre.

1771   Benjamin Franklin begins his *Autobiography.*
Battle of Alamance, North Carolina, between western Regulators and eastern militia led by the governor.

1772   British schooner *Gaspée* burned in Rhode Island.
Boston Committee of Correspondence formed.

1773   Tea Act imposed.
Boston Tea Party.

1774   Coercive Acts.
Continental Congress meets in Philadelphia.
Galloway's Plan of Union.
Continental Association.

SUGGESTED READINGS

A convenient guide to the historical literature on the American Revolution can be found in Jack P. Greene, ed., *The Reinterpretation of the American Revolution, 1763–1789* (1968). Although there are many short accounts of the Revolution, the student ought to begin with R. R. Palmer's monumental *The Age of the Democratic Revolution: A Political History of Europe and America, 1760–1800* (2 vols; 1959, 1964), which places the American Revolution in a Western perspective. Stephen G. Kurtz and James H. Hutson, eds., *Essays on the American Revolution* (1973); Alfred F. Young, ed., *The American Revolution* (1976); and the five volumes from the Library of Congress, *Symposia on the American Revolution* (1972–76) are collections of original essays on various aspects of the Revolution.

Among the early attempts to treat the coming of the Revolution from an imperial viewpoint, George Louis Beer, *British Colonial Policy, 1754–1765* (1907), is still informative. Charles M. Andrews summarized his ideas on the causes of the Revolution in *The Colonial Background of the American Revolution* (1931). The most detailed narrative of the political events leading up to the Revolution, written from an imperial perspective, is Lawrence H. Gipson, *The British Empire before the American Revolution* (15 vols., 1936–70). Gipson has summarized his point of view in *The Coming of the Revolution, 1763–1775* (1954). Merrill Jensen, *The Founding of a Nation* (1968), is the fullest single volume of the pre-Revolutionary years written from an American perspective; it is especially rich in its description of the factional struggles within the separate colonies. An ingenious but sound study that combines the views of a British and an American historian on the causes of the Revolution is Ian R. Christie and Benjamin W. Labaree, *Empire or Independence, 1760–1776* (1976).

The appropriate chapters of James A. Henretta, *The Evolution of American Society, 1700–1815* (1973), discuss American society on the eve of the Revolution. Jackson T. Main, in *The Social Structure of Revolutionary America* (1965), has attempted to describe the distribution of wealth and the nature of "classes" in American society. Carl Bridenbaugh, *Cities in Revolt* (1955), attributes the Revolutionary impulse to the cities. Gary B. Nash, *The Urban Crucible: Social Change, Political Consciousness, and the Origins of the American Revolution* (1979), stresses urban class conflict in bringing on the Revolution. The extent of westward migration is ably recounted in Jack M. Sosin, *Revolutionary Frontier, 1763–1783* (1967). Carl Bridenbaugh, *Mitre and*

Sceptre (1962), describes the growth of Anglicanism and the effort to establish an American episcopacy in the decades leading up to the Revolution. For the American reaction to these efforts, see Charles W. Akers, *Called unto Liberty: A Life of Jonathan Mayhew, 1720–1766* (1964).

The opening years of the reign of George III have been the subject of some of the most exciting historical scholarship in the twentieth century—largely the work of Sir Lewis Namier and his students. Namier and his followers have exhaustively demonstrated that George III was not seeking to destroy the British constitution, as nineteenth-century historians had argued, and that in 1760 party government with ministerial responsibility to Parliament lay very much in the future. Namier's chief works include *The Structure of Politics at the Accession of George III* (2d ed., 1957), and *England in the Age of the American Revolution* (2d ed., 1961). For detailed studies of British politics in the Revolutionary era, see P. D. G. Thomas, *British Politics and the Stamp Act Crisis* (1975); Paul Langford, *The First Rockingham Administration: 1765–1766* (1973); John Brooke, *The Chatham Administration, 1766–1768* (1956); Bernard Donoughue, *British Politics and the American Revolution: The Path to War, 1773–1775* (1964). The best biography of George III is John Brooke, *King George III* (1972). An excellent summary of British politics is George H. Guttridge, *English Whiggism and the American Revolution* (2d ed., 1963); but for a more recent study that reconciles the Whig and Namierite interpretations, see John Brewer, *Party Ideology and Popular Politics at the Accession of George III* (1976).

Other important studies of British imperial policy in the period 1760–1775 include Jack M. Sosin, *Whitehall and the Wilderness . . . 1763–1775* (1961); Michael Kammen, *A Rope of Sand: The Colonial Agents, British Politics, and the American Revolution* (1968); and Franklin B. Wickwire, *British Subministers and Colonial America, 1763–1783* (1966). On the military in America, see John Shy, *Toward Lexington: The Role of the British Army in the Coming of the American Revolution* (1965); and Neil R. Stout, *The Royal Navy in America, 1760–1775* (1973).

On American resistance, see especially Edmund S. Morgan and Helen M. Morgan, *The Stamp Act Crisis* (1953), which emphasizes the colonists' appeal to constitutional principles. Pauline Maier, *From Resistance to Revolution* (1972), stresses the limited and controlled character of American opposition. But see Dirk Hoerder, *Crowd Action in Revolutionary Massachusetts, 1765–1780* (1977). Oliver M. Dickerson, *The Navigation Acts and the American Revolution* (1951), argues that Americans accepted the navigation system until "customs racketeering" was introduced in the late 1760s. For a more balanced view of the navigation system, see Thomas C. Barrow, *Trade and Empire: The British Customs Service in Colonial America, 1660–1775* (1967).

On other irritants and incidents in the imperial relation, see Joseph A. Ernst, *Money and Politics in America, 1755–1775* (1973); Carl Ubbelohde, *The Vice-Admiralty Courts and the American Revolution* (1960); M. H. Smith, *The Writs of Assistance Case* (1978); Hiller Zobel, *The Boston Massacre* (1970); Benjamin W. Labaree, *The Boston Tea Party* (1964); and David Ammerman, *In the Common Cause: American Response to the Coercive Acts of 1774* (1974). Arthur M. Schlesinger, *The Colonial Merchants and the American Revolution, 1763–1776* (1918), schematically traces the responses of an important social group.

The loyalist reaction is analyzed in William H. Nelson, *The American Tory* (1961); Robert M. Calhoon, *The Loyalists in Revolutionary America: 1760–1781* (1973); and Bernard Bailyn, *The Ordeal of Thomas Hutchinson* (1974). A vitriolic account by a loyalist of the causes of the Revolution is Peter Oliver, *Origin and Progress of the American Rebellion,* ed. Douglass Adair and John A. Schutz (1961).

Among the many local studies of American resistance are Carl Becker, *The History of Political Parties in the Province of New York, 1760–1776* (1909); David S. Lovejoy, *Rhode Island Politics and the American Revolution, 1760–1776* (1958); Theodore Thayer, *Pennsylvania Politics and the Growth of Democracy, 1740–1776* (1954); Richard Ryerson, *The Revolution Is Now Begun: The Radical Committees of Philadelphia, 1765–1776* (1978); Patricia Bonomi, *A Factious People: . . . New York* (1971); Jere R. Daniel, *Experiment in Republicanism: New Hampshire Politics and the American Revolution, 1741–1794* (1970); Richard H. Brown, *Revolutionary Politics in Massachusetts* (1970); Stephen E. Patterson, *Political Parties in Revolutionary Massachusetts* (1973); and Ronald Hoffman, *A Spirit of Dissension: Economics, Politics, and the Revolution in Maryland* (1973). For biographical analyses of some of the leading Revolutionaries, see John C. Miller, *Sam Adams* (1936); Richard R. Beeman, *Patrick Henry* (1974); Merrill Peterson, *Thomas Jefferson and the New Nation* (1970); Eric Foner, *Tom Paine and Revolutionary America* (1976); Peter Shaw, *The Character of John Adams* (1976); and John R. Howe, Jr., *The Changing Political Thought of John Adams* (1966).

CHAPTER 8

The Revolution: Ideology and War

*W*ithin the short span of a dozen years or so following the introduction of the imperial reforms, Americans who had celebrated the accession of George III were in open rebellion against Great Britain. The speed with which Americans moved into rebellion astonished their contemporaries, and it has astonished historians ever since. A series of trade acts and tax levies, however far-reaching in their implications, do not seem to justify revolution. Yet many Americans by 1776 agreed with John Adams that the colonists were "in the very midst of a revolution, the most complete, unexpected, and remarkable, of any in the history of nations." What accounts for this revolution? How was it justified?

It was not the particular acts of the British government in themselves but the meaning the colonists gave to those acts that explains the Revolution. From the outset of the controversy, Americans sought to understand the intentions of the British government and to determine their rights and liberties. The result was an outpouring of political writings and an interest in political ideas unequaled in the nation's history. The colonists' extraordinary efforts to discover the meaning of what was happening made the Revolution an unusually intellectual affair and ultimately gave it worldwide importance.

An Asylum for Liberty

Throughout their writings, American patriot leaders insisted they were rebelling, not against the principles of the English constitution, but on behalf of them. They invoked historic English party designations and called themselves "Whigs," and branded the supporters of the crown "Tories" in order to express their continuity with the great struggles for political liberty in seventeenth-century England. By emphasizing that it was the letter and spirit of the British constitution that justified their resistance, Americans could easily believe they were simply preserving what Englishmen had valued from time immemorial; they thereby gave a conservative coloring to their Revolution.

Yet the colonists were mistaken in believing that they were struggling only to return to the essentials

AN ENGLISH RADICAL

John Wilkes was the most popular hero of the age in the Anglo-American world. Although a gentleman himself, he came to symbolize for middling and lowly sorts of people all their pent-up hostilities toward established authority. Note the references in the engraving to the seventeenth-century libertarian philosophers, John Locke and Algernon Sidney. Silver bowl by Paul Revere (1735–1818), Boston, 1768. Note No. 45, Wilkes and Liberty engraving. (*Print: American Antiquarian Society; Bowl: Courtesy, Museum of Fine Arts, Boston*)

of the English constitution. The historical traditions of the English constitution they invoked were not the principles held by English officials in the mid-eighteenth century, but were in fact, as the Tories and royal officials tried to indicate, "revolution principles" outside the mainstream of English thought. Since the colonists seemed to be reading the same literature as other Englishmen, they were hardly aware that they were seeing the English heritage differently. Amid their breadth of reading and references, however, was a concentration on a strain of thought that ultimately implicated them in a peculiar conception of English life and in an extraordinary radical perspective on the English constitution they were so fervently defending.

The Country-Whig Tradition of Opposition. The heritage of liberal thought the colonists drew upon was composed not simply of the political treatises of notable philosophers like John Locke but also of the writings of such influential coffee-house pamphleteers as John Trenchard and Thomas Gordon. Many

of these pamphleteers were on the extreme edges of the political spectrum and wrote out of a deep and bitter hostility to the great political, social, and economic changes taking place in England during the first half of the eighteenth century. These critics thought that the general commercialization of English life, seen in the rise of the Bank of England, powerful trading companies, stock markets, and the huge public debt, was corrupting traditional values and threatening England with ruin. Believing that the crown was ultimately responsible for these changes, such writers promoted a so-called "country" opposition to the deceit and luxury of the "court" party associated with the crown. They were obsessively fearful of the capacity of executive or state power—particularly as it had operated under the ministries of Sir Robert Walpole—to corrupt Parliament and English society. Throughout the first half of the eighteenth century these defenders of political liberties made ringing proposals to reduce and control what seemed to be the enormously inflated powers of the crown in order to recover the rights of the people and the original principles of the English constitution.

Many of the reforms they proposed were ahead of their time for England—reforms that advocated the right to vote for all adult males and not just well-to-do property-holders, more liberty for the press, and greater freedom of religion. Other suggested reforms aimed at prohibiting salaried government puppets ("placemen") from sitting in the House of Commons, at reducing the public debt, and at obtaining such popular rights as equal representation for more people, the power to instruct members of Parliament, and shorter Parliaments. All of these reform proposals combined into a widely shared conception about how English life should ideally be organized. In this ideal nation, the parts of the constitution would be independent of one another, and members of Parliament would be independent of any connection or party. In other words, there would exist a political world in which no one would be controlled by anyone else.

The colonists had long felt the relevance of these "country" ideas more keenly than the English themselves. These ideas had made good sense of both the simple character of American life in contrast with a sophisticated England and of the colonists' antagonism to royal power; and during the conflicts between their assemblies and governors during the first half of the eighteenth century Americans had invoked these ideas off and on. Now, however, in the years after 1763 the need to explain the growing controversy with Britain gave this country-opposition ideology a new and comprehensive importance. It not only prepared the colonists intellectually for resistance but offered them a powerful justification of their many differences from a decayed and corrupted mother country.

A Conspiracy Against Liberty. These inherited ideas contained an elaborate set of rules for political action by the people. How were the people to identify a tyrant? How long should the people put up with abuses? How much force should be used? The answers to these questions came logically as events unfolded and led the colonists almost irresistibly from

resistance to rebellion. Step by step the colonists became convinced that the obnoxious efforts of crown officials to reform the empire were not simply the result of insensitivity to peculiar American conditions or mistakes of well-meant policy but were rather the intended consequences of grand tyrannical design. In Thomas Jefferson's words, the British reforms by 1774 were nothing less than "a deliberate systematical plan of reducing us to slavery."

America, the colonists believed, was the primary object of this tyrannical conspiracy, but the goals of this conspiracy ranged far beyond the colonies. Americans were involved not simply in a defense of their own rights but in a worldwide struggle for the salvation of liberty itself. The crucial turning point came in the late 1760s. Americans had earlier read of the prosecution of the English radical John Wilkes for criticizing His Majesty's government in his *North Briton* No. 45 and had made Wilkes and the number "45" part of their political symbolism. Then in 1768 Wilkes's four successive expulsions from the House of Commons, despite his repeated reelections by the voters of Middlesex outside London, seemed to many Americans to mark the twilight of representative government in Great Britain. Everywhere liberty seemed to be in retreat before the forces of tyranny. As Americans learned of the desperate struggles of the Sons of Liberty in Ireland and the failure of the freedom fighter Pascal Paoli to establish the independence of Corsica, they became convinced that America was the only place where a free popular press still existed, the only place where the people could still elect representatives who spoke for them and them only.

By 1776 their picture of the immensity of the struggle they were involved in was complete. And they could respond enthusiastically, as lovers of mankind and haters of tyranny, to the passionate appeal of Thomas Paine's *Common Sense* to stand forth for liberty:

Every spot of the old world is overrun with oppression. Freedom hath been hunted round the globe. Asia and Africa have long expelled her. Europe regards her like a stranger, and England hath given her warning to depart. O! receive the fugitive, and prepare in time an asylum for mankind.

THOMAS PAINE, BY JOHN WESLEY JARVIS
Paine was probably the first detached "intellectual" in American history. He belonged to no country, lived by his pen, and saw his role as the stimulator of revolutions. (*The National Gallery of Art, Washington, D.C.*)

The Imperial Debate

The belief that America was destined to redeem and make free not just its own people but the entire world helped to create a distinctive identity that is still an important part of American awareness. Indeed, much of what Americans believe about themselves, their governments, and their rights and liberties derives from the Revolutionary experience. The Revolutionary era was the most creative period in the history of American political thought. During three decades of intense controversy, intricate argument, and political experimentation, Americans made lasting contributions to constitutional thought everywhere. The immediate origins of this rich intellectual achievement lay in the debate that accompanied the colonists' rising resistance to British authority. This debate compelled the colonists to put into words for the

first time their own peculiar political experience and to lay the intellectual foundations for their subsequent constitution-making.

Virtual vs. Actual Representation.   With the Stamp Act, the first unmistakable tax levy by Parliament, American intellectual resistance was immediately elevated to the highest plane of principle. "It is inseparably essential to the freedom of a people, and the undoubted rights of Englishmen," the Stamp Act Congress declared in 1765, "that no taxes should be imposed on them, but with their own consent, given personally, or by their representatives." And since "the people of these colonies are not, and from their local circumstances, cannot be represented in the House of Commons in Great Britain," the colonists could only be represented and taxed by persons, known and chosen by themselves, in their respective legislatures. This statement defined the American position at the outset of the controversy, and despite subsequent confusion and stumbling this essential point was never shaken.

Once the British ministry sensed a stirring of colonial opposition to the Stamp Act, a group of English government pamphleteers set out to explain and justify parliamentary taxation of the colonies. Although the arguments of these writers differed, they all eventually agreed that the Americans, like all Englishmen everywhere, were embraced by acts of Parliament through a system of "virtual" representation. It was this concept of virtual representation, as distinct from actual representation, these writers argued, that gave Parliament its supreme authority or sovereignty. Even though the colonists, like "nine-tenths of the people of Britain," did not in fact choose any representative to the House of Commons, one government pamphleteer wrote, they were undoubtedly "a part, and an important part of the Commons of Great Britain: they are represented in Parliament in the same manner as those inhabitants of Britain are who have not voices in elections." During the eighteenth century, England's electorate comprised only a tiny proportion of its population. Since English electoral districts were a hodgepodge left over from centuries of history, ancient "rotten boroughs," completely depopulated by the eighteenth century, continued to send members to Parliament while newer large cities like Manchester and Birmingham sent none. What made such peculiarities intelligible to Englishmen was the assumption, classically voiced by Edmund Burke in 1774, that each member of Parliament represented the whole community, not just a particular locality. Hence representation in England was proper and effective not because of the process of election, but rather because of the mutual interests presumably shared by members of Parliament and the Englishmen for whom they spoke, including those, like the colonists, who did not actually vote for them.

The Americans immediately and emphatically rejected these British claims that they were "virtually" represented in the House of Commons in the same way that the nonvoters of cities like Manchester and Birmingham were. In the most notable colonial pamphlet written in opposition to the Stamp Act, *Considerations on the Propriety of Imposing Taxes* (1765), Daniel Dulany of Maryland conceded the relevance in England of virtual representation, but denied its applicability to America. For America, he wrote, was a distinct community from England and thus could hardly be represented by Members of Parliament with whom it had no common interests. Others pushed beyond Dulany's argument, however, and challenged the very idea of virtual representation. If the people were to be properly represented in a legislature, many colonists said, they not only had to vote directly for the members of the legislature but had to be represented by members whose numbers were proportionate to the size of the population they spoke for. What purpose is served, asked James Otis of Massachusetts in 1765, by the continual attempts of Englishmen to justify the lack of American representation in Parliament by citing the examples of Manchester and Birmingham who returned no members to the House of Commons? "If those now so considerable places are not represented, they ought to be."

In the New World, electoral districts were not the products of history going back to time immemorial but recent and regular creations related to changes in population and the formation of new towns and counties. As a consequence, many Americans had come to believe in a very different kind of representation

from that of the English. Their belief in "actual" representation made election not incidental but central to representation; it stressed the closest possible connection between the local electors and the elected agent. For them it was only proper that representatives be residents of the localities they spoke for and that people of the locality have the right to instruct their representatives; and it was only fair that localities be represented in proportion to their population. In short, the American belief in actual representation pointed toward the fullest and most equal participation of the people in the process of government that the modern world had ever seen.

"THE BRUTAL TREATMENT OF JOHN MALCOMB...."
This print from a London paper shows John Malcomb, commissioner of customs at Boston, being tarred and feathered in 1774 for trying to collect customs duties. Note the number "45" on the patriot's hat, a symbol of liberty since John Wilke's imprisonment for printing the *North Briton No. 45*. (*The John Carter Brown Library, Brown University*)

THE PATRIOTIC AMERICAN FARMER.

J—N D-K-NS—N, Esq; BARRISTER at LAW.

Who with Attic Eloquence, and Roman Spirit, hath afferted the Liberties of the BRITISH Colonies in America.

'Tis nobly done to Stem Taxations Rage,
And raife the Thoughts of a degenerate Age,
For Happinefs and Joy, from Freedom fpring;
But Life in Bondage is a worthlefs Thing.

JOHN DICKINSON'S
"THE PATRIOTIC AMERICAN FARMER"
In the 1760s Dickinson was the most famous patriot-writer in all America. But by 1776 his unwillingness to endorse American independence diminished his reputation, which posterity has not yet restored.
(*American Antiquarian Society*)

The Problem of Sovereignty. Yet while Americans were denying Parliament's right to tax them because they were not represented in the House of Commons, they knew that Parliament had exercised some authority over their affairs during the previous century, and they groped to explain what that authority should be. What was the "due subordination" that the Stamp Act Congress admitted Americans owed Parliament?

Could the colonists accept parliamentary legislation but not taxation—"external" customs duties but not "internal" stamp taxes? In his famous *Letters from a Pennsylvania Farmer* (1767–68), John Dickinson repudiated the idea that Parliament could rightly impose "external" or "internal" taxes, and made clear once and for all that the colonists opposed *all* forms of parliamentary taxation. Dickinson recognized nevertheless that the empire required some sort of central regulatory authority, particularly for commerce, and conceded Parliament's superintending legislative power so far as it preserved "the connection between the several parts of the British empire." The empire, it seemed to many colonists, was a unitary body for some affairs but not for others.

To all of these halting and fumbling efforts to divide parliamentary authority, the British offered a simple, formidable argument. Since they could not conceive of the empire as anything but a single, homogeneous community, they found absurd and meaningless all these American distinctions between trade regulation and taxation, between "external" and "internal" taxes, or between separate spheres of authority. If Parliament even "in one instance" was as supreme over the colonists as over the people of England, then, wrote William Knox in a crucial ministerial pamphlet of 1769, the Americans were members "of the same community with the people of England." On the other hand, if Parliament's authority over the colonists were denied "in any particular," then it must be denied in "all instances" and the union between Great Britain and the colonies dissolved. "There is no alternative," Knox concluded; "either the colonies are part of the community of Great Britain or they are in a state of nature with respect to her, and in no case can be subject to the jurisdiction of that legislative power which represents her community, which is the British Parliament."

What made this British argument so powerful was its basis in the widely accepted doctrine of sovereignty—the belief that in every state there could be only one final, indivisible, and uncontestable supreme authority. This was the most important concept of English political theory in the eighteenth century; and it became the issue over which the empire was finally broken.

This idea that every state had to have in the end one single supreme undivided authority somewhere had been the basis of the British position from the beginning. The concept of sovereignty was best expressed in the Declaratory Act of 1766, which, following the repeal of the Stamp Act, affirmed Parliament's authority to make laws binding the colonists "in all cases whatsoever." But now in the early 1770s its implications were drawn out fully. In 1773 Massachusetts Governor Thomas Hutchinson was provoked into directly challenging the radical movement and its belief in the *limited* nature of Parliament's power. In a dramatic and well-publicized speech to the Massachusetts legislature, Hutchinson attempted to clarify the central constitutional issue between America and Great Britain once and for all and to show the colonists how unreasonable their views were. "I know of no line," he declared, "that can be drawn between the supreme authority of Parliament and the total independence of the colonies, as it is impossible there should be two independent legislatures in one and the same state."

By then many Americans despaired of trying to divide what royal officials told them could not be divided. The Massachusetts House of Representatives had a simple answer to Hutchinson's position. If there were no middle ground between the supreme authority of Parliament and the total independence of the colonies from Parliament, as Governor Hutchinson said, then, the House declared, there could be no doubt that "we were thus independent." The logic of sovereignty therefore forced a fundamental shift in the American position. By 1774 the leading colonists, including Thomas Jefferson and John Adams, were arguing that sovereignty resided only in the separate American legislatures. Thus Parliament had no final authority over America, and the colonies were connected to the empire solely through the king. The most the colonists would concede was that Parliament had the right to regulate their external commerce, as the Declaration and Resolves of the First Continental Congress put it, "from the necessity of the case, and a regard to the mutual interest of both countries." But the British government remained committed to the principle of the Declaratory Act, which no leader of the Revolution could any longer take seriously.

The War for Independence

However necessary ideas were in making events meaningful and in mobilizing people into resistance and rebellion, they could not by themselves achieve independence. Once Britain determined to enforce its authority with troops, Americans had to take up arms to support their beliefs.

By the beginning of 1775, the English government was already preparing for military action. In February Lord North got Parliament to pass what he regarded as a conciliatory measure. He proposed that any colony contributing its proportionate share to the common defense would not be subject to parliamentary taxation. But since the British government did nothing to resolve the issues raised by the Coercive Acts and the declarations of the Continental Congress, the colonists regarded North's efforts at reconciliation as an insidious attempt to divide them. By this date North's supporters and the king himself saw no alternative to force in bringing the colonists back into line. George III had told North as early as November 1774, "Blows must decide whether they are to be subject to the Country or Independent." The British government thus increased the army and navy and began restraining the commerce first of New England and then of the other colonies.

In May 1775 delegates from the colonies met in Philadelphia for the Second Continental Congress to take up where the First Congress left off. Outwardly the Congress continued the policy of resolves and reconciliation. In July, at the urging of John Dickinson, Congress in an Olive Branch Petition professed loyalty to the king and humbly asked him to disavow his "artful and cruel" ministers who were blamed for the oppressive measures. At the same time, the Congress issued a "Declaration of the Causes and Necessities of Taking Up Arms" (largely the work of Dickinson and Thomas Jefferson), in which the colonies denied they had any "ambitious design of separating from Great Britain, and establishing independent states." As this superb summary of the American case against Britain demonstrated, the time for paper solutions had passed. Fighting had broken out at Lexington and Concord, Massachusetts, in April 1775, and the Second Congress now had to assume some

THE BATTLE OF CONCORD, MASSACHUSETTS

In their march to and from Concord on April 19, 1775 73 British soldiers were killed and 200 wounded out of a total force of 1800. Of the nearly 4000 colonial militia who fought sometime during the day, 49 were killed and 46 were wounded. (*State Street Trust Company*)

of the responsibilities of a central government for the colonies. It created a continental army, appointed George Washington of Virginia as commander, issued paper money for the support of the troops, and formed a committee to negotiate with foreign countries.

By the summer of 1775 the escalation of actions and reactions was out of control. On August 23, George III, ignoring the colonists' Olive Branch Petition, proclaimed the colonies in open rebellion. In October he publicly accused them of aiming at independence. By December the British government declared all American shipping liable to seizure by British warships. As early as May 1775, American forces had captured Fort Ticonderoga at the head of Lake Champlain. Out of a desire to bring the Canadians into the struggle against Britain, the Congress ordered makeshift forces under Richard Montgomery and Benedict Arnold to invade Canada. Although by the beginning of 1776 no official American body had as yet formally endorsed independence, the idea was obviously in the air. It was left to Thomas Paine to express in January 1776 in his *Common Sense* the accumulated American rage against George III, whom Paine now called the "Royal Brute." In the early spring of 1776, the Congress threw open America's ports to the world and prepared for the Declaration of Independence, which it formally approved on July 4, 1776. In this famous thirteen-hundred word document, largely written by the graceful hand of Jefferson, the king, as the only remaining link between the colonists and Great Britain, was now held accountable for every grievance suffered by Americans since 1763. The reign of George III, Americans declared "to a candid world," was "a history of repeated injuries and usurpations, all having in direct object the establishment of an absolute Tyranny over these States."*

The Declaration of Independence was not an American call to arms but a consequence of arms already taken up. For over a year, beginning with the hostilities in Massachusetts in the spring of 1775 and including the ill-fated American attack on Quebec in the winter of 1775–76, the American and British forces had been at war. It was a war that would eventually go on for nearly eight years—the longest war in American history, until that of Vietnam two centuries later.

*For the Declaration of Independence, see Appendix.

The War in the North, 1775–1776.   This war for independence passed through a series of distinct phases, growing and widening until what had begun in British eyes as a breakdown in governmental authority in a section of their empire became in time a world struggle. Great Britain found itself for the first time in the eighteenth century diplomatically isolated and at one point, in 1779, even threatened with French invasion. The war for American independence thus eventually became an important episode in Britain's long struggle with France for global supremacy, a struggle that went back a century and would continue for another generation into the nineteenth century.

The British military actions of 1775 grew logically out of the coercive policies of 1774, for both rested on the assumption by the British government that Boston was the center of the disruption and needed to be isolated and punished. The British thought at first that they were dealing with mobs led by a few seditious instigators who had to be arrested and tried and

"THE DECLARATION OF INDEPENDENCE," BY JOHN TRUMBULL

The committee that drafted the Declaration of Independence included from left to right; John Adams, Roger Sherman, Robert R. Livingston, Thomas Jefferson, and Benjamin Franklin.   (*Copyright Yale University Art Gallery*)

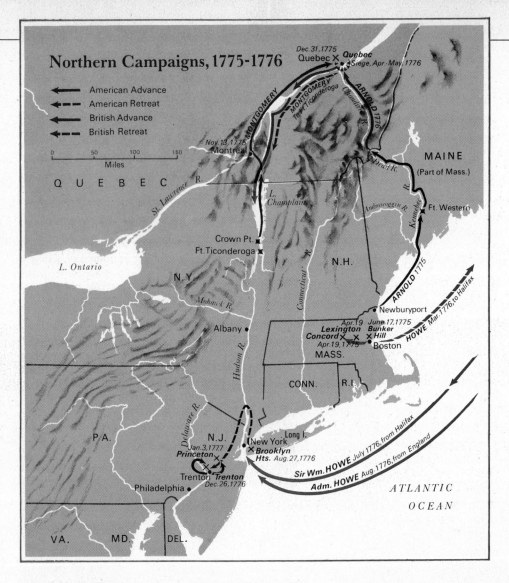

Northern Campaigns, 1775-1776

→ American Advance
- -→ American Retreat
→ British Advance
←- British Retreat

whose bases of insurgency had to be broken up. This view of the situation led General Gage on April 19, 1775, to attempt to seize rebel munitions stored at Concord, Massachusetts. As a result the colonial militia was called out. It stopped the British at Lexington and harassed them on their march back to the besieged town of Boston. By surrounding Boston from positions in Charlestown and Dorchester Heights, the colonists raised doubts that all that was required to quell the struggle was police action.

Two months later in June 1775, British soldiers attempted to dislodge American fortifications on a spur of Bunker Hill in Charlestown overlooking Boston. Assuming, in General John Burgoyne's words, that no numbers of "untrained rabble" could ever stand up against "trained troops," the British under General William Howe attempted a series of frontal assaults on the American position that were eventually successful but only at a terrible cost of one thousand British casualties, over 40 percent of Howe's troops. In this battle at Bunker Hill—the first formal engagement of the Revolution—the British suffered their heaviest losses of the entire war. This experience convinced the British government that it was not simply a New England mob they were up against, and it swept away almost every objection among the ministers to a conquest of the colonies.

The appointment of generals by the Continental Congress, the organization of a Continental field army under George Washington in the summer of 1775, and the American expedition to Canada were evidence to the British that they were involved in a military rather than a police action, which in turn dictated a conventional eighteenth-century policy of maneuver and battle. This change of strategy required that the British evacuate Boston in favor of New York, with its presumably more sympathetic population, its superior port, and its central position. Accordingly, in the summer of 1776 Howe, who replaced Gage as commander in chief of the British army in North America, sailed into New York harbor with a force of over 30,000 men. Howe aimed to cut New England off from the other rebels and to defeat Washington's army in a decisive battle. It was a plan that Howe was to spend the next two frustrating years trying to realize.

On the face of it, a military struggle seemed to promise all the advantage to Great Britain. Britain was the most powerful nation in the world with a population of about 11 million, compared with only 2.5 million colonists. The British navy was the largest in the world, with nearly half its ships initially committed to the American struggle. The British army was a well-trained professional force, having at one point in 1778 nearly 50,000 troops in North America alone; to this force were added during the war over 30,000 hired German mercenaries. To confront this military might the Americans had to start from scratch, creating eventually a small continental army numbering at times less than 5,000 troops, supplemented by state militia units of varying sizes. The whole motley collection was led mostly by inexperienced, amateur officers. The commander in chief, Washington, for example, had been only a regimental colonel on the Virginia frontier, and had little first-hand knowledge of combat. Not surprisingly, then, most British officers thought that the Americans would be no match for His Majesty's troops. A veteran of many North American campaigns told the

GEORGE WASHINGTON, BY CHARLES WILSON PEALE
Washington's genuis lay not in his military expertise in the field but in his coolness and determination and in his extraordinary political skills. Although he lost most of his battles, he never lost the support of his officers or the Congress. (*The Brooklyn Museum, Dick S. Ramsay Fund*)

House of Commons in 1774 that with 5,000 regulars he could easily march from one end of the country to the other.

Yet such a contrast of numbers was deceptive, for the British disadvantages were immense and perhaps overwhelming, even at the beginning when their opportunities to put down the rebellion were greatest. Great Britain not only had to carry on the war three thousand miles across the Atlantic with consequent problems of communications and logistics, but also had to wage a different kind of war from any other the country had fought in the eighteenth century. A well-trained army might have been able to conquer the American forces, but, as one French officer observed at the end, America itself was unconquerable. The great breadth of territory and the wild nature of the terrain made conventional maneuverings and operations difficult and cumbersome. The fragmented and local character of authority in America inhibited decisive action by the British; there was no nerve center anywhere whose capture would destroy the rebellion. In such circumstances the prevalence of amateur militia and the weakness of America's organized army made the Americans more dangerous than if they had a trained professional army. The British never clearly understood what they were up

RECRUITING FOR THE AMERICAN CAUSE

Privateers were privately-owned armed vessels sailing under license (letters of marque) issued by a state or by the Continental Congress. There were more than 2,000 of them during the Revolution. Enemy vessels captured by privateers became the captors' "prizes." (*American Antiquarian Society*)

Now fitting for a

Privateer,

In the Harbour of *BEVERLY*,

The BRIGANTINE

Washington,

A strong, good vessel for that purpose and a prime sailer.

Any Seamen or Landmen that have an inclination to

Make their Fortunes in a few Months,

May have an Opportunity, by applying to

JOHN DYSON.

Beverly, September 17th, 1776.

against—a revolutionary struggle involving widespread support in the population. Hence they continually underestimated the staying power of the rebels and overestimated the strength of the loyalists. And in the end, independence came to mean more to the Americans than reconquest did to the English.

From the outset, the English objective could never be as simple and clear-cut as the Americans' desire for independence. Conquest by itself could not restore political relations and imperial harmony. Many people in England were reluctant to engage in a civil war, and several officers actually refused out of conscience to serve in America. Although the bulk of the Parliament and the English ministry were intent on subjugating America by force, the British commanders appointed in 1775, Sir William Howe and his brother Admiral Richard, Lord Howe, in charge of the navy, never shared this overriding urge for outright coercion. The brothers, particularly Lord Howe, saw themselves not simply as conquerors but also as conciliators. They interrupted their military operations with peace feelers to Washington and the Continental Congress, and they tried to avoid plundering and ravaging the American countryside and ports out of fear of destroying all hope for reconciliation. Such "a sentimental manner of waging war," as Lord George Germain, head of the American Department, called it, weakened the morale of British officers and troops and left the loyalists confused and disillusioned.

The Howes' policy was not as ineffectual initially as it later appeared. After defeating Washington at Brooklyn Heights on Long Island in August 1776 and driving him in the fall of 1776 from New York City, General Howe drove Washington into pell-mell retreat southward. Instead of pursuing Washington across the Delaware River, Howe resorted to a piecemeal occupation of New Jersey, extending his lines and deploying brigade garrisons at a half-dozen towns around the area with the aim of gradually convincing the rebels of British invincibility. Loyalist militiamen emerged from hiding and through a series of ferocious local struggles with patriot groups began to assume control of northern New Jersey. Nearly 5,000 Americans came forward to accept Howe's

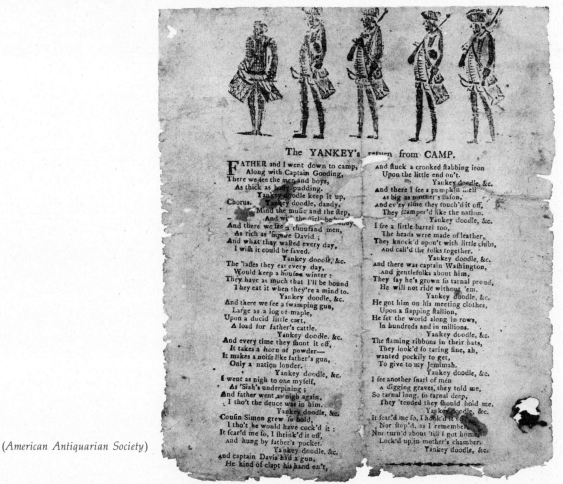

The YANKEY's return from CAMP.

FATHER and I went down to camp,
  Along with Captain Gooding,
There we see the men and boys,
  As thick as hasty-pudding.
    Yankey doodle keep it up,
Chorus. Yankey doodle, dandy,
    Mind the music and the step,
    And with the girls be handy.
And there we see a thousand men,
  As rich as 'Squire David ;
And what they wasted every day,
  I wish it could be saved.
    Yankey doodle, &c.
The 'lasses they eat every day,
  Would keep a house a winter :
They have as much that I'll be bound
  They eat it when they're a mind to.
    Yankey doodle, &c.
And there we see a swamping gun,
  Large as a log of maple,
Upon a ducid little cart,
  A load for father's cattle.
    Yankey doodle, &c.
And every time they shoot it off,
  It takes a horn of powder——
It makes a noise like father's gun,
  Only a nation louder.
    Yankey doodle, &c.
I went as nigh to one myself,
  As 'Siah's underpining ;
And father went as nigh again,
  I tho't the deuce was in him.
    Yankey doodle, &c.
Cousin Simon grew so bold,
  I tho't he would have cock'd it :
It scar'd me so, I shrink'd it off,
  And hung by father's pocket.
    Yankey doodle, &c.
and captain Davis had a gun,
He kind of clapt his hand on't,

and stuck a crooked stabbing iron
  Upon the little end on't.
    Yankey doodle, &c.
And there I see a pumpkin shell
  as big as mother's bason,
And ev'ry time they touch'd it off,
  They scamper'd like the nation.
    Yankey doodle, &c.
I see a little barrel too,
  The heads were made of leather,
They knock'd upon't with little clubs,
  and call'd the folks together.
    Yankey doodle, &c.
and there was captain Washington,
  and gentlefolks about him,
They say he's grown so tarnal proud,
  He will not ride without 'em.
    Yankey doodle, &c.
He got him on his meeting clothes,
  Upon a slapping stallion,
He set the world along in rows,
  In hundreds and in millions.
    Yankey doodle, &c.
The flaming ribbons in their hats,
  They look'd so taring fine, ah,
wanted pockily to get,
  To give to my Jemimah.
    Yankey doodle, &c.
I see another snarl of men
  a digging graves, they told me,
So tarnal long, so tarnal deep,
  They 'tended they should hold me.
    Yankey doodle, &c.
It scar'd me so, I hook'd it off,
  Nor stop'd, as I remember,
Nor turn'd about 'till I got home,
  Lock'd up in mother's chamber.
    Yankey doodle, &c.

(American Antiquarian Society)

offer of pardon and to swear loyalty to the crown. American prospects at the end of 1776 were as low as they ever would be during the war. These were, as Thomas Paine wrote, "times that try men's souls."

The Howes' policy of leniency and pacification, however, was marred by plundering by British troops and by loyalist recriminations against the rebels. But even more important in undermining the British successes of 1776 were Washington's brilliant strokes in picking off two of General Howe's extended outposts, at Trenton on December 26, 1776, and at Princeton on January 3, 1777. With these victories Washington forced the British to withdraw from the banks of the Delaware and to leave the newly formed bands of loyalists to fend for themselves. Patriot morale soared, oaths of loyalty to the king declined, and patriot militia moved back into control of local areas vacated by the withdrawing British troops. The British again had to reconsider their plans.

Burgoyne and Saratoga, 1777. The British strategy for 1777 involved sending an army of 8,000 under General John Burgoyne southward from Canada through Lake Champlain to recapture Fort Ticonderoga. Near Albany, Burgoyne was to join a secondary force under Lieutenant Colonel Barry St. Leger

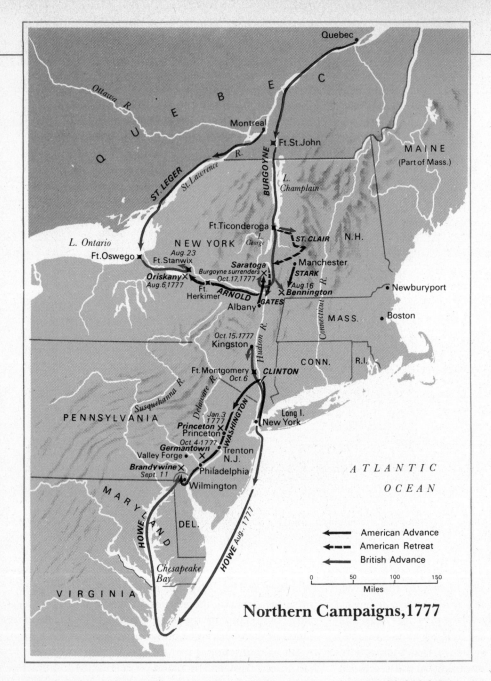

Northern Campaigns, 1777

moving eastward through the Mohawk Valley, and General Howe, advancing northward from New York City through the Hudson Valley. The ultimate aim of the campaign was to isolate New England and break the back of the rebellion. It was assumed in England that General Howe would join with Burgoyne. But Howe continued to believe that there was widespread loyalist support in the middle states and decided to capture Philadelphia, the seat of the Continental government. He moved on Philadelphia by sea, landing after much delay at the head of Chesapeake Bay at the end of August 1777. Washington, believing he should not give up the Continental capital without a struggle, confronted Howe at Brandywine and later at Germantown and was defeated in both battles. But his defeats were not disastrous; they proved that the

American army was capable of organized combat, and they prevented Howe from moving north to help Burgoyne. Howe's capture of Philadelphia demonstrated that loyalist sentiment reached only as far as British arms, and it scarcely justified what happened to Burgoyne's army in the North.

After St. Leger's force was turned back at Oriskany, New York, in the summer of 1777, Burgoyne and his huge slow-moving entourage from Canada increasingly found their supply lines stretched thin and their flanks harassed by patriot militia from New England. While Burgoyne's slow advance gave the American forces in the Hudson Valley needed time to collect themselves, the British army was diminishing. When 900 of Burgoyne's men attempted to seize provisions from a patriot arsenal in Bennington, Vermont, they were overcome and destroyed by 2,000 New England militia under John Stark. Another 900 British redcoats were detached to garrison Ticonderoga. Burgoyne determined to press on. On September 13–14 he crossed to the west side of the Hudson, cutting off communications with his rear. When he reached Saratoga, he confronted a growing American force of over 10,000 men under General Horatio Gates. Two bloody battles convinced Burgoyne of the hopelessness of his situation, and in October 1777 he surrendered his entire army to the Americans.

Saratoga was the turning point. It suggested that reconquest of America might be beyond British strength. It brought France openly into the struggle. And it led to changes in the British command and a fundamental alteration in strategy.

From the beginning of the rebellion France had been secretly supplying money and arms to the Americans in the hope of revenging its defeat by Britain in the Seven Years' War. By 1777 French ports had been opened to American privateers, and French officers were joining Washington's army. It seemed only a matter of time before France recognized the new republic. The British ministry realized at once the significance of Burgoyne's surrender, and by appointing the Carlisle Commission early in 1778 made new efforts to negotiate a settlement. The British government now offered the rebels a return to the imperial status before 1763, indeed everything the Americans had originally wanted. These British over-

HORATIO GATES (1728–1806)

This low-born former officer in the British army was appointed Washington's adjutant-general in 1775. After his victory at Saratoga, some members of Congress and several officers, including General Thomas Conway, thought about replacing Washington with Gates. These suggestions, which became known as the "Conway Cabal," were stifled by Washington's political shrewdness. (*Library of Congress*)

tures, which Franklin skillfully used in Paris to play on French fears of an Anglo-American reconciliation, led Louis XVI's government in February 1778 to sign two treaties with the United States: one a commercial arrangement, the other a military alliance pledged to American independence. In 1779 Spain, in hopes of recovering its earlier losses from England, especially Gibraltar, became allied with France. And in 1780 Russia formed a League of Armed Neutrality to which nearly all of the maritime states of Europe eventually acceded—leaving England diplomatically isolated for the first time in the eighteenth century.

The War in the South, 1778–1781. After 1778, putting down the rebellion became secondary to Britain's global struggle with France and Spain. The center of the war effort in America shifted seaward and southward as Britain sought to protect its stake in the West Indies. General Howe was replaced by Sir Henry Clinton, and a more ruthless policy was adopted, including the bombardment of American ports and marauding expeditions in the countryside. Philadelphia was abandoned, and the British assumed a defensive position from their northern bases in New York and Rhode Island. From its concentration in the West Indies, the British force now aimed to secure military control of ports in the American South, restore civil royal government with loyalist support, and then methodically move the army northward as a screen behind which the gradual pacification of rebel territory by local loyalists would proceed. This strategy was based on an assumption that the South, with its scattered, presumably more loyalist population living in fear of Indian raids and slave uprisings, was especially vulnerable to the reassertion of British authority.

At the end of 1778, the British captured Savannah, and on May 12, 1780, with the surrender of General Benjamin Lincoln and an American army of 5,500 men, the British took Charleston. It was the greatest American loss of soldiers in the entire war. A new, hastily assembled American southern army under General Gates—the victor of Saratoga—rashly moved into South Carolina to stop the British advance. On August 16, 1780, at Camden, South Carolina, Gates suffered a devastating defeat, which destroyed not only his new American army but his military reputation as well. But the British were not able to consolidate their gains and give the loyalists the military protection they needed to pacify the countryside. Loyalist retaliations against Whigs for past harsh treatment and British depredations, particularly those by Colonel Banastre Tarleton, drove countless Georgians and Carolinians into support of the Revolution. Irregular bands of patriots, sometimes organized under colorful leaders like Francis Marion, "the Swamp Fox," harassed the loyalists and the British army, and turned the war in the Lower South into a series of guerrilla skirmishes.

Lord Cornwallis, now in command of the British forces in the South, was impatient with the gradual policy of pacification and was eager to demonstrate British strength to the undecided by dramatically carrying the war into North Carolina. With his army constantly bedeviled by patriot guerrillas, he had just begun moving north when word of the destruction of his left flank at King's Mountain on October 7, 1780, forced him to return to South Carolina. In the meantime, the Americans had begun organizing a third southern army under the command of a thirty-eight-year-old ex-Quaker from Rhode Island, Nathanael Greene, recently quartermaster general of the Continental army. Shrewdly avoiding a direct confrontation with Cornwallis, Greene compelled the British to divide their forces. On January 17, 1781, at Cowpens in western South Carolina a detached corps of Greene's army under Daniel Morgan defeated "Bloody" Tarleton's Tory Legion and changed the course of British strategy in the South. Cornwallis cut his ties with his base in Charleston and set out after the elusive American army. After an indecisive battle with Greene at Guilford Courthouse on March 15, 1781, Cornwallis's tired and battered soldiers withdrew to Wilmington on the coast of North Carolina with the intention of moving the seat of war northward into Virginia. Thus ended the British experiment with a thorough program of pacification. During the spring and summer of 1781, patriot forces regained control of the entire Lower South except for a narrow strip between Charleston and Savannah.

Although marauding by British forces in the summer of 1781 frightened Virginians and humiliated Governor Thomas Jefferson, Cornwallis could not convince his commander in chief, Clinton, in New York to make Virginia the center of British military

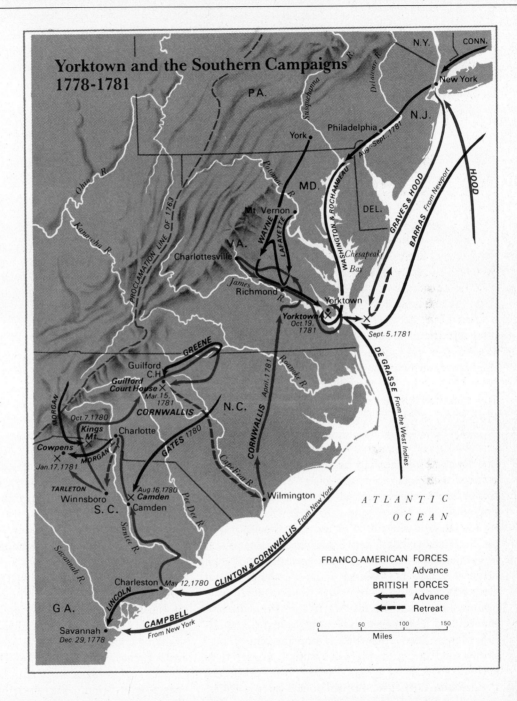

Yorktown and the Southern Campaigns 1778-1781

JOHN TRUMBULL'S "SURRENDER OF LORD CORNWALLIS"

General Benjamin Lincoln of Massachusetts leads the surrendered British troops between the French and American forces. Rochambeau and Washington, the two allied command-ers in chief, are on horseback to the rear. Lafayette is the second figure from Washington's left. To Lafayette's immediate left is Baron von Steuben, the Prussian army captain who in 1778 was made a major-general in the Continental Army. (*Courtesy of Yale University Art Gallery*)

operations. The haggling between the two generals enabled the Americans to bolster their Virginian troops under the command of the dashing French nobleman, the Marquis de Lafayette, who had been in the struggle since 1777. Cornwallis's withdrawal to the Virginia coast and his eventual isolation at Yorktown gave the combined American and French army of nearly 17,000 men under Washington and the Comte de Rochambeau the opportunity it was looking for. The French fleet under Admiral de Grasse moved into Chesapeake Bay and blocked Cornwal-lis's plans to escape by sea. Thus surrounded and bombarded in Yorktown, Cornwallis was forced to surrender his army of 8,000 troops to Washington in October 1781. The British policy since 1778 of spreading their control along the entire Atlantic sea-board depended on maintaining naval superiority; and when this superiority was temporarily lost in

1781, the entire plan collapsed. Although the war dragged on for several months, everyone knew that Yorktown meant American independence.

The Peace Treaty.   The peace, nevertheless, still had to be won. The main objective of the new nation —independence from Great Britain—was clear and straightforward. But this objective and others con-cerning America's territorial boundaries and its rights to the Newfoundland fisheries had to be reconciled with the aims of America's ally, France, and with the aims of France's ally, Spain, which had been at war with Great Britain since 1779. The United States and France had pledged in 1778 not to make a separate peace with Britain. But since France was bound to Spain against Britain until Gibraltar was recovered, there was great danger of American interests' getting lost in the machinations of the European powers.

Despite the desire of France and Spain to humiliate Britain, neither monarchy really wanted a strong and independent American republic. Spain in particular feared the spread of republicanism among its South American colonies and sought to protect its interests in the Mississippi Valley.

Although Franklin, John Adams, and John Jay, the American negotiators in Europe, were only "militia diplomats," in Adams's words, they wound their way through the intricate problems of international politics with professional diplomatic skill. Despite instructions from the Congress to do nothing without consulting the French, the American diplomats decided to negotiate with Britain alone. By hinting at the possibility of weakening the Franco-American alliance, they induced Great Britain to recognize the independence of the United States and to agree to generous boundaries for the new country: on the west, the Mississippi River; on the south, the thirty-first parallel; and on the north, roughly the present boundary with Canada. The American negotiators then presented this preliminary Anglo-American treaty to France as an accomplished fact and persuaded the French to accept it by suggesting that allies must conceal their differences from their enemies. The prospect of American peace with Britain now compelled Spain to abandon its demands for Gibraltar and to settle for Minorca and East and West Florida. In the final treaty signed on September 3, 1783, the United States, by shrewdly playing off the mutual fears of the European powers, gained independence and concessions that stunned the French and indeed all of Europe.

Republicanism

From 1775, when independence and hence the formation of new governments became imminent, and continuing throughout the war, nearly every piece of writing about the future of the new states was filled with extraordinarily idealistic hopes for the

PRELIMINARY PEACE NEGOTIATIONS WITH GREAT BRITAIN, BY BENJAMIN WEST

Although history painter to George III, the American-born Benjamin West actually toyed with the idea of painting the great events of the American Revolution. But this unfinished picture of the peace negotiators was the only one he attempted. The picture includes John Jay, John Adams, Benjamin Franklin, Temple Franklin (Franklin's grandson and secretary to the delegation), and Henry Laurens, who did not sign the final treaty. (*Courtesy, The Henry Francis du Pont Winterthur Museum*) transformation of America. Americans had come to believe that the Revolution meant nothing less than the reordering of eighteenth-century politics and society—a reordering summed up in the conception of republicanism.

This republicanism was in every way a radical ideology, comparable in the eighteenth century to Marxism in the nineteenth. It meant more than simply eliminating a king and instituting an elective system of government. It added a moral and indeed utopian dimension to the political separation from England—a dimension that promised a fundamental shift in values and a change in the very character of American society.

Republicanism intensified the radicalism of the "country" ideology Americans had borrowed from opposition groups in English society and linked it with older and deeper European currents of thought. This republican tradition reached back through the brief commonwealth period in seventeenth-century England and the writings of James Harrington, John Milton, and Algernon Sidney to its classical beginnings in antiquity. By the eighteenth century this republican tradition had become a kind of counter-culture for many dissatisfied Europeans. In countless writings and translations, eighteenth-century European and English intellectuals evoked the image of an earlier Roman republican world of simple yeomen-citizens enjoying liberty and pastoral virtue. They viewed this idealized ancient world as an alternative to the sprawling monarchies, with their hierarchies, pervasive luxury, and corruption, that they had come to despise in their own time.

In the excitement of the Revolutionary movement, these classical republican values merged with the long-existing image of Americans as a simple, egalitarian, liberty-loving people to form one of the most coherent and powerful ideologies the Western world had yet seen. Many of the ambiguities Americans had felt about the rustic provincial character of their society were now clarified. What some people had seen as the crudities and deficiencies of American life could now be viewed as advantages for republican government. Independent American farmers who owned their own land were now regarded not as primitive folk living on the edges of European society and in the backwaters of history, but as citizens naturally equipped to realize the republican values intellectuals had espoused for centuries.

Independent Citizens. Inevitably then the new American states in 1776 became republics. Everyone knew that these new republics with their elective systems had not only political but moral and social significance. Republicanism struck directly at the traditional society in which heredity, patronage, and dependency were essential. Believing that the social evils of the Old World—encrusted privilege, inflated aristocracy, and pervasive poverty—all flowed from the abuses of government, republican liberals aimed to reduce if not destroy government's overarching power. They were determined that government no longer be able to squeeze money from the people, create titles of distinction, grant monopolies, shore up religious establishments, dispense offices, and do all those other things that ate away at the moral vitality of the people. In place of strong government, republicanism promised a society in which relations would be based on natural merit and the equality of independent citizens linked to one another in harmony. Although republicanism was based on individual property-holding, it repudiated a narrow, selfish individualism and stressed a morality of social cohesion and devotion to the common welfare. Several of the states, Massachusetts, Pennsylvania, and Virginia, in 1776 even adopted the designation "commonwealth" to express better this new dedication to the public good.

Such republican communities of independent citizens presented an inspiring ideal. But history had shown republics to be the most unstable kind of state, highly susceptible to faction and internal disorder. Theorists thus concluded that republics had to be small in territory and homogeneous in character. The only existing European republican models—the Netherlands, and the Italian and Swiss city-states—were small and compact. When a large country attempted to establish a republic, as England had tried to do in the seventeenth century, the experiment was sure to end in some sort of dictatorship, like that of Oliver Cromwell. Unlike monarchies, whose executive power and numerous dependent ranks maintained public order even over a large and diverse population, republics had to be held together from below, by the people themselves.

The Need for Virtue. Republicanism was radical precisely because it demanded an extraordinary degree of moral virtue in the people. If only the society could be organized so as to allow the moral strength of people to express itself, then there would be little need for excessive monarchlike government. But if the society developed in such a manner as to lessen the people's virtue, if the people became selfish and luxury-loving as the ancient Romans had, then the society's ability to sustain a republic would be lost and the transformation of the republican state into a monarchy or dictatorship would inevitably follow.

Americans, however, seemed naturally virtuous and thus ideally suited for republican government. Did they not possess the same hardy egalitarian character that the ancient republican citizens had had? Were not the remarkable displays of popular order in the face of disintegrating royal governments in 1774–75 evidence of the willingness of the American people to obey their governments without coercion? The Revolutionary leaders exhorted the American people to act patriotically, telling them, as Samuel Adams did, that "a Citizen owes everything to the Commonwealth." The citizen was in fact, as the Philadelphia physician Benjamin Rush said, "public property. His time and talents—his youth—his manhood—his old age—nay more, life, all belong to his country."

Republican citizens, in short, had to be patriots, and patriots were not simply those who loved their country but those who were free from the control of others. As Jefferson wrote in his *Notes on Virginia*, "Dependence begets subservience and venality, suffocates the germ of virtue, and prepares fit tools for the designs of ambition." Hence the sturdy independent yeomen, Jefferson's "chosen people of God," were regarded as the most incorruptible and the best citizens for a republic.

The individual ownership of property, especially land, was essential for a republic, both as a source of independence and as evidence of a permanent attachment to the community. Those who were propertyless and dependent, like women and servants, could thus be justifiably denied the vote because they could have no wills of their own. In Europe, corruption and dependency were common because only a few people possessed property. But, as one Carolinian wrote in 1777, "The people of America are a people of property; almost every man is a freeholder." Jefferson was so keen on this point that he proposed in 1776 that the new commonwealth of Virginia grant fifty acres of land to every citizen who did not have that many.

Equality. At the heart of this republican emphasis on virtue and independence lay equality, the most powerful and influential concept in American history. Equality was the necessary basis for the anticipated harmony and public virtue of the New World. The incessant squabbling over position and rank and the bitter contentions of factional politics in the colonies had been due, it was said, to the artificial inequality of colonial society, created and nourished largely through the influence and patronage of the British crown. In a republic individuals were no longer doomed to be what their fathers had been. It was ability not birth that mattered. But republican equality did not mean the elimination of distinctions. Republics would still have an aristocracy, said Jefferson, but it would be a natural not an artificial one. A republican elite would resemble not the luxury-loving, money-mongering lackeys of the British court but the stoical and disinterested heroes of antiquity—men like George Washington, who seemed to Americans to embody perfectly the classical ideal of a republican leader.

Obviously these ideals of Revolutionary republicanism could not be wholly realized. Much of its communitarian emphasis flew in the face of the surging individualism of American life. Yet whatever the practical results, republicanism as it was idealized by Jefferson's generation colored the entire Revolutionary movement. Eventually it would come to shape much of what Americans believe and value.

CHRONOLOGY

1775   Battle of Lexington and Concord.
Fort Ticonderoga taken by American forces.
Second Continental Congress meets in
Philadelphia.
George Washington appointed commander in
chief of Continental army.
Battle of Bunker Hill.
Congress adopts its "Declaration of the Causes
and Necessities of Taking Up Arms."
George III proclaims colonists in open
rebellion.
American forces fail to take Quebec; General
Montgomery killed.
Pennsylvania Quakers form first antislavery
society in world.

1776   Thomas Paine's *Common Sense.*
British troops evacuate Boston.
Congress calls on colonies to suppress all
crown authority and establish governments
under authority of the people.
Declaration of Independence.
Battle of Long Island, New York; Americans
defeated by General Howe.
British take New York City.
Battle of Trenton.
New Hampshire, New Jersey, Pennsylvania,
Delaware, Maryland, Virginia, North Carolina,
and South Carolina write state constitutions.
Rhode Island and Connecticut change their
colonial charters.

1777   Battle of Princeton.
Battle of Monmouth, New Jersey. Although
outcome indecisive, Washington's troops stand
up to British regulars.
Battle of Brandywine, Pennsylvania;
Washington defeated.

British occupy Philadelphia.
Battle of Germantown, Pennsylvania; Howe
repulses Washington's attack.
Burgoyne surrenders at Saratoga.
Articles of Confederation adopted by
Continental Congress, but not ratified by all
states until 1781.
Washington retires to Valley Forge for winter.
New York and Georgia write state constitutions.

1778   United States concludes military alliance and
commercial treaty with France. First and only
military alliance by United States until North
Atlantic Treaty Organization, 1949.
British evacuate Philadelphia.
British seize Savannah, Georgia.

1779   Spain enters the war against Britain.
George Rogers Clark captures Vincennes and
ends British rule in Northwest.

1780   Americans surrender 5,500 men and the city
of Charleston, South Carolina.
Battle of Camden, South Carolina; Gates
defeated by Cornwallis.
Battle of King's Mountain, South Carolina;
British and Tories defeated.
Creation of Massachusetts constitution.

1781   Battle of Cowpens, South Carolina; British
under Tarleton defeated by Morgan.
Battle of Guilford Courthouse, North Carolina;
outcome indecisive, but Cornwallis withdraws
to coast.
Cornwallis surrenders to Washington at
Yorktown, Virginia.

SUGGESTED READINGS

Modern interest in the ideas of the Revolution dates back to the 1920s and 1930s with the studies of constitutional law and natural rights philosophy by Carl Becker, *The Declaration of Independence* (1922); Charles H. McIlwain, *The American Revolution: A Constitutional Interpretation* (1923); Randolph G. Adams, *Political Ideas of the American Revolution* (1922); William S. Carpenter, *The Development of American Political Thought* (1930); and Benjamin F. Wright, Jr., *American Interpretations of Natural Law* (1931). While these books emphasized formal political theory, others explicitly treated the ideas as propaganda. See Philip Davidson, *Propaganda and the American Revolution, 1763–1783* (1941); and Arthur M. Schlesinger, *Prelude to Independence: The Newspaper War on Britain, 1764–1776* (1958).

In the 1950s serious attention was paid to the determinative influence of ideas in Clinton Rossiter, *Seedtime of the Republic* (1953); and especially in Edmund S. Morgan and Helen M. Morgan, *The Stamp Act Crisis* (1953). The Morgan book focuses on parliamentary sovereignty.

Only in the 1960s, however, did historians comprehend the Revolutionary ideas as ideology and begin to recover the distinctiveness of the late eighteenth-century world. The starting point now for analyzing the ideology of the Revolution—as a configuration of ideas giving meaning and force to events—is Bernard Bailyn, *The Ideological Origins of the American Revolution* (1967). Bailyn's book, which appeared initially as the introduction to the first of a four-volume edition of *Pamphlets of the American Revolution, 1750–1776* (1965–   ), was partly based on the rediscovery of the radical Whig tradition by Caroline Robbins, *The Eighteenth-Century Commonwealthmen* (1959). J. G. A. Pocock, *The Machiavellian Moment* (1975); J. R. Pole, *Political Representation in England and the Origins of the American Republic* (1966); Trevor H. Colbourn, *The Lamp of Experience: Whig History and the Beginnings of the American Revolution* (1965); and Isaac F. Kramnick, *Bolingbroke and His Circle* (1968), have further contributed to an understanding of the sources of the Revolutionary tradition. Pauline Maier, *From Resistance to Revolution* (1972), details the escalation of American fears of British policy between 1765 and 1776.

On the military actions of the Revolutionary War, the best brief account is Willard M. Wallace, *Appeal to Arms* (1951). Don Higginbotham, *The War of American Independence* (1971), and John Shy, *A People Numerous and Armed: Reflections on the Military Struggle for American Independence* (1976), best appreciate the unconventional and guerrilla character of the war. Two books edited by George A. Billias, *George Washington's Generals* (1964) and *George Washington's Opponents* (1969), contain excellent essays written by various historians on the military leaders of both sides. Eric Robeson, *The American Revolution in Its Political and Military Aspects, 1763–1783* (1955), has some penetrating chapters on the conduct of the war. For naval operations, see Gardner W. Allen, *A Naval History of the American Revolution* (2 vols., 1913). The fullest account of British strategy is Piers Mackesy, *The War for America, 1775–1783* (1964). On the British commanders in chief, see Ira Gruber, *The Howe Brothers and the American Revolution* (1972); and William Willcox, *Portrait of a General: Sir Henry Clinton in the War of Independence* (1964). Paul H. Smith, *Loyalists and Redcoats* (1964), describes British attempts to mobilize the loyalists.

On diplomacy the standard account is Samuel Flagg Bemis, *The Diplomacy of the American Revolution* (1935). See also William C. Stinchcombe, *The American Revolution and the French Alliance* (1969). Richard B. Morris, *The Peacemakers* (1965), is a full study of the peace negotiations.

For a summary of the history writing covering the eighteenth-century tradition of republicanism, see Robert E. Shalhope, "Toward a Republican Synthesis: The Emergence of an Understanding of Republicanism in American Historiography," *Wm. and Mary Q.*, 3d. ser., 29 (1975). Studies emphasizing the peculiar character of this tradition include Bernard Bailyn, *The Ideological Origins of the American Revolution* (1967); J. G. A. Pocock, *The Machiavellian Moment* (1975); Franco Venturi, *Utopia and Reform in the Enlightenment* (1971); Gerald Stourzh, *Alexander Hamilton and the Idea of Republican Government* (1970); and Gordon S. Wood, *The Creation of the American Republic, 1776–1787* (1969). Garry Wills, *Inventing America: Jefferson's Declaration of Independence* (1978), stresses the importance of Scottish moral sense philosophy and the natural sociableness of people in Jefferson's thought. On the origins of the Americans' conception of the individual's relationship to the state, see James H. Kettner, *The Development of American Citizenship, 1608–1870* (1978). For the influence of antiquity, see Richard Gummere, *The American Colonial Mind and the Classical Tradition* (1963); and Meyer Reinhold, ed., *The Classick Pages* (1975). For the way in which many Europeans viewed the New World in the eighteenth century, see Durand Echeverria, *Mirage in the West* (1957).

CHAPTER 9

The States and the Confederation

"How few of the human race have ever enjoyed an opportunity of making an election of government," rejoiced John Adams, like many others in 1776. Indeed, it was in the spirit of being able to control their own destiny that the Revolutionaries approached the immense task ahead of them. They had an acute sense that the entire world was watching to see how they would put their ideals into practice when they established governments for the new country. Their investigations into the abuses of power and the protection of liberty that had begun during the imperial debate now shaped the new governments they formed, in what proved to be the most creative period of constitutionalism in American history.

State Constitution-Making

From the time royal authority disintegrated, Americans began thinking about creating new governments. During the summer of 1775 Samuel Adams and John Adams of Massachusetts, together with the Virginia delegation to the Continental Congress led by Richard Henry Lee, worked out a program for independence. They made plans to establish foreign alliances, to create a confederation, and most important, to frame new state governments. The climax of their efforts came with the congressional resolutions of May 1776, advising the colonies to adopt new governments "under the authority of people," and declaring "that the exercise of every kind of authority under the . . . Crown should be totally suppressed." Even before the Declaration of Independence, the Congress had created a committee to form a confederation, and some of the states—New Hampshire, South Carolina and Virginia—had begun working on new constitutions. With the May resolves and the Declaration of Independence, the other states followed successively; by the end of 1776 New Jersey, Delaware, Pennsylvania, Maryland, and North Carolina had formed new constitutions. Because the corporate colonies, Rhode Island and Connecticut, were already republics in fact, they simply confined themselves to the elimination of all mention of royal authority in their existing charters. Because of war conditions Georgia and New York delayed their constitution-making until 1777. Massachusetts had recovered its old charter that the British had abrogated, and was busy preparing to write a more permanent constitution.

In 1776–77, most of the Americans' attention and much of their energies were concentrated on establishing these new state constitutions. The states, not the central government or Congress, were to test the Revolutionary hopes. In fact, forming new state governments, as Jefferson said in the spring of 1776, was "the whole object of the present controversy." For the aim of the Revolution had become not simply independence from British tyranny, but the prevention of future tyrannies.

Constitutions as Written Documents. It was inevitable that Americans would embody their constitutions in written documents. By the word "constitution," most eighteenth-century Englishmen meant not a written document but the existing arrangements of government, that is, laws, customs, and institutions, together with the principles they embodied. Americans, however, had come to view a constitution in a different way. From the seventeenth century, they had repeatedly used their colonial charters as defensive barriers against royal authority; and during the debate with Britain, they had been compelled to recognize that laws made by Parliament were not necessarily constitutional, or in accord with fundamental principles of rightness and justice. If the constitutional principles were to be asserted against a too powerful government, then somehow they had to be lifted out of the machinery of government and set above it. The Americans' new state constitutions would therefore have to be fixed plans—written documents as the British constitution never had been—prescibing the powers of government and specifying the rights of citizens.

Fear of Executive Power. As they wrote these new state constitutions, the Americans set about to institutionalize all that they had learned from their colonial experience and from the recent struggle with England. Although they knew they would establish republics, they did not know precisely what forms the new governments should take. Their central aim was to prevent power, which they identified with the rulers or governors, from encroaching upon liberty, which they identified with the people or their representatives in the legislatures. Only the Americans' deep fear of executive power can explain the radical changes they made in the authority of their now elected governors.

In their desire to root out tyranny once and for all, the members of the state congresses who drafted the new constitutions reduced the governors' powers to a pale reflection of those that had been exercised by the royal governors. No longer would governors have the authority to create electoral districts, control the meeting of the assemblies, veto legislation, grant lands, erect courts, issue charters of incorporation, or in some states pardon crimes. All the new state governors were surrounded by controlling councils elected by the assemblies. These governors were to be elected annually, generally by the assemblies, limited in the number of times they could be reelected, and subject to impeachment.

However radical these changes in executive authority may have been, many Americans believed that they did not get to the heart of the matter. They did not destroy the most insidious and dangerous source of despotism—the executive's power of appointment to office. Since in a traditional, monarchical society the disposal of offices, honors, and favors affected the social order, American republicans were determined that their governors would never again have the capacity to dominate public life. Exclusive control over appointments to executive and judicial offices was now wrested from the traditional hands of the governors and shared with the legislatures. This change was justified by the familiar principle of "separation of powers." This emphasis in the new state constitutions on keeping the executive, legislative, and judicial parts of the government separate and distinct was invoked in 1776, not to protect each power from the others, but to keep the judiciary and especially the legislature free from executive manipulation, the very kind of manipulation that had corrupted the English Parliament. Hence the new constitutions categorically barred all executive office-holders and those receiving salaries from the government from sitting in the legislatures. As a consequence, parliamentary cabinet government such as existed in England was forever prohibited in America, and constitutional development moved off in a direction independent of the former mother country.

Strengthening of the Legislatures.　The powers and prerogatives taken from the governors in the new state constitutions of 1776 were granted to the legislatures. This marked a radical shift in the responsibility of government. Traditionally in English history the "government" had mainly been identified with the executive; representative bodies had generally been confined to voting taxes and passing corrective and exceptional legislation. But the new American state legislatures, in particular the lower houses of the assemblies, were no longer to be merely adjuncts of governmental power or checks on it. They were now given powers formerly reserved to magistrates, including the making of alliances and the granting of pardons.

To ensure that the state legislatures fully embodied the will of the people, the ideas and experiences behind the Americans' view of representation were now drawn out and implemented. The Revolutionary state constitutions put a new emphasis on actual representation and explicit consent: on equal electoral districts, on annual elections, on a broadened suffrage, on residential requirements for both electors and elected, and on the right of constituents to instruct their representatives. The royal authority's prohibition against extending representation to newly settled areas was now dramatically reversed. Towns and counties, particularly in the backcountry, were granted either new or additional representation in the state legislatures, in a belated recognition of the legitimacy of the western uprisings of the 1760s. Some of the new constitutions even explicitly recognized the principle that population was the basis of representation. Five states wrote into fundamental law specific plans for periodic adjustments of their representation, so that, as the New York constitution of 1777 stated, it "shall for ever remain proportionate and adequate."

In light of what would happen in the coming dec-ade, the confidence of the Revolutionaries in 1776 in their representative legislatures was remarkable. Except for some disgruntled Tories, few people expected these state legislatures to become tyrannical; for in the Whig theory of politics it did not seem possible for the people to tyrannize over themselves. Of course the people were apt to be licentious or headstrong; hence the republics needed not only governors but upper houses in the legislatures to counterbalance the popular lower houses of representatives. All the states, except Pennsylvania, Georgia, and the new state of Vermont, therefore provided for upper houses or senates, the designation taken from Roman history. The senators in these bicameral state legislatures were not to be a legally defined nobility but the wisest and best members of the society, who would revise and correct the well-intentioned but often careless measures of the people represented in the lower houses.

This Revolutionary state constitution-making was an extraordinary achievement. Nothing quite like it had occurred before in modern history. Foreign intellectuals thought that the new American state constitutions were concrete realizations of Enlightenment ideas. In the decade following Independence the state constitutions were translated, published, and republished in France and other European countries, and their features were avidly examined and debated. More than anything else in 1776 these new written state constitutions gave people everywhere a sense that a new era in history was beginning.

The Articles of Confederation

At the same time that the Revolutionaries were creating their state constitutions, they were drafting a central government. Yet in marked contrast to the rich and exciting public explorations of political theory accompanying the formation of the state constitutions, there was little discussion of the plans for a central government. In 1776 the loyalties of most people were still concentrated on their particular provinces. The Declaration of Independence, drawn up by the Continental Congress, was actually a declaration by "thirteen united States of America" proclaiming that as "Free and Independent States, they have full Power to levy War, conclude Peace, contract Alliances, establish Commerce, and to do all other Acts and Things which independent States may of right do." Despite all the talk of union, few Americans in 1776 could conceive of creating a single full-fledged Continental republic.

Still, the Congress needed some legal basis for its authority. Like the various provincial conventions, it had been created in 1774 simply out of necessity, and was exercising an extraordinary degree of political, military, and economic power over Americans. It had adopted commercial codes, established and maintained an army, issued a Continental currency, erected a military code of law, defined crimes against the union, and negotiated abroad. With the approach of Independence it was obvious to many leaders that a more permanent and legitimate union of the states was necessary. Although a draft of a confederation was ready for consideration by the Congress as early

as mid-July 1776, not until November 1777, after heated controversy, did Congress present a document of union to the states for their separate approval or rejection. It took nearly four years, until March 1781, for all the states to accept this document and thereby legally establish the Articles of Confederation.

The Nature of the Union.   The Articles created a confederacy, called "The United States of America," that was essentially a continuation of the Second Continental Congress. Delegates from each state were to be sent annually to the Congress, and each state delegation was to have only a single vote. In Article 9 Congress was granted the authority to determine diplomatic relations, requisition the states for men and money, coin and borrow money, regulate Indian affairs, and settle disputes between the states. While a simple majority of seven states was needed for minor matters, a larger majority, nine states, was required for important matters, including engaging in

PAPER CURRENCY ISSUED BY THE CONTINENTAL CONGRESS

(*American Antiquarian Society*)

war, making treaties, and coining and borrowing money. There was no real executive but only congressional committees with fluctuating memberships.

This union was stronger than many people expected. The states were specifically forbidden to conduct foreign affairs, make treaties, or declare war. The citizens of each state were entitled to the privileges and immunities of the citizens of all states. All travel and discriminatory trade restrictions between the states were eliminated. Judicial proceedings of each state were honored by all states. These stipulations, together with the substantial grant of powers to the Congress, made the United States of America as strong as any similar republican confederation in history. The Articles marked a big step toward a genuine national government.

Nevertheless, the Americans' fear of distant central authority, intensified by a century of experience in the British empire, left no doubt that this Confederation would remain something less than a full national government. Under the Articles, the crucial powers of commercial regulation and taxation, indeed all final lawmaking authority, remained with the states. Congressional resolutions continued to be, as they had been under the Continental Congress, recommendations which, it was assumed, the states would enforce. And should there be any doubts of the decentralized nature of the Confederation, Article 2 stated bluntly that "each State retains its sovereignty, freedom and independence, and every power, jurisdiction, and right, which is not by this confederation expressly delegated to the United States, in Congress assembled."

The "United States of America" thus possessed a literal meaning that is hard to appreciate today. The Confederation, based on equal representation of each state, necessarily resembled more a treaty among closely cooperating sovereign states than a single government. It was intended to be and remained, as Article 3 declared, "a firm league of friendship" among states jealous of their individuality. Not only ratification of the Articles of Confederation but any subsequent changes in it required consent of all states.*

*For the Articles of Confederation, see Appendix.

State Rivalries and the Disposition of the Western Lands. The local self-interests of the states prolonged the congressional debates over the adoption of the Articles and delayed its unanimous ratification until 1781. The major disputes—over representation, the apportionment of the states' contribution to the union, and the disposition of the western lands—involved concrete state interests. Large populous states like Virginia argued for proportional representation in the Congress, but had to give way to the small states' determination to maintain equal representation. The original draft of the Articles provided that each state's financial contribution to the general treasury be based on its population, including slaves. Strenuous opposition from the southern states, however, forced the Congress to shift the basis for a state's financial contribution to the value of its land. This was done against the wishes of the New England states where land values were high.

The states' rivalries were most evident in the long controversy over the disposition of the western lands between the Appalachians and the Mississippi. The Articles sent to the states in 1778 for ratification gave Congress no authority over the unsettled lands of the interior, and this delayed its approval. While states like Virginia and Massachusetts with charter claims to this western territory wanted to maintain control over the disposal of their land, states like Maryland and Rhode Island without such claims wanted the western land pooled in a common national domain under the authority of Congress. By March 1779, however, all the states had ratified the Articles except Maryland, which, under the influence of land speculators, refused to join the union until all the states had ceded their western lands to the central government. When Virginia, the state with charter rights to the largest amount of western territory, finally agreed on January 2, 1781, to surrender its claims to the United States, the way was prepared for other land cessions and for ratification of the Articles of Confederation by all the states. But the Confederation had to promise, in return for the cession of claims by Virginia and the other states, that this huge national domain in the West would "be settled and formed into distinct republican states."

BRITISH POSSESSIONS

Disputed With Great Britain until 1842

MAINE (Part of Mass.)

L. Superior

St. Lawrence R.

(Claimed by Virginia) Ceded 1784

L. Michigan

(by N.Y. and Va.)

L. Huron

L. Ontario

NEW YORK   VT   N.H.

(Claimed by Mass. and Va.) Ceded 1785, 1784

(by Mass., Va. and N.Y.)

N.Y.

L. Erie

(Ceded to N.Y. 1786)

(Claimed by N.Y. and Mass.)

MASS.

CONN.   R.I.

Claimed by Conn., N.Y. and Va. Ceded 1786, 1782

PENNSYLVANIA

N.J.

S P A N I S H

(Claimed by Virginia and New York) Ceded 1784, 1782

Ohio R.

A L L E G H E N Y   M T S.

MD.

DEL.

VIRGINIA

L O U I S I A N A

Mississippi R.

(Claimed by Spain)

(Claimed by N.Y. and N.C.) Ceded 1790

NORTH CAROLINA

(Claimed by S. Carolina)

SOUTH CAROLINA

(Claimed by Spain and Georgia) Ceded 1802

GEORGIA

(Claimed by Spain, U.S. and Ga.)

SPANISH   FLORIDA

State Claims to Western Lands and Cessions

Western Claims
Western Reserve, Ceded 1800

Ordinances for the West.

The Congress drew up land ordinances in 1784 and 1785, and in 1787 it adopted the famous Northwest Ordinance which acknowledged, as the British in the 1760s had not, the settlers' destiny in the West. The land ordinances of 1784 and 1785 provided for the land north of the Ohio River and west of the Appalachians to be surveyed and formed into townships of six miles square along lines running east–west and north–south. Each township was divided into thirty-six numbered lots, or sections of 640 acres. The Confederation favored speculators and large groups by providing for the sale of the land by auction and by stipulating that a section was to be the smallest unit purchased, at a price of no less than a dollar an acre. In each township Congress retained four sections for future sale and set aside one other for the support of public education. The Ordinance of 1787 dealt with the political organization of the Northwest. It guaranteed to the settlers basic political and legal rights and arranged for the area to be divided into not less than three nor more than five territories. When each territory reached a population of 60,000 it was to be admitted to the Union on equal terms with the existing states.

These remarkable ordinances were the greatest achievement of the Confederation outside of winning the war. They solved at a stroke the problem, which Britain had been unable to solve, of relating "colonies" or dependencies to the central government. In the succeeding decades the Land Ordinance of 1785 and the Ordinance of 1787 remained the bases for the surveying, sale, and the political evolution of America's western territories. Settlers could leave the older states assured that they were not abandoning their political liberties and know that they would be allowed eventually to form new republics as sovereign and independent as the other states in the Union. Thus even the organization of this great national landed resource by the Congress was immediately devoted to the dispersion of central authority by the anticipated creation of more states, the only political units most Americans seemed to value.

Republican Society

At the same time that efforts to establish governments and constitutions were being made, unsettling changes in American society were taking place. To be sure, there was no immediate collapse of the social order and no abrupt and wholesale destruction of familiar social institutions. But everywhere there were alterations in the way people related to government, to the economy, and to each other. Many of these changes were the results of deeply rooted forces long in motion, some since the beginning of the colonial period. But others were the sudden effects of the Revolution itself.

The Departure of the Loyalists. One such sudden effect was the departure of tens of thousands of loyalists. The loyalists may have numbered close to half a million, or 20 percent of white Americans. Nearly twenty thousand of them fought for the crown in regiments of His Majesty's army, and thousands of others served in local loyalist militia bodies. As many as sixty to eighty thousand loyalists, it is estimated, left America during the Revolution for Canada and

Great Britain, although many of these returned after the war and were reintegrated into American society. Although the loyalists came from all ranks and occupations of the society, a disproportionate number of them belonged to the upper political and social levels. Many had been officeholders and overseas merchants involved with government contracting; in the North, most were Anglicans. Their regional distribution was likewise uneven. In New England and Virginia they were a tiny minority. But in western frontier areas, where hostility to eastern encroachment went back to the pre-Revolutionary times, and in the regions of New York, New Jersey, and Pennsylvania, and the Deep South where the British army offered protection, loyalists made up a considerable part of the population. Their flight, displacement, and retirements created a vacuum at the top that was rapidly filled by patriots. The effects were widespread. Crown and Tory property and lands valued at millions of pounds were confiscated by the Revolutionary governments and almost immediately thrown onto the market. The resulting speculation accentuated the sudden rise and fall of fortunes during the Revolutionary years.

Economic Effects of the Revolution. Economic disruptions created the most social disorder. Suddenly Americans found themselves outside the protective walls of the British mercantile empire which had nurtured their commercial life for over a century. Exports dropped drastically. Traditional markets in Britain, and especially in the British West Indies, were closed. Bounties paid on particular colonial products were now gone. Colonial ships could no longer be sold to Britain and prewar sources of credit were upset. Such changes were devastating to particular groups and individuals, but overall the results of the break from Britain were beneficial and stimulating. Simply by destroying old encrusted habits and relationships the Revolution released new energies.

The South suffered the greatest dislocations from the war. Not only did it lose established markets for its tobacco and other staples, but tens of thousands of its slaves were freed by the British and taken out of the country. Indeed, the British army was perhaps the greatest single instrument of emancipation in

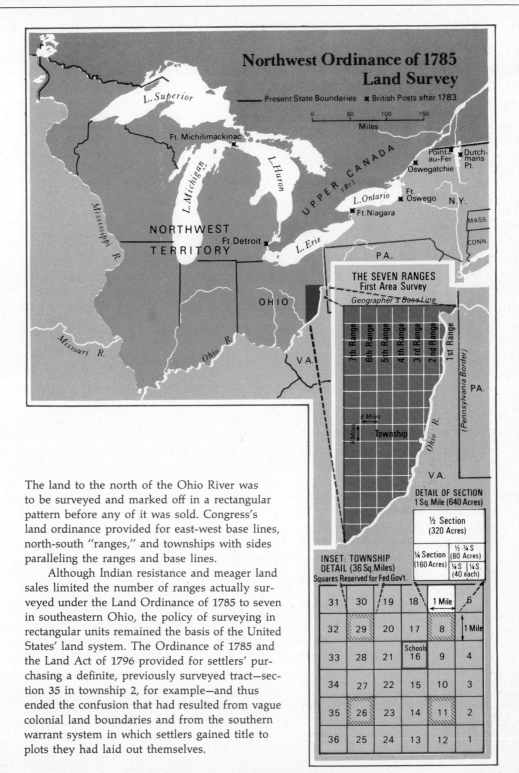

Northwest Ordinance of 1785 Land Survey

— Present State Boundaries ■ British Posts after 1783

0 · · 50 · · 100 · · 150
Miles

L. Superior

Ft. Michilimackinac

L. Michigan

L. Huron

UPPER CANADA (Br.)

Point au-Fer · Dutchmans Pt.
Oswegatchie

L. Ontario · Ft. Oswego

Ft. Niagara

N.Y.

MASS.

CONN.

NORTHWEST TERRITORY

Ft. Detroit

L. Erie

Mississippi R.

OHIO

PA.

THE SEVEN RANGES
First Area Survey

Geographer's Base Line

7th Range · 6th Range · 5th Range · 4th Range · 3rd Range · 2nd Range · 1st Range

Missouri R.

Ohio R.

V.A.

(Pennsylvania Border)

6 Miles
6 Miles
Township

PA.

Ohio R.

V.A.

DETAIL OF SECTION
1 Sq. Mile (640 Acres)

½ Section (320 Acres)	
¼ Section (160 Acres)	½-¼ S (80 Acres)
	¼ S ¦ ¼ S. (40 each)

INSET: TOWNSHIP DETAIL (36 Sq. Miles)
Squares Reserved for Fed. Gov't.

31	30	19	18	1 Mile	6
32	29	20	17	8	1 Mile
33	28	21	Schools 16	9	4
34	27	22	15	10	3
35	26	23	14	11	2
36	25	24	13	12	1

The land to the north of the Ohio River was to be surveyed and marked off in a rectangular pattern before any of it was sold. Congress's land ordinance provided for east-west base lines, north-south "ranges," and townships with sides paralleling the ranges and base lines.

Although Indian resistance and meager land sales limited the number of ranges actually surveyed under the Land Ordinance of 1785 to seven in southeastern Ohio, the policy of surveying in rectangular units remained the basis of the United States' land system. The Ordinance of 1785 and the Land Act of 1796 provided for settlers' purchasing a definite, previously surveyed tract—section 35 in township 2, for example—and thus ended the confusion that had resulted from vague colonial land boundaries and from the southern warrant system in which settlers gained title to plots they had laid out themselves.

"THE TONTINE COFFEE HOUSE," BY GUY FRANCIS, 1797
During the Revolution fire had ravaged much of the commercial section of New York. In the following years New York's merchants enlarged the harbor facilities and rebuilt the business district, including this busy corner of Wall and Water streets. By 1797 New York had surpassed rival Philadelphia in both imports and exports. (*Courtesy of The New-York Historical Society, New York City*)

America until the Civil War. But these dislocations only accelerated an agricultural diversification that had begun before the Revolution. The Upper South in particular recovered rapidly. Tobacco production in the 1780s equaled prewar levels, and involved many new participants and new marketing arrangements.

In the North divisions within the merchant communities that had been apparent before the Revolution now widened, and merchants who had previously been on the periphery of economic activity were granted new opportunities at the center of things. In Massachusetts, for example, provincial families like the Higginsons, Cabots, and Lowells quickly moved into Boston and formed the basis of a new Massachusetts elite. The same process was duplicated

less notably but no less importantly elsewhere. New merchants pushed out in all directions in search of new markets, not only into the restricted colonial areas of the West Indies and South America, but throughout Europe and even as far away as China.

After the war trade with Great Britain quickly reached its earlier levels; by the 1780s aggregate figures show an amazing recovery of commerce. Yet such gross statistics do not do justice to the extent of change involved; for in all the states there were new sources of supply, new commercial configurations, and new and increased numbers of participants in the market. Although exports soon surpassed their prewar levels, they now represented a smaller part of America's total economic activity. The wartime collapse of British imports had encouraged domestic manufacturing, and though purchasing of British goods resumed with the return of peace, societies were now formed to promote American manufacturing and to secure protective legislation. Already the economy was beginning to turn inward with a remarkable spread of interstate and interregional trade that would soon generate demands for new roads and canals. In these changing circumstances, towns without hinterlands to exploit began a relative decline. Newport, Rhode Island, for example, had been a flourishing colonial port but, without an inland area for supply and marketing, it rapidly slipped into insignificance.

The Revolutionary War itself was at once a disrupting and a creative force. Like all wars, it destroyed familiar channels of trade and produced new sources of wealth. Almost overnight the machinery of governmental finance was overhauled. During the war the Congress and the states became gigantic borrowers and buyers and dominated economic life in ways that were unfamiliar to eighteenth-century Americans. Since there were no mechanisms for assessing and taxing wealth, and since Congress did not even have the legal authority to tax, American governments had to rely largely on borrowing to pay for the war. But government borrowing could scarcely raise the sums needed. Both the Congress and the state governments therefore resorted to the extensive printing of noninterest-bearing paper currency, which took on the character of forced loans. These bills of credit, which the governments promised to redeem by taxes at some future time, were given to citizens in return for supplies and services.

This currency issued by the congressional and state governments eventually totaled nearly $400 million in paper value and led to a socially disintegrating inflation. By 1781, $167 of congressional paper money was worth only $1 in specie, and the depreciation of the states' bills was nearly as bad. While creditors, wage earners, and those on relatively fixed incomes were hurt by this inflation, many of those who were most active in the economy, buying and selling goods rapidly, were able to profit. These circulating government bills enabled countless commodity farmers and traders to break out of a barter economy and to specialize and participate more independently in the market. Throughout the war, government buying was generally a commercial stimulant; army purchasing agencies became new centers of economic activity and breeding grounds for both petty entrepreneurs and powerful postwar capitalists.

(*American Antiquarian Society*)

Long-Range Social Change. These were the immediate social and economic effects of the war. But there were other, deeper, and more long-lasting conditions that were greatly affected by the Revolution and by republicanism. Despite a slackening of immigration and the loss of tens of thousands of loyalist emigrés, the population continued to grow. The 1780s saw the fastest rate of demographic growth of any decade in American history. This swelling population, after being delayed for several years in the late 70s by intermittent warfare against the British and Indians, resumed its movement westward. By the early 1780s there were over twenty thousand inhabitants in the Kentucky territory; within a decade it had become more populous than most of the colonies had been at the time of the Revolution.

This spectacular growth and movement of people further weakened the traditional forms of social organization. Such a mobile population, one Kentuckian told James Madison in 1792, "must make a very different mass from one which is composed of men born and raised on the same spot. . . . They see none about them to whom or to whose families they have been accustomed to think themselves inferior." And the ideology of republicanism intensified these tendencies. In a republic, declared a writer in 1787 in the *American Museum* (the most important of several new American magazines founded in the postwar years), "the idea of equality breathes through the whole and every individual feels ambitious to be in a situation not inferior to his neighbour."

This republican equality became a rallying cry

FRONTIER FARM IN 1793

Even at the end of the eighteenth century, many American farmers continued to grow their crops Indian style, girdling and burning trees, planting between tree stumps, and allowing the fields to revert to forest when their fertility gave out. Such wasteful and shifting methods of agriculture shocked foreign observers but made sense where land was so abundant. (*Harvard College Library*)

NICHOLAS BOYLSTON, BY JOHN
SINGLETON COPLEY, 1760

Boylston represented those wealthy and fashionable circles surrounding royal authority that ambitious men like John Adams simultaneously admired and resented. "Dined at Mr. Nick Boylstones . . . ," Adams in 1766 confided to his diary with wide-eyed excitement. "An elegant dinner indeed! Went over the house to view the furniture, which alone cost a thousand pounds sterling. A seat it is for a noble man, a prince, the turkey carpets, the painted hangings, the marble tables, the rich beds with crimson damask curtains and counterpanes, the beautiful chimney clock, the spacious garden, are the most magnificent of any thing I have ever seen." (*Fogg Art Museum, Harvard University*)

ularly bitter hostility. Some fervent citizens attacked distinctions of all kinds, including membership in private social clubs and the wearing of imported finery. Gentlemen in some areas of the North found that the traditional attributes of social authority—breeding, education, gentility—were becoming liabilities for political leadership. In this new republican society no one would admit being dependent on anyone else. Every citizen now claimed for himself or herself the titles that had once belonged only to the gentry—"Mr." and "Mrs." Foreign visitors were stunned by the unwillingness of American servants to address their masters and mistresses as superiors and by the servants' refusal to admit they were anything but "help." For many Americans, never having to doff one's cap to anyone was what living in a free country meant.

This growing egalitarianism did not mean that in post-Revolutionary America wealth was distributed more equitably. On the contrary: the inequality of wealth was greater after the Revolution than before. What it did mean was that the way people related to one another was being transformed. Relationships came to be based on money rather than on social position. Towns, for example, stopped assigning seats in their churches by age and status and began auctioning the pews to the highest bidders. Self-earned wealth gave men the independence that republicanism celebrated and seemed a more appropriate source of achievement than patronage or influence. For many Americans wealth soon became the sole and, in the new republican society, the proper means of distinguishing one person from another.

By the end of the eighteenth century the character of all sorts of former paternalistic dependencies was changing. Many apprentices no longer became "children" in the master's family but were trainees in a business, now often conducted outside the household. Paternalism in labor relations was now replaced by impersonal cash payments, and journeymen moved more frequently from one master to another. Both masters and journeymen in many of the crafts were beginning to perceive their interests as more distinct and conflicting than they had before; and as employers and employees they were forming new class-conscious organizations to protect these interests. Be-

for people in the aspiring middle ranks who were now more openly resentful than ever before of those who presumed to be their social superiors. The formation in 1783 of the hereditary Order of the Cincinnati by Revolutionary army officers aroused partic-

PLEDGE OF SOLIDARITY
This pledge of solidarity between worker and employer
in 1795 represented the tradition of the past when journeymen and masters of a particular craft worked together in the same shop. Already, the interests of artisan
employers and employees were becoming separate and
distinct. (*Library of Congress*)

PAUL REVERE, BY JOHN SINGLETON COPLEY
Urban artisans and craftsmen like the silversmith Paul
Revere were the most important social group in the
cities that emerged into political consciousness during
the Revolutionary era. (*Courtesy, Museum of Fine Arts,
Boston. Gift of Joseph W., William B., and Edward H. R.
Revere*)

tween 1786 and 1816 at least twelve strikes by various
craftsmen occurred (the first major strikes by employees against employers in American history), and
masters were now resorting more and more to the
courts to enforce what had once been seen largely as
a mutual and personal relationship.

The Destruction of Corporate Privilege. Many of
the individual and face-to-face relationships of the
older society gradually gave way to larger and more
impersonal business associations. While only a half-
dozen business charters had been granted in the entire colonial period, in the years after the Revolution
corporate grants rapidly multiplied. The republican
states created private banks, insurance companies,
and manufactures, and licensed entrepreneurs to
operate bridges, roads, and canals.

Eleven charters of incorporation were issued by
the states between 1781 and 1785, 22 between 1786
and 1790, and 114 between 1791 and 1795. Between

1800 and 1817 the states granted nearly 1,800 corporate charters; the single state of Massachusetts had more corporations than existed in all of Europe. If one town had an incorporated bank, it seemed that every town wanted one, and the annually elected popular legislatures of the states, beset by hosts of new interests, were readily pressured into granting them.

This rapid creation of corporations typified the increasingly fragmented nature of the public interest under popularly elected governments. As far back as the Virginia Company, at the time of the original settlements, governmentally chartered corporations had been instruments by which the state harnessed private enterprise to carry out such desirable public goals as founding a colony, maintaining a college, or building a bridge. In the new republican society, however, not only had such forms of legal privilege become suspect, but it had become no longer clear to whom the state ought to grant its legal authority. So mistrusted was legal privilege in the egalitarian atmosphere of the early republic that such corporate monopolies could only be justified by making them available to practically everybody. This practice, of course, destroyed their exclusiveness. If nearly everyone had access to these corporate powers granted by the state, then what had once been a privilege now became a right. And as rights, these corporate charters, even though issued by state legislatures, were immune from future legislative tampering—a view eventually endorsed by the Supreme Court in the *Dartmouth College* case of 1819.

In this famous case the Court decided that the charter of Dartmouth College, although it was originally granted by the New Hampshire legislature and had a public purpose, was a private contract that could not be violated by the legislature. The states in the post-Revolutionary years therefore not only parceled out their legal authority to individuals and groups in the society but at the same time lost control of what they dispersed. Unexpected and disturbing as these disintegrating developments were to devout republicans like Jefferson, they were only the logical consequence of the Revolution's promise to break up politically supported privilege in order to allow the free expression of individual talent and energy.

The Betterment of Humanity

The republicanism of the Revolutionary era was not just exhilarating; it was contagious as well. Its optimistic liberalism, its promise of beginning everything anew, could not be confined to governmental reform or to the invigoration of manufacturing and commerce; inevitably it spilled out into all areas of American life.

In the years following the Revolution there was a suddenly aroused enthusiasm for putting the humanitarian hopes of the Enlightenment into practice. Drawing upon the thoughts of the great seventeenth-century English philosopher John Locke, eighteenth-century liberals stressed the capacity of human nature to be shaped by experience and external circumstances. People were not born to be corrupt. Placed in a proper republican environment, people could develop in healthy ways that the encrusted society of the Old World had not permitted. From these enlightened assumptions flowed the reforming liberalism that would affect the Revolutionary era and all subsequent American history as well.

Educational and Social Reform.   Since republicanism depended upon a knowledgeable citizenry, the Revolution immediately inspired educational efforts of every conceivable sort. American leaders formed scores of scientific organizations and medical societies, and produced many scholarly magazines. Gentlemen-scientists and amateur philosophers gave lectures and wrote essays on everything from raising Merino sheep to expelling noxious vapors from wells. They compiled geographical and historical studies of the states. And they concocted elaborate plans for educational structures ranging from elementary schools to a national university.

Although by 1776 there were only nine colleges in America, by 1800 sixteen more had been founded; and by the early nineteenth century colleges—mostly religiously inspired and short-lived—were being created by the dozens. Yet in the decades immediately following the Revolution most of the high hopes of the Revolutionary leaders for the establishment of publicly supported educational systems were not fulfilled, largely because of penny-pinching legislatures and religious jealousies. Even in New England, which had a long tradition of public education, privately endowed academies sprang up in the post-Revolutionary years to replace the older town supported grammar schools. Nevertheless, the republican ideal that the state had a fundamental responsibility to educate all its citizens remained alive to be eventually realized by the Common School movement during the second quarter of the nineteenth century.

Not only education but all social institutions were affected by this Revolutionary idealism. Americans grasped at the possibility that they might change their environment, even their natural environment, and thus their character. When the fast-growing

BENJAMIN RUSH, 1745–1813

One of the most versatile figures of the American Enlightenment, Rush was a physician, scientist, and humanitarian reformer of unbounded optimism. By the early nineteenth-century however, his earlier confidence in liberal rationalism was gone. The country's reliance on liberty "has already disappointed the expectations of its most sanguine and ardent friends." "Nothing but the gospel of Jesus Christ" could save republicanism. (*Courtesy, Pennsylvania Hospital*)

cities were afflicted by epidemics of yellow fever, Americans cleaned the streets and built public water works for sanitation. If the heat and cold of America's climate were too excessive, they cleared forests and drained marshes, and congratulated themselves on having moderated the weather. They now regarded virtually every sort of social victim as salvageable. Societies for assisting widows, immigrants, debtors, and other distressed groups were formed in the cities. More such philanthropic organizations were established in the decade and a half following Independence than in the entire colonial period. Revolutionary leaders like Jefferson drew up plans for liberalizing the harsh penal codes inherited from the colonial period. Pennsylvania led the way in the 1790s in abolishing the death penalty for all crimes other than murder, and began the experiment of confining criminals in specially designed penitentiaries instead of, as in the past, publicly punishing their bodies by whipping, mutilation, and execution.

The Family and Women. Republicanism even affected the transformation of the family that was taking place in many parts of the Western world at the end of the eighteenth century. In a republican society children could no longer be regarded simply as a means of making money for and bringing honor to the family; everyone in the family had to be treated individually and equally. Thus the new Revolutionary state governments struck out against aristocratic colonial laws that had confined the inheritance of property to the eldest sons (primogeniture) and to special lines of heirs (entail). Family-arranged marriages increasingly gave way to ties based on romantic love, and writings and novels in the post-Revolutionary years stressed the importance of raising children to become rational and independent citizens.

Republicanism also enhanced the status of women. It was now said that women as wives and mothers had a special role in cultivating in their husbands and children the moral feelings—virtue and social affection—necessary to hold a sprawling and competitive republican society together. Although some American leaders like the physician and humanitarian Benjamin Rush concluded that republi-

ABIGAIL ADAMS, BY MATHER BROWN
Though unschooled, the wife of John Adams was a confident, intelligent and widely-read woman. Occasionally she expressed her resentment at the circumscribed role allowed to women in the eighteenth century, playfully urging John in 1776 to "remember the ladies" in his plans for enhancing liberty. But generally she was very willing to sacrifice herself for her husband and to accept her femininity "as a punishment for the transgression of Eve." *(New York State Historical Association, Cooperstown, New York)*

MERCY OTIS WARREN (1728-1814), BY JOHN SINGLETON COPLEY
Warren, a sister of James Otis and the wife of the Massachusetts patriot James Warren, was an important intellectual figure in her own right. She wrote a number of satiric plays and a three-volume devoutly republican history of the Revolution. *(Courtesy, Museum of Fine Arts, Boston)*

canism required women to be educated along with men, others feared that female education would lead only to vanity and a false ornamental gentility. Besides, asked Timothy Dwight, president of Yale, if women were educated, "Who will make our puddings?"

At the same time that a distinct sphere of domestic usefulness was being urged on women, they were becoming more economically important and indepen-

dent. Economic developments made it possible for women to earn their own incomes by working in handicrafts at home, hence enabling them to purchase more and more "conveniences." Once they had become more independent by earning money at home, women found it easier to work outside the household, in factories and later as teachers. Although the development of a new sphere of domestic usefulness for women may seem regressive by modern standards, it was at the time liberating, and it intensified the advance begun in the colonial period over the dependent, inferior position traditionally held by women.

Antislavery. Perhaps the institution most directly and substantially affected by the liberalizing spirit of republicanism was chattel slavery. To be sure, the enslavement of nearly a half a million blacks was not eradicated at the Revolution, and in modern eyes this failure, amid all the high-blown talk of liberty and equality, becomes the one glaring and hypocritical inconsistency of the Revolutionary era. Nevertheless, the Revolution did suddenly and effectively end the social and intellectual climate that had allowed black slavery to exist in the colonies for over a century without substantial questioning. The colonists had generally taken slavery for granted as part of the natural order of society and as one aspect of the general brutality and cheapness of life in those premodern and prehumanitarian times. Bondage and servitude in many forms had continued to exist in pre-Revolutionary America, and the colonists had felt little need to question or defend slavery any more than other forms of debasement. Now, however, republican citizenship suddenly brought into question all kinds of personal dependency. For the first time

THE OLD PLANTATION, c. 1774–1794

"On Sundays," wrote a British visitor to the Chesapeake in 1774, "the slaves generally meet together and amuse themselves with Dancing to the Banjo. This musical instrument . . . is made of a Gourd something in imitation of a guitar, with only four strings. . . . Their Dancing is most violent exercise, but so irregular and grotesque. I am not able to describe it." (*Abby Aldrich Rockefeller Folk Art Center, Williamsburg*)

Americans were compelled to confront the slavery in their midst, to recognize that it was an aberration, a "peculiar institution," and, if they were to retain it, to explain and justify it.

Even before the Declaration of Independence, the colonists' struggle against political "slavery" had exposed the contradiction of tolerating chattel slavery. The initial efforts to end the contradiction were directed at the slave trade. In 1774 the Continental Congress urged abolishing the slave trade, and a half-dozen states quickly followed this advice. In 1775 the Quakers of Philadelphia formed the first antislavery society in the world, and soon similar societies were organized elsewhere, even in the South. During the war Congress and the northern states together with Maryland gave freedom to black slaves who enlisted in their armies. In various ways the Revolution worked to weaken the institution.

In the North, where slavery of a less harsh sort than existed in the South had been widespread but not deeply rooted in the society or economy, the institution was susceptible to political pressure, and it slowly began to recede. In the decades following the Revolution, most of the northern states moved to destroy slavery. By 1830 there were less than 3,000 slaves out of a northern black population of over 125,000. The Revolutionary vision of a society of independent freeholders led Congress in the 1780s to forbid slavery in the newly organized Northwest Territory between the Appalachians and the Mississippi. The new federal Constitution of 1787 promised an end to the slave trade after twenty years (1808), which many hoped would cripple the institution.

In the South, however, despite initial criticism by Jefferson and Madison and other enlightened social thinkers, slavery was too entrenched to be legislatively or judicially abolished. Southern whites who had been in the vanguard of the Revolutionary movement and among the most fervent spokesmen for its liberalism now began to develop a self-conscious sense of difference from the rest of America that they had never had before. By the 1790s the South was living with a growing realization, fed by the black insurrections in Santo Domingo, that the American presumption that people everywhere had a right to seek their freedom meant all people, white or black.

Democratic Despotism

Post-Revolutionary America was not all exhilaration and optimism however. Despite the victory over Great Britain and the achievement of independence, many of the Revolutionary leaders soon became disillusioned in the 1780s with the way the Revolution was developing. The very success of the Revolution in opening up opportunities for economic prosperity to new elements of the population made the 1780s a critical period for some members of the Revolutionary elite. Some even thought the entire experiment in republicanism was in danger. Too many ordinary people, some felt, were perverting republican equality, defying legitimate authority, and confounding those natural distinctions that all gentlemen, even republican gentlemen, thought essential for social order. Everywhere, even among the sturdy independent yeomen farmers—Jefferson's "chosen people of God"—private interests, selfishness, and money-making seemed to be eclipsing social affection and public spirit and indicating that Americans lacked the qualities required of republicans. If this were true, America, some feared, was doomed to share the fate that had befallen the ancient republics, Britain, and other corrupt nations. Americans, William Livingston, governor of New Jersey concluded in 1787, "do not exhibit the virtue that is necessary to support a republican government." This unrepublican character of the people seemed most clearly revealed in the behavior of the greatly strengthened state legislatures.

Democratization of the State Legislatures. The radical changes in representation that accompanied the Revolution had democratized the state assemblies by increasing the number of members and by altering their social character. Men of more humble, more rural origins, and less educated than those who sat in the colonial legislatures, now became representatives. In New Hamshire, for example, in 1765 the colonial house of representatives had contained only thirty-four members, almost all well-to-do gentry from the coastal region around Portsmouth. By 1786 the state's house of representatives had increased to eighty-eight members. Most of these men were ordinary farmers or men of moderate wealth, and many were from the western areas of the state. In other states, the change was much less dramatic but no less important. It was reflected in the shifts, or in the attempted shifts, of many of the state capitals from their former colonial locations on the eastern seaboard to new sites in the interior—from Portsmouth to Concord, from New York to Albany, from Williamsburg to Richmond, from New Bern to Raleigh, from Charleston to Columbia, from Savannah to Augusta.

Everywhere electioneering and the open competition for office increased, along with demands for greater popular access to governmental activities. Assembly proceedings were opened to the public, and a growing number of newspapers, which now included dailies, began to report legislative debates. Self-appointed leaders, speaking for newly aroused groups and localities, took advantage of the enlarged suffrage and the annual elections of the legislatures (a radical innovation in most states) to seek membership in the assemblies. New petty entrepreneurs like Abraham Yates, a part-time lawyer and cobbler of Albany, and William Findley, a Scotch-Irish ex-weaver of western Pennsylvania, bypassed the traditional social hierarchy and vaulted into political leadership in the states. The number of contested elections and the turnover of legislative seats multiplied.

Local Factionalism. Under these circumstances many of the state legislatures could scarcely fulfill what many Revolutionaries in 1776 had assumed was their republican responsibility to promote the general good. In every state decisions had to be made about what to do with the loyalists and their confiscated property, about the distribution of taxes among the citizens, and about the economy. Yet with the general political instability, the common welfare in the various states was increasingly difficult to define. By the 1780s James Madison concluded that "a spirit of *locality*" in the state legislatures was destroying "the aggregate interests of the community,"

and that this localist spirit was "inseparable" from elections by small districts and towns. Each representative, said Ezra Stiles, president of Yale College, was concerned only with the special interests of his electors. Whenever a bill was read in the legislature, "every one instantly thinks how it will affect his constituents."

Such narrow-interest politics was not new to America. But the multiplication of economic and social interests in the post-Revolutionary years and the heightened sensitivity of the enlarged popular assemblies to the conflicting demands of these interests now dramatically increased its intensity and importance. Debtor farmers urged low taxes, the staying of court actions to recover debts, and the printing of paper money. Merchants and creditors called for high taxes on land, the protection of private contracts, and the encouragement of foreign trade. Artisans pleaded for price regulation of agricultural products, the abolition of mercantile monopolies, and tariff protection against imported manufactures. And entrepreneurs everywhere petitioned for legal privileges and corporate grants.

All this political scrambling among contending interests made lawmaking in the states seem chaotic. Laws, as the Vermont Council of Censors said in 1786 in a common complaint, were "altered—realtered—made better—made worse; and kept in such a fluctuating position, that persons in civil commission scarce know what is law." As James Madison pointed out, more laws were enacted by the states in the decade following Independence than in the entire colonial period. Many of them were simply private acts for individuals or resolves that redressed minor grievances. Every effort of the legislatures to respond to the excited pleas and pressures of all the various groups alienated as many as it satisfied and brought lawmaking itself into contempt.

By the mid-1780s many American leaders had come to believe that the state legislatures, not the governors, were the political authority to be most feared. Not only were some of the legislators violating the individual rights of property through their excessive printing of paper money and their various acts on behalf of debtors, but in all the states the assemblies pushed beyond the generous grants of legisla-

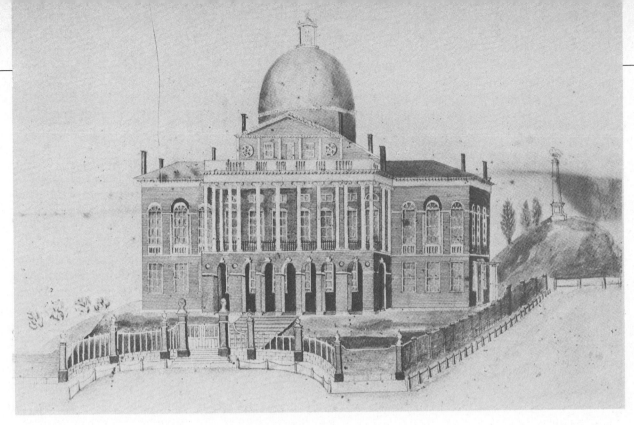

MASSACHUSETTS STATE HOUSE AND MEMORIAL COLUMN, 1795–1798
Charles Bulfinch (1763–1844) was one of the first Americans to move from being a leisured gentleman with an amateur interest in building to becoming a professional architect. Everything about his State House, one of many public buildings he designed, celebrates the new classical grandeur of republican America. (*The Bostonian Society*)

tive authority of the 1776 Revolutionary constitutions and were absorbing numerous executive and judicial duties. It began to seem that the legislative power of the people was no more trustworthy than the detested royal power had been. Legislators were supposedly the representatives of the people who annually elected them; but "173 despots would surely be as oppressive as one," wrote Jefferson in 1785 in his *Notes on Virginia*. "An *elective despotism* was not the government we fought for."

Revision of the State Constitutions. Such growing fears of tyrannical legislatures forced many leaders to have second thoughts about their popularly elected assemblies. Indeed, the ink was scarcely dry on the Revolutionary state constitutions before some were suggesting that they needed to be revised. Beginning with the New York constitution in 1777 and proceeding through the constitutions of Massachusetts in

1780 and New Hampshire in 1784, constitution-makers now sought a very different distribution of powers of government from that made in 1776.

Instead of placing all power in the legislatures, particularly in the lower houses, and draining all power from the governors as the early state constitutions had done, these later constitutions strengthened the executives, senates, and judiciaries. The Massachusetts constitution of 1780 especially seemed to many to have recaptured some of the best characteristics of the English constitutional balance, which had been forgotten during the popular enthusiasm of 1776. The new Massachusetts governor, with a fixed salary and elected directly by the people, now assumed more of the independence and some of the powers of the old royal governors, including those of appointing to offices and vetoing legislation.

With the Massachusetts constitution as a model, other constitutional reformers worked to revise their own state constitutions. The popular legislatures were reduced in size and their authority curbed. Senates or upper houses were instituted where they did not exist, as in Pennsylvania, Georgia, and Vermont; and where they did exist, they were made more stable by lengthening their terms and by requiring higher property qualifications for their members. The governors were freed of their dependence on the legislatures, and given a clearer responsibility for government. And judges became independent guardians of the constitutions. By 1790 Pennsylvania, South Carolina, and Georgia had reformed their constitutions along these more conservative lines; New Hampshire, Delaware, and Vermont soon followed in the early 1790s.

At the same time that political leaders were trying to restrengthen the authority of governors, senators, and judges that had been diluted in the state constitutions created in 1776, they also were trying to limit the powers of the legislatures by appealing to the fundamental law that was presumably embodied in these written documents. Since many of the constitutions had been created by simple legislative act, the distinction between fundamental and ordinary law was not easily sustained. At first several of the states had grappled with various devices to ensure the fundamentality of their constitutions. Some simply declared their constitutions to be fundamental; others required a special majority or successive acts of the legislature for amending the constitution. But none of these measures proved effective against recurrent legislative encroachments.

Out of these kinds of pressures, both logical and political, Americans gradually moved toward institutionalizing the belief that if the constitution was to be truly immune from legislative tampering, it would have to be created, as Jefferson said in 1783, "by a power superior to that of the ordinary legislature."

For a solution, Americans fell back on the institution of the convention. In 1775–76, the convention had been merely a legally deficient legislature made necessary by the crown's refusal to call together the regular representatives of the people. Now, however, the convention became a special alternative representation of the people with the exclusive authority to frame or amend a constitution. When Massachusetts and New Hampshire came to write new constitutions in the late 1770s and early 1780s the proper pattern of constitution-making and constitution-altering had become clear. Constitutions were formed by specially elected conventions and then placed before the people for ratification.

With this idea of a constitution as fundamental law immune from legislative encroachment firmly in hand, some state judges during the 1780s began cautiously moving in isolated cases to impose restraints on what the assemblies were enacting as law. In effect they said to the legislatures, as George Wythe, judge of the Virginia supreme court, did in 1782, "Here is the limit of your authority; and hither shall you go, but no further." These were the hesitant beginnings of what would come to be called "judicial review." But as yet many leaders were unwilling to allow appointed judges to set aside laws made by the people represented in democratically elected legislatures. It appeared obviously unrepublican.

As vigorously as all these state reforms were tried in the 1780s, however, to many they did not seem sufficient. By the mid-eighties some reformers were thinking of shifting the arena of constitutional change from the state to the nation and were considering some sort of modification of the structure of the central government as the best and perhaps only answer to America's political and social problems.

SUGGESTED READINGS

The fullest account of state constitution-making and politics is Allan Nevins, *The American States during and after the Revolution, 1775–1789* (1924). Elisha P. Douglass, *Rebels and Democrats* (1955), is important in emphasizing the radical and populist impulses in the states. Among the most significant of the state studies are Philip A. Crowl, *Maryland during and after the Revolution* (1943); Richard P. McCormick, *Experiment in Independence: New Jersey in the Critical Period, 1781–1789* (1950); Irwin H. Polishook, *Rhode Island and the Union, 1774–1795* (1969); Robert J. Taylor,

Western Massachusetts in the Revolution (1954); and Alfred F. Young, *The Democratic Republicans of New York: The Origins, 1763–1797* (1967). Jackson T. Main, *The Sovereign States, 1775–1783* (1973), describes state affairs during the war. J. R. Pole, *Political Representation in England and the Origins of the American Republic* (1966), has some excellent chapters on state politics during the Revolutionary and immediate post-Revolutionary years. Merrill Jensen, in *The Articles of Confederation . . . 1774–1781* (1940), and *The New Nation . . . 1781–1789* (1950), describes the political and social conflicts within the Confederation government and stresses the achievements of the Articles. H. James Henderson, *Party Politics in the Continental Congress* (1974), emphasizes a sectional rather than a social division among the delegates to the national government. The best history of the congress is Jack N. Rakove, *The Beginnings of National Politics* (1979).

The starting point for appreciating the social changes of the Revolution is the short essay by J. Franklin Jameson, *The American Revolution Considered as a Social Movement* (1926). The last two chapters of James A. Henretta, *The Evolution of American Society, 1700–1815* (1973), summarize the social effects of the war and the Revolution. J. Kirby Martin, *Men in Rebellion: Higher Government Leaders and the Coming of the American Revolution* (1973); Jackson T. Main, *The Upper House in Revolutionary America, 1763–1788* (1967); and Main, "Government by the People: The American Revolution and the Democratization of the Legislatures," *Wm. and Mary Q.*, 3d ser., 28 (1966), document the displacement of elites in politics during the Revolution. Chilton Williamson, *American Suffrage from Property to Democracy, 1760–1860* (1960), describes the expansion of voting rights. A neat account of Concord, Massachusetts in the Revolution is Robert A. Gross, *The Minutemen and Their World* (1976).

A helpful survey of American social history is Rowland Berthoff, *An Unsettled People* (1971). But it has not replaced the encyclopedic History of American Life Series edited by Arthur M. Schlesinger and Dixon Ryan Fox. The two volumes covering the Revolutionary era are Evarts B. Greene, *The Revolutionary Generation, 1763–1790* (1943); and John Allen Krout and Dixon Ryan Fox, *The Completion of Independence, 1790–1830* (1944). Population developments are summarized by J. Potter, "The Growth of Population in America, 1700–1860," in David Glass and D. E. Eversley, eds., *Population in History* (1965). An important social history that goes well beyond its title is David J. Rothman, *The Discovery of the Asylum: Social Order and Disorder in the New Republic* (1971).

Two surveys of economic life are useful: Stuart Bruchey, *The Roots of American Economic Growth, 1607–1861* (1965); and Douglass C. North, *The Economic Growth of the United States, 1790–1860* (1961). To understand the interrelated nature of the social, economic, and political processes in this period, the student can find no better work than Oscar Handlin and Mary Handlin, *Commonwealth: A Study of the Role of Government in the American Economy: Massachusetts, 1774–1861* (rev. ed., 1969). It is especially important for its analysis of the changing nature of the corporation.

On the commercial effects of the Revolution, see Curtis P. Nettles, *The Emergence of a National Economy, 1775–1815* (1962); and Robert A. East, *Business Enterprise in the American Revolutionary Era* (1938). On the plight of the loyalists, see Wallace Brown, *The Good Americans* (1969), and Mary Beth Norton, *The British-Americans: The Loyalist Exiles in England, 1774–1789* (1972).

On the Enlightenment, see Henry May, *The Enlightenment in America* (1976) and Henry S. Commager, *Empire of Reason* (1977). The standard survey is Russel B. Nye, *The Cultural Life of the New Nation, 1776–1830* (1960). See also Joseph J. Ellis, *After the Revolution: Profiles of Early American Culture* (1979). A particularly important study of education is Carl F. Kaestle, *The Evolution of an Urban School System* (1973). See also Rush Welter, *Popular Education and Democratic Thought in America* (1962), and Douglas Sloan, *The Scottish Enlightenment and the American College Ideal* (1971). On women, see Mary Beth Norton, *Liberty's Daughters: The Revolutionary Experience of American Women, 1750–1800* (1980); and Nancy Cott, *The Bonds of Womanhood* (1977). Benjamin Quarles, *The Negro in the American Revolution* (1961), is the best study of the contribution of blacks to the Revolution. On slavery and opposition to it, see Winthrop Jordan, *White over Black: American Attitudes toward the Negro, 1550–1812* (1968); and David Brion Davis, *The Problem of Slavery in the Age of Revolution, 1770–1823* (1975). On the abolition of slavery in the North, see Arthur Zilversmit, *The First Emancipation* (1967).

CHAPTER 10

The Federalist Age

The American Revolution, like all revolutions, could not fulfill all the highest hopes of its leaders. Within a decade after the Declaration of Independence was signed many of the Revolutionary leaders had come to doubt the direction America was taking. Not only were they anxious to lessen the power of the state legislatures, but at the same time they were becoming increasingly aware that the Confederation Congress was too weak to accomplish its tasks both at home and abroad. In the mid-1780s frustration with piecemeal changes in the Articles of Confederation came together with mounting concern over the political and social conditions in the states to produce a powerful momentum for drastic constitutional change. The federal Constitution of 1787 was the result.

This new national Constitution, which supplanted the Articles of Confederation, both limited the authority of the states and created an unprecedented concentration of power. Many Americans could only conclude that this new Constitution represented as radical a change as the Revolution itself. At last, in the eyes of some, the inauguration of a new federal government promised the harmony and stability that would allow America to become a great and glorious nation.

The Critical Period

Even before the Articles of Confederation were ratified in 1781, the experiences of the war had exposed the weakness of the Congress and encouraged some Americans to think about making changes in the central government. By 1780 the war was dragging on longer than anyone had expected, and the skyrocketing inflation of the paper money used to finance it was unsettling commerce and business. Congressional delegates were barred from serving more than three years in six, and leadership in the Confederation was fluctuating and confused. The states were ignoring congressional resolutions and were refusing to supply their allotted financial requisitions to the federal government. The Congress stopped paying interest on the public debt. The Continental army was smoldering with resentment at the lack of pay and was falling apart through desertions and even outbreaks of mutiny. All these circumstances were forcing mercantile and creditor interests, especially those centered in the mid-Atlantic states, to seek to add to the powers of the Congress—by broad interpretation of the Articles; by direct amendment, which required the consent of all states; and even by the threat of military force.

Domestic Weakness of the Confederation.   A shift in congressional leadership in the early 1780s expressed the increasing influence of these concerned groups. Older popular radicals such as Richard Henry Lee and Arthur Lee of Virginia and Samuel Adams of Massachusetts were replaced by younger men such as James Madison of Virginia and Alexander Hamilton of New York, who were more interested in authority and stability than popular liberty. Disillusioned by the ineffectiveness of the Confederation, these nationalists in the Congress set about reversing the localist and power-weakening thrust of the Revolution. They strengthened the regular army at the expense of the militia and promised pensions to the Continental army officers. They reorganized the departments of war, foreign affairs, and finance in the Congress and appointed individuals in place of committees to run them.

The key individual in the nationalists' program was Robert Morris, a wealthy Philadelphia merchant who was made superintendent of finance and virtual head of the confederacy in 1781. Morris undertook to stabilize the economy and to involve financial and commercial groups with the central government. He induced Congress to recommend to the states that paper money laws be repealed and to require that the states' contributions to the general expenses be paid in specie. And he sought to establish a bank and to make federal bonds more secure for investors.

This nationalist program depended upon amending the Articles so that the Confederation would have the power to levy a five percent duty on imports. Once Congress had adequate revenues independent of the states, the Confederation could pay its debts and would become more attractive to prospective

ROBERT MORRIS

Morris, a wealthy Philadelphia merchant, has been called "the financier of the Revolution." Land speculation in the 1790s ruined him, and he ended his career in debtors prison.   (*National Portrait Gallery, Smithsonian Institution, Washington, D.C.*)

buyers of its bonds. Although Morris was able to induce Congress to charter the Bank of North America, the rest of the nationalists' economic proposals narrowly failed. Not only did the states refuse to grant the unanimous consent required for the tax amendment, but many were delinquent in supplying requisitioned funds to Congress. Nor was Congress able to get even a restricted authority to regulate commerce.

After the victory at Yorktown in October 1781 and the opening of peace negotiations with Great Britain, interest in the Congress declined and some individuals became desperate. The prospect of Congress's demobilizing the army without fulfilling its promises of back pay and pensions created a crisis that brought the United States as close to a military coup d'état as it has ever been. In March 1783 the officers of Washington's army encamped at Newburgh on the Hudson issued an address to the Congress concerning their pay, and actually considered some sort of military action against the Confederation. Only when Washington personally intervened and refused to support a movement designed, as he said, "to open the floodgates of civil discord, and deluge our rising empire in blood" was the crisis averted.

News of the peace in 1783 shattered much of the unionist sentiment that had existed during the war. By December 1783 the Congress, in Jefferson's opinion, had lost much of its usefulness. "The constant session of Congress," he said, "can not be necessary in time of peace." After clearing up the most urgent business, the delegates should "separate and return to our respective states, leaving only a Committee of the states," and thus "destroy the strange idea of their being a permanent body, which has unaccountably taken possession of the heads of their constituents."

Congressional power, which had been substantial during the war years, now began to disintegrate, and delegates increasingly complained how difficult it was even to gather a quorum. Congress could not even agree on a permanent home for itself, but wandered from Philadelphia to Princeton, to Annapolis, to Trenton, and finally to New York. The states reasserted their authority and began taking over the payment of the federal debt that many had earlier hoped to make the cement of union. By 1786 nearly one-third of the federal securities had been converted into state bonds, thus creating a vested interest among

public creditors in the sovereignty of the individual states. Under these circumstances the influence of those, in Hamilton's term, "who think continentally" rapidly declined, and the chances of amending the Confederation piecemeal declined with them. The only hope of reform now seemed to lie in some sort of convention of all the states.

International Weakness of the Confederation. In Europe the reputation of the United States dwindled as rapidly as did its credit. Loans from the Dutch and French were extracted only at extraordinary rates of interest. Since American ships now lacked the protection of the British flag, they were seized by the Barbary states in the Mediterranean and their crews sold as slaves. Congress had no money to pay the

THE OLD STATE HOUSE OF PENNSYLVANIA (UNTIL 1799) LATER CALLED INDEPENDENCE HALL.

Both the Second Continental Congress and the federal Convention of 1787 met here. The tower was added in the middle of the eighteenth century to house the Liberty Bell. (*By permission of the Houghton Library, Harvard University*)

necessary tribute and ransoms to these North African pirates.

Amid a world of hostile empires it was even difficult for the new republican confederacy to maintain its territorial integrity. Britain refused to send a minister to the United States and ignored its treaty obligations to evacuate its military posts in the Northwest, claiming that the United States had not honored its commitments. The treaty of peace had stipulated that the Confederation would recommend to the states that loyalist property confiscated during the Revolution be restored and that neither side would make laws that obstructed the recovery of prewar debts. When the states flouted these treaty obligations, the impotent Confederation could do nothing.

Britain was known to be intriguing with the Indians and encouraging separatist movements in the Northwest and in the Vermont borderlands, and Spain was doing the same in the Southwest. Spain in fact refused to recognize American claims in the territory between the Ohio River and Florida. In 1784, in an effort to influence the American settlers moving into Kentucky and Tennessee, Spain closed the Mississippi to American trade. Ready to deal with any government that could ensure access to the sea for their agricultural produce, many of the westerners were, as Washington noted in 1784, "on a pivot. The touch of a feather would turn them any way."

In 1785–86 John Jay, a New York aristocrat and the secretary of foreign affairs, negotiated a treaty with the Spanish minister to the United States, Diego de Gardoqui. By the terms of this agreement Spain was opened to American trade in return for America's renunciation of its right to navigate the Mississippi for several decades. Out of fear of being denied an outlet to the sea in the West, the southern states prevented the necessary nine-state majority in the Congress from agreeing to the treaty. But the willingness of a majority of seven states to sacrifice western interests for the sake of northern merchants brought long-existing sectional jealousies into play and threatened to shatter the Union.

Toward the Philadelphia Convention. The inability of the Confederation to regulate commerce finally precipitated reform of the Articles. Jefferson, Madison, and other agrarian-minded leaders feared that if American farmers were prohibited from selling their surplus crops freely in Europe not only would the industrious character of the farmers be undermined, but the United States would be unable to pay for manufactured goods imported from Europe and would therefore be compelled to enter into large-scale manufacturing for itself. This in turn would eventually destroy the yeoman-citizenry on which republicanism was based and create in America the same kind of corrupt, stratified, and dependent society that existed in Europe.

Yet, in the 1780s, despite strenuous diplomatic efforts like those of John Adams in Britain and Jefferson in France to develop new international commercial relationships involving the free exchange of goods, the mercantilist empires of the major European nations remained generally closed to the new republic. The French were unwilling to take as much American produce as expected, and Britain effectively closed its markets to competitive American goods while recapturing American consumer markets for its own goods. The Confederation lacked any authority to retaliate with trade regulations, and several attempts to grant Congress a restricted power over commerce were lost amid state and sectional jealousies. The Confederation Congress watched helplessly as the separate states attempted to pass conflicting navigation acts of their own; by the mid-eighties Connecticut was laying heavier duties on goods from Massachusetts than on those from Great Britain.

By 1786 these accumulated pressures made some sort of revision of the Articles inevitable. Virginia's desire for trade regulation led to a convention of several states at Annapolis in September 1786. Those who attended this meeting quickly realized that commerce could not be considered apart from other problems and called for a larger convention in Philadelphia the following year. After several states agreed to send delegates to Philadelphia, the Confederation Congress belatedly recognized the approaching convention and in February 1787 authorized it to revise and amend the Articles of Confederation.

DANIEL SHAYS AND JACOBB SHATTUCKS
Shays and Shattucks, former militia officers, were leaders of the uprising of aggrieved western Massachusetts farmers in 1786. The farmers, calling themselves "Regulators," protested the shortage of money and the foreclosures of mortgages and imprisonments for debt. Shays's Rebellion had a powerful effect on conservative leaders and helped compel reform of the national government. (*National Portrait Gallery, Smithsonian Institution, Washington, D.C.*)

Although by 1787 nearly all of America's political leaders agreed that some reform of the Articles was necessary, few expected what the Philadelphia Convention eventually created—a new Constitution that utterly transformed the structure of the central government and promised a radical weakening of the power of the states. The extraordinarily powerful national government that emerged from Philadelphia went well beyond what was demanded in additional congressional powers by the difficulties of credit and commerce and the humiliations in foreign affairs. Given the Revolutionaries' loyalty to their states and their deep-rooted fears of centralized governmental authority, the formation of the new Constitution was a truly remarkable achievement that cannot be explained simply by the obvious weaknesses of the Articles of Confederation.

In the end it was the problems within the separate states during the 1780s that made constitutional reform of the central government possible. The confusing and unjust laws coming out of the state governments, Madison informed Jefferson in 1787, had become "so frequent and so flagrant as to alarm the most stedfast friends of Republicanism." It was these state vices, said Madison, that "contributed more to that uneasiness which produced the Convention, and prepared the public mind for a general reform, than

those which accrued to our national character and interest from the inadequacy of the Confederation to its immediate objects."

In 1786 a rebellion of nearly two thousand debtor farmers threatened with foreclosure of their property broke out in western Massachusetts. This rebellion, led by a former militia captain, Daniel Shays, confirmed many of these anxieties about state politics. For the insurrection, which temporarily closed the courts and threatened a federal arsenal, occurred in the state considered to have the best balanced constitution. Although Shays's insurgents were defeated by militia troops, his sympathizers were victorious at the polls early in 1787, and they enacted debtor relief legislation that added to the growing fears of legislative tyranny.

Thus by 1786–87 the reconstruction of the central government was being sought as a means of correcting not only the weaknesses of the Articles but the internal political vices of the states. A new central government, some believed, could save both Congress from the states and the states from themselves. And new groups joined those already working to invigorate the national government. Urban artisans hoped a stronger national government would prevent competition from British imports. Southerners, particularly in Virginia, wanted to gain representation in the national government proportional to their growing population. And most important, gentry up and down the continent momentarily submerged their sectional and economic differences in the face of what seemed a threat to individual liberty from the tyranny of legislative majorities within the states. Creating a new central government was no longer simply a matter of cementing the Union, or of standing up strong in foreign affairs, or of satisfying the demands of particular creditor, mercantile, and army interests. It was now a matter, as Madison declared, that would "decide forever the fate of republican government."

The Federal Constitution

The convocation of the Philadelphia Convention that drafted the federal Constitution in the summer of 1787 was very much a revolutionary movement. Yet such were the circumstances and climate of the post-Revolutionary years in America that the sudden calling of a constitutional convention and the creation of an entirely new and different sort of federal republican government in 1787 seemed remarkably natural and legitimate.

Fifty-five delegates representing twelve states attended the Philadelphia Convention in the summer of 1787. (Rhode Island refused to have anything to do with efforts to revise the Articles.) Although many of the delegates were young men—their average age was forty-two—most were well educated and experienced members of America's political elite. Thirty-nine had served in Congress at one time or another, eight had worked in the state constitutional conventions, seven had been state governors, and thirty-four were lawyers. One-third were veterans of the Continental army, that "great dissolvent of state loyalties," as Washington once called it. Nearly all were gentlemen, "natural aristocrats," who took their political superiority for granted as an inevitable consequence of their social and economic position. Washington was made president of the Convention. Some of the outstanding figures of the Revolution were not present: Samuel Adams was ill; Jefferson and John Adams

were serving as ministers abroad; and Richard Henry Lee and Patrick Henry, although selected by the Virginia legislature, refused to attend the Convention, Henry saying, "I smelt a rat." The most influential delegations were those of Pennsylvania and Virginia, which included Gouverneur Morris and James Wilson of Pennsylvania and Edmund Randolph, George Mason, and James Madison of Virginia.

The Virginia Plan. The Virginia delegation took the lead, presenting the Convention with its first working proposal. This, the Virginia Plan, was largely the effort of the thirty-six-year-old Madison, who

JAMES MADISON, 1751–1836

Madison was the greatest political thinker of the Revolutionary era and perhaps of all American history. His was the most critical and undogmatic mind of the Revolutionary leaders. More than anyone else he formulated the theory that underlaid the new expanded republic of 1787. (*The Thomas Gilcrease Institute of American History and Art, Tulsa, Oklahoma*)

more than any other person deserves the title "father of the Constitution." Short, shy, and soft-spoken, habitually dressed in black, trained to no profession but widely read and possessing an acute and questioning mind, Madison devoted his life to public service. He understood clearly the historical significance of the meeting of the Convention, and it is because he decided to make a detailed private record of the Convention debates that so much is known of what was said that summer in Philadelphia.

Madison's initial proposals for reform were truly radical. They were not, as he pointed out, mere expedients or simple revisions of the Articles; they promised "systematic change" of government. What Madison had in mind was to create a general government that would not be a confederation of independent republics but a national republic in its own right. It would operate directly on individuals and be organized as the state governments had been organized, with a single executive, a bicameral legislature, and a separate judiciary.

This national republic would be superimposed on the states, which would now stand to the central government, in John Jay's words, "in the same light in which counties stand to the state of which they are parts, viz., merely as districts to facilitate the purposes of domestic order of good government." Thus the radical Virginia Plan provided for a two-house national legislature with the authority to legislate "in all cases to which the states are incompetent" and "to negative all laws passed by the several states, contravening in the opinion of the national legislature, the articles of union." If the national government had the power to veto all state laws, Madison believed, it could then play the same role the English crown had been supposed to play in the empire—that of a "disinterested umpire" over clashing interests.

The New Jersey Plan.   For many in the Philadelphia Convention, however, this Virginia Plan was much too extreme. Most delegates were prepared to grant substantial power to the federal government, including the right to tax, regulate commerce, and execute federal laws; but many did not want to allow such a weakening of state authority as the Virginia Plan proposed. Opponents of the nationalists, led by dele-

gates from New Jersey, Connecticut, New York, and Delaware, countered with their own proposal, the New Jersey Plan (so-called because William Paterson of New Jersey introduced it). This plan essentially amended the Articles of Confederation by increasing the powers of Congress but at the same time maintained the basic sovereignty of the states. With two such opposite proposals before it, the Convention, in the middle of June 1787, approached a crisis.

Provisions of the Constitution.   During the debate that followed, the nationalists, led by Madison and Wilson, were able to retain the basic features of the Virginia Plan. Although the Convention refused to grant the national legislature a blanket authority "to legislate in all cases to which the separate States are incompetent," it granted the Congress (in Article I, Section 8, of the Constitution) a list of enumerated powers, including the powers to tax, to borrow and coin money, and to regulate commerce. Instead of giving the national legislature the right to veto harmful state laws, as Madison wanted, the Convention forbade the states to exercise particular sovereign powers whose abuse lay behind the crisis of the 1780s. In Article I, Section 10, of the final Constitution the states were barred from carrying on foreign relations, levying tariffs, coining money, issuing bills of credit, passing *ex post facto* laws (which punished actions that were not illegal when they were committed), or doing anything to relieve debtors of the obligations of their contracts.*

In contrast to the extensive fiscal powers given to the Congress, the state governments were rendered nearly economically impotent. Not only did the new federal Constitution prohibit the states from imposing customs duties—the eighteenth century's most common and efficient form of taxation—but it denied the states the authority to issue paper money and succeeded in doing what the British government's several currency acts had earlier tried to do.

The Convention decided on a strong and single executive. The president stood alone, unencumbered by an executive council except of his own choosing.

---

*For the Constitution, see Appendix.

With command over the armed forces, with the authority to direct diplomatic relations, with power over appointments to the executive and judicial branches, and with a four-year term of office and perpetual eligibility for reelection, the president was a magistrate who, as Patrick Henry later charged, could "easily become king."

To ensure the president's independence, he was not to be elected by the legislature, as the Virginia Plan had proposed. Since the framers of the Constitution believed that only a few presidential candidates in the future would be known to the people throughout the country, they provided for local elections of "electors" equal in number to the representatives and senators from each state. These electors would cast ballots for the president, but if any candidate failed to get a majority—which in the absence of political parties and organized electioneering was normally expected—the final selection from the five candidates with the most votes would be made by the House of Representatives, with each state delegation having one vote.

The Virginia Plan's suggestion of a separate national judiciary to hold office "during good behavior" was accepted without dispute; the structure of the national judiciary was left to the Congress to devise. The right of this judiciary, however, to nullify acts of the Congress or of the state legislatures was as yet by no means clear.

The nationalists in the Convention reluctantly gave way on several crucial issues, particularly on the national legislature's authority to veto state legislation. But they fought longest and hardest to hold on to the principle of proportional representation in both houses of the legislature, and almost stalemated the Convention. It was decided that both taxation and representation, at least in the House of Representatives, would be based not on states as such or on landed wealth, but on population, with the slaves each counting as three-fifths of a person. The nationalists like Madison and Wilson, however, wanted representation in the Senate also to rest on population. Any semblance of representing the separate sovereignty of the states smacked too much of the Articles of Confederation. Hence they came to regard the eventual "Connecticut Compromise" by which

ROGER SHERMAN, BY RALPH EARL

Roger Sherman (1721–1793) began as a cobbler, but well before the Revolution he had become a lawyer, merchant, and substantial Connecticut official. He is best known for his introduction in the Philadelphia Convention of the "compromise" granting each state two senators. (*Yale University Art Gallery, Gift of Roger Sherman White*)

each state secured two senators in the upper house of the legislature as a defeat.

Although Madison and Wilson lost the battles over the congressional veto of state laws and proportional representation in both houses, the Federalists (as those who supported the Constitution came to call themselves) had won the war even before the Convention adjourned. Once the New Jersey Plan, which embodied the essentials of the Articles of Confederation, was rejected in favor of the Virginia Plan, the opponents, or Antifederalists, found themselves forced, as Richard Henry Lee complained, to accept "this or nothing."

Although the Articles of Confederation stipulated that amendments be made by the unanimous consent of the state legislatures, the delegates to the Philadelphia Convention decided to bypass the state legislatures and submit the Constitution to specially elected state conventions for ratification. Approval of only nine of the thirteen states was necessary for the new government to take effect. This transgression of earlier political principles was only one of many to which the Antifederalists objected.

The Federalist-Antifederalist Debate.   The federal government established by the Philadelphia Convention seemed severely to violate the maxims of 1776 that had guided the Revolutionary constitution-makers. Not only did the new Constitution provide for a strong government with an extraordinary amount of power given to the president and the Senate, but it created a single republican state that would span the continent and encompass all the diverse and scattered interests of the whole of American society—an impossibility for a republic, according to the best political science of the day.

During the debates over ratification in the fall and winter of 1787–88, the Antifederalists seized on these Federalist violations of the earlier Revolutionary assumptions. They charged that the new federal government with its concentration of power at the expense of liberty resembled a monarchy, and that because of the extensive and heterogeneous nature of the society it was to govern, it would have to act tyrannically. Inevitably America would become a single consolidated state, with the individuality of the separate states sacrificed to a powerful government. And this would happen, the Antifederalists argued, because of the logic of sovereignty—that powerful principle of eighteenth-century political science, earlier maintained by the English in the imperial debate, that said that no society could long possess two legislatures but must inevitably have one final, indivisible, lawmaking authority. The Antifederalists argued that if the new national government was to be more powerful than the state governments, and the Constitution was to be the "Supreme Law of the Land," then, according to the doctrine of sovereignty, the legislative authority of the separate states would eventually be annihilated.

Despite these formidable Antifederalist arguments, the Federalists did not believe that the Constitution repudiated the Revolution and the prin-

ciples of 1776. During the decade since Independence the political world had been transformed. Americans, it now appeared clear, had effectively transferred the location of this final lawmaking authority called sovereignty from the institutions of government to the people at large.

In the years since the Revolution many Americans had continued to act outside of all official institutions of government. During the 1780s they had organized various committees, conventions, and other extralegal bodies of the people as they had during the Revolution, to voice grievances and to seek political goals. Vigilante actions of various kinds had done quickly and efficiently what the new state governments often were unable to do, whether it was controlling prices, preventing profiteering, or punishing Tories. Everywhere people had drawn out the logic of "actual" representation and had sought to instruct and control the institutions of government. By 1787–88 all of this activity of the people at large tended to give reality to the idea that sovereignty in America resided in the people, and not in any institution of government. Only by believing that sovereignty was held by the people outside of government could Americans make theoretical sense of their recent remarkable political inventions—their conception of a written constitution immune from legislative tampering, their special constitution-making conventions, and their unusual ideas of "actual" representation.

The Federalists were now determined to use this new understanding of the ultimate power of the people to meet all the Antifederalist arguments against the Constitution. True, they said, the Philadelphia Convention had gone beyond its instructions to amend the Articles of Confederation; it had drawn up an entirely new government, and had provided for its ratification by special state conventions. But had not Americans learned during the previous decade that legislatures were not competent to create or change a constitution? If the Constitution were to be truly a fundamental law, then, Federalists like Madison argued, it had to be ratified "by the supreme authority of the people themselves." Hence it was "We the people of the United States," and not the

The Federal Plan Most Solid & Secure
Americans Their Freedom Will Endure
All Arts Shall Flourish in Columbia's Land
And All her Sons Join as One Social Band.

SOCIETY OF PEWTERERS

SOLID AND PURE

SILK BANNER OF
SOCIETY OF PEWTERERS

The pewterers, like other artisans, favored the new Constitution and in several cities in July 1788 joined in huge parades celebrating the birth of the new federal government. Such craftsmen were worried about imported foreign manufactures and thought the new national government could better levy tariffs than the separate states. Their support of the Constitution was important for ratification in several northern states. (*Courtesy of The New York Historical Society, New York City*)

states, that ordained and established the Constitution.

By locating sovereignty in the people rather than in any particular institution, the Federalists could now conceive of what had hitherto been a contradiction in politics—two legislatures operating simultaneously over the same community—and could thus answer the principal objection to the Constitution. Only by making the people themselves the final lawmaking authority could the Federalists explain this emerging conception of federalism, or that peculiar division of legislative responsibilities between the national and state governments that still amazes the world.

This new understanding of the relation of the society to government now enabled the Federalists to explain the expansion of a single republican state over a large continent of diverse groups and interests. Seizing on the English philosopher David Hume's radical suggestion that a republican government might operate better in a large territory than in a small one, the Federalists, and in particular James Madison, ingeniously turned upside down the older assumptions about the appropriate size of a republic.

Experience in America after 1776 had demonstrated that no republic could be made small enough to avoid the clashing of rival parties and interests (tiny Rhode Island was the most faction-ridden of all). The extended territory of the new national republic, Madison wrote in a series of publications, especially in his most famous piece, *The Federalist* No. 10, was actually its greatest source of strength.* In a large society, Madison concluded, there were so many interests and parties that no one faction could triumph and the threat of majoritarian tyranny would be eliminated. Furthermore, election by the people

---

The Federalist was a series of eighty-five essays published in New York in the winter of 1787–88 in defense of the Constitution. They were written under the pseudonym "Publius" largely by Madison and Alexander Hamilton, with five essays contributed by John Jay. The essays were quickly published as a book and became the most famous work of political philosophy in American history, labeled by Jefferson in 1788 as "the best commentary on the principles of government, which ever was written."

in the large districts of the national government would inhibit demagoguery and crass electioneering. If the people of a state—New York, for example—had to select only ten men to the federal Congress in contrast to the sixty-six they elected to their state assembly, they were more likely to ignore ordinary men and elect those who were experienced, well educated, and well known. In this way the new federal government would avoid the problems the states had suffered from in the 1780s.

In the ratifying conventions held in the states throughout the fall, winter, and spring of 1787–88, the Antifederalists were little match for the arguments and the array of talents that the Federalists gathered in support of the Constitution. Many of the Antifederalists were state-centered men with local interests and loyalties, politicians without the influence and education of the Federalists, and often without social and intellectual confidence. They had difficulty making themselves heard because they had very few influential leaders and because much of the press was closed to them: out of a hundred or more newspapers printed in the late 1780s only a dozen supported the Antifederalists.

Many of the small states—Delaware, New Jersey, Connecticut, and Georgia—which were commercially dependent on their neighbors or militarily exposed, ratified immediately. The critical struggles took place in the large states of Massachusetts, Virginia, and New York, and acceptance of the Constitution in these states was achieved only by narrow margins and by the promise of future amendments. North Carolina and Rhode Island rejected the Constitution, but after New York's ratification in July 1788 the country was ready to go ahead and organize the new government without them.

Despite the difficulties and the close votes in some states, the country's eventual acceptance of the Constitution was nearly preordained, for the alternative was governmental chaos. Yet in the face of the preponderance of wealth and respectability in support of the Constitution, what in the end remains extraordinary is not the political weakness and disunity of Antifederalism but its strength. That

large numbers of Americans could actually reject a plan of government created by the leaders of the nation and backed by George Washington and nearly the whole of the "natural aristocracy" of the country said more about the changing character of American politics and society than did the Constitution's acceptance. It was indeed a portent of what was to come.

The Hamiltonian Program

The Constitution created only the outline of the new government; it remained for Americans to fill in the details of the government and make something of it. During the succeeding decade the government leaders, that is, the Federalists—who clung to the name used by the supporters of the Constitution—sought to build a consolidated empire that few Americans in 1776 had ever envisioned. The consequence of their efforts was to make the 1790s the most awkward decade in American history, bearing little relation to what went on immediately before or after.

Because the Federalists stood in the way of democracy as it was emerging in the United States, everything seemed to turn against them. They despised political parties, yet parties nonetheless emerged, shattering the remarkable harmony of 1790 and producing one of the most divisive and passionate eras in American history. They sought desperately to avoid conflict with England to the point where they appeared to be compromising the independence of the new nation. In the end the war with Great Britain that they sought to avoid had to be fought anyway in 1812. By the early nineteenth century Alexander Hamilton, the brilliant leader of the Federalists, who more than anyone else pursued the heroic dreams of the age, was not alone in his despairing conclusion "that this American world was not made for me."

Organizing the Government.   There was more consensus when the new government was inaugurated in 1789–90 than at any time since the Declaration of Independence. Regional differences were temporarily obscured by a common enthusiasm for the new Constitution. And the unanimous election of Washington as the first president gave the new government an immediate respectability. Washington, with his tall, imposing figure and his Roman nose and stern, thin-lipped face, was already at age fifty-eight an internationally famous classical hero. Like Cincinnatus the Roman conqueror, he had returned to his farm at the moment of military victory. He was understandably reluctant to take up one more burden for his country and thus risk shattering the reputation he had so painstakingly earned as commander in chief; yet his severe sense of duty made refusal of the presidency impossible. He possessed the dignity, patience, and restraint that the untried but potentially powerful office needed at the outset. Despite the strong-minded, talented people around him, particularly Hamilton as secretary of the treasury and Jefferson as secretary of state, Washington was very much the leader of his administration.

Immediately Madison, as the government's leader in the House of Representatives, sought to fulfill earlier promises to the Antifederalists and quiet their fears by proposing amendments to the Constitution. He beat back Antifederalist efforts to change fundamentally the character of the Constitution and extracted from the variety of suggested amendments those least likely to sap the energy of the new government. To the chagrin of some former Antifederalists, the ten amendments that were ratified in 1791 —the Bill of Rights—were mostly concerned with protecting from the federal government the rights of *individuals* rather than the rights of the *states.* They included the guarantees of freedom of speech, press, religion, petition, and assembly and a number of protections for accused persons. Only the Tenth Amendment, reserving to the states or the people powers not delegated to the United States, was a concession to the main Antifederalist fear.*

With the inauguration of Washington and the establishment of the new government, many Americans began to feel a sense of beginning anew, of

*For the fist ten amendments, see Appendix.

EDWARD SAVAGE'S "LIBERTY"

This 1796 engraving combines the two most important symbols of the early Republic, the goddess "Liberty" giving support to the eagle, representing power and unity. The print was very popular and for years appeared in a wide variety of adaptations, including embroidery. Note the liberty cap on the flag staff in the background. (*Library of Congress*) putting the republican experiment on a new and stronger foundation. They talked of benevolence, glory, and heroism, and foresaw the inevitable westward movement of the arts and sciences across the Atlantic to the New World. The outlook was cosmopolitan, liberal, and humanitarian; America was entering a new age.

Yet despite all this optimism the Americans of the 1790s never lost their Revolutionary sense of the novel and fragile nature of their boldly extended republican government. Except in the epic poems of a few excited patriots such as Joel Barlow and Timothy Dwight, America in the 1790s was far from being a consolidated nation in any modern sense. Already separatist movements in the West threatened to break up the new country. Some Westerners even considered an allegiance to Spain in return for access to the Gulf of Mexico. The entire Mississippi River basin was susceptible to exploitation by ambitious adventurers willing to sell their services to European nations, including William Blount, senator from Tennessee and George Rogers Clark, frontier hero during the Revolution. Fear of this kind of intrigue and influence led to the hasty admission into the Union during the 1790s of Vermont, Kentucky, and Tennessee. But the danger of splintering remained.

Only in this context of uncertainty and awesome responsibility for the future of republican government can the Federalist aims and the conflicting passions they aroused be properly appreciated. The very character of America's emerging republican state was at issue in the 1790s. The Federalist leaders sought to maintain the momentum that had begun in the late 1780s when the Constitution was formed. In place of the impotent confederation of chaotic states, they envisioned a strong, consolidated, commercial empire led by an energetic government composed of the best men in the society.

In order to bolster the dignity of the new republic with some of the ceremony and majesty of monarchy, some Federalists in the Senate, led by Vice-President John Adams, tried to make "His Highness" the proper title for addressing the president. Because the future of the new republic was so unformed and problematical, such an issue seemed loaded with significance and occupied the Congress in a month of debate. Although the Federalists lost this monarchical title to the republican simplicity of "Mr. President," they drew up elaborate rules concerning government receptions and the proper behavior at what soon came to be called the "republican court" located in New York and, after 1790, in Philadelphia. At the same time, plans were begun for erecting a monumental "federal city" as the permanent capital. Always acutely sensitive to the precedents being established, the Federalists also worked out the relations between the president and the Congress. Before the end of the first session of the Congress in 1789, the sparse frame of government provided by the Constitution had been filled in. Congress created the executive departments of state, war, and treasury, and a federal judiciary consisting of the Supreme Court and a hierarchy of inferior courts.

Hamilton's Financial Program.   Alexander Hamilton, then thirty-five years old, was the moving force in the new government. As a military aide to Washington during the Revolutionary War, he had earned the president's admiration. In fact, despite his short stature, Hamilton impressed everyone who met him. Unlike Washington, he was quick-witted, excitable, and knowledgeable about public finance. Born in the West Indies an illegitimate son of a Scottish merchant, Hamilton was anxious to enter and enjoy the polite world of the rich and wellborn. But despite his concern for the commercial prosperity of the United States he cannot be regarded simply as a capitalist promoter of America's later business culture. He was willing to allow ordinary men their profits and property, but it was fame and honor he wanted for himself and for his country. As the secretary of the treasury he was now in a crucial position to put his ideas into effect.

Since British "country-opposition" groups had traditionally considered the treasury as the source of political corruption, the new secretary of the treasury was regarded by the first Congress with some suspicion, and with good reason. The treasury was by far the largest department, with dozens of officers and well over two thousand customs officials, revenue agents, and postmasters; and although Congress limited the capacity of these officials to engage in business or trade or to buy public lands or government securities, they were an important source of patronage and influence. Hamilton, in fact, saw his role in eighteenth-century English terms—as a kind of prime minister to President Washington. Hamilton felt justified in meddling in the affairs of the other departments and of the Congress and in taking the lead in organizing and administering the government. While denying that he was creating a "court" party, he set out to duplicate the great financial achievements of the early eighteenth-century English governments that had laid the basis for England's stability and commercial supremacy.

Hamilton worked out his program in a series of four reports to the Congress in 1790–91: on credit, on duties and taxes, on a national bank, and on manufactures. Nearly everyone admitted that the new government needed to put its finances in order and to settle the Revolutionary War debts of the United States. Hamilton was determined to establish the credit of the United States, but he was not at all interested in paying off what the American governments, state and national, owed their citizens and others in the world. Instead of extinguishing these public debts, which in 1790 totaled $42 million for the federal government and $21 million for the several state governments, Hamilton proposed that the United States government "fund" them, that is, collect all the government bonds and loan certificates, both federal and state, into a single package and issue new federal securities in their place.

In this way the central government would create a consolidated and permanent national debt that would strengthen America in the same way that the English national debt had strengthened England. Regular interest payments on the refunded debt were to be backed by the new government's revenues from customs duties and excise taxes; indeed, over 40 percent of these revenues in the 1790s went to pay interest on the debt. These interest payments not only would make the United States the best credit risk in the world, but would create a system of investment

ALEXANDER HAMILTON (1757–1804)
Hamilton is the most controversial of the Founding Fathers. Certainly he was the least taken with radical Whig ideology and the most adventurous and heroic. As Gouverneur Morris said, "he was more covetous of glory than of wealth or power." His talents, his energy, and his clear sense of direction awed his contemporaries, friends and enemies alike. (*Library of Congress*)

for American moneyed groups who lacked the stable alternatives for speculation that Europeans had.

Besides giving investors a secure stake in the new national government, these new bonds would become the basis of the nation's money supply. Not only would the securities themselves be negotiable instruments in business transactions, but Hamilton's program provided for their forming two-thirds of the capital of a new national bank patterned on the Bank of England. This Bank of the United States and its branches (to be established in select cities) would serve as the government's depository and fiscal agent and act as a central control on the operation of the state banks, which numbered thirty-two by 1801. But most important, it would create paper money.

The Bank would issue its notes as loans to private

FIRST BANK OF THE UNITED STATES, PHILADELPHIA
Designed by an unsuccessful businessman from New Hampshire, Samuel Blodget, this building was essentially a three-story New England brick house with a classical portico, decorated, the *Gazette of the United States* reported excitedly, in the style of "Palmyra and Rome when architecture was at its zenith in the Augustan age." (*Library of Congress*)

citizens, and these notes along with those of the state-chartered banks would become the principal circulating medium for a society that lacked an adequate supply of specie, that is, gold and silver coin. Above all, Hamilton wanted a paper money that would hold its value in relation to specie. By guaranteeing that the federal government would receive the Bank's notes at face value for all taxes, holders of the notes would be less likely to redeem them in coin. The notes would pass from hand to hand without depreciating, even though only a fraction of their value was available in specie at any one time. Although many American leaders continued to believe, as John Adams did, that "every dollar of a bank bill that is issued beyond the quantity of gold and silver in the vaults, represents nothing, and is therefore a cheat upon

somebody," these multiplying bank notes quickly broadened the foundation of the nation's economy.

In his final report, that on manufactures, Hamilton laid out plans for eventually industrializing the United States. He and some other Federalists hoped to transform America from an agricultural nation into precisely the complicated and stratified country that agrarians such as Jefferson and Madison feared. He proposed incentives and bounties for the development of large-scale manufacturing that would be very different from the small household industry most Americans were used to. Yet because the Federalist government needed the revenue from customs duties on imported manufactures, and because most businessmen's energies were still absorbed in overseas shipping and land speculation, these proposals for stimulating manufacturing went unfulfilled. The rest of Hamilton's extraordinary financial program, however, was adopted by Congress early in the 1790s.

Hamilton's Political Program. As much as Hamilton and other Federalist leaders planned for and celebrated the commercial prosperity of the United States, their ultimate goals were more political than economic. Like many other Federalists, Hamilton had no faith in the idealistic hopes of the Revolutionaries that American society could be held together solely by "virtue," by the people's willingness to sacrifice their private interests for the sake of the public good. Instead of virtue and the natural sociability of men, Hamilton saw only the ordinary individual's selfish pursuit of his own private happiness. Social stability therefore required the harnessing of this self-interest. The Federalists thus tried to use the new economic and fiscal measures to re-create in America traditional kinds of eighteenth-century connections to knit the sprawling society together.

In effect, Hamilton sought to reverse the egalitarian thrust of the Revolutionary movement. He and other Federalists believed that the national government could influence and manipulate the economic and social leaders of the country, and these leaders in turn would use economic interest to bring along the groups and individuals dependent upon them in support of the new central government. Not only did the Federalists expect the new national financial program to draw people's affections away from the now economically weakened state governments, but they deliberately set out to "corrupt" the society (in the language of eighteenth-century opposition thinking) into paying allegiance to the central government. In local areas they exploited previous military camaraderie and the Society of the Cincinnati, the organization of Revolutionary War officers; they appointed important and respectable individuals to the federal judiciary and other federal offices; they carefully managed the Bank of the United States and other parts of the national economic program; and they had President Washington in 1791 make a regal tour of the country.

By 1793, through the shrewd use of these kinds of influence or "corruption" on key individuals, the Federalists had formed groups of "friends of government" in most of the states. The lines of connection of these centers of economic and political patronage ran from the various localities through the Congress to the federal executive, and created a vested interest in what opponents called "a court faction"—the very thing that Madison in *The Federalist* No. 10 had deemed unlikely in an expanded republic.

Ultimately Hamilton believed, as he declared in 1794, that "government can never [be] said to be established until some signal display has manifested its power of military coercion." From the beginning many Federalists, such as Secretary of War Henry Knox, regarded a cohesive militia and a regular army as "a strong corrective arm" necessary for the federal government to meet all crises "whether arising from internal or external causes." In 1791 the Federalists imposed a federal excise tax on whiskey—a profitable and transportable product for many inland grain farmers—to ensure that all citizens, however far-removed from the seaports, felt the weight of the new national government. When in 1794 some western Pennsylvania farmers rebelled against this hated internal tax, they seemed to fall into the government's plans, as Madison charged, to "establish the principle that a standing army was necessary for enforcing the laws." The national government raised nearly fifteen thousand militia troops to meet this Whiskey Rebellion. Such an excessive show of force was essential, President Washington declared, because "we had given no testimony to the world of being able or willing to support our government and laws."

Dealing with external problems was not as easy as putting down internal rebellions. Both Great Britain and Spain maintained positions on the borderlands of the United States and traded and plotted with the Indians, who still occupied huge areas of the trans-Appalachian West. From its base in Canada, Britain encouraged the Indians to join forces and resist American encroachments. In the South, Spain held the Floridas, New Orleans, and the Louisiana territory, refused to recognize American boundaries,

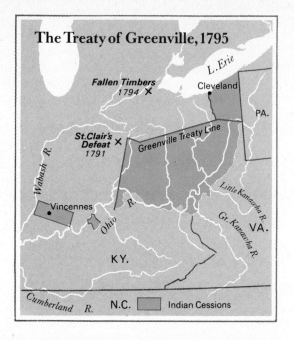

The Treaty of Greenville, 1795

controlled navigation down the Mississippi, and offered protection to the Creeks and Cherokees of the Southwest. Much of the diplomacy of the early Republic was devoted to the removal of these barriers to western expansion.

Major breakthroughs came in 1795. In 1790–91 the Indians of the Northwest inflicted several defeats on American soldiers, mostly militia, in the area along the present boundary between Ohio and Indiana, climaxing in November 1791 with the annihilation of a motley collection of troops under the command of Arthur St. Clair, the territorial governor of the Northwest. These devastating defeats gave the Federalists the opportunity to overhaul the War Department and to create the regular standing army that many of them wanted.

With a reorganized professional army, General Anthony Wayne in 1794 smashed the Indians at Fallen Timbers, near present-day Toledo, Ohio, and temporarily broke Indian resistance and British influence in the Old Northwest. In the Treaty of Greenville in 1795 the Indians ceded much of the Ohio territory to the United States and made inevitable

the British evacuation of the Northwest posts that was promised in a treaty negotiated by John Jay and ratified in 1795.

In another treaty that Thomas Pinckney negotiated in the same year, Spain finally recognized American claims to the Florida boundary and to navigation of the Mississippi. Both Jay's and Pinckney's treaties thus secured the territorial integrity of the United States in a way the diplomacy of the Confederation had been unable to do.

But the United States was still far from being a world power. Measuring American strength by European standards, the Federalists were acutely conscious of the country's weakness in the world, and this consciousness largely determined their foreign policy. Unlike England and France, the United States as yet lacked the essential elements of state power and greatness—commercial strength and military might. Since to build the United States into a strong and prosperous nation rivaling the powers of Europe might take fifty years or more, the new nation had to buy time by maintaining harmonious relations with Great Britain.

Britain was the only power that could seriously hinder American development; duties on British imports supplied the national revenue on which Hamilton's entire financial program depended. Until the United States could stand up to Great Britain, the Federalists believed that the country ought to concentrate on acquiring or controlling the New World possessions of a decrepit Spain and on dominating the Western Hemisphere. The Federalists' policy of reconciliation with Britain thus became another means toward the ultimate fulfillment of their grandiose dreams of American glory.

The Republican Opposition

Opposition to the Federalist program was slow in developing. Since the only alternative to the new national government was the prospect of disunity and anarchy, Alexander Hamilton and the Federalists were in a position to build up their system without great difficulty. During the first year of the new government (1789–90), James Madison acted as congressional leader of those anxious to counteract Antifederalist sentiment and eager to build a strong and independent executive. Not only did Madison write President Washington's first inaugural address, but he argued for the president's exclusive power to remove executive officials and worked hard to create a Treasury Department with a single head. Indeed, Hamilton, thinking of the collaborative atmosphere of 1787–88 in which he and Madison had written *The Federalist* papers, was so confident of Madison's nationalism and that of the southern representatives in the Congress that he felt betrayed when they did not unquestionably support his program.

On the refunding of the debt and on the national assumption of the states' debts Madison broke with the administration. On the refunding issue he urged some sort of discrimination between the original purchasers of the federal bonds and their present, often northern, speculative holders who had bought them cheaply. Madison was also convinced that national assumption of the outstanding state debts would penalize those states, particularly Virginia, that had already liquidated a large portion of their debts. Yet in 1790 congressmen who were opposed to these measures were still capable of compromising for the sake of federal union. Jefferson, Madison, and other southern representatives were even willing to support national assumption of state debts in return for locating the new federal city on the Potomac on the border between Virginia and Maryland.

With the government's effort to charter the Bank of the United States in December 1790, the opposition began to assume a more strident and ideological character. Madison in the House of Representatives and Jefferson in the cabinet as secretary of state both urged a strict construction of the Constitution as a defense against what seemed to have become the dangerous consolidating implications of Hamilton's program. They argued that the Constitution had not expressly granted the federal government the authority to charter a bank. Washington, after asking the opinions of his cabinet members on the constitution-

ality of the Bank, rejected Jefferson's view in favor of Hamilton's broad construction of the Constitution. Hamilton argued that Congress's authority to charter a bank was implied by the clause in the Constitution that gave Congress the right to make all laws "necessary and proper" to carry out its delegated powers. But this presidential decision in favor of the Bank did not quiet the opposition.

By 1791 a "republican interest" was emerging in the Congress and in the country, with Madison and Jefferson as its spokesmen. By 1792 this "interest" had begun to form into a Republican "party." This Republican party now saw itself representing the "country opposition" of the people against the corrupt influence of the Federalist "court." It was the 1760s and 1770s all over again.

The Republican Party. The Republican party was composed of and supported by a variety of social elements. Foremost were southern planters who were becoming increasingly conscious of the distinctiveness of their section of the country and more and more estranged from the business world Hamilton's system seemed to be generating. Unlike Federalist gentlemen in the North these southern gentry retained the earlier Whig confidence in what Jefferson called the "honest heart" of the common man. Part of this faith in democracy shared by Jefferson and his southern colleagues came from their relative insulation from it. With the increasing questioning of black slavery in the North and throughout the world, small white farmers in the South found a common identity with large planters. Most of the leading planters therefore did not feel threatened by the democratic electoral politics that was eating away popular deference to "the better sort" in the North.

In the North, especially in the rapidly growing middle states, ambitious individuals and new groups without political connections were finding that the Republican party was a means by which they could challenge entrenched leaders. Therefore, while the Republican opposition to the Federalist program in the South was largely the response of rural gentry committed to a nostalgic image of independent free-

1 Jon.ª Dayton, speaker. Congressional Pugilists. *2 Jon.ª W. Condy, Clerk*

He in a trice struck Lyon thrice
Upon his head, enrag'd sir,

Who seiz'd the tongs to ease his wrongs,
And Griswold thus engag'd sir.

Congress Hall.
in Philad.ª Feb. 15. 1798
S. E. to.

CARTOON LAMPOONING THE
LYON-GRISWOLD TANGLE IN
CONGRESS IN 1797
With the wrestling on the floor
of the House of Representatives
in 1797 between Republican
Matthew Lyon of Vermont and
Federalist Roger Griswold of
Connecticut, followed by Lyon's
"outrageous" and "indecent"
defense (he was reported in the
Annals of Congress to have said,
"I did not come here to have
my —— kicked by everybody"),
some members concluded that
Congress had become no better
than a "tavern," filled with
"beasts, and not gentlemen,"
and contemptible in the eyes of
all "polite or genteel" societies.
(*New York Public Library*)

holders, the Republican party in the North was the political expression of new egalitarian social forces released and intensified by the Revolution. Such rising entrepreneurs were in fact the principal contributors to the very kind of world the southern Republicans were coming to fear.

These diverse and ultimately incompatible sectional and social elements were brought together in a national Republican party by a comprehensive and common ideology. This Republican ideology, involving a deep hatred of bloated state power and of the political and financial mechanisms that created such power, had been inherited from the English "country-opposition" tradition, sharpened and Americanized during the Revolutionary years. Now, during the 1790s, it was given a new and heightened relevance by the policies of the federal administration.

To those steeped in country-Whig ideology, Hamilton's system threatened to re-create the kind of government and society Americans had presumably eradicated in 1776—a society of patronage connections and artificial privilege sustained by executive powers that would in time destroy the independence of the republican citizenry. Hamilton appeared to be another Walpole, using the new economic program to corrupt the Congress and the country and create a swelling phalanx of "stock-jobbers and king-jobbers" (in Jefferson's words) in order to build up executive power at the expense of the people.

Once the Republicans grasped this ideological pattern, all the Federalist measures fell into place. The high-toned pageantry of the "court," the aristocratic talk of titles, the defense of corporate monopolies, the enlargement of the military forces, the growth of taxes, the reliance on the monarchical president and the aristocratic Senate, all pointed toward a systematic plan, as Caroline County of Virginia declared in 1793, of "assimilating the American government to the form and spirit of the British monarchy." Most basic and insidious of all was the Federalist creation of a huge perpetual federal debt, which, as George Clinton, the Republican governor of New York, explained, not only would poison the morals of the people through speculation, but would "add an artificial support to the administration, and by a species of bribery enlist the monied men of the community on the side of the measures of government. . . . Look to Great Britain."

The French Revolution. The eruption of the French Revolution in 1789 and its subsequent expansion in 1792 into a European war pitting monarchical Britain and republican France against one another added to the quarrel Americans were having among themselves over the direction of their society and government. The meaning of the American Revolution and the capacity of the United States to sustain its grand republican experiment now seemed tied to the fate of Britain and France.

President Washington proclaimed America's neutrality in the spring of 1793. The United States quickly tried to take advantage of its position and to gain recognition of its neutral rights by the belligerents. Unable to control the seas, France threw open its empire in the West Indies to American commerce, and American merchants soon developed a profitable shipping trade between the French and Spanish West Indies and Europe. Britain retaliated by invoking what was called the Rule of 1756. This rule, first set forth during the Seven Years' War, enabled British prize courts (that is, courts that judged the legitimacy of the seizure of enemy ships or goods) to deny the right of neutral nations in time of war to trade with belligerent ports that had been closed to them in time of peace. During 1793 and 1794 Britain seized over three hundred American merchant ships.

Although Washington had proclaimed the United States' neutrality, the Federalists and their Republican opponents both sought to favor whichever power—Britain or France—they thought would better promote American interests. The Federalists attempted strenuously to overcome the natural sympathy most Americans had for France, their former Revolutionary ally and new sister republic. Citizen Genêt, the new French minister to the United States, in 1793 began arming privateers in the United States for use against the British and seemed to be appealing over the head of the government to the American people for support. These clumsy actions helped the Federalists win over many Americans otherwise sympathetic to the French Revolution. Aided by the increasing fears of antireligious sentiments and of social upheaval, both associated with the French Revolution, the Federalists recruited growing numbers of Protestant clergy and conservative groups to their cause. While the Republicans were calling for stiff commercial retaliation against Britain for its seizing of American ships and sailors and for its continued occupation of posts in the Northwest, the Federalists hoped to head off war with Britain by negotiation. In the spring of 1794 Washington appointed John Jay, chief justice of the Supreme Court, to be a special minister to Great Britain.

Jay's Treaty. The treaty negotiated by Jay with Britain diplomatically expressed both the Federalist fears of France and the Federalist reliance on the British connection. In the treaty Britain finally agreed to evacuate the Northwest posts, to open parts of her empire to American commerce, and to set up joint arbitration commissions to settle the outstanding issues of prewar debts, boundaries, and compensation for illegal seizures. The United States was compelled to abandon principles concerning freedom of the seas and broad neutral rights that it had promoted since 1776. The treaty in effect recognized the British Rule of 1756. Moreover, by granting Britain more favorable trade conditions than it gave to any other nation, the United States ceded the power to make any future commercial discrimination against Britain, the one great weapon the Republicans counted on to weaken the former mother country's hold on American commerce.

The Republicans were aghast at the treaty. Jay was burned in effigy, and Republicans in the House of Representatives tried to prevent implementation of the treaty, which the Senate reluctantly ratified in 1795 after a bitter struggle. Although the Republicans thought that Britain had conceded to America little more than peace, for most Federalists this was enough. War with Britain would end the imports of English goods and the customs revenues on which Hamilton's financial program depended and would only increase the influence of what Federalist Senator George Cabot of Massachusetts called "French principles [that] would destroy us as a society."

The Quasi-War with France. Washington's decision to retire from the presidency at the end of his second term created an important precedent for the future. The New Englander and vice-president John Adams was widely regarded as Washington's natural successor, but he was elected in 1796 by only a narrow margin of electoral votes, seventy-one to sixty-eight, over the Republican leader, Thomas Jefferson, who became vice-president. Before Washington left office, he with the aid of Hamilton prepared a Farewell Address that became an important political testament of American history, laying the basis for later American "isolationism." In the address, Washington urged Americans "to steer clear of permanent alliances" with any foreign power. Republicans rightly thought that Washington was rejecting the idea that the United States and France were naturally linked in the common cause of bringing revolutionary republicanism to the world.

The Federalist government's pro-British policies expressed in Jay's treaty now drove the embattled French into a series of attacks on American shipping and a refusal to deal with the United States until the new American connection with Britain was broken. President Adams dealt with the crisis in 1797 by sending a special mission to France. The French government, using agents designated as X, Y, and Z,

JOHN ADAMS (1735–1826)
Adams is perhaps the most neglected of the Founding Fathers; he certainly felt himself to be. He seemed to court unpopularity with his displays of jealously, vanity, and pomposity. Yet as his diaries reveal, he was at heart a vulnerable, amiable, and very likeable person. (*The Metropolitan Museum of Art. Gift of William H. Huntington, 1883*)

tried to extort a payment from the American diplomats as a precondition for negotiations. This humiliating "XYZ Affair" further aroused American antagonism to France and led to the repudiation of the Franco-American treaties of 1778, the outbreak in 1798 of an undeclared "quasi-war" on the seas with France, and the opportunity for some extreme Federalists led by Hamilton to strengthen the central government once and for all.

Jefferson, as the leader of the Republican party, saw the world differently. Whether in or out of office, he never let the growing anti-French atmosphere weaken his faith in the cause of the French revolu-

"The Gore Children" c. 1753 by John Singleton Copley. Courtesy, The H. F. du Pont Winterthur Museum

The Rising Glory of America

*L*ate eighteenth century American gentry were confident that the United States would eventually exceed Europe in artistic grandeur and taste. Yet the fine arts had so long been associated with European court life and social decadence that many Americans thought them incompatible with republican simplicity and virtue. Hence any art that Americans developed would have to be a peculiarly republican one.

Americans found the sources for such a republican art in a revolutionary artistic movement that swept through Europe in the latter half of the eighteenth century. This movement, later called neoclassicism, sought to emulate the severe and rational standards of classical antiquity and to infuse art with new moral seriousness and idealistic virtue. Drawing its subjects from history, art would become an instrument for public reform and refinement. Artists would no longer be craftsmen amusing a few rich aristocratic patrons; they would become philosophers instructing a whole society eager to uplift its taste and cultivate its manners.

John Singleton Copley (1738–1815) of Boston had longed to express these new ideas in his art, but the provinciality of colonial society had compelled him to devote his immense talent to painting portraits of the colonial gentry. In 1774, in frustration, he sailed for England. He left a moment too soon, for the Revolution changed everything.

"The Battle of Bunker's Hill" by John Trumbull. Copyright Yale University Art Gallery

John Trumbull (1756–1843), member of a distinguished Connecticut family, quickly grasped that the Revolution was as much a cultural as a political event. He knew only too well that being an artist, "as it is generally practiced, is frivolous, little useful to society, and unworthy of a man who has talents for more serious pursuits. But, to preserve and diffuse the memory of the noblest series of actions which have ever presented themselves in the history of man"—that was a task that "gave dignity to the profession" and justified any gentleman's devotion.

Trumbull's use of the grand style and his attempt at an ennobling effect from history painting can be seen vividly in his *The Battle of Bunker's Hill* (1786). Trumbull thought he would make a

fortune from the sale of engravings of his paintings of the Revolution, but after an initial encouraging reception, subscriptions soon ceased. Early nineteenth-century Americans were not much interested in history paintings, and Trumbull even had trouble getting Congress to pay for the huge commemorative scenes of the Revolution he painted in the rotunda of the Capitol.

No one responded to neoclassical ideas about art with more enthusiasm than did Thomas Jefferson. Since architecture to Jefferson was "an art which shows so much," it was particularly important for the new republican nation that appropriate inspirational forms be used. He cursed the Georgian buildings of colonial Virginia as barbaric, and aimed, through a new symbolic architecture, "to improve the taste of my countrymen, to increase their reputation, to reconcile to them the respect of the world and procure them its praise." He wanted Americans to emulate a classical art that "has pleased universally for nearly 2000 years," even at the expense of functional requirements. From France in the 1780s Jefferson badgered his Virginia colleagues into erecting as the new state capitol a magnificent copy of the Maison Carrée, a Roman temple at Nîmes from the first century A.D., and thus almost singlehandedly introduced the classical style to American public buildings. In fact there was nothing like this use of a Roman temple anywhere in the world. No matter that Richmond was still a backwoods town with mud-lined streets. No matter that a model of a Roman temple was hard to heat and acoustically impossible. For Americans other considerations counted more. By 1820 Roman and Greek revival architecture had become the official style of public buildings in the new nation.

Detail of Virginia State Capitol. *Library of Congress*

View of Richmond from Bushrod Washington's Island in the James River *by Benjamin Henry Latrobe. The Papers of Benjamin Henry Latrobe, Maryland Historical Society*

Excited by the new ideas about art, the Revolutionaries created a sudden outpouring of iconographic works. Statues and monuments were planned; plays, prints, and pageants were employed in support of the Revolution and the new republic. The Revolutionaries continually interrupted their constitution-making and military campaigning to design all sorts of emblems and commemorative medals and to sit for long hours having their portraits painted for history's sake.

When compared to the later extravagant French Revolutionary achievement, under the direction of Jacques Louis David, of putting the arts into the service of republicanism, the American artistic efforts seem pale and feeble. But given America's provincialism and its lack of artists and artistic experience, the Revolutionaries' aims and accomplishments are astonishing. That a monumental city like Washington, D.C., with its sweeping scale, its huge boulevards, and its magnificent parks, could have been conceived and begun in the midst of a swampy wilderness is an extraordinary tribute to the neoclassical aspirations of the Revolutionary leaders.

Yet the classical spirit that inspired Washington, D.C., the ancient place names, the Roman and Greek buildings, and the many emblems and devices was being lost even as these things were being created. Soon few Americans would know the meaning behind the Latin mottoes and the Masonic pyramid and eye appearing on the Great Seal. Indeed, many of the cultural artifacts that Americans inherited from the Revolutionary and early republican eras remain only as awkward reminders of the brevity of America's classical age.

Plan of Washington, D.C., 1791, by Pierre Charles L'Enfant (Library of Congress); Great Seal of the United States of America, front and back; House of Representatives colonnade and design for female figure for the Capitol, drawn by Benjamin Latrobe, 1815 (Library of Congress); Capitol building, east and west wings, drawn by W. Thornton, 1794 (Library of Congress).

The symbol-making of American neo-classical art reached its height with the various depictions of Washington, who came to represent all the great republican virtues Americans ought to value. This oil painting on glass shows the great hero, no longer a man but a symbol, being borne to heaven in a dramatic apotheosis. Such pictures were supposed to fill viewers with awe and inspiration and make them conscious of their national identity.

The concept of art as high-minded moral instruction lingered into the new democratic age of the 1820s. Like earlier American artists, Samuel F. B. Morse (1791–1872) sought to escape from the vulgarity of painting portraits. Instead he wanted to "elevate and refine public feelings by turning the thoughts of his countrymen from sensuality and luxury to intellectual pleasures" by painting great historical subjects, like his *The Old House of Representatives* (1821). The canvas measured nearly seven feet by twelve feet and cost Morse a year of labor. Although the painting was photographic in its meticulous detail, in its emphasis on classical sobriety, dignity, and decorum, it hopelessly idealized the brawling and rowdy House of Representatives that had emerged by the 1820s. Morse put the painting on tour, but the public would not pay to see its elected officials, and Congress would not buy it. In disillusionment Morse eventually turned to photography and the invention of the telegraph and the code which bears his name.

(Opposite) Oil painting on glass, made in China. *Courtesy, The Henry Francis du Pont Winterthur Museum*

(Below) "The Old House of Representatives" *by Samuel F. B. Morse. In the collection of the Corcoran Gallery of Art*

"Pat Lyon at the Forge" by John Neagle. Courtesy of Museum of Fine Arts, Boston

This new kind of republican portrait reveals just how far behind early nineteenth-century America had left its patrician colonial hierarchy. Although Lyon by 1826 was a rich and prominent businessman, he wanted his portrait, as he said, to depict his humble origins as a blacksmith in Philadelphia, "at work at my anvil, with my sleeves rolled up and a leather apron on." The artist, John Neagle (1796–1865), was himself something of a self-made man. His father came from County Cork and his mother was a New Jersey yeoman's daughter. He managed, however, to marry the stepdaughter of the well-known and successful portrait painter, Thomas Sully (1783–1872).

As different as the new bourgeois leaders of the early republic were from the eighteenth-century gentry, in wanting from art mainly pictures of themselves they were much the same. By the 1820s many American intellectuals were still anxiously awaiting the long-predicted westward transit of the arts across the Atlantic.

tionary republic. While he supported the outward neutrality of the United States in the European war between Britain and France, he and other Republicans were bitterly opposed to Jay's treaty and convinced they could not remain impartial in a cause on which "the liberty of the whole earth was depending." Even knowledge of the bloody excesses of the French Revolution did not dampen Jefferson's enthusiasm for it. "Rather than it should have failed," he wrote in 1793, "I would have seen half the earth desolate; were there but an Adam and Eve left in every country, and left free, it would be better than it now is."

Convinced that the very meaning of the United States as a republic was directly related to the conflict between Britain and France, some American public officials of both political persuasions were led into extraordinarily improper diplomatic behavior during the 1790s. Hamilton as secretary of the treasury secretly passed on information about United States plans to the British government. Jefferson, as secretary of state under Washington, Edmund Randolph, his successor in that office, and James Monroe as minister to France, all indiscreetly tried to undermine the pro-British stand of the administration they were serving and came very close to becoming unwitting tools of French policy.

The Crisis of 1798–1799.   In such an inflamed atmosphere political passions ran as high as they ever have in American history. Every aspect of American life—business groups, banks, dance assemblies, even funerals—became politicized. People who had known each other their whole lives now crossed streets to avoid meeting. As personal and social ties fell apart, differences easily spilled into violence, and fighting broke out in the state legislatures and even in the Congress.

Amid such passions the political parties that emerged in the 1790s were unlike any later American parties. Although by 1796 the Federalists and the Republicans had organized to win the presidency for their respective candidates, Adams and Jefferson, both parties saw themselves in an increasingly revolu-

tionary situation. The Federalists thought of themselves as the most enlightened and socially established members of the natural aristocracy, who by their very respectability were best able to carry out the responsibility of ruling the country. They thus affirmed that they were the government, not a "party." Parties, as Washington warned in his Farewell Address, were equivalent to factions and could lead only to sedition and the disruption of the state.

Jefferson and many other Republicans shared this traditional eighteenth-century abhorrence of party, but under the extraordinary circumstances of the 1790s they had come to believe that organized opposition was justified. Because the Republicans thought the normal processes of American politics had become corrupted and poisoned by a Federalist government that had detached itself from the people, they felt pressed to create popular organizations of political opposition similar to those the Whigs had formed during the pre-Revolutionary crisis. Their goal in forming caucuses, corresponding committees, and Democratic-Republican societies was to band people together and use what they increasingly called "public opinion" to influence elections and counteract the weight of prominent Federalist individuals in national politics. The extralegal opposition of the Republican party, they believed, would be a temporary but necessary instrument that would save the people's liberties from Federalist monarchism.

Nothing was more important in mobilizing the the people into political consciousness than the press. Newspapers multiplied dramatically, from fewer than 100 in 1790 to over 230 by 1800; by 1810 Americans were buying over 22 million copies of 376 papers annually, the largest aggregate circulation of newspapers in any country in the world. By the late 1790s these papers, many of them Republican, were lowering their prices and adopting eye-catching typography and cartoons in order to reach new readers. By popularizing political affairs as never before and by relentlessly criticizing Federalist officials, the press seemed to be single-handedly shaping American political life.

Although the Federalists began to adopt some

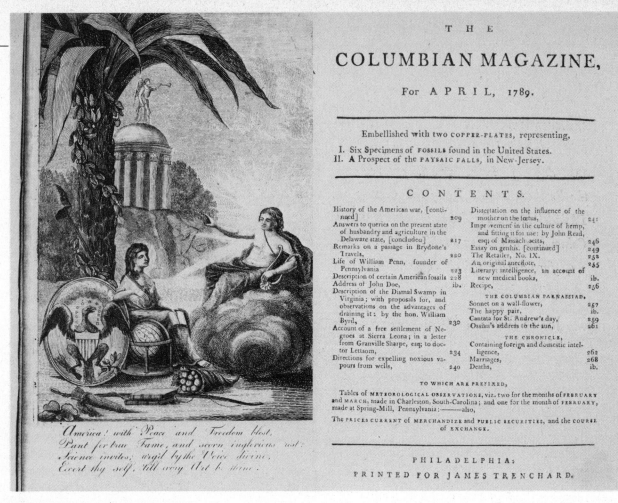

THE

COLUMBIAN MAGAZINE,

For APRIL, 1789.

Embellished with two COPPER-PLATES, representing,

I. Six Specimens of FOSSILS found in the United States.
II. A Prospect of the PAYSAIC FALLS, in New-Jersey.

CONTENTS.

TO WHICH ARE PREFIXED,

Tables of METEOROLOGICAL OBSERVATIONS, viz. two for the months of FEBRUARY
and MARCH, made in Charleston, South-Carolina; and one for the month of FEBRUARY,
made at Spring-Mill, Pennsylvania;———also,

The PRICES CURRENT of MERCHANDIZE and PUBLIC SECURITIES, and the COURSE
of EXCHANGE.

PHILADELPHIA;
PRINTED FOR JAMES TRENCHARD.

*America! with Peace and Freedom blest,
Pant for true Fame, and scorn inglorious rest:
Science invites; urged by the Voice divine,
Exert thy self, till every Art be thine.*

PAGES FROM "COLUMBIAN MAGAZINE"

Between 1775 and 1795 twenty-seven learned and gentlemanly magazines like this one were begun, six more than in the entire colonial period. The creation of these new journals was a remarkable testimony to the cultural promise of the Revolution.   (*American Antiquarian Society*)

of what they called the "petty electioneering arts" of the Republican opposition, they were not comfortable with the new democratic politics. They saw themselves in traditional eighteenth-century terms as gentleman leaders to whom ordinary people, if they were only left alone, would naturally defer. The Federalists attributed the difficulties and disorder of the 1790s to the influence of newspapers, demagogues, and extralegal political associations. Republican upstarts and factions, they believed, were stirring up the people against their natural rulers. They spread radical French principles, interfered with the

electoral process, and herded the people, including recent immigrants, into political activity. New kinds of writers and publishers, like the former indentured servant and now congressman and editor Matthew Lyon of Vermont, were reaching out to influence an audience as obscure and ordinary as themselves. Through the coarse language and slander of their publications they were destroying the governing gentry's personal reputation for character on which popular respect for the entire political order was presumably based.

By the late 1790s, amid an economic depression

and the "quasi-war" with France, all these Federalists' fears climaxed in their desperate repressive measures of 1798—measures which more than anything else have tarnished the historical reputation of the Federalists. In control of both the executive and the Congress, the Federalists contemplated various plans for strengthening the Continental union. They sought to broaden the power of the federal judiciary, to increase the transportation network throughout the country, and to enlarge the army and navy. Above all, the Federalists aimed to end the Republicans' political exploitation of new immigrants and to stop the flow of Republican literature that was poisoning the relations between rulers and ruled.

In 1798 the Federalist-dominated Congress enacted Alien and Sedition Acts, which lengthened the naturalization process for foreigners, gave the president extraordinary powers to deal with aliens, and provided the central government with the authority to punish as crimes seditious libels against federal officials. At the same time, the Congress ordered the immediate enlistment of a new regular army of twelve thousand and laid plans for provisional armies numbering in the tens of thousands. Washington was to be called out of retirement as commander in chief of the new army, but Hamilton was to be actually in command. Presumably all this was done to meet the threat of a French invasion, but some people believed that it was to deal with the domestic disorder of the United States. When the United States army quickly suppressed an armed rebellion of several northeastern Pennsylvania counties led by John Fries in protest against the new federal tax on houses, land, and slaves, the advantages of federal strength were confirmed in some Federalist eyes.

For their part, the Republicans in 1798–99 thought the very success of the American Revolution was at stake. In response to the Federalist repression, particularly the Alien and Sedition Acts, the Virginia and Kentucky legislatures issued resolutions, drawn up by Madison and Jefferson respectively. These resolutions proclaimed the right of the states to judge the constitutionality of federal acts and to interpose themselves between the citizenry and the unconstitutional actions of the central government. Although the other states declined to support Virginia and Kentucky, the stand taken by the two states opened a question about the nature of the union that would trouble the country for many years to come.

By the end of the decade several developments brought a measure of reconciliation. Both Madison and Jefferson were unwilling to resort to force to support their resolutions. British Admiral Horatio Nelson's naval victory over the French at the Battle of the Nile in October 1798 lessened the threat of a French invasion of either England or America. But most important in calming the crisis was the action of President John Adams.

Adams's presidency had been contentious, and he was never in command of his own cabinet, let alone the government. This short, puffy, and sensitive man, who wore his heart on his sleeve, was much too honest, impulsive, and independent-minded to handle the growing division among the Federalists over the military buildup; but he had an abiding fear of standing armies and a stubborn courage. In 1799 against the wishes of his advisers he decided to send another peace message to France despite the humiliating failure of his earlier effort in the XYZ Affair. France, now under Napoleon as first consul, agreed to make terms, and in 1800 signed an agreement with the United States that brought the quasi-war to a close.

Adams's independent action irreparably split the Federalist leadership between the moderates who supported the president and the High Federalists who supported Hamilton, and thus crippled Adams's chances of winning the presidential election of 1800. Adams, always ready to bemoan his country's neglect of his achievements, considered his decision to negotiate with France "the most disinterested, most determined and most successful of my whole life." His controversial decision ended the war crisis and undermined the attempts of the extremist Federalists to strengthen the central government and the military forces of the United States. Although the worst was over, that was not yet clear to everyone at the time. In 1800 the British ambassador still thought the "whole system of American Government" was "tottering to its foundations."

CHRONOLOGY

1781 Articles of Confederation ratified.
Congress establishes Bank of North America.

1782 Fall of Lord North's ministry.

1783 Newburgh conspiracy of American army
officers.
Society of Cincinnati founded.
Pennsylvania Evening Post, first daily newspaper
in United States, begins publication.
Treaty of Peace with Britain signed.

1785 Land Ordinance for Northwest Territory
adopted by Congress.

1786 Jay-Gardoqui Treaty; rejected by Congress.
Virginia Statute for Religious Freedom.
Shays's Rebellion in western Massachusetts.
Annapolis Convention; adopts plan to meet in
Philadelphia to revise Articles of Confederation.

1787 Federal Constitutional Convention meets in
Philadelphia and drafts Constitution.
Northwest Ordinance enacted by Congress.
The Federalist papers begun by Madison,
Hamilton, and Jay.

1788 Ratification of United States Constitution by
all the states except Rhode Island and
North Carolina.

1789 First session of Congress meets.
Washington inaugurated as first president.
Capitol at Richmond, Virginia, built from
model of Maison Carrée supplied by Jefferson.
Outbreak of French Revolution.

1790 Hamilton's Report on Public Credit; Funding
Bill; Assumption Bill.
Father John Carroll made first Roman Catholic
bishop of United States with See in Baltimore.

1791 Bank of the United States established.

First ten amendments to Constitution
(Bill of Rights) adopted.
Defeat of General Arthur St. Clair by
Ohio Indians.

1793 Execution of Louis XVI and outbreak of
European war.
Washington inaugurated for second term.
Proclamation of Neutrality by Washington.
Citizen Genêt Affair.
Samuel Slater erects first cotton mill at
Pawtucket, Rhode Island.
Eli Whitney applies for patent on cotton gin.
Yellow fever epidemic in Philadelphia.

1794 Whiskey Rebellion in western Pennsylvania.
Battle of Fallen Timbers, Ohio; General
Anthony Wayne defeats Indians.
Philadelphia-Lancaster turnpike completed.

1795 Jay's Treaty with Britain.
Treaty of Greenville, between United States
and Indians of Northwest.
Pinckney's Treaty with Spain.

1796 Washington's Farewell Address, warning
against foreign entanglements and domestic
factionalism.
John Adams elected president.

1798 XYZ Affair reported by Adams to Congress.
Quasi-war with France on high seas.
Alien and Sedition Acts enacted by Federalists
in Congress.
Virginia and Kentucky resolutions.
Eleventh Amendment to Constitution ratified.

1799 *American Review and Literary Journal*, first
quarterly literary review in America, established
by the novelist Charles Brockden Brown.
Fries uprising in Pennsylvania.

SUGGESTED READINGS

John Fiske, *The Critical Period of American History* (1888), popularized the Federalist view of the Confederation for the nineteenth century. Merrill Jensen, *The New Nation* (1950), minimizes the crisis of the 1780s, and explains the movement for the Constitution as the work of a small but dynamic minority. E. James Ferguson, *The Power of the Purse . . . ,1776—1790* (1961), also stresses the nationalists' efforts to strengthen the Confederation. Clarence L. Ver Steeg, *Robert Morris, Revolutionary Financier* (1954), is the major study of that important figure. Forrest McDonald, *E Pluribus Unum: The Formation of the American Republic, 1776-1790* (1965), describes the commercial scrambling by Americans in the 1780s. The best account of the army and the Newburgh Conspiracy is Richard H. Kohn, *Eagle and Sword: The Federalists and the Creation of the Military Establishment in America, 1783–1802* (1975). Frederick W. Marks III, *Independence on Trial* (1973), analyzes the foreign problems contributing to the Constitution. The best short survey of the Confederation period is still Andrew C. McLaughlin, *The Confederation and the Constitution, 1783–1789* (1905).

Charles Beard's *An Economic Interpretation of the Constitution* (1913) sought to explain the Constitution as something other than the consequence of high-minded idealism. It became the most influential history book ever written in America. Beard saw the struggle over the Constitution as "a deep-seated conflict between a popular party based on paper money and agrarian interests and a conservative party centered in the towns and resting on financial, mercantile, and personal property interests generally." While Beard's particular proof for his thesis—that the Founders held federal securities that they expected would appreciate in value under a new national government—has been demolished, especially by Forrest McDonald, *We the People* (1958), his general interpretation of the origins of the Constitution still casts a long shadow. Jackson T. Main, *Political Parities before the Constitution* (1974), finds a "cosmopolitan"-"localist" split within the states over the Constitution. Gordon S. Wood, *The Creation of the American Republic, 1776–1787* (1969), working through the ideas, discovers a similar social, but not strictly speaking a "class," division over the Constitution.

For a different emphasis on the origins of the Constitution, see Robert E. Brown, *Reinterpretation of the Formation of the American Constitution* (1963); and Benjamin F. Wright, Jr., *Consensus and Continuity, 1776–1787* (1958). The best history of the Convention is still Max Farrand, *The Framing of the Constitution of the United States* (1913), which sees the Constitution as "a bundle of compromises" designed to meet specific defects of the Articles. Irving Brant's third volume of his biography of *James Madison* (6 vols., 1941–61) has a sure-footed description of the Convention.

Max Farrand, ed., *The Records of the Federal Convention of 1787* (4 vols.; 1911, 1937); and Jonathan Elliot, ed., *The Debates in the Several State Conventions on the Adoption of the Federal Constitution* (5 vols., 1876), are collections of the important documents. Jacob Cooke, ed., *The Federalist* (1961), is the best edition of these papers. Two sympathetic studies of the Antifederalists are Jackson T. Main, *The Antifederalists . . . , 1781–1788* (1961); and Robert A. Rut-

land, *The Ordeal of the Constitution* (1966). See also Robert A. Rutland, *The Birth of the Bill of Rights, 1776–1791* (1955). The papers of the Founders—Jefferson, Franklin, Hamilton, John Adams, Madison, and others—are currently being published in mammoth scholarly editions.

Politics in the 1790s is ably summarized in John C. Miller, *The Federalist Era, 1789–1801* (1960). Richard Buel, Jr., *Securing the Revolution: Ideology in American Politics, 1789–1815* (1972), however, better recaptures the distinctiveness of the age and the problematical character of the new national government. John C. Miller, *Alexander Hamilton, Portrait in Paradox* (1959), is the fullest biography; but Gerald Stourzh, *Alexander Hamilton and the Idea of Republican Government* (1970), better places this leading Federalist in an eighteenth-century context. In this respect, see also the collected essays of Douglass Adair, *Fame and the Founding Fathers* (1974). A concise study is Forrest McDonald, *The Presidency of George Washington* (1974). For single-volume biographies of Washington, see Marcus Cunliffe, *George Washington: Man and Monument* (1958); and James Thomas Flexner, *Washington: The Indispensable Man* (1974).

Leonard D. White, *The Federalists: A Study in Administrative History* (1948), is the standard account of the creation of the governmental bureaucracy. See also Carl Prince, *The Federalists and the Origins of the U.S. Civil Service* (1978). Lisle A. Rose, *Prologue to Democracy* (1968), describes the formation of Federalist influence in the South during the 1790s. Richard H. Kohn, *Eagle and Sword: The Federalists and the Creation of the Military Establishment in America, 1783–1802* (1975), is important for understanding the Federalist goals. On foreign policy, see Samuel Flagg Bemis, *Jay's Treaty* (1923), and *Pinckney's Treaty* (1926). Jerald A. Combs, *The Jay Treaty* (1970), is broader than its title would suggest. A good survey is Lawrence S. Kaplan, *Colonies into Nation: American Diplomacy, 1763–1801* (1972).

Much of the literature on the history of the 1790s treats the opposition of the Republicans as ordinary party activity. See William N. Chambers, *Political Parties in a New Nation . . . , 1776–1809* (1963); and Noble E. Cunningham, Jr., *The Jeffersonian Republicans: The Formation of Party Organization, 1789–1801* (1957). Notable exceptions are Richard Buel, Jr., *Securing the Revolution* (1972), and Lance Banning, *The Jeffersonian Persuasion* (1978). See also John Zvesper, *Political Philosophy and Rhetoric: A Study of the Origins of American Party Politics* (1977). On the formation of extralegal organizations, all we have is Eugene P. Link, *Democratic Republican Societies, 1790–1800* (1942). There are a number of studies of the growth of the Republican party in the separate states. See especially Paul Goodman, *The*

Democratic Republicans of Massachusetts (1964); Alfred F. Young, *The Democratic Republicans of New York* (1967); Sanford W. Higgenbotham, *The Keystone in the Democratic Arch: Pennsylvania Politics 1800–1816* (1952); Carl E. Prince, *New Jersey's Jeffersonian Republicans* (1967); and Norman K. Risjord, *Chesapeake Politics, 1781–1800* (1978). On the Whiskey Rebellion, see Leland D. Baldwin, *Whiskey Rebels* (1939).

On the foreign crisis of the late 1790s, see Alexander De Conde, *The Quasi-War: Politics and Diplomacy of the Undeclared War with France, 1797–1801* (1966). Manning J. Dauer, *The Adams Federalists* (1953), captures some of the desperation of the Federalists in 1798. The fullest study of the Alien and Sedition Acts is James Morton Smith, *Freedom's Fetters* (1956); but for a proper appreciation of the special eighteenth-century context in which freedom of speech and of the press has to be viewed, see Leonard W. Levy, *Legacy of Suppression* (1960). Stephen G. Kurtz is solid on *The Presidency of John Adams . . . , 1795–1800* (1957).

The Federalist world, born in the reaction to the excesses of Revolutionary populism, could not endure. It ran too much against the grain of fast-moving social developments. The Federalists of the 1790s refused to recognize that the people's position in American politics was no longer a debatable issue. Convinced that people feared disunion so much that almost any sort of strong national government within a republican framework would be acceptable, the Federalists tried to revive some of the energy and authority of executive government that had been lost in the turbulence of the Revolution. America was increasingly more prosperous, and the Federalists counted on this to justify both their program and their reliance on rule by a traditional gentlemanly elite. But so out of touch were they with the rapid developments of American life, so counter to the impulse of the Revolutionary ideology was their program, that they provoked a second revolutionary movement that threatened to tear the Republic apart.

Only the electoral victory of the Republicans in 1800 ended this threat and brought, in the eyes of many Americans, the entire Revolutionary venture of two and a half decades to successful completion. Indeed, "the Revolution of 1800," as the Republican leader and third president of the United States, Thomas Jefferson, described it, "was as real a revolution in the principles of our government as that of 1776 was in its form."

The Revolution of 1800

Thomas Jefferson was an unlikely popular radical. He was a well-connected and highly cultivated southern planter who never had to scramble for his position in Virginia. The wealth and leisure that made possible his great contributions to liberty were supported by the labor of a hundred or more slaves. He was tall, gangling, red-haired, and unlike his fellow Revolutionary John Adams, whom he fought and befriended for fifty years, he was reserved, self-possessed, and incurably optimistic. He disliked personal controversy and was always charming in face-to-face relations with both friends and enemies. But at a distance

CHAPTER 11

The Revolution Recovered

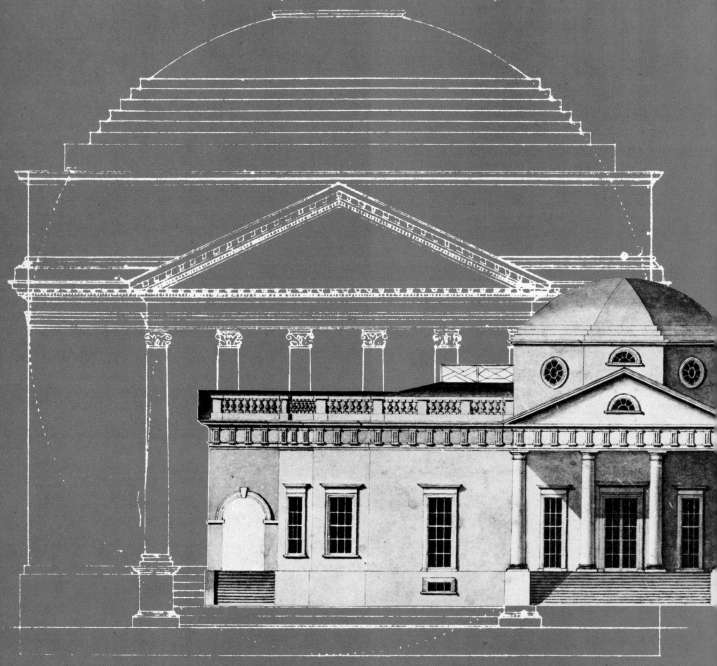

THOMAS JEFFERSON, ARCHITECT; MONTICELLO; AND SKETCH OF THE ROTUNDA OF THE
UNIVERSITY OF VIRGINIA

"Architecture," Thomas Jefferson once said, "is my delight, and putting up and pulling
down one of my favorite amusements." Even as a young man, Jefferson was absorbed in
designing and building his home at Monticello. He went at architecture with a mathe-
matical precision; no detail of building—from the chemistry of mortar to the proper technique of laying bricks—was too insignificant for his attention.   *(Portrait by R. Peale. Courtesy,
The New-York Historical Society, New York City; Monticello, Massachusetts Historical Society)*

he could hate, and thus many of his opponents concluded that he was two-faced. He was undeniably complicated. He mingled the most lofty visions with astute backroom politicking. He was a sophisticated man-of-the-world, who loved no place better than his native Virginia. This complex slaveholding aristocrat became the most important apostle for democratic idealism in American history.

Thomas Jefferson's narrow victory in the presidential election of 1800 confirmed the changing course of national developments. Jefferson received seventy-three electoral votes, to the sixty-four of the Federalist candidate, John Adams, who was opposed by the Hamiltonians within his own party. For a moment even that close victory was in doubt. Because the Constitution did not provide that the electors distinguish between their votes for president and vice-president, both Jefferson and the Republican vice-presidential candidate Aaron Burr had received the same number of electoral votes, thus throwing the election into the House of Representatives. After thirty-five deadlocked ballots, Hamilton and other Federalist leaders, preferring Jefferson to Burr and thinking they had assurances from Jefferson to continue Federalist policies, allowed the acknowledged Republican leader to become president. To avoid a repetition of this electoral impasse, the country adopted the Twelfth Amendment to the Constitution, which allowed the electors to designate the president and vice-president separately in their ballots.*

In these confused electoral circumstances it is difficult to see the bold and revolutionary character of Jefferson's election. It was one of the first popular elections in modern history that resulted in the peaceful transfer of governmental power from one "party" to another. At the outset Jefferson himself struck a note of conciliation: "We are all republicans—we are all federalists," he said in his inaugural address. Many Federalists were soon absorbed into the Republican cause. And the Republican administration did subsequently deviate from strict Republican principles. Thus the continuities are impressive, and the Jeffersonian "Revolution of 1800" has blended nearly im-

*For the Twelfth Amendment, see Appendix.

THOMAS JEFFERSON'S VICTORY BANNER, 1800
(Ralph E. Becker Collection, Smithsonian Institution, Division of Political History)

perceptibly into the main democratic currents of American history. However, when compared with the consolidated state the Federalists tried to build in the 1790s, what the Republicans did after 1800 proved that a real revolution—as Jefferson said it was—took place.

Government Without Power.   Believing that most of the evils afflicting mankind in the past had flowed from the abuses of political establishments, the Republicans in 1800 set about deliberately to carry out what they rightly believed was the original aim of the Revolution—to reduce the overawing and dangerous power of government. They wanted to form a national republic based on the country-Whig opposition ideology and formed in the image of the Revolutionary state governments of 1776. They envisioned a central state whose authority would resemble that of the old Articles of Confederation more than that of the European type of state the Federalists had thought essential. They wanted in fact to create a general government that would rule without the traditional attributes of power.

From the outset Jefferson was determined that the new government would lack even the usual rituals of power. At the very beginning he purposefully set a new tone of republican simplicity in contrast to the stiff formality and regal ceremony with which the Federalists, in imitation of European court life, had surrounded the presidency. Since the Federalist presidents, like the English monarchs, had personally delivered their addresses to the legislature "from the throne," Jefferson chose to submit his in writing. Unlike Washington and Adams, he made himself easily accessible to visitors, all of whom, no matter how distinguished, he received, as the British chargé reported, "with a most perfect disregard to ceremony both in his dress and manner." Much to the shock of foreign dignitaries, at American state occasions he replaced the protocol and distinctions of European court life with the egalitarian rules of what he called "pell-mell."

While Jefferson's dignity and gentlemanly tastes scarcely allowed any actual leveling in social gatherings, his transformation of manners at the capital harmonized with changes in society. For the Republican revolution soon brought to the national government men who, unlike Jefferson, were without the attributes of gentlemen, who did not know one another, and who were decidedly not at home in polite society. During the following years of the early nineteenth century, life in the national capital became steadily vulgarized by the growing presence in drawing rooms of muddy boots, unkempt hair, and the constant chawing and spitting of tobacco.

Even the removal of the national capital in 1800 from Philadelphia, the bustling intellectual and commercial center of the country, to the rural wilderness of the "federal city" on the Potomac accentuated the transformation of power that was taking place. It dramatized the Republicans' attempt to separate the national government from intimate involvement in the society and their aim to erect the very kind of general government Hamilton, in *The Federalist* No.

27, had warned against, "a government at a distance and out of sight" that could "hardly be expected to interest the sensations of the people." The new and remote capital, Washington, D.C., utterly failed to attract the population, the commerce, and the social and cultural life needed to make it what its original planners had boldly expected, the Rome of the New World. By 1820 Washington was an out-of-the-way village of less than ten thousand inhabitants whose principal business was keeping boardinghouses. Situated in a marsh, the federal city fully deserved the gibes of the visiting Irish poet, Thomas Moore:

> This embryo capital
> where Fancy sees
> Squares in Morasses,
> obelisks in trees.

Political Reform. The Republicans in fact meant to have an insignificant national government. The federal government, Jefferson declared in his first message to Congress in 1801, was "charged with the external and mutual relations only of these states." All the rest—the "principal care of our persons, our property, and our reputation, constituting the great field of human concerns"—was to be left to the states. Such a limited national government required turning back a decade of Federalist policy. The Sedition Act of 1798 was allowed to lapse, a new liberal naturalization law was adopted, and rigorous economy was invoked to root out Federalist corruption.

The inherited Federalist governmental establishment was minuscule by modern standards and was small even by eighteenth-century European standards; in 1801 the headquarters of the War Department, for example, consisted of only the secretary, an accountant, fourteen clerks, and two messengers; and the attorney general did not have even a clerk. Nevertheless, in Jefferson's eyes, this tiny federal bureaucracy had become "too complicated, too expensive," and offices under the Federalists had "unnecessarily multiplied." Thus the roll of federal officials was severely cut back. All tax inspectors and collectors were eliminated. The diplomatic establishment was reduced to three missions—in Britain,

REPUBLICANS

Turn out, turn out and save your Country from ruin !

From an *Emperor*—from a *King*—from the iron grasp of a *British Tory Faction*—an unprincipled banditti of British speculators. The hireling tools and emissaries of his majesty king George the 3d have thronged our city and diffused the poison of principles among us.

DOWN WITH THE TORIES, DOWN WITH THE BRITISH FACTION,

Before they have it in their power to enslave you, and reduce your families to distress by heavy taxation. Republicans want no Tribute-liars—they want no ship Ocean-liars—they want no Rufus King's for Lords —they want no Varick to lord it over them—they want no Jones for senator, who fought with the British against the Americans in time of the war.—But they want in their places such men as

Jefferson & Clinton,

who fought their Country's Battles in the year '76

(Courtesy of the New-York Historical Society, New York City)

France, and Spain. The Federalist dream of creating a modern army and navy in emulation of Europe disappeared; the military budget was cut in half. The army, stationed only in the West, was left with 3,000 regulars and only 172 officers. The navy had but a half-dozen frigates, and by 1807 these were replaced with several hundred gunboats designed only to defend the coast or to deal with the Barbary pirates in the Mediterranean. The benefits of a standing military establishment, the Jeffersonians believed, were not worth the cost either in money or in the threat to liberty such an establishment posed.

Since Hamilton's financial program had formed the basis of the heightened political power of the federal government, it above all had to be dismantled. All the internal excise taxes the Federalists had designed to make the people feel the energy of the national government were eliminated. For many citizens the federal presence was now reduced to the delivery of the mails.

Although Jefferson's extremely able secretary of the treasury, Albert Gallatin, persuaded the reluctant president to keep the Bank of the United States, the government was under continual pressure to reduce the Bank's influence. The growing numbers of state banking interests were resentful of the privileged and restraining authority of the national Bank. By 1811 state bankers and southern planters, who hated all banks, eventually prevented a renewal of the Bank's charter. The federal government then distributed its patronage among twenty-one state banks and effectively diluted its authority to control by that means either the society or the economy. It was in fact the proliferation of these state-chartered banks and their issuing of notes that enabled the states to have paper money after all, in spite of the Constitution's prohibition against the states' issuing bills of credit.

Just as Hamilton had regarded the permanent federal debt as a principal source of support for the federal government, so the Republicans were determined to pay off the debt, and quickly. By 1810 the federal debt had been reduced to nearly half of the $80 million it had been when the Republicans took office. Jefferson's lifelong desire to reduce the government's debt was not simply a matter of prohibiting a present generation from burdening posterity, but a matter of destroying what he considered an insidious and dangerous instrument of political influence. His aim was to create a new kind of government, one without privilege or patronage.

Perhaps nothing illustrates Jefferson's radical conception of government better than his problems with patronage. Not all Republicans took his assault on patronage as seriously as he did, and many were often reluctant to join a government in which they would have no sources of influence. Time and again Jefferson found himself caught between his conscientious determination to avoid any semblance of Hamiltonian political patronage or "corruption" and the pressing demands of his fellow Republicans that he give them a share in the government and oust the enemy. Once the Federalists were replaced by Republicans, however, there was no need for compromise on this issue. Removals from office for political reasons came to an end. By the end of the administrations of Jefferson's Republican successors, James Madison (1809–17), James Monroe (1817–25), and John Quincy Adams (1825–29) the holders of government appointments had become a permanent officialdom of men grown old in their positions. Until the

Jacksonian revolution of 1828 patronage as a means of influence in government virtually ceased.

Republican Politics.   Jefferson, through a combination of this initial patronage and some improvised forms of political influence (in particular his nightly legislative dinner parties and the use of confidential legislative agents), was able personally to direct the Congress and the Republican party to an extraordinary degree. Yet Jefferson's personal strength and his notable achievements as president cannot hide the remarkable transformation in the traditional meaning of government that the Republican revolution of 1800 created. During the opening three decades of the nineteenth century, particularly after Jefferson retired from the presidency, the United States government was weaker than at any other time in its national history.

The alignments of politics became increasingly confused. The Federalists in 1800–1801 surrendered the national ruling authority without a fight. Because the Federalist leaders considered themselves gentlemen for whom politics was not an exclusive concern, they were prepared to retire to their businesses and private lives and await what they assumed would soon be the people's desperate call for the return of the "wise and good" and the "natural rulers." But the popular reaction they expected to the Republican revolution never came. Some, like John Jay and John Adams, retired to their country estates. Others, like John Quincy Adams, the son of the former president, eventually joined the Republican movement. Others, like Robert Goodloe Harper of South Carolina, clung to their principles and their minority status in politics. And still others, like Timothy Pickering, secretary of state under Adams, dreamed of revenge and fomented separatist plots in New England. But as a national party Federalism slowly withered under the relentless democratization of American society.

Although the Federalists and Republicans continued to compete for election and worked successfully to increase voter participation, neither was a party in any modern sense; and it is probably anachronistic to call their electoral competition, as many historians have done, "the first party system." Though the Federalists continued to put up presidential candidates, their electoral strength was generally negligible and mostly confined to New England. In 1820 they were too weak even to nominate a candidate.

While the declining Federalist gentry regarded themselves less as a party than as dispossessed rulers, the Republicans saw themselves as leaders of a revolutionary movement eager to incorporate the bulk of the opposition into their fold. Only as long as the Federalists posed a threat to the principles of free government could the Republicans remain a unified party. Therefore as the possibility of a Federalist resurgence receded, the Republican party gradually fell apart. A variety of Republican factions and groups arose in the Congress and in the country organized around particular individuals (the "Burrites," the "Clintonians"), around states and sections (the "Pennsylvania Quids," the "Old Republicans" of Virginia), or around ideology ("the Principles of '98," the "Invisibles," the "War Hawks"). Individual politicians continued to pride themselves on their independence from influence of any sort, and "party" remained a disparaging term. In fact, until the Jacksonian era nothing approaching a stable party system developed in the Congress.

By the end of Jefferson's presidency in 1809 the balance of governmental power had slipped to the Congress, which was unequipped to exercise it. Because of the great increase in the size of Congress and its growing disintegration into diverse voting blocs, neither Madison nor Monroe was able to use any of the personal presidential charm and influence that Jefferson had used. By 1808 caucuses of Republicans within the Congress had taken over nomination of the party's candidates for the presidency, and Republican presidential aspirants soon became dependent on the legislature in the way governors in the Revolutionary state constitutions of 1776 had been.

While Secretary of State James Madison was able with Jefferson's private blessing to secure the Republican nomination in 1808 and again in 1812 against only some divided opposition, in 1816 Madison's secretary of state, James Monroe, had to contend strenuously with Secretary of War William H. Crawford of Georgia for the nomination. By the early 1820s Secretary of State John Quincy Adams, Secretary of War John C. Calhoun, and Secretary of the Treasury Crawford were all feuding with one another and seeking support in the Congress for the presidential nomination. If such political realities did not dictate presidential subservience to the legislature, Republican ideology did. Except in foreign affairs, both Presidents Madison and Monroe, the second and third members of the "Virginia Dynasty," regarded Congress as the rightful determinant of the public will, free of executive influence.

As the Congress in Madison's and Monroe's administrations (1809–25) gathered up the power passing from the executive, it sought to organize itself into committees in order to initiate and supervise policy. But the rise of the committee system only further fragmented the government into contending interests. The executive authority itself broke apart into competing departments, each seeking its own support in the Congress and becoming a rival of the president. Congress now fought with the president for control of the cabinet and connived with executive department heads behind the president's back. At one point the Congress actually forced Madison to accept a secretary of state who was plotting against him, and its meddling drove Monroe into bitter hostility against his secretary of the treasury, with whom he stopped speaking. Until the congressional caucus system of presidential nomination collapsed in 1824 and a new kind of democratic presidency emerged in 1828 with the election of Andrew Jackson, the energy of the national executive remained weak.

But despite this concentration on strict republican principles there were by the second decade of the nineteenth century many Americans who sought to reclaim and reenact some of the abandoned Federalist measures. A new generation of politicians, less attached to the ideology and fears of the eighteenth century and with none of Hamilton's dream to create a consolidated European-like state, now began urging a new national bank, protective tariffs, and a federally sponsored program of internal improvements. By 1815 the nation had grown faster than anyone had expected, and new states, new interests, and new outlooks had to be taken into account. By then it was becoming clear that the future of the country lay in the West.

(Abby Aldrich Rockefeller Folk Art Center, Williamsburg, Virginia)

An Empire of Liberty

While Hamilton and the Federalists had looked eastward across the Atlantic to Europe for their image of the destiny of the United States, the Republicans from the beginning had had their eyes on the West. Only by moving westward, Jefferson thought, could Americans maintain their republican society of independent yeomen-farmers and avoid the miseries of the concentrated urban working classes of Europe. Jefferson was indeed the most expansionist-minded president in American history. He dreamed of Americans endowed with republican principles eventually swarming over the continent and creating an "empire of liberty." Yet even Jefferson did not anticipate how suddenly and chaotically Americans would scatter westward.

The population grew from almost 4 million in 1790 to over 7 million in 1810 and nearly 10 million by 1820, and much of it was moving west. By the 1790s the population in some of the tidewater counties of the Chesapeake already was declining. The advance over the Allegheny Plateau that had been a trickle before the Revolution and had swelled during the 1780s now became a flood. Within a single generation following the Revolution more territory was occupied than during the entire colonial period. By 1810 westward-moving Americans had created a great triangular wedge of settlement to the Mississippi. The northern side ran from New York along the Ohio River, the southern side from east Georgia through Tennessee, and the two lines met at the tip of the wedge at St. Louis. Within this huge triangle of settlement people were distributed haphazardly, and huge pockets remained virtually uninhabited.

National leaders had expected migration westward, but not the way it happened. The carefully drawn plans of the 1780s for the orderly surveying and settlement of the West were simply overwhelmed by the massive and chaotic movement of people. Many settlers ignored land ordinances and titles, squatted on the land, and claimed rights to it. For decades beginning in 1796 the federal government steadily lowered the price of land, reduced the size of purchasable tracts, and relaxed the terms of credit in ever-more desperate efforts to bring the public land laws into line with the speed with which they were being settled. There was more land than people could use, and still they kept moving; some moved three and four times in a lifetime. Speculators and land companies that had counted on land values rising through neat and orderly settlement, as in colonial days, were now wiped out. Many of the most prominent and wealthy Revolutionary leaders, including Robert Morris, financier during the Confederation, Henry Knox, Washington's secretary of war, and James Wilson, justice of the Supreme Court,

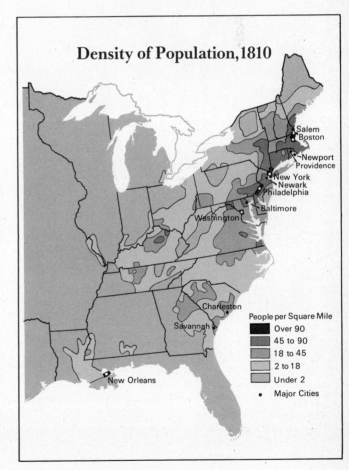

Density of Population, 1810

People per Square Mile
- Over 90
- 45 to 90
- 18 to 45
- 2 to 18
- Under 2
- • Major Cities

MERIWEATHER LEWIS (1774-1809)
President Jefferson in 1801 made this soldier and explorer his private secretary and thought so highly of his scientific as well as military qualifications that he appointed him the leader of the long-planned expedition to the Pacific. Together with his friend William Clark, Lewis led a party of fifty in a two-year exploration of western North America. It is one of the great heroic events of American history. *(National Portrait Gallery, Smithsonian Institution, Washington, D.C.)*

speculated heavily in land and ended their careers in bankruptcy. Even Washington died with his estate tied up in speculative land that no one would pay for.

The Louisiana Purchase. Nothing in Jefferson's administration contributed more to this astonishing expansion than his sudden acquisition in 1803 of the entire Louisiana territory, which, extending from the Mississippi to the Rockies, doubled the size of the United States. For decades Jefferson and other American leaders had foreseen that this young and thriving nation would expand naturally and "piece by piece" take over the feebly held Spanish possessions in North America. Some even thought that British-held Canada would eventually pass to the United States. When the Revolutionary War ended in 1783, Jefferson was already dreaming of explorations to the Pacific. And when he became president, well before he had any inkling that America would purchase the whole Louisiana territory, he laid plans for scientific—and also military and commercial—expeditions into the foreign-held trans-Mississippi West. The most famous of these expeditions was that of Lewis and Clark, eventually undertaken in 1803–06.

When in 1800, in the Treaty of San Ildefonso, a weak Spain ceded back to a powerful France the Louisiana territory, including New Orleans, it had formerly held west of the Mississippi these dreams of expansion were suddenly placed in doubt. The livelihood of the western farmers depended on the free navigation of the Mississippi, and Jefferson was determined to maintain it. He immediately began strengthening fortifications in the West and preparing for the worst. "The day that France takes possession of New Orleans," he informed his American minister to France, Robert Livingston, in April 1802, "we must marry ourselves to the British fleet and nation." This prospect of an American-British alliance threatened the French; Napoleon was already appraising the difficulties of reestablishing the French empire in the New World if war should break out again in Europe. As a result, in 1803 the French government decided to sell to the United States not just New Orleans, which Jefferson had sought to purchase, but all of Louisiana for $15 million.

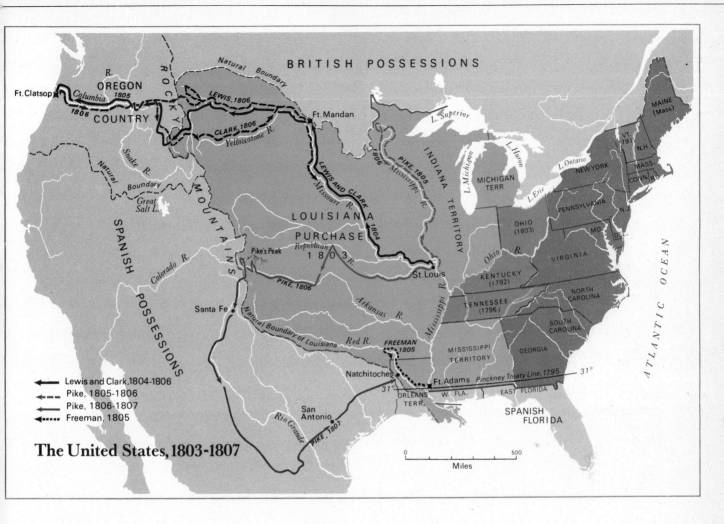

The United States, 1803–1807

- Lewis and Clark, 1804–1806
- Pike, 1805–1806
- Pike, 1806–1807
- Freeman, 1805

Jefferson hesitated over what to do; he feared that the purchase of Louisiana by the federal government would exceed the limited powers granted to it by the Constitution. He considered amending the Constitution in order to acquire this new territory, but finally and regretfully, under intense pressure, he allowed his constitutional scruples to be passed over in silence. Despite its fulfillment of his grandest dreams for America, Jefferson's agonized decision did not suggest that he was conceding in any way to a broad Federalist interpretation of the Constitution. His hesitation only showed the extreme seriousness with which he took his strict construction of the Constitution.

The purchase of Louisiana was the most popular and momentous event of Jefferson's presidency. Not only did it end the long struggle for control of the Mississippi's outlet to the sea, but it also, as Jefferson exulted, freed America from Europe's colonial entanglements and prepared the way for the eventual dominance of the United States in the Western Hemisphere. Its most immediate consequence, however, was to raise fears once again of the country's splitting apart. The borders of the new territory were so vague, the Spanish hold on Mexico and the Floridas so weak, and the rough and unruly frontier inhab-

UNDER MY WINGS EVERY THING PROSPERS

VIEW OF NEW ORLEANS, 1803
"There is on the globe one single spot, the possessor of which is our natural and habitual enemy," said President Jefferson in 1802. "It is New Orleans, through which the produce of three-eighths of our territory must pass to market." It was the American desire to control this port that led to the Louisiana Purchase. *(Chicago Historical Society)*

itants so captivated by the dreams of America's destined expansion that adventurers, filibustering expeditions, and rumors of plots and conspiracies flourished throughout the South and the West.

The Burr Conspiracy. The most grandiose of these schemes was that of 1806–7. It involved Aaron Burr, Jefferson's former vice-president, and (until he turned state's evidence) General James Wilkinson, commanding general of the United States Army secretly in the pay of the Spanish government and one of the most unscrupulous and skillful adventurers in American history. In the summer of 1806 Burr and sixty men in flatboats floated down the Ohio and Mississippi toward New Orleans to make contact with the Spanish. When Burr learned that Wilkinson had

denounced him, he fled toward Florida, probably on his way to Europe, but was captured and brought east to be tried for treason. Although Burr was acquitted because no overt act of treason could be constitutionally proved, he undoubtedly had had in mind some sort of conspiracy, involving a number of American military and civil officials, directed toward an attack on Mexico or a separation of the western areas of the United States. These kinds of activities and the danger of the country's splintering caused the Congress to incorporate into the Union as fast as possible the underdeveloped frontier territories of Ohio (1803), Louisiana (1810), Indiana (1816), Mississippi (1817), Illinois (1818), and Alabama (1819). These new western states were firmly Republican and created constitutions that were more democratic than those of the older eastern states. Most provided for weak executives, white adult male suffrage, annually elected legislatures, no property qualifications for officeholders, and popular election for a host of offices, including judges.

Indians. The Indians in these western territories were no match for the hordes of advancing settlers. By 1800 Ohio had 45,000 inhabitants; by 1810 it had over 230,000 and was already bursting its boundaries. Although the Greenville Treaty of 1795 had drawn a definite line between Indians and whites, most Americans, including President Jefferson, assumed that the vast Indian hunting grounds between Ohio and the Mississippi must sooner or later belong to the advancing Americans. Jefferson expected the Indians willingly to cede their lands to the United States and either become farmers and partake of the blessings of republican civilization or move west beyond the Mississippi.

American pressure on the Indians to surrender their lands was immense, and under Presidents Jefferson and Madison fifty-three treaties of land cession were made. Finally in 1805 the Shawnee Chief Tecumseh and his brother The Prophet attempted to halt this steady encroachment of whites by forming an Indian confederacy. This tribal effort at organized resistance was broken by the governor of the Indiana Territory, General William Henry Harrison, in a battle between 600 Indians and a mixed force of 1,000 American army troops and Kentucky frontiersmen at Tippecanoe in 1811. Sporadic Indian fighting and raiding in the Old Northwest continued, however, but it did not stop the waves of settlers. By 1815 the Indiana Territory had nearly 60,000 settlers.

In the southwestern territories the Indian presence was even more formidable. Still, by 1810, the Mississippi Territory (much of present-day Alabama and Mississippi) had over 40,000 people, including 17,000 slaves, mainly clustered along the Mississippi River counties south of Natchez, which was fast becoming a bustling trade center. In 1810 the Territory of Orleans (modern Louisiana) had over 76,000 inhabitants, more than half of whom were slaves. New Orleans with its mixture of Spanish, French, and other nationalites in a population of over 10,000 was by far the largest and most flamboyant city of the Mississippi Valley and on its way to becoming one of the great ports of the country. By 1810 pioneers were rapidly pushing beyond the Mississippi River into what are now the states of Arkansas and Missouri, leaving behind huge pockets of Indians—Creeks in

TECUMSEH (c. 1768–1813)

Tecumseh, a Shawnee chief, was perhaps the most extraordinary Indian leader in American history. Together with his brother, the Prophet, he attempted in the early nineteenth century to organize a huge confederation of Indians in the Northwest. The Indians were to refuse to cede any more lands to the Americans and were to abandon the white man's ways and goods. But after the battle of Tippecanoe in 1811, organized Indian resistance gave way to sporadic warfare. Tecumseh was killed fighting for the British at the battle of the Thames (1813). *(Courtesy, Field Museum of Natural History, Chicago)*

Georgia, and Cherokees in Tennessee. By 1815 the Missouri Territory had over 20,000 people.

All the while eastern Federalists expressed alarm at this expanding "empire of liberty." With their vision of the United States as a homogeneous and integrated nation-state like those of Europe, the Federalists found it inconceivable that such a gigantic republic could long hold together. To the Republicans, however, who thought of the United States as a loosely bound confederation of states, the huge expanse of territory posed no problems. "Who can limit the extent to which the federative principle may operate effectively?" asked Jefferson in his second inaugural address. Jefferson's "empire of liberty" was always one of like principles, not of like boundaries; and he was at times remarkably indifferent to the possibility that a western confederacy might break away from the eastern United States. What did it matter? he asked in 1804. "Those of the western confederacy will be as much our children and descendants as those of the eastern."

The Federalists called it "a most visionary theory," and believed the consequence would eventually be anarchy. But in the Republican conception, Americans were creating new bonds of social cohesion, not the virtue of classical republicanism perhaps, but, as Jefferson said, "that progress of opinion which is tending to unite them in object and in will."

The Origins of Judical Review

At Jefferson's election in 1800 no institution of the national government was more detested by the Republicans than the judiciary. The appointed federal judges were less susceptible to popular rule than were other government officials, and during the 1790s the Federalists had consciously tried to strengthen the federal courts in order to extend the central government's presence among the people. Since there was not a single Republican judge in the entire national judiciary during the 1790s, Republican newspaper editors had often been brought before the federal courts on charges of sedition. Moreover, Federalist land speculators with interests that spanned

state lines had used the more sympathetic federal courts to resolve their conflicting claims, often to the anger of Republican-controlled state courts. Even after the Federalists had lost the election of 1800, the lame duck Congress dominated by Federalists had passed a new judiciary act creating a system of circuit courts and broadening the jurisdiction of the federal courts. And before surrendering the presidency to Jefferson, John Adams had hastily appointed a number of judges, including John Marshall as chief justice of the United States. This convinced Jefferson that "the remains of federalism" had "retired into the judiciary as a stronghold . . . , and from that battery all the works of republicanism are to be beaten down and erased."

To complete "the revolution," therefore, as a fellow Virginian told Jefferson, "the enemy" had to be routed from "that strong fortress." After a bitter debate in the Congress, the Republicans repealed the Federalist Judiciary Act of 1801. They thus destroyed the newly created circuit courts and for the first and only time in United States history revoked the tenure of federal judges as well. In order to bring the entire judicial establishment under greater congressional control, some Republicans proposed amending the Constitution. Others, however, fixed on impeachment for "high crimes and misdemeanors" as the best constitutional device available for removing obnoxious Federalist judges. The Republicans in the House of Representatives first impeached and the Senate then convicted John Pickering, an alcoholic and insane judge of the federal district court of New Hampshire, even though he had committed no crimes or misdemeanors.

With this broad construction of the criminal meaning of impeachment in hand, the most rabid Republicans under the leadership of John Randolph of Virginia, next attempted to bring down Supreme Court Justice Samuel Chase, the most overbearing Federalist on the Court. However, this perversion of the impeachment process into a mode of removal was too much for some Republicans. While a majority of the Senate in 1805 found Chase guilty, the Republicans could not muster the necessary two-thirds majority. Not only did Chase's acquittal hurt

JOHN MARSHALL, 1755–1835, BY CEPHAS THOMPSON
Marshall is the most famous Chief Justice of the Supreme
Court in American history. During his long tenure on
the Court from 1801 to his death, this Virginia Federalist
participated in more than 1,000 decisions, writing over
half himself. In effect Marshall created for America what
came to be called constitutional law and transformed
the meaning and role of the Supreme Court. (*The Bettmann Archive, Inc.*)

Randolph's reputation, driving him to the extremist
edges of the Republican party, but it ended any further direct assault by the Republicans on the national
judiciary.

Marbury v. Madison. In the meantime John Marshall from his position as chief justice of the Supreme
Court managed to drain some of the bitterness from
the controversy over the judiciary. Marshall was the
most important chief justice in American history.
During his long career (1801–35), which spanned the
administrations of five presidents, he laid the foundations both for the Court's eventual independence
and for the constitutional supremacy of the national
government over the states.

In 1801, however, the Court was very weak. Although Marshall solidified the Court by making one
justice's opinion, usually his own, stand for the decision of the whole Court, he had to move very cautiously. Instead of confronting the Republicans head-
on by declaring the Congress's repeal of the Judiciary
Act of 1801 unconstitutional, as many Federalists
had urged, Marshall chose to act indirectly. In the
case of *Marbury* v. *Madison* (1803), the Marshall Court
decided that Marbury, one of the "midnight judges"
President Adams had appointed, was entitled to his
commission, which Secretary of State Madison had
withheld. Yet if unenforced by the president, such
a bold decision would obviously have discredited the
Court. Marshall avoided a losing clash with the executive branch by going on to state that, although Marbury deserved his commission, the Court had no
authority to order the president to grant it. The provision of the earlier Federalist-enacted Judiciary Act
of 1789 that gave the Court such original authority, he
said, was unconstitutional. Thus Marshall obliquely
asserted the Court's role in overseeing the Constitution without the serious political repercussions involved in opposing the Republicans. Since the American people regarded their written Constitution as
"the fundamental and paramount law of the nation,"
wrote Marshall for the Court, then it followed that
"a law repugnant to the Constitution," such as part of
the Judiciary Act of 1789, "is void; and that courts, as
well as other departments, are bound by that instrument."

Although Marshall's decision in *Marbury* v.
Madison has since taken on immense historical significance as the first judicial assertion by the Supreme
Court of its right to declare acts of Congress unconstitutional, few in 1803 saw its momentous implications. Such a right was nowhere explicitly recognized
in the Constitution, and it was by no means established in American thinking at the end of the eighteenth century. To be sure, some like Hamilton in *The
Federalist* No. 78 tried to justify this ultimate judicial
authority by invoking the supremacy of the Constitution created by the sovereignty of the people and
protected by the courts.

By asserting in the *Marbury* decision that the

Court had a right and duty to declare what the fundamental law was, Marshall obviously drew upon this earlier thinking. But he did not say unequivocally that the Court was the only part of the national government with such a right and duty. Indeed, Marshall's assertion of judicial authority in the *Marbury* decision was limited and ambiguous and implied that the other departments in the government had an equal obligation with the courts to construe the law in accord with the Constitution. Jefferson certainly believed that the executive and the legislature had the same ultimate right as the judiciary to interpret the Constitution, and he always explicitly denied the "exclusive" authority of the judiciary to decide what laws were constitutional. Such a monopoly of interpretative power, he said in 1804, "would make the judiciary a despotic branch." *Marbury* v. *Madison* was in fact the only time in Marshall's long tenure in which the Supreme Court declared an act of Congress unconstitutional.

Constitutional Nationalism.

What the Marshall Court did do in its long career was declare a large number of *state* judicial interpretations and *state* laws in violation of the federal Constitution. In a series of decisions beginning with the *United States* v. *Peters* (1809) and proceeding through *Martin* v. *Hunter's Lessee* (1816) and *Cohens* v. *Virginia* (1821), the Supreme Court established its right to review and reverse decisions of state courts involving interpretations of federal law and the federal Constitution. At the same time, following the first test in *Fletcher* v. *Peck* (1810), the Court overturned a series of state laws that interfered with private contracts and hence violated the Constitution.

Marshall, however, was not content merely with these negative restraints on state power; he sought positively to enhance the supremacy of the national government. In the greatest decision of his career, *McCulloch* v. *Maryland* (1819), Marshall upheld the right of Congress to charter a national bank even though that right was not expressly mentioned in the Constitution. The power to charter a bank, said Marshall, was implied by the "necessary and proper" authority the Constitution granted to Congress to carry its delegated powers into effect. Hence the

attempt by the Maryland legislature to destroy the Bank by taxation was unconstitutional. No decision of Marshall's was more important to the future of America and none asserted the supremacy of the Constitution more unequivocally. By 1820 the Court had already become—even for James Madison—something resembling that "disinterested umpire" he had wanted in 1787 the entire federal government to be.

The Manipulative Tradition of American Law.

Yet as important as Marshall's decisions were in establishing that the Court had final authority over the states to interpret the Constitution, they do not by themselves explain the origins of the extraordinary authority wielded by all American judges. Nineteenth-century Americans inherited an unusual manipulative attitude toward law from the colonial period. Since the colonists had derived their law haphazardly both from their colonial legislatures and courts and from various English sources, they tended to equate law not with what English judges and legal authorities said it was, but with what made sense in America's local circumstances. Time and again eighteenth-century Americans had justified minor deviations and irregularities in their laws in the name of reason, justice, or utility. They thus developed a particularly pragmatic attitude toward law that became stronger in the decades that followed the Revolution.

In the emerging business society of early nineteenth-century America, the desired predictability of law came not from strict adherence to precedent but from rapid adaptability to changing commercial circumstances. To mold the law to fit the needs of America's expanding enterprise, judges increasingly abandoned the customs and technicalities of the inherited English common law and replaced them with useful and prudent regulations. By the second decade of the nineteenth century, American law was coming to be thought of as a man-made creative instrument of social policy. And judges under fast-moving economic pressures were becoming the chief agents of legal change. The judicial interpretative power inherent in the flexibility of American law from the beginning was now starkly revealed and liberally expanded.

Despite continued efforts in the early nineteenth

century to weaken this remarkable judicial authority, law in America maintained its pliable and instrumental quality. Although judges continued to deny that they made law in the way legislatures did, it was obvious that they did something more than simply discover it in the precedents and customs of the past. Law in America, rooted in the consent and sovereignty of the people, was designed to serve the needs of that people, and when it did not, it was the obligation of judges to construe it in such a way that it did. In fact, if neither legislatures nor judges could act fast enough to shape the law to changing circumstances, then some Americans thought that the people themselves, in extralegal groups and "mobs," had the right to take the law into their own hands and mold it as their situation demanded. The peculiarly American practices of judicial review and vigilantism were actually two sides of the same legal coin.

Republican Religion

Although politics and constitutionalism dominated the Revolutionary era, most ordinary Americans still conceived of the world in religious terms. Hence the Revolution and even republicanism had a religious dimension. Indeed, the Revolution marked an important point in the history of American religion. It endorsed the Enlightenment's faith in liberty of conscience, severed the already tenuous connection between church and state, and advanced America into a religious world of competing denominations that was unique to Christendom.

Religious Liberty in the Revolution. From the outset of the Revolutionary controversy, Americans had argued that the dark forces of civic tyranny and religious tyranny were linked. All the new Revolutionary constitutions of 1776 in some way affirmed religious freedom. Yet the constitutional declarations "that all men have a natural and unalienable right to worship Almighty God according to the dictates of their own consciences" did not necessarily mean that the state would abandon its traditional role in religious matters. To be sure, the establishment of the Church of England that existed in several of the colo-

nies was immediately eliminated. But the Maryland, South Carolina, and Georgia Revolutionary constitutions authorized their state legislatures to create in place of the Anglican church a kind of multiple establishment using tax money to support "the Christian religion."

Virginians especially were divided over the meaning of their 1776 declaration of religious liberty. Liberals like Jefferson and Madison joined growing numbers of Presbyterian and Baptist dissenters to oppose the Anglican clergy and planters in a fierce but eventually successful struggle for the complete disestablishment of the Church of England. In 1786 this Virginia struggle was climaxed by the passage of Jefferson's memorable Act for Establishing Religious Freedom. Many of the states, however, retained some vague or general religious qualifications for public office, and both Connecticut and Massachusetts continued to maintain their modified Congregational establishments.

In short, unlike the church in Europe, the American churches, developing as they had in the colonial period, perceived no threat from revolution or republicanism. Except for the Anglican clergy, Protestant ministers were in the vanguard of the Revolutionary movement. In fact, it was the clergy who made the Revolution meaningful for most common people. For every gentleman who read a scholarly pamphlet and delved into Whig and ancient history for an explanation of events, there were dozens of ordinary people who read the Bible and looked to their ministers for an interpretation of what the Revolution meant. Evangelical Protestantism blended with republicanism in a common effort to rid America of sin and luxury and to build a new society of benevolence and virtue.

Despite these hopes, however, the immediate effect of the Revolution on church organization was devastating. The Revolution destroyed churches, scattered congregations, and led to a sharp decline in church membership. By the 1790s perhaps only one in twenty Americans was affiliated with a church. The earlier revivalistic enthusiasm receded under the pressure of a spreading religious rationalism, or deism, which sought to substitute reason for revelation and the science of Newton for the mysteries of

LEMUEL HAYNES, 1753–1833, FIRST BLACK MINISTER OF THE CONGREGATIONAL CHURCH IN AMERICA
Haynes fought in the Revolutionary War, and after he was ordained in 1785 he became minister of the west parish of Rutland, Vermont, where he remained for thirty years. *(Museum of Art, Rhode Island School of Design, Gift of Lucy T. Aldrich)*

traditional Christianity. In 1784 Ethan Allen published his deistic work *Reason the Only Oracle of Man*, which boldly attacked the Bible and the clergy and defended natural religion. With Thomas Paine's *Age of Reason* (1794), the Comte de Volney's *Ruins of Empire* (1791), and Elihu Palmer's attempts to organize deistic societies among urban workingmen in the 1790s, it seemed to many religious leaders that republicanism was breeding infidelity.

As long as the enlightened deism of Jefferson and the other Revolutionary leaders had been confined to the drawing rooms of the gentry and was not publicized, it had posed little threat to Protestant orthodoxy. But with the dissemination of rational and natural religion among ordinary people at the time of the French Revolution, the clergy, especially the older Calvinistic clergy, became alarmed and began a countermovement on behalf of orthodox Christianity. So identified with the excesses of the French Revolution and hence the Republican party was this rational deism that even Hamilton toyed with the idea of enlisting Christianity on behalf of the beleaguered Federalists. In the end this countermovement by conservative Congregationalists and Presbyterians in the 1790s transcended its creators. It became an eastern version of the revivalism that had continued throughout the South and West during the Revolutionary era, and it eventually fused into the early nineteenth-century evangelical movement known as the Second Great Awakening.

The Second Great Awakening.   The Second Great Awakening was a radical expansion and extension of the earlier eighteenth-century revivals. It did not simply intensify the religious feeling of existing church members; more important, it mobilized unprecedented numbers of hitherto unchurched people into religious communions. By popularizing religion as never before and by bringing Christianity into the remotest areas of America, this great revival marked the beginning of the republicanizing and nationalizing of American religion. Thousands upon thousands of ordinary people found in evangelical religion new sources of order and community.

In the decades following the Revolution the various Protestant churches reorganized themselves nationally and entered a period of denominational rivalry. With the decline in the number of college graduates among the gentry now willing to enter the ministry, the older Calvinist churches, Presbyterians and Congregationalists, were forced to form separate colleges and seminaries for the professional education of clergymen and to recruit increasing numbers of their ministers from lower social levels. The newer denominations, the Methodists and the Baptists, recruited their preachers even more informally. Rejecting as they did the idea of a settled and learned ministry, they were more capable than the older churches of speaking the language of the common people they sought to evangelize. By 1820 the Baptists and Methodists had become the largest denominations in America.

Although evangelism spread throughout America, it was most successful in the West, where the dynamic process of revivalism was better able to deal with a mobile population than were the traditional churchly institutions. In the first twelve years of the nineteenth century the Methodists in Tennessee, Kentucky, and Ohio grew from less than 3,000 to well over 30,000. In the short period between 1800 and 1802 the Baptists in Kentucky alone increased from 4,700 to 13,500. In these fast-growing new territories the need for some kind of community, however loose and voluntary, among isolated men and women was most intense; there the need for building barriers against barbarism and licentiousness was most keenly felt.

In the summer of 1801 at Cane Ridge, Kentucky, unbelievable numbers of these Westerners, together with dozens of clergymen of several denominations, came together in what some thought was the greatest outpouring of the Holy Spirit since the beginning of Christianity. Crowds estimated at 12–25,000 participated in a week of frenzied conversions. The heat, the noise, and the confusion were overwhelming: ministers shouted sermons from wagons and tree stumps; people fell to the ground moaning and wailing in remorse, and they sang, laughed, barked, rolled, and jerked in excitement. This gigantic camp meeting at Cane Ridge immediately became a symbol of the promises and the excesses of the new kind of evangelical Protestantism spreading throughout the South and West. Although the conservative Presbyterians and Congregationalists in the East did not hold camp meetings, they too were compelled to adopt some of the new revivalistic methods. By 1820 there were already clearly revealed a number of basic and interrelated characteristics of American religious life whose roots went back to the colonial period and which underlay the emerging Evangelical Age.

Evangelical Denominationalism.   First, the number of religions multiplied, and whatever lingering sense of orthodoxy there was disintegrated; the legal residues of establishment in Connecticut (1818) and Massachusetts (1833) were eliminated. American religions became denominations and abandoned once and for all the traditional belief that any of them could be the true and exclusive church for the society. Each religious association, called or *denominated* by a particular name, now saw itself simply as one limited and imperfect representative of the larger Christian community; each denomination was equal to and in competition with the others. No other society in the world had ever conceived of religion in this way.

By abandoning all expectation of maintaining any special identity with the society, religion in America became an entirely personal and voluntary affair in which all individuals who wished to could bring about their own salvation. Even the Calvinists, who believed that God had already chosen those who were to be saved, nevertheless managed to stress the responsibility of each individual for his or her own conversion. Sin was no longer thought of as inherent in human beings but as a kind of failure of individual will. Thus each person was fully capable of eliminating sin through his or her individual exertion. With such an assumption the numbers who could be saved were no longer limited by God's election, and all the denominations began to sound remarkably like the new denomination, the Universalists, who democratically promised salvation for everyone.

Since religion was now clearly personal and voluntary, people were free to join and change religious associations whenever they wished. This meant that the churches were less capable than they had been in the eighteenth century of reflecting the variety of social ranks within their own community. Particular denominations became identified with particular social classes; for example, the Episcopalians (the former Anglicans) and the Unitarians (liberal Congregationalists) became largely the preserve of social elites. If the role of the denominations was to contend with one another for souls in the religious marketplace, then it was important that each denomination be as united, tightly organized, and homogeneous as possible. Dissenters and schismatics were thus allowed to go their separate ways without the struggles that had marked earlier American religious life. The consequence was a further splintering of religion and the proliferation of new, peculiar religious groups, like the Stonites and Campbellites, with no connection whatever to the Old World.

The divisive effects of this fragmentation were offset by a conscious blurring of theological distinctions among the competing denominations. Some extreme evangelicals urged the creation of a simple Christian religion based only on the gospel. They denounced in the name of the American Revolution all the paraphernalia of organized Christianity, including even the clergy, and claimed the right of every individual to be his own theologian. Within a few decades some of these fundamentalist Christians came together as the Disciples of Christ, which soon emerged as the third-largest Protestant religious group in nineteenth-century America.

Despite the competition among them, all the denominations identified themselves with the nation and worked to unify American culture under evangelical Protestantism. Clergymen were determined to prove that America's separation of church and state would not result in the infidelity and religious neglect that most Europeans expected. Evangelicals emphasized over and over that America, though without a state supported church, was nonetheless a nation of God. Throughout the early nineteenth century, religious groups resisted the secularizing effects of the Enlightenment and the First Amendment, and urged the Republic to recognize its basis in Christianity by instituting chaplains in Congress, proclaiming days of fasting and prayer, and ending mail delivery on the Sabbath. Clergymen, said Nathaniel William Taylor of Connecticut, the most important theologian of the Second Great Awakening, had no intention of creating a new governmental establishment or denying the rights of conscience. "We only ask for those provisions in law . . . in behalf of a common Christianity, which are its due as a nation's strength and a nation's glory."

By 1800 the fate of Christianity and the fate of the nation were tied together by a belief in millennialism. Many evangelical clergymen had come to believe that America was leading humanity into earth's final thousand years of glory and happiness before the Second Coming of Christ and the Day of Judgment predicted in the Bible. The apocalyptic hopes of these clergymen focused on contemporary historical events occurring in America as signs of the approaching age of perfection. The millennium thus became more than a vague promise of Christian theology; it was to be an actual phase in the history of the American republic. Every advance in America's worldly progress—even new inventions and canals—was interpreted in millennial terms. By giving the millennium such a concrete temporal and material character and by identifying the Kingdom of God with the prospects of the United States, the Protestant clergy contributed greatly to nineteenth-century Americans' growing sense of mission. By improving and prospering, the United States—it was thought—was destined to redeem the world.

Republican Diplomacy

The dramatic culmination of the Republicans' revolution of 1800 came in the War of 1812. It was an unusual war, a war on which the entire experiment in free government seemed to rest. It was a war that few wanted but that many had made inevitable. It was a war that in the end solved nothing, but that was widely regarded as a glorious American victory.

The origins of the War of 1812 lay in the American principles of foreign relations first expressed at the time of the Revolution. The American Revolution had been centrally concerned with power, not only power within a state, but power among states in their international relations. Throughout the eighteenth century liberal intellectuals had looked forward to a rational world in which corrupt monarchical diplomacy and secret alliances, balances of power, and dynastic conflicts would be eliminated. In short, they had dreamed of nothing less than an end of war and a new era of peace based on natural commercial relations among nations. If the people of the various nations were left alone to exchange goods freely among themselves, it was believed, then international politics would become republicanized and pacified.

Suddenly in 1776, with the United States isolated outside the European mercantile empires, the Americans had an opportunity and a need to put these liberal ideas about the free exchange of goods into practice. Thus commercial interest and Revolutionary idealism blended to form the basis for American thinking about foreign affairs that lasted until well into the first half of the twentieth century. America first expressed these principles during discussions over the prospective treaty with France at the time of Independence. Many in the Congress in 1776 at-

BUILDING THE FRIGATE "PHILADELPHIA"

All seven of the frigates of the United States Navy that fought the War of 1812 were built in the 1790s, when war with France threatened. The Federalists also wanted to build some ships of the line, which had more decks and nearly twice as many guns as frigates. Although the Federalists acquired timber and six navy yards, the accession of the Republicans in 1801 ended their plans for enlarging the Navy.   (I. N. Phelps Stokes Collection, The New York Public Library)

tempted to work out a model treaty to be applied to France and eventually to other states that would avoid the traditional kinds of political and military commitments and focus instead on exclusively commercial connections. Although in the treaties of 1778 with France the United States was unable to implement its desired commercial plan, and in fact had to settle for a customary European kind of military alliance, many Americans never lost their enlightened hope that international politics might be made over by new liberal commercial relationships.

By the 1790s, however, the Federalists had rejected many of these enlightened dreams for international relations. Hamilton in particular denied the liberal assumptions that republics were naturally peaceful and that commerce was an adequate substitute for the power politics of traditional diplomacy. He put no stock in the idealistic Republican conviction that Britain's great power could be dealt with solely by a policy of commercial discrimination and economic coercion.

The Republicans therefore emerged as the preservers of the visionary principles of diplomacy they identified with the Revolution of 1776. In contrast to the Federalists, who thought the only way to prepare for war was to build up the government and armed forces in a European manner, the Republicans believed that the United States did not need, nor could safely afford, enlarged state power and a traditional army and navy; it did not even need an elaborate diplomatic establishment. While some Republicans in the 1790s urged eliminating all American diplomatic posts except those in London and Paris, others favored replacing the entire American representation abroad with consuls, who were all that were required to handle matters of international trade. At times Jefferson even talked wistfully of abandoning all international commerce so that the United States might "stand, with respect to Europe, precisely on the footing of China." More often, however, he and other Republicans saw American commerce not simply as something to be protected by national policy, as the Federalists did, but as a political weapon to be used as an alternative to war in the way the colonists had used nonimportation in the pre-Revolutionary crisis with Great Britain.

Republicans and the War in Europe.   When the conflict between Britain and France resumed in 1803, the Republicans, now in control of the national government, at last had an opportunity to put their policies to a test. Since Britain was unable to contest on land Napoleon's domination of the continent of Europe, it was determined to exploit its supremacy on the seas to blockade France into submission.

American commerce, once again caught between these two Goliaths, prospered magnificently. Ever since the outbreak of the European war in the early 1790s, American merchants had gained access to the European mercantile empires formerly barred to them and had made the United States the largest neutral carrier of goods in the world. Between 1793 and 1807 American ship tonnage tripled, and the value of American exports increased fivefold. Particularly profitable was the growth of America's wartime shipping between the Spanish and French possessions in the New World and Europe. The value of this trade increased from $300,000 in 1790 to nearly $60 million by 1807. This commerce, however, violated the British Rule of 1756, which prohibited neutrals in time of war to trade within a mercantile empire closed to them in time of peace. To protect this carrying trade, therefore, American merchants developed a legal fiction. By carrying belligerent goods from, say, the French West Indies to American ports, unloading and paying duties on them, then reloading and getting a rebate on the duties before taking them on to France, American traders broke their voyages and thus technically conformed to the British Rule of 1756. The British now resolved to put a stop to this reexport trade. The *Essex* decision of 1805, in which a British admiralty court held that belligerent goods reexported in this fictitious manner were liable to seizure, opened the way to increased British attacks on American shipping.

At the same time, Britain expanded its impressment, or the forcible removal, of seamen from American vessels on the grounds that they were British subjects. Many of these seamen were deserters from the British navy, and since Great Britain refused to recognize the right of expatriation, which was an essential right for a nation of immigrants, conflict over the nationality of American seamen was inevita-

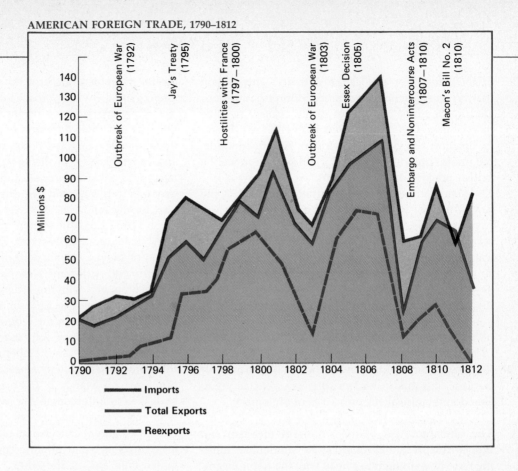

ble. "This authorized system of kidnapping upon the ocean," as John Quincy Adams called it, continued until it was ended by the general European peace of 1815 and resulted in an estimated ten thousand sailors being forcibly taken from American ships. Such provocative practices now dissolved the cordial relations between Britain and America that had begun with Jay's Treaty in 1795.

Napoleon responded to the British blockade with commercial restrictions of his own—a "continental system" designed essentially to deprive England of markets in Europe. In his Berlin Decree of 1806, he ruled that any neutral vessel stopping at an English port would be denied access to all European ports under French control. The British retaliated by requiring all neutral ships trading in the blockaded zones of Europe to stop at English ports to secure licenses. Napoleon then countered with his Milan Decree of 1807, which declared that all neutral ships submitting to British search or entering British ports

to secure licenses would be confiscated by the French. The net effect of these belligerent regulations was to render all neutral commerce illegal and liable to seizure by one power or the other. Although by 1807 the French were rigorously confiscating American ships in European ports, Britain's greater ability to capture American vessels (it was plundering about one of every eight American ships that put to sea) and its humiliating practice of impressment made Britain appear the greater culprit in American eyes. British regulations seemed to strike at the heart of American independence. "They assume the principle," said John Quincy Adams in 1808, "that we shall have no commerce in time of war, but with her dominion, and as tributaries to her."

The immediate response of the Jeffersonian administration to the British seizures was the Nonimportation Act of 1806, threatening a prohibition of certain British imports unless an Anglo-American agreement could be reached. Jefferson refused to send to the Senate for ratification a treaty with Britain that William Pinckney and James Monroe had negotiated in December 1806, not only because its commercial provisions scarcely went beyond Jay's Treaty in opening the British empire to American trade, but, more important, because it did not renounce the British practice of impressment.

Almost immediately thereafter, in June 1807, the British man-of-war *Leopard* fired upon the American warship *Chesapeake* as it sailed out of Norfolk, killing several seamen; the British then boarded the American ship and impressed four sailors, including three Americans alleged to be deserters from the British navy. Waves of patriotic indignation swept through the United States and brought Anglo-American relations to the breaking point. "Never since the battle of Lexington," said Jefferson, "have I seen the country in such a state of exasperation as at present." Although the United States was emotionally primed for war, the Republican leaders were reluctant as yet to abandon their idealistic principles of diplomacy.

The Embargo. All of the strains of idealism and utopianism present in American Revolutionary thinking were now brought to a head with the Republicans' resort to a general embargo. In 1807 Congress passed a sweeping prohibition of all American shipping with the outside world. Jefferson determined to see this "candid and liberal experiment" in "peaceful coercion" through to the end. From December 1807 to March 1809 in the face of mounting opposition, particularly from New England, Jefferson's government desperately stuck by—indeed, used ever-harsher measures to enforce—its embargo policy.

While Britain and France showed few ill effects from this self-imposed stoppage of American shipping, American commerce was thrown into disarray. The American export and reexport trade, which between 1805-7 had doubled to over $108 million in value, suddenly fell to $22 million during 1808; and American imports declined in value from $138 million to $56 million. Yet the economic effects were far from disastrous. Not only did numerous loopholes and violations—especially toward the end of 1808— mitigate the embargo's depressing effect on the economy, but America's growing reliance on its own domestic manufacturers and its internal markets was strengthened by the cutbacks in international trade. Yet while many areas of the United States could fall back on their domestic overland and coastwide trade, the New England ports, such as Boston, Salem, and Providence, with their relatively meager hinterlands and their disproportionate investment in the overseas carrying and reexport trade, were badly hurt by the embargo.

In New England the embargo had the political effect of temporarily reviving Federalism. With hundreds of New England petitions flooding in on the government, with some New Englanders on the verge of rebellion, and with the Federalist governor of Connecticut claiming the right of the state to interpose its authority between the federal government and its citizens, some sort of retreat from the embargo became a matter of time. Hopeful of salvaging something from their policy of peaceful coercion, the Republicans on March 1, 1809, replaced the embargo with the Nonintercourse Act, which prohibited trade with just France and Britain and provided that if either belligerent canceled its blockade against American shipping, then nonintercourse would be maintained only against the other.

President Madison was just as determined as Jefferson had been to maintain this Republican experiment in commercial warfare, but difficulties in enforcing the Nonintercourse Act and growing governmental deficits from the loss of duties on trade forced the Madison administration to turn its commercial restrictions inside out. Macon's Bill No. 2, which passed Congress in May 1810, once again opened American shipping with both Britain and France, with the provision that if either belligerent revoked its restrictions on neutral commerce, nonintercourse would be restored against the other. Signs of a change in Napoleon's policy against American shipping and Madison's eagerness to prove the workability of the experiment in peaceful coercion led the Republican administration in March 1811 into a hasty invocation of nonintercourse against Great Britain.

If the United States had to go to war, the Republicans thought, then better to fight the country that had symbolized resistance to the experiment in popular self-government from the beginning. Despite some strong misgivings over Napoleon's dictatorship and some weak suggestions that America fight both belligerents simultaneously, it was virtually inconceivable that the Republicans would have gone to war against France. The threat of Federalist "monarchism" tied to Great Britain was still so real to Republicans that war with Britain became a necessary product of the Republican revolution of 1800 and thus of the original Revolution itself. "We are going to fight for the re-establishment of our national character," declared Andrew Jackson.

The War of 1812

War was declared in June 1812, and it was strictly a Republican party war. The congressional vote for war was solidly opposed by the Federalists and it temporarily unified the splintered Republican party. Many Republican congressmen newly elected in 1810, such as Henry Clay of Kentucky, Felix Grundy of Tennessee, and John C. Calhoun of South Carolina, were so eager to fight that they earned the label of "War Hawks." Although many of the Republican congress-

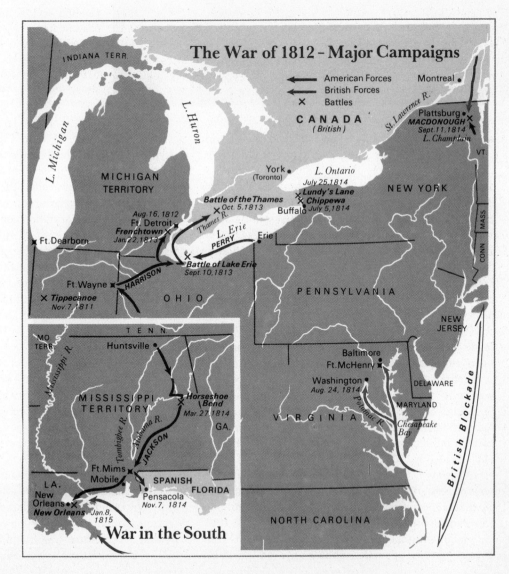

The War of 1812 – Major Campaigns

← American Forces
← British Forces
× Battles

PERRY'S VICTORY ON LAKE ERIE, BY AN UNKNOWN ARTIST

Oliver Hazard Perry (1785–1819) commanded a fleet of nine vessels built in Erie, Pa., to challenge British control of the Great Lakes in the War of 1812. During the battle on Sept. 10, 1813 Perry's flagship was disabled, and, as the painting depicts, he transferred to the *Niagara.* Then he sailed directly into the British line and destroyed the British ships, inspiring his famous dispatch: "We have met the enemy and they are ours." *(New York State Historical Association, Cooperstown, N.Y.)*

men came from areas far removed from the eastern trading ports, they represented farmers who were interested in commerce and in the marketing of their agricultural produce. Moreover, many backcountry Americans deeply resented British and Spanish intrigue among the Indians of the Northwest and Southwest and were convinced, especially by the recent battle with Tecumseh's Indians at Tippecanoe in November 1811, that the frontier would never be at peace until the British and Spanish bases in Canada and Florida were eliminated. War offered an opportunity to do just that.

Yet in the end the war came because the Republicans' foreign policy left no alternative. America had been engaged in a kind of war with the European belligerents since 1806. The actual fighting of 1812 was only the logical consequence of the failure of "peaceful coercion." Still, many Republicans hesitated to commit the United States to a traditional sort of military conflict. They realized, as Jefferson had warned in 1806, that "our constitution is a peace establishment—it is not calculated for war." War, they feared, would lead to a Hamiltonian enlargement of taxes, debt, military forces, and the executive branch; far from saving the Jeffersonian revolution of 1800, war might ultimately destroy republican principles. Therefore, even as the Republicans moved inevitably

toward war, many of them opposed all efforts to strengthen the government's capacity to wage it. While Nathaniel Macon of North Carolina, for example, reluctantly conceded the necessity of war, he like other Republicans urged reduction of the navy, indeed suggested abolition of the army, opposed raising taxes, and resisted all efforts to add two assistant secretaries to the War Department. Not only was the regular army cut back in favor of the militia, but the Bank of the United States, the government's chief financial agency, was allowed to expire in 1811 on the eve of hostilities. With such deliberate lack of preparation the war was bound to be very different from any known before.

The Invasions of Canada. Though woefully unprepared for war, many Americans in 1812 were confident of victory. Since two out of every three persons in Upper Canada (present-day Ontario) came from America, Canada seemed ripe for American "liberation." It would be, said Jefferson, "a mere matter of marching." But the American militia campaigns against Canada in 1812 were all dismal failures; General William Hull surrendered his entire army at Detroit without a fight. William Henry Harrison, the hero at Tippecanoe, was then appointed commander of the northwestern army; but before he could get very far, part of his army was wiped out at French-town near Detroit in January 1813.

In April 1813 invading Americans captured York (present-day Toronto), the capital of Upper Canada, and burned its public buildings; but within two months the American forces were in retreat once again. After Oliver Perry secured naval control of Lake Erie, Harrison finally defeated combined British and Indian forces on the Thames River north of the Lake in October 1813. Although this victory broke up the Indian confederacy, American leaders thought it was too far west to have any strategic significance and did not follow it up. During the summer of 1814 Americans tried to invade Canada again, but withdrew after several tough but indecisive battles in the Niagara region. After two years of repeated forays, the American position on the Canadian frontier remained what it had been at the beginning.

On the sea American frigates, including the U.S.S. *Constitution,* initially won some notable single-ship engagements, and American privateers, the navy's militia, captured more than thirteen hundred British merchant vessels. Eventually, however, Britain's great naval superiority made itself felt, and by 1813 most of the American warships were bottled up in their ports and American commerce was effectively blockaded. When Napoleon abdicated early in 1814, Britain was able to concentrate its military attention on America. It planned several major assaults, one designed to move down the Lake Champlain route that Burgoyne had followed in the Revolutionary War, and another aimed at New Orleans. During the summer of 1814 a British marauding force landed in the Chesapeake, entered Washington, and burned the Capitol and the White House. The government's credit collapsed and the nation's finances were thrown into chaos. Without a national bank the government was unable to transfer funds across the country or to pay its mounting bills.

The Treaty of Ghent. Despite these humiliating circumstances, however, the American peace commissioners sent to negotiate with the British in August 1814 in Ghent, Belgium, were unwilling to make any concessions. The British, learning that their invasion from Canada had turned back as a result of

an American naval victory on Lake Champlain in September 1814 and increasingly anxious about the shifting situation in Europe, came to realize once again that a decentralized government and a spacious continent were not easily conquered. The peace signed on Christmas Eve, 1814, restored the status quo as it was before the war and said nothing about impressment and maritime rights. Andrew Jackson's smashing victory over the British invasion at New Orleans at the beginning of 1815 came after the treaty was signed and clinched it. Although the Americans had gained nothing tangible from the war, it was widely and rightly regarded as a great success for the Republican party and the nation.

URBAN SOCIETY
"Worldly folk" questioning chimney sweeps and their master before Christ Church, Philadelphia, by Pavel Petrovich Svinin. *(The Metropolitan Museum of Art, Rogers Fund, 1942)*

The Hartford Convention and the End of the Federalists.   The peace effectively destroyed Federalism as a national movement. The northeastern Federalists had repeatedly obstructed the war, refusing to comply with federal militia requisitions and discouraging loans to the United States government. Some New England extremists talked of separating from the Union. Other Federalists were convinced that the Republican failures in the war would justify their opposition and that a disillusioned people would catapult the Federalists back into national dominance.

Hence the Federalist convention that met in Hartford, Connecticut, at the end of 1814 disavowed secession and contented itself with proposing a series of amendments to the Constitution. These amendments were designed to curb the power of the South in the federal government by eliminating the three-fifths representation of slaves; to prevent the admission of new states, future embargoes, and declarations of war without a two-thirds majority of Congress; and to end Virginia's dominance of the executive by prohibiting the president from serving two terms and the same state from providing two presidents in succession. The national exuberance following the Treaty of Ghent and Jackson's victory discredited these Federalist hopes and led to the enthusiastic election in 1816 of still another Republican and Virginian president, James Monroe. Thus was vindicated the Republicans' remarkable experiment in governing a huge country and fighting a war without the traditional instruments of power.

Although the war seemed to settle nothing, actually it settled everything. "Notwithstanding a thousand faults and blunders," John Adams told Jefferson in 1817, Madison's administration had "acquired more glory, and established more Union than all his three predecessors, Washington, Adams, Jefferson, put together." The Revolution, which had begun nearly a half century earlier, at last seemed to be over and to have succeeded. The Federalist attempt to build a strong central government had been halted. The new national government the Republicans had created was unlike any the eighteenth century traditionally understood to be a government. Its capital was isolated from the main social and economic cen-

DETAIL OF "ELECTION DAY AT THE STATE HOUSE," PENCIL BY JOHN LEWIS KRIMMEL, 1813.
(Historical Society of Pennsylvania)

ters of the country; its influence was diffused throughout a rapidly expanding geographical sphere; and its effect on the daily lives of its citizens was negligible.

By 1817–18 Jefferson was exultant. "Our government," he wrote in those years to his old French ally, the Marquis de Lafayette, "is now so firmly put on its republican tack, that it will not be easily monarchised by forms." The War of 1812 and the disgrace of the Federalists, he said, had ended the need for his revolutionary party, and had in fact resulted in the "complete suppression of party." In the new "Era of Good Feelings" symbolized by Monroe's uncontested election to the presidency in 1820, the ideological passions and divisions aroused by the Revolution could at last subside. Americans could begin celebrating their own common national identity.

CHRONOLOGY

1800 Washington, D.C., becomes capital.
Library of Congress established.
Convention of 1800, supplanting treaties of 1778 with France.
Thomas Jefferson elected president.

1801 Plan of Union between Presbyterians and Congregationalists to bring religion to frontier.
War with Barbary states.
Cane Ridge, Kentucky, revival meeting.
John Marshall becomes chief justice.

1802 Republican Congress repeals Judiciary Act of 1801.

1803 *Marbury* v. *Madison*, Supreme Court upholds right of judicial review.
Louisiana Purchase.
War resumed in Europe.
Lewis and Clark expedition begun.

1804 Hamilton killed by Vice-President Aaron Burr in duel.
Impeachment of judges Pickering and Chase.
Twelfth Amendment to Constitution ratified.
Jefferson elected for second term.

1805 Pennsylvania Academy of Fine Arts formed.
Essex decision by British prize court increases British seizures of American neutral ships.

1806 Monroe-Pinckney treaty with Britain, which Jefferson refuses to send to Senate for ratification.
Burr conspiracy.

1807 *Chesapeake-Leopard* affair.
Embargo Act.
Robert Fulton's steamboat *Clermont* travels on Hudson River from Albany to New York in 30 hours.

1808 Congress prohibits Americans from participating in African slave trade.

1809 James Madison elected president.
Embargo repealed; Nonintercourse Act passed, prohibiting trade with Britain and France.

1810 Macon's Bill No. 2 passed, restoring trade with Britain and France, but providing for trade restrictions to be reimposed on one of the powers if other should abandon its seizure of American ships.
Connecticut Moral Society formed to combat infidelity and drinking.
West Florida annexed by Madison.
American Board of Commissioners for Foreign Missions formed.
In *Fletcher* v. *Peck*, Supreme Court invalidates state law re *Yazoo* land claims because of impairment of contracts.

1811 Madison, believing Napoleon has removed restrictions on American commerce, prohibits trade with Britain.
Battle of Tippecanoe, Indiana, in which William Henry Harrison defeats Tecumseh and prevents formation of Indian confederacy.
Charter of the Bank of the United States allowed to lapse by Congress.

1812 Congress declares war against Britain.
Americans surrender Detroit to British.
Madison elected for second term.

1813 Battle of Lake Erie, in which Captain Oliver Perry defeats British naval forces.
Battle of the Thames, in which General Harrison defeats British and their Indian allies.

1814 Battle of Horseshoe Bend, Alabama; General Andrew Jackson defeats Creek Indians fighting for British.
British burn Washington, D.C.
Commander Thomas Macdonough defeats British fleet on Lake Champlain; invading British turned back at Plattsburgh, New York.
Hartford Convention of Federalist delegates from New England states meets.
Treaty of Ghent signed between United States and Great Britain.

1815 Battle of New Orleans; Jackson defeats British.
North American Review founded in Boston; soon becomes leading literary review in America.

1816 Second Bank of the United States chartered by Congress.
American Bible Society founded.
Protective tariff passed.
James Monroe elected president.

1817 Bonus Bill establishing fund for building roads and canals vetoed by Madison.
American Tract Society formed to circulate religious literature in the West.
Seminole War on Georgia-Florida border.

| 1818 | General Jackson invades Florida to end Seminole War. | Adams-Onis Treaty signed between United States and Spain; Spain cedes Florida to the United States and recognizes the western limits of the Louisiana Purchase. |

1818   General Jackson invades Florida to end Seminole War.

Rush-Bagot convention between Britain and United States establishes American fishing rights and boundary between United States and Canada.

1819   Commercial panic with many bank failures.

Adams-Onis Treaty signed between United States and Spain; Spain cedes Florida to the United States and recognizes the western limits of the Louisiana Purchase.

Dartmouth College case.

McCulloch v. *Maryland.*

1820   Missouri Compromise.

James Monroe reelected president.

SUGGESTED READINGS

The classic account of the Republican administrations is Henry Adams, *History of the United States of America during the Administration of Thomas Jefferson [and] of James Madison* (9 vols., 1889–1891). It is artful, but its obsession with the ironic turn of Jeffersonian policies subtly distorts the period. Marshall Smelser, *The Democratic Republic, 1801–1815* (1968), is a one-volume survey. Daniel Sisson, *The American Revolution of 1800* (1974), tries to recapture the radical meaning of Jefferson's election; but it does not succeed as well as James S. Young, *The Washington Community, 1800–1828* (1966), which despite an unhistorical focus rightly stresses the Republicans' fear of power. On the Republican party, see Noble E. Cunningham, Jr., *The Jeffersonian Republicans in Power: Party Operations, 1801–1809* (1963). Richard Hofstadter, *The Idea of a Party System: The Rise of Legitimate Opposition in the United States, 1740–1840* (1969), is a lucid essay that tries but does not quite break from the party conception of the secondary sources on which it is based. David Hackett Fischer, *The Revolution of American Conservatism: The Federalist Party in the Era of Jeffersonian Democracy* (1965), is an important book that compels a new look at the Republicans as well as the Federalists. A tough-minded study is Forrest McDonald's *The Presidency of Thomas Jefferson* (1976). See also James H. Broussard, *The Southern Federalists, 1800–1816* (1979). On the Republicans' dismantling of the Federalist bureaucracy, see Leonard D. White, *The Jeffersonians: A Study in Administrative History, 1801–1829* (1951). See also Noble E. Cunningham, Jr., *The Process of Government under Jefferson* (1979), and Robert M. Johnstone, Jr., *Jefferson and the Presidency* (1979). On Jefferson and Madison, see the monumental multivolumed biographies by Dumas Malone and Irving Brant.

Daniel Boorstin, *The Lost World of Thomas Jefferson* (1948), describes the rigidities of intellectual life in Republican circles, while Linda K. Kerber analyzes the Federalists' cultural problems in *Federalists in Dissent* (1970).

On the development of the West, see Reginald Horsman, *The Frontier in the Formative Years, 1783–1815* (1970). On the new cities of the West, see Richard C. Wade, *The Urban Frontier* (1959). Beverley W. Bond, *The Civilization of the Old Northwest: A Study of Political, Social and Economic Development, 1788–1812* (1934) is a good compilation. Land policy and land laws are covered in Malcom J. Rohrbough, *The Land Office Business . . . 1789–1837* (1968).

On the Louisiana Purchase, see Alexander De Conde, *The Affair of Louisiana* (1976); and the appropriate chapters of George Dangerfield, *Chancellor Robert R. Livingston of New York, 1746–1803* (1960). On Indian affairs, see Reginald Horsman, *Expansion and American Indian Policy, 1783–1812* (1967). For the tragic irony in the story of American relations with the Indians, see Bernard W. Sheehan, *Seeds of Extinction: Jeffersonian Philanthropy and the American Indian* (1973). A good, short, though unsympathetic, account of the Burr conspiracy can be found in Thomas Abernathy, *The South in the New Nation, 1789–1819* (1961).

On the politics of the judiciary, see Richard E. Ellis, *The Jeffersonian Crisis* (1971). The best biography of Marshall is still Albert J. Beveridge, *The Life of John Marshall* (4 vols., 1919). The origins of judicial review are treated in Edward S. Corwin, *The "Higher Law" Background of American Constitutional Law* (1955); and Charles G. Haines, *The American Doctrine of Judicial Supremacy* (1932). But despite all that has been written, the sources of judicial review remain perplexing. Understanding the problem requires less work on the Supreme Court and more on colonial jurisprudence. For a significant study of changes in law during the Revolution, and after, see William E. Nelson, *Americanization of the Common Law: The Impact of Legal Change on Massachusetts Society, 1760–1830* (1975); and Morton J.

Horowitz, *The Transformation of American Law, 1780–1860* (1977).

On religion and the Revolution, see William W. Sweet, *Religion in the Development of American Culture, 1765–1840* (1952). On the varying definitions of the American Enlightenment and its relation to Protestantism, see the superb study by Henry F. May, *The Enlightenment in America* (1976). The opening chapters of Perry Miller, *The Life of the Mind in America* (1965), are very helpful for understanding the emergence of evangelicism. The essays collected in Elwyn A. Smith, ed., *The Religion of the Republic* (1971), are important in relating evangelical Protestantism and republicanism. Older studies that need updating are Catherine C. Cleveland, *The Great Revival in the West, 1797–1805* (1916); and Oliver W. Elsbree, *The Rise of the Missionary Spirit in America, 1790–1815* (1928). See also John Bole, *The Great Revival in the South, 1787–1805* (1972); Howard Miller, *The Revolutionary College: American Presbyterian Higher Education, 1707–1837* (1976); and especially Donald G. Mathews, *Religion in the Old South* (1977). For secular-minded approaches to evangelicism, see Charles I. Foster, *An Errand of Mercy: The Evangelical United Front, 1790–1837* (1960); and Clifford S. Griffin, *Their Brothers' Keepers: Moral Stewardship in the United States, 1800–1865* (1960). On the changing role of the ministry, see Donald M. Scott, *From Office to Profession: The New England Ministry, 1750–1850* (1978). On deism, see Gustav A. Koch, *Republican Religion* (1933); and Herbert M. Morais, *Deism in Eighteenth-Century America* (1934). On millennialism, see Ernest Lee Tuveson, *Redeemer Nation: The Idea of America's Millennial Role* (1968); James W. Davidson, *The Logic of Millennial Thought* (1977); and Nathan O. Hatch, *The Sacred Cause of Liberty* (1977).

The underlying eighteenth-century liberal assumptions about international politics are explored in Felix Gilbert, *To the Farewell Address: Ideas of Early American Foreign Policy* (1961). Lawrence S. Kaplan, *Jefferson and France: An Essay on Politics and Political Ideas* (1967), captures the idealism of Jefferson. The best discussion of the diplomatic steps into war is Bradford Perkins, *Prologue to War: England and the United States, 1805–1812* (1961). Burton Spivak, *Jefferson's English Crisis: Commerce, Embargo and the Republican Revolution* (1979), is the best study of the embargo. Julius W. Pratt, *Expansionists of 1812* (1925), stresses how the desire of Westerners and Southerners for land caused the war. However, A. L. Burt, *The United States, Great Britain and British North America* (1940), emphasizes the issues of impressment and neutral rights. Roger H. Brown, *The Republic in Peril: 1812* (1964), and Norman K. Risjord, *The Old Republicans* (1965), offer the best perspective on the logic of the Republicans' foreign policy that led to war.

Harry L. Coles, *The War of 1812* (1965), and Reginald Horsman, *The War of 1812* (1969), are good brief surveys. Irving Brant, *James Madison: The Commander in Chief, 1812–1836* (1961), defends Madison's wartime leadership, but Ralph Ketcham, *James Madison* (1971), is better in recovering the peculiar character of Madison's republican aims. On the Treaty of Ghent, see Bradford Perkins, *Castlereagh and Adams: England and the United States, 1812–1823* (1964). James M. Banner, *To the Hartford Convention: The Federalist and the Origins of Party Politics in Massachusetts, 1789–1815* (1970), superbly describes the Federalists' attitudes and stresses their conservative purposes in calling the Convention.

PART THREE

David Brion Davis

Expanding the Republic

1820–1860

The end of the American Enlightenment also marked the end of attempts to model American society on European blueprints. By the 1820s it was becoming clear that the American people would quickly overleap restraints and limits of every kind. Expansive, self-assertive, extravagantly optimistic, they believed they had a God-given right to pursue happiness. In a nation of supposedly infinite promise, there could be no permanent barriers to the people's aspirations for wealth and self-improvement.

This absence of barriers, of distinctions of rank, and of prescribed identities was what Alexis de Tocqueville meant by "the general equality of condition among the people." Nothing struck Tocqueville more forcibly when he visited the United States in 1831 than this leveling of ancient and inherited distinctions of rank. He took it to be "the fundamental fact" about American society from which all other facts seemed "to be derived." Tocqueville was aware of the economic and racial inequalities of American society. Indeed, he suggested that it was precisely the lack of traditional restraints, such as those associated with a landed aristocracy, that opened the way for racial oppression and for a new kind of aristocracy created by business and manufacturing.

All societies require a system of rules, restraints, and limits. In a traditional, premodern society, such as the feudal regime to which Tocqueville looked back with some nostalgia, there was a certain stability to the territorial boundaries of a kingdom, an estate, or a people. Similarly, few people questioned the customary rules that defined social rank, the rights and duties of lords and peasants, the inheritance of land, the limits of political power and economic enterprise, and the expectations appropriate for each individual. Men and women knew what they had been born to, what place they had been assigned by fate. A close relation prevailed between the narrow boundaries of the physical environment and the social boundaries that political, legal, and religious institutions imposed.

The United States, as Tocqueville repeatedly emphasized, had thus far managed to avoid anarchy while greatly expanding most people's possibilities of life. From the time of the first colonial settlements, Americans had evolved institutions that had ensured a degree of order and stability to social life, protecting the public good from the worst excesses of acquisitive self-interest. By the early nineteenth century, however, there was a growing faith that the public good would best be served by allowing maximum freedom to the individual pursuit of self-interest.

In the period 1820–60 this drive for individual self-betterment led to an unprecedented economic and territorial expansion, to the migration of millions

Overleaf: "View of Baltimore from Federal Hill, 1850" by Fitz Hugh Lane. *(Courtesy, Shelburne Museum, Shelburne, Vermont)*

of Europeans to America, and to the settlement of millions of Americans in the new states and territories of the West. Much of the nation's foreign policy was devoted to extending territorial boundaries and to preventing European attempts to impose future barriers to American influence and expansion in the Western Hemisphere. Federal land policy encouraged rapid settlement of the West. Both national and state governments committed a large share of public resources to the construction of roads, canals, and railroads that surmounted the barriers of mountains and increasing distance. Government at all levels actively sought to stimulate growth and economic opportunity. Much of the political ideology of the period was directed against forces and institutions, such as the Second Bank of the United States, which could be portrayed as restricting individual opportunity.

But for many thoughtful Americans, reformers as well as conservatives, there was a danger that these expansive energies would erode all respect for order, balance, and community purpose; that the competitive spirit would lead to an atomized society ruled by the principle, "Every man for himself and the devil take the hindmost"; that the American people would become enslaved to money, success, and material gratification; and that the centrifugal forces of expansion would cause the nation to fly apart.

Most of the proposed remedies centered on the critical need to shape and reform individual character. Instead of looking to political institutions and governmental programs, most Americans sought social change through the moral reformation of individuals. They believed that if self-interest could be enlightened by a sense of social responsibility, the nation could be saved from the dehumanizing effects of commercialism and competitive strife. This was the great goal of the public schools, the religious revivals, and most of the new reform movements. It was a mission that gave a new importance and an educational role to mothers and to the middle-class home. In one sense, these efforts at shaping character embodied a nostalgic desire to restore a lost sense of community and united purpose. But the crusades for moral improvement were also instruments of modernization that encouraged predictable and responsible behavior and that aimed at ennobling and legitimating a market-oriented society.

It was the issue of Negro slavery that finally dramatized the conflict between self-interest and the ideal of a righteous society—a society that could think of itself as "under God." And it was the westward expansion of Negro slavery that ultimately became the testing ground for defining and challenging limits—the territorial limits of slavery, the limits of federal power, and the limits of popular sovereignty and self-determination. For most of the period an ambiguity on all these matters allowed the North and South to expand together and to resolve periodic conflicts by compromise. By the 1850s, however, southern leaders insisted that the equal rights of slaveholders would be subverted unless the federal government guaranteed the protection of slave property in the common territories. Northern leaders, including eventually many moderates who had always favored compromise, drew a firm line against imposing slavery on a territory against the wishes of the majority of settlers. To paraphrase the poet Robert Frost, the territorial question came down to what Americans were willing to wall in or wall out. In one form or another, Americans had to face the question whether, in a free society, any limits could be imposed on the total dominion of one person over another.

To understand American experience during the four decades preceding the Civil War, one must grasp the dimensions of demographic and economic change. Other nations have undergone periods of rapid growth and industrialization, accompanied by painful cultural adjustment and social conflict. In general, however, this modernizing experience has occurred in long-settled communities with traditions, customs, and class interests that served at once as barriers to change and as stabilizers of society. What distinguished American history, in the period 1820–60, was that a modern market economy emerged in conjunction with the rapid settlement of virgin land and the unprecedented expansion of the western frontier.

There were few barriers to this double process, and the American people were determined to test, push back, and overcome what barriers there were. The American economy showed a remarkable freedom in the flow of goods, people, and capital in response to market forces. No laws restricted the influx of European and Asian laborers. The Constitution ruled out any taxes on American exports. Thanks largely to southern pressure, the federal government gradually lowered protective tariffs on imports. The federal government's sale and donation of immense tracts of public land were intended to encourage individual enterprise in a free and unregulated market. Political stability, even in the rapidly created new states, helped to guarantee the security of private property and the legal enforcement of contracts. The states themselves actively promoted economic growth, but no other society had imposed so few fiscal, political, religious, and social restraints on the marketplace. No other society had been so confident that market forces constituted the "invisible hand" of a higher, cosmic order. No other society had become so committed to the goals of maximizing individual profits by increasing productivity and lowering costs.

The result of this extraordinary freedom from limitations, along with the availability of land, labor, and capital, was extremely rapid economic growth. As perceived and experienced by living human beings, however, this growth was both liberating and extremely disruptive. It destroyed family self-suffi-

CHAPTER 12

Population: Expansion and Exploitation

ciency, pride in craftsmanship, and personal and family ties that unified residential communities with local economic markets. Though the growth of national markets broadened the range of individual choice for businessmen, there was little choice for the Indians, slaves, unskilled laborers, landless farmers, and domestic servants; in short, for all those who were excluded by force or circumstance from the benefits of the market. Despite a generally rising standard of living, Americans in the pre-Civil War decades witnessed growing economic inequalities. Moreover, the nation's triumphs in economic and territorial expansion depended on two forms of outright racial exploitation: the coercive removal of the Indian people from the rich land east of the Great Plains; and the forced labor of black slaves who produced invaluable exports, mainly cotton, that helped finance America's economic growth.

Population Growth, Immigration, and Urbanization

From 1820 to 1860 America's population maintained the extraordinary rate of growth that had characterized the colonial and early national periods. The average increase by decade amounted to nearly 35 percent; the total population continued to double every twenty-three years. The United States sustained this high rate of growth until the 1860s. During the nineteenth century no European nation achieved a growth rate one-half as high as America's for even two decades.

America's population growth cannot be attributed to any single, consistent cause. Before the mid-1840s most of the population growth resulted from the remarkable fertility of the American people, reinforced by a relatively low rate of infant mortality. Like many countries in modern Africa and South America, the United States literally swarmed with children. In 1830 nearly one-third of the total white population was under the age of ten. Yet in most parts of the country the birthrate had actually begun to decline before 1810 and continued to fall throughout the century. By the 1840s it was only the influx of European immigrants, who accounted for one-

quarter of the total population increase in that decade, that maintained the previous rate of national growth.

Imigration was partly the result of economic distress in Europe. Few Europeans would have left their homes if population growth had not pressed hard on available supplies of land, food, and jobs, and if they had not been displaced and defined as expendable by the forces of a market economy. The disastrous failure of Ireland's potato crop in 1845, followed by five years of famine, gave many Irish little choice but to emigrate or starve. And the British landlords who controlled Ireland helped to subsidize emigration in the hope of reducing taxes for the support of workhouses, which were spilling over with starving laborers evicted from the land. In parts of Germany and Scandinavia, governments encouraged emigration as a way of draining off unemployed farmers and artisans, who had been displaced by the modernization of agriculture and by competition from imported machine-made goods.

But the most important stimulus to immigration

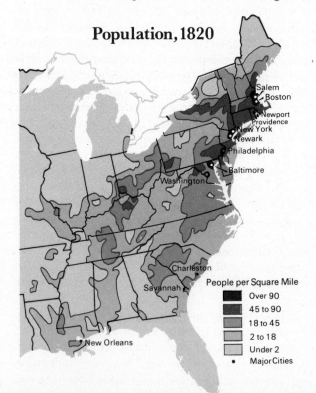

Population, 1820

Salem
Boston
Newport
Providence
New York
Newark
Philadelphia
Baltimore
Washington
Charleston
Savannah
New Orleans

People per Square Mile

■ Over 90
■ 45 to 90
■ 18 to 45
□ 2 to 18
□ Under 2
• Major Cities

was the promise of jobs in America. Immigration rose to high levels during America's years of greatest prosperity, and lagged during years of economic recession. Mass emigration from Europe was a direct response to the sudden demand in America for labor in construction and manufacturing, and to the supposedly limitless opportunity for land ownership in the West. American promoters, representing shipping firms, labor contractors, manufacturers, and even the governments of western states, enticed Europeans with glowing accounts of the United States. More persuasive were the reports of fellow villagers or family members who had already crossed the Atlantic and tested the terrain. In the 1830s when northwestern Europe became aware of America's economic boom, of the North's shortage of labor, and of the opening of vast tracts of farmland in the West, the number of immigrants rose to nearly 600,000, approximately a fourfold increase over the previous decade. In the 1840s the number soared to about 1.5 million, and in the 1850s to about 2.8 million.

The swelling stream, although it originated almost entirely from northwestern Europe, was anything but homogeneous. It included illiterate peasants from Germany and Ireland, highly skilled artisans from England, Germany, Belgium, and Switzerland, political refugees escaping the repression that followed the abortive European revolutions of 1830 and 1848, and Jews and other victims of religious discrimination. The Germans amounted to about 1.3 million immigrants, and many had sufficient funds to purchase farms in the West or at least to make their way to thriving German communities in Cincinnati, St. Louis, and Milwaukee. The Irish, numbering some 1.7 million, had few skills and often arrived penniless, traveling steerage in the holds of westbound ships that had carried American lumber, grain, cotton, and other bulk products to Europe. Cast off by Britain as an unwanted population, the Irish peasants were in effect dumped in the northeastern port cities or sometimes in Canada, from which they migrated southward. Gradually they found employment in heavy

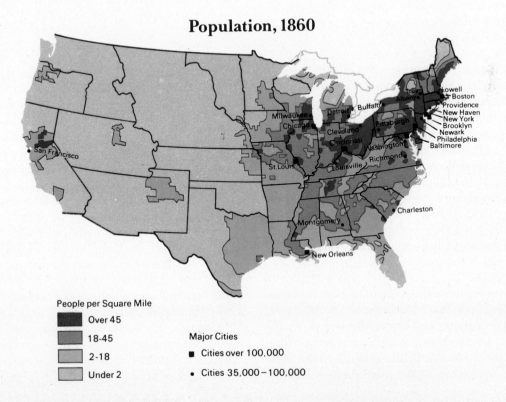

Population, 1860

People per Square Mile

- Over 45
- 18-45
- 2-18
- Under 2

Major Cities

- ■ Cities over 100,000
- • Cities 35,000 – 100,000

EMIGRATION AGENT'S OFFICE
By the 1840s the expansion of transatlantic commerce had greatly reduced the westbound steerage fare from Europe to America. Nevertheless, many emigrants, such as the Irish portrayed here, had to depend on loans, charitable gifts, or funds sent from relatives in America. *(Library of Congress)*

construction work, in foundries and factories, and in domestic service, though for a time they enormously swelled the ranks of paupers and recipients of public and private welfare.

Before the Civil War the proportion of foreign-born in the population as a whole never rose above 15 percent, but in Boston and New York City by the 1850s the figure had climbed to over 50 percent. Over half the foreign-born lived in Ohio, Pennsylvania, and New York. This concentration of immigrants greatly accelerated the growth of cities in the Northeast and towns and villages along the Great Lakes and the Ohio and Mississippi rivers.

In 1860 four out of five Americans still lived in rural environments, that is, on farms or in settlements of less than 2,500. Nevertheless, by 1850 over half the populations of Massachusetts and Rhode Island lived in urban centers, a proportion the nation at large did not reach until the 1920s. By 1860 eight American cities, three of them west of the Appala-

chians, had more than 150,000 inhabitants, a population exceeded at that time by only seven cities in industrial England. Although America could boast of no metropolis equivalent to London, in 1860 the combined populations of Manhattan and Brooklyn exceeded 1 million. New York City, endowed with a superior harbor and with the Hudson River, which provided deep-water navigation into the interior, had won a further competitive advantage over other seaboard cities when in 1818 its merchants established the first regular, scheduled sailings to Europe. Seven years later the Erie Canal opened cheap access to the Great Lakes and to the markets of the West. Immigrants arrived and stayed in New York because it was America's great seaport and commercial center, a crucible of risk and opportunity.

Overall, the declining birthrate resulted in a slightly higher average age for the American population, but the influx of immigrants greatly enlarged the number of Northeasterners between the ages of twenty and thirty. In 1850 over 70 percent of the American people were still under thirty, a figure that takes on greater meaning when compared with the 63 percent for England and the 52 percent for France. Before the Civil War the Americans remained an extraordinarily youthful people, a circumstance that helps to account for their restlessness, their venturesomeness, and their impatience with boundaries of any kind.

Alexis de Tocqueville echoed the amazement of many Europeans at the "strange unrest" of a people who could be seen "continually to change their track for fear of missing the shortest cut to happiness":

In the United States a man builds a house in which to spend his old age, and he sells it before the roof is on . . . he brings a field into tillage and leaves other men to gather the crops; he embraces a profession and gives it up; he settles in a place, which he soon afterwards leaves to carry his changeable longings elsewhere . . . and if at the end of a year of unremitting labor he finds he has a few days' vacation, his eager curiosity whirls him over the vast extent of the United States, and he will travel fifteen hundred miles in a few days to shake off his happiness. Death at length overtakes him, but it is before he is weary of his bootless chase of that complete felicity which forever escapes him.

This sense of limitless possibility helps to explain the feverish westward rush of population. By 1860 the settled area of the United States was five times what it had been in 1790, and nearly half the people lived beyond the 1790 boundaries of settlement. As late as 1820 many Americans had thought it would take at least a century to settle the vast territory west of the Mississippi. In 1860 the United States had firmly established its present continental boundaries, except for Alaska. No other nation had populated so much new territory in so short a time or absorbed so many immigrants. No other had combined rapid urbanization with the dramatic expansion of an agricultural frontier.

Farmers and the Land

Before the Civil War the majority of American families made their livings by supplying the primary human needs for food and clothing. Agriculture dominated the economy and provided the commodities for most of the nation's domestic and foreign trade. Even in towns and cities families customarily kept a vegetable garden and perhaps a pig, a cow,

**The United States
1820-1860**

☐ States Admitted Before 1820
■ New States with Dates of Admission

and chickens. Many of the most seasoned urbanites could at least remember the smell of a barnyard from their childhoods.

Agricultural Expansion. What distinguished the period 1820–60 were two trends that might seem at first to be contradictory. On the one hand, the quickening pace of urbanization and industrialization brought a decisive shift toward nonagricultural employment. This shift had actually begun in the late eighteenth century but had started to slow before 1820, when approximately 79 percent of the labor force was gainfully employed in agriculture. By 1850, however, the proportion had fallen to 55 percent. This was the most rapid structural change in the economy during the entire nineteenth century. On the other hand, the same period saw a phenomenal expansion of agriculture into the "virgin lands" of the West and Old Southwest, accompanied by revolutionary changes in transportation and marketing. The two trends were intimately related. The urban East provided the capital and markets that made the agricultural expansion possible. The food and fiber of the West and Old Southwest were indispensable for the industries and urban growth of the East. Western farming, fur trapping, mining, and lumbering were the spearheads of an expansive capitalist economy increasingly integrated with the great markets of the world.

A nation of farmers is almost by definition a nation at an early stage of economic development. Yet in nineteenth-century America, agriculture did not suggest a conservative way of life limited by the entrenched customs of a feudalistic past. Farming increasingly took on the characteristics of a speculative business. The very isolation of individual farms, posted like sentries along lonely country roads, indicated that Americans placed efficiency above community solidarity. The individual family, practically imprisoned near the fields it worked and usually owned, had proved to be the most effective unit of production.

Four central conditions shaped America's unprecedented expansion of cultivated land. First, public policy continued to favor rapid settlement of the im-

mense public domain, amounting to a billion acres if one includes the territorial acquisitions of the 1840s. There was no countervailing interest in conserving resources and future revenue. Second, despite population growth, agricultural labor remained scarce and expensive, especially in frontier regions. Most farm owners had to rely on an occasional hired hand to supplement the labor of their own families or of tenant families. In the South the price of slaves continued to rise. Third, the dispersion of settlement made farmers heavily dependent, for many decades, on navigable rivers and waterways for transportation. Fourth, the real estate mentality of earlier periods burgeoned into a national mania as the westward movement and the mushrooming of towns brought spectacular rises in land values. Great land companies and private investors, representing eastern and European capital, purchased virtual empires of western land and then used every possible device to promote rapid settlement. Even the small farmers saw that it was more agreeable to make money by speculating in land than by removing stumps or plowing up the resistant bluestem grass of the prairies.

From one point of view the pioneering outlook was progressive. There can be no doubt that Americans who moved west were inventive, hardy, and willing to take risks. Often moving ahead of roads and organized government, the frontier farmers engaged in a struggle by trial and error to succeed in the face of unfamiliar climate, insects, soil conditions, and drainage. In time they experimented with different crops, livestock, and transportation routes, searching for the commodity and market that would bring a predictable cash return. Although the federal government supplied little direct information to farmers, it continued Jefferson's tradition of promoting land surveys and sending expeditions into land west of the Mississippi to collect information on flora and fauna, geology, watersheds, and Indians. This enterprising spirit, evident in both public and private endeavors, led to the discovery and exploitation of undreamed of resources, confirming Tocqueville's judgment that "Nature herself favors the cause of the people."

But the quest for immediate returns also led to a

ruthless stripping of natural resources. In the absence of national legislation and national power, the timber, grasses, and minerals of the public domain invited a headlong scramble by the pioneers to cut trees, graze their cattle, and dig for ore. The government actually bought gold and silver that miners took from public property. European visitors were astonished at the American conviction that forests were a hostile element to be destroyed without regard for need. Trees, like the buffalo and beaver of the West, seemed so plentiful that few Americans could foresee a time of diminishing supply.

The soil itself, the most valuable of all resources, fared no better. Americans generally lacked the incentives and patience to conserve the soil by using fertilizers and carefully rotating crops. They tended to look on land as a temporary and expendable resource that should be mined as rapidly as possible. This attitude, especially prevalent in the South and the West, reflected the common need to produce the most profitable single crop, whether wheat, corn, rice, tobacco, or cotton, in order to pay for land that they had purchased or settled on credit.

The entrepreneurial character of American agriculture owed much to the way new lands were originally settled. For Americans of the late twentieth century it is difficult to grasp the significance of the fact that the chief business of the federal government, before the Civil War, was the management and disposal of public land. The government, wanting revenue as well as rapid settlement, hastily surveyed tracts of western land, which were then sold to the highest bidder at public auction; the remainder was offered at the minimum price of $1.25 per acre. Since there was no limit to how many acres an individual or company might buy, investors eagerly bought blocks of thousands of acres. The great peaks of speculation coincided with the expansion of bank credit in the early 1830s and in the mid-1850s. The profitable resale of such land depended on promoting settlement.

Speculators and Squatters.   Speculators had always helped to shape the character of American agriculture. The great theme of American settlement was

the continuing contest of will between absentee owners and the squatters who first developed the land and who often had some partial claim of title. Although squatters often sold their own claims to succeeding waves of migrants, they tended to picture wealthier speculators as rapacious vampires. Yet the large speculators played a key role in financing the rapid settlement of the public lands. Pooling private capital, they loaned money to squatters, often at illegally high interest rates, to finance the purchase of tools, livestock, and supplies. They extended credit for buying farms. They pressured local and national governments to subsidize canals and railroads. Such speculation often involved considerable risk; the returns on investment depended on the speculators' ability to predict business conditions accurately and on how fast settlement took place.

Squatters for their part yearned for economic independence. They successfully agitated for state "occupancy laws" favoring the claims of actual settlers and guaranteeing them compensation, if evicted, for their cabins, fences, outbuildings, and other improvements. Squatters also pressed for a lowered minimum in the amount of public land that could be purchased, a restriction that had fallen by 1832 to 40 acres. Above all, squatters called on the federal government to sanction squatting, formally allowing settlers to clear and cultivate tracts of public land prior to purchase. This policy of preemption, developed in limited acts in the 1830s and finally established in a general law of 1841, gave squatters the chance to settle land and then purchase as much as 160 acres at the minimum price in advance of public auction.

In practice the federal land system was a compromise between the interests of farmers and those of speculators. Government measures did nothing to curb speculators, who were in fact favored by the requirement, beginning in 1820, of full cash payment for public land; by lavish donations of land to military veterans, railroads, and state governments; and by eventual pricing of land long unsold for as little as 12.5¢ an acre. Federal land policy allowed speculators to amass great private fortunes by acquiring valuable tracts of the public domain. Yet the wide dispersion of freehold farms gave some substance to the myth that any American could become an owner of property and an independent producer for the capitalist market.

Southern agriculture remained strikingly distinctive, though it was influenced by the same public land policies that applied to the rest of the country and the same democratic pressures for widespread property ownership in the form of family farms. As in the North, owners of family farms tried to combine relative self-sufficiency with a cash income from marketable staples. By 1820 the long depression in tobacco prices had induced many planters in the coastal area of Virginia and Maryland to shift to the cultivation of wheat and corn. Having suffered a relative decline in income during the decades following Independence, white Southerners had led the way in the rush for western land.

Demand for Better Transportation.   Access to growing markets was the overriding concern of the commercial farmer. Unlike southern cotton, most of the North's commercial crops were perishable and had to be marketed fairly quickly. Yet the teams of horses that hauled wagons of freight over the nation's turnpikes averaged no better than two miles an hour. The craze during the early nineteenth century for building turnpikes, bridges, and plank roads failed to reduce significantly the cost of long-distance freight. It was not until canals began to link together other inland waterways that northern farmers could think of concentrating on the production of corn and wheat for distant markets.

The Erie Canal, completed in 1825, united Northeast and West by providing a continuous waterway from Lake Erie to the Atlantic. In 1817 it had cost 19.2¢ per mile to ship a ton of freight overland from Buffalo to New York. By the late 1850s the cost per mile, via the canal, had dropped to 0.81¢. New York State had directed and financed this prodigious undertaking, by far the longest canal in the world, and

THE JUNCTION OF THE ERIE AND NORTHERN CANALS, c. 1830–1832
Although canals greatly reduced the cost of overland freight, it was a slow and arduous task negotiating multiple locks and pulling barges by rope from the "tow path" alongside. *(Courtesy of the New-York Historical Society, New York City)*

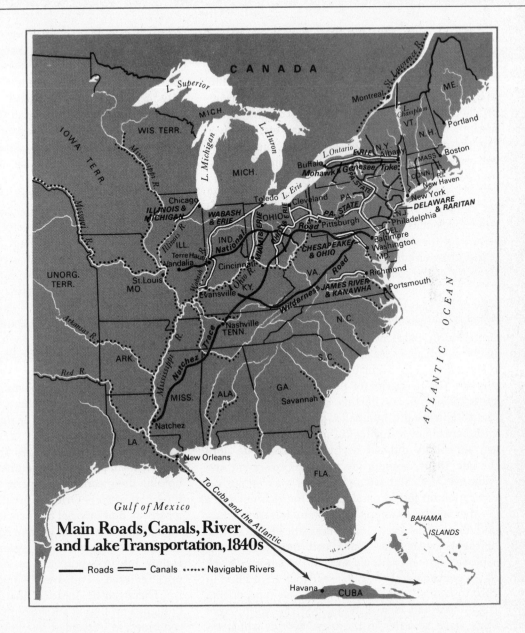

Main Roads, Canals, River and Lake Transportation, 1840s

— Roads ═ Canals ••••• Navigable Rivers

soon reaped spectacular rewards. Foreign capital quickly flowed into the country to meet the demand of other state and municipal governments, setting off a canal-building mania that soon linked Pittsburgh with Philadelphia, and the Ohio River with the Great Lakes. The high cost of building this network of wa-

terways, undertaken for the most part by the states themselves, severely strained the credit of Ohio, Pennsylvania, and Indiana. But by dramatically lowering the costs of transport, the most successful canals had an enormous effect on northern agriculture and industry.

By the mid-1830s the basic pattern of internal transportation began to shift away from the traditional routes that had led from the Ohio and upper Mississippi valleys to New Orleans and ocean shipment via the Gulf of Mexico. Ohio Valley farmers would continue to ship grain and pork down the Mississippi by flatboat. The richest markets, however, lay east of the Great Lakes, and for a time the richest commercial agriculture developed in regions accessible by canal to Lake Erie. By 1840 Rochester, New York, had become the leading flour-milling center of the country. The marketing of grain became more efficient as brokers and other middlemen began to arrange for storage, transport, sale, and credit. This transformation preceded the East–West railroad connections of the early 1850s.

Rise of the Cotton Kingdom.   From 1820 on, Southerners benefited from three advantages unavailable in the North. First, the climate and soil of large parts of the South were ideally suited to growing cotton, the indispensable raw material for the Industrial Revolution. The perfection of the cotton gin and screw press, devices for extracting cotton from the plant and compressing it into bales, provided Southerners with benefits of technological innovation that northern agriculture did not begin to approximate until the late 1850s. Second, the rapid improvement and wide use of steamboats opened the way to upriver navigation on the Mississippi and the rich networks of other southern waterways, thereby lowering transportation costs even more dramatically than the northern canals did. Third and most important, southern agriculture could exploit the labor of black slaves, whose numbers increased from 1.5 million in 1820 to nearly 4 million in 1860. A self-reproducing labor force had long distinguished the South from other slave societies in the New World, which remained dependent on the continuing importation of slaves from Africa. It was the unprecedented natural increase in the slave population that enabled white Southerners to clear and settle the vast Cotton Kingdom extending from Georgia to Louisiana, Arkansas, and eventually, eastern Texas.

While the economics of slavery is still subject to much dispute, one must begin by emphasizing the shortage of white labor as a crucial condition affecting both northern and southern agriculture. All American farmers wanted the independence and relative security of owning their own land. Since land was generally accessible, especially in the West, this meant that it was difficult to hire nonfamily labor in order to expand production and take advantage of a rising demand for cash crops, such as wheat, cotton, and corn.

In the North, this labor shortage led to improved transportation, labor-saving machinery, and promotional schemes to attract immigrants. But in the South, black slaves provided a highly mobile and elastic supply of labor. Large planters and speculators could quickly transport an army of involuntary workers to clear rich western land, or sell slaves to meet the labor demands of expanding areas. Even prospering family farmers could buy or rent a few slaves in order to increase their output of cotton or other cash crops. The flexibility of the system also enabled planters to allocate needed labor to raising livestock and growing foodstuffs for domestic consumption; and when market conditions improved, to increase the proportion of time devoted to cotton or other staples.

These various advantages also meant that slaves became the major form of southern wealth, and slaveholding the means to prosperity. Except for the bustling port of New Orleans, great urban centers failed to appear, and internal markets languished. European immigrants, having no wish to compete with slave labor, generally shunned the region. Investment flowed mainly into the purchase of slaves, whose soaring price reflected an apparently limitless demand.

There can be no doubt that investment in slaves brought a profitable return, or that the slave economy continued to expand throughout the pre-Civil War decades. Yet, essentially, the system depended on the world's demand for cotton as it entered the age of industrialization, led by the British textile industry. At times the South's production of cotton outran international demand; cotton prices fell sharply following the Panics of 1819 and 1837. But until the Civil War, the world market for cotton textiles grew

"GEESE IN FLIGHT"

This imaginative painting by Leila T. Bauman captures some of the mid-nineteenth-century excitement over movement and improved transport—the steam from the train and riverboat harmonizing with the movement of horses, geese, and wind. *(Courtesy, National Gallery of Art)*

at such a phenomenal rate that both southern planters and British manufacturers thought only of infinite expansion. By 1840 the South grew over 60 percent of the world's cotton; during the pre-Civil War boom, more than three-fourths of the South's cotton was exported. Much of it went to Britain, amounting to over 70 percent of that country's cotton imports. In addition, the South also shipped cotton to the rising industries of continental Europe, including Russia. Throughout the antebellum period cotton accounted for well over half the value of all American exports, and thus paid for the major share of the nation's imports. A stimulant to northern industry, cotton also contributed to the growth of New York City as a distributing and exporting center that drew income from commissions, freight charges, interest, insurance, and other services connected with the marketing of America's number one commodity.

Neither American sellers nor British buyers felt comfortable over such a single source of prosperity.

British manufacturers searched unsuccessfully for alternative sources of high-grade cotton. Though the South continued to export large quantities of rice, tobacco, and other staples, southern commercial conventions unsuccessfully called for a more balanced economy. In Louisiana wealthy sugar planters expanded production by using new technology for the processing of cane. Planters effectively applied slave labor to cultivating hemp, corn, and grain; to mining and lumbering; to building canals and railroads; and even to manufacturing textiles, iron, and other industrial products. Yet the South's economic growth and prosperity depended ultimately on foreign markets.

Paradoxically, no other American region contained so many farmers who merely subsisted on their own produce; yet in no other region had agriculture become so speculative and commercial—for small cotton famers who could not afford slaves as well as for the planter elite. Like some of the later Third World regions where involuntary labor produced raw materials for industrial nations, the South was intimately connected with industrial capitalism and yet cut off from its liberalizing and diversifying influences.

Indians

This rapid expansion in agriculture, North and South, depended initially on the displacement of the native population. The white Americans, determined to go where they pleased and to seize any chance for quick profit, regarded the millions of acres of western land as a well-deserved inheritance that should be exploited as quickly as possible. But in 1820 the prairies and forests east of the Mississippi still contained approximately 125,000 Indians. Although millions of acres had been legally cleared of Indian occupancy rights, the physical presence of the Indians blocked the way to government sale of much public land that could lead to increased revenue, to profits from land speculation, and to the creation of private farms and plantations.

The Indians, hopelessly outnumbered by an invader with superior technology, had little room for maneuver. Though they had long sought trade and alliances with whites, Indians had learned that advancing white settlements undermined tribal culture and destroyed the fish and game on which their economy depended. If the Indians had little understanding of the whites' conceptions of private property and competitive individualism, the whites were just as blind to the diversity and complexity of Indian cultures, to the natives' traditions of mutual obligation and communal ownership of land, and to the peculiarly advanced position of Indian women. Iroquois women, for example, played a crucial role in political and economic decisions. Such cultural barriers made it easier for whites to think of Indians in terms of negative stereotypes—as deceitful and bloodthirsty savages or as a weak and "childlike" race doomed to extinction. In fact, the Indian responses to white encroachments were complex, ranging from skillful warfare and stubborn negotiation to resigned acquiescence in the face of treachery and superior force.

The Indians had proved to be the major losers in the War of 1812. This war, by ending the long conflict between Western settlers and European sovereigns, had removed the Indians' last hope of finding white allies who could slow the advance of white America. The decisive victories of William Henry Harrison over the Shawnees in the Old Northwest, and of Andrew Jackson over the Creeks in the Old Southwest, had also shattered the hope of a union between northern and southern Indian confederations. These triumphs opened the way for exploiting tribal divisions and for gradually abandoning what Jackson termed "the farce of treating with Indian tribes" as units. Jackson thought that all Indians should be required as individuals to submit to the laws of the states, like everyone else, or to migrate beyond the Mississippi, where they could progress toward civilization at their own pace.

Federal Indian Policy.   The land-hungry frontiersmen faced the constraints of a federal Indian policy that had evolved from imperial, colonial, and early national precedents. This makeshift policy rested on four premises that were becoming increasingly contradictory. First, in line with Old World legal concepts the federal government continued to acknowledge that Indian tribes, while lacking many of the attributes of sovereignty, were in some sense independent nations that had acquired rights of possession by prior occupancy of the land. The continuing efforts to negotiate treaties, to purchase land, and to mark off territorial boundaries demonstrated that legitimate settlement by whites required at least symbolic consent from Indians. The same Old World model allowed the United States to punish "aggressor" tribes by demanding the cession of land as a legal indemnity for the damages of war.

The second premise, a product of New World experience, was that Indian "occupancy" must inevitably give way to white settlement. White Americans, like the heirs of a dying relative, had an "expectancy"—to use Jefferson's phrase—in the property that Indians held. In theory this preemptive claim did not infringe on the existing property rights of Indians. It simply gave the American government an exclusive right to purchase Indian lands, thereby blocking any future imperial designs by European powers. In practice, however, the doctrine of preemption led to the third premise of supreme federal authority over Indian affairs. Knowing the dangers of alliances between hostile Indians and foreign nations, the federal government had from its beginning assumed powers that would have been unthinkable in any other domestic sphere. It subjected all trade with Indians to federal licensing and regulation. It invalidated any sale or transfer of Indian lands, even to a state, unless made in accordance with a federal treaty. It guaranteed that Indians would be protected from encroachments on unceded land. Unfortunately, no federal administration had the will or military power to protect Indian rights while supervising the equitable acquisition of land by whites. In a government increasingly attuned to the voice of the people, the Indians had no voice of their own.

The fourth premise, which Jefferson had articulated and which gained momentum after the War of 1812, was that Indian culture, or "savagery," and American civilization could not permanently coexist. President James Monroe expressed the common conviction in a letter of 1817 to Andrew Jackson: "The hunter or savage state requires a greater extent of territory to sustain it, than is compatible with the progress and just claims of civilized life, and must yield to it." The government actively promoted schools, agriculture, and various "useful arts" among the Indians, hoping to convert nomadic hunters into settled farmers. This hope drew nourishment from the progress of the more populous southern tribes, particularly the Cherokees, whose achievements in agriculture, in developing a written alphabet, and in adopting white technology seemed to meet the American tests of capability. But the government also pressured the Cherokees into ceding tracts of valuable eastern land in exchange for lands west of the Mississippi. By 1824 it was becoming clear that the five southern confederations—Cherokees, Creeks, Choctaws, Chickasaws, and Seminoles—could not survive as even temporary enclaves without federal protection against white exploiters. The southern tribes occupied western Georgia and North Carolina, and major portions of Tennessee, Florida, Alabama, and Mississippi, including the heart of the future Cotton Kingdom. In 1825 President Monroe officially proposed that these and all other remaining tribes should be persuaded to move west of the Mississippi, a plan that Jefferson and others had long regarded as the only way of saving America's original inhabitants from ultimate extinction.

Conflict of Federal and State Laws. In Georgia, white speculators, squatters, and gold miners had no desire to see civilized Indians living on choice ancestral land. In 1828, when the Cherokees adopted a constitution and claimed sovereign jurisdiction over their own territory, the state declared them to be mere tenants on state land, subject to the state's laws and authority. In 1832, in the case of *Worcester* v. *Georgia*, Chief Justice John Marshall ruled against the state. Georgia, he said, had no right to extend state laws to the Cherokees or their territory. "The several Indian nations," he maintained, were "distinct political communities, having territorial boundaries, within which their authority is exclusive, and having a right to all lands within those boundaries, which is not only acknowledged, but guaranteed by the United

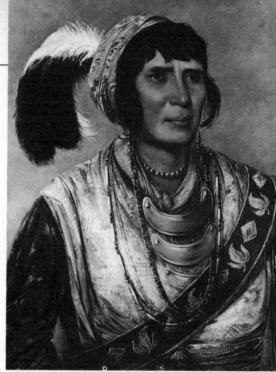

CATLIN'S AMERICAN INDIANS

Although Americans were continually reminded of the Indians' acts of cruelty, as in this scene of initiation rites in a Mandan tent, there was also a growing fascination with Indians as representatives of the exotic. Even by the early 1830s George Catlin had created a prototype for the commercial Wild West show. An accomplished painter of Plains tribesmen, Catlin also created the heroic image of Osceola, the Seminole chief who had been captured by American treachery and who posed for this portrait in prison, shortly before his death. For over two centuries Anglo-American settlers had magnified Indian violence in order to justify their own aggression against Indians. The Seminole War presented the opportunity for dramatizing the ultimate racial nightmare—the specter of supposedly docile blacks uniting with Indians to slaughter "defenseless" whites. Such images appealed to deep-seated racial fears and helped to justify the most extreme measures for removing "wild" Indians far beyond the geographic boundaries of a "civilized" slave society. *(Top left, courtesy of the American Museum of Natural History; top right, National Portrait Gallery, Smithsonian Institution; bottom, American Antiquarian Society; opposite page, Library of Congress)*

CATLIN'S INDIAN GALLERY,
(FOR A FEW EVENINGS ONLY,) AT
AMORY HALL,
CORNER OF WASHINGTON AND WEST STREETS.

Mr. CATLIN, who has been for seven years traversing the Prairies of the "Far West," procuring the Portraits of the most distinguished Indians of those uncivilized regions, together with Paintings of their

VILLAGES, BUFFALO HUNTS, DANCES
LANDSCAPES OF THE COUNTRY, &c. &c.

Will endeavour to entertain and instruct the Citizens of Boston and its vicinity, for a short time, with an Exhibition of his

PAINTINGS, COSTUMES, &c.
——CONSISTING OF——

330 Portraits, and numerous other Paintings,

Which he has collected from 36 different Tribes, speaking different languages, all of whom he has been among, and Painted his Pictures from Life.——IN HIS COLLECTION ARE

Portraits of BLACK HAWK and Nine of his Principal Warriors,

Painted at Jefferson Barracks, while prisoners of war, in their War Dress and War Paint.

OSCEOLA, MICK-E-NO-PAH, CLOUD, COA-HA-JO & KING PHILIP,
Chiefs of the Seminoles.

ALSO, FOUR PAINTINGS, REPRESENTING THE

Annual Religious Ceremony of the Mandans,

Doing Penance, by inflicting the most cruel tortures upon their own bodies—passing knives and splints through their flesh, and suspending their bodies by their wounds, &c.

AND A SERIES OF

TWELVE BUFFALO HUNTING SCENES,
TOGETHER WITH
SPLENDID SPECIMENS OF COSTUME,
AND OTHER ARTICLES OF THEIR MANUFACTURE.

The great interest of this collection consists in its being a representation of the *wildest Tribes of Indians* in America, and entirely in their Native Habits and Customs: consisting of Sioux, Pawnees, Konzas, Shiennes, Crows, Ojibbeways, Assinaboins, Mandans, Crees, Blackfeet, Snakes, Mohus, Ottos, Ioways, Flatheads, Weahs, Puncas, Sacs, Foxes, Winnebagoes, Menomonies, Minatarees, Rickarees, Oneidas, Comanches, Wacos, Pawnee-Picts, Kioways, Seminoles, Euchees and others.

In order to render the Exhibition more *instructive* than it could otherwise be, the Paintings will be exhibited one at a time, and such *explanations* of their Dress, Customs, Traditions, &c. given by Mr. Catlin, as will enable the public to form a just idea of the Customs, Numbers and Cremation of the Savages (?) in a state of nature in North America.

The EXHIBITION, with EXPLANATIONS, will commence this Evening, (Wednesday,) August 15, and on several successive Evenings, at 8 o'clock precisely—and it is hoped that visitors will be in and seated as *near the hour as possible*, that they may see the whole collection as they are passed over.

Two Evenings will constitute the course, so that persons attending on any two successive Evenings will see the whole, and form general and just notions of the Manners and Customs of the Indians to the Rocky Mountains.

EACH ADMITTANCE 50 CENTS, CHILDREN HALF PRICE.

States." But President Jackson, who had already withdrawn the federal troops earlier sent to protect Cherokee lands from intrusion, had no intention of enforcing the Supreme Court's decision.

Jackson firmly believed that Indians should be subject to state law and to the forces of a free market economy. To deal with tribes as privileged corporate groups, he thought, was simply to reinforce the power of corrupt chiefs and cunning half-breeds, who prevented tribesmen from following their own best interest. Jackson had no doubt that the vast majority of Indians, when liberated from tribal tyranny, would willingly emigrate to the West. The civilized few would be free to cultivate modest tracts of land and become responsible citizens of state and nation.

Jackson's denial of federal protection provided the needed incentives for a supposedly voluntary migration. Following Georgia's lead, other southern states harassed Indians with laws that few tribesmen could comprehend. White traders and lawyers descended like locusts on Indian lands, destroying tribal unity and authority. In 1830 Congress supported Jackson's policy by appropriating funds that would enable the president to negotiate treaties for the removal of all Indian tribes then living east of the Mississippi. The government still considered it necessary to purchase title to Indian land and to grant allotments of land to individual tribal leaders who could prove a legitimate claim. Federal officials even sought to protect Indians by supervising private contracts for sale. The majority of Indians, however, had no concept of land as a measurable and salable commodity. A few of the more experienced Chickasaws and other tribesmen secured good prices for rich cotton land, but white speculators, who swiftly cornered between 80 and 90 percent of southern allotments, reaped windfall profits.

The government thus furthered its goal of removal by dispossessing the Indians of their land. Victims of wholesale fraud, chicanery, and intimidation, the great mass of southern Indians had no choice but to follow the "Trail of Tears" to the vacant territory of Oklahoma. Subjected to disease, starvation, and winter cold, thousands died along the way.

Massacre of the Whites by the Indians and Blacks in Florida.

The above is intended to represent the horrid Massacre of the Whites in Florida, in December 1835, and January, February, March and April 1836, when near Four Hundred (including women and children) fell victims to the barbarity of the Negroes and Indians.

Military force gave a cutting edge to removal deadlines; in 1838 federal troops herded fifteen thousand Cherokees into detention camps. Meanwhile, Indians north of the Ohio River had earlier been demoralized as whites had cut down the supply of game, negotiated treaties with the more acculturated factions of certain tribes, and ensnared primitive societies with unfamiliar mechanisms of debt and credit. In 1832 the government crushed the resistance of Sac and Fox Indians in Illinois and Wisconsin, and in 1835 launched a long and costly war against the Seminoles in Florida. By 1844, except for a few remaining pockets mainly in the backcountry of New York, Michigan, and Florida, the mission of removal had been accomplished.

In his Farewell Address of March 4, 1837, Jackson applauded Indian removal as a great humanitarian achievement that had also happily removed the main impediment to America's economic growth:

While the safety and comfort of our own citizens have been greatly promoted by their removal, the philanthropist will rejoice that the remnant of that ill-fated race has been at length placed beyond the reach of injury or oppression, and that paternal care of the General Government will hereafter watch over them and protect them.

The Beginning of Indian Reservations. Ten years later, however, the government had recognized the impossibility of a "permanent Indian barrier" west of the Mississippi. Having defeated all Indian attempts to build dikes against the tides of westward migration, the government now began moving toward

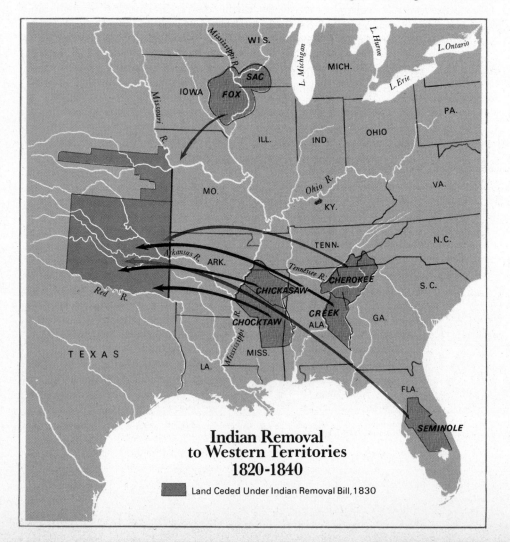

Indian Removal to Western Territories 1820-1840

■ Land Ceded Under Indian Removal Bill, 1830

a policy of fencing Indians within specified "reservations" and opening the otherwise boundless territory of the great West to wagon trains, cavalry, miners, farmers, surveyors, and railroads. Even in the 1820s a few perceptive Indian chieftains had foreseen that western lands would be no more invulnerable than the lands in the East, a conclusion soon confirmed by the destruction of tribal game reserves and by the purchase of remaining Indian lands in Missouri and Iowa. The Anglo-Saxon settlers in Texas, who won independence from Mexico in 1836, asserted the unprecedented claim that Indians had no right whatever to possession of the land. Texas reaffirmed this doctrine after being annexed as a state in 1845, and even demanded that some twenty-five thousand Apaches and other tribesmen be removed or face extermination. Years of border warfare finally led in 1854 to the Texans' acceptance of Indian reservations under federal jurisdiction. But the federal government found that it could not protect Texas tribes from being slaughtered by marauding whites, and therefore authorized their removal to the territory north of the Red River.

Meanwhile, from 1846 to 1860 government policy began to settle the fate of the strong western tribes that had previously been free to roam prairies and mountain parks without concern for the conflicting claims of white nations. The American invasion and occupation of New Mexico, in the Mexican War, led to brutal punitive expeditions against the Navajo. In 1851 Congress passed the critically important Indian Appropriations Act, designed to consolidate western tribes on agricultural reservations, thereby lessening the danger to the tens of thousands of emigrants streaming toward California and Oregon and also to the proposed transcontinental railroad.

The degradation reached its climax in California, in the 1850s, where federal restraints on white aggression disappeared. Whites molested the Diggers and other primitive Indians, shooting the males for sport and enslaving the women and children. Farther east, the Apaches and powerful Plains tribes would continue to offer sporadic and sometimes spectacular resistance. The famed encounters between Indians and the United States Cavalry came after the Civil War. But even by 1860 the western tribes had been

demoralized, their economy had been fatally weakened when buffalo and other game became depleted, and increasing numbers of Indians had been herded into compounds with boundaries that moved only inward.

The Slave's World

The native Americans were not the only or the most numerous racial victims of the nation's expansion in the pre-Civil War years. Millions of black laborers were even more systematically exploited in the expansion of southern agriculture.

The Slave Masters.   In theory, the southern slaveholder possessed all the power of any owner of chattel property. This power was limited only by state laws, which were generally unenforceable, protecting slaves from murder and mutilation; setting minimal standards for food, clothing, and shelter; and prohibiting masters from teaching slaves to read or allowing them to carry firearms or roam about the countryside. These slave codes acknowledged that bondsmen were human beings who were capable of plotting, stealing, fleeing, or rebelling, and who were likely to be a less "troublesome property" if well cared for under a regimen of strict discipline. Yet the laws also insisted that the slave was a piece of property that could be sold, traded, rented, mortgaged, and inherited. They did not recognize the interests and institutions of the slave community, or the slave's right to marry, to hold property, or to testify in court.

In practice, it proved impossible to treat human beings as no more than possessions or as the mere instruments of an owner's will. Most masters were primarily motivated by the desire for profit. They wanted to maximize their slaves' productivity while protecting the value of their capital investment, a value that kept rising with the generally escalating trend in slave prices. Accordingly, it made sense to provide a material standard of living that would promote good health and a natural increase in the size of slave families, and thus increase capital gains. It also made sense to keep the morale of slaves as high as possible, and to encourage them to do willingly

COTTON PLANTATION, BY C. GIROUX
Although southern slaves cultivated sugar, rice, hemp, tobacco, and other crops, it was the cotton plantation that gave a distinctive stamp to nineteenth-century American slavery. *(Courtesy, Museum of Fine Arts, Boston)*

and even cheerfully the work they would be forced to do in the last resort. Convinced of the moral legitimacy of the system, most planters sincerely believed that their own best interests were identical with their slaves' best interests. They therefore sought to convince slaves of the essential justice of slavery, and expected gratitude for their acts of kindness, indulgence, and generosity, or even for their restraint in inflicting physical punishment.

But slaves were not passive, compliant puppets who could be manipulated at will. As human beings they had one overriding objective: self-preservation at a minimal cost of degradation and loss of self-respect. To avoid punishment and win rewards, they carried out with varying degrees of thoroughness their owners' demands. But black slaves became cunningly expert at testing their masters' will. They learned how

to mock while seeming to flatter; how to lighten unending work with moments of spontaneity, song, intimacy, and relaxation; how to exploit the whites' dependence on black field drivers and household servants; and how to play on the conflicts between their masters and white overseers. In short, they learned through constant experiment and struggle how to preserve a core of dignity and self-respect.

Although slavery "worked" as an economic system, its fundamental conflict of interests created a highly unstable and violent society. The great sugar planters in Louisiana and cotton planters in the delta country of Mississippi, often employing over one hundred slaves on a productive unit, tried to merge Christian paternalism with a kind of welfare capitalism. They provided professional medical care, offered monetary rewards for extra productivity, and granted a week or more of Christmas vacation. Yet these same plantations were essentially ruled by terror.

Even the most humane and kindly planters knew that only the threat of violence could force gangs of field hands to work from dawn to dusk "with the discipline," as one contemporary observer put it, "of a regular trained army." Frequent public floggings reminded every slave of the penalty for inefficient labor, insubordination, or disorderly conduct. Bennet H. Barrow, a particularly harsh Louisiana planter, maintained discipline by ordering occasional mass whippings of all his field hands, by chaining offenders or ducking them under water, and even by shooting a black who was about to run away. Barrow also distributed generous monetary bonuses to his slaves and bought them Christmas presents in New Orleans. The South could point to far gentler masters who seldom inflicted physical punishment. Slaves understood, however, that even the mildest of whites could become cruel despots when faced with the deception or ingratitude of people who, regardless of pretenses to the contrary, were kept down by force.

Masters also uneasily sensed that circumstances might transform a loyal and devoted slave into a vengeful enemy. It is true that white Southerners could congratulate themselves on the infrequency of serious insurrections, especially when the South was compared with Brazil and most of the Caribbean. Yet the French colony of St. Domingue had enjoyed an even more secure history than the American South until 1791, when the greatest of all slave revolts had led to the creation of the black republic of Haiti. Toussaint L'Ouverture, the brilliant Haitian military leader, was until the age of forty-five the trusted, docile, and privileged slave of an unusually kind and indulgent master. The record showed that the South had no magic immunity from slave revolts. In 1822 South Carolina hanged thirty-five blacks after uncovering Denmark Vesey's plot for a full-scale insurrection, a plot that involved some of Charleston's most trusted household servants. Nine years later Nat Turner led some seventy slaves on a bloody rampage through Southampton County, Virginia. To the outside world Southerners presented a brave façade of self-confidence, and individual planters reassured

themselves that their own slaves were happy and loyal. But rumors of arson, poisoning, and suppressed revolts continued to flourish. Alarmists frequently warned that outside agitators were secretly sowing discontent among the slaves. This widespread fantasy at least hinted at the truth; slavery not only had little sanction in the outside world, but the institution ultimately depended on the sheer weight of superior force.

The difficulties in generalizing about the slave's world are compounded by the geographic, climatic, and cultural diversities of the "South"—a region in which mountain highlands, pine forests, and swampy lowlands are all frequently traversed within a few hundred miles.

Almost half of the southern slaveholders owned fewer than five slaves; 72 percent owned fewer than ten. The typical master could thus devote close personal attention to his human property. Many small farmers worked side by side with their slaves, an arrangement that might have been far more humiliating for the slaves than working in a field gang under black "drivers." From the slave's point of view, much depended on the character of an owner, on the norms of a given locality, on the accidents of sale, and on the relative difficulty of harvesting cotton, rice, tobacco, or sugar.

Slave experiences covered a wide range from remarkable physical comfort and lack of restraint to the most savage and unrelieved exploitation. But to dwell on contrasting examples of physical treatment is to risk losing sight of the central horror of human bondage. As the Quaker John Woolman pointed out in the eighteenth century, no human is saintly enough to be entrusted with total power over another. The slave was an inviting target for the hidden anger, passion, frustration, and revenge from which no human is exempt; a slave's work, leisure, movement, and daily fate depended on the will of another person.

Moreover, despite the numerical predominance of small slaveholders, most southern slaves were concentrated on large farms and plantations. Over half belonged to owners who held twenty or more slaves; one-quarter belonged to productive units of over fifty slaves. In the South, slave ownership was the

primary route to wealth, and the most successful planters cornered an increasing share of the growing but limited human capital. Therefore, most slaves experienced fairly standardized patterns of plantation life.

Life on the Plantation.   By sunrise black drivers had herded gangs of men and women into the fields. The older children served as water carriers or began to learn the lighter tasks of field work. Slaves too old for field work tended small children, along with the stables, gardens, and kitchens. This full employment of all available hands was one of the economies of the system that increased the total output from a planter's

SCULPTURED FIGURE

Excavated at the site of a plantation forge in Virginia, this iron figure is an excellent example of eighteenth-century Afro-American sculpture.   *(Collection Adele Earnest)*

AFRO-CAROLINIAN FACE VESSEL

Recent research in art history has demonstrated a profound African influence on the folk sculpture of American slaves in such states as Georgia and South Carolina. This cultural continuity was always modified by the slaves' gift for improvisation and by their need to respond expressively to a new physical and social environment. *(Courtesy Augusta Richmond County Museum)*

capital investment. Nevertheless, slaves often succeeded in maintaining their own work rhythm and in helping to define the amount of labor a planter could reasonably expect. Bursts of intense effort required during cotton picking, corn shucking, or the eighteen-hour-a-day sugar harvest were followed by periods of festivity and relaxation. Even in relatively slack seasons, however, there were cattle to be tended, fences mended, forests cleared, and food crops planted.

Black slaves were saved from becoming mere robots in the field by the strength of their own community and evolving culture. There has long been controversy over the survival in North America of African cultural patterns. In contrast to Brazil, where continuing slave importations sustained a living bond with African cultures, the vast majority of southern blacks were removed by several generations from an African-born ancestor. Yet recent research has uncovered striking examples of African influence in the southern slaves' oral traditions, folklore, songs, dances, language, sculpture, religion, and kinship patterns. The question at issue is not the purity or even persistence of distinct African forms. In the New World all imported cultures have undergone blending, adaptation, and synthesis. The point is that slaves created their own Afro-American culture, which preserved the most crucial areas of life and thought from white domination. Within such a culture, sustained by strong community ties, slaves were able to maintain a sense of apartness, of pride, and of independent identity.

African kinship patterns seem to have been the main vehicle for cultural continuity. As in West Africa, children were frequently named for grandparents, who were revered even in memory. Kinship patterns survived even the breakup of families. Strangers often took on the functions and responsibilities of grandparents, uncles, and aunts. The fictional portrayals of Uncle Tom and Aunt Jemima were not figments of the imagination; many younger slaves were cared for and protected by "aunts" and "uncles" who were not blood kin. These older teachers and guardians passed on knowledge of a historical time, before the fateful crossing of the sea, when their ancestors had not been slaves. This historical awareness inspired hope in a future time of deliverance, a deliver-

ance that slaves associated with the Jews' biblical flight from Egypt, with the sweet land of Canaan, and with the Day of Jubilee. In the words of one spiritual:

> *Dear Lord, dear Lord, when slavery'll cease*
> *Then we poor souls will have our peace;—*
> *There's a better day a-coming,*
> *Will you go along with me?*
> *There's a better day a-coming,*
> *Go sound the jubilee!*

Historians have recently recognized how important the slave family was as a refuge from the dehumanizing effects of being treated as chattel property. The strength of family bonds is suggested by

MOSS PICKERS, SAVANNAH, GEORGIA
This remarkable photograph of American-born slaves depicts generational continuity from childhood to old age and also suggests the kind of household utensils and living quarters that could be seen in antebellum Georgia. *(Courtesy, Lightfoot Collection)*

the thousands of slaves who ran away from their owners in search of family members separated by sale. The myth of weak family attachments is also countered by the swarms of freedmen who roamed the South at the end of the Civil War in search of their spouses, parents, or children, and by the eager desire of freedmen to legalize their marriages.

Nevertheless, the slave family was a highly vulnerable institution. Though many slaveholders had moral scruples against separating husbands from wives or small children from their mothers, even the strongest scruples frequently gave way to economic need. The forced sale of individual slaves in order to pay a deceased owner's debts further increased the chances of family breakups. In some parts of the South, it was common for a slave to be married to another slave on a neighboring or even distant plantation, an arrangement that left visitation at the discretion of the two owners.

In sexual relations there was a similar gap between moral scruples and actual practice. White planter society officially condemned miscegenation, and tended to blame lower-class whites for fathering mulatto children. Yet there is abundant evidence that many planters, sons of planters, and overseers took black mistresses or sexually exploited the wives and daughters of slave families. This abuse of power was not as universal as abolitionists claimed, but it was common enough to humiliate black women, to instill rage in black men, and to arouse shame and bitterness in white women. At best, slave marriage was a precarious bond, unprotected by law and vulnerable to the will of whites.

The larger slave community provided some stability and continuity for the thousands of blacks who were sold and shipped to new environments. On the larger plantations one could find conjurers whose magic powers were thought to ward off sickness, soften a master's heart, or hasten the success of a courtship. There were black preachers who mixed Christianity with elements of West African religion and folklore. In the slave quarters particular prestige was attached to those who excelled at the traditional memorizing of songs, riddles, folktales, superstitions, and herb cures—who were carriers, in short, of Afro-

American culture. These forms of oral communication allowed free play to the imagination, enabling slaves to comment on the pathos, humor, absurdity, sorrow, and warmth of the scenes they experienced. Together with the ceremonial rituals, especially at weddings and funerals, the oral traditions preserved a sanctuary of human dignity that enabled slaves to survive the humiliations, debasement, and self-contempt that were inseparable from human bondage.

Population Distribution and Opportunity

As we have seen, America's spectacular expansion in agriculture, which fueled other forms of economic growth, depended in large measure on the dispossession of Indians and on the exploitation of black slave labor. There can be no question that the nation's overall economic growth brought impressive gains in income and standard of living. By 1860, in per capita income, the United States was well ahead of western Europe; even the South was richer than most nations of Europe. But much is yet to be learned about the actual distribution of wealth in the pre-Civil War decades, to say nothing of the opportunity to acquire property or to move upward in status and occupation.

Discussions of America's economic opportunities generally omit three groups: the Indians; the black slaves; and the free blacks in both North and South whose small economic gains in various skilled trades and service industries were severely damaged by competition from white immigrants. Even excluding these oppressed minorities, one finds many indications that economic inequality increased substantially from 1820 to 1860.

The Rich Grow Richer, 1820–1860. According to the best recent estimates, by 1860 the upper 5 percent of families owned over half the nation's wealth. The disparity was far greater than this in parts of the South, where the wealth of the average slaveholder was growing far more rapidly than that of the average nonslaveholder. The average slaveholder was not only more than five times as wealthy as the average

FIVE POINTS, NEW YORK CITY, 1827
For many decades the region around "Five Points," the intersection of five streets in lower Manhatten, epitomized the worst of urban degradation: poverty, prostitution, crime, drunkenness, and mob violence. Fashionably dressed gentlemen and racially mixed crowds mingled with prostitutes and pigs. *(Brown Brothers)*

Northerner, but more than ten times as wealthy as the average nonslaveholding southern farmer. Even in the relatively egalitarian farming country of the eastern North Central states, the upper 10 percent of landholders owned nearly 40 percent of taxable wealth. The national centers of inequality, however, were the growing urban regions from Boston to New Orleans. Although much statistical research remains to be done, it is clear that between 1820 and 1860 the big cities led the nation toward the increasing dominance of the very rich. By 1860, according to

one estimate, Philadelphia's richest 1 percent of population owned half the city's wealth; the lower 80 percent of the city's population had to be content with 3 percent of the wealth. According to a relatively modest estimate, the richest 5 percent of American families in 1860 received between 25 and 35 percent of the national income. While these figures indicate an inequality far greater than that estimated for modern America, they are roughly comparable to the inequalities in northern Europe in the late nineteenth century.

This conclusion would not be startling if America's pre–Civil War decades had not been claimed and almost universally accepted as "the age of the common man." American politicians and journalists eagerly expanded on the theme "equality of condition," supposedly confirmed by the observations of Alexis de Tocqueville and other European travelers. On closer inspection, however, Tocqueville and other travelers claimed only that American fortunes were "scanty" compared with fortunes in Europe; that in America "most of the rich men were formerly poor"; and that in America "any man's son may become the equal of any other man's son." In other words, American inequalities were thought to be temporary and to enhance the incentives of a race to success in which all were free to compete.

This belief in America's unique fluidity was especially reassuring by 1850, when European industrialism had produced undeniable evidence of misery, class conflict, and seething revolution. By that date American leaders could not hide their alarm over similar contrasts of wealth and squalor, particularly when the urban poor congregated in slums beyond the reach of traditional religious and social discipline. Yet affluent Americans persuaded themselves that the poor were free to climb the ladder of success, and that the wealthiest citizens were, in the words of Senator Henry Clay, "enterprising self-made men, who have whatever wealth they possess by patient and diligent labor."

In truth, however, the fortunes of John Jacob Astor and other leading American families compared favorably with the fortunes of the richest Europeans. Notwithstanding a few astonishing examples of rags-to-riches achievement, the great majority of America's rich and successful men had benefited from inherited wealth, an affluent childhood, or a prestigious family tradition. Between 1820 and 1860 there was a marked persistence of family wealth; in effect, the rich grew richer. In the cities, at least, they constituted an elite that became increasingly segregated by exclusive clubs, high social life, intermarriage, foreign travel, and business alliances.

At the other end of the spectrum was the mass of unskilled day laborers, who took what temporary jobs they could find and whose wages, even if regular, could not possibly support a family unless supplemented by the income of wives and children. No one knows the size of this unskilled, propertyless population, which drifted in and out of mill towns, flocked to the construction sites of canals and railroads, and gravitated to urban slums. In the 1840s and 1850s the largest cities attracted the chronic failures and castoffs who had no other place to turn. They jammed themselves into the attics and dank, windowless basements of Boston's Half Moon Place, where as many as one hundred people might share the same overflowing privy; or into New York's notorious Old Brewery, a noxious tenement that supposedly housed over a thousand beggars, pickpockets, whores, robbers, alcoholics, and starving children. In contrast to mid-nineteenth-century England, the relatively unstructured society of America provided very few public agencies that could enforce minimal standards of health, welfare, and safety.

Social Mobility. The extremes of wealth and poverty tell little about the amount of upward movement from one class to another. Thus far, however, the available evidence indicates that the odds were heavily against an unskilled laborer's acquiring a higher occupational status. The overwhelming majority of unskilled workers remained unskilled workers. It is true that in the 1850s many of the sons of unskilled workers moved into semiskilled factory jobs. But this generational advance was almost always limited to the next rung on the ladder. It was extremely rare for the children of manual workers, even skilled manual workers, to rise to the levels of clerical, managerial, or professional employment.

Despite growing signs in the pre–Civil War decades of semipermanent boundaries between occupational groups, there were remarkably few expressions of class consciousness or class interest. Historians have sometimes been misled by the labor rhetoric of the Jacksonian period, a time when the rich felt it necessary to prove their humble origins and when everybody who could do so laid claim to the proud title of "workingman." The labor leaders of the era were typically artisan proprietors and small businessmen intent on fixing prices and reducing the hazards of interregional competition. This is not to deny the importance of immigrant British artisans who had been displaced by the British factory system, who reinforced the preindustrial craft traditions in the United States, and who were schooled in the techniques of secret organization and industrial warfare. Nor can one deny the courage of union organizers who faced conspiracy trials in the 1820s and 30s, who saw their gains wiped out by the depression of 1837–42, and who finally formed city federations of craft unions and national trades unions in the 1850s. Yet the great strikes for higher wages and for the ten-hour day were staged by skilled printers, typographers, hatters, tailors, and other artisans. Employers, who were mostly supported by the courts and who benefited from fresh supplies of cheap immigrant labor, had little difficulty in breaking strikes. Although the Massachusetts Supreme Court led the way, in *Commonwealth* v. *Hunt* (1842), in ruling that trade unions were not in themselves conspiracies in restraint of trade, in 1860 only 0.1 percent of the American labor force was organized.

Even by the 1840s America's relative freedom from class consciousness and class conflict evoked considerable comment. According to Karl Marx and other European observers, the explanation could be found in the fresh lands of the American frontier, which provided an outlet for surplus population. In America, George Henry Evans's National Reform Association referred to the West as a "safety valve" that could and should provide an escape for workers whose opportunities were limited in the East. Evans contended in the 1840s that the nation owned enough land in the West to guarantee every family a farm. In the 1850s Horace Greeley, editor of the enormously influential New York *Tribune*, popularized the Republican party's slogan, "Vote yourself a farm." More than a generation later, the historian Frederick Jackson Turner and his followers evolved a detailed historical theory that pictured the frontier as both a safety valve for the pressures of the industrializing East and a wellspring of rejuvenating opportunity.

The theory, in its simplest and crudest form, has been thoroughly demolished. The eastern laborer, earning a dollar a day or less, could not afford to travel to the frontier and borrow funds for a farm and tools, even if he possessed the skills for western farming. The evidence shows that western land sales lagged in hard times, when a safety valve would be most needed, and increased when prosperity drove up the prices of wheat and cotton. Except for a few cooperative settlement associations and a few hundred wage earners sent by antislavery groups to settle Kansas, there are no records to show that industrial workers were transformed into frontier farmers.

On the other hand, the westward surge of millions of Americans intensified and dramatized the central fact of American life: physical mobility. Wages in the Northeast might well have been lower if the farmers, shopkeepers, artisans, and small businessmen who did go West had stayed put. Some of these aspiring adventurers might have been forced to seek factory employment. Some might have become America's counterparts to Europe's labor organizers. Ironically, since young males predominated in the migration away from industrial New England, an increasing number of women had no prospect for marriage and thus became part of a permanent industrial labor force. These women found themselves living permanently on the low wages from jobs they had taken while awaiting marriage.

Intense geographic mobility reinforced the myth of America's boundlessness, of America's infinite promise. By 1850 one-quarter of the entire population born in New England had moved to other states. The South Atlantic states experienced a no less striking westward drain of whites and of black slaves. In each decade the northern cities, towns, and factories witnessed an extraordinary inflow and outflow of population. Although few of these mobile Americans had a chance to acquire farms, they moved because they had hope of finding it better someplace else. And the hope may have been more significant than the reality they found. For unskilled laborers the reality was often grim, but the factories and towns they left behind had no need to worry about their accumulating grievances. The more fortunate and competitive movers could not doubt that Illinois was preferable to Ohio, or that New York City offered

VICTUALLERS IN PHILADELPHIA
Victuallers were licensed suppliers of food, drink, and provisions. This parade of Philadelphia victuallers was typical of the ceremonial processions of various trades and crafts, proud of their ancient emblems and symbols of public service, but concerned, even by the 1820s, over economic changes which threatened their distinctive identity. *(Courtesy, The Historical Society of Pennsylvania)*

more opportunities than the rocky hillsides of Vermont.

It was obvious that the condition of most white Americans, except for the floating population of impoverished laborers, was improving. Even the lowliest Irish laborers in a factory town like Newburyport, Massachusetts, found that they could accumulate property if they stuck to their jobs for a decade or more. To maintain a savings account or eventually to buy a house required discipline, frugality, and multiple income from family members at the expense of education and leisure. The Irish put a greater premium on home ownership than on education or occupational achievement. The Jews, on the other hand, tended to make every sacrifice for their children's education. The gains, particularly for the families of manual workers, were extremely limited. But these gains engendered pride in achieving what others had not achieved, and were sufficient to prevent even a permanent working class from becoming a permanent and propertyless proletariat.

The incessant turnover of population, the lack of physical roots, also gave force to the ideology of an open and boundless society—an ideology repeatedly stressed by newspapers, sermons, and political speeches. Who could tell what had become of all one's former neighbors and fellow workers? No doubt some had hit it rich. The mystery of everyone's past made it believable that most men's positions had been won according to talent and performance—that in America, where the only limits were individual will and ability, most men got what they were worth. If in time a manual worker could finally boast of a savings account of $300, of owning the roof over his head, or of a son who had moved up to the next rung on the ladder, why should he doubt the common claim, "This is a country of self-made men," where most of the rich had once been poor?

SUGGESTED READINGS

For informative surveys and detailed bibliographies, see George Dangerfield, *The Awakening of American Nationalism, 1815–1828* (1965); Glyndon G. Van Deusen, *The Jacksonian Era* (1959); Edward Pessen, *Jacksonian America: Society, Personality, and Politics* (1969); and Russel B. Nye, *Society and Culture in America, 1830–1860* (1974). Louis Hartz, *The Liberal Tradition in America* (1955), presents a brilliant and provocative interpretation of America's divergence from Old World norms. Hartz, like most interpreters of the period, draws heavily on Alexis de Tocqueville's classic work, *Democracy in America*, of which there are many editions. Daniel J. Boorstin's *The Americans: The National Experience* (1965), also emphasizes America's uniqueness. The period is illuminated in different ways by Yehoshua Arieli, *Individualism and Nationalism in American Ideology* (1964); Rowland Berthoff, *An Unsettled People: Social Order and Disorder in American History* (1971); and Fred Somkin, *Unquiet Eagle: Memory and Desire in the Idea of American Freedom, 1815–1860* (1967). An anthology of primary source material, accompanied by extensive commentary, is David B. Davis, ed., *Antebellum American Culture: An Interpretive Anthology* (1979).

Population growth is analyzed by J. Potter, "The Growth of Population in America, 1700–1860," in *Population and History...*, eds. D. V. Glass and D. E. C. Eversley (1965); and Richard A. Easterlin, *Population, Labor Force, and Long Swings in Economic Growth: The American Experience* (1968). Maldwyn A. Jones, *American Immigration* (1960), is a useful introduction to the subject; it should be supplemented by Marcus L. Hansen, *The Atlantic Migration, 1607–1860* (1940); Oscar Handlin, *Boston's Immigrants* (1959); Charlotte Erickson, *Invisible Immigrants*; Robert Ernst, *Immigrant Life in New York City, 1825–1863* (1949); Kathleen N. Conzen, *Immigrant Milwaukee, 1836–1860* (1977); and Carl Wittke, *The Irish in America* (1956). For urbanization, see Sam Bass Warner, Jr., *The Urban Wilderness* (1972); Richard C. Wade, *The Urban Frontier* (1964); and Paul Boyer, *Urban Masses and Moral Order in America, 1820–1920* (1978).

The best introduction to current views of economic growth can be found in W. Elliot Brownlee, *Dynamics of Ascent* (1974), and Stuart Bruchey, *Growth of the Modern American Economy* (1975). For a fascinating discussion of the economic thought of the pre–Civil War period, see Joseph Dorfman, *The Economic Mind in American Civilization*. Vol. 2 (3 vols., 1946–49).

The best introduction to Indian removal is Wilcomb E. Washburn, *The Indian in America* (1975). Francis P. Prucha, *American Indian Policy in the Formative Years* (1962), is sympathetic to government policy-makers. Ronald N. Satz, *American Indian Policy in the Jacksonian Era* (1975), provides an informative account of the subsequent period. The most recent and comprehensive study of the so-called civilized tribes is Charles Hudson, *The Southeastern Indians* (1976); for the Far West, see Sherburne F. Cook, *The Conflict between the California and White Civilization* (1976). An outstanding work which corrects the mythology regarding the relation between Indians and western pioneers is John Unruh, *The Plains Across: The Overland Emigrants and the Trans-Mississippi West* (1979). There are three valuable related works in intellectual history: Roy H. Pearce, *The Savages of America* (1965); Richard Slotkin, *Regeneration through Violence: The Mythology of the American Frontier, 1600–1860* (1973); and Roderick Nash, *Wilderness in the American Mind* (1967).

Ray A. Billington, *Westward Expansion* (1974), presents an excellent survey of western history as well as a comprehensive bibliography. The fullest histories of agriculture are Percy W. Bidwell and John I. Falconer, *History of Agriculture in the Northern United States, 1620–1860* (1925), and Lewis C. Gray, *History of Agriculture in the Southern United States to 1860* (2 vols., 1933). A briefer and outstanding survey is Paul W. Gates, *The Farmer's Age: Agriculture, 1815–1860* (1960), which can be supplemented by Clarence H. Danhof, *Change in Agriculture in the Northern United States, 1820–1870* (1969).

The classic study of transportation is George R. Taylor, *The Transportation Revolution, 1815–1860* (1951). A monumental work, confined to New England, is Edward Kirkland, *Men, Cities, and Transportation* (2 vols., 1948). For canals, see Harry N. Scheiber, *Ohio Canal Era* (1969), and R. E. Shaw, *Erie Water West* (1966).

Eugene D. Genovese, *Roll, Jordan, Roll* (1974), is a monumental study of Negro slavery in the South. Herbert G. Gutman, *The Black Family in Slavery and Freedom, 1750–1925* (1976), is no less impressive and innovative. For a briefer and illuminating discussion of the slaves' society, based mainly on slave narratives, see John W. Blassingame, *The Slave Community* (rev. ed., 1979). Two rich collections of source material are Willie Lee Rose, ed., *A Documentary History of Slavery in North America* (1976); and John W. Blassingame, ed., *Slave Testimony* (1977). As an overall survey of slavery as an institution Kenneth Stampp's *The Peculiar Institution* (1956) has not been superseded.

A highly controversial work on the economics of Negro slavery is Robert W. Fogel and Stanley L. Engerman, *Time on the Cross: The Economics of American Negro Slavery* (1974). For important criticisms of this work, as well as for new information, see Paul A. David *et al.*, *Reckoning with Slavery* (1976), and Herbert G. Gutman, *Slavery and the Numbers Game* (1975). An excellent survey of the more traditional literature is Harold D. Woodman, ed., *Slavery and the Southern Economy* (1966). For the use of slaves in nonagricultural employment, see Robert S. Starobin, *Industrial Slavery in the Old South* (1970). The synthesis of African and Christian religious forms is carefully studied in Albert J. Raboteau, *Slave Religion: The "Invisible Institution" in the Antebellum South* (1978). A brilliant and comprehensive study of black folklore and culture is Lawrence W. Levine, *Black Culture and Black Consciousness: Afro-American Folk Thought from Slavery to Freedom* (1977).

A pioneering study of social and economic mobility is Stephan Thernstrom, *Poverty and Progress* (1964). For disparities in the distribution of wealth and income, see Edward Pessen, *Riches, Class, and Power before the Civil War* (1973), and Lee Soltow, "Economic Inequality in the United States in the Period from 1790 to 1860," *Journal of Economic History*, 31 (December 1971), 822–839. The discovery of poverty is analyzed in Robert H. Bremner, *From the Depths* (1956), and Raymond A. Mohl, *Poverty in New York, 1783–1825* (1971). On working-class culture, the best guides are Alan Dawley, *Class and Community: The Industrial Revolution in Lynn* (1977); James Henretta, "Families and Farms: Mentalité in Pre-Industrial America," *Wm. and Mary Q.*, 3d. ser., vol. 35 (1978); Bruce Laurie, *The Peoples of Philadelphia* (1973); Paul Faler, "Cultural Aspects of the Industrial Revolution: Lynn, Massachusetts, Shoemakers and Industrial Morality, 1826–1860," *Labor History*, 15 (Winter 1974); Herbert G. Gutman, *Work, Culture, and Society in Industrializing America* (1976); Howard M. Gitelman, *Workingmen of Waltham* (1974); Peter R. Knights, *The Plain People of Boston* (1971); and Norman Ware, *The Industrial Worker, 1840–1860* (1959). For labor movements and protests, see David Montgomery, "Workers' Control of Machine Production in the Nineteenth Century," *Labor History*, 17 (1976); David Montgomery, "The Shuttle and the Cross: Weavers and Artisans in the Kensington Riots of 1844," *Journal of Social History* (Summer 1972); Joseph Rayback, *A History of American Labor* (1966); Walter Hugins, *Jacksonian Democracy and the Working Class* (1960). Two good studies of the ideology of the self-made man, Irvin G. Wyllie, *The Self-Made Man in America* (1954), and John G. Cawelti, *Apostles of the Self-Made Man* (1965), should be supplemented by Daniel T. Rodgers, *The Work Ethic in Industrial America, 1850–1920* (1978). Though dealing with a later period, Richard Weiss, *The American Myth of Success* (1969), also sheds light on the earlier history of the subject.

CHAPTER 13

Politics: Cohesion and Division

*T*he generation that came to maturity in the early nineteenth century carried a unique burden. As "children of the Founding Fathers," they could not achieve immortal fame by winning independence from British tyranny. Instead, their assigned mission was vigilant preservation—the preservation of what the famous lawyer Rufus Choate called the "beautiful house of our fathers" against divisive ambition, corruption, and arbitrary power.

For a time it seemed that Liberty and Union could be preserved by patriotic rhetoric honoring hallowed figures like Thomas Jefferson and John Adams (who both died on July 4, 1826, exactly fifty years after the adoption of the Declaration of Independence) and by electing "Virginia Dynasty" presidents. The last in that succession, James Monroe, still appeared in public dressed in his Revolutionary War uniform. The collapse of the Federalist party, after the War of 1812, fostered the illusion of an "Era of Good Feelings" in which a single national party would guarantee republican simplicity, order, and self-restraint. President Monroe, in his second inaugural address (1821), invoked the image of harmony. The American people, he affirmed, constituted "one great family with a common interest." Four years later President John Quincy Adams, also a Republican, voiced similar sentiments and happily observed that "the baneful weed of party strife" had been uprooted. Most Americans still associated political parties with the self-serving, aristocratic factions that had dominated British politics. In a republican nation, as in a republican family, no room could be allowed for selfish alliances representing separate interests.

This ideal of family unity was, however, far removed from social and economic realities. Between 1819 and 1821 Congress faced the most dangerous crisis it had yet experienced when northern and southern representatives deadlocked over the admission of Missouri as a new slave state. Simultaneously, the financial panic of 1819, followed by a severe depression, aroused widespread hostility toward banking corporations and other groups that had used political influence to gain economic privilege. Economic recovery and expansion only intensified demands for equality of opportunity, as various competing classes, localities, and social groups became

GEORGE CALEB BINGHAM'S "VERDICT OF THE PEOPLE"
Politics became the Americans' major public ritual. Like religious revivals, political events provided the occasion for sociability and for emotional expression. But politics also evoked the excitement that springs from looking upon or touching the levers of power. *(Courtesy, The Boatman's National Bank of St. Louis)*

THE TWO-PARTY SYSTEM

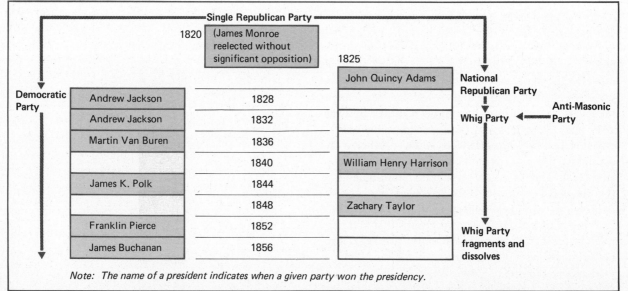

Democratic Party			National Republican Party / Whig Party
		1820 (James Monroe reelected without significant opposition)	1825
			John Quincy Adams
Andrew Jackson	1828		
Andrew Jackson	1832		Whig Party ◄ Anti-Masonic Party
Martin Van Buren	1836		
	1840		William Henry Harrison
James K. Polk	1844		
	1848		Zachary Taylor
Franklin Pierce	1852		
James Buchanan	1856		Whig Party fragments and dissolves

Single Republican Party

Note: The name of a president indicates when a given party won the presidency.

increasingly aware of the unequal effects of government policies concerning tariffs, banking and currency, and public land sales. By the mid-1820s it was becoming painfully clear that widening opportunities for some Americans meant constricting opportunities for others. Paradoxically, the post-Revolutionary generation found a way of containing the many factions that had arisen by *institutionalizing* division in the form of political parties. From the early 1830s to the early 1850s, this two-party system helped preserve national cohesion. The Democrats and the National Republicans—succeeded later by the Whigs—were national coalitions of sectional, class, economic, ethnic, and religious interests, held together by compromise and cooperation. To maximize votes, politicians had to find ways of arousing the apathetic on more than immediate local issues. The basic political style that emerged in antebellum America, in the South and West as well as in the North, centered on the portrayal of some self-serving, privileged interest that had secretly consolidated power and had begun to shut off equal access to the rewards of national growth. In an era of relative security from foreign dangers, politicians continued to portray their opponents as heirs of the British and Tories who were seeking to undermine American liberties and betray the heritage of the Founding Fathers. The Democrats and Whigs survived as national coalitions as long as they drew significant support from both the slaveholding and nonslaveholding states. But when black slavery, the institution that most flagrantly subverted liberty and opportunity, was seriously questioned in a national forum, the unifying force of the parties was destroyed.

"A Fire Bell in the Night": The Missouri Compromise

From the time of the Continental Congress, American leaders had realized that a serious dispute over slavery could jeopardize their bold experiment in self-government. Beginning with the Constitutional Convention, the entire structure of national politics had been designed to prevent any faction from directly threatening southern slaveholders and thereby subverting common national interests. It is therefore not surprising that before 1819 slavery never became a central issue in national politics. But it was an issue that sat like an unactivated bomb in the minds of the foremost political leaders.

The agreement to keep the bomb unactivated rested on two unwritten understandings: the North would recognize the property rights of southern slaveholders and the South would recognize slavery as an evil that should be discouraged and eventually abolished whenever it became safe and practicable to do so. Changing circumstances, including the shifting balance of sectional power, forced repeated challenges to these understandings. The challenges took the form of clashes in Congress, during which representatives from the Lower South threatened to dissolve the Union and even hinted at the possibility of civil war. On each occasion the resulting compromise strongly favored the South. This political process demonstrated the Americans' remarkable ability to make pragmatic adjustments in the interest of national stability. Yet these successful compromises depended on the dangerous assumption that southern threats of disunion would always be met by northern concessions.

The militancy of the Lower South's congressional leaders rested on a realistic estimate of the future. For a time the North could afford to make concessions because slavery seemed to endanger no vital northern interests. But after 1815, humanitarian causes had increasing appeal in the North and more and more Northerners expressed moral and patriotic misgivings over the westward expansion of slavery. Sooner or later, as Southerners like John Randolph predicted, such northern antislavery sentiments would become strong enough to create new sectional parties. Even by 1820, as a result of rapid population growth in the North, the major slaveholding states held only 42 percent of the seats in the House of Representatives. Only the Senate could provide a firm bulwark against potential northern encroachments, and the key to the Senate was new slave states. In the Senate, following the admission of Mississippi and Alabama (1817, 1819), eleven slave states balanced eleven free states.

Sectional Conflict.   The Missouri crisis erupted in February 1819, when the House was considering a bill that would enable the people of Missouri to draft a constitution and be admitted as a slave state. Slaves constituted nearly one-sixth of the territory's population. James Tallmadge, Jr., a New York Jeffersonian Republican, offered an amendment that prohibited the further introduction of slaves into Missouri and provided for the emancipation, at age twenty-five, of all children of slaves born after Missouri's admission as a state. After a prolonged and often violent debate, the House approved Tallmadge's amendment by an ominously sectional vote. The Senate, after equally violent debates, passed a Missouri statehood bill without any restrictions on slavery. The issue seemed hopelessly deadlocked.

Virginia now took the lead in militancy, trying to arouse a generally apathetic South to a common peril. "This momentous question," Jefferson announced from Monticello, where he had retired, "like a fire bell in the night, awakened and filled me with terror." Along with Madison and other Virginia statesmen, Jefferson was convinced that the attempt to exclude slavery from Missouri was part of a Federalist conspiracy to create a sectional party and destroy the Union.

The Missouri crisis was aggravated by a sense that understandings had been broken, veils torn off, and true and threatening motives exposed. The congressional debates rekindled the most divisive issues that had supposedly been settled in the Constitutional Convention, and thus raised the hypothetical question of disunion. This reenactment of 1787 was underscored by the prominence in the congressional debates of two of the Convention's surviving antagonists —Charles Pinckney of South Carolina, who now insisted that Congress had no power to exclude slavery from even the unsettled territories; and Rufus King of New York, the alleged leader of the Federalist conspiracy, who now announced that any laws upholding slavery were "absolutely void, because [they are] contrary to the law of nature, which is the law of God."

It was a new generation of Northerners, however, who had to reaffirm or reject the kinds of compro-mises over slavery that had created the original Union. Like the Founders, the northern majority in Congress could do nothing about slavery in the existing states. But there had been an understood national policy, they believed, enshrined in the Northwest Ordinance, committing the government to restrict slavery in every feasible way. This understanding had seemingly been confirmed by southern avowals that slavery was an evil bequeathed by the past. The North had accepted the original slave states' expectations that migrating slaveholders would not be barred from bringing their most valuable property into the territories south of the Ohio River and east of the Mississippi. But Missouri occupied the same latitudes as Illinois, Indiana, and Ohio (as well as Kentucky and Virginia). To allow slavery to become legally entrenched in Missouri might thus encourage its spread throughout the entire West, to the detriment of free labor and industry. Southerners had long argued, however illogically, that if slavery were diffused over a large geographical area, it would weaken as an institution and the likelihood of slave insurrections would diminish. In 1820 Daniel Raymond, a prominent political economist, gave the obvious reply: "Diffusion is about as effectual a remedy for slavery as it would be for the smallpox, or the plague."

Southerners were particularly alarmed by the argument of northern congressmen that the constitutional guarantee to every state of "a Republican Form of Government" meant that Missouri could not be admitted as a slave state. The argument implied that Virginia and other southern states fell short of "a Republican Form of Government" and would therefore not be admissible to a new Union. If this were true, the southern states would be reduced to a second-class status. If they accepted the northern definition of a republican form of government, they had no choice but to take steps toward abolishing slavery or to face, like colonies, the punitive measures of an imperial authority.

The Terms of Compromise.   Henry Clay, the Speaker of the House of Representatives, by exerting all the powers of his office and of his magnetic personality, finally achieved a compromise. A small

The Missouri Compromise, 1820-1821

Admitted as a free state in 1820 — MAINE

OREGON COUNTRY
Occupied jointly by Great Britain and U.S.

UNORGANIZED TERRITORY
Made free by the Missouri Compromise 1820

SPANISH POSSESSIONS

MICHIGAN TERR.

MISSOURI
Admitted as slave state 1821

36°30' — Line of the Missouri Compromise

ARKANSAS TERR.

VT. N.H. N.Y. MASS. R.I. CONN.
PA. N.J.
OHIO MD. DEL.
ILL. IND. VA.
KY.
TENN. N.C.
S.C.
MISS. ALA. GA.
LA.
FLORIDA TERR.

Free States and Territories   Slave States and Territories

minority of northern congressmen agreed to drop the antislavery provision for Missouri, while a small minority of Southerners agreed that slavery should be excluded from the remaining and unsettled portions of the Louisiana Purchase north of latitude 3°30', the same latitude as the southern border of Missouri. In effect, this measure limited to Arkansas and the future territory of Oklahoma any further expansion of slavery within the Louisiana Purchase. Given the sectional balance of power, the swing vote favoring these concessions was sufficient to carry the compromise. The way was now opened for admitting Maine as a free state, since the Senate had refused to accept Maine's statehood until the House had abandoned efforts to restrict slavery in Missouri.

The press and legislatures of the North generally interpreted the Missouri Compromise as a victory for the South. A new hope arose that public pressure could force Missouri to adopt a constitution providing for gradual emancipation. But the defiant Missourians drafted a constitution that prohibited the state legislature from emancipating slaves without the consent of their owners and that barred free blacks and mu-

lattoes from entering the state. Since free blacks had been recognized as citizens by some of the eastern states, this second provision violated the constitutional guarantee that "the Citizens of each State shall be entitled to all Privileges and Immunities of Citizens in the several States." Northern congressmen now stood firm in rejecting the Missouri constitution and in effect the entire compromise. Eventually, in 1821, Clay's skillful manipulation of committees produced a second compromise prohibiting Missouri from discriminating against citizens of other states—an abstract resolution that still left citizenship undefined. The country applauded Clay for saving the Union.

But the Union would never be the same. In southern eyes the uninhibited debates on slavery had opened a Pandora's box of dangers. The free blacks of Washington had packed the galleries of the House and had listened intently to antislavery speeches. In 1822, during the trial of the conspirators associated with Denmark Vesey, a Charleston slave testified that Vesey had shown him an antislavery speech delivered by Rufus King, "the black man's friend." The link between the Missouri debates and a sizable slave conspiracy stunned South Carolina, confirming its worst fears. The cumulative effect was twofold: to unite all whites in the suppression of dangerous discussion, and to strengthen the hand of states' rights extremists and of the defenders of slavery as a positive good.

The End of Republican Unity

The Missouri crisis alerted politicians to the perils of sectional division. The North's unexpected outrage over the admission of a new slave state convinced many Southerners that they needed to cultivate rising northern leaders like Martin Van Buren, whose faction of young "Bucktails" had captured control of the New York Republican party by 1820. Van Buren, whose shrewdness, ambition, and personal charm made up for his lack of family prestige and connections, viewed the clamor over slavery as evidence of a dangerous breakdown in party loyalty. New national organizations were needed that could prevent sectional conflict. Party distinctions, he said, were infinitely safer than geographic ones. If party distinctions were suppressed, "geographical differences founded on local instincts or what is worse, prejudices between free and slaveholding states" would inevitably take their place.

The Van Buren faction also stated a new conception of political parties as agencies of the people. When the Bucktails were attacked by their opponents as the "Albany Regency," a label suggesting the oppressive British regency of the Prince of Wales (1811–20), they replied with a strong defense of political parties, a defense that later Democrats and Whigs would echo. In America, they claimed, political parties drew their power from the people instead of from kings or aristocratic cliques; therefore, the American people could safely extend their loyalty to parties. American parties, far from being self-serving, required a selfless submission to the will of the organization. This respect for party discipline was later summed up by a prominent Whig who declared that he "would vote for a dog, if he was the candidate of my party." In theory, the excesses of one party would inevitably be exposed by the other party, and public opinion would decide between them. Responsiveness to the people would thus be ensured as each party strove to win the largest possible mandate from the people.

Van Buren's appeal for disciplined national parties came at an opportune time. As early as 1821 it was evident that the Virginia Dynasty of presidents would end in 1825 with Monroe's second term. The Republicans, no longer confronted by Federalist opponents, were splintering into personal and sectional factions. One group responded to the vibrant nationalism of Henry Clay's "American System"—a policy for economic expansion based on protective tariffs, a national bank, and federal aid for internal improvements. Other "Old Republicans," including Van Buren, viewed government intervention in the economy as a revival of the kinds of alliances between political power and special privilege that had corrupted Britain. By the early 1820s many Americans, especially in the South and West, had ample grounds for fearing that a northeastern elite would gain economic control of the nation's banks and system of credit.

Election of 1824. Monroe's second administration was dominated by political maneuvering to determine who would be his successor. Three of the leading contenders—William H. Crawford, John Quincy Adams, and John C. Calhoun—were nationally distinguished members of Monroe's cabinet. Crawford, secretary of the treasury during several administrations, a Georgian born in Virginia, would be heavily favored in any congressional party caucus. He had won prestige as America's minister to France during the War of 1812 and as an advocate of state rights and limited federal power, he was supported by the aged Thomas Jefferson and other influential Virginians. Van Buren led the Crawford forces in Congress. But the skeleton congressional caucus that nominated Crawford carried little weight, and an incapacitating illness further diminished his chances.

The other leading candidates bypassed the established procedure of nomination by congressional party caucus and sought support from state legisla-

HENRY CLAY
Henry Clay's campaign posters stressed national economic growth and public welfare, goals to be directly fostered by protective tariffs and a national bank. *(Library of Congress)*

native New England but would always be aloof from the rough-and-tumble electioneering of the South and West. John C. Calhoun, the secretary of war, had little support outside his native South Carolina. A graduate of Yale and a product of America's first small law school, in Connecticut, Calhoun was one of the few political leaders of his time who could be described as an "intellectual." Calhoun withdrew from the presidential race before the election, assuming that his almost certain choice as vice-president would help him win the highest office in 1828. Henry Clay, the popular "Harry of the West," had won national prestige as a parliamentarian and engineer of compromise in the House of Representatives. It was expected that if no candidate should win the electoral majority, the House would elect Clay president. But despite his appeal in Kentucky and other western states, Clay ran fourth in electoral votes and was therefore excluded by the Twelfth Amendment from further consideration.

The fifth candidate, Andrew Jackson, entered the contest unexpectedly and at a late stage. Unlike the other candidates, he had taken no clear stand on the controversial issues of the day, and his brief terms in the House and Senate had been undistinguished. Jackson's national fame arose from his victory over the British at the Battle of New Orleans in the War of 1812, and from his unswerving efforts to clear the West of Indians, thus promising limitless opportunity for white Americans. But "Old Hickory" was a good bit more than a military hero and an Indian fighter. Born on the Carolina frontier and orphaned at age fourteen, Jackson had studied law and had finally emigrated to Nashville, Tennessee, where he became attached by marriage and business connections to the local network of leading families. He prospered as an attorney, land speculator, and planter, and became the owner of over one hundred slaves. The Tennessee leaders who originally promoted Jackson for the presidency did not take his candidacy seriously, hoping only to use his popularity for their own local purposes. In 1823 Jackson's backers were astonished when the movement caught fire in Pennsylvania and other states. The Old Hero turned out to be an astute politician, who perfectly gauged the national temper

tures. Three of the remaining aspirants were closely associated with the economic nationalism that had alienated the Old Republicans. John Quincy Adams, the secretary of state and the nation's most experienced diplomat, could expect solid support from his and who, once launched on the road to the presidency, skillfully took charge of his own campaign.

In the election of 1824 Jackson won a plurality of both the popular and the electoral votes, and could therefore legitimately claim to be the choice of the people. But because no candidate had won an electoral majority, the responsibility of electing a president fell to the House of Representatives. There, Clay threw his decisive support behind Adams, who was elected president and who soon appointed Clay secretary of state. This so-called corrupt bargain deeply embittered Calhoun, who was already beginning to defect from his former colleagues' economic nationalism. It also infuriated Jackson, who almost immediately launched a campaign to unseat Adams in 1828.

John Quincy Adams as President. This final collapse of Republican unity proved to be a disaster for Adams's presidency. Adams inaugurated his administration by proposing a sweeping program of federal support for internal improvements, science, education, and the arts. For example, he hoped that Congress would subsidize western explorations and an astronomical observatory. He soon discovered, however, that he lacked the mandate and the power for even the simple tasks of government. One of the most intelligent and farseeing presidents, Adams was also one of the least successful. Unfairly accused of being a monarchist with arrogant contempt for the people, he had the misfortune of inheriting the presidency when it had fallen into decay. His own experience with the realities of American political life helped to make him the unmourned victim, in 1828, of the first modern presidential contest.

Jackson's Rise to Power

Andrew Jackson, the leader of the rising Democratic coalition, precisely fitted the need for a popular national political leader. His stately bearing and natural dignity befitted one of "nature's noblemen," someone who had risen to greatness without benefit of family, formal education, or subservience to any faction. Jackson's promoters disseminated the roman-

J. Q. ADAMS, BY THOMAS GIMBREDE
John Quincy Adams personified the intellectual as statesman. A man of learning and of wide diplomatic experience, he was more at home in the courts and capitals of Europe than in the caucuses and public forums of American politics. *(National Portrait Gallery, Smithsonian Institution, Washington, D.C.)*

tic mythology by every conceivable means: ballads, broadsides, barbecues, liberty pole-raisings, local committees, and militia companies. In contrast to the office-grubbing politicians and to the austere, highly cultivated John Quincy Adams, here was a frontiersman, a truly self-made man, a soldier of iron will who personified the will of the people, a man without artifice or pretension who moved decisively in the light of simple moral truths. The Jackson image, in short, was an image of reassuring stability in the face of bewildering social and economic change.

Jackson also fitted the need for a leader who

comprehended the new meaning of party politics. Against the Adams-Clay alliance he molded a coalition that included among other groups the followers of Calhoun (who became his running mate in 1828), Virginia's Old Republicans, influential Westerners who had become disillusioned with Clay, former Federalists who had lost office in New Jersey, and Van Buren's powerful Albany Regency. This new Democratic party appealed to many urban workers and immigrants, to frontier expansionists and Indian haters, to many southern planters, and to various northeastern editors, bankers, and manufacturers who built local Democratic machines as the means of gaining or preserving power.

The "Tariff of Abominations."

Jackson's state organizers, looking ahead to 1828, bypassed the local ruling gentry and concentrated for the first time on mobilizing the necessary popular vote to capture the full electoral vote of critical states. Because the new coalition contained Pennsylvanians who clamored for higher tariffs and South Carolinians who detested tariffs, keeping unity required delicate manipulation. In 1828 Jackson's leaders in Congress helped to pass the so-called Tariff of Abominations, an opportunistic bill which made arbitrary concessions to various groups demanding protection. They assumed that southern support for Jackson was secure, that the new duties on raw materials would win votes from northern and western protectionists, and that the most objectionable provisions could be blamed on the Adams administration. The subsequent outrage in the South suggested that Jackson as president could no longer get by with vague statements favoring a "judicious" tariff. Yet Southerners knew that a Jackson-Calhoun alliance was far more promising than the economic nationalism of Adams and Clay, who were now known as National Republicans.

The Election of 1828.

In a general sense, the election of 1828 affirmed the people's rejection of policies that seemed to encourage special privilege, except for the privilege of owning slaves and counting three-fifths of the slave population for purposes of representation. In the South, Jackson's 200,000 supporters,

accounting for 73 percent of that section's vote, gave him 105 electoral votes; in the North, where he won only slightly more than half the popular vote, his 400,000 supporters gave him only 73 electoral votes. The election also proved the effectiveness of campaign organization and of the promotional techniques that Jackson's managers, particularly Van Buren, had perfected.

Once in power, the Democrats soon adopted two instruments that solidified popular support for party rule. The first was a system of patronage, or "spoils," which continued practices begun during previous administrations and tried to give them legitimacy. Jackson ardently defended the theory that most public offices required no special abilities or experience, that they should frequently rotate among loyal deserving party workers, and that party rule should prevent the establishment of a permanent and parasitic class of civil servants. In fact, however, he actually removed no more than one-fifth of the surviving federal officeholders.

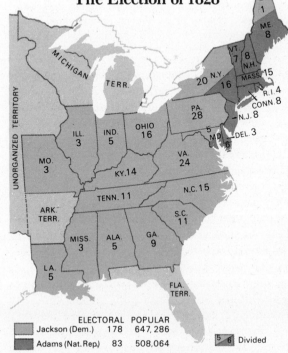

The Election of 1828

	ELECTORAL	POPULAR
Jackson (Dem.)	178	647,286
Adams (Nat. Rep.)	83	508,064

5 6 Divided

JACKSON TICKET

Honor and gratitude to the man who has filled the measure of his country's glory—*Jefferson*

FOR THE ASSEMBLY
GEORGE H. STEUART,
JOHN V. L. McMAHON.

JACKSON POSTER, 1828
In the presidential campaign of 1828, Andrew Jackson appeared as a symbol of patriotism, military honor, and faithful preservation of the ideals of the Founding Fathers. *(Library of Congress)*

The second mechanism was the national party convention, which, like various Jacksonian measures, had earlier been initiated by anti-Jacksonian forces. As an alternative to nomination by legislative caucus, the "convention," by its name, suggested a return to fundamental law, to the direct voice of the people assembled in a constitution-framing body. Although party conventions could do no more than frame partisan platforms and nominate partisan candidates, they pretended to represent the true interests of the people. In theory, since they drew representatives from a broad spectrum of society, they were more democratic than legislative caucuses. In practice, they were more subject to manipulation by political machines. But like the partisan spoils system, the party convention symbolized the central appeal of Jackson's party. It promised to break the congealing crust of privilege and eliminate all institutional barriers to individual opportunity. It also provided the assurance of solidarity with a party headed by a man of the people, a man who magnified the idealized self-image of millions of Americans.

Certain principles and aspirations distinguished the Jacksonian Democrats from their National Republican (later Whig) opponents. Jackson had long given voice to the West's demand for territorial expansion as a way to ensure economic opportunity. As the first Westerner elected to the presidency, he symbolized a geographical shift in political power. Of course, not all Westerners supported Jackson. Those who understood that western economic expansion depended on access to eastern markets and on investment capital from the East and Europe favored federal aid for internal improvements, a program that Henry Clay championed. But though Jackson vetoed the Maysville Road Bill, which authorized funds to build a road in Kentucky, suggesting that federal support for internal improvements was unconstitutional, he did not lose the majority of western voters. Many Westerners had come to view federally supported internal improvements as sources of waste and corruption. Others learned that despite Jackson's pronouncements federal support for roads and canals continued to pour in from a Congress less concerned with constitutional theory than with constituents' needs. On the whole, the West cheered for Jackson because it had come to see itself as the repository of values that Jackson fought for: an agrarian society of independent farmers, committed to individual enterprise and local self-determination.

To say Jacksonian Democrats were advocates of laissez-faire is accurate but insufficient. They knew that on the local and state levels, economic opportunity hinged on political power. And Jackson was the most forceful and aggressive president since Washington. During preceding administrations the chief executive's powers had been siphoned off by cabinet rivals and a jealous Congress. With the aid of party discipline, Jackson soon exerted his dominance over Congress by an unprecedented use of vetoes and pocket vetoes (the refusal to sign a bill during the last ten days of a congressional session). Except for Van Buren, whom he chose as secretary of state,

ANDREW JACKSON
In this homey carving President Jackson appears as a gaunt, stern, rough-hewn man of the people, a democratized Washington. *(Museum of the City of New York)*

Jackson treated his cabinet in the manner of the army's commander in chief. Unlike his predecessors, Jackson escaped the coercion of disloyal and powerful cabinet members by relying on a group of informal advisers, the so-called Kitchen Cabinet, who could be trusted or dismissed at will.

The Threat of National Division: Tariffs, Nullification, and the Gag Rule

Protective Tariffs. Tariffs and fiscal policy were obvious testing grounds for defining the role of the federal government in national economic life. Because the economy was still more regional than national and because the national government had so few functions, the critical issues of the era grew out of the commitment to protective tariffs and a national bank that had resulted from the War of 1812. The Middle Atlantic states, the most vulnerable to competition from European manufactured goods, had long been the political stronghold of protectionism. During the 1820s, as New England's economy became increasingly dependent on the production of wool and on textile manufacturing, Daniel Webster and other New England leaders abandoned their traditional defense of free trade and portrayed protective tariffs as the key to economic growth and individual opportunity. Simultaneously, the Lower South became increasingly hostile to tariffs that threatened to raise the price of manufactured goods and to curtail foreign markets for rice and cotton. For a time the Democrats successfully arranged compromises among the various interests and regions represented in the party. In 1832, however, Congress passed a tariff bill that was unresponsive to the demands of the Lower South. South Carolina thereupon defied federal authority and sought to arouse the rest of the slaveholding South to the dangers of being victimized economically by the federal government. South Carolinians believed that acceptance of such dependence would reduce the state to the status of a colony and deprive it of any effective protection against antislavery ideas.

South Carolina's sudden threat of disunion severely tested the American political system, and it involved issues that went far beyond the protective tariff. In no other state had a planter aristocracy succeeded so well in commanding the allegiance of small farmers, both slaveholding and nonslaveholding, and in preventing the development of an effective two-party system. Despite continuing conflicts between the coastal and upcountry regions, there were few checks on state-rights extremists who were able to exploit fears of slave insurrection and anger over persisting agricultural depression, high consumer prices, and sagging prices for rice and cotton in foreign markets.

Moreover, of all the southern states South Carolina had the closest historical, geographical, and cultural ties with the British West Indies. Like those British colonies, South Carolina had a dense concentration of slaves, and its merchants and planters had continued to import African slaves until 1808, when the slave trade was prohibited by federal law. South Carolinians were acutely aware that in Britain a seemingly innocuous movement to end the slave trade had been transformed, by 1823, into a crusade for slave emancipation. And they knew that the West Indians, though still a powerful faction in Parliament, had found no way of countering commercial policies that had hastened their economic decline. The lesson was clear. The West Indian colonies had once been far richer and more valued than Canada or New England; in 1832 they faced possible devastation—a massive slave revolt broke out in Jamaica after Christmas 1831—and certain economic ruin.

Theory of Nullification. South Carolina could escape a similar fate, the state's leaders believed, only by reasserting state sovereignty and insisting on the strict limitation of national power. The tariff issue made an ideal testing ground for the defense of slavery without risking the explosive effects of debating the morality of slaveholding. Because the power to tax and regulate trade could also be used to undermine slavery, the two questions had been linked in the Constitutional Convention of 1787 and in the Missouri debates. Conversely, a state's power to nullify a tariff would be a guarantee not only against economic exploitation but also against direct or in-

JOHN C. CALHOUN, 1782–1850
(National Archives)

direct interference with slavery. Calhoun, in his anonymous *Exposition* (1828), refined the theoretical arguments that were being put forth by South Carolina's most militant leaders. According to Calhoun the ultimate appeal, in any dispute between federal and state interests, must be directed to a state convention, the same power that originally enabled the state to ratify the Constitution. Otherwise, a national majority, controlling the federal courts as well as Congress, would have unlimited power. The tyranny of the majority could be curbed only if each state retained the right to consent or to nullify, within its own jurisdiction, the national majority's decisions. Calhoun carefully distinguished nullification from secession. He looked for means by which states might exercise an authentic, though limited, sovereignty while remaining within the Union.

The nullification controversy was complicated by the shifting pressures of state, sectional, and national politics. Calhoun, the vice-president, hoped to succeed Jackson as president, and many South Carolinians still believed they could achieve their goals through the Democratic party. Calhoun did not divulge his authorship of the *Exposition* until 1831, when he had split with Jackson over various personal and political issues. When Jackson purged Calhoun's followers from his cabinet and administration, Van Buren became in effect the president's chosen successor. Nevertheless, Calhoun continued to aspire to the presidency. He believed nullification would be a means of satisfying South Carolina's "fire-eater" extremists and of establishing the Union on a more secure basis, while still preserving his own national following.

By 1832, however, South Carolina had become increasingly isolated from the rest of the South and had also failed to unite the West against an alleged northeastern conspiracy to discourage western settlement. Though many Southerners detested protective tariffs and maintained that states had a right to secede from the Union, southern legislatures turned a stony face to nullification. As a result, there was no regional convention of southern delegates that might have moderated South Carolina's suicidal course by reinforcing the hand of the South Carolina unionists who risked their lives and reputations in a violent and losing struggle with the extremists. In the fall of 1832 South Carolina held a state convention that directly challenged federal authority by making it unlawful after February 1, 1833, to collect tariff duties within the state.

South Carolina chose the wrong president to test. Andrew Jackson was a wealthy slaveholder but he was also a shrewd politician. Though his maturing views on tariffs and internal improvements were close to those of South Carolina's oligarchy, he had fought for the military supremacy of the United States, crushing British and Indian armies; had hanged English meddlers in Spanish Florida; and had ordered the execution of an unruly teenage soldier. He was probably the toughest of America's presidents. When South Carolina nullified the tariff of 1832, the old

general privately threatened to lead an invation of the state and to have Calhoun hanged. He sent reinforcements to the Federal forts in Charleston harbor, but publicly sought to avoid armed conflict by relying on civilian revenue agents to enforce the law and by warning that armed resistance would be punished as treason.

As in 1820, the crisis ended in a compromise which failed to resolve fundamental conflicts of interest and ideology. In an attempt to head off civil war, Henry Clay, assisted by Calhoun, secured the passing of a compromise bill that would gradually reduce tariff duties over a period of nine years. But this measure was accompanied by a "force bill," reaffirming the president's authority to use the army and navy when necessary, to enforce Federal laws. South Carolina's fire-eaters continued to call for armed resistance; the governor recruited a volunteer army. Early in 1833, however, the state convention repealed its earlier nullification of the tariff and, to save face, nullified the force bill. Jackson ignored this defiant gesture. He had already proscribed as unlawful and unconstitutional the claim that any state could annul the laws of the United States. In effect, he had told rebellious states that secession was their only escape, and that secession would be met with armed force.

"Gag Rules." The compromise did not allay South Carolina's suspicions and anxieties. The nullification controversy had failed to provide the assurance of constitutional safeguards against a hostile national majority. Southern extremists demanded ironclad guarantees that would permanently bar the abolitionists' "incendiary publications" from the mails and prevent Congress from receiving petitions calling for the abolition of slavery in the District of Columbia. In actuality, the Democratic party fulfilled these objectives in a less formal way. The Jackson and Van Buren administrations, dependent on the large Democratic vote in the South, encouraged federal postmasters to stop abolitionist literature at its point of origin. Despite continuing protest from northern Whigs, northern Democrats also provided southern congressmen of both parties with enough votes to maintain "gag rules" from 1836 to 1844, a procedure that automatically tabled abolitionist petitions in Congress and helped prevent explosive debates on the subject of slavery. Many Northerners were outraged by these infringements on civil and political liberties. But South Carolinians were also dissatisfied with pragmatic mechanisms for security that depended on the continuing support of the national Democratic party. Without further constitutional protections, they feared that a shift in northern opinion might induce Congress to withdraw all federal sanction and protection for slavery.

The Bank War, The Panic of 1837, and Political Realignments

The Bank War. Meanwhile, President Jackson had enhanced his national popularity by declaring "war" on the Second Bank of the United States (BUS). Jackson had long harbored a mistrust of banks in general, especially of the BUS. Van Buren, Senator Thomas Hart Benton of Missouri, Amos Kendall of the Kitchen Cabinet, and other key presidential advisers shared these sentiments. To understand their "hard-money" position, it is important to remember that the national government issued no "paper money" like that in circulation today. Payment for goods and services might be in gold or silver coin (specie) or, more likely, in paper notes issued by private commercial banks. The value of such paper currency fluctuated greatly. The hard-money Democrats realized that large commercial transactions could not be carried on with specie. But they believed that the common people, including small businessmen as well as farmers and wage earners, should not be saddled with the risk of being cheated by a speculative currency. They also knew that a policy favoring the greater circulation of gold and silver coin, which seemed magically endowed with some fixed and "natural" value, would win votes for the party.

To a large degree, however, the reserves and transfers of specie were controlled by the BUS. The BUS performed many of the functions of a truly national bank. Its own notes could be exchanged for specie, and they were accepted by the government

as legal payment for all debts to the United States. Because the BUS had large capital reserves and because it limited the issue of its own highly stable notes, it occupied a creditor position relative to the hundreds of state-chartered banks throughout the country. It served as a clearinghouse and regulatory agency for their money, refusing to accept notes that were not backed by sufficient reserves of specie. By promoting monetary stability, the BUS helped to improve the public reputation of banks in general and eased the difficulties of long-distance transfers of goods and credit. It also mobilized a national reserve of capital on which other banks could draw. Consequently most state banks favored congressional renewal of the BUS charter, which was scheduled to expire in 1836.

Opponents of the bank feared the concentration of so much economic power in a few hands and worried that the federal government had practically no control over the bank, although it provided one-fifth of the bank's capital. The bank's critics complained that, even under the expert presidency of Nicholas Biddle, this partly public institution was far more oriented to the interests of its private investors than to the interests of the general public. Senator Daniel Webster, the main lobbyist for rechartering the BUS, not only was the director of the Boston branch (the BUS headquarters was in Philadelphia), but relied heavily on Biddle for private loans and fees for legal and political services. In Jackson's eyes the BUS had become a "monster institution," unconstitutionally diverting public funds for private profit.

The celebrated "Bank War" erupted into open conflict in 1832, when Webster and Clay launched a legislative offensive, partly to prevent Jackson's reelection. Knowing that they could win support from many Democrats for the passage of a bill rechartering the BUS, they were confident that the president could not veto the measure without fatally damaging his chances for reelection in the fall. Jackson took up the challenge. In a masterful veto message he spelled out the principles that would be a touchstone for "Jacksonian democracy" and for populist politics in the decades to come. He denounced the BUS as a

"THE DOWNFALL OF MOTHER BANK"

In this popular cartoon Jackson's removal of federal deposits from the Bank of the United States carries overtones of Christ's chasing the money lenders from the ancient temple. Biddle, in the form of the devil, flees along with Webster, Clay, and the various minions of the Money Power. *(Library of Congress)*

priviliged monopoly, and vowed to take a stand "against all new grants of monopolies and exclusive privileges, against any prostitution of our Government to the advancement of the few at the expense of the many." Jackson in no way favored leveling wealth or other distinctions derived from "natural and just advantages." "Equality of talents, of education, or of wealth," he affirmed, "cannot be produced by human institutions." But government should provide "equal protection, and, as heaven does its rains, shower its favors alike on the high and the low, the rich and the poor." The BUS, he declared, represented a flagrant example of government subsidy to the privileged, of laws that made "the rich richer and the potent more powerful." Jackson also warned of the dangerous provisions that allowed foreigners to buy BUS stock and thus to acquire influence over American policy. In

defiance of the Supreme Court's decision in *McCulloch v. Maryland* (1819), he argued that the BUS was unconstitutional.

Although Webster and other conservative leaders immediately cried that the president was trying "to stir up the poor against the rich," the election of 1832 decisively vindicated Jackson's bold leadership and political shrewdness. Old Hickory would have won a sweeping victory even if the opposition votes had not been divided between Henry Clay, the National Republican candidate, and William Wirt, the reluctant leader of the Anti-Masons. Confident now that the supporters of the BUS could never override his veto, Jackson vowed to defang the "monster institution" by removing all of the deposits placed in the bank by the federal government.

This aggressive policy was opposed by many of

DANIEL WEBSTER, 1782–1852
(Culver Pictures, Inc.)

ever, without adding to popular hostility to the bank. In the winter of 1832–33 Biddle did retrench, but the constriction of credit was not serious enough to shake Jackson's resolution. The president also gained political leverage through his discriminating choice of pet banks. Many bankers who had earlier hoped to keep clear of the political struggle were eager for interest-free federal funds that would allow them to expand loans and other commercial operations. Jackson's victory was fairly complete by the spring of 1834.

Jackson's Hard-Money Policy.   Like many triumphs, the destruction of the BUS enmeshed the victors in a web of problems. The Democrats claimed that by slaying the "monster," they had purged the nation of a moral evil. Yet the deposit of federal funds in pet banks encouraged the expansion of credit, and in the mid-1830s the nation reeled from the intoxication of a speculative boom. Some of the orthodox Jacksonian officials even bemoaned the growing federal surplus— an unimaginable phenomenon to later generations who have only known federal deficits and mounting public debts—because there seemed to be no place to put the funds that would not corrupt the Republic. Whatever the administration did invited trouble. On the one hand, if it distributed funds to the states, it fed the speculative boom by encouraging further construction of roads and canals and other kinds of "improvements." On the other hand, if it kept the funds in the pet banks, these banks clearly had to be regulated by the federal government, lest they too feed inflation by issuing vast quantities of paper money based on this reserve.

Slowly Jackson and his successor, Van Buren, who was elected in 1836, moved toward a policy of hard money. They tried to reduce or eliminate the circulation of small-denomination bank notes and to set a minimal requirement for the pet banks' specie reserves. In 1836 Jackson also issued an executive order, the so-called "specie circular," requiring payments in specie for purchase of public land. The specie circular represented a direct federal effort to curb speculation and thus to manage the fluctuations of the economy. This controversial measure signaled the

the president's advisers, since the BUS already appeared to be doomed. The removal policy also raised new problems. According to Jackson's plan, which his secretary of the treasury, Roger B. Taney, soon put into execution, federal funds would be dispersed among chosen state-chartered banks that were soon dubbed "pet" banks. For the policy to succeed, Jackson had to persuade the banking community that decentralization would not bring economic disaster. Nicholas Biddle, on the other hand, needed to produce a minor financial panic to underscore the powerful role of the BUS in maintaining financial stability. Biddle could not exert his full financial powers, how-

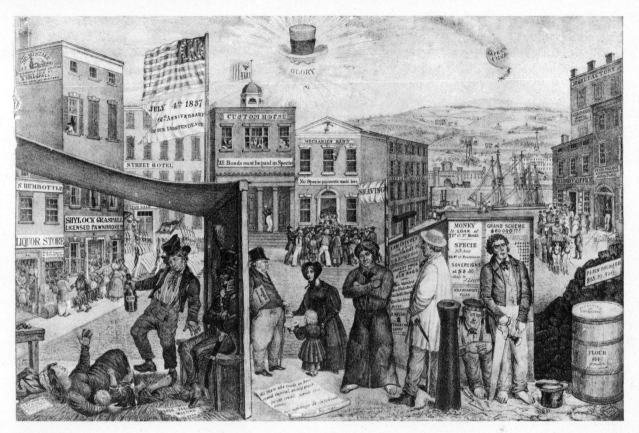

"THE TIMES"

This complex cartoon portrays the allegedly disastrous results of the Democratic rule: the government's hard money policy leads to a run on the bank, which has suspended specie payments; the custom house is deserted; debtors are herded into the sheriff's office; beggars and unemployed artisans crowd the streets; scenes of drunkenness are linked with the unruliness of immigrants and Locofoco radicals. *(Library of Congress)*

growing dominance of the antibank and hard-money factions in the Democratic party. The subsequent nomination and election of Van Buren strengthened the hand of those Democrats who found hostility to all banks politically effective.

The Panic of 1837. In 1837 a banking panic brought an abrupt end to the speculative boom, and by 1839 a severe depression had developed that persisted to the mid-1840s. This painful downturn in investment, prices, and employment was mainly the product of a business cycle still tied to agriculture (especially cotton), and related to English demand, English in-

vestment, and the international flow of silver. In many respects the American economy still resembled that of a colony or underdeveloped nation dependent on foreign investment and on raw material exports. Hence it was vulnerable to sudden contractions of British credit coupled with temporary drops in the British demand for cotton. As bankruptcies multiplied, the business community blamed the widespread suffering on Jacksonian fiscal policies which had first fueled reckless expansion by destroying the BUS and then had suddenly curtailed credit by requiring specie for the purchase of public land. But as bankers and businessmen deserted the Democratic party, the reigning hard-money, laissez-faire faction argued that the economic collapse proved the folly of government partnership with even pet banks.

After three years of bitter intraparty struggle, President Van Buren finally achieved a "divorce of bank and state" with the passage of the Independent Treasury Act (1840). By locking federal funds in "independent" subtreasuries of the United States government insulated from the banking community, this measure deprived the banking system of reserves that might have encouraged loans and aided economic recovery.

Laissez-faire Capitalism.   In summary, the Democrats' program can be illuminated by pointing to two inconsistencies. First, their economic policies did little to aid the groups of farmers and artisans the Democrats claimed to represent. If the political attacks on special privilege served to revitalize democratic ideology, the ultimate beneficiaries were the southern planters who were aided by Indian removal, lowered tariffs, and the suppression of antislavery literature and petitions. Moreover, the policy of economic laissez-faire seemed to offer the South assurance that the federal government would not interfere with the interstate movement of slave labor. By 1838 Calhoun and his followers, who had earlier seceded from the Democratic party, returned to the fold, and as it turned out, Calhoun's return paved the way for southern domination of the party in the two decades to come.

Second, the nation's banking continued to grow into an integrated system, and the nation's economy continued to grow with serene disregard for the fluctuations of politics. The attempts of Jackson and Van Buren to withdraw the government from what they saw as a corrupting economy had little effect on the general trends of economic development.

Whigs and the Two-Party System

For most of the thirty years following Jackson's 1828 victory the Democrats ruled the White House. Between 1828 and 1856 their presidential nominees defeated every opposition candidate except William Henry Harrison (1840) and Zachary Taylor (1848), both of whom died in office. John Tyler, the vice-president who succeeded Harrison only a month after the latter's inauguration, soon returned to his original Virginia Democratic loyalties and principles. Millard Fillmore, Zachary Taylor's successor, was a genial but colorless Whig party hack who began his political career as an Anti-Mason and ended it by running for president in 1856 on the nativist and anti-Catholic "Know-Nothing" or American party ticket.

But the Democrats' dominance of the presidency is deceptive. By the late 1830s Whigs could match Democratic strength in most parts of the country. Though the South has commonly been pictured as a preserve for state-rights Democrats, Whigs predominated as the South's representatives in three out of five Congresses elected between 1832 and 1842. Whig strength was particularly evident on local, county, and state levels. For the viability of the two-party system depended essentially on vigorous local conflict—on the ability of a second party to challenge incumbents by convincing voters that a genuine alternative was available. To maintain partisan loyalties, leaders tried to exploit or manufacture conflicts, to dramatize party differences, and to be responsive enough to public demands to convince voters that their grievances could be resolved through the ballot. Whigs, like the Democrats, claimed to represent the interests of the *excluded* people against a privileged and self-serving "power." Since no incumbent party could possibly avoid patronage, the game of two-party politics consisted of proving that incumbents were partial to their friends and thus insincere in professing to serve the common good. In effect, both parties were torn between a desire to battle for the special interests of their permanent constituency and a need to advocate bland, lofty goals that would attract the widest possible national following.

Webster, Clay, and Calhoun.   Like the Democratic party, the Whigs were a wholly new coalition. They were not, as the Democrats charged, simply Federalists in disguise—the Democrats themselves recruited an impressive number of ex-Federalist leaders. In

"KING ANDREW THE FIRST"
The Whig image of Jackson as an autocratic king, brandishing the veto and trampling the Constitution under foot. *(Library of Congress)*

Congress the Whigs first began to emerge in a legislative rebellion against Jackson's "Executive Usurpation." During the summer of 1832 Jackson's veto of the bill rechartering the BUS led to the temporary coalition of three of the most formidable senators in American history. All three longed for the presidency. By 1832 they had won fame as three mythical gods, deliverers of Olympian oratory that dazzled aspiring young men.

Daniel Webster struck the keynote when he attacked "King Andrew" as a reincarnation of the French monarch who had declared, "I am the State." A man of humble New Hampshire origins and aristocratic Boston tastes, Webster had risen in the legal profession by emulating and paying deference to New England's commercial elite. He was a heavy drinker, given to extravagant living and continual debt. His sonorous voice and commanding physical presence could never quite convey the moral sincerity that most northeastern Whigs expected of their leaders. Yet Webster upheld their traditional mistrust of divisive parties and their traditional ideal of government by "disinterested gentlemen." He succeeded in blending this conservative tradition with a celebration of material and moral progess. As the agent of commercial and manufacturing interests in Massachusetts, he was flexible enough to shift his style of argument from the forums of the Supreme Court and the Senate to the stump of popular politics, always pleading for the natural harmony of interests that the Democratic party threatened to undermine.

Henry Clay considered himself a Jeffersonian Republican and the leader of the National Republicans, the label originally applied to Jackson's opponents. The author of the American System, designed to maximize federal support for industry, economic growth, and national self-sufficiency, Clay joined Webster's assaults on Jackson's alleged despotism. Clay was a Kentuckian of Virginia birth, and had also risen from humble origin. Like Webster, he was notorious for extravagant living, though Clay's self-indulgence took the typically southern forms of gambling, dueling, and horse-racing. A slave-owning planter and brilliant courtroom lawyer, Clay assumed two contradictory political roles. He competed with Jackson as a western man of the people, a coonskin man of nature. But Clay had also helped to negotiate the Treaty of Ghent ending the War of 1812; he had been Adams's secretary of state; and he represented the western business and commercial interests that demanded federal aid for internal improvements. One of the greatest political manipulators in nineteenth-century America, Clay had talents unequaled in caucuses, committee rooms, and all-night boardinghouse negotiations.

The most unpredictable member of the anti-Jackson triumvirate was John C. Calhoun, who had shifted in the 1820s from militant nationalism to a militant defense of slavery and state rights, and who had been Jackson's nominal ally until personal conflicts had provoked a fatal split. Despite Calhoun's dramatic turnabouts, contemporaries admired the clarity and logical force of his arguments and respected his earlier distinguished service as secretary of war. But Calhoun's role in the nullification controversy made him a dangerous ally in the developing Whig coalition. Most southern Whig leaders shared the economic and nationalistic views of their northern brethren; Calhoun did not.

Whig Philosophy.   The Whig outlook on the world was almost too diffuse to be termed an ideology. Like the Democrats, Whigs gloried in the dream of America's future as the greatest nation the world had ever seen, and they found confirmation for that dream in the measurable growth of population, wealth, and power. Far more than the Democrats, they associated the "spirit of improvement" with concrete technological and social inventions. They assumed that steam power, the telegraph, railroads, banks, corporations, prisons, factories, asylums, and public schools all contributed to an advancing civilization and to an increasing equality of opportunity. On both social and individual levels, they advocated saving from income, capital accumulation, budgetary planning, and fiscal responsibility. They opposed aggressive territorial expansion as a cure-all for economic problems. They insisted that America's expansion and power should be harnessed to social ends and stabilized by publicly acknowledged moral boundaries. Alarmed by the excesses of rampant individualism, they expressed continuing and sometimes hysterical concern over the loss of community—over the demagogues who won support by inciting the poor against the rich, children against parents, wives against husbands, and geographic section against geographic section.

Whigs thought of themselves as conservatives and often invoked European theories that stressed the organic unity of society and the necessity of balancing human rights with social duties. Yet the Whig ideal of government was essentially optimistic and progressive. In 1825, long before the Whig party began to coalesce, John Quincy Adams advanced the central Whig proposition that the Constitution had given the central government both the duty and the necessary powers to promote "the progressive improvement of the condition of the governed."

On a popular level the Whig party began to appear by 1834 as a loose coalition of state and local groups opposed to Jacksonian Democrats. Reluctant to allow the Jacksonians a monopoly of the popular label "democrat," the anti-Jacksonians sometimes called themselves Democratic Whigs. The final acceptance of the term "Whig" was significant. Superficially the label suggested an identity with the British "country" party which had allegedly defended the British constitution against the despotism of the pro-Catholic Stuart kings and the later executive encroachments of George III. This imagery linked "King Andrew" with the various reactionary and demagogic monarchs of Europe. Such parallels may seem far-fetched, but the very act of drawing parallels with Europe contained a deeper significance. Unlike the Democrats, the Whigs tended to deny the uniqueness of the American experience and to place less faith in political institutions than in economic and cultural progress. They also tended to look on Britain, despite its monarchic and aristocratic institutions, as a model of economic and cultural progress. For the most thoughtful Whig spokesmen, America was less a revolutionary departure from the rest of the world than a testing ground for progressive forces that were universal and depended essentially on moral character.

The Whig Constituency.   In all parts of the country Whigs attracted a broad cross section of the electorate, a cross section, however, often weighted in favor of the wealthy, the privileged, and the aspiring, but including—paradoxically—the victims of overt discrimination. In the North this constituency included most of the free blacks; British and German Protestant immigrants; manual laborers sympathetic with their employers' interests; business-oriented farmers; educators, reformers, and professional people; well-to-do merchants, bankers, and manufacturers; and active members of the Presbyterian, Unitarian, and Congregationalist churches. In the South the party had particular appeal to urban merchants, editors, bankers, and to those farmers and planters who associated progress with expanding commerce, capital accumulation, railroads, and economic partnership with the North.

During their initial stages of organization the Whigs faced three formidable problems. First, in the populous northern states like New York, Pennsylvania, and Massachusetts they had to find strategies for uniting the economic interests of the National Republicans with the moral and cultural aspirations of various groups alienated by the incumbent Democrats. Second, they had to get rid of the elitist stigma that had been fastened on John Quincy Adams and then on the defenders of the BUS, and somehow prove that they were better democrats than the Democrats. Finally, they had to find delicate maneuvers for bypassing senatorial prima donnas like Webster and Clay and selecting less controversial presidential candidates who could appeal to the nation without arousing dissension and jealousy among the various state party organizations.

The way these problems were met is well illustrated by the career of Thurlow Weed of New York, who became the prototype of the nineteenth-century political boss and manipulator. A self-made man, Weed first acquired a voice in New York politics as editor of the Rochester *Telegraph* and as a bitter foe of Van Buren's Albany Regency. In 1827 Weed and his young protégé William H. Seward took up the cause of Anti-Masonry as a means of embarrassing the ruling Van Buren machine. In western New York, Anti-Masonry had suddenly erupted as a kind of religious crusade after the abduction and probable murder of a former Freemason who was thought to have divulged the secrets of the fraternal society. The crusade expressed widespread popular resentment against an organization that knit many of the wealthier and more powerful urban leaders of the state into a secret brotherhood pledged to mutual aid and support. Weed and Seward succeeded in portraying the Van Buren regime as the agent of Freemasonry—a "monster institution"—intent on suppressing legal investigation and prosecution of the alleged murder, and on disguising statewide links

between Masonic political influence and economic privilege. This antielitist rhetoric helped to counteract the Democrats' claims of being the true champions of the people against the unpopular Adams administration in Washington. By 1830 Anti-Masons captured approximately one-half the popular vote in New York State. When the movement showed increasing signs of strength in other northern states, Weed and other strategists worked to absorb the National Republicans into a new anti-Jackson coalition.

But though the Anti-Masons organized the first national political convention in American history, Weed began to sense that the movement could be no more than a springboard for a successful national party. Weed launched his powerful Albany *Evening Journal* as an Anti-Masonic organ, but he increasingly downplayed Masonry and combined blistering attacks on the Albany Regency with the advocacy of various social reforms. To his political cronies and businessmen backers Weed kept insisting that the Jacksonians could never be beaten so long as they continued to persuade the people that they represented "the principle of democracy . . . the poor against the rich." By 1834 Weed had abandoned Anti-Masonry and had succeeded in organizing a New York Whig coalition.

In 1836, when the Whigs tried to broaden their appeal by nominating various regional candidates for president, including Daniel Webster of Massachusetts and Hugh White of Tennessee, it was Weed's candidate, William Henry Harrison of Ohio, who won the most electoral votes. "Old Tippecanoe," famous for his military defeat of the Shawnee Indians in 1811, appealed to many former Anti-Masons and won strong support in the South as well as in New York, Ohio, and Pennsylvania. After years of patient organizing, wire-pulling, and passing out cigars, Weed finally came into his own in 1838 when he succeeded in getting Seward elected governor of New York. As the master of patronage, the official state printer, and the "dictator" of the New York machine, Weed was now in a position to challenge his old archrival Van Buren, who claimed to be the president of the common people.

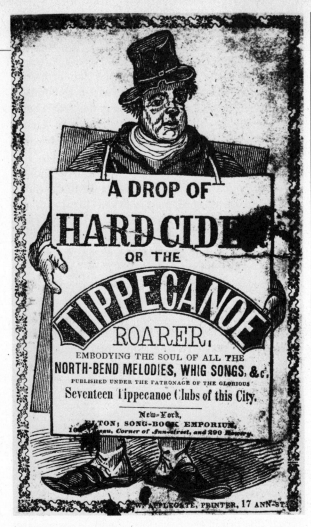

TIPPECANOE ROARER
By 1840 the Whigs could match the Democrats as a popular people's party with their own distinctive songs, clubs, and political symbols. *(Courtesy, The Cincinnati Historical Society)*

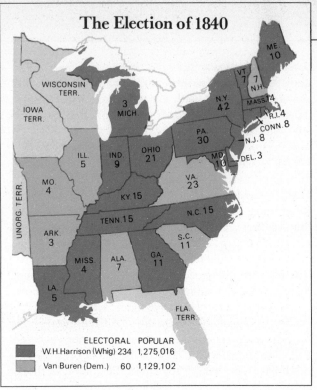

The Election of 1840

ELECTORAL POPULAR
W.H.Harrison (Whig) 234 1,275,016
Van Buren (Dem.) 60 1,129,102

The Election of 1840. In 1840 Weed played a key role in blocking the Whigs' nomination of Clay and in opening the way for Harrison. Weed's young protégé, Horace Greeley, edited the Whigs' most influential paper, *The Log Cabin,* which set the pace by attacking President Van Buren as an affected dandy who had transformed the White House into a palace of effeminate luxury. Greeley and others cast Harrison as a frontiersman of simple tastes; his symbols were a barrel of cider (whether hard or soft depended on the locality), and a log cabin with a welcoming

coonskin at the door. Harrison's victory seemed to show that strategists like Weed had overcome the Whigs' political liabilities. They could rival the Democrats in populistic appeals, in carnival-like hucksterism, and above all, in grass-roots organization.

Nevertheless, the Whigs never found a magnetic national leader who, like Jackson for the Democrats, could become a unifying symbol for their party. John Tyler, the vice-president who succeeded Harrison, soon betrayed the economic principles of the party. In 1844 Clay went down to defeat for a third time, after which the Whigs returned to the tested expedient of nominating apolitical military heroes, Zachary Taylor in 1848 and Winfield Scott in 1852.

The Whigs' difficulties went beyond the weakness of their presidential candidates. Despite their political pragmatism and impressive party discipline, the Whigs contained a militant, reform-minded element that resented the compromises necessary for a national party. Anti-Masonry had been one of the early expressions of such reformist and issue-oriented politics, and many of the Anti-Masons who joined the Whigs had never been comfortable with the opportunism of leaders like Thurlow Weed, who placed victory above principle. In addition to the Anti-Masons, the Whig party became the uneasy lodging place for people who wanted laws enforcing a stricter Sabbath, laws prohibiting the sale of alcohol, laws barring slavery in the territories and abolishing slavery in the District of Columbia, and laws prolonging the time before an immigrant could be naturalized or allowed to vote. These causes were nourished by the spread of Protestant religious revivals in the North. Among southern Whigs and hard-headed supporters of Clay's American System they had little appeal.

Limitations of the Two-Party System.   Nevertheless, while a national party's strength depended on a continuing sensitivity to the needs of its constituent groups, it also served as a disciplining and educational force, imposing definite limits to individual, local, and regional self-assertion. The political issues of the 1840s tended to reinforce such party loyalty.

The majority of state legislators adhered to a strict Whig or Democratic vote even when a different position might have harmonized more with local or personal interests. The appointment of loyal party men to positions in local land offices, post offices, and customhouses established Whig or Democratic nerve centers at the grass-roots level. Until the early 1850s, when voters became disillusioned with traditional alternatives and when the Whig party began to fall apart, the two-party system worked as a powerful cohesive force in American society. Unfortunately this political stability rested on the illusion of consistent and sharply defined differences between two parties which were intended to represent the interests of only white Americans. If the existence of national parties succeeded in moderating sectional conflict, it was at the cost of suppressing alternatives to the expansion of slavery and of stifling national debate over America's most dangerous conflict of interest.

CHRONOLOGY

1820   Missouri Compromise.
Maine admitted as 23rd state.
Reelection of James Monroe without opposition symbolizes "Era of Good Feelings."

1821   Henry Clay effects "Second Missouri Compromise."
Missouri admitted as 24th state.

1822   Denmark Vesey's conspiracy to lead massive slave uprising in South Carolina exposed.

1824   John Quincy Adams elected president by House of Representatives after failure of any candidate to win electoral majority.

1827   Thurlow Weed takes up cause of anti-Masonry

1828   John C. Calhoun's anonymous *South Carolina Exposition and Protest.*
Congress passes "Tariff of Abominations."
Election of Andrew Jackson as president brings triumphant victory to new Democratic party.

1830   Jackson vetoes Maysville Road Bill.
Anti-Masonic party holds first national party convention.

1832   Beginning of Jackson's "war" against Second Bank of the United States (BUS).
Special convention in South Carolina nullifies new protective tariff.
Jackson reelected president.

1833   Congress provides for a gradual lowering of tariffs, but passes Force Bill authorizing Jackson to enforce federal law in South Carolina.

1836   Jackson's "specie circular."
Martin Van Buren elected president.

1837   Financial panic brings many bank failures and suspension of specie payment.

1839   A major depression begins, leading to widespread bankruptcies and default of several states.

1840   Congress passes Van Buren's Independent Treasury Act.
William H. Harrison elected president; Whigs in power.

1841   John Tyler becomes president upon Harrison's death.

SUGGESTED READINGS

Arthur M. Schlesinger, Jr., *The Age of Jackson* (1945), should be used with caution, but is still an indispensable introduction to political democratization. Other studies that illuminate the same subject are Shaw Livermore, Jr., *The Twilight of Federalism* (1962); Chilton Williamson, *American Suffrage: From Property to Democracy* (1960); Henry Christman, *Tin Horns and Calico: A Decisive Episode in the Emergence of Democracy* (1945); David M. Ludlum, *Social Ferment in Vermont* (1939); and Marvin E. Gettleman, *The Dorr Rebellion* (1973).

Lee Benson, *The Concept of Jacksonian Democracy: New York as a Test Case* (1961), challenges the traditional historical categories of liberalism and conservatism. Richard P. McCormick, *The Second American Party System: Party Formation in the Jacksonian Era* (1966), also deemphasizes political issues and ideology. These pioneering works should be supplemented by Richard Hofstadter, *The Idea of a Party System* (1969); Ronald Formisano, *The Birth of Mass Political Parties: Michigan, 1827–1861* (1971); Joel Silbey, ed., *Transformation of American Politics, 1840–1860* (1967); Douglas T. Miller, *Jacksonian Aristocracy: Class and Democracy in New York, 1830–1860* (1967); and Michael F. Holt, "The Antimasonic and Know-Nothing Parties," and Holt, "The Democratic Party," in *History of U.S. Political Parties,* ed. Arthur M. Schlesinger, Jr., Vol. 1 (1789–1860: *From Factions to Parties),* (4 vols., 1973). Michael F. Holt, *The Political Crisis of the 1850s* (1978), while dealing mainly with a later period, points to connections between political ideology and the working of the party system.

For the election of 1828, see R. V. Remini, *The Election of Andrew Jackson* (1963). Two imaginative studies of Jacksonian ideology are Marvin Meyers, *The Jacksonian Persuasion* (1957); and John W. Ward, *Andrew Jackson: Symbol for an Age* (1955). For a comprehensive portrait of Jackson's early years, see R. V. Remini, *Andrew Jackson and the Course of American Empire* (1977); for his presidency, see Richard B. Latner, *The Presidency of Andrew Jackson: White House Politics* (1979). Informative essays on all of the presidential elections can be found in Arthur M. Schlesinger, Jr., ed., *History of American Presidential Elections, 1789–1968.* Vol. 1 (4 vols., 1971)

The standard work on the tariff issue is Frank W. Taussig, *The Tariff History of the United States* (1931). The best introduction to the banking controversy is R. V. Remini, *Andrew Jackson and the Bank War* (1967). The main authorities on the history of banking are Bray Hammond,

Banks and Politics in America from the Revolution to the Civil War (1957); J. Van Fenstermaker, *The Development of American Commercial Banking, 1782–1837* (1965); and Fritz Redlich, *The Molding of American Banking* (2 vols., 1947–51). Thomas P. Govan, *Nicholas Biddle* (1959), presents a strong defense of the president of the Bank of the United States. The wider political ramifications of the controversy are examined in William G. Shade, *Banks or No Banks: The Money Question in Western Politics* (1972), and John M. McFaul, *The Politics of Jacksonian Finance* (1972).

On the Missouri crisis of 1820, Glover Moore, *The Missouri Controversy* (1953), is still the most thorough and convincing account. William W. Freehling, *Prelude to Civil War* (1966), presents a masterful interpretation of South Carolina's growing militancy, and of the nullification and gag-rule controversies. For the general question of sectionalism, see William J. Cooper, *The South and the Politics of Slavery, 1828–1856* (1978).

There is still no adequate history of the Whig party and its antecedents, but Daniel W. Howe, *The Political Culture of the American Whigs* (1980), brilliantly illuminates the Whig ideology. See also Lynn L. Marshall, "The Strange Stillbirth of the Whig Party," *American Historical Review,* 62 (January 1967), 445–68; Charles G. Sellers, Jr., "Who Were the Southern Whigs?" *American Historical Review,* 59 (January 1954), 335–46; Glyndon G. Van Deusen, "Some Aspects of Whig Thought and Theory in the Jacksonian Period," *American Historical Review,* 63 (January 1958), 305–32; and Thomas H. O'Connor, *Lords of the Loom: The Cotton Whigs and the Coming of the Civil War* (1968).

Political history is always illuminated by the biographies of influential figures. Richard Hofstadter, *The American Political Tradition* (1948), provides brilliant sketches of a number of pre–Civil War leaders. Among the best biographies are Martin Duberman, *Charles Francis Adams, 1807–1886* (1961); Samuel F. Bemis, *John Quincy Adams and the Foundations of American Foreign Policy* (1949), and *John Quincy Adams and the Union* (1956); W. N. Chambers, *Old Bullion Benton: Senator from the New West* (1956); William E. Smith, *The Francis Preston Blair Family in Politics* (2 vols., 1933); Richard N. Current, *John C. Calhoun* (1966); C. M. Wiltse, *John C. Calhoun: Nationalist, 1782–1828* (1944); *Nullifier, 1829–1839* (1949); *Sectionalist, 1840–1850* (1951); Clement Eaton, *Henry Clay and the Art of American Politics* (1957); Marquis James, *Life of Andrew Jackson* (1938); Harry Ammon,

James Monroe: The Quest for National Identity (1971); Charles G. Sellers, Jr., *James K. Polk: Jacksonian, 1795–1843* (1957); *Continentalist, 1843–1846* (1966); Robert Dawidoff, *The Education of John Randolph* (1979); Glyndon G. Van Deusen, *William Henry Seward* (1967); David H. Donald, *Charles Sumner and the Coming of the Civil War* (1960); Carl B. Swisher, *Roger B. Taney* (1935); Holman Hamilton, *Zachary Taylor* (1951); William Y. Thompson, *Robert Toombs of Georgia* (1966); James P. Shenton, *Robert John Walker: A Politician from Jackson to Lincoln* (1961); Robert F. Dalzell, Jr., *Daniel Webster and the Trial of American Nationalism, 1843–1852* (1973); Sydney Nathans, *Daniel Webster and Jacksonian Democracy* (1973); Glyndon G. Van Deusen, *Thurlow Weed: Wizard of the Lobby* (1947); and John W. DuBose, *The Life and Times of William Lowndes Yancey* (2 vols., 1892).

Of the many editions of diaries and collected papers, the following deserve special notice: C. F. Adams, ed., *The Memoirs of John Quincy Adams* (12 vols., 1874–77); Thomas Hart Benton, *Thirty Years' View* (1857); Allan Nevins, ed., *The Diary of Philip Hone, 1828–1851* (2 vols., 1927); Allan Nevins and Milton H. Thomas, eds., *The Diary of George Templeton Strong* (4 vols., 1952); Horace Greeley, *Recollections of a Busy Life* (2 vols., 1868); Milo M. Quaife, ed., *The Diary of James K. Polk* (4 vols., 1910); and J. C. Fitzpatrick, ed., *The Autobiography of Martin Van Buren* (1920).

CHAPTER 14

Attempts to Shape the American Character

Duuring the pre–Civil War decades political and religious leaders repeatedly warned that the fate of free institutions depended on the moral and intellectual character of the American people. Religious beliefs continued to differ about man's sinfulness or inherent capacity for love and social harmony. But Americans of various persuasions agreed that human nature was much like clay that can be molded to any shape before it hardens.

This conviction could be inspiring. In 1823, for example, Charles Jared Ingersoll, a Philadelphia lawyer and former congressman, delivered the influential *Discourse Concerning the Influence of America on the Mind.* Ingersoll was confident that the average American, as a result of the free and republican environment, stood far above the average European in both intelligence and virtue. He promised that American achievements in the arts and sciences would soon show the world the full potentialities of human nature when it was not hobbled by despotism and aristocratic privilege.

But a capacity for infinite improvement might also be a capacity for infinite corruption. Even the optimists tended to worry over the growing inadequacy of local religious and social institutions in the face of America's sensational expansion. The need to shape or change individual character gave a new social importance to educators, religious revivalists, popular essayists, phrenologists, and other promoters of self-improvement.

"We Must Educate or Perish"

Shaping character, whether by school, church, prison, or asylum, seemed to be the only means of ensuring moral stability in an expansive and increasingly individualistic society. Lyman Beecher, best-known today as the father of Harriet Beecher Stowe but in his own day the most prominent Protestant minister in the North, viewed the rapid settlement of the West with a mixture of exhilaration and alarm. By 1835 the states west of the Appalachians had grown so rapidly that he could predict a population of 100 million by 1900: "A day which some of our children may live to see." As a "young empire of mind, and power, and wealth, and free institutions, " the West, Beecher believed, contained the potential for nothing less than "the emancipation of the world." Beecher had no doubts about the West's material progress. The danger was "that our intelligence and virtue will falter and fall back into a dark minded, vicious populace—a poor, uneducated reckless mass of infuriated animalism." Aroused particularly by the supposed threat of Catholic immigrants, whom he pictured as the agents of foreign despots intent on subverting republican institutions, Beecher urged an immediate crusade to evangelize and educate the West: "For population will not wait, and commerce will not cast anchor, and manufacturers will not shut off the steam nor shut down the gate, and agriculture, pushed by millions of freemen on their fertile soil, will not withhold her corrupting abundance. We must educate! We must educate! or we must perish by our own prosperity."

The State of Education.

Educational reformers had some reason for alarm. Even Massachusetts, which in 1837 established the nation's first state board of education, suffered from dilapidated school buildings, untrained and incompetent teachers, and dependence on unequal and unpredictable local funding. The one-room country schoolhouse, often idealized in later years, was not only dirty, drafty, and overheated, but commonly packed with children of all ages, some old and rowdy enough to inflict beatings on male teachers and to prompt some women teachers to hide a pistol in a desk drawer. The soaring growth of eastern cities made middle-class citizens suddenly aware of begging street urchins, teenage prostitutes, gangs of juvenile delinquents, and vagrant children who, like Mark Twain's Huckleberry Finn, had little desire to be "civilized."

Until the second quarter of the nineteenth century, the education of Americans was informal, unsystematic, and dependent on parental initiative and ability to pay. Even so, compared with most Europeans, white American males had always enjoyed a high rate of literacy, especially in New England. During the 1790s a surprising number of artisans and skilled laborers had sent their children to the "com-mon pay schools" in New York City, where children of rich and poor backgrounds mingled. By the early nineteenth century illiteracy was rapidly disappearing among white females. Boys and girls frequently attended the same schools, despite prejudices against sexual integration. Some "free" schools expected parents to pay a small fee, and most tax-supported schools were intended only for the children of paupers. Aside from school attendance, apprenticeship long served as a noteworthy educational institution, providing the vocational skills that could not be learned in any school. Not until the mid-nineteenth century—and in the South not until after the Civil War—did education become increasingly confined to specialized institutions segregated from the mainstreams of adult social life.

Working-Class Demands.

Middle-class religious reformers were not the only ones to demand educational reform. In 1828 the organized mechanics and journeymen of Philadelphia, most of whom were skilled artisans and craftsmen who had served their apprenticeship, began to protest. As in other northeastern cities, these workers were angered by depressed wage levels, by the substitution of temporary child "apprentices" for skilled adult labor, and by the erosion of the traditional craft system that allowed apprentices and journeymen to rise within a given trade. The Philadelphia Working Men's party pressed for a broad range of economic and social reforms. "The original element of despotism, " proclaimed a committee in 1829, "is a monopoly of talent, which consigns the multitude to comparative ignorance, and secures the balance of knowledge on the side of the rich and the rulers."

The demand for free tax-supported schools became a rallying cry for the workingmen's parties and associations that sprang up in New York, Boston, and dozens of small towns throughout the country. A group of New York workers expressed the typical rhetoric when they asked in 1830 "if many of the monopolists and aristocrats in our city would not consider it disgraceful to their noble children to have them placed in our public schools by the side of poor yet industrious mechanics?" Though many of the

"POPERY UNDERMINING FREE SCHOOLS"
A typical example of anti-Catholic iconography. While the American eagle hovers over the schoolhouse, this bulwark of democratic institutions is being literally undermined by sappers working under the directions of a priest, who in turn is executing the orders of the pope, pictured here as a foreign potentate. *(American Antiquarian Society)*

leaders of these groups were not manual laborers, the short-lived workingmen's movement reflected an authentic desire for equal educational opportunity on the part of skilled laborers whose economic and social condition had begun to deteriorate.

For most workingmen economic grievances soon took precedence over education. The economic growth of the pre–Civil War decades called for more and more unskilled laborers, but not for a significant increase in the number of skilled and nonmanual workers who might benefit materially from an education beyond the "Three Rs." In New York City, where the proportion of nonmanual and professional jobs changed very little from 1796 to 1855, many working-class parents questioned whether they should sacrifice family income in order to educate their children for jobs that did not exist.

As early as 1832 the New York Public School Society pointed out: "The labouring classes of society will, to a great extent, withhold their children from school, the moment they arrive at an age that renders their services in the least available in contributing to the support of the family." Later evidence indicated that children under fifteen earned as much as 20 percent of the income of working-class families in Newburyport, Massachusetts. For such families compulsory attendance laws often threatened an unbearable drop in already subsistence-level income. Not surprisingly, 40 percent of Newburyport's laborers admitted to the census takers of 1850 that their school-age children had not been enrolled in any school during the previous year. And many children who were enrolled could not attend regularly.

Moreover, by the 1840s the working class in the Northeast was becoming increasingly Roman Catholic. Though the public schools were theoretically secular—in New York and elsewhere denominational schools had been deprived of public funding—the values and teachings of the schools were unmistakably Protestant. Most Americans in the mid-nineteenth century still regarded Americanism as synonymous with Protestantism. Protestant clergymen played a critical role on school committees and in school reform. They saw nothing sectarian about public school teachers reading aloud from the King James Bible or teaching that the Protestant Reformation represented a liberation from Popish despotism. Bishop John Hughes and other Catholic leaders saw the matter differently. In 1840 New York Catholics launched a political offensive against the Protestant monopoly of public education. As a result of this conflict, the Catholic church decided to construct its own separate system of schools, a costly program that took many decades to complete.

For many immigrants, Catholics, and working-class parents the Protestant school reformers threatened to impose a uniform set of values on all segments of American society. Resistance also arose from local authorities who feared any centralizing interference from a state board of education. Many conservatives insisted that parents should pay for education, if they could afford it, just as they would for any other service or commodity. Others, brought up on the tradition of church schools, feared that the teaching of value-laden subjects would be catastrophic if guided only by a vaguely Protestant and nondenominational spirit.

Educational Reformers. These obstacles to the expansion of public education were finally overcome by reformers like Horace Mann, who as the chief officer of the Massachusetts Board of Education from 1837 to 1848 became the nation's leading champion of public schools. An ascetic, humorless puritan, Mann denounced intemperance, profanity, and ballet dancing along with ignorance, violence, and Negro slavery. Having personally struggled with the terrors of his New England Calvinist heritage, he had finally concluded that children were capable of infinite improvement and goodness. As a kind of secular minister, still intent on saving souls, he insisted that there must have been a time in the childhood of the worst criminal when, "ere he was irrecoverably lost, ere he plunged into the abyss of infamy and guilt, he might have been recalled." Mann offended the religiously orthodox by winning the fight in Massachusetts against specific religious instruction in the public schools. He outraged conservatives by asserting that private property is not an absolute right but rather

a trusteeship for society and future generations. Trained as a lawyer, he decided as a young man that "the next generation" should be his clients. In pleading the cause of generations to come, he held that school taxes were not a "confiscation" from the rich, but rather a collection of the debt the rich owed to society.

Reformers placed a stupendous moral burden on the public schools. Horace Mann proclaimed the common school to be "the greatest discovery ever made by man." "Other social organizations are curative and remedial," he said; "this is a preventive and antidote." This characteristic argument suggests that the schools were to be a bulwark against undesirable change, preserving the cherished values of a simpler, more homogeneous America. Educators spoke of the frenzied pace of American life, of the diminishing influence of church and home. They held that the school should thus serve as a substitute for both church and home, preventing American democracy from degenerating into what Mann called "the spectacle of gladiatorial contests." The school, representing the highest instincts of society, could alone be counted on for cultivating decency, cooperation, and a respect for others. Women, it was believed, were best suited as teachers because they exemplified the noncombative and noncompetitive instincts. Because they also could be employed for lower wages than men, women teachers soon predominated in New England's elementary schools.

The character traits most esteemed by educational reformers were precisely those alleged to bring material success in a competitive and market-oriented society: punctuality, cheerful obedience, honesty, responsibility, perseverance, and foresightedness. Public schools seemed to promise opportunity by providing the means of acquiring such traits. In the words of one school committee, the children "entered the race, aware that the prize was equally before all, and attainable only by personal exertion." The famed McGuffey's "Eclectic" series of readers, which after 1836 were used in countless schoolrooms and of which well over 100 million copies were eventually sold, taught young readers that no possession was more important for getting on in the world than reputation, or "a good name." On the other hand, the readers held out little hope of rags-to-riches success. When the good little poor boy sees other children "riding on pretty horses, or in coaches, or walking with ladies and gentlemen, and having on very fine clothes, he does not envy them, nor wish to be like them." For he has been taught "that it is God who makes some poor, and others rich; that the rich have many troubles which we know nothing of; and that the poor, if they are but good, may be very happy."

From a present-day viewpoint, the educational reformers were often insensitive to the needs of the non-Protestants, non-Christians, nonwhites, and women. Throughout the North, except in a few scattered communities, the public schools excluded black children. Many localities made no provision for blacks to be educated. Other towns and cities, including New York and Boston, distributed a small portion of public funds to segregated and highly inferior schools for blacks. By 1850 blacks constituted no more than 1.5 percent of Boston's population,

EDUCATING WOMEN

The pre-Civil War decades opened unprecedented opportunities for middle-class girls to advance beyond an elementary level of education. The price of this opportunity, however, was a system of strict discipline and of constant supervision of manners and morals. *(Left, American Antiquarian Society; Right, The Metropolitan Museum of Art, Gift of I. N. Phelps Stokes, Edward S. Hawes, Alice Mary Hawes, and Marion Augusta Hawes, 1937)*

REGULATIONS

OF THE

FEMALE CLASSICAL SEMINARY, BROOKFIELD.

THE Principal expects of the young Ladies attending his Seminary,

1. That they will attend at the Academy, regularly and punctually, at the hours appointed by the Principal.

2.—That all noise and disorder in the house, before the Principal arrives, and after the exercises are closed, will be carefully avoided.

3.—That, during the hours of instruction, they will give constant and diligent attention to the exercises prescribed, avoiding every thing which would be an interruption to the teacher or pupils.

4.—That, during the recitations, all the members of a class will close their books, except the nature of the recitation requires their being open.

5.—That the young Ladies will constantly attend public worship on the Sabbath.

6.—That they will always board in those families, which have the approbation of the Principal.

7.—That they will not attend balls, assemblies, or other parties for the indulgence of frivolous mirth.

8.—That the social visits of the young Ladies, among the families of the village, will be arranged by the Principal, whenever invitations are extended.

9.—That they will avoid walking or riding, with persons of the other sex, at unseasonable hours.

10.—That they will not leave town, without permission from the Principal.

11.—That they will be subject in all respects to the superintendence and direction of the Principal, while belonging to his school.

TUITION, for each term. Arithmetic, Grammar, or Geography, $3,50.— Rhetoric, History, or Latin, $4,50.——Geometry, Natural Philosophy, Chemistry, Algebra, Euclid, Logic, Intellectual Philosophy, or Moral Philosophy, $5,00.——French, Music, and Painting will probably be taught the ensuing spring.

Sept. 1825.

E. AND G. MERRIAM, PRINTERS, BROOKFIELD.

but it still required a prolonged struggle on the part of militant blacks and white abolitionists to achieve legal desegregation. In 1855 Massachusetts became the single state in which no applicant to a public school could be excluded on account of "race, color or religious opinions." In marked contrast to the public schools, Oberlin, Harvard, Bowdoin, Dartmouth and some other private colleges opened their doors to a few black students. In 1837 Oberlin also became America's first coeducational college. In general, however, American women had no opportunities for higher education except in female seminaries and, by the 1850s, in a few western state universities.

By the 1850s Massachusetts had acquired all the essentials of a modern educational system: special "normal schools" for training female teachers; the grading of pupils according to age and ability; standardized procedures for advancement from one grade to another; uniform textbooks; and a bureaucracy extending from the board of education to superintendents, principals, and teachers. Although Massachusetts led the nation, by the 1850s it was possible for a New York City male child to proceed from an "infant school" to a college degree without paying tuition. Educational reformers, many of them originally New Englanders, had helped to create state-supported and state-supervised school systems from Pennsylvania to the new states of the Upper Mississippi Valley. In the 1850s the same cause made some headway in the South, particularly in Virginia and North Carolina.

Whatever prejudices and blind spots the public school movement may have had, it aroused the enthusiam of hundreds of idealistic men and women who devoted time and energy to the cause. Northern legislators committed an impressive proportion of public spending to the education of succeeding generations. The movement, particularly in the 1850s, trained a young generation of teacher-missionaries, who in time would descend on the devastated South, equipped with an ideology for "reconstruction." Above all, the movement reinforced the American faith that social problems could be solved by individual enterprise, a diffusion of knowledge, and a reconstruction of moral character.

The Evangelical Age

Americans continued to look on the church, no less than the public school, as a decisive instrument for shaping the national character. As in the early national period, religion appeared to thrive the more it achieved independence from the state.* Despite the officially secular stance of American governments, evangelical Protestantism became increasingly identified with patriotism, democracy, and America's mission in the world. Despite the continuing division and competition among religious denominations, Americans increasingly appealed to religion as the only adhesive force that could preserve a sense of community and united purpose.

Religious Revivals.   Between 1820 and 1860 religious revivalism became a powerful organizing and nationalizing force, permeating all parts of American life, in the South as well as the North, in the cities as well as on the western frontier. Although church membership figures can be misleading, since many people who regularly attended church could not meet the religious or financial obligations required for formal membership, it has been stated that by 1835 as many as three out of four adult Americans maintained some nominal relationship to a church. Most foreign observers agreed with Tocqueville that by the 1830s there was no country in the world in which the Christian religion retained "a greater influence over the souls of men."

For the majority of adults evangelical Protestantism provided a common language and a common frame of reference. It explained not only the nature and destiny of man but the meaning of democracy and of American nationality. In the words of a non-church member, a young self-made man and future president of the United States, Andrew Johnson, "Man can become more and more endowed with divinity; and as he does he becomes more God-like in his character and capable of governing himself." Like millions of other Americans, Johnson believed

---

*In 1833 Massachusetts became the last state to give up an established church.

CAMP MEETING, ca. 1835
The religious camp meeting, originally associated with the boisterous and unruly West, became an established and well-organized institution throughout rural America. *(Courtesy of the New York Historical Society, New York City)*

that Christianity and political democracy were together elevating and purifying the people, working toward the day when it could be proclaimed: "The millennial morning has dawned and the time has come when the lion and the lamb shall lie down together, when . . . the glad tidings shall be proclaimed . . . of man's political and religious redemption, and there is 'on earth, peace, good will toward men.'"

In some ways this evangelical vision transcended boundaries of class and section. Although it is possible to think of America as undergoing a single Great Revival during the six decades preceding the Civil War, the revival's social significance differed according to time and place. Some socioeconomic groups were more susceptible to religious enthusiasm than others. Some personality types were likely to view revivalists as self-righteous zealots who threatened to remove all fun from life. Others were likely to

seize the chance to profess faith in Christ crucified, to announce repentance for their sins, to experience the liberation of rebirth, and as the popular hymn put it, to "stand up, stand up for Jesus!" For many Americans religion provided the key to social identity. It was not that people flocked to churches to meet the right kind of people, although some no doubt did. It was rather that the "right" kind of religion, as defined by employers, slaveholders, and other wielders of power, was often considered to bestow the "right" kind of character.

Religious revivalism depended on sensitivity to the community's norms and vital interests. In the South leaders of various denominations discovered that any open criticism of slavery could threaten the very survival of a church. The Baptist and Methodist churches thus gradually retreated from their cautious antislavery pronouncements of the late eighteenth century, which had supposedly bred discontent if not insurrection among Negro slaves. By the 1830s the most influential southern churches had begun to deny that there was any moral contradiction between slavery and Christianity. They also insisted that Christianity, rightly understood, posed no danger to "the peculiar institution."

As a result of the evangelical revivals, southern planters increasingly promoted the religious conversion of their slaves. Even by the first decades of the nineteenth century, a growing number of churchmen and planters had argued that religious instruction would make slaves more obedient, industrious, and faithful. The ideal Christian master would treat his slaves with charity and understanding. The ideal Christian slave would humbly accept his assigned position in this world, knowing that his patience and faithfulness would be rewarded in heaven. Servitude, in short, could be softened, humanized, and perfected by Christianity. The reality of slavery fell far short of the ideal. Religion may have induced many masters to take a sincere interest in their slaves' welfare, but it could not eliminate the cruelty and injustice inherent in the system.

No white preachers could entirely purge Christianity of its subversive overtones, or prevent black preachers from converting it into a source of self-respect, dignity, and faith in eventual deliverance—the longed-for Day of Jubilee. In both North and South, free blacks responded to growing racial discrimination by forming their own "African" churches, usually Baptist or Methodist. And despite the efforts by whites to control every aspect of their slaves' religion, the slaves created their own folk religion and shaped it to their own needs and interests. As one ex-slave from Texas recalled, "The whites preached to the niggers and the niggers preached to theyselves."

MEETING IN THE AFRICAN CHURCH

Although most illustrators tended to caricature American blacks, this wood engraving conveys some of the fervor and emotional intensity of the black churches, the churches that did so much in preserving a sense of hope and communal identity. *(Library of Congress)*

Civilizing the West.　Revivalism also served as a socializing force in the nonslaveholding West, but the context and consequences were different. In the opinion of Easterners, the West was both lawless and sinful. From the lumber camps of Wisconsin to the mining camps of California, the image of Westerners was essentially the same: rough dirty men who swore, gambled, got drunk, frequented houses of prostitution, and relished savage eye-gouging, knife-slashing fights. Although the stereotypes were exaggerated, there was no doubt that frontier communities were a challenge to nineteenth-century notions of decency and civilization.

The challenge of the West could not be met simply by building churches where none had existed before. When Theron Baldwin, a member of a Yale missionary group, arrived in Illinois in 1830, he was horrified by the ignorance of the settlers. Even in Vandalia, the state's capital, Baldwin discovered that most of the pupils in his Sunday school class were illiterate. Nor could he find a literate adult in over half the families he visited in the region. Religion, Baldwin concluded, could make no headway without education and an institutional rebuilding of society. Appealing for funds from the East, he expressed the New England ideal: "We wish to see the school house and church go up side by side and the land filled with Christian teachers as well as preachers." He added, significantly, that young men could come there "and in a short time get enough by teaching to purchase a farm that would ever after fill their barns with plenty and their hands with good things." Baldwin himself worked to secure from the legislature a charter for the first three colleges in the state. As a result of the labors of Baldwin and other young missionaries, the Old Northwest became dotted with academies, seminaries, and small denominational colleges.

Easterners who still thought of churches as fixed institutions within an ordered society did not understand that religious revivals were an effective instrument for shaping and controlling character. The frank emotionalism and homespun informality of the western and southern revivals disguised the fact that even the camp meetings were soon stabilized by rules, regulations, and the most careful advance planning. And camp meetings were by no means the most important tool of the revivals. The power of the movement flowed from the dynamic balance between popular participation and the control of leaders. According to the evangelical message, every man and woman, no matter how humble or mired in sin, had the capacity to say "Yes!" to Christ's offer of salvation—to reject what was called "cannot-ism," and along with it an unsatisfying identity. Even for the poor and uneducated, consent opened the way for participation and decision-making.

Peter Cartwright, for example, grew up in one of the most violent and lawless regions of Kentucky; his brother was hanged for murder, and his sister was said to have "led a life of debauchery." At the age of sixteen Cartwright repented his sins at a Methodist camp meeting; at seventeen he became an exhorter; at eighteen a traveling preacher; at twenty-one a deacon; and at twenty-three a presiding elder of the church. Each upward step required a probationary period, followed by an examination of the candidate's conduct, ability, and purity of doctrine. The Methodists showed particular skill in devising a system that encouraged widespread participation and upward mobility under hierarchical authority. But all the evangelical churches displayed the great American gift for organization. Revivals, they believed, could not be had by waiting for God to stir human hearts. Revivals required planning, efficient techniques, and coordinated effort. The need was not for educated theologians but for professional promoters.

Christianity and the Social Order.　While revivalism was an organizing and socializing movement, it was also by definition selective. The people most likely to be converted were those who had some Christian upbringing or those who were already disturbed by excessive drinking, gambling, fighting, disorder, and irresponsibility. Conversion itself reinforced crucial social distinctions. For one part of the community, religion became more than a matter of going to church on Sunday. The obligations of a new religious life required sobriety and responsibility from friends, family, employees, and business associates. The weekly "class meetings" and "love feasts" provided fellowship and helped to prevent backsliding. No doubt the solidarity of the converted brought order and discipline to the community at large. But if the evangelicals always insisted that every man and woman could say "Yes!", there were always those who said "No!" The congregations that loved to hear their preachers "pouring hot shot into Satan's ranks" knew that Satan's ranks were concentrated on the other side of the tracks.

Religious revivals could accentuate social distinctions by forging an alliance among the more ambitious, self-disciplined, and future-oriented members of a community. In the fall of 1830, for example, the leaders of Rochester, New York, invited Charles Grandison Finney to save that booming city from sin. By far the most commanding and influential evangelist of the pre–Civil War period, Finney was a tall, athletic spellbinder, a former lawyer who had undergone a dramatic religious conversion in 1823. Though lacking formal seminary training, Finney had been ordained as a Prebyterian minister and in 1825 had begun a series of highly unorthodox and spectacular revivals along the route of the newly constructed Erie Canal.

In 1831 Finney's triumphs in Rochester stunned Christian America; communities from Ohio to Boston appealed to him to save their collective souls. Finney's converts in Rochester were largely manufacturers, merchants, lawyers, shopkeepers, master artisans, and skilled journeymen. He appealed to people who had profited from the commercial revolution initiated by the building of the Erie Canal but who had become deeply disturbed by the immense influx of young transient laborers looking for work. Rochester's leaders had no control over the behavior of these youths. Significantly, during Rochester's revival years church membership declined among the hotel proprietors and tavern keepers who catered to the floating population of young males traveling the Erie Canal. Rochester's Protestant churches, interpreting the revival as a sweeping popular mandate, launched a crusade to purge the city of its dens of vice and unholy amusement. They also offered a "free church" —free of pew rents and other financial obligations—

to the workers on the canal. Increasingly Rochester became divided between a Christian minority dedicated to education and upward advancement and an essentially nonpolitical, free-floating majority of disoriented and unskilled young men.

Philadelphia differed from Rochester in important respects, but there, too, religious revivals eventually redefined the boundaries of respectable and "modern" behavior. Unlike Rochester, which grew by 512 percent in the 1820s, Philadelphia was not a new boom town. An old city by American standards, Philadelphia was relatively resistant to religious enthusiasm. Revivalism had little appeal to the wealthy Quakers and conservative Presbyterian clergy who dominated the city's religious life. Evangelical morality was even less appealing to Philadelphia's workingmen, who preserved and cherished a traditional artisan, preindustrial culture. Largely because of irregular and undeveloped transportation to interior markets, Philadelphia workers suffered periodic layoffs. This forced leisure allowed them to enjoy traveling circuses, cockfights, drinking and gambling at the local taverns, and above all, the boisterous comradeship of voluntary fire companies. Until 1837 neither the revival nor the closely related temperance movement made much headway among Philadelphia's manual workers. The people who reformed their drinking habits and who joined the reform-minded wing of the Presbyterian church were the professional and business groups who were ushering in the new industrial order. But in 1837 the financial panic and subsequent depression began to undermine the traditional habits and culture of the working class. Waves of religious revivalism, often Methodist in character, reached working-class neighborhoods. A new and more powerful temperance movement developed spontaneously from the ranks of master craftsmen, journeymen, shopkeepers, and the most ambitious unskilled laborers. In Philadelphia, as in Rochester, the decision to abstain from all alcohol was the key symbol of a new morality and of a commitment to self-improvement. By the 1840s the evangelical workingmen could contrast their own sobriety and self-discipline with the moral laxity of mounting numbers of Irish immigrants. Not surpris-

RIOT IN PHILADELPHIA
In 1844 anti-Catholic violence reached a climax in Philadelphia, where the Catholic bishop had persuaded school officials to allow the use of both the King James and Latin vulgate Bibles. After Protestant mobs had burned two Catholic churches, a full-scale riot required the intervention of state militia. *(The Library Company of Philadelphia)*

ingly, the revivalism that bolstered the self-respect of blue-collar native workers also contributed to virulent anti-Catholicism and to nativist prejudice against a population that seemed to threaten the newly won dignity of manual labor.

Revivalism and Economic Prosperity.   Revivals appeared to be the only hopeful counterforce against rampant individualism, self-serving politics, and corrupting luxury. As Finney put it, "the great political and other worldly excitements" of the time distracted attention from the interests of the soul. He held, accordingly, that these excitements could "only

be counteracted by *religious* excitements." Only revivals could prevent the United States from sliding into the decay and collapse of ancient Greece and Rome, and prepare the nation "to lead the way," in Lyman Beecher's phrase, "in the moral and political emancipation of the world."

Revivalism was fed by the moral doubts that inevitably accompanied rapid economic growth, the disruption of older modes of work and responsibility, the sudden accumulation of wealth, and the appearance of new class divisions. Revivalist preachers denounced atheism far less than "mammonism," the greedy pursuit of riches. They voiced repeated concern over the frantic pace of American life, the disintegration of family and community, and the worship of material success.

But revivalism seldom led to ascetic withdrawal or to spiritualistic contemplation. Evangelical religion was above all activist, pragmatic, and oriented toward measurable results. The fame of Finney and the other great exhorters depended on the body count, or soul count, of converts. Finney proclaimed: "The results justify my methods"—a motto that could as well have come from John D. Rockefeller or other entrepreneurs in more worldly spheres. Finney confidently predicted: "If the church will do her duty, the millennium may come in this country in three years." He knew, however, that a millennium would require no revivals, and that as a revivalist, though dedicated to virtue, he needed sin much as a soldier needs war.

There was a close relation between the revivals and America's expansive economy. The exuberant materialism of American life furnished revivalists with continuing targets for attack and with vivid symbols of communal strife and moral shortcoming. Without moral crises there would be no cause for national rededication, and calls for rededication have long been America's way of responding to social change. But on another level, the revivalists had merged their cause with America's secular destiny. They had repeatedly warned that without religion, American democracy would speedily dissolve into "a common field of unbridled appetite and lust." Yet instead of dissolving, the nation continued to prosper, expand, and reveal new marvels. Sometimes clergymen hailed the achievements as signs of national virtue and divine favor. More important, as a reflection of their increasing respect for efficient methods and material results, they applauded technological improvements as the instruments that God had provided for saving the world.

The telegraph, railroad, and steamship all quickened the way for spreading the gospel around the world, and could thus be interpreted as portents of the coming millennium. But America's technology and rapid westward expansion could be justified only if America took seriously the burdens of a missionary nation. Samuel Fisher, the president of Hamilton College, elaborated on the message in an address to the American Board of Commissioners for Foreign Missions:

Material activity, quickened and guided by moral principle, is absolutely essential to the development of a strong and manly character. . . . The product of this devotion to material interests is capital diffused through the masses; and capital is one of the means God uses to convert the world.

The diffusion of capital through the masses seemed to falter in 1857, when a financial crash brought a severe depression and unprecedented unemployment among factory workers. Economic insecurity formed the backdrop of what many took to be "the event of the century," the great urban revival of late 1857 and 1858. What distinguished the event from earlier religious revivals was the absence of revivalists. In Philadelphia and New York thousands of clerks and businessmen began to unite spontaneously for midday prayer. The New York *Herald* and the New York *Tribune* devoted special issues to the remarkable events—wealthy stockbrokers praying and singing next to messenger boys; revivals in the public high schools; joint services by Methodists, Episcopalians, Presbyterians, Baptists, and even the traditionally antirevivalist Unitarians. The spirit rapidly spread to manufacturing towns throughout the Northeast. Unscheduled and unconventional religious meetings sprang up in small towns and rural areas from Indiana to Quebec. "It would seem," wrote one enthusiast, "that the mighty crash was just what was wanted . . . to startle men from their golden dreams." Americans had become too overbearing, too self-confident, too complacent in their success. Yet if God had shown His displeasure, as countless interpreters maintained, He had also chosen means that underscored America's promise. He had punished Americans with economic loss, which even the hardest head among the business community could understand.

The great revival of 1858 gave a new sense of unity to Northerners who had become increasingly divided by class and religious conflict, to say nothing of the issue of slavery. It also signified the maturity of an urban, industrial Protestantism committed to material progress and self-improvement. For good or for ill, the revivals reinvigorated America's official ideal of *Novus Ordo Seclorum*—a phrase stamped on every dollar bill, conveying the message that a new social order is to exist, that Americans carry the high burden of helping to create a better world.

The Cult of Self-Improvement

What made public schools and religious revivals seem so indispensable by the 1830s was the relative absense of authoritative institutions that could define social roles, rules of conduct, and models of character. There was no standing army, for example, that could train a military class or enforce unpopular public policy. The disestablishment of the churches gave semiliterate evangelists the same official status as college-trained theologians. Some states guaranteed any citizen, regardless of training, the right to practice law in any court. Increasingly Americans showed little respect for any intellectual elite, religious or secular, or for any group of self-perpetuating masters who claimed to preserve and monopolize a body of knowledge that the public at large could not understand.

Not only had American law rejected Old World notions of privileged social orders, but as time went on courts swept away most of the legal barriers that had restrained individuals from entering into certain kinds of risky or inequitable agreements. In other words, the law assumed that all society was a market of competitive exchange in which each individual calculated the probable risks of a given choice of action. This burden of individual freedom and responsibility placed an enormous premium on acquiring effective skills and up-to-date knowledge. Continuous self-improvement became the great ideal of the age.

Lyceums and Learning. To Americans of the late twentieth century there is nothing novel about fads, cults, and nostrums that promise the solution to life's problems. But in the 1830s and 1840s the cult of self-improvement was unprecedented in both the boldness and variety of its appeals. Some conservatives expressed alarm over the credulity of public opinion, assuming that fads and quackery posed a threat to public order. But the pervasive desire of the people was not for restructuring society but for self-knowledge and self-advancement. Numerous respectable societies and institutes for adult education and "mutual improvement" began to spread in the 1820s from England to the United States. Tens of thousands of adults, first in New England and then in the Old Northwest, grew accustomed to attending lyceums—public lectures, concerts, and cultural events. Lyceum lectures covered a vast range of subjects, but tended during the early years of the movement to concentrate on "useful knowledge" associated with moral improvement and popular science.

Americans generally equated the advance of science with the advance of human liberty, a linkage that was part of the heritage of the European Enlightenment. They believed that everyone could benefit from the scientific method; the marvels and secrets of nature were open to all. But what most impressed and fascinated American audiences were lectures and books on the applications of science, demonstrating the ingenious ways that human beings could master nature. As early as 1829 Jacob Bigelow's *Elements of Technology* not only helped to popularize a

new word but gave impetus to the general public's growing inclination to see invention as the key to national progress. Excitement over the uses of technology and steam power was matched by a new curiosity about the human mind, which had shown that it could unlock nature's secrets.

Mind Control.   The gap between public ignorance and the achievements of science could be bridged if someone invented the supreme technology, a technology for controlling the human mind. The quest for such power united many of the popular cults and fads. Mesmerists, for example, claimed to have discovered the laws of magnetic attraction and repulsion that governed relations between people. Spiritualists convinced hundreds of thousands that they had found techniques and apparatus for communicating with the dead and probing the laws of the occult. Even the manuals on self-improvement and character building, directed mainly at the young, presumed definitive knowledge of the mechanics of the brain. The Reverend John Todd's *Student's Manual* (1835), which sold by the hundreds of thousands, maintained that mental power depends on a strict conservation of bodily and especially sexual energies. Todd's thesis, repeated by countless physicians and other experts, was that masturbation or sexual excess of any kind posed the

gravest threats to sanity, social order, and individual achievement. Self-improvement required the rigorous avoidance of unwholesome thoughts and tempting situations.

Phrenology.   Phrenology, however, was the most ambitious and institutionalized science of the mind. The invention of Franz Joseph Gall, a Viennese physician, phrenology identified the supposed physical location in the brain of a large assortment of human "faculties," such as firmness, benevolence, acquisitiveness, destructiveness, and platonic love. Phrenologists claimed that they could precisely measure character from the form and shape of a head. Americans first responded to phrenology as a promising medical breakthrough. Gall's leading disciple, Johann Gaspar Spurzheim, became the first missionary for the cause. On a visit to America in 1832, he was lionized by New England dignitaries, including Justice Joseph Story and the Yale chemist Benjamin Silliman. For a time the support of Horace Mann, the famous Unitarian preacher William Ellery Channing, and business leaders like Abbott Lawrence gave phrenology intellectual prestige. As usual, however, the American public displayed far more interest in practical application than in theory. Two skillful promoters, Orson and Lorenzo Fowler, helped to convert

LYCEUM LECTURE
A caricature of the early
man-of-science, pontificating
to an audience of attentive
women and to a few apparently inattentive men. *(Museum of the City of New York)*

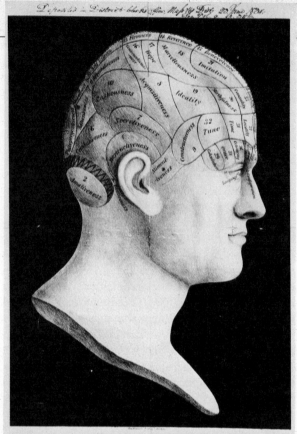

DR. SPURZHEIM.
Divisions of the Organs of Phrenology marked externally

PHRENOLOGY CHART
This widely circulated bust of Dr. Johann Spurzheim illustrated the physical location of an amazing assortment of abilities, inclinations, and character traits.
(Library of Congress)

phrenology into a major business enterprise. In the cities audiences of thousands paid fees for lengthy lecture series expounding the new science. Thousands more flocked to salons to have their characters analyzed. Itinerant lecturers and mail-order courses enlightened the countryside. By the mid-1850s the *American Phrenological Journal* had a circulation of over fifty thousand.

In many ways phrenology perfectly suited the needs of a people devoted to technique and uncertain of their own character. In an expansive and socially disruptive economy, it provided a new set of guidelines that reduced the fear of risk. Employers, for example, no longer able to rely on long-term apprenticeships, on personal knowledge of an employee's family, or even on a worker's reputation in the community, could request a phrenological examination. Young men who dreamed of many careers but who could decide on none welcomed a science that would measure their talents and capabilities. The great message of phrenology was individual adjustment. In a world of confusing and fluid expectations, it furnished boundaries and specific identities. It told the individual which traits to cultivate and which to restrain. For the faithful it also made life more predictable. Criminologists not only found a physical explanation for deviant behavior, but discovered a new hope for preventing crime by identifying potential criminals and by teaching convicts to control their overdeveloped antisocial faculties. Although Americans gradually came to realize that the results of phrenology could not substantiate its high promise, they had expressed an ardent desire, which would continue to our own time, for a popular science of human behavior.

Emerson. Like phrenology, the essays and lyceum lectures of Ralph Waldo Emerson, who came closer than anyone else to being America's official philosopher of the nineteenth century, offered something for everyone and thus nourished hope for reduced friction and for social harmony. While there is no way of knowing how much influence Emerson actually had on American thought and culture, he helped to stimulate the great literary renaissance of the 1850s. For decades to come his writing was a source of inspiration for reformers, businessmen, and countless ordinary folk. It can be argued that Emerson's worship of power and of self-improvement provided the spiritual backdrop for the entire progressive era of the early twentieth century.

Yet Emerson's thought eludes all attempts at classification or categorization. His words awakened reformers but he wrote the most penetrating critiques of reform of his generation. He was at once the most homespun, down-to-earth, and yet stratospheric of American thinkers. An ardent champion of cultural independence, he defined the mission of native artists and writers, yet exploited his knowledge of the newest currents of German and English thought. He was the leading figure in a group that domesticated German idealistic philosophy, usually referred to by Immanuel Kant's awkward term "Transcendentalism"; but he championed an extreme form of individualism and never felt comfortable as a member of any association. His pithy maxims on self-reliance were quoted by anarchists and yet were framed on the walls of the nation's business leaders.

Emerson's spongelike capacity to absorb ideas and the common attitudes of his time, and his empathy for all sides and commitment to none, had much in common with America's greatest weaknesses and strengths. To various audiences he proclaimed that "who so would be a man, must be a noncon-

RALPH WALDO EMERSON, 1803–1882
(Library of Congress)

formist." To the youth of America he delivered the reassuring thought: "We but half express ourselves, and are ashamed of the divine idea which each of us represents. . . . Trust thyself: every heart vibrates to that iron string." He upbraided Americans for their single-minded pursuit of wealth and fame, for their obsession with material things. But the point of this protest against materialism and conformity—which became clearer as both Emerson and his audiences grew older—was the need for a continuing reshaping and reinvigoration of the American character.

To Emerson the great peril that threatened the American people was not injustice but a fragmentation of soul: "The reason why the world lacks unity and lies broken and in heaps, is because man is disunited with himself." The essential problem, then, was one of reconstituting character, of recovering a sense of the whole. By self-reliance Emerson really meant a detachment from society in order to achieve the sense of wholeness that flowed from unity with God, or as Emerson put it, "the Oversoul." This notion that every "private man" possesses infinite and godlike capacities was an inspiring ideal, perfectly suited to the fantasies and aspirations of many Americans. At times, however, this doctrine meant that Emerson had no standard beyond power and success: "Power is, in nature, the essential measure of right."

The Tensions of Democratic Art

The continuing democratization of American culture produced a profound ambivalence about the artistic standards and precedents of European culture. On the one hand, American writers and artists felt the need to proclaim their independence from Europe and to create a genuinely native art, stripped of aristocratic associations. On the other hand, by the 1820s it was becoming clear that political independence did not guarantee cultural independence and that republican institutions would not automatically give birth to the Great American Masterwork. Improved transportation, coupled with a prolonged period of peace in Europe, made it easier for Americans to cross the Atlantic in search of inspiration and training.

"THE GREEK SLAVE" AT THE DUSSELDORF GALLERY

The traveling exhibition of Hiram Powers's "The Greek Slave" created the greatest artistic sensation of the pre-Civil War decades. The daring—and to some, immoral—display of female nudity was justified by the "ideality" of the form and by the assumption that the enslaved girl had been immodestly stripped by her brutal Turkish captors. *(The New York Public Library)*

LOOKING NORTH TO KINGSTON

An example of the Hudson River School of landscape painting in which human settlement and transport are blended into a dreamy, spiritualized Nature. *(Courtesy, Smith College Museum of Art)*

Even the more ardent cultural nationalists viewed Europe with awe and fascination. Often shocked by European contrasts between elegance and squalor, they were also dazzled by the great cathedrals, castles, spacious parks, monumental public buildings, museums, and villas. From Washington Irving's *Alhambra* (1832) to Nathaniel Hawthorne's *Marble Faun* (1860), American writers expressed their enchantment with castles and ruins, with places that had been steeped in centuries of history. Whatever its evils, Europe teemed with associations that fed the imagination. It was the continent of mystery, of beauty, of romance, and in short, of culture. For many American artists it was also at least a temporary refuge from the materialism, vulgarity, and hurried pace of life they found in the United States. It is significant that Washington Irving was living in England when he created the classic American tales "Rip Van Winkle" and "The Legend of Sleepy Hollow" (1819–20). James Fenimore Cooper was living in Paris when he wrote *The Prairie* (1827). Horatio Greenough, America's first professional sculptor and a champion of democratic artistic theory, completed his gigantic, half-draped statue of George Washington, a statue commissioned by the United States government, in his studio in Florence.

It would be a mistake, however, to think of American art of the period as slavishly imitative. Although Americans tended to express native subject matter in conventional artistic forms, they became increasingly skilled and sophisticated in their mastery of the forms. The choice of native material also affected the total character of a work. For example, space, nature, and the wilderness took on new qualities as Thomas Cole, Asher B. Durand, and other painters of the Hudson River school sought to idealize the American landscape. Cooper's five "Leatherstocking Tales," *The Pioneers* (1823), *The Last of the Mohicans* (1826), *The Prairie* (1827), *The Pathfinder* (1840), and *The Deerslayer* (1841), were far more than American versions of Sir Walter Scott's "Waverley novels." Like William Gilmore Simms's tales of the southern frontier and backcountry, they gave imaginative expression to a distinctively American experience with Indians, violence, the law, and the meaning of social bonds in a wilderness setting. The popular New England poets and men-of-letters chose homey, unpretentious subjects that disguised both their literary skill and erudition. Thus Henry Wadsworth Longfellow, a translator of Dante and a master of meter, celebrated the village blacksmith. John Greenleaf Whittier sang of the barefoot boy. The highly cultivated James Russell Lowell delivered political satire in the homespun Yankee dialect of an imaginary Hosea Biglow.

Art as Product.   By the 1820s it was becoming clear that art in America would have to be marketed like any other commodity, and that the ideal of the dabbling gentleman amateur would have to give way to the reality of the professional who wrote, carved, or painted for a living. Federal, state, and local governments did award a few commissions for patriotic and historical subjects, but political squabbles over art (including the seminudity of Greenough's Washington) dampened artists' desire for government patronage. The need to compete for middle-class customers and audiences helps to explain the dominant patriotic, didactic, and sentimental themes of popular American culture.

Art as Character Shaper.   A self-consciously democratic art, as opposed to the remnants of folk art that it began to replace, had to justify itself by serving such essentially nonartistic needs as shaping of character. Before the Civil War, both literature and the so-called fine arts claimed to perform educational, quasi-religious functions. They provided models to imitate, they trained and refined the emotions and they taught that sin is always punished and virtue rewarded. Art promoted patriotism by glorifying the American Revolution and deifying George Washington. It defined idealized sex roles by identifying the American male as the man of action and conquerer of nature—hunter, trapper, scout, mountain man, sea-faring adventurer—and by associating the American female with refinement of emotions—physical frailty, periods of melancholy, and a sensitivity expressed by sudden blushing, paleness, tears, and fainting—and confinement in a home. Above all, art furnished models of speech, manners, courtship, friendship, and grief that helped to establish standards of middle-class respectability.

A few writers achieved the imaginative indepen-

THE TALCOTT FAMILY
This "primitive" watercolor of the Talcott family by Deborah Goldsmith captures the ideal of the home as a private refuge, surrounded by trees and green space. Note that the father and mother share the responsibilities of parenthood, and that the grandmother seems detached in space as well as by her old-fashioned dress. *(Courtesy, Abby Aldrich Rockefeller Folk Art Center, Williamsburg, Virginia)*

dence to interpret character and sensibility in new ways. Edgar Allan Poe, who strove for commercial success while remaining committed to the ideal of art as an autonomous craft, gave a dark transmutation to the stock themes of sentimental poetry and fiction. In a different way Nathaniel Hawthorne subtly transcended the conventions of sentimental moralism in *The Scarlet Letter* (1850), *The House of the Seven Gables* (1851), and *The Blithedale Romance* (1852). This period of creativity, later termed the American Renaissance, included Walt Whitman's *Leaves of Grass* (1855), which not only celebrated the boundless potentialities of American experience but took joy in defying the conventional limits of poetic language. Herman Melville's *Moby Dick* (1851), one of the world's great novels, also fused native subject matter with new and distinctively American artistic forms. Henry David Thoreau's *Walden* (1854) stated a goal that could be applied to many of the best works of the period. Thoreau had nothing but contempt for the conventional efforts to shape character in the interest of social conformity. But Thoreau's decision to live by himself on Walden Pond was an experiment in self-improvement. The goal of his experiment, and of the art it produced, was to break free from the distractions and artificialities that disguised "the essential facts of life"—"to drive life into a corner, and reduce it to its lowest terms." "For most men, it appears to me," he said, "are in a strange uncertainty about it, whether it is of the devil or of God."

SUGGESTED READINGS

An excellent collection of source material on children can be found in the first volume of Robert H. Bremner, ed., *Children and Youth in America: A Documentary History* (1970–71). Two recent studies of the history of juvenile delinquency are Joseph M. Hawes, *Children in Urban Society* (1971), and Robert M. Mennel, *Thorns and Thistles* (1973).

Michael Katz, *The Irony of Early School Reform* (1968), sharply challenges the self-congratulatory tradition of educational history. Two important studies, also critical but more balanced, are: Carl F. Kaestle, *The Evolution of an Urban School System: New York City, 1750–1850* (1973), and Stanley K. Schultz, *The Culture Factory: Boston Public Schools, 1789–1860* (1973). Rush Welter, *Popular Education and Democratic Thought in America* (1962), presents a more traditional approach, and so does the excellent biography by Jonathan Messerli, *Horace Mann* (1972). Among the special studies of note are Bernard Wishy, *The Child and the Republic: The Dawn of Modern American Child Nurture* (1968); Marianna C. Brown, *The Sunday School Movement in America* (1961); Ruth Elson, *Guardians of Tradition: American Schoolbooks of the Nineteenth Century* (1964); Vincent P. Lannie, *Public Money and Parochial Education* (1968); and Merle Curti, *The Social Ideas of American Educators* (1935). The best introduction to higher education is Frederick Rudolph, *The American College and University* (1962), which can be supplemented by Theodore R. Crane, ed., *The Colleges and the Public, 1767–1862* (1963), and by Richard Hofstadter and Wilson Smith, *American Higher Education: A Documentary History* (2 vols., 1961).

The most imaginative treatment of revivalism is the first section of Perry Miller, *The Life of the Mind in America* (1965). William G. McLoughlin, Jr., *Modern Revivalism* (1959), gives a more detailed and systematic account of individual revivalists and more recently McLoughlin has written a stimulating interpretive essay, *Revivals, Awakenings, and Reform: An Essay on Religion and Social Change in America, 1607–1977* (1978). Charles A. Johnson, *The Frontier Camp Meeting* (1955), is the standard history of the subject. The wider social impact of revivalism in New York State is brilliantly traced in Whitney Cross, *The Burned-Over District* (1950), but this must now be supplemented by Paul E. Johnson's *A Shopkeeper's Millennium: Society and Revivals in Rochester, New York, 1815–1837* (1978).

The fullest general history of American religion is Sydney E. Ahlstrom, *A Religious History of the American People* (1972). A provocative study analyzing the cultural alliance between Protestant ministers and middle-class women is Ann Douglas, *The Feminization of American Culture* (1977). Among the special studies of unusual interest are Henri Desroche, *The American Shakers from Neo-Christianity to Pre-Socialism* (1971); Nathan Glazer, *American Judaism* (1957); Daniel W. Howe, *The Unitarian Conscience* (1970); Martin Marty, *The Infidel: Freethought in American Religion* (1961); William G. McLoughlin, Jr., *The Meaning of Henry Ward Beecher* (1970); Theodore Maynard, *The Story of American Catholicism* (1960); Ernest L. Tuveson, *Redeemer Nation:*

The Idea of America's Millennial Role (1968). D. H. Meyer, *The Instructed Conscience: The Shaping of the American National Ethic* (1972); T. D. Bozeman, *Protestants in an Age of Science: The Baconian Ideal and Antebellum American Religious Thought* (1977); and Winton U. Solberg, *Redeem the Time: The Puritan Sabbath in Early America* (1977).

Perry Miller, *Life of the Mind in America* (1965), contains a brilliant analysis of legal thought in America. A masterly interpretive work is James W. Hurst, *Law and Social Order in the United States* (1977), which should be contrasted with the challenging and highly innovative work by Morton J. Horwitz, *The Transformation of American Law, 1780–1860* (1977). An important aspect of constitutional development is traced in Bernard Schwartz, *From Confederation to Nation: The American Constitution, 1835–1877* (1973). Leonard W. Levy, *The Law of the Commonwealth and Chief Justice Shaw* (1957), is an outstanding study of a leading jurist. The standard biographies of Marshall and Taney are Albert J. Beveridge, *The Life of John Marshall* (4 vols., 1916–19), and Carl B. Swisher, *Roger B. Taney* (1936).

On science, the last section of Perry Miller's *Life of the Mind* contains important insights. The best general work is George Daniels, *American Science in the Age of Jackson* (1968). For medicine, see Richard H. Shryock, *Medicine and Society in America* (1960); and Martin Kaufman, *Homeopathy in America: The Rise and Fall of a Medical Heresy* (1971). Among the best biographies of individual scientists are Edward Lurie, *Agassiz: A Life of Science in America* (1960), and Frances Williams, *Matthew Fontaine Maury* (1963).

John D. Davies, *Phrenology: Fad and Science* (1955), is highly informative. Carl Bode treats the popularization of knowledge in *The American Lyceum* (1956), and reveals popular taste and culture in *The Anatomy of American Popular Culture* (1959).

The most illuminating studies of Emerson's thought are Joel Porte, *Representative Man: Ralph Waldo Emerson in His Time* (1979), and Stephen Whicher, *Freedom and Fate: An Inner Life of Ralph Waldo Emerson* (1953). O. B. Frothingham, *Transcendentalism in New England* (1876), conveys a young participant's memories of the liberating excitement of the Transcendentalist movement. Perry Miller, ed., *The Transcendentalists* (1950), is a difficult but magnificent anthology. Walter Harding's *Thoreau: Man of Concord* (1960), and Joseph W. Krutch, *Henry David Thoreau* (1948), can be supplemented with profit by Richard Lebeaux, *Young Man Thoreau* (1977). For individual Transcendentalists, see Charles Crowe, *George Ripley* (1967); Odell Shepard, *Pilgrim's Progress: The Life of Bronson Alcott* (1937); and Arthur M. Schlesinger, Jr., *Orestes A. Brownson* (1939). F. O. Matthiessen, *American Renaissance* (1941), is a brilliant and unsurpassed study of Emerson, Thoreau, Hawthorne, Melville, and Whitman.

Of the numerous studies of important literary figures, the following have special value for the historian: Richard Chase, *The American Novel and Its Tradition* (1957); Joel Porte, *The Romance in America: Studies in Cooper, Poe, Hawthorne, Melville, and James* (1969); Charles Feidelson, Jr., *Symbolism and American Literature* (1953); A. N. Kaul, *The American Vision: Actual and Ideal Society in Nineteenth-Century Fiction* (1963); R. W. B. Lewis, *The American Adam: Innocence, Tragedy, and Tradition in the Nineteenth Century* (1955); and David Levin, *History as Romantic Art* (1959). For Whitman, see Gay Allen, *The Solitary Singer* (1967). The best introduction to Poe is Edward Wagenknecht, *Edgar Allan Poe: The Man Behind the Legend* (1963). Newton Arvin has written two fine literary biographies: *Herman Melville* (1950); and *Longfellow: His Life and Work* (1963). For Hawthorne, see Edward Wagenknecht, *Nathaniel Hawthorne: Man and Writer* (1961).

Van Wyck Brooks, *The Flowering of New England, 1815–1865* (1936), is still highly readable and informative. On the South, the best guide is Jay B. Hubbell, *The South in American Literature, 1607–1900* (1954). Henry Nash Smith, *Virgin Land: The American West as Symbol and Myth* (1950), is a brilliant study of the imaginative portrayal of the West. The early publishing industry is analyzed in William Charvat, *Literary Publishing in America, 1790–1850* (1959). For popular literature, see James Hart, *The Popular Book in America* (1950); Herbert R. Brown, *The Sentimental Novel in America, 1798–1860* (1940); and Frank L. Mott, *Golden Multitudes: The Story of Best Sellers in the United States* (1947). Mott, *American Journalism* (1962), is the standard source on newspapers. The first volume of Mott's monumental *A History of American Magazines* (5 vols., 1957), is a mine of information. For folk songs, see Alan Lomax, *The Folk Song in North America* (1969).

Oliver W. Larkin, *Art and Life in America* (1949), is the fullest study of the early history of art and architecture. On painting it should be supplemented by Barbara Novak's superb study, *Nature and Culture: American Landscape and Painting, 1825–1875* (1980), as well as David C. Huntington, *Art and the Excited Spirit: America in the Romantic Period* (1972); and James T. Flexner, *That Wilder Image: The Painting of America's Native School from Thomas Cole to Winslow Homer* (1962). Neil Harris, *The Artist in American Society: The Formative Years, 1790–1860* (1966), is a sensitive study of art as a profession. Arthur H. Quinn, *American Drama* (2 vols., 1955), is a comprehensive introduction to the theater. A more imaginative work is David Grimstead, *Melodrama Unveiled* (1968). On architecture, see Talbot F. Hamlin, *Greek Revival Architecture in America* (1944); and Wayne Andrews, *Architecture in America* (1960). The best guides to early American music are Gilbert Chase, *America's Music* (1955); H. Wiley Hitchcock, *Music in the United States* (1969); and Dena J. Epstein, *Sinful Tunes and Spirituals: Black Folk Music through the Civil War* (1977).

CHAPTER 15

Dissent, Protest, and Reform

*T*he desire to transform character lay at the heart of American reform. Like other Americans, reformers rejoiced in the nation's freedom from kings and nobles, from aristocratic institutions, and from status and roles defined at birth. They were cheered by the absence or removal of traditional barriers to human progress. But in pursuing the good life that had supposedly been made accessible by the sacrifices of the Founders, Americans had somehow created a society of astounding moral and physical contrasts—a society of luxury and of squalor, of spiritual uplift and of degradation, of freedom and of bondage. In the eyes of dissenters and reformers, it often seemed that America was ruled only by the principles of ruthless self-interest and power.

The spirit of dissent and reform centered in the Northeast and particularly in New England. During the years before the Civil War, this region spawned numerous crusades to regenerate the social order—to substitute love, harmony, and cooperation for what William Ellery Channing termed the "jarring interests and passions, invasions of rights, resistance of authority, violence, force" that were deforming the entire society. Whether these movements were religious or secular, most of them sought to orient American culture to a "higher law," "the moral government of God," as a means of preventing anarchy. Though reformers differed in their specific objectives, they shared a common desire to channel spiritual aspirations into the secular world of power.

Their procedures—the character of the reform movement of the pre–Civil War period—were unique. Throughout the ages religious reformers had sent out missionaries to convert the heathen, and had sought to provide the world with models of ascetic life, dietary discipline, and selfless commitment. But they had never created the kind of highly professional reform organizations that began to spring up in Britain and America in the early nineteenth century. These organizations were devoted to various goals—to abolishing slavery, to building model penitentiaries, to persuading people to abstain from alcoholic drinks. The objectives were uncompromising, and the systematic techniques for mobilizing public opinion and exerting pressure on public officials were altogether novel.

Nevertheless, these reform movements usually embodied a nostalgia for a supposedly simpler and more harmonious past. Members of the movements believed that the evils they combated had multiplied because of an alarming disintegration of family authority and community cohesiveness and of traditional morality. The various programs, therefore, had a dual objective for change and improvement. On the one hand, they attacked institutions, lifestyles, and traditional social roles that seemed to limit individual opportunity and to block the path of progress. On the other hand, they attempted to restore and revitalize a sense of purity, simplicity, and wholeness which had been lost in the headlong pursuit of modernity and material improvement.

The Mormons as a Test Case

The history of the Mormons is seldom included in discussions of American dissent and reform. Yet, not only was Mormonism America's first truly indigenous religion, it began as a radical expression of dissent—so radical that Mormons found that they could survive only by building their own asylum in the remote deserts of the Far West. Because the early history of Mormonism exemplifies so many of the aspirations and difficulties of other dissenters—who wished to live in their own ways in accordance with a higher moral law, free from the religious and political contaminations of their time—the Mormon experience can serve as an introduction or "test case." What the Mormons tested, essentially, were the outermost limits of permissible dissent, and the ability of any group or subculture to withstand the pressures of American secular society.

Joseph Smith, Founder. In 1830 Joseph Smith, Jr., published The Book of Mormon in Palmyra, New York. He said the work was a translation of mysterious golden plates containing the history of an ancient Christian civilization in the New World. It also portrayed the American Indians as the degenerate but salvageable descendants of an ancient Hebrew tribe, and foresaw a new American prophet who would

discover the lost history and reestablish Christ's pure and undefiled kingdom in the New World. In 1830 Smith was an athletic, gregarious, cheerful, intensely imaginative man of twenty-four, who was subject to visions and claimed revelations. He was the son of one of America's many families of drifters, debtors, and habitual losers, whose poverty worsened as they drew closer to belts of commercial prosperity. Smith had been born in the hills of Vermont, and his parents had migrated to that caldron of progress and poverty, of religious revivalism and new social movements, in upstate New York that was soon to be known as the "Burned-Over District." Shortly after the publication of The Book of Mormon, Smith organized the Church of Christ, which in 1834 would be renamed the Church of Jesus Christ of Latter-Day Saints.

Faced from the outset with religious persecution, Smith knew that the saints must ultimately move westward and build their city of Zion at some divinely appointed spot near the Indian tribes they were commissioned to convert. As he was told to do in his revelations, he dispatched missionaries to scout out the Missouri frontier. In 1831 a few Mormons established an outpost near Independence, Missouri, which Smith designated as the site of the New Jerusalem, and which was then the eastern entry to the Santa Fe Trail. During the same year Smith and his New York followers migrated to Kirtland, Ohio, near Cleveland, where Mormon missionaries had converted an entire community.

Persecution of Mormons. By 1839 the Mormons had met defeat in both Ohio and Missouri and were fleeing to a refuge of swampy Illinois farmland that Smith had bought along the eastern shore of the Mississippi. In Ohio the Mormons had experimented with communal ownership of property and with an illegal, wildcat banking venture that had brought disaster during the Panic of 1837. In Missouri pro-southern mobs, hostile to any group of nonslaveholding Yankees, and infuriated by reports that Mormons intended to bring free blacks into the state, had destroyed the settlements around Independence. A series of armed encounters, beginning with an attempt to bar Mormons from voting, led to outright warfare and to Governor L. W. Boggs's proclamation that the Mormons had to be treated as enemies, and "had to be exterminated, or driven from the state." At Haun's Mill a band of Missourians massacred nineteen Mormon men and boys. Smith himself was convicted of treason and sentenced to be shot. But he managed to escape, and in Illinois the Mormons finally built their model city of Nauvoo, which the legislature incorporated in 1840 as a virtually independent city-state. The Mormon's political power derived from the decisive weight they could throw in state elections that were fairly evenly balanced between Whigs and Democrats. Beginning in 1840 their numbers grew not only as the result of missionary work in the East, but as the result of the immigra-

tion of thousands who had been converted to Mormonism in the manufacturing districts of England. The English converts' route to the American Zion was eased by the church's highly efficient planning authority that took care of the details of travel.

By the early 1840s visitors to Nauvoo marveled at the city's broad streets, carefully laid out in neat squares; at the steam sawmills and flour mill, the factories, hotel, and schools. Though the Nauvoo temple, supported by thirty gigantic pillars and walls of hewn stone, was not yet complete, it promised to be, in the words of the poet John Greenleaf Whittier, "the most splendid and imposing architectural monument in the new world." Dressed in the uniform of a lieutenant general, Smith presided over a Nauvoo legion of 2,000 troops. In 1843 he dictated the official

JOSEPH SMITH, REVIEWING TROOPS
While this painting exaggerates the machine-like discipline of the Nauvoo legion, it suggests why many non-Mormons could feel concern over Joseph Smith's private army. *(Church Archives, The Church of Jesus Christ of Latter-Day Saints)*

revelation, which he never made public, justifying the practice of plural marriage or polygamy. In 1844 he established the secret Council of Fifty, a secular authority independent of the church, and gave it the mission of building a world government that would prepare the way for Christ's kingdom.

But Smith felt the American world closing in on him and his fellow Mormons. Sensing that the surrounding society would not long tolerate Mormon power, he unsuccessfully tried to persuade the new Republic of Texas to sponsor an independent Mormon colony along the contested border with Mexico. While also sending secret diplomatic missions to Russia and France, he tried to influence the established order through normal political channels. But neither the federal government nor the 1844 presidential candidates would defend the Mormons' claims against Missouri outlaws who had seized thousands of Mormon farms and buildings. As a gesture of protest, Smith finally announced his own candidacy for the highest office in the land. But long before the election, Smith ordered the destruction of a printing press set up by Mormon dissidents who had declared: "We will not acknowledge any man as king or lawgiver to the church." Illinois then charged Smith with treason and locked him and his brother in the Carthage jail. On June 27, 1844, a "mob" that included many prominent non-Mormon citizens stormed the jail and killed them both.

To the Mormons the Prophet's martyrdom brought shock, division, and a struggle for power. It also temporarily appeased the aggression of anti-Mormons and gave Smith's followers time to plan an exodus. Brigham Young, like Smith a man of humble Vermont origin, soon emerged as the leader of the church and as one of the nineteenth century's greatest organizers. Aided by the elite Quorum of the Twelve Apostles and the Council of Fifty, he preserved order and morale while considering and rejecting possible refuges in British and Mexican territory. Before the end of 1845, the Mormon leadership had decided to send an advance company of 1,500 men to the valley of the Great Salt Lake, then still part of Mexico. As a result of mounting persecution and harassment, the Mormons soon concentrated

their energies on evacuating Nauvoo, on selling property at tremendous sacrifice, and on setting up refugee camps from eastern Iowa to Winter Quarters, a temporary destination in eastern Nebraska. The last refugees crossed the Mississippi at gunpoint, leaving Nauvoo a ghost town. During the summer of 1846 some 12,000 Mormons were on the road; 3,700 wagon teams stretched out across the prairies of Iowa.

In the summer of 1847 Brigham Young led a vanguard of picked men across the barren wastes of Nebraska and Wyoming to the Great Salt Lake Valley of Utah. In September a second party of 2,000 weary Mormons found home in the new Zion. During the same year the American defeat of Mexico brought Utah within the dominion of the United States. The Mormons had contributed a battalion of 500 men who had marched with the American army across New Mexico to southern California, and whose pay had helped to finance the migration to Utah. Yet by 1848 the Mormons occupied an inland mountain fortress, a thousand miles beyond the Kansas frontier, and seemed at last to be the masters of their own destiny. When federal judges and other officials arrived in the territory, they found that the Mormons had held a census, adopted a constitution, elected Young governor, and established a "State of Deseret," complete with its own currency and army. The theocratic government was responsible for the remarkably rapid and orderly settlement of the valley, for the collective labor and central economic planning that brought irrigation to the dry but fertile land, and for the coordinated expansion that planted ninety-six colonies in ten years, extending in a corridor from Salt Lake City to San Diego.

Ten years before the time when South Carolina defied federal authority by firing on Fort Sumter and thus precipitating the Civil War, federal officials fled from Utah, denouncing Young's government as a theocracy fundamentally disloyal to the United States. Although the Mormons professed loyalty to the Constitution and acknowledged their territorial status, they intended to pay little attention to authorities sent from Washington. When Young publicly proclaimed the sacred doctrine of polygamy, which Mormon leaders had privately practiced for over a

MORMONS EXPELLED FROM NAUVOO

Despite its inaccuracies, this romanticized view of the Mormons being expelled from Nauvoo conveys the reality of white American families being driven out of the city they built. The building on the horizon is the famous Nauvoo temple. *(Church Archives, The Church of Jesus Christ of Latter-Day Saints)*

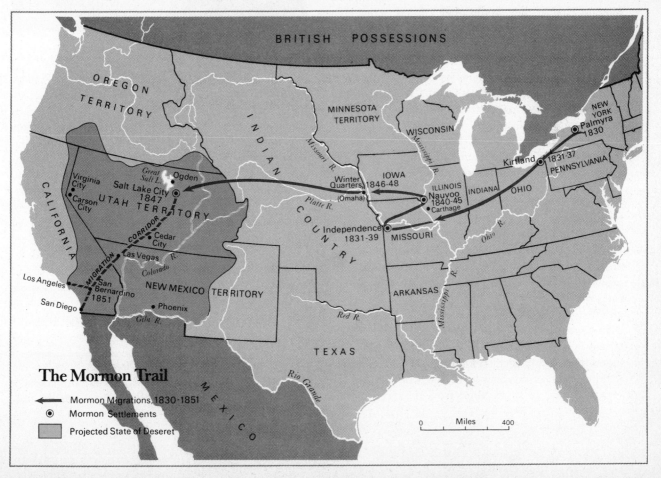

BRITISH POSSESSIONS

OREGON TERRITORY

MINNESOTA TERRITORY

WISCONSIN

NEW YORK
Palmyra
1830

Kirtland
1831-37

PENNSYLVANIA

INDIAN COUNTRY

Missouri R.

Platte R.

Winter
Quarters
1846-48

(Omaha)

IOWA

Mississippi R.

ILLINOIS
Nauvoo
1840-45

INDIANA

OHIO

Ohio R.

Carthage

CALIFORNIA

Virginia
City

Great Salt L.

Ogden

Salt Lake City
1847

UTAH TERRITORY

Carson
City

CORRIDOR

Cedar
City

Las Vegas

Colorado R.

Los Angeles

San
Bernardino
1851

MIGRATION

NEW MEXICO TERRITORY

San Diego

Phoenix

Gila R.

Independence
1831-39

MISSOURI

ARKANSAS

Mississippi R.

TEXAS

Red R.

Rio Grande

MEXICO

The Mormon Trail

➤ Mormon Migrations, 1830-1851

⊙ Mormon Settlements

Projected State of Deseret

0 — Miles — 400

decade, he presented a ready-made issue to outraged reformers, clergymen, and politicians. President Buchanan felt the need of appeasing this popular clamor and of forcibly establishing federal authority in Utah. In 1857 he dispatched a regular army force of 2,500 men to impose federal law on the Mormons; they were led, in an irony of history, by Albert Sidney Johnston, who would soon be a Confederate general resisting an invasion by the United States.

Fortunately for the Mormons, winter snows trapped the expedition in the Rocky Mountains, allowing time for behind-the-scenes negotiations. Governor Young proclaimed martial law and threatened to burn Salt Lake City to the ground and "to utterly lay waste" the land if Utah were invaded. State-rights Democrats had little enthusiasm for setting precedents that might be turned against southern slavery, and though Buchanan had sworn that he would "put down the Mormon rebellion," he decided early in 1858 to proclaim a "pardon" to the inhabitants of Utah if they would obey United States laws and cooperate with federal officials. To prove their strength, however, the Mormons evacuated Salt Lake City. Johnston's army entered a deserted city, greeted only by squads of tough police, "glowering from beneath their hat-brims, with clubs in their hands, and pistols ready slung at their belts." The later withdrawal of federal troops concluded the so-called Mormon War, which brought no change in the actual government of Utah. When Buchanan's successor, Abraham Lincoln, was asked what he proposed to do about the Mormons, he answered, "I propose to let them alone." Lincoln, of course, had other problems on his hands.

No story in American history is more incredible. From the outset, Mormonism embodied the longings and aspirations of people who had not shared in the growing prosperity and social modernization of the early nineteenth century. The poet Whittier observed, after listening to a Mormon service in Massachusetts: "They speak a language of hope and promise to weak, weary hearts, tossed and troubled, who have wandered from sect to sect, seeking in vain for the primal manifestation of the divine power." The new church recruited most of its members from the more remote

BRIGHAM YOUNG, 1801–1877
(Library of Congress)

and isolated parts of New England; from the sparsely populated southern districts of New York and adjacent parts of Pennsylvania; from the rural backcountry of the Upper South and frontier Midwest; and eventually from both rural and manufacturing districts of Wales, Lancashire, and Scandinavia. Few of these converts were well-to-do, well educated, or well established in settled communities. They were mainly small farmers who had been displaced by commercial agriculture, and footloose tradesmen and mechanics who had been bypassed by expanding markets, a people already uprooted and highly mobile, long engaged in a search for communal and religious security.

The Meaning of Mormon Dissent. Because the Mormon search for authority took religious form, it is easy to miss its radical challenge to American secular values and institutions. Against a pluralistic permissive, and individualistic society, the Mormons pitted a higher authority that rested on a rock of unswerving certainty and conviction. Their institutions, based on divine authority, cast doubt on the legitimacy of popular sovereignty, secular law, and established government. The claim that divine revelation sanctioned such a practice as polygamy challenged the basic premises of secular law and morality. And according to their enemies, the Mormons' communal economy subverted private property, encouraged wholesale theft, and excluded non-Mormon enterprise from Utah. Far worse, the Mormons had shown little Christian forbearance in response to persecution. If like the earliest Christians they had looked for strength from the blood of their martyrs, they had also promised retaliation, or "blood atonement," to their enemies.

But the Mormons were not revolutionaries. Despite many points of dissent, Mormonism had much in common with the developing culture of pre–Civil War America. No other American denomination so fully incorporated the "Protestant ethic" of work, or the rule of abstaining from tobacco and all alcoholic drinks as a symbol of their own self-discipline and modernized values. In many respects, the Mormons' theocratic ideal was an extreme version of the ideal of Lyman Beecher, the New England revivalist reformer, and of countless other evangelists who insisted that rampant democracy must be guided by a higher moral force.

In sum, Mormonism was both a radical protest against the values of an individualistic, competitive, uprooting, and disinheriting world, and a vehicle of solidarity and authority that enabled its members to adjust to that world. During the pre–Civil War decades no other movement, with the exception of the southern crusade to vindicate black slavery, posed so serious a challenge to the ideology of the industrializing, urbanizing, and modernizing North. The Mormons probed the outermost limits of tolerance, the violent limits where dissent verged on treason, and finally established their own fragile asylum beyond— but soon within—America's geographical frontiers. Unlike the South, they escaped the major confronta-

tion of civil war. But their unique success required a prolonged accommodation and ultimate capitulation to the civilization against which the South finally waged civil war.

The Benevolent Empire

Like the founders of Mormonism, the reformers of the early nineteenth century were responding to the breakdown of social rules and moral authority associated with a traditional society. To restore "the moral government of God" was the supreme goal of the so-called Benevolent Empire—an informal coalition of home and foreign missionary societies, the American Tract Society, the American Sunday School Union, the American Society for the Promotion of Temperance, the American Colonization Society, the Prison Discipline Society, and the General Union for Promoting the Observance of the Christian Sabbath. Even William Lloyd Garrison, who later came to symbolize radical abolitionism and a defiance of both church and state, began his career in the 1820s as a lowly but ardent champion of these seemingly conservative reform organizations. Like many clergymen and wealthy philanthropists, young Garrison deplored the rising "mobocracy," the "lawless multitude" who enjoyed liquor, violence, profanity, sexual vice, and vulgar entertainment. American social reform originated in the crusade to purify public morals and to find new means, such as the asylum and penitentiary, for instilling habits of regularity, sobriety, obedience, and responsibility.

The Reform of Society. Ideals of purification and the exclusion of undesirables dominated the activities of the Benevolent Empire. Having already provided for the abolition of slavery in the northern states, many antislavery reformers wanted to send the free blacks back to Africa, an idea that had gained increasing support during the early nineteenth century, especially among missionary groups who assumed that American blacks would help to Christianize the land of their ancestors. Drunkards were to be banished from the sight of respectable society.

STATE PENITENTIARY, PENNSYLVANIA
The early nineteenth century witnessed the creation of asylums—totally planned and manipulated environments—which were intended to cure the insane, reform criminals, and liberate the handicapped from the effects of deafness and blindness. Whether liberating or repressive, these institutions exemplified the prevailing faith in the malleability of human nature. *(Courtesy, The Pennsylvania Prison Society)*

Criminals and deviants of various kinds were to be walled off in prisons and asylums, where in the words of some New York reformers of 1822, "their stubborn spirits are subdued, and their depraved hearts softened, by mental suffering." When deviants were institutionalized, they could neither disturb nor contaminate a society that needed to concentrate on business and moral virtue. Some enthusiastic prison reformers even argued that society itself should be modeled on "the regularity, and temperance, and sobriety of a good prison."

Unlike the Mormons, these reformers aspired to be leaders and transformers of the dominant secular society. Although they sought to gather together like-minded promoters of virtue, they originally gave no thought to withdrawing from a sinful society in order to practice virtue. Most of the leaders of the Benevolent Empire were men of economic and educational attainment. They could think of themselves, under "normal" circumstances, as the natural leaders of their communities. They tended to idealize the New England heritage of ordered and homogeneous communities governed by educated clergy and magistrates. Above all, they looked increasingly to Britain

for models of "practical Christianity" and organized reform.

Organized philanthropy had a long history in Britain, but during the Napoleonic wars (1798–1815) it grew dramatically. A vast campaign was set afoot in Britain to reform public morals, to Christianize the world, and to unite rich and poor by an affectionate bond of philanthropy that would replace the traditional deference to the upper classes that even in England had begun to decay. The British and Foreign Bible Society, founded in 1804, became the model for nonsectarian organizations committed to the ideal of "Christian unity." The Bible Society also became a pioneer in highly specialized organization as it acquired women's auxiliaries, skilled professional agents, and teams of "visitors" assigned to specific towns, districts, and streets to collect funds, interview poor families, and distribute Bibles. This kind of systematic division of labor, later to form the core of Mormon community organization in Utah, was soon adopted by hundreds of British societies.

There were societies to promote Christianity among the Jews, observance of the Christian Sabbath, universal peace, and the abolition of slavery;

societies to suppress immorality, infidel publications, juvenile delinquency, and cruelty to animals; societies to aid the indigent blind, the industrious poor, orphans of soldiers and sailors, and "Poor, Infirm, Aged Widows, and Single Women, of Good Character, Who Have Seen Better Days." The English, who seem to have outdone the Americans as a nation of joiners, even launched the Society for Returning Young Women to Their Friends in the Country.

By the 1820s Britain appeared suddenly to have moved into the vanguard of humanitarianism. The evangelical reformers won particular prestige from the leadership they took in the successful campaign to abolish the African slave trade. Most Americans, however, remembering the British invasions of the United States during the War of 1812, continued to think of England as a nation of tyranny and political corruption, and remained suspicious of any alleged humanitarian change of heart. But the New England clergy welcomed any news of England's moral transformation. Confronted by the collapse of Federalist political power, by the growing political force of public opinion, and by irresistible demands for the separation of church and state, many New England clergymen seized on the organizational apparatus of British benevolence as a means for securing control of American culture. With the aid of allies from other parts of the Northeast, these New England ministers and reformers succeeded in capturing and Americanizing the British evangelical spirit and in institutionalizing it in New York City, Philadelphia, and regions stretching west to Illinois.

From about 1810 to 1830 the Benevolent Empire developed gradually as local societies for the reformation of morals enlarged their objectives through various interstate and interlocking personal networks. A remarkable number of the original promoters of benevolent societies were students or recent graduates of Andover Theological Seminary in Massachusetts, founded by Congregationalists in 1809 in opposition to Harvard's drift toward liberal, rationalistic religion (Unitarianism). Andover was a seedbed for missionary work in Asia, Africa, and the American West. Many of the seminary's alumni took up such secular causes as black colonization, prison

reform, and the suppression of intemperance. Louis Dwight, for example, who traveled the country as an agent for the American Bible Society, was so shocked by the squalor and disorder of jails that he became a leading crusader for the penitentiary system of total silence, close surveillance, and solitary confinement at night used in the Auburn, New York, prison. This Auburn system, Dwight maintained, "would greatly promote order, seriousness, and purity in large families, male and female boarding schools, and colleges."

These Andover reformers worked closely with serious-minded young ministers and laymen who had attended Yale or Princeton, as well as with rich and pious businessmen like Edward C. Delavan, Gerrit Smith, and the Tappan brothers. Delavan, a former wine merchant and Albany real estate magnate, contributed a fortune to the temperance cause. Gerrit Smith, a land baron in upstate New York, promoted innumerable reforms ranging from Sunday schools, penitentiaries, and temperance to radical abolitionism, women's rights, and world peace. Arthur and Lewis Tappan, who were wealthy importers and retail merchants in New York City, contributed money and leadership to a whole galaxy of local and national reform societies.

The Sabbatarian Movement. The movement to enforce the Christian Sabbath reveals some of the basic concerns of the Benevolent Empire as well as the obstacles that prevented the emergence of a much hoped-for "Christian party in politics." In 1810 Congress had passed a law requiring the mail to flow seven days a week, in order to meet the critical business demands for faster communication. Sunday mail service immediately drew fire from Lyman Beecher and other New Englanders, and subsequently provoked national debate. For devout Christians the Sabbath evoked memories of a less hurried, agrarian past. This was true even for some harried merchants who were uneasy over their own success and total immersion in worldly pursuits; the silent Sabbath became a reassuring symbol of spiritual goals which justified the previous six days of worldly cares and ambition.

It is significant that Sabbatarian reform orig-

"GO YE INTO ALL THE WORLD"
A certificate given to contributors to the Presbyterian Board of Foreign Missions. At the left are pictured a New England church and factories; at the right, scenes from Burma, the site of the most publicized early American mission. (*American Antiquarian Society*)

inated in the boom town of Rochester, not in the long-settled urban areas of the seaboard. Rochester's established clergy had come from New England and New Jersey, where a quiet Sabbath had been enforced by custom and law. But the Erie Canal passed directly under the windows of Rochester's First Presbyterian Church, and the rowdy boatmen made no effort to lower their voices during the hours of Sunday prayer. In 1828 the town's leading ministers, real estate magnates, and entrepreneurs enlisted Lyman Beecher and Lewis Tappan in a national crusade to persuade

Congress to enforce the laws of God. Although unsuccessful, the movement was historically important because it polarized "serious Christians" against the multitude; because it prepared the way for collaboration between wealthy New York philanthropists and social activists inspired by the revivals of Charles Grandison Finney; and because it marked the transition between distributing Bibles and resorting to direct political and economic action. It should also be emphasized that Rochester lay at the heart of the Burned-Over District and that the Sabbatarian movement coincided with the anti-Masonic crusade, Finney's revivals, the perfection and extension of the Auburn penitentiary system, and the birth of Mormonism.

Although the various causes taken up by the Benevolent Empire appear conservative when compared with later abolitionism, feminism, and perfectionism, they challenged vested interests and provoked immediate and furious resistance. The Sabbatarian movement, for example, threatened loss to owners of boat lines, ferries, taverns, theaters, and stores, much as the temperance movement threatened not only brewers, distillers, and distributors but also thousands of grocers and storekeepers whose customers expected a free pick-me-up as a sign of hospitality. Like the more militant temperance reformers, the Sabbatarians urged true Christians to boycott offending proprietors. Between Buffalo and Albany they also established their own six-days-a-week Pioneer Stage Line, a counterpart of the special temperance hotels and of the abolitionist shops that sold only produce made by free labor. These "anti"-institutions, which were almost uniformly unsuccessful, were intended to be sanctuaries—virtuous, disciplined environments set off from a chaotic and corrupting society—and models for the world to imitate. But like other reformers, the Sabbatarians were also committed to an imperial mission. Setting a precedent for later abolitionists, they organized a great petition campaign to persuade Congress to stop the Sunday mails. Like the abolitionists, they warned that unless Congress acknowledged a "higher law," the nation had little chance for survival:

If this nation fails in her vast experiment, the world's last hope expires; and without the moral energies of the Sabbath it will fail. You might as well put out the sun, and think to enlighten the world with tapers . . . as to extinguish the moral illumination of the Sabbath, and break this glorious mainspring of the moral government of God.

As the Mormons later discovered, many Americans were suspicious of people who laid claim to the moral government of God. By 1831 the Benevolent Empire had failed in its most daring and secular missionary efforts to regenerate society. Lyman Beecher

had early defined the supreme goal of the missionary and benevolent societies: to produce "a sameness of views, and feelings, interests, which would lay the foundation of our empire upon a rock." But this purpose smashed against the rocklike resistance of people who refused to be homogenized, especially under Yankee direction. In response to the Sabbatarians' petitions, Congress agreed with a Kentucky senator who drafted a report stating that the national legislature was not "a proper tribunal to determine the laws of God." The colonization movement—the movement to send free blacks to Africa—did much to unite northern urban blacks, who angrily affirmed that they would not accept a foreign asylum as a substitute for justice: "We will never separate ourselves voluntarily from the slave population of this country." "Let not a purpose be assisted which will stay the cause of the entire abolition of slavery." Resistance to the Benevolent Empire also appeared in the South and Southwest, paradoxically, where an antimission movement appealed to "Hard-Shell" Baptists and rural Methodists. These groups found no biblical sanction for benevolent societies and bitterly resented any attempts to bring religious instruction to the blacks. Further, as one Baptist declared, "our backwoods folks" simply could not understand the pretentious talk of the "young men come from the eastern schools."

The Benevolent Empire solved no social problems. It received no credit for legislative triumphs of the magnitude of Britain's abolition of the slave trade (1807) and gradual emancipation of West Indian slaves (1833). By 1837, moreover, internal conflicts had shattered all hope of a united front among evangelical reformers. Growing divisions over slavery simply intensified suspicions and grievances that had long been festering on every level. Sectarian rivalry weakened the supposedly nondenominational societies that northern Presbyterians and Congregationalists had always controlled. In 1837, when the Presbyterian church separated into conservative Old School and liberal New School camps, the economic depression also sharply reduced philanthropic gifts and thus further weakened the various organizations of the Benevolent Empire. The major Protestant churches, however, continued much of the work under denominational auspices.

Waging the War. It can be argued that the true revolution in American reform began in the 1820s with the militancy, the dedication, the towering expectations, and the phenomenal organization of the nonsectarian, evangelical societies. It began, that is, when an agent of the Sunday School Union, addressing the well-to-do members of the Bible Society, repeated a British motto: "Not by exactions from the opulent but by the contributions from all"; when the organizers of foreign missions called for a "vast body like a host prepared for war"; and when the benevolent societies developed the techniques of modern fund-raising campaigns. The real revolution began with the mass production of literally millions of moralistic tracts, priced cheaply enough to undersell all commercial publications and marketed by discounts and other techniques that were far ahead of commercial practice. By 1830, in short, the evangelicals had devised all the apparatus needed for a massive conquest of American culture.

Although the conquest had ethnic, class, and geographical boundaries, few invading armies or political revolutions have had such a far-reaching effect on an entire society as the Benevolent Empire did. In 1834 the Temperance Society estimated that they had over 1.25 million members; in 1836 the American Tract Society alone sold over 3 million publications. In 1843, in response to the depression that had filled New York City's streets with thousands of beggars and vagrants, the New York Association for Improving the Condition of the Poor imitated the earlier models and sent teams of agents to gather information district by district and to distribute food, fuel, and clothing. The needy recipients could not help but be influenced, one way or another, by the association's links with the temperance movement, its conviction that poverty was a problem of individual morality, and its commitment to make the poor "respectable." If the reformers harbored little sympathy for sinners who refused to be saved, their ideology rested on a belief in human perfectibility, strongly laced with hopes for an American millennium.

The reformers' confidence in human perfectibil-ity inspired a multitude of efforts, especially in the 1840s, to liberate individuals from all coercive forces and institutions. Perfectionism—the belief that people are capable of unlimited moral improvement—took both religious and secular forms. Suddenly new things seemed possible, new ways of thinking and acting seemed worth trying. The nation had never before witnessed such frothy experimentation, such gusty defiance of traditional wisdom, or such faith in spontaneous love and harmony. Some reformers won fame for their success in emancipating individual victims of deafness, blindness, and insanity. Samuel Gridley Howe, best known for his pioneering work with the blind and deaf-blind, expressed the growing view that even criminals were "thrown upon society as a sacred charge." "Society," Howe said, "is false to its trust, if it neglects any means of reformation." Prison reformers tried, with little success, to transform penitentiaries into communities of rehabilitation and to persuade society of the need for parole, indeterminate sentences, and sympathetic care for discharged convicts. Nativists, who were alarmed by the increasing number of Catholic immigrants, publicized cases of Catholic women who had escaped from supposedly tyrannical and immoral nunneries, and demanded laws that would liberate Catholic laymen from the control of their priests.

Temperance. The temperance movement, a direct outgrowth of the Benevolent Empire, illustrates this mixture of humanitarianism, intolerance, progressivism, and self-righteousness. Though sometimes portrayed as religious cranks and killjoys, the temperance reformers were responding to a genuine social problem. During the early nineteenth century, per capita consumption of hard liquor far exceeded even the highest twentieth-century levels; alcohol abuse undoubtedly contributed to family discord and child abuse, to public disorder, and to lowered productivity and rising social costs of all kinds. By the mid-1830s various groups of urban artisans and northern free blacks endorsed temperance as a prerequisite for self-improvement. At the same time, middle-class champions of total abstinence became embroiled in bitter disputes over biblical sanctions for drinking wine.

"Fur Traders Descending the Missouri" by John Caleb Bingham. The Metropolitan Museum of Art, Morris K. Jesup Fund, 1933

The Perils of Civilization

By the second quarter of the nineteenth century a growing number of artists were giving imaginative expression to the changing American experience. Some of these artists drew on the rich resources of primitive painting and popular folklore; an increasing number had received formal training in Europe and in the new artistic academies of the East. Apart from training and talent, American artists were becoming more sensitive to the opportunities and coercions of a market economy in which art competed with other luxuries. They were becoming more responsive to the exotic and romantic fashions of the time, largely derived from Europe and, above all, to America's dramatic expansion, which seemed at once exhilarating and dangerous. For the central legacy of Old World culture, running like a blinking danger light from the ancient Greeks to Shakespeare and Milton, was the message that destruction inevitably follows excessive human pride, arrogance, or a defiance of the boundaries that God and nature had imposed on humankind.

Nature became the central theme of American art in the pre–Civil War era. It was still a nature that stood above and apart from humankind—a source of inspiration, a force to be conquered, but not a *resource* to be preserved in parks or commemorated in museums. George Caleb Bingham, who grew up on the frontier, could portray the penetration and exploitation of nature as an idyllic moment of harmony. He depicts fur traders descending the great Missouri River (not fishermen or hunters in a protected game preserve). The boat

"Death Struggle" by Charles Deas. Shelburne Museum, Inc., Shelburne, Vt.

is laden with pelts and a live fox is chained to the bow. The young trapper lounges over his gun and a dead waterfowl. The colorful detail and sharp, angular lines of the men and boat stand out against the feathery trees in the background. Yet Bingham has skillfully blended the human forms with the watery reflections and mist of the wild landscape. His trappers are less intruders upon nature than converts to its serenity.

Even when conflict became explicit, nature re-tained a sense of transcendence or "otherness." Civilization had not yet won supremacy. In Charles Deas's melodramatic painting, *Death Struggle*, a white trapper, still clutching a mink he has caught in a trap, is locked in combat with an Indian. In contrast to Bingham's peaceful mist and mirror-like river, nature now assumes the beautiful awe and terror that romantics termed the "sublime"—a boiling conflict between light and darkness that re-calls nineteenth-century illustrations of Dante's

Divine Comedy and Milton's *Paradise Lost*. Deas's painting also echoes the themes of the contemporary *Leather-Stocking Tales* of James Fenimore Cooper. Deas's trapper, like Cooper's heroes, is in dire peril, but the white audience can confidently assume that his Indian foe will plunge into the dark abyss below.

Yet there was open space in the West that remained unconquered. The first pictorial images of conquest focused on trading posts that enclosed small fortified spaces in the midst of boundless plains and barren mountains. Alfred Jacob Miller's views of Fort Laramie represented a compromise between the harmonious blending of Bingham and the stark combat of Deas. Miller, enlisted in 1837 as the official artist for an expedition led by a British explorer and army officer, made the first on-the-spot paintings of the Rocky Mountains fur-

trapping region. Fort Laramie had been built on the North Platte River (northeast of the later town of Laramie, Wyoming), at the crossroads of Indian trading routes and in the direct path of the future Oregon Trail. Miller depicted it as an outpost of white civilization, a protected space filled with rectangular lines and jutting towers reminiscent of medieval European castles. A secure oasis for tens of thousands of future overland emigrants, it was also surrounded by the tepees of nomadic Oglala Sioux. As portrayed here in *The Interior of Fort Laramie* by Miller, the fort stakes off a physical space for controlled intercourse between whites and Indians—the Indians who were sometimes allowed to enter the gate, trade, stare at the cannon, and be exploited, sexually and otherwise, by a superior power.

"The Interior of Fort Laramie" by Alfred Jacob Miller. Walters Art Gallery, Baltimore

For pre–Civil War Americans, the Far West represented only one aspect of nature, a raw nature that sometimes seemed to threaten the moral and psychological foundations of civilization. East of the Mississippi, where civilization faced no more than a mopping-up operation, the victors could afford a certain nostalgia for the wilderness landscape that was being transformed and enclosed. Most of the East was still woodland, swamp, and pasture, but "nature," in the sense of an environment that affects man more than it is affected by man, seemed increasingly vulnerable. It could therefore be enshrined and for a time preserved in its precarious autonomy by landscape painting, a form of art that enjoyed increasing popularity. The reverent imagery of the so-called Hudson River School suggested a divine spirit within hills, brooks, forests, rocks, clouds, and illuminated skies. Building on this tradition, Martin Heade evolved an eerie realism that captured fleeting moments of changing light and atmosphere, often set off by wide horizons where civilized land gives way to a wild and ominous sea. In his *The Coming Storm*, the luminous sailboat and human figures seem almost frozen in place, yet threatened by the distant flash of lightning and heavy rain clouds. In the works of Heade and other landscape painters, nature could startle viewers, bringing a delight of recognition as well as a moment of humility. As the symbol of something beyond human reach, nature could thus serve as an aesthetic counterweight to civilization's demands for predictability, mastery, and control.

"The Coming Storm" by Martin J. Heade. The Metropolitan Museum of Art, Gift of Irving Wolf Foundation

"The Lackawanna Valley" by George Innes. The National Gallery of Art, Washington, D.C., Gift of Mrs. Huttleston Rogers

In a way, however, American culture demanded that nature somehow assimilate and give legitimacy to the machine. This demand was most imaginatively met by George Innes, who in 1854 accepted a commission from the Lackawanna Railroad Company to paint such unorthodox subjects as a railroad roundhouse and steam locomotive. In Innes's *The Lackawanna Valley*, a pastoral landscape seems to embrace and merge with civilization's smoke and iron. A lone spectator, similar to the contemplative figure in Heade's *The Coming Storm*, looks out upon a peaceful valley. The train's plume of smoke is echoed by a distant wisp beyond the church steeple. The curving track links the background hills with the tall tree in the foreground. Despite the stumps, despite the signs of encroaching industry, the human intrusion on nature appears to be in harmony with nature's rhythms.

But antebellum artists evolved no similar formula for romanticizing the city, a subject they generally shunned. A few anonymous painters did succeed in documenting the squalor, moral degradation, and jostling confusion of New York's growing slums. It was Thomas Cole, however, the original leader of the Hudson River School and the painter who did the most to popularize the American landscape, who expressed the era's most striking vision of the consequences of "overcivilization."

Cole painted his five canvases on *The Course of Empire* after returning from a residence in Europe, where he had contemplated the ruins of antiquity. His choice of classical imagery had special meaning for a modern republic that had taken so many of its moral and aesthetic models from classical Rome. Cole's first two canvases show the evolution from primitive origins of a pastoral, creative, classical society. In *The Consummation of Empire*, however, chasteness and innocence have given way to luxurious decadence. The scene represents a total subjugation and defiance of nature. Except for a jutting cliff in the background, the landscape has become wholly encrusted with marble temples and monuments. An imperial procession on the bridge suggests the arrogance of unlimited power. The sinuous fountain and voluptuous setting at the lower right suggest moral decay.

"The Consummation of Empire" by Thomas Cole. Courtesy of the New York Historical Society, New York City

"The Destruction of Empire" by Thomas Cole. Courtesy of the New York Historical Society, New York City

In *The Destruction of Empire* the viewer's perspective has shifted to the right and rear. The jutting cliff is still visible in the distance, and is the only landmark certain to survive the catastrophic destruction. Civilization is engulfed in a storm of flame and swirling smoke. People spill like ants from the bridge, while in the foreground the statue of a gigantic headless warrior holds his helpless shield above the scene of pillage and rape. On the base of the statue Cole inscribed the large numbers "1836," which was not only the date of the painting but a year when financial panic caused many Americans to ponder the future course of their own empire.

Cole's final canvas presents lifeless ruins and rubble covered by creeping vegetation—a view of nature unperturbed by the extinction of civilization. A similar theme of catastrophism, qualifying the exuberant optimism of antebellum society, was not uncommon in American literature and art. It drew on traditions of religious millennarianism as well as on the fear that any republic, no matter how virtuous its origins, might share the fate of Rome. Both models suggested the spasmodic anxieties of a people who continued to defy the limits and boundaries of their Old World heritage.

In 1840 the movement took a new direction when groups of reformed alcoholics began organizing "Washingtonian Societies" that appealed to working-class people and to members of subcultures that had not been reached by the traditional and elitist temperance organizations. At Society meetings former drunkards told rapt audiences what hell was really like, sometimes reenacting the agonies of delirium tremens. Old guard temperance leaders tried to use and patronize the Washingtonians, much as some white abolitionists tried to use and patronize fugitive slaves. But the middle-class societies never felt comfortable with the former victims of intemperance, or with the boisterous showmanship that induced thousands of disreputable-looking people to pledge themselves, at least temporarily, to total abstinence.

Faith in "moral suasion," or individual conversion to abstinence, disintegrated in the face of hundreds of thousands of German and Irish immigrants who had little taste for Yankee moralism. The celebrated "Maine law" of 1851, which outlawed the manufacture and sale of alcoholic beverages, marked the maturing of a new campaign for legal coercion in the form of statewide prohibition. On both local and state levels, bitter political conflicts erupted over the passage, repeal, and enforcement of prohibition laws. For temperance reformers of the 1850s, it was no longer safe to rely on the individual's mastery of temptation. The crucial act of will was now to be made by the state, which would attempt to remove the temptation. In less than thirty years one of the crucial goals of the Benevolent Empire had been consigned to the realm of political power; faith in moral influence and liberation had yielded to what the *American Temperance Magazine* hailed as the only force that drunkards could comprehend—"the instrumentality of the law."

Radical Abolitionism

Black slavery was the first issue to expose the limitations of the Benevolent Empire. Even by 1830 there was a striking discrepancy between the public optimism of the evangelical philanthropists and their whispered despair concerning black slavery. Harsh facts made the discrepancy increasingly noticeable. Despite the legal prohibition in 1808 of slave imports from Africa, the natural increase of the American slave population exceeded all earlier expectations. The number of slaves in the United States increased from approximately 1.5 million in 1820 to over 2 million in 1830. This figure represented almost one-sixth of the total United States population and more than twice the number of slaves in the British and French West Indies. The number of free blacks grew during the 1820s from about 234,000 to 320,000.

Failure of Black Colonization. In 1830 the American Colonization Society transported a total of only 259 free blacks to Liberia, the West African colony that the society had established as a refuge for American blacks. Yet most reformers still regarded colonization as the only solution: "We must save the Negro," as one missionary put it, "or the Negro will ruin us." Racial prejudice permeated the Benevolent Empire, and was by no means foreign to later radical abolitionists. But the new and significant fact was the rising tide of virulent racism among the working classes of the North. Prejudiced as they may have been, many leaders of the colonization movement were sincere opponents of slavery who abhorred the growing racism of the northern masses and who saw deportation as the only realistic means for preventing racial war in the North and for inducing southern planters to free their slaves.

A series of events reinforced the realization that white America could not solve its racial problem by shipping a few hundred free blacks each year to Liberia. In 1829 David Walker, a Boston black who belonged to the Massachusetts General Colored Association, published his revolutionary *Appeal to the Colored Citizens of the World*, which justified slave rebellion and warned white Americans that if justice were delayed blacks would win their liberty "by the crushing arm of power." The pamphlet created a furor and copies soon appeared among blacks in the Deep South. Then in 1831 Nat Turner, a trusted Virginia slave, led the bloodiest slave revolt the South had yet experienced. At the end of the same year a far larger insurrection rocked the British colony of Jamaica. In Britain, mass demonstrations continued to demand the immediate and unconditional emancipation of West Indian slaves. When Parliament responded in 1833 with monetary compensation to slaveowners to cover part of the financial loss of emancipation, and with an apprenticeship plan to prepare slaves for freedom, a few Americans concluded that effective political action of any kind required a mammoth mobilization of public opinion.

The Ethical Basis of Abolitionism.   To the young abolitionists who began to appear in the early 1830s, black slavery was the great national sin. Theodore Dwight Weld, the son of a Connecticut minister and a convert and close associate of Charles Grandison Finney in upstate New York, personally symbolized the fusion of American revivalism with British anti-slavery influence. His most intimate friend and religious model was Charles Stuart, a visiting British reformer who worked with Finney's disciples in the Burned-Over District and then in 1829 returned to England to throw himself into the battle for slave emancipation. After being urged by Stuart to take up the cause in America, Weld shifted from temperance and educational reforms to abolitionism, becoming one of the most fearless and powerful lecturers in the area from Ohio to Vermont. Early in 1833 he wrote a letter to William Lloyd Garrison, whom he knew only by reputation, illuminating the meaning of slavery as sin:

That no condition of birth, no shade of color, no mere misfortune of circumstances, can annul the birth-right charter, which God has bequeathed to every being upon whom he has stamped his own image, by making him a *free moral agent,* and that he who robs his fellow man of this tramples upon right, subverts justice, outrages humanity, unsettles the foundations of human safety, and sacrilegiously assumes the prerogative of God; and further, tho' he who retains by force, and refuses to surrender that which was originally obtained by violence or fraud, is joint partner in the original sin, becomes its apologist and makes it the business of every moment to perpetuate it afresh, however he may lull his conscience by the vain plea of expediency or necessity.

Weld's statement sums up an ethical imperative that sprang from three fundamental convictions: that

all men and women have the ability to do what is right, and are therefore morally accountable for their actions; that the intolerable social evils are those that degrade the image of God in man, stunting or corrupting the individual's capacities for self-control and self-respect; and that the goal of all reform is to free individuals from being manipulated like physical objects. As one Garrisonian put it, the goal of abolitionism was *"the redemption of man from the dominion of man."*

That abolitionists like Weld were almost wholly concerned with ideals was at once their greatest strength and greatest weakness. America was supposedly a nation of doers, of practical builders, framers, drafters, organizers, and technicians. The overriding question, in abolitionist eyes, was whether the nation would continue to accommodate itself to a social system based on sheer violence. To propose rational plans or to get embroiled in debates over the precise means and timing of emancipation would only play into the hands of slavery's apologists. What the times required, therefore, was "an original motive power" that would shock and awaken public opinion, create a new moral perspective, and require legislators to work out the details, however imperfectly, of practical emancipation. In 1831 William Lloyd Garrison admitted: "Urge immediate abolition as earnestly as we may, it will alas! be gradual abolition in the end. We have never said that slavery would be overthrown by a single blow; that it ought to be we shall always contend."

The Abolitionists.   On one level, the abolitionists realistically saw that the nation had reached a dead end on slavery. Instead of gradually withering away, as earlier optimists had hoped, the evil had grown and had won increasing acquiescence from the nation's political leaders and most powerful institutions. Therefore, the abolitionists took on the unpopular role of agitators, of courageous critics who stood outside the popular refuges of delusion, hypocrisy, and rationalization. In 1830 Garrison went to jail for writing libelous attacks against a New England merchant who was shipping slaves from Baltimore to New Orleans. After Arthur Tappan had paid his fine and

secured his release, Garrison in 1831 founded the newspaper *The Liberator* in Boston, hurling out the famous pledge: *"I will be* as harsh as truth, and as uncompromising as justice. . . . I am in earnest—I will not equivocate—I will not excuse—I will not retreat a single inch—AND I WILL BE HEARD."

Although *The Liberator* had an extremely small circulation and derived most of its support from black subscribers in the Northeast, Garrison succeeded in being heard. In the South especially, newspaper editors seized the chance to reprint specimens of New England's radicalism, accompanied by their own furious rebuttals. Even before the end of 1831, the Georgia legislature proposed a reward of $5,000 for anyone who would kidnap Garrison and bring him south for trial. Garrison also championed the free blacks' grievances against the Colonization Society, which he had once supported, and mounted a blistering attack against the whole conception of colonization. He pointed out that the hope for colonization confirmed and reinforced white racial prejudice and that it was racial prejudice that was the main barrier the abolitionists faced in the North. Largely as a result of Garrison's early and independent leadership, the American Anti-Slavery Society, founded in 1833, committed itself to at least a vague legal equality of whites and blacks and to a total repudiation of colonization.

Even though they had practically declared war

WILLIAM LLOYD GARRISON, 1805–1879
(Harvard College Library)

against the values, institutions, and power structure of Jacksonian America, the abolitionists continued to think of their reform societies as simple extensions of the Benevolent Empire. They assumed that they could quickly win support from churches and ministers; that they could persuade the pious, influential, and respectable community leaders that racial prejudice was as harmful as intemperance. Then, after mobilizing righteous opinion in the North, they could shame the South into repentance. Abolitionists did not think of themselves as provokers of violence and disunion. Rather, it was slavery that had brought increasing violence and threats of disunion. A national commitment to emancipation, they believed, would ensure harmony and national union.

Like the wealthy British philanthropists, Arthur and Lewis Tappan moved from various benevolent causes to the cause of immediate emancipation. By 1833 philanthropists in Great Britain had won the support of the established order as well as of middle-class public opinion. But in America, precisely because the Tappans had wealth and prestige, they were viciously attacked for encouraging radicals like Garrison and for betraying the common interests that had allowed leaders in different sections to do business with one another. Mass rallies in the South pledged as much as $50,000 for the delivery of Arthur Tappan's body, dead or alive. In New York City, business leaders vainly pleaded with the two brothers, whose lives were being repeatedly threatened by 1834, to give up their radical activities. In that year, prominent New Yorkers cheered on a mob of butcher-boys and day laborers who smashed up Lewis Tappan's house and burned the furnishings. Only the unexpected arrival of troops prevented an armed assault on the Tappans' store.

Antiabolitionists played on popular suspicions of England, charging that men like George Thompson, an English friend of Garrison's, had been sent "to foment discord among our people, array brother against brother . . . to excite treasonable opposition to our government . . . to excite our slave population to rise and butcher their masters; to render the South a desert, and the country at large the scene of fraternal war." Abolitionists continually invoked the ideals of

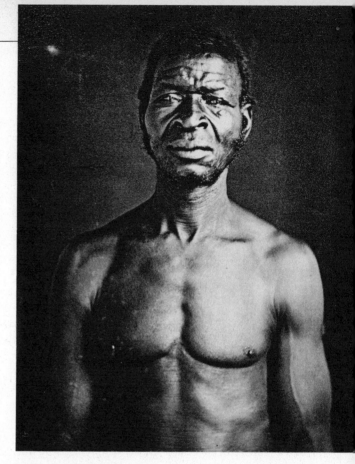

JACK, A SLAVE DRIVER
This remarkable photograph portrays "Jack," an African-born driver on B. F. Taylor's South Carolina plantation. It was recently discovered, along with other daguerreotypes of African-born slaves, at Harvard's Peabody Museum of Archaeology and Ethnology. The pictures were originally commissioned in 1850 by Louis Agassiz, a celebrated Swiss-born scientist eager to prove that God had created Africans as a distinct and separate species. It is ironic that Agassiz, who wanted to give scientific support to the enemies of abolitionism, could gather documents that were far more eloquent indictments of slavery than any of the literary evidence available to abolitionists. *(Peabody Museum, Harvard University)*

the Declaration of Independence and portrayed themselves as fulfilling the Revolution's promise. But their enemies styled themselves as Minute Men defending American liberties. The mob riots of the Revolutionary periods appeared to sanction the antiabolitionist riots that spread across the North in the 1830s. For the most part this mob violence was carefully planned, organized, and directed toward specific goals, such as the destruction of printing presses and the intimidation of free blacks. The leaders were "gentlemen of property and standing"—prominent lawyers, bankers, merchants, doctors, and local political leaders of both parties. In most towns and cities the white abolitionists and free blacks had little protection from the forces of law and order. The colonizationists, already weakened by financial difficulties and internal division, took the lead in accusing the abolitionists of being "amalgamationists" who would not stop short of encouraging black men to woo the daughters of white America.

Abolitionism and Freedom of Speech. It was this bugaboo that brought the northern crowds into the streets and that also lay behind the abolitionists' most dramatic break with the Benevolent Empire. Lane Theological Seminary, in Cincinnati, was meant to be one of the Empire's crowning achievements, a beachhead of benevolence on the Ohio River, a staging ground for the missionary conquest of the West. Arthur Tappan paid Lyman Beecher's salary as president of the seminary. He also paid the way for Theodore Weld, then thirty-one, to attend the school as a student. Early in 1834 Weld conducted at Lane an eighteen-day soul-searching revival on the question of slavery. After converting many students and nonstudents to the doctrine of immediate emancipation, Weld led his band into the slums where the black residents of Cincinnati lived. There they set up libraries, conducted evening classes, and fraternized with the city's "untouchable" caste. In Weld's view, educational institutions had a duty to train minds for the new "era of disposable power and practical accomplishment."

To the Tappans' dismay, Lane's board of trustees voted to get rid of Weld and the other antislavery leaders, and Lyman Beecher, who was still a supporter of colonization, acquiesced in the decision. Various leaders of American higher education agreed that antislavery agitation endangered the fundamental purposes of American colleges. In response, almost all the Lane students walked out of the seminary with

Weld. Some ended up in Arthur Tappan's newly financed college, Oberlin. But many joined Weld as traveling agents for the American Anti-Slavery Society, of which Arthur Tappan was president, braving showers of rotten eggs and stones in order to address the American people.

As a product of the Benevolent Empire, abolitionism drew on and perfected techniques of mass communication that gave the nation its first taste of modern "public relations." By 1835 the new steam printing press and other technological improvements had reduced the cost and increased the volume of mass publication. In 1834 the Anti-Slavery Society distributed 122,000 pieces of literature; in 1835 the figure rose to 1.1 million. President Jackson and various national and local authorities expressed alarm over this attempt to apply the methods of the Bible and tract societies to a revolutionary purpose—a purpose that threatened one of the nation's chief capital investments as well as a national system for racial control. But though the government encouraged the destruction of abolitionist mail, it could do nothing about the itinerant abolitionist lecturers in the North, the "antislavery bazaars" held to raise funds and distribute literature, the auxiliary societies for ladies and children, or the flood of propaganda in the form of medals, emblems, broadsides, bandannas, chocolate wrappers, songs, and children's readers.

The rapid growth of abolitionist societies, coupled with violent efforts to suppress them, led to sharp divisions of opinion over abolitionist principles and tactics. One turning point was the celebrated martyrdom in 1837 of Elijah P. Lovejoy, a New England abolitionist who, like the Mormons, had been driven out of Missouri and had established a refuge in Illinois. While trying to defend a new printing press from an antiabolitionist mob, Lovejoy was shot and killed. His violent death dramatized the issue of civil liberties and won new support for the abolitionists; it also forced abolitionists to debate the proper response to violence, since Lovejoy and his men had used arms in self-defense.

Nonresistance. Garrison, who had nearly been lynched in 1835 by a Boston mob, had become convinced that violence was a disease infecting the entire body of American society. Whenever the nation faced any issue of fundamental morality, such as the treatment of Indians, blacks, or dissenters, it resorted to the principle that might makes right. The only Christain response, Garrison maintained, was to renounce all coercion and adhere to the perfectionist ideal of absolute nonresistance. If abolitionists tried to oppose power with power, as Lovejoy had done, they were certain to be crushed. They would also dilute their moral argument, since the essence of slavery was the forcible dominion of man over man. In 1838 Garrison and his followers formed the New England Non-Resistance Society, a group which condemned every kind of coercion including not only defensive war and capital punishment, but lawsuits, prisons, and insane asylums, unless designed solely for "cure and restoration."

What began to emerge in New England abolitionism, then, was a radical repudiation of all limits imposed on the individual by the threat of force. Negro slavery and racial oppression were merely extreme manifestations of an evil embodied in the patriarchal family, the criminal law, and the police power of the state. By 1843 Garrison concluded that the majority rule was simply the rule of superior power, with no protection for human rights, that the Union had always been a compact for the preservation of slavery, and that the Constitution was therefore "a covenant with death, and an agreement with Hell." The Garrisonians demanded withdrawal from corrupt churches and from all complicity with the corrupt government. Calling for disunion with the South, they also crossed the threshold of symbolic treason and declared themselves enemies of the Republic.

In interesting ways the Garrisonians' rhetoric paralleled the rhetoric of the Mormons. "The governments of the world," Garrison announced in 1837, "are all anti-Christ." Yet by 1845 he also cast off the Old Testament, arguing that God could never have sanctioned slavery and violence. Instead of moving beyond the geographic frontiers, as the Mormons had done, to establish the kingdom of God, Garrison defended his own fortress of moral independence within a hostile society.

Feminism, Perfectionism, and Political Consolidation

Radical abolitionism was part of a much broader protest against forms of oppression and inequality that had long been accepted as inevitable. In the 1830s abolitionism became intertwined with attacks against the traditional subordination of women. The founders of the feminist movement, like the male abolitionists, had mostly served apprenticeships in the moral reform and temperance societies of the Benevolent Empire.

Women were not only deprived of higher education, barred from the professions, and denied the right to vote; most women upon marriage also surrendered any legal right to their own earnings and property. Harriet Robinson, who began working in a Massachusetts textile mill at age eleven and who participated in 1836 in one of the first women's strikes against wage-cutting, recalled that many workers were "fugitives" from oppressive husbands and had thus assumed false names in order to prevent their husbands from legally seizing their wages. Such conditions evoked mounting protest from writers like Catharine Beecher, a daughter of Lyman Beecher and sister of Harriet Beecher Stowe. While conceding that women should not infringe upon the "male sphere" of business and politics, Catharine Beecher exposed the oppression of mill girls, fought for improved female education, and attempted to enlist thousands of American women as teachers in a vast crusade "to secure a proper education to the vast multitude of neglected American children all over our land." Such agitation focused attention on women's collective interests, problems, and responsibilities, and thus contributed to a new feminist consciousness.

Female Abolitionists. Abolitionism provided female reformers with an egalitarian ethic and with a public forum for attacking entrenched injustice. From the outset, the Garrisonian movement attracted a group of exceptionally talented writers and lecturers such as Maria Weston Chapman, Lydia Maria Child, Abby Kelly, and Lucretia Mott. Among Garrison's most important converts were Sarah and An-

HARRIET BEECHER STOWE, 1811–1896

The daughter of Lyman Beecher, Harriet Beecher Stowe, *above,* suddenly became not only the most famous member of an illustrious family but also the world's most admired and hated woman. Bitterly attacked in the South, she was lionized in England and soon became an international literary celebrity. *(The Metropolitan Museum of Art. Gift of I. N. Phelps Stokes, Edward S. Hawes, Alice Mary Hawes, and Marion Augusta Hawes, 1937)*

ELIZABETH CADY STANTON

In 1840 she traveled to London with her husband, abolitionist Henry Brewster Stanton, to the first World's Antislavery Convention where the issue of women's participation sharply divided the convention. Subsequently, she and Lucretia Mott led the first women's rights convention in the United States held at Seneca Falls, New York, in July, 1848. *(American Antiquarian Society)*

gelina Grimké, two articulate sisters who had abandoned their father's South Carolina plantation and had then been converted to Quakerism and abolitionism in Philadelphia. Because they could speak of southern slavery from personal experience, the Grimkés had a striking effect on New England audiences. In 1837 they boldly lectured to mixed audiences of men and women, an offense that outraged clergymen and conservative reformers who believed that women should move within a precisely limited "sphere." The Grimkés attacked the hypocrisy of conservative abolitionists who scoffed at biblical justifications for slavery but who invoked the Bible when defending

female subservience. The Garrisonians convinced the Grimkés that the Christian "principles of peace" were at the root of all reform; the Grimkés helped to convince the Garrisonians that the same principles applied to the "domestic slavery" of women to men.

In 1840 the issue of women's participation in abolitionist conventions brought an irreparable split in the American Anti-Slavery Society, which the more conservative Tappan faction abandoned to the Garrisonian radicals. Female abolitionists increasingly stressed the parallels between their own powerlessness and the legal status of slaves. In 1848 Elizabeth Cady Stanton and Lucretia Mott finally organized at

Seneca Falls, New York, the first convention in history devoted to women's rights. The convention's Declaration of Sentiments, modeled on the Declaration of Independence, proclaimed that "the history of mankind is a history of repeated injuries and usurpations on the part of man toward woman, having in direct object the establishment of an absolute tyranny over her." Among the list of specific grievances, Stanton insisted on including the exclusion of woman from "her inalienable right to the elective franchise."

Despite this demand for political rights, the National Women's Rights conventions of the 1850s devoted more attention to legal and economic disabilities, and to challenging the clergy's insistence that the Bible defined a subordinate "sphere" for the "weaker sex." "Leave woman," Lucy Stone, a radical feminist leader, demanded, "to find her own sphere."

Although abolitionism provided the feminists with a sympathetic audience and with ready-made channels of communication, the relationship was also limiting in the sense that women's rights were always subordinate to the seemingly more urgent cause of slave emancipation. This dependence is evident even in the rhetoric of radical feminists who compared the prevailing system of marriage to a private plantation in which every woman was a slave breeder and a slave in the eyes of her husband.

Communitarianism. The quest for social equality led some reformers, including radical abolitionists, to join experimental communities where they could escape from the coercions and frustrations of competitive labor and of the private, isolated family. Some of these communities were inspired by secular social theories. In the 1820s, for example, the socialist experiment at New Harmony, Indiana, was based on the doctrines of Robert Owen, a wealthy Scottish philanthropist. In the 1840s a wide scattering of projects drew on the theories of Charles Fourier, a French social philosopher. The most successful communities, however, were those of religious sects like the Rappites and Shakers, or those disciplined by the authority of extraordinary leaders such as John Humphrey Noyes.

THE FUGITIVE SLAVE'S SONG, 1845
Frederick Douglass's escape from slavery was celebrated in a popular song. The illustration, however lacking in skill, is notable because it broke away from the standard racist caricature of blacks. (*American Antiquarian Society*)

Noyes, who had studied theology at Andover and Yale, was a perfectionist who believed that the millennium had already begun and that the time had arrived for "renouncing all allegiance to the government of the United States, and asserting the title of

Jesus Christ to the throne of the world." Garrison's repudiation of all coercive government owed much to the influence of Noyes, who had proclaimed: "As the doctrine of temperance is total abstinence from alcoholic drinks, and the doctrine of antislavery is immediate abolition of human bondage, so the doctrine of perfectionism is the immediate and total cessation from sin." For Noyes and his followers there was no point in attacking a single sin like slavery when all Americans were enslaved by the bonds of private property and monogamous marriage, both of which imprisoned the human spirit behind walls of sinful possessiveness. At Putney, Vermont, and then at Oneida, New York, Noyes and his growing group of disciples developed a cohesive community based on a form of plural marriage, the collective ownership of property, and the discipline of "mutual criticism." The Oneida experiment, which flourished from 1847 to 1879, posed a radical alternative to the economic, sexual, and educational practices of the surrounding society.

Political Antislavery: From the Liberty Party to Free Soil. By the 1840s, however, most reformers expressed new hopes for transforming the dominant society by means of the political process. There were various indications of this growing involvement in political action. During the late 1830s thousands of antislavery petitions poured into Congress as a popular challenge to the "gag rule."* John Quincy Adams, then a Whig congressman from Massachusetts, used every parliamentary trick to defend the petitioners' rights. Antislavery Whigs like Congressmen Joshua Giddings and Salmon P. Chase, both of Ohio, capitalized on their constituencies' resentment of the "gag rule" and other sectional compromises that sacrificed moral principle. Liberal Democrats, such as Senators Thomas Morris of Ohio and John P. Hale of New Hampshire, voiced growing dissatisfaction with a party which professed to attack economic privilege while serving the interests of wealthy slaveholding planters. And after 1842, when the Supreme Court

*See p. 351–52.

ruled that the Fugitive Slave Law of 1793 applied solely to the federal government's responsibility in helping to recover fugitives, five northern states enacted "personal liberty laws" prohibiting state officials from assisting in the recapture of runaway slaves.

For most part, political abolitionists hoped to pursue their goals by promoting antislavery candidates and by subjecting the two major parties to well-organized public pressure in behalf of such measures as prohibiting the interstate slave trade, abolishing slavery in the District of Columbia, and preventing any further expansion of slavery in western states and territories. In 1839, however, Alvan Stewart, a lawyer and president of the New York State Anti-Slavery Society, converted most of the non-Garrisonian abolitionists to a temporary third party (the Garrisonians opposed political activism). It was hoped that this Liberty party, which ran James G. Birney for president in 1840, would win a balance of power in closely contested regions of the North and thus free Whigs and Democrats from the stranglehold of the "Slave Power"—an alleged conspiratorial alliance of southern planters and their northern minions.

The Libertymen blamed the Slave Power for the depression, for the undermining of civil liberties, and for most of the ills that the nation had suffered. Although Birney captured only a small fraction of the potential antislavery vote in the elections of 1840 and 1844, the Liberty party succeeded in popularizing the belief in a Slave Power conspiracy. By offering voters an abolitionist alternative to even moderately antislavery Whigs and Democrats, the Libertymen also stimulated figures like Giddings, Chase, and Hale to make a bolder appeal for antislavery votes.

By 1848 the more extreme political abolitionists had arrived at the position that the Constitution gave Congress both the power and duty to abolish slavery in the southern states. But in that year most abolitionists saw more hope in the more moderate, broadly coalitionist Free Soil party, which promised only to remove all federal sanctions for slavery by abolishing the institution in the District of Columbia, by excluding it from the territories, and by employing all

HARRIET TUBMAN
Born into slavery in Maryland, Harriet Tubman escaped to the North and then became the most celebrated leader of the Underground Railroad. Fearlessly returning on many trips to the South, she guided hundreds of slaves to freedom in the North or in Canada. She appears at the extreme left in this photograph with a group of blacks whom she rescued from slavery. *(The Bettmann Archive, Inc.)*

other constitutional means to deprive it of national support.

The Free Soil platform of 1848, unlike the platform of the Liberty party, ignored the legal discriminations that free blacks suffered. Many of the dissident northern Democrats who helped form the party had consistently opposed black suffrage and had exploited white racist prejudices. And indeed abolitionism in general became more acceptable in the North by accommodating itself to white racism. Many blacks increasingly resented the attention given to women's rights, nonresistance, and communitarian experiments, to say nothing of the hypocrisy of many reformers regarding racial equality in the North. They also resented the patronizing attitudes of white abolitionists who might defend abstract equality while treating blacks as inferiors who had to be led.

Black Abolitionists. From the beginning, black abolitionists had worked closely with the antislavery societies in New England and New York. Beginning with Frederick Douglass's celebrated escape from slavery in 1838 and enlistment as a lecturer for Garrison's Massachusetts Anti-Slavery Society in 1841, fugitive slaves performed the indispensable task of translating the abolitionists' abstract images into concrete human experience. The lectures and printed narratives of Douglass, William Wells Brown, Ellen Craft, Henry Bibb, Solomon Northup, and other escaped slaves did much to undermine whatever belief there was in the North that slaves were kindly treated and contented with their lot. The wit and articulate militancy of black abolitionists like Henry Highland Garnet and Charles Lenox Remond, coupled with the towering dignity of Douglass, also helped to shake confidence in the popular stereotypes of Negro inferiority.

Yet black abolitionists faced constricting walls and physical dangers that made the difficulties of white abolitionists seem like child's play. When Douglass and Garrison traveled together on lecture tours, it was Douglass who experienced constant insult, humiliation, and harassment. Black vigilance committees could help a small number of fugitives find their way to Canada and relative security—and blacks were the main conductors on the so-called Underground Railroad—but except in Massachusetts, black abolitionists had little leverage for loosening the rocklike edifice of discriminatory law. Instead, white abolitionists kept pressuring blacks to keep a low profile, to act the part assigned them by white directors, who presumably knew the tastes of an all-white audience, and to do nothing that might spoil the show.

In the 1840s black leaders gradually cast off the yoke that had bound them to a white man's cause and tried to assert their own leadership. In 1843, at the Convention of the Free People of Color held at Buffalo, Garnet openly called for a slave rebellion, arguing that it was a sin to submit voluntarily to human bondage. Douglass adhered to his own version of nonresistance until 1847, when he broke with Garrison over the propriety of founding a black abolitionist newspaper, the *North Star.* In the same year Garrison sadly reported that Remond had proclaimed that "the slaves were bound, by their love of justice, to RISE AT ONCE, en masse, and THROW OFF THEIR FETTERS."

But speeches were one thing, action another. Black abolitionists had always looked to voting, a right few blacks possessed, as the most promising route to power. For the most part, therefore, they supported the Liberty party in 1840 and 1844, and the Free Soil party in 1848. The drift of antislavery politics, however, was away from black civil rights in the North and emancipation in the southern states and toward a walling off of the western territories—a walling off, in all probability, of free blacks as well as slaves. It is not surprising that by 1854 a few black leaders like Martin Delaney were talking of a separate black nation, or that blacks who had proudly defended their American heritage and right to American citizenship were beginning to reconsider voluntary colonization.

But by 1854 many northern whites had also con-cluded that the Slave Power had seized control of America's manifest destiny, thereby appropriating and nullifying the entire evangelical and millennial mission.* Moreover, the Fugitive Slave Law of 1850, requiring federal agents to recover fugitive slaves from their sanctuaries in the North, directly challenged the North's integrity and its new self-image as an asylum of liberty. The arrival of federal "kidnappers" and the spectacle of blacks being seized in the streets invited demonstrations of defiance and civil disobedience. Increasing numbers of former moderates echoed Garrison's rhetoric of disunion, and an increasing number of former nonresistants called for a slave insurrection or predicted that the streets of Boston might "yet run with blood." Wendell Phillips, a Boston aristocrat and the most powerful of all abolitionist orators, rejoiced in the knowledge "that every five minutes gave birth to a black baby," for in its infant wail he recognized the voice that should "yet shout the war cry of insurrection; its baby hand would one day hold the dagger which should reach the master's heart."

In the 1850s northern abolitionists finally concluded that if the Slave Power were not crushed by insurrection or expelled from the Union, it would surmount every legal and constitutional barrier and destroy the physical ability of Northerners to act in accordance with the moral ability that had been the main legacy of revivals. The western territories were thus the critical testing ground that would determine whether America would stand for something more than selfish interest, exploitation, and rule by brutal power. All of the aspirations of the Benevolent Empire, of evangelical reformers, and of perfectionists of every kind could be channeled in a single and vast crusade to keep the territories free, to confine and seal in the Slave Power, and thus to open the way for an expansion of righteous liberty and opportunity that would transcend all worldly limits.

*For this critical contest over admitting Kansas as a slave state, see Chapter 17, pp. 447–51.

SUGGESTED READINGS

David B. Davis, ed., *Ante-Bellum Reform* (1967), presents differing interpretations of reform and also an annotated bibliography. Though out of date, Alice F. Tyler, *Freedom's Ferment* (1944), is the only comprehensive survey. Whitney R. Cross, *The Burned-Over District* (1950), analyzes the origins of secular reform as well as of Mormonism and other religious movements.

Thomas F. O'Dea, *The Mormons* (1957), is the best introduction to Mormonism. Fawn M. Brodie, *No Man Knows My History: The Life of Joseph Smith* (1945), is also indispensable. Klaus J. Hansen, *Quest for Empire* (1967), is a brilliant account of the Mormons' efforts to prepare for a worldly Kingdom of God. Robert B. Flanders, *Nauvoo: Kingdom on the Mississippi* (1965), is a fascinating study of the Mormons' city-state in Illinois. A dramatic and authoritative narrative of the westward migration is Wallace Stegner, *The Gathering of Zion: The Story of the Mormon Trail* (1964). Leonard J. Arrington's two works, *Great Basin Kingdom* (1958) and *Building the City of God: Community and Cooperation among the Mormons* (1976), are masterly accounts of the Mormon settlement of Utah. On polygamy, see Kimball Young, *Isn't One Wife Enough?* (1954). Norman F. Furniss, *The Mormon Conflict, 1850–1859* (1960), covers the so-called Mormon War.

There are no satisfactory general works on the relation between religion and secular reform. Important aspects of the subject are examined in Carroll Smith-Rosenberg, *Religion and the Rise of the American City: The New York Mission Movement* (1971); Paul E. Johnson, *A Shopkeeper's Millennium: Society and Revivals in Rochester, New York, 1815–1837* (1978); Charles I. Foster, *An Errand of Mercy: The Evangelical United Front* (1960); Clifford S. Griffin, *Their Brothers' Keepers: Moral Stewardship in the United States* (1960); Timothy L. Smith, *Revivalism and Social Reform* (1957); and Bertram Wyatt-Brown, "Prelude to Abolitionism: Sabbatarian Politics and the Rise of the Second Party System," *Journal of American History*, 58 (1971), 316–41. The temperance movement, a critical link between evangelical religion and secular reform, is well described in John A. Krout, *The Origins of Prohibition* (1925). For American drinking habits, see W. J. Rorabaugh, *The Alcoholic Republic: An American Tradition* (1979).

The literature on abolitionism is voluminous. The historical precedents and background are covered in David B. Davis, *The Problem of Slavery in Western Culture* (1966); and *The Problem of Slavery in the Age of Revolution,*

1770–1823 (1975). The best brief account of later abolitionism is James B. Stewart, *Holy Warriors: The Abolitionists and American Slavery* (1976). Gilbert H. Barnes, *The Anti-Slavery Impulse* (1933), is a dramatic and readable study, emphasizing the role of Theodore Weld and the Lane Seminary rebels. For an opposing and brilliantly argued view, see Aileen S. Kraditor, *Means and Ends in American Abolitionism: Garrison and His Critics on Strategy and Tactics* (1967). A similarly powerful and creative work is Lewis Perry, *Radical Abolitionism: Anarchy and the Government of God in Antislavery Thought* (1973). Provacative new approaches can be found in Lewis Perry and Michael Fellman, eds., *Antislavery Reconsidered: New Perspectives on the Abolitionists* (1979). Leonard L. Richards, *"Gentlemen of Property and Standing": Anti-Abolition Mobs in Jacksonian America* (1970), keenly analyzes antiabolition violence. Concerning civil liberties, see Russel B. Nye, *Fettered Freedom: Civil Liberties and the Slavery Controversy* (1963); and Thomas O. Morris, *Free Men All: The Personal Liberty Laws of the North, 1780–1861* (1974).

For the politics of antislavery, see Richard H. Sewell, *Ballots for Freedom* (1976), as well as the following biographical studies: Bertram Wyatt-Brown, *Lewis Tappan and the Evangelical War against Slavery* (1969); Betty Fladeland, *James Gillespie Birney: Slaveholder to Abolitionist* (1955); James B. Stewart, *Joshua R. Giddings and the Tactics of Radical Politics* (1970); Richard H. Sewell, *John P. Hale and the Politics of Abolition* (1965); Frank O. Gatell, *John Gorham Palfrey and the New England Conscience* (1963); Ralph V. Harlow, *Gerrit Smith* (1939); Edward Magdol, *Owen Lovejoy, Abolitionist in Congress* (1967); and David Donald, *Charles Sumner and the Coming of the Civil War* (1960). William Lloyd Garrison, who tried to abstain from political involvement, is the subject of two fine biographies: John L. Thomas, *The Liberator: William Lloyd Garrison* (1963); and Walter M. Merrill, *Against Wind and Tide: A Biography of William Lloyd Garrison* (1963).

Benjamin Quarles, *Black Abolitionists* (1969), is a pioneering study of a subject long neglected by historians. An important recent work is Jane H. Pease and William H. Pease, *They Who Would Be Free: Blacks' Search for Freedom, 1830–1861* (1974). For Frederick Douglass, see Arna Bontemps, *Free at Last: The Life of Frederick Douglass* (1971), and Douglass, *Life and Times of Frederick Douglass, Written by Himself* (1881).

An original work that is indispensable for understanding the changing status of women and the origins of feminism is Nancy F. Cott, *The Bonds of Womanhood: "Woman's Sphere" in New England, 1780–1835* (1977), which should be supplemented by Barbara J. Berg, *The Remembered Gate: Origins of American Feminism—The Woman and the City, 1800–1860* (1977) and Keith M. Melder, *Beginnings of Sisterhood: The American Woman's Rights Movement, 1800–1850* (1977). Aileen S. Kraditor, ed., *Up from the Pedestal: Selected Writings in the History of American Feminism* (1968), is an excellent anthology. The best overall survey is Carl N. Degler, *At Odds: Women and the Family in America from the Revolution to the Present* (1980). Other useful works are Ellen C. DuBois, *Feminism and Suffrage: The Emergence of an Independent Women's Movement in America, 1848–1869* (1978); W. L. O'Neill, *Everyone Was Brave: The Rise and Fall of Feminism in America* (1970); Andrew Sinclair, *The Better Half: The Emancipation of the American Woman* (1965); and Page Smith, *Daughters of the Promised Land* (1970). For individual biographies, see Alma Lutz, *Created Equal: A Biography of Elizabeth Cady Stanton* (1973); Otelia Cromwell, *Lucretia Mott* (1971); Katharine Du Pre Lumpkin, *The Emancipation of Angelina Grimké* (1974); and Gerda Lerner, *The Grimké Sisters from South Carolina: Rebels against Slavery* (1967).

David S. Rothman, *The Discovery of the Asylum* (1971), is a brilliant interpretation of reformatory institutions. The most imaginative study of early prisons is W. David Lewis, *From Newgate to Dannemora: The Rise of the Penitentiary in New York* (1965). Black McKelvey, *American Prisons* (1936), is a more comprehensive reference. On the insane, the best guides are Helen E. Marshall, *Dorothea Dix: Forgotten Samaritan* (1937); and Gerald N. Grob, *Mental Institutions in America: Social Policy to 1875* (1973). For the reformer who did most for the deaf and blind, see Harold Schwartz, *Samuel Gridley Howe* (1956).

The classic work on the peace movement is Merle Curti, *The American Peace Crusade, 1815–1860* (1929), which should be supplemented by Peter Brock, *Pacifism in the United States: From the Colonial Era to the First World War* (1968).

On communitarian settlements, the best general works are Mark Holloway, *Heavens on Earth* (1951), and the relevant chapters in Donald D. Egbert and Stow Persons, *Socialism and American Life* (2 vols., 1952). The communitarian phase inspired by Robert Owen is masterfully covered by J. F. C. Harrison, *Quest for the New Moral World: Robert Owen and the Owenites in Britain and America* (1969). For the New Harmony experiment, see also William Wilson, *The Angel and the Serpent* (1964); and Arthur Bestor, *Backwoods Utopias* (1950). The best introduction to the Oneida community is Maren L. Carden, *Oneida: Utopian Community to Modern Corporation* (1969); Robert D. Thomas, *The Man Who Would Be Perfect: John Humphrey Noyes and the Utopian Impulse* (1977). Three other studies of unusual importance are Lawrence Veysey, ed., *The Perfectionists: Radical Social Thought in the North, 1815–1860* (1973); Michael Fellman, *The Unbounded Frame: Freedom and Community in Nineteenth-Century Utopianism* (1973); and William H. Pease, *Black Utopia: Negro Communal Experiment in America* (1963).

CHAPTER 16

Expansion and New Boundaries

*T*he 1840s marked the beginning of a new era. In the North, recovery from a long depression was accompanied by rapid urban growth, the extension of machine production and of the factory system, the influx of hundreds of thousands of immigrants, and the construction of vast railway networks linking western farms with eastern markets. In the South, the remarkable profitability of cotton and sugar plantations confirmed a whole region's unapologetic commitment to slave labor. The moral discomforts that had troubled Jefferson's generation of Southerners had finally given way to a proud and self-conscious identity as a "progressive slave society." This sectional confidence was bolstered not only by the world's demand for cotton but by the annexation of Texas. The resulting Mexican War, which extended America's boundaries to the Pacific, led some southern leaders to dream of a vast tropical empire based on the slave labor of an "inferior race." These spectacular fulfillments of trends and aspirations that had been developing since the War of 1812 posed grave challenges to governmental policy and to the nation's sense of its own character.

Industrialization and Economic Growth

There is still much controversy over the stages of America's economic growth. Some economists have advanced the theory of a dramatic "takeoff" starting in the 1840s, in which the growth of the nation's productivity shot dramatically ahead of the growth of population. The best recent evidence suggests that a pattern of long-term accelerated growth preceded significant industrialization and probably originated in the 1820s from the interaction between urbanization and western agriculture. In those years manufacturing still mostly conformed to the literal meaning of the word—goods that were made by hand in households and in small shops or mills. Blacksmiths, coopers, cobblers, curriers, hatters, tailors, weavers—these and other artisans and apprentices worked in central shops, mills, and stores, or moved as itinerants through the more sparsely settled countryside. Yet the 1820s marked the beginning of rapid urbanization, a decisive shift toward nonagricultural employment, and perhaps the fastest economic growth of the pre–Civil War era.

Manufacturing. As had happened in England, cotton textiles became the leading industrial innovation. Aided somewhat by protective tariffs, a group of wealthy Boston merchants pooled their capital and in the 1820s extended the Waltham system of large-scale factory production to new manufacturing centers like Lowell and Chicopee, in Massachusetts. The Waltham system, which had been created by New England merchants when the War of 1812 had curtailed international trade, exploited the latest English technology, such as the power loom, and continued to draw on the expertise of immigrant English artisans.

If their products were to compete successfully with imported English textiles, New England manufacturers had to lower the cost and increase the efficiency of labor. Traditionally, American manufacturers had cut costs by employing children or families including children who increased the labor force without increasing wages. It soon became apparent, however, that children could not handle the frequent breakdowns of the new machinery or conform to the regimen necessary for increased labor productivity.

By the late 1840s immigrants had begun to ease the general shortage of factory labor. But for a few decades the Boston merchants relied on the unique expedient of employing adult young women who were attracted to the factories by chaperoned dormitories and various cultural amenities. The merchant-manufacturers desired, no doubt sincerely, to avoid the moral degradation that had stigmatized the English factory system. As economy-minded entrepreneurs, they also hoped to exert influence over their employees' leisure time, preventing the binges and self-proclaimed holidays that had always led to irregular work habits and absenteeism among the preindustrial folk. New England farm girls could also be hired for less than half the wages of male factory hands, since they were secondary earners for their families and since the factory was virtually the only possible liberation from the farm.

From 1815 to 1833 the cotton textile industry increased average annual output at the phenomenal

rate of 16 percent. Although slackening demand soon reduced the annual rate of growth to about 5 percent, textile producers, including wool and carpet manufacturers, continued to be pioneers in mechanization, in efficiency, and in the use of steam power.

New England also gave birth to the so-called "American system of manufacturing." This innovation consisted of imaginatively applying and reaping the benefits from a machine-tool technology that had first been developed in England. Unlike the English, American manufacturers could not draw on a plentiful supply of highly skilled craftsmen with many years of training in an established craft tradition. They therefore encouraged the perfection of light machine tools that not only eliminated many hand operations but also allowed ordinary mechanics to measure within one-thousandth of an inch and to mill or cut metal with great precision. At the English Crystal Palace exhibition of 1851, American machinery astonished European experts. In 1854 one of the English commissions sent to study American achievements exclaimed over "the extraordinary ingenuity displayed in many of their labour-saving machines, where automatic action so completely supplies the place of the more abundant hand labour of older manufacturing countries."

The English investigators understood the significance for the future of such seemingly prosaic devices as a machine that produced 180 ladies' hairpins every minute. As early as 1853 an exuberant writer for the *United States Review* could predict that within a half-century machines would liberate Americans from the restraints of work: "Machinery will perform all work —automata will direct them. The only tasks of the human race will be to make love, study and be happy."

In 1860 American industry was still at an early stage of transition, showing sharp contrasts according to product and level of regional development. The American iron industry, despite an impressive expansion in output, was not, for example, nearly as successful as the cotton textile industry in adopting and improving the latest English technology. The continued use of small blast furnaces that used charcoal to produce malleable iron has been explained by the cheapness and availability of wood for charcoal; by the absence of bituminous coal east of the

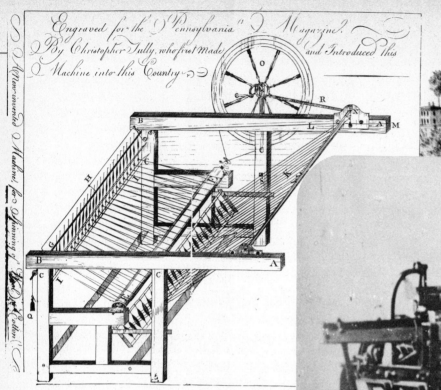

INDUSTRY IN NEW ENGLAND

Americans expressed an absorbing interest in diagrams of new machines, such as Christopher Tully's eighteenth-century spinning machine for wool; even young boys became expert in grasping the principles by which gears transmitted power to moving rollers and other parts. The woman tending a machine in the illustration at right is weaving cloth on a power loom. The lithograph of the Pontoosuc Woolen Mills in Pittsfield, Massachusetts, dramatizes the rural setting of early American industry. *(Top left, American Antiquarian Society; others, Merrimack Valley Textile Museum)*

Alleghenies; by the belated discovery and use of anthracite; and by the particular needs of local blacksmiths. Whatever the reasons, American industry in the 1850s heavily depended on imported English wrought iron and railroad rails, and lagged far behind England in exploiting coal, iron, and steam.

In the West, manufacturing often reverted to preindustrial methods that had almost disappeared in the East. But even in the Northeast many goods were produced not in factories but by merchants who still relied on the "putting-out" system, distributing raw materials to laborers who often owned their own tools and worked at home. Other merchant capitalists hired laborers essentially as instruments of produc-

tion—they had no share in the ownership of tools and machines, in managerial decisions, in the risks of marketing, or in the industrial product.

In 1860 American manufacturing still depended largely on water power, not steam. The typical firm employed a handful of workers, was unincorporated, and engaged in the small-scale processing of raw materials. Few industries processed the products of other industries. The nation's largest industries included some that were thoroughly mechanized, such as the production of cotton goods, flour, and meal; some that were partly mechanized, such as the manufacture of boots and shoes; and some that were characterized by premodern technology and low labor productivity, such as lumbering and the making of men's clothing.

Agriculture.   The expansion and commercialization of agriculture, in both North and South, provided the impetus for the economy's accelerated growth and modernization.* During the 1840s the United States began to export an increasing proportion of its agricultural output, partly in response to poor harvests in Europe and to England's repeal of the protective "Corn Laws" that had excluded American and other

*See Chapter 12, pp. 315–22.

foreign grain. This outflow helped to pay for America's imports of manufactured products and the immense interest charges on foreign investment in American land, cotton, and railroads. Much of America's economic expansion depended on the ability to attract such investment from Europe. By preventing glutted domestic markets, agricultural exports also helped to raise the price of domestic farm products, thereby encouraging the further expansion of cash crops.

Continuing improvements in transportation enabled agricultural regions to specialize in the search for competitive advantages in response to the pressures of an increasingly national market. In the states of the Old Northwest, north of the Ohio River, farmers began to buy trademarked tools and machines from authorized distributors. Steel plows, invented in the 1830s but widely accepted only in the 1850s, made it possible to break the tough sod and cultivate the rich but sticky soil of the prairies. Mechanical reapers had also been invented in the 1830s, but only in the 1850s did Cyrus McCormick's Chicago factory begin large-scale production and employ modern techniques of advertising and promotion. As the Old Northwest proved its superiority in producing wheat and other grains, along with wool, corn, pork, and beef, farmers in the East, no longer able to compete with their western counterparts, had to be content to produce hay for horses and perishable foodstuffs for urban markets.

Railroad Building.   The great railroad boom of the late 1840s and 1850s dramatized the growing links between agriculture and industry. Although the nation's railroads equaled the canals in mileage as early as 1840, canal barges and river steamboats continued to carry a significant proportion of freight throughout the antebellum period. By providing speedy access to isolated farms and distant markets, railroads opened new horizons and extended the risks and promises of a commercial society.

The development of railway networks was long delayed by primitive technology, a high incidence of breakdowns and accidents, and construction costs that required unprecedented amounts of capital investment. As early as 1828, Baltimore promoters began building the first trans-Appalachian railroad to compete with New York's Erie Canal, which threatened to channel much of the western trade toward New York City. But it was not until 1853 that this Baltimore and Ohio road reached the Ohio River. As late as 1860 there were still hundreds of small, independent lines with different widths of track. Nevertheless, by the early 1850s construction engineers were improving rails, roadbeds, bridges, and locomotives. Railroad corporations had amassed immense reserves of capital, and their managers were learning how to administer complex bureaucracies that employed thousands of workers and required instant interstate communication by means of the recently perfected electric telegraph. By 1854 tracks extended from New York City to the Mississippi, and, by 1860, to the Missouri at St. Joseph. This burst of western railroad construction led to the beginning of consolidation into trunk lines that further cemented economic ties between the West and the Northeast. By 1860 railroads had become the nation's

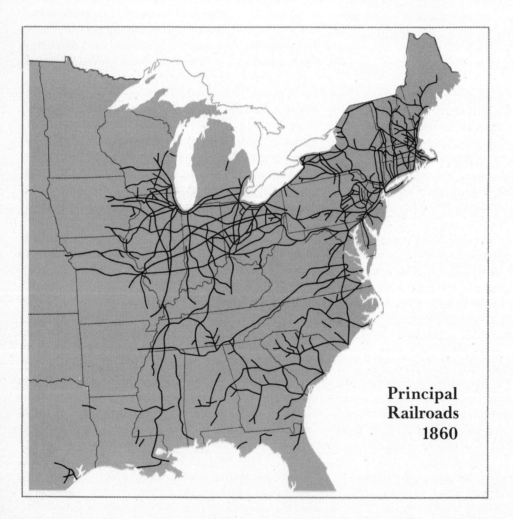

**Principal
Railroads
1860**

first billion-dollar industry, spawning the first giant corporations, linking cash-crop farming with the production of iron, coal, lumber, and machine tools.

Panic of 1857. There were dark shadows, however, in this overall picture of growth and economic integration. The mid-1850s brought a slowing down of investment and of industrial production, culminating in the financial panic of 1857. For the first time the business cycle seemed to be primarily geared to the fluctuations of nonagricultural forces, such as speculative investment in railroads, in the domestic economy. Significantly the South suffered little from the essentially industrial depression of the late 1850s. Southern leaders could not refrain from gloating over the economic vulnerability of northern industry and the insecurities of "wage slavery." Northern leaders angrily accused the South of contributing to the depression by defeating northern moves for protective tariffs and free homesteads. Slave-grown cotton remained an important contributor to the North's industrial growth. But many Northerners perceived the South as a vestige of colonial dependency—a dependency on English markets that blocked the way to national self-sufficiency.

The South as a "Slave Society"

By the 1830s the institution of black slavery had come to dominate all aspects of southern society. Apologies for slavery as an unfortunate though necessary evil were beginning to give way to aggressive self-justification. Paradoxically, as the South became increasingly isolated from the free-labor ideology of the Western world, the expansion of cotton cultivation helped to assure southern leaders that slavery was indispensable to northern and British industry. Accordingly, slaveholders regarded their critics as ungrateful hypocrites who would bite the hand that fed them.

The meaning of the term "slave society" is best illustrated by the West Indian colonies of the eigh-

teenth and early nineteenth centuries. There Negro slaves typically made up 90 percent or more of an island's population; political and social life was wholly dominated by large planters, their managers and agents, and the merchants who lived off the system. On the question of black slavery there was almost no dissent.

Parts of the South almost approximated this model: the swampy lowcountry of South Carolina and the Sea Islands; the fertile Black Belt, extending from Georgia to Mississippi; the delta counties of Mississippi and the sugar parishes of Louisiana. But unlike the small and isolated West Indian islands, the sprawling South was anything but a uniform and monolithic society. In 1860 roughly 10,000 families belonged to the planter aristocracy, out of a white population of some 8 million. Fewer than 3,000 families owned over one hundred slaves. Barely one out of four white Southerners owned a slave or belonged to a family that did. There were extensive regions of eastern Tennessee and western Virginia where blacks, slave or free, were a rarity. Slavery had declined sharply in most of the Upper South (by 1860 fewer than 2,000 slaves remained in Delaware). Nor could most of the nonslaveholding majority be classed as hillbillies and poor whites. In addition to artisans, factory workers, and professionals, there were millions of small farmers in the South who worked their own land or who grazed herds of cattle, pigs, and horses in the forests and open range of the public domain.

Nevertheless, except for a few isolated pockets, the South did become a slave society dominated politically and ideologically by a planter oligarchy. Throughout the period, slaveholding remained the most widespread and obvious route to wealth and status. By 1860 millions of nonslaveholders believed that any serious threat to slavery was sufficient justification for southern independence; many of them, especially in the Southwest, had reasonable hopes of acquiring land and becoming planters. And small farmers often depended on a neighboring planter's cotton gin or political patronage; they knew that in turn he depended for security on their services as armed patrols that searched the countryside for any unauthorized movement of blacks.

Dominance of the Planter Class.   The planter class could also draw on a rich tradition of political leadership. In the South—but not in the North—the eighteenth-century connection between wealth and personal political power endured. Political leadership sprang directly from the ownership of slaves, which was supposed to provide leisure, a concern for public order, and a certain paternalistic self-assurance in exercising authority. The planter elite demonstrated skill in commanding the loyalty of nonslaveholding whites and also in disciplining dissent within the white population. By the 1830s numerous southern abolitionists and Southerners with simply a strong distaste for slavery had emigrated to the North or West after abandoning hope of challenging the dogma that Negro slavery was a necessary evil that should be discussed as little as possible. They left behind them a planter elite solidified in its defense of slavery and militantly intolerant of dissent.

The key to southern white unity was race. The South was an amorphous society dedicated to the ideal of equality of opportunity as long as the ideal applied only to whites. It was also a region that depended economically on a system of labor exploitation that was difficult to square with republican and libertarian principles. Racial doctrine, the supposed innate inferiority of blacks, became the primary instrument for justifying the persistence of slavery, for rallying the support of nonslaveholding whites, and for defining the limits of dissent.

Southern Free Blacks.   The key to racial policy was the status of free blacks. Before the nineteenth century this status had been ambiguous, and the number of free blacks was insignificant. By 1810, however, as a result of the emancipations that had accompanied and followed the Revolution, there were 100,000 free blacks and mulattoes in the southern states. This group, the fastest growing element in the southern population, was beginning to acquire property, to found "African" churches and schools, and to assert its independence, especially in the Upper South. In

response, white legislators tightened restrictions on private acts of freeing slaves in an effort to curb the growth of an unwanted population. A rash of new laws, similar to the later black codes of Reconstruction, reduced free Negroes almost to the status of slaves without masters. The new laws regulated their freedom of movement; prohibited their fraternization with slaves; subjected them to surveillance and discipline by whites; denied them the legal right to testify against whites; required them to work at approved employments; and threatened them with penal labor if not actual reenslavement. Paradoxically, in the Deep South free blacks continued to benefit from a more flexible status because they were fewer than elsewhere in the South and, as in the West Indies, could serve as valued intermediaries between a white minority and a slave majority. Racial discrimination was most flagrant in the Upper South, precisely because slavery was economically less secure in that region.

Decline of Antislavery in the South.   From the time of the Revolution a cautious, genteel distaste for slavery had been fashionable among the planters of the Upper South. This Jeffersonian tradition persisted even after the more militant abolitionists had been driven from the region and after Methodist and Baptist leaders had backtracked on various resolutions encouraging gradual emancipation. The desire to find some way of ridding the South of its "burden" or "curse," as the Jeffersonian reformers called it, was perpetuated by some of the sons of affluent planters who went to the North or to Europe to study.

The hope of removing the South's burden also won assent from a few cosmopolitan planters, mostly Whigs, who were troubled by the soil depletion and economic decline of eastern Virginia and Maryland, and by the continuing loss of population to the Southwest. In 1832 the belief that slavery was "ruinous to the whites" received unexpected support in the Virginia legislature from nonslaveholders who lived west of the Blue Ridge and who had various motives for challenging the political control of tidewater planters. But in the end, their arguments, in a notable legislative debate of 1832 which arose in response to Nat

Turner's insurrection, demonstrated the power of racism. Even the nonslaveholding rebels acknowledged that bondage had benefits for blacks, and that its detrimental effects on white society could be ended only by gradually freeing and deporting the entire black population. The antislavery delegates failed even to carry a resolution that would have stigmatized slavery as an evil to be dealt with at some future time.

The Proslavery Argument. By the 1840s—less than a decade later—such a public debate would have been inconceivable in any southern state. By then regional loyalty, intensified by sectional conflict, required that Southerners believe slavery to be a "positive good." The proslavery argument ranged from appeals to ancient Greek and Roman precedents to elaborate biblical interpretations designed to prove that slavery had never been contrary to the laws of God. Drawing on the romantic and chivalric literary fashions of the time, southern writers represented the plantation as a feudal manor blessed with human warmth, reciprocal duties, knightly virtues, and a loyalty to blood and soil.

The most striking part of the proslavery ideology was its indictment of liberalism and capitalism, its well-documented charge that the prevailing rule in so-called free societies, as George Fitzhugh put it, was "every man for himself, and the devil take the hindmost." In his *Sociology for the South* (1854) and *Cannibals All!* (1857), Fitzhugh incisively criticized the philosophic premises of an individualistic, egalitarian society. He also examined the destructive historical consequences of dissolving the social and psychological networks that had once given humanity a sense of place and purpose. Fitzhugh, the most rigorous and consistent proslavery theorist, presented the master-slave relation as the only alternative to a world in which rampant self-interest had subjected propertyless workers to the impersonal exploitation of "wage-slavery." He was consistent enough to renounce *racial* justifications for actual slavery and to propose that the benefits of the institution he boasted of be extended to white workers. But these arguments, however interesting theoretically, only showed how far Fitzhugh had moved from social reality. Racism lay at the heart of the South's unity; the enslavement of whites was unthinkable, and in the 1850s the South even rejected extremist proposals for expelling or reenslaving a quarter-million free blacks. Fitzhugh's theories did more to expose the moral dilemmas of free society than to illuminate the actual complexities and contradictions of the South.

It is true that moral doubts persisted, especially in the Upper South. But after the 1830s such doubts were more than counterbalanced by the conviction that emancipation in any form would be a disaster, for blacks as well as whites. Southerners channeled their moral concern into dedicated efforts to reform, improve, and defend the peculiar institution. To own slaves, according to the reigning dogma, meant to have a sense of duty and a burden—a duty and a burden that defined the moral superiority of the South; a duty and a burden nonslaveholders in the South respected and were prepared to defend with their lives. That, perhaps, was the ultimate meaning of a "slave society."

Foreign Dangers, American Expansion, and the Monroe Doctrine

America's foreign policy had always presupposed a commitment by the national government to protect and support the South's peculiar institution. It is true, however, that American foreign policy reflected many other interests and motives, and that until 1844 protecting slavery was not explicitly acknowledged as a vital objective. The overriding objective in the early nineteenth century, as in the post-Revolutionary period, was to prevent England or France from acquiring a foothold in the increasingly vulnerable Spanish territories of North America. But those territories, including Cuba, East and West Florida, and Texas, were a threat mainly to the slaveholding South. The War of 1812 made clear that possession of the Floridas was essential for the security of the entire Lower South. From bases in supposedly neutral Spanish Florida, the British had incited Indian raids, had encouraged slave desertions, and had originally planned to launch an invasion inland to cut off New Orleans from the rest of the United States. The Haitian revolution of 1791–1804 had also shown that war could ignite a massive slave insurrection and totally destroy a slaveholding society.

Decline of New World Slavery. One of the consequences of the Napoleonic wars was the fatal weakening of slaveholding regimes in most parts of the New World. Not only did France lose Haiti, the richest sugar colony in the world, but Napoleon's seizure of Spain opened the way for independence movements in the immense Spanish territories from Mexico to Chile. The prolonged wars of liberation undermined the institution of slavery and committed the future Spanish American republics to programs of gradual emancipation. After the British abolished the slave trade to their own colonies, they embarked on a long-term policy of suppressing the slave trade of other nations. By 1823, when little remained of the former Spanish, Portuguese, and French New World empires, slavery was a declining institution except in Brazil, Cuba (still a Spanish colony), and the United States.

This wider context dramatizes a momentous paradox of American foreign policy from the time of Jefferson's presidency to the Civil War. The extension of what Jefferson termed an "empire for liberty" was also the extension of an empire for slavery and thus a counterweight to the forces that threatened to erode slavery throughout the hemisphere. Jefferson himself initiated the policy of trying to quarantine Haiti, economically and diplomatically, to end the contagion of black revolution. In 1820, in the midst of the Missouri crisis and in response to Spain's delay in ratifying the Transcontinental Treaty of 1819 ceding East Florida, Jefferson privately assured President Monroe that the United States could soon acquire not only East Florida but Cuba—then on the road to becoming the world's greatest producer of slave-grown sugar—and Texas. Texas, he confidently predicted, would be the richest state of the Union, partly because it would produce more sugar than the country could consume.

There is no reason to think that American statesmen consciously plotted to create a vast empire for slavery—at least until the 1840s. From the annexation of Florida (1821) to the annexation of Texas (1845), the United States acquired no new territory that could upset the balance between free states and slave states achieved by the Missouri Compromise. The Old Southwest contained immense tracts of uncleared and uncultivated land, and many Southerners feared that reckless expansion would lead to excessive production that would lower the price of cotton and other staples.

Slavery and Territorial Expansion. The connections between slavery and national expansion were more indirect. They involved two basic and continuing premises that governed foreign policy. The first premise was that territorial expansion was the only means of protecting and extending the principles of the American Revolution in a generally hostile world. "The larger our association," Jefferson had predicted, "the less will it be shaken by local passions." According to this nationalist view, Americans could deal with domestic imperfections once the nation had achieved sufficient power to be secure. Thus for ardent nationalists like John Quincy Adams any personal misgivings over slavery had to give way to the need for a united front against the monarchic despots of Europe. During the Missouri crisis the antislavery forces could never overcome the unfair charge that they were serving Britain's interests by fomenting sectional discord and blocking the westward expansion of the United States.

The second premise, held with passionate conviction by every president from Jefferson to Polk, was that England was America's "natural enemy," a kingdom ruled by selfish interest, filled with a deep-rooted hatred for everything America represented, and committed to the humiliation and subjugation of her former colonies. Anglophobia had much to do with the swift demise of the Federalist party. It was nourished by contemptuous anti-American essays in British periodicals and by unflattering descriptions by English travelers which were widely reprinted in the United States. Many Americans blamed England for the eco-

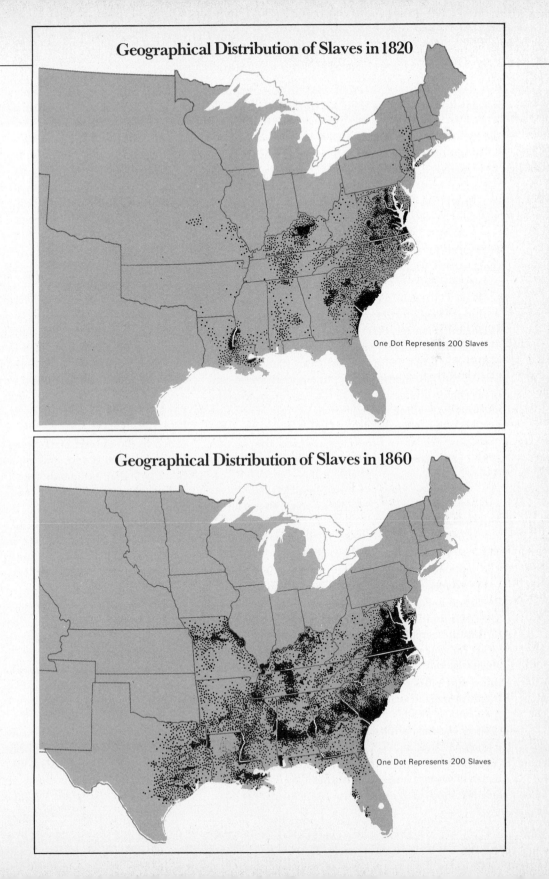

Geographical Distribution of Slaves in 1820

One Dot Represents 200 Slaves

Geographical Distribution of Slaves in 1860

One Dot Represents 200 Slaves

nomic depressions of 1819 and 1837. Irish immigrants regarded the English as their hereditary enemies. No American politician could risk even the suspicion of being an unintentional agent of British interests. It was thus an unhappy coincidence that British interests veered increasingly toward antislavery which American leaders interpreted, not without some reason, as a cloak for new forms of economic and ideological imperialism.

It was the takeover of Florida that established the precedents for the future and that also coincided with the dramatic southwestward expansion of cotton and slavery. As early as 1786 Jefferson had warned against pressing "too soon on the Spaniards." He held that East and West Florida could not be in better hands. He feared, however, that the Spanish were, as he said, "too feeble to hold them till our population can be sufficiently advanced to gain it from them piece by piece." By 1810 there were enough American settlers in the Baton Rouge district of West Florida to stage an armed rebellion against Spanish rule. President Madison, affirming that West Florida was part of the Louisiana Purchase, promptly annexed the section of the Gulf coast extending eastward to the Perdido River. To prevent any possible transfer of West Florida to England, Congress sanctioned Madison's annexation but balked at plans to seize East Florida during the War of 1812.

The Transcontinental Treaty of 1819.   The postwar negotiations with Spain involved not only Florida but the entire western boundary of the United States. Spain had never recognized the validity of Napoleon's sale of Louisiana, a sale prohibited by the treaty transferring the territory from Spain to France. Luis de Onís, the Spanish minister, tried to limit American claims to the narrowest strip possible west of the Mississippi. But as the negotiations dragged on, the South American wars of independence increasingly undermined Spain's position. Secretary of State John Quincy Adams proved to be a tough and skillful bargainer, and in 1818 Andrew Jackson, then the American military commander in the South, immensely strengthened Adams's hand. Without official authorization, Jackson invaded East Florida, captured the main Spanish forts, deposed the governor, and hanged two English troublemakers. The excuse was that Florida had become a refuge for fugitive slaves and a base for Seminole Indian raids on American settlements.

Faced with the temporary seizure of his main bargaining card and fearful that the United States would begin aiding the rebellious Spanish colonies, Onís, agreed in the Transcontinental Treaty of 1819 to cede the Floridas to the United States in return for America's relinquishing the questionable claim that Texas was part of the Louisiana Purchase. In actuality, Onís had been desperate enough to give up most of Texas. But as President Monroe assured General Jackson, "We ought to be content with Florida, for the present, and until the public opinion . . . [in the Northeast] shall be reconciled to any further change."

For Adams the Transcontinental Treaty (or Adams-Onís Treaty, ratified in 1821) was "a great epoch in our history." Not only did it transfer the Floridas to the United States, but it extended American territorial claims to the Pacific Ocean. Spain ceded to the United States her rather weak claims to the Pacific Northwest, and agreed to an international boundary that extended from the Sabine River, dividing Texas from Louisiana, westward along the Red and Arkansas rivers to the Rocky Mountains, and then along the forty-second parallel to the Pacific. Spain had hardly ratified this momentous treaty before the burden of defending its boundaries fell upon an independent, weak, and war-torn Mexico.

Events Leading to Monroe Doctrine.   The collapse of the Spanish empire led directly to the Monroe Doctrine. By 1823 it was clear that Spain could never reduce her rebellious colonies to their former status, and Britain and America shared a common interest in preventing Europe's Holy Alliance of autocratic nations from intervening in Spain's behalf. Under pressure from the Russian czar, France was about to invade Spain, where a revolution had established a constitutional monarchy, in order to restore the absolutist regime of Ferdinand VII. The French foreign minister was known to have grandiose schemes for extending to the New World the Holy Alliance's

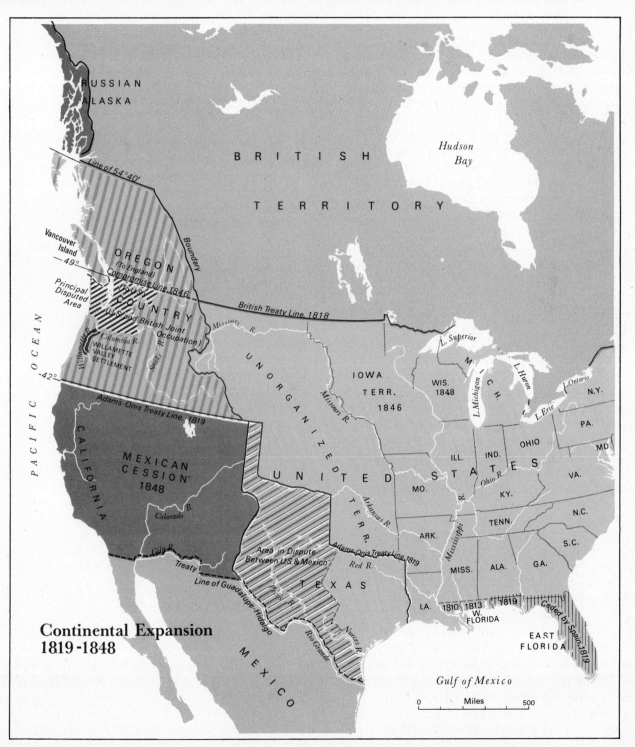

RUSSIAN ALASKA

BRITISH

TERRITORY

Hudson Bay

Line of 54°40'

Boundary

Vancouver Island
— 49°

OREGON
(To England)
Compromise Line 1846
(To U.S.)

COUNTRY

Principal Disputed Area

British Treaty Line, 1818

Missouri R.

L. Superior

(U.S. and British Joint Occupation)

Columbia R.
WILLAMETTE VALLEY SETTLEMENT
Snake R.
Willamette R.

— 42°

U N O R G A N I Z E D

IOWA TERR. 1846

WIS. 1848

M I C H.

L. Michigan
L. Huron

L. Ontario

N.Y.

Adams-Onis Treaty Line, 1819

Missouri R.

L. Erie

PA.

PACIFIC OCEAN

CALIFORNIA

MEXICAN CESSION 1848

Colorado R.

U N I T E D

T E R R.

Arkansas R.

ILL.

IND.

OHIO

Ohio R.

MD.

S T A T E S

MO.

VA.

KY.

Gila R.

Treaty

Adams-Onis Treaty Line 1819

Area in Dispute Between U.S. & Mexico

Red R.

ARK.

TENN.

N.C.

S.C.

Line of Guadalupe-Hidalgo

TEXAS

MISS.

ALA.

GA.

M E X I C O

Rio Grande

Nueces R.

LA.

1810 1813 1819
W. FLORIDA

Ceded by Spain, 1819

EAST FLORIDA

Gulf of Mexico

Continental Expansion 1819-1848

0   Miles   500

crusade for monarchic government. England, though not willing to risk war, strongly opposed this French intervention in Spain. And while not a promoter of independent republics, England also had no intention of allowing antirevolutionary zeal to interfere with her growing commercial dominance in the former Spanish empire. George Canning, the English foreign minister, therefore proposed a joint British-American declaration that would disavow any British or American designs on former Spanish territory and that would warn other nations against intervention.

The British offer presented the Monroe administration with a serious dilemma. The United States was the only nation that had begun to recognize the independent republics of Spanish America, but only Britain could deter a Franco-Spanish expeditionary force from trying to subdue them. Moreover, in 1821 Russia, which was leading the crusade to reestablish monarchic rule and which had earlier expanded from Siberia into Alaska, had issued a decree claiming a monopoly over the North Pacific. Russian traders were becoming more active in the Oregon country, a region that England and the United States had agreed to occupy jointly at least until 1828. Although accepting Canning's offer to issue a joint declaration would have the drawback of temporarily preventing America's annexation of Cuba, the idea appealed to the elder statesmen, Jefferson and Madison, as well as to Monroe and most of his cabinet.

The question was complicated further by the forthcoming presidential election of 1824. The nationalist, anti-English vote was much on the minds of the leading candidates. John Quincy Adams, the secretary of state, was already being portrayed by his rivals as a former Federalist and secret Anglophile. Despite his proved nationalism and loyal service to Republican administrations, Adams was vulnerable to such charges because of his New England and Federalist background. He was also the only candidate who was not a slaveholding planter. He knew that as secretary of state he would bear the largest share of political liability resulting from any Anglo-American alliance. He had long gone out of his way to publicize his resistance to English pressure for an antislave trade treaty. Adams now insisted on a uni-

lateral declaration against European intervention in the New World, much as he insisted on a unilateral policy against the slave trade. It would be more candid and dignified, Adams pointed out, to declare United States principles directly to Russia and France than "to come in as a cock-boat in the wake of the British man-of-war."

Adams's arguments prevailed, and the famous Monroe Doctrine reaffirmed America's diplomatic independence from Europe. By disavowing any American interference in the "internal concerns" of European states, Monroe in effect repudiated the popular clamor for aiding various revolutionary struggles against despotism, including the Greek war for independence from Turkey. But America's warning to Europe against future colonization in the New World extended to Britain as well as to Russia and France. And the Monroe Doctrine in no way precluded America's own expansion in the New World.

For some time the Monroe Doctrine had little practical consequence, except perhaps in vindicating Adams's reputation as a nationalist and thus in helping him win the presidency. Regardless of American pronouncements, it was British naval power that ensured the independence of Spanish America. Yet the Monroe administration, by spurning an Anglo-American alliance, also set a precedent for opposing any foreign attempts to limit the expansion of slavery. No doubt Monroe was thinking only of monarchic institutions when he warned that the United States would consider any European attempt to extend "their system" to any portions of the Western Hemisphere dangerous to America's peace and safety. By the 1830s, however, antislavery was an integral part of the British "system," and many Southerners regarded the expansion of slavery as vital to America's "peace and safety."

Annexation of Texas. The Texas issue eventually tested this point and led to a proslavery reformulation of the Monroe Doctrine. For abolitionists in both Britain and the United States it was not inevitable that Texas should become a slave state. In 1829 Mexico abolished slavery in all provinces (including California), providing loopholes only for the stubborn

SAM HOUSTON, 1793–1863
Leader of the badly outnumbered Texans whose spectacular victory at San Jacinto in 1836 secured Texas's independence from Mexico, Houston went on to become president of the new republic, then senator from the new state. In 1861 as governor, Houston's stand against Texas's secession from the Union forced him out of office. *(Library of Congress)*

Anglo-American settlers in Texas. By 1830 the Mexican government had become alarmed by the growing autonomy of the Anglo-American settlements, by the intrigue accompanying the American government's secret efforts to purchase Texas, and by the agitation for annexation in the Jacksonian press. Consequently in 1830 the Mexican government tried to prohibit the further immigration of Anglo-Americans as well

as the further importation of slaves, and sought to promote the colonization of Europeans as a buffer against encroachments from the United States. Since Negro slavery had only begun to take root in Texas, English reformers were beginning to look on the province as a promising site for cultivating cotton with free labor. Benjamin Lundy, an American Quaker abolitionist, even tried in the early 1830s to establish an asylum in Texas for free blacks from the United States.

But during his travels in Texas Lundy found evidence of growing proslavery sentiment and of various plots to throw off Mexican rule and annex Texas to the United States. The Mexican government was in fact incapable of either governing or satisfying the needs of the Anglo-Texans. In 1836, after President Antonio López de Santa Anna had succeeded in abolishing Mexico's federal constitution and in asserting centralized rule, the Texans proclaimed their independence. Their new constitution, modeled on the United States Constitution, specifically legalized Negro slavery. Meanwhile, Santa Anna's army had wiped out a small band of Texas rebels at San Antonio's Alamo Mission, thereby provoking cries for revenge in the American press. Aided by a great influx of volunteers from the officially neutral United States, the Texans, led by General Sam Houston, crushed the Mexican army at San Jacinto, captured Santa Anna, and soon voted overwhelmingly to join the United States.

As late as 1835 President Jackson had tried to buy not only Texas but all the Mexican territory stretching northwestward to the Pacific; his main object was to secure "within our limits the whole bay of St. Francisco." By then Americans had long been engaged in trade along the Santa Fe Trail and settlers were beginning to arrive by sea in sparsely populated California. After the Texan Revolution, however, Jackson knew that a premature attempt at annexation would in all likelihood bring on a war with Mexico, which refused to acknowledge Texan independence. It would also arouse the fury of the Northeast and lead to a sectional division within the Democratic party in the election year of 1836. But Jackson knew that California was important to the whaling and

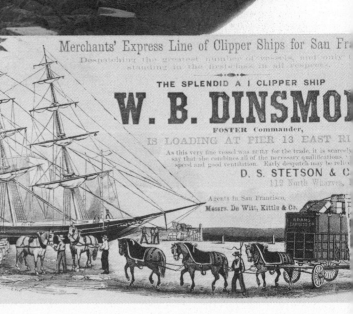

McKAY'S SHIPYARD

Donald McKay's shipyard in East Boston, established in 1845, constructed some of the fastest, most graceful, and most beautiful sailing ships ever made. McKay's clipper, the *Flying Cloud*, made San Francisco in less than 90 days from New York. The *James Baines* set a world record of 12 days 6 hours from Boston to Liverpool. McKay's best clippers could average more than 400 nautical miles in a day. *(Courtesy, Richard Parker Collection. Photograph from George Eastman House)*

"THE SPLENDID, A1 CLIPPER SHIP"

An advertisement for the highly competitive clipper ship travel to San Francisco. *(Museum of the City of New York.)*

maritime interests of the Northeast. New England whalers and cargo ships had begun to make portions of the Pacific an American preserve. Jackson therefore secretly advised Texans to bide their time and to establish a claim to California, "to paralyze the opposition of the North and East to Annexation." He assumed that such opposition would wane as soon as Northerners concluded that annexing Texas would lead to the acquisition of California.

The passage of time, however, encouraged the hopes of American and British opponents of slavery. Jackson's Democratic successor, Martin Van Buren, was too dependent on northeastern support to risk agitating the public with the question of annexation. John Quincy Adams's eloquent speeches in the House of Representatives, in which he served for seventeen years after he retired as president, popularized the view that the southern Slave Power had engineered the Texas Revolution and the drive for annexation. In 1838 Adams carried on a three-week filibuster, presented hundreds of antislavery petitions, and finally defeated a move to annex Texas by joint resolution. The rebuffed Texan leaders withdrew their formal proposal for annexation and began to think seriously of building an independent empire. As time went on, they looked to Britain and France for financial support and for diplomatic aid in ending the perilous state of war with Mexico.

The spring and summer of 1843 marked a decisive turn of events. John Tyler, who had been elected as Harrison's vice-president in 1840 and had then become president after Harrison's death, had been disowned by the Whig party. He was therefore courting southern Democrats and searching for an issue that would win him reelection. Daniel Webster, the last of the Whig cabinet members, finally resigned as secretary of state after negotiating with Britain the Webster-Ashburton Treaty; this treaty settled disputed borders with Canada, provided for cooperative measures in suppressing the Atlantic slave trade, and was immediately attacked by Democrats for betraying America's interests. Through Calhoun's influence, Webster was replaced by Abel P. Upshur, a Virginian who had defended slavery as a "positive good." For the first time, an entire administration was in the hands of ardent proslavery Southerners who saw territorial expansion as the key to southern security.

Britain and Texas. Although British leaders did not want to antagonize the South, on which England depended for cotton, they were sensitive to one abolitionist argument. An independent Texas might begin importing slaves from Africa, thereby adding to Britain's difficulties in suppressing the Atlantic slave trade. The British had evidence that American officials in Cuba were conniving with slave smugglers and that American ships predominated in the illegal trade to Cuba. Texas might open another rich market for the same interests. Therefore, when Britain offered Texas a treaty of recognition and trade, it included a secret agreement to outlaw the slave trade. Otherwise, under close questioning from a delegation of abolitionists, Lord Aberdeen, the foreign secretary, conceded only two points: that in serving as mediator between Texas and Mexico, Britain hoped that any peace agreement would include a commitment to slave emancipation; and that as everyone knew, the British public and government hoped for the abolition of slavery throughout the world.

In Washington these words brought anger and alarm. The Tyler administration was convinced that West Indian emancipation had proved to be an economic and social disaster. The British, according to the prevailing southern theory, were now determined to undermine slavery in other nations to improve the competitive advantage of their own colonies, including India. But Southerners never comprehended the depth of antislavery sentiment among the British middle class. Having subsidized West Indian emancipation by paying £20 million in compensation to planters, British taxpayers wanted assurance that Britain's short-term sacrifices would not lead to the expansion of plantation slavery in neighboring regions of the Caribbean and Gulf of Mexico.

Regardless of the truth, however, Southerners had long been predisposed to believe that British antislavery was part of a long-term diplomatic plot to seal off and contain the United States within a crescent of British influence extending from Cuba and Texas to California, Oregon, and Canada. In 1843 this conviction was seemingly confirmed by the exaggerated reports of Duff Green, an intimate of Calhoun's and President Tyler's secret agent in England and France. According to Green, the British government was about to guarantee interest on a loan to Texas on the condition that Texas abolish slavery. The plan would make Texas a British satellite and an asylum, like Canada, for fugitive slaves from the United States. The British, by erecting a barrier of freedom across the southwestern flank of the slave-holding states, could effectively join northern abolitionists in destroying both slavery and the federal Union.

Like many myths, this elaborate fantasy rested on a thin foundation of truth. It interpreted every event as part of a master plan, and justified national desires that were otherwise difficult to justify. It furnished the pretext for the grand strategy that would govern American expansionist policy for the next five years. In response to an appeal for advice from Secretary of State Upshur, Calhoun in 1843 secretly spelled out the steps for implementing this policy. He called for private assurances to Texas that as soon as a propaganda campaign had been launched to soften northern opposition, the administration would secure annexation. In order to win support from the land-hungry farmers of the Old Northwest, Calhoun also suggested linking Texas annexation with the assertion of American claims to Oregon. As a preliminary step toward this plan, he wanted to demand a formal explanation from Britain for policies that threatened "the safety of the Union and the very existence of the South."

Calhoun himself soon had the power to begin implementing this grand design. Early in 1844 Upshur was killed in an accident, and Calhoun succeeded him as secretary of state. Soon afterwards a Whig newspaper revealed that the administration had been engaged for months in secret negotiations with Texas and that Tyler was about to sign an annexation treaty. In response to growing northern furor, Calhoun seized on and made public the British government's private avowal that Britain "desires, and is constantly exerting herself to procure, the general abolition of slavery throughout the world."

By skillfully distorting and publicizing the British diplomatic notes, Calhoun tried to identify the anti-annexation cause with a British plot to destroy the Union. He lectured the British on the blessings of Negro slavery, employing faulty statistics from the census of 1840 to argue that emancipation in the North had produced Negro insanity, crime, suicide, and degeneracy. He also informed Mexico that because of the British conspiracy to subvert southern slavery, the United States was forced to annex Texas in self-defense.

The Expansionist Issue and Election of 1844. This open defense of slavery by an American secretary of state marked the beginning of a sectional conflict over slavery and expansionism that severely tested the party system. President Tyler's defection from the Whigs, in addition to Calhoun's presidential ambitions and independence from party discipline, complicated the political maneuvering that set the stage for the 1844 campaign. With an eye to northern votes, both Henry Clay and Van Buren, the leading Whig and Democratic contenders, felt compelled by April 1844 to express their opposition to the immediate annexation of Texas.

In the Senate the Missouri Democrat Thomas Hart Benton led the onslaught against the duplicity of Tyler and Calhoun. Seven other Democratic senators, all Northerners, joined the Whigs in decisively rejecting the annexation treaty. Yet the Whig opposition to expansion encouraged the Democratic party to close ranks and rally behind patriotic demands for the "reannexation of Texas" (which assumed that Texas had been part of the Louisiana Purchase), and the "reoccupation of Oregon" (which assumed that Britain had never had legitimate claims to the region south of 54°40', the border of Russian Alaska). The issue of expansion diverted attention from the Democrats' internal disputes over banking and fiscal policy, and also enabled a southern-dominated coalition to defeat Van Buren and nominate James K. Polk, a Jacksonian expansionist from Tennessee, as the Democratic candidate.

As Calhoun had predicted, the Oregon question became an ideal means for exploiting national Anglophobia and winning northern support for national expansion. For decades the British Hudson's Bay Company had ruled the region north of the Columbia River, although the United States had strong claims to the Columbia itself and to the territory extending southward to latitude 42°. New England ships had long frequented the entire Pacific Northwest in search of sea otter furs for the China trade, and since the 1820s American trappers had developed a thriving trade in beaver and other furs within the region west of the Rockies. As American traders challenged the political and judicial authority of the powerful Hudson's Bay Company, it became more difficult to resolve conflicting Anglo-American claims. Moreover, in 1827, when the two nations had renewed a "joint occupation" agreement that simply deferred any settlement of national boundaries, no one could fore-

see the future appeal of the fertile Willamette Valley to farmers in the Old Northwest. Glowing reports from American missionaries to the Indians of the rich farmland there helped to spread the "Oregon fever" of the 1840s, inducing thousands of families to risk the perils and hardships of overland travel to the Pacific. In 1843 the first of the great overland wagon migrations along the Oregon Trail took place, and the resulting claims to "All Oregon" acted as a political balance wheel for the annexation of Texas.

In 1844, as in other elections of the time, voter preference depended less on issues than on ethnic, religious, and party loyalty. And so, concerned about the crucial swing vote, Clay, the Whig candidate, retreated from his earlier stand against Texas annexation. His last-minute gestures for southern support persuaded thousands of northern Whigs to vote for

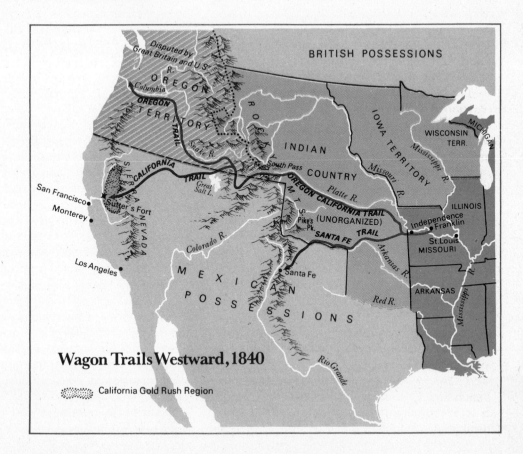

Wagon Trails Westward, 1840

California Gold Rush Region

James G. Birney, the Liberty party candidate, who stood firm against annexation. More popular votes were actually cast against Polk than for him, and although he won the election, he would certainly have lost it if Birney's votes in New York and Michigan had gone to Clay.

Nevertheless, the incumbent President Tyler and the triumphant Democrats interpreted the election as a mandate for immediate annexation. The Democrats in Congress united in championing the new expansionism, allowing the retiring Tyler administration to secure annexation by joint resolution of both houses of Congress. After a tense period of international intrigue, the Republic of Texas rejected offers of peace from Mexico and mediation from Britain. In December 1845, having bypassed territorial status, Texas entered the Union as a new slave state.

The Mexican War and Manifest Destiny

The admission of Texas coincided with President Polk's aggressive reformulation of the Monroe Doctrine. In his annual message of December 2, 1845, Polk warned that henceforth the United States would not tolerate any kind of European interferences designed to limit the spread of the American form of government or the right of any of the peoples of North America "to decide their own destiny," by which Polk meant the right to be annexed to the United States. In the case of Texas, whose boundaries were still extremely controversial, such annexation meant a federal commitment to support the restoration of slavery in a region in which it had earlier been outlawed by Mexico. Only the future could determine the fate of Cuba, California, and Oregon—provinces that Polk had very much in mind. And the future too would determine precisely how the people would "decide their own destiny," an ideal soon to be known as "popular sovereignty."

Oregon and California. President Polk's warnings about European interference were directed mainly at Britain. He emphasized that the danger of British

The Election of 1844

	ELECTORAL	POPULAR
Polk (Dem.)	170	1,337,243
Clay (Whig)	105	1,299,062

economic or political interference, even apart from physical colonization, justified an indefinite expansion of America's boundaries. He also spurned further negotiation with Britain over the Oregon question and asked Congress to give notice of the termination of the 1827 joint occupation agreement. The dismayed British government ignored the belligerent rhetoric but commissioned new steam warships and ordered a naval force to the northeast Pacific.

While Polk hoped to force concessions from Britain on Oregon, his primary objective was California. In 1845 a British consul correctly observed that California, which contained no more than ten thousand white inhabitants, was at the mercy of whoever might choose to take possession of it. Polk feared that the British might appropriate the province as compensation for Mexican debts. Months before his December message, orders had been sent to the commodore of the American Pacific Squadron, instructing him to seize San Francisco and other ports if he could "ascertain with certainty" that Mexico had declared war against the United States.

Polk's secretary of state, James Buchanan, also sent secret instructions to Thomas Larkin, the American consul at Monterey, telling him to foil British plots and to foment, as cautiously as possible, a spirit of rebellion among the Spanish Californians. Finally, only days after Polk's belligerent message, America's dashing "Pathfinder," Captain John C. Frémont, arrived in California at the head of a "scientific expedition" of heavily armed engineers. Frémont had been exploring the Mexican West without permission from Mexico, and would soon defy the Mexican authorities in California and encourage the Anglo-American settlers in an uprising, supposedly in their own self-defense.

Slidell's Mission. December 1845 also marked the arrival in Mexico City of Polk's secret minister, John Slidell, who had orders to win Mexican acceptance of the Rio Grande River as the new border with the United States, and to purchase as much of New Mexico and California as possible. The instructions emphasized the determination of the United States to

A DRUGSTORE, A BOOKSTORE, AND AN "INTELIGENCE" OFFICE: SONORA, CALIFORNIA
In such outposts as Sonora, California, the general store was a gathering place for people of all classes and occupations. *(Wells Fargo Bank History Room, San Francisco)*

prevent California from becoming a British or French colony, and authorized Slidell to offer Mexico as much as $25 million for the territories desired, with the additional proviso that the United States would assume the debts owed by Mexico to American citizens.

The Mexican government had earlier shown a willingness to settle the Texas dispute, but by December, when one of Mexico's numerous revolutions was about to erupt, the unstable government could not dare recognize an American envoy who made such sweeping demands, demands that had already been leaked to the American press. Mexican nationalists considered Texas a "stolen province," and especially resented the wholly unfounded claim that Texas extended to the Rio Grande. In 1816 Spain had designated the Nueces River, 130 miles north and east of the Rio Grande, as the boundary between Tamaulipas and the province of Texas; this was the boundary that appeared on American and European maps. In 1836, however, when the Texans had captured the Mexican president, Santa Anna, he had been forced to agree to the Rio Grande boundary as a condition for his release. The Mexican government had promptly repudiated this extortionary agreement. By the end of 1845, Mexican nationalists, hoping for European support, were eager for a war of revenge against American imperialists.

War with Mexico. On learning of Slidell's failure, the Polk administration was also eager for war but wanted a pretext that would justify seizing California. In January 1846 the president ordered General Zachary Taylor, who had been poised for the move, to march to the Rio Grande. Without opposition, American ships blockaded the river and Taylor took up a position across from the Mexican town of Matamoros, toward which he aimed his cannons. By early May, however, Washington had heard no news of hostilities and the impatient president and cabinet decided that Mexico's unpaid debts and the rebuff to Slidell were sufficient grounds for war. Then just as Polk had drafted a war message to Congress, news arrived that a minor skirmish had occurred between Mexican and American patrols. Polk could now indignantly

inform Congress that war already existed. He said, "Notwithstanding all our efforts to avoid it [war] exists by the act of Mexico herself. [Mexico] has passed the boundary of the United States, has invaded our territory and shed American blood upon the American soil."

By any objective interpretation, Americans had crossed the Mexican boundary and had shed Mexican blood on Mexican soil. For American expansionists, however, the protests from Europe simply substantiated the fact that the growth of the United States was a blow to political and religious tyranny. It was America's mission to liberate the peoples of California, Mexico, Cuba, Central America, and even Canada, allowing them to share in the blessings of republican government, religious freedom, and modern technology. In 1845 an influential Democratic editor had coined the electric phrase "manifest destiny," while denouncing the policy of other nations of

hampering our power, limiting our greatness and checking the fulfillment of our manifest destiny to overspread the continent allotted by Providence for the free development of our yearly multiplying millions.

But the crusade to prevent Europe from imposing a "balance of power" in North America strained the fragile balance on which the Union had always depended, the balance of power between North and South. In the Northeast and particularly in New England the Mexican War provoked thunderous outrage. It was denounced from press and pulpit as a war of brutal aggression, plotted by the Slave Power to extend slavery and secure permanent control over the free states. The Massachusetts legislature went so far as to proclaim the war unconstitutional.

The war remained unpopular with the great majority of Whig leaders, even in the South, who objected to Polk's devious tactics and to the way in which Congress had been stampeded into a declaration of war in order to rescue Zachary Taylor's army, which was erroneously said to be endangered.

Settlement of Oregon Controversy. By June 1846, a month after the war began, even the prowar western Democrats were angered when Polk allowed the

Gen. Wool's staff
Calle Real del Sur.

AMERICAN SOLDIERS HEADING SOUTH

General Thomas John Wood, a member of Zachary Taylor's staff, leads American troops through the streets of Saltillo, the capital of Coahuila province in northern Mexico. *(Yale University Library)*

Senate to assume full responsibility for approving a treaty that gave Britain Vancouver Island and all of the Oregon country north of the forty-ninth parallel. As the western expansionists rightly suspected, Southerners had never been enthusiastic about adding probable free states in the Pacific Northwest, and Polk had no wish to risk war with England when he was intent on dismembering Mexico.

Yet the nation as a whole supported the war. Mindful that opposition to the War of 1812 had split and destroyed the Federalist party, Whigs in Congress dutifully voted for military appropriations and congratulated themselves on the fact that the army's two leading generals, Zachary Taylor and Winfield Scott, were also Whigs. Taylor was the first to win glory. Within a few months, and with incredibly few American casualties, he defeated Mexican armies much larger than his own, crossed the Rio Grande, and captured the strategic town of Monterrey, thereby commanding northeastern Mexico. According to Democratic critics, he then settled down to prepare for the presidential campaign of 1848, which he won. In

February 1847, however, in the battle of Buena Vista, Taylor crushed another Mexican army over three times the size of his own. It was led by Santa Anna, who had earlier been exiled from Mexico. Polk had allowed Santa Anna to enter Mexico from Cuba because he believed that this self-styled Napoleon of the West would persuade Mexico to sue for peace.

Meanwhile, by early 1847 Polk's professed objectives had been achieved. Mexico's defense of California collapsed so rapidly that the only serious conflicts stemmed from the rival and uncoordinated American onslaughts: Consul Larkin's efforts to mobilize the restive Spanish Californians; Frémont's leadership of the Anglo-American settlers; the American navy's capture of the port towns; and the arrival of an overland force, led by Stephen W. Kearny, which conquered New Mexico on the way to San Diego.

But the war was far from over. What the Mexicans lacked in leadership and modern armament, they made up for in national pride and determination. The United States could hardly claim an efficient military machine, but the army sparkled with talent. The roster of young officers read like a gallery of later Union and Confederate heroes: Lee, Grant, Sherman, Meade, McClellan, Beauregard, Stonewall Jackson, and even Jefferson Davis. For Europeans, whose memories of Napoleonic battles had receded into more than thirty years of romantic haze, the American triumphs were stupendous—without parallel, according to the Manchester *Guardian*, "except in that of Alexander the Great through Persia, Hannibal from Spain

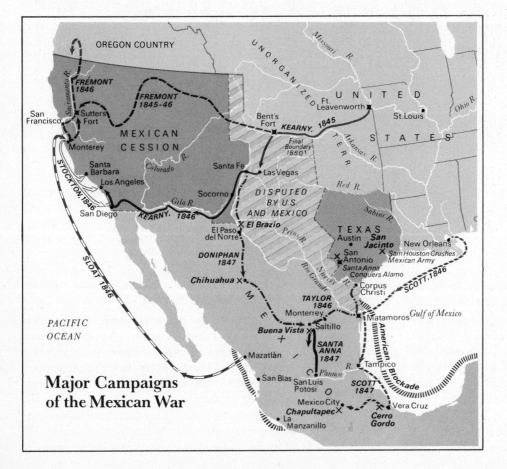

Major Campaigns of the Mexican War

"THE OCCUPATION OF THE CAPITAL OF MEXICO BY THE AMERICAN ARMY" BY P.S. DAVAL
Americans enter the historic square, or Zocalo, of Mexico City, March 1847. *(American Antiquarian Society)*

to the gates of Rome, or Napoleon over the Alps into Italy." Instead of one Napoleon, America had them "by the dozen."

Treaty of Guadalupe Hidalgo. The events that astonished even hostile Europeans began with General Scott's invasion of central Mexico in March 1847. By September, after winning a series of hotly contested battles, American troops had captured Mexico City and were relaxing in the halls of the Montezumas. Still, the Mexicans refused to surrender. In the United States Americans were becoming increasingly divided over the meaning of Manifest Destiny. As the American army pushed upward to the Mexican plateau, in the caustic words of James Russell Lowell, "our Destiny higher an' higher kep' mountin'." Some Southerners believed that slavery could be extended at least into the northern states of Mexico; some antislavery Northerners believed that Mexico would be

a force for freedom, and therefore favored annexing the whole country. In general, however, the Democratic leaders—Polk, Buchanan, Lewis Cass, Stephen Douglas, Sam Houston, Jefferson Davis—demanded and expected to get no less than a third of the country south and west of the Rio Grande. They were therefore outraged when Nicholas Trist, whom Polk had angrily recalled as America's negotiator, proceeded to conclude the unauthorized Treaty of Guadalupe Hidalgo. Instead of capitalizing on America's conquests, Trist settled for the same terms that Slidell had been prepared to offer before the war: the United States was to pay Mexico $15 million and assume up to $3.25 million in Mexican debts to American citizens in return for California, New Mexico, and the Rio Grande boundary. Polk would have liked to repudiate the treaty, but feared that further war and prolonged negotiations would split the Democratic party in an election year. Alarmed by the growing antiwar and Free Soil movement among northern Democrats, he reluctantly submitted the treaty to the Senate, which approved it in March 1848.

Attempts to Acquire Cuba. But Polk had other cards up his sleeve. In 1848 the Democratic expansionists launched an intense propaganda campaign to annex the Yucatán Peninsula, a rebellious province that had seceded from Mexico and that contained white inhabitants in danger of being exterminated by hostile Indians. Polk, fearing British intervention and mindful of the virtually unemployed American army in Mexico, invited Congress to act. But enthusiasm waned when news arrived that the Yucatán racial crisis had subsided.

Polk was actually far more interested in acquiring Cuba. Like the Yucatán Peninsula, Cuba guarded access to the Gulf of Mexico; its traditional strategic importance would be increased by any future canal, about which there was already much discussion, connecting the Gulf of Mexico with the Pacific. In 1848 England was on the verge of war with Spain, and might at any time gain control of Cuba. Many of Cuba's sugar planters, resenting England's growing interference with their labor system and fearing the continuing spread of emancipation in the West Indies, believed that annexation to the United States was their only guarantee of remaining a prosperous slave society.

The Polk administration knew, however, that the North would not approve the use of military force to acquire over one-third of a million additional Negro slaves. Polk's only alternative was to try, with the utmost caution and secrecy, to persuade Spain that $100 million was a good price for a colony that was about to rebel or be lost to England. But Spain greatly prized the only rich remnant of her once great empire, and contemptuously rejected the bungled overtures of Polk's minister. The prospects for annexing Cuba were further dashed when, in the fall of 1848 Lewis Cass, the Democratic candidate who favored the purchase of Cuba and the annexation of Yucatán, was defeated for the presidency by the nonexpansionist Zachary Taylor.

Southern hopes for acquiring Cuba now turned to encouraging a Cuban revolution against Spain. Groups of Cuban emigrés, aided by American expansionists, led a series of "filibustering" invasions to liberate the Cuban people. By 1850, however, the anxieties of Cuban planters had subsided and their desire to be taken over by the United States had waned. In 1851, in an episode that strangely anticipated the Bay of Pigs disaster in 1961, Cubans captured the entire expedition of Narciso Lopez, a southern hero, and executed him and fifty of his American followers.

Serious efforts to acquire Cuba revived under the Democratic administration of Franklin Pierce (1853–57), which contained many of Polk's more ardent expansionists. In 1854 the diplomatic intrigues culminated in the secret meetings of America's ministers to Spain, France, and England, who drafted a long memorandum to the State Department justifying the forcible seizure of Cuba if the island could not be purchased from Spain. Labeled the Ostend Manifesto, the secret memorandum was leaked to the American public at a moment of explosive sectional conflict, confirming the conviction of many Northerners that the Slave Power would continue to expand unless checked by political might. One of the authors of the Manifesto, the minister to Britain, was James Buchanan. His platform, as the Democratic presidential candidate in 1856, openly called for annexing Cuba. By this time, however, the heated controversy over legalizing slavery in Kansas had diverted attention from further national expansion.

CHRONOLOGY

1819 Transcontinental (Adams-Onís) Treaty. Spain renounces claims to the Floridas and Pacific Northwest; United States renounces claims to Texas.

1823 President issues Monroe Doctrine.

1829 Mexico abolishes slavery.

1831 Nat Turner's slave insurrection in Virginia.

1832 Virginia legislative debates whether to allow a committee to report on future abolition of slavery.

1836 Texas proclaims its independence from Mexico. Martin Van Buren elected president.

1838 John Quincy Adams's filibuster defeats move to annex Texas.

1841 John Tyler becomes president on death of Harrison.

1842 Webster-Ashburton Treaty settles disputed U.S.-Canada boundary; provides for extradition of fugitives.

1843 "Oregon Fever"; first overland caravans to Oregon.
Duff Green, Calhoun, and others begin planning imperial expansion to thwart British plots to undermine American slavery.

1844 Senate rejects Calhoun's Texas annexation treaty. James K. Polk elected president.

1845 Texas enters Union as slave state.
Polk gives aggressive reformulation to Monroe Doctrine.
John Slidell's unsuccessful mission to Mexico to negotiate purchase of New Mexico and California.

1846 Beginning of Mexican War. General Zachary Taylor invades Mexico from the north.
Treaty with Britain divides Oregon Territory along 49th parallel.

1847 General Winfield Scott captures Vera Cruz and Mexico City.

1848 Treaty of Guadalupe Hidalgo ends Mexican War, establishes Rio Grande as border.
Secret attempts to purchase Cuba from Spain.
Zachary Taylor elected president.

1854 Ostend Manifesto favors U.S. purchase or annexation of Cuba.
Railroads link New York City with the Mississippi River.
George Fitzhugh's *Sociology for the South.*

1857 Financial panic and depression.

SUGGESTED READINGS

For overviews of antebellum economic growth, see W. Elliot Brownlee, *Dynamics of Ascent* (1974), and Stuart Bruchey, *Growth of the Modern American Economy* (1975). A more technical but useful summary of the new economic history is Lance E. Davis *et al., American Economic Growth: An Economist's History of the United States* (1972). Douglass C. North, *The Economic Growth of the United States, 1790–1860* (1961), stresses the importance of international trade. Peter Temin, *The Jacksonian Economy* (1969), challenges many of the traditional beliefs of historians.

For the general subject of transportation, see George R. Taylor, *The Transportation Revolution, 1815–1860* (1951). For railroads, see Albert Fishlow, *American Railroads and the Transformation of the Ante-Bellum Economy* (1965); Alfred D. Chandler, Jr., ed., *The Railroads: The Nation's First Big*

Business (1965); and Thomas C. Cochran, *Railroad Leaders, 1845–1890* (1953). The organization and management of railroad corporations is masterfully analyzed in Alfred D. Chandler, Jr., *The Visible Hand: The Managerial Revolution in American Business* (1977). The role of government is treated in Carter Goodrich, *Government Promotion of American Canals and Railroads, 1800–1890* (1960); Louis Hartz, *Economic Policy and Democratic Thought* (1954); and Oscar Handlin and Mary F. Handlin, *Commonwealth: A Study of the Role of Government in the American Economy* (1969).

The best works on maritime trade are Robert G. Albion, *The Rise of New York Port* (1939), and Samuel E. Morison, *Maritime History of Massachusetts, 1789–1860* (1921). For the clipper ships, see C. C. Cutler, *Greyhounds of the Sea* (1930), and A. H. Clark, *The Clipper Ship Era* (1910). L. H.

Battistini, *The Rise of American Influence in Asia and the Pacific* (1960), treats an important aspect of America's commercial expansion.

On manufacturing, Victor S. Clark, *History of Manufactures in the United States, 1607–1860* (3 vols., 1929), remains indispensable. The best specialized studies are Peter Temin, *Iron and Steel in Nineteenth-Century America* (1964); Caroline F. Ware, *The Early New England Cotton Manufacture* (1931); Arthur H. Cole, *The American Wool Manufacture* (2 vols., 1926); and Nathan Rosenberg, ed., *The American System of Manufactures* (1969). Siegfried Giedion, *Mechanization Takes Command* (1948), contains a fascinating account of American technological innovation. A brilliant study of the significance of the new technology is Merritt R. Smith, *Harpers Ferry Armory and the New Technology: The Challenge of Change* (1977). H. J. Habakkuk, *American and British Technology in the Nineteenth Century* (1962), places American invention in a larger context, as does Carroll W. Pursell, Jr., *Early Stationary Steam Engines in America: A Study in the Migration of Technology* (1969). For a comprehensive reference work, see Melvin Kranzberg and Carroll W. Pursell, Jr., eds., *Technology in Western Civilization* (2 vols., 1967). The ideological impact of technology is imaginatively treated in John F. Kasson, *Civilizing the Machine: Technology and Republican Values in America, 1776–1900* (1976). The social implications of industrialization are admirably traced in Alan Dawley, *Class and Community: The Industrial Revolution in Lynn* (1977).

The best general guide to sectional conflict and the coming of the Civil War is David M. Potter, *The Impending Crisis, 1848–1861* (completed and edited by Don E. Fehrenbacher, 1976). Allan Nevins, *Ordeal of the Union* (2 vols., 1947), is a highly readable and informative survey of the same subject.

A comprehensive picture of the South as a slave society can be found in Clement Eaton, *A History of the Old South: The Emergence of a Reluctant Nation* (1975); and Eaton, *Freedom of Thought in the Old South* (1940). The growth of sectional feeling is outlined in more detail in Charles S. Sydnor, *The Development of Southern Sectionalism, 1819–1848* (1948); and Avery O. Craven, *The Growth of Southern Nationalism, 1848–1861* (1953). Carl N. Degler, *The Other South: Southern Dissenters in the Nineteenth Century* (1974), traces the decline of antislavery protest. H. Shelton Smith, *In His Image, But . . .* (1972), is a fine study of the growing racism in the southern churches. Frank Owsley, *Plain Folk of the Old South* (1949), contains valuable information on the nonslaveholding whites. A penetrating study of the mythology of the Old South, often northern in origin, is

William R. Taylor, *Cavalier and Yankee* (1961). C. Vann Woodward's essays in *The Burden of Southern History* (1960) and *American Counterpoint* (1971) are indispensable for understanding the South. The mind of the planter class is brilliantly illuminated by two accounts contemporary with the period: Mary B. Chestnut, *A Diary from Dixie* (1949); and Robert M. Myers, ed., *The Children of Pride: A True Story of Georgia and the Civil War* (1972).

The standard work on proslavery thought is William S. Jenkins, *Pro-Slavery Thought in the Old South* (1935), which can be supplemented by Harvey Wish, *George Fitzhugh* (1943), and Drew Gilpin Faust, *A Sacred Circle: The Dilemma of the Intellectual in the Old South, 1840–1860* (1977). Ira Berlin, *Slaves without Masters* (1975), is a superb analysis of free blacks in the South. John H. Franklin, *From Slavery to Freedom* (1974), is the best introduction to the history of the blacks. George M. Fredrickson, *The Black Image in the White Mind: The Debate on Afro-American Character and Destiny, 1817–1914* (1971), is a brilliant study of racism in America. More specialized works of importance are Eugene H. Berwanger, *The Frontier against Slavery: Western Anti-Negro Prejudice and the Slavery Extension Controversy* (1967); and William Stanton, *The Leopard's Spots: Scientific Attitudes toward Race in America, 1815–1859* (1960).

The fullest history of the origins of the Monroe Doctrine is Dexter Perkins, *The Monroe Doctrine, 1823–1826* (1927). Ernest R. May, *The Making of the Monroe Doctrine* (1975), stresses the importance of domestic politics preceding the presidential election of 1824. For the European background, see E. H. Tatum, Jr., *The United States and Europe, 1815–1823* (1936); and C. C. Griffin, *The United States and the Disruption of the Spanish Empire* (1937). For a general introduction to American foreign policy, see Lloyd C. Gardner *et al.*, *Creation of the American Empire* (1973); and for a more traditional view, Samuel F. Bemis, *A Diplomatic History of the United States* (1965). The standard work on Asia is A. Whitney Griswold, *The Far Eastern Policy of the United States* (1938).

Ray A. Billington, *Westward Expansion* (1974), covers every aspect of America's westward expansion and contains an encyclopedic, relatively up-to-date bibliography. Albert K. Weinberg, *Manifest Destiny* (1935), is a fascinating study in intellectual history, but it should be supplemented by Edward M. Burns, *The American Idea of Mission: Concepts of National Purpose and Destiny* (1957). In three outstanding, revisionist studies, Frederick W. Merk reemphasizes the importance of slavery and the fear of British encroachments on the West: *Manifest Destiny and Mission in American History: A Reinterpretation* (1963); *The Monroe Doctrine and*

American Expansionism, 1843–1849 (1966); and *Slavery and the Annexation of Texas* (1972). For a detailed treatment of the diplomatic history, see D. M. Pletcher, *The Diplomacy of Annexation: Texas, Oregon and the Mexican War* (1973).

On Texas two of the standard works are by William C. Binkley: *The Texas Revolution* (1952); and *The Expansionist Movement in Texas, 1836–1850* (1925). Much can still be learned from the older, nationalistic studies: J. H. Smith, *The Annexation of Texas* (1911); and E. C. Barker, *Mexico and Texas, 1821–1835* (1928). For a meticulous portrayal of the Mexican point of view, see Gene M. Brack, *Mexico Views Manifest Destiny, 1821–1846* (1976).

Frederick W. Merk has written several superb essays on the Anglo-American diplomacy regarding Oregon: *Albert Gallatin and the Oregon Problem* (1950); and *The Oregon Question: Essays in Anglo-American Diplomacy and Politics* (1967). For general histories of the Northwest, see Norman A. Graebner, *Empire on the Pacific* (1955); Oscar O. Winther, *The Great Northwest* (1947); and Earl Pomeroy, *The Pacific Slope: A History* (1965).

Ray A. Billington, *The Far Western Frontier, 1830–1860* (1956), is a lively and scholarly survey of the exploration and settlement of the Great West. By far the best account of the overland emigration to the Far West is John D. Unruh, Jr., *The Overland Emigrants and the Trans-Mississippi West, 1840–1860* (1979). The fascinating story of government exploration is described with admirable care in William H. Goetzmann, *Army Exploration in the American West, 1803–1863* (1959). Gloria G. Cline, *Exploring the Great Basin* (1963), is an invaluable study. H. M. Chittenden, *The American Fur Trade of the Far West* (3 vols., 1935), is still the most comprehensive story of the fur trade, although important new work has long been in progress. Though sometimes scorned by professional historians, Bernard DeVoto's *Across the Wide Missouri* (1947), which deals with the Mountain Men and fur trade, and DeVoto's *The Year of Decision, 1846* (1943), which deals with the political, social, and cultural events surrounding America's war with Mexico, are exciting, readable, and basically accurate accounts of the early West.

J. H. Smith, *The War with Mexico* (2 vols., 1919), remains the fullest account of the Mexican War. Of the studies listed at the end of the previous chapter, Gene M. Brack, *Mexico Views Manifest Destiny* (1976), deserves special mention for its insight into the Mexican motives for war. The best recent account of the military campaigns is K. Jack Bauer, *The Mexican War, 1846–1848* (1974). For Mexican-American relations, see G. L. Rives, *The United States and Mexico: 1821–1848* (2 vols., 1913). John H. Schroeder, *Mr. Polk's War: American Opposition and Dissent, 1846–1848* (1973), is an excellent study of antiwar sentiment.

CHAPTER 17

Compromise and Conflict

On the surface the two-party system resolved the dangerous sectional conflicts unleashed by the annexation of Texas, the Mexican War, and the acquisition of a new continental empire. By the early 1850s cohesion and compromise seemed to have triumphed over division. Americans, more prosperous than they had ever been before, were able for the most part to ignore or rationalize evidence of continuing injustice and exploitation. Public interest in further empire building waned, despite attempts by Democratic leaders to revive the people's enthusiasm. There was sufficient challenge, it seemed, in building railroads, settling a continent, and extending American commerce. In 1854, for example, Commodore Matthew C. Perry, through diplomatic tact and a display of naval power, persuaded the rulers of Japan to open that country to trade and Western influence. In the opinion of political realists, the North had neither the will nor the desire to interfere with slavery in the South; nor was there any reason for the North to fear that slavery would expand beyond its "natural limits" in Missouri, Arkansas, and Texas.

There were hazards, however, in this very triumph of moderation. The stormy passions that culminated in the Compromise of 1850 gave way to political apathy and disenchantment. Voters complained that Whigs and Democrats were indistinguishable in their self-serving lust for office, in their mouthing of stale rhetoric on stale issues, and in their unresponsiveness to public needs and fears. For reasons that varied in each state and locality, significant numbers of voters abandoned their former party allegiance. One consequence of this realignment was the rapid disintegration of the Whigs, especially in the South. By 1855 the anti-Catholic Know-Nothing party had replaced the Whigs as the dominant anti-Democratic alternative in the Northeast. In all sections the weakening of balanced national parties opened the way for new and more extreme appeals to resist the encroachments of some supposedly antirepublican "power."

The American fear of unchecked power was deeply rooted in the colonial and Revolutionary past. The fear acquired new dimensions, however, as the restraints of local customs, traditions, and privileges gave way to individual enterprise and the dominance of market forces. For a time the party system succeeded in channeling and moderating public alarm over the rise of various "powers," such as Freemasons, the "Monster Bank," the "Money Power," Jackson's "monarchic" presidency, and the alleged British conspiracy to block American expansion. By the mid-1850s, however, the controversy over slavery in the territories began to distract attention from anti-Catholic nativism, and the Americans' diffuse fears of unchecked power became grounded in the concrete conflict of interests between free and slave societies.

Like a magnetic field, Negro slavery polarized opposing clusters of values, interests, and aspirations. Southerners believed that any withdrawal of federal sanction and protection for slavery would expose private property to the tyranny of a national majority, undermine the equal sovereignty of states, and lead America in the direction of European "wage-slavery" and class warfare, to say nothing of black insurrection and racial amalgamation.

By the mid-1850s a growing number of Northerners had become convinced that black slavery, by supporting "idle planters" and by associating work with servility, undermined the dignity of labor. As an alternative to the whips and chains of the South, the North offered an idealized vision of prosperity and progress without exploitation—a vision of industrious farmers and proud artisans, of schoolhouses, churches, town meetings, and self-made men. The vast territories of the West, unfenced and jointly owned by the American people, would thus become the critical testing ground for two competing versions of the American dream.

Free Soil and the Challenge of California

Once the vast Mexican territories were acquired, national decisions had to be made. These decisions reactivated all the constitutional issues as well as the political and moral arguments of the Missouri crisis of 1819–21. Would the South be able to maintain its balance of power in the Senate? What was the precise nature of congressional power over territories and the creation of new states? Would the government impose limits on the further expansion of slavery? Or would it adopt a policy of noninterference? Or would it, perhaps, openly sanction slavery by guaranteeing all free Americans equal protection if they took into the common territories property, such as slaves, protected by the laws of their former states?

The Wilmot Proviso.   It was predictable that a move would be made in Congress to prohibit slavery in any of the territories acquired by the Mexican War; similar moves had been made since 1784 concerning the trans-Appalachian West, Mississippi, Louisiana, Arkansas, and Missouri. In 1846 the motion came from David Wilmot, a Pennsylvania Democrat, in the form of a proposed amendment to an appropriation bill. The Wilmot Proviso was extraordinarily significant because it was used to challenge "Mr. Polk's War" and all that it signified. The legislatures of fourteen free states eventually endorsed the Proviso's principle; and while many northern senators ignored the instructions of their states, the House of Representatives several times approved the measure, which antislavery members continued to offer.

From 1847 to 1850 this sectional insistence that the territories ceded by Mexico remain "free soil" raised a challenge to Whig and Democratic party unity. Many southern Whigs denounced any proposal for excluding slavery from the territories as a direct violation of southern rights and of state equality. The more extreme Calhounites tried to erode national party loyalty by uniting all Southerners in defense of sectional rights and in opposition to any candidate who failed to repudiate the Wilmot Proviso. In the North in the election of 1848 both Whigs and Democrats suffered losses to the new Free Soil party, which nominated Martin Van Buren for president. "Conscience Whigs," centered in Massachusetts, refused to vote for Zachary Taylor, the former general and Louisiana slaveholder nominated by the Whigs. They claimed that moral protest against the further expansion of slavery should take precedence over the material and political advantages of a united Whig party.

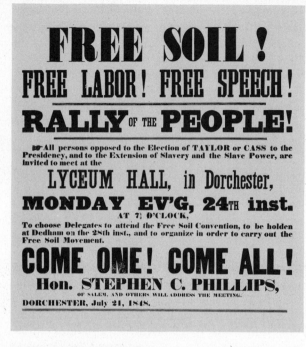

POSTER FOR FREE SOIL RALLY
(American Antiquarian Society)

Free Soil Democrats were led by New York "Barn-burners," politicians who had been angered when the Democrats rejected Van Buren in 1844 and had then been further alienated when Polk's administration had favored rival Democratic factions in distributing patronage.

But this upsurge of sectional politics proved to be singularly unsuccessful in undermining the two-party system. Both the Whig and the Democratic parties evaded official commitment on the territorial issue and unashamedly made contradictory appeals to northern and southern voters. In the election of 1848 Van Buren received only 14 percent of the popular vote in the North and won no electoral votes for his Free Soil party. Taylor carried even Massachusetts, where the Whig defections seemed most threatening; Whigs actually gained strength in the South. As a result of this defeat, Van Buren and most of his Democratic followers returned to the national party which now shared common interests in opposing a new Whig administration. The Conscience Whigs, for their part, mostly returned to their uneasy alliance

with the "Cotton Whigs," led by such powerful New England textile manufacturers as Abbott Lawrence and Nathan Appleton, who looked to a continuation of their profitable trade relations with the cotton-producing South. Early in 1849 it became clear that the Calhounites had little hope of winning support for a new southern rights coalition.

The survival of national parties did nothing, however, to resolve the territorial issue or to break the congressional deadlock over the Wilmot Proviso. Northern Democrats had favored either extending the Missouri Compromise line of 36°30′ to the Pacific, or leaving the question of slavery to territorial legislatures (popular sovereignty) without congressional interference. President Taylor, on the other hand, tried to prevent further sectional confrontations by urging California and New Mexico to draft constitutions and apply for immediate statehood. This strategy would have avoided congressional action either sanctioning or banning slavery. Both Taylor and his southern opponents recognized that the inhabitants of the Far West, if allowed to organize state governments, would almost certainly vote to exclude Negro slavery. These settlers, most of whom had lived in the intensely racist states of the Old Northwest, cared little about the fate of the slaves in the South, but feared the competition of slave labor in a "land of promise" supposedly reserved for aspiring whites.

Suddenly antiblack feeling became acute in California. The great gold rush of 1849 brought tens of thousands of settlers who resented the prolongation of ineffective military government and who clamored for instant statehood. It also brought a small number of southern masters and slaves and of free black prospectors who, according to hostile whites, were "proverbially lucky." White miners considered it unfair to compete with slave labor, and also considered it degrading "to swing a pick side by side with the Negro," whether free or slave. Fear and hatred of blacks, particularly in the mining regions, led the California constitutional convention of 1849 to copy the sections of the newly written Iowa constitution that prohibited slavery.

In Oregon, which was organized as a separate territory south of the Columbia River, the fusion of

SLUICING FOR GOLD
Gold miners pose beside a
"long tom" sluice near
Auburn, California, in 1852.
(Courtesy, California State
Library)

racism with antislavery was even more clear-cut. Though few blacks had arrived in the region by 1844, the provisional government followed the models of the Old Northwest and ordered the removal of both slaves and free blacks. The South succeeded in delaying Oregon's elevation to territorial status until 1848, and as late as 1857 there was a concerted drive to legalize slavery in the Oregon Territory. After heated public debate, a referendum decisively rejected slavery but approved even more decisively the constitutional exclusion of free black settlers—a measure Congress accepted as part of the state's constitution.

By 1849, however, Southerners tended to construe even such dubious forms of antislavery as abolitionism in disguise. Most southern leaders, whether Whig or Democrat, had moved from a defensive policy of censorship and gag rules to an aggressive hostility toward any barrier, however theoretical, to the expansion of slavery. They feared that enactment of the Proviso would swing the full weight of the federal government against an institution it had always protected. By 1849 Free Soil and antislavery congressmen had already linked the Proviso with demands for abolishing slavery in the District of Columbia, which,

like the territories, was subject to federal legislation. The new personal liberty laws of the northern states raised the prospect that the North would become as secure a refuge for runaway slaves as British Canada, to which a small number of blacks had successfully escaped.

Indeed, for a growing number of southern diehards, the Northeast of the late 1840s was becoming a perfect replica of the British enemy that had first exploited her own slave colonies, and then ruined them under the influence of misguided philanthropy, finally using antislavery as a mask of righteousness in assuming commercial and ideological domination of the globe. The Northeast, like England, was attracting millions of immigrant wage earners, was developing vast urban centers, and was gaining mastery over the mysterious sources of credit and investment capital. Unless Dixie made her stand, she would therefore share the fate of the exploited, debt-ridden, and ravaged West Indies. If the South were deprived of land and labor for expansion, its boundaries pushed back from the west and the Gulf of Mexico as well as from the north, it would then be subjected by a tyrannical government to slave emancipation and racial amalgamation.

The Crisis of 1850

The Taylor administration faced a succession of problems that exposed irreconcilable divisions within the Whig party. Zachary Taylor was a recent convert to Whiggery (previously, he had never even voted) who had run for president as a military hero and as a man "above party." As president he aggravated the mistrust of Old Whigs when, seeking to broaden the administration's constituency, he bypassed party stalwarts in distributing patronage. Taylor also seemed to betray traditional Whig principles when he tried to build a broad coalition that could compete with the Democrats, who were gaining enormous strength from the votes of recent immigrants.

The preceding Polk administration had reestablished the Independent Treasury, reaffirming the Democrats' opposition to any alliance between government and banks. It had also enacted the Walker Tariff that drastically reduced the duties Whigs had established in 1842. To the dismay of Old Whigs, Taylor balked at proposals to repeal the treasury and tariff acts and advocated compromises that would avoid unnecessary conflict. Simultaneously southern Whigs who had thought they could trust a Louisiana planter were shocked to discover that the president had no objections to admitting California as a free state. In fact, Taylor even dumbfounded his powerful Georgia backer, Robert Toombs, by saying that if Congress saw fit to pass the Wilmot Proviso, "I will not veto it."

When the Thirty-First Congress convened in December 1849, there was a prolonged and ominous conflict over electing the Speaker of the House. It soon became clear that Taylor's program for admitting California and New Mexico as states would receive no support from southern Whigs or even from such party chieftains as Clay, Webster, and Seward. Tensions were heightened by the knowledge that all northern legislatures, with one exception, had instructed their senators to insist on the Wilmot Proviso in any agreement respecting the territories. Also, a growing number of southern legislatures were appointing delegates to a convention at Nashville in June 1850 to consider potentially revolutionary measures for the defense of southern rights.

Clay's Resolutions. In January 1850 the aging Henry Clay temporarily recovered leadership of the Whig Party by offering a series of compromise resolutions to the Senate. As an alternative to the Wilmot Proviso and to the popular southern plan which would extend the Missouri Compromise line to the Pacific, Clay favored admitting California as a free state. He also proposed that no restrictions on slavery be imposed in the rest of the territory acquired from Mexico. Clay also attempted to resolve the critical Texas issue. Texas claimed a western boundary that included more than half of the present state of New Mexico. As a result there was an imminent danger of border conflict between the armed forces of Texas and the United States, a conflict that could easily escalate into civil war. Further, when Texas became an American state it had lost its former customs revenue, which was a matter of considerable concern to the influential holders of Texas bonds. To resolve these problems, Clay proposed that the government assume the Texas debt—which promised windfall profits to Texas bondholders—as compensation for Texas's acceptance of New Mexico's territorial claims.

In a gesture to northern sensibilities, Clay recommended that Congress prohibit professional slave trading in the District of Columbia, and thereby rid the national capital of the moral eyesore of slave pens and public auctions. But he also urged that Congress should allay southern fears of an abolitionist "entering wedge" by formally denying that it had authority to interfere with the interstate slave trade and by promising that slavery would never be abolished in the District of Columbia without the consent of its citizens as well as the consent of neighboring Maryland. Finally, Clay proposed that Congress adopt a fugitive slave law that provided severe punishment for anyone who obstructed the efforts of slave owners to recover runaway slaves in any part of the United States.

Such was Clay's contribution to the Compromise

of 1850. The ensuing congressional struggle took place on two distinct levels. On the loftiest level, the Senate became a public forum for some of the most famous and eloquent speeches in American history, speeches that clarified conflicting principles, conflicting political philosophies, and conflicting visions of America's heritage, mission, and destiny. Calhoun, so ill and so near death that he could not personally deliver his farewell address to the nation, argued that a tyrannical northern majority had gradually excluded Southerners from 1.25 million square miles of territory. No further compromises could save the South from a continuing loss of power or prevent the day when a hostile and increasingly centralized government would execute the demands of the abolitionists. The Union might be preserved if the North agreed to open all the territories to slaveholders and to restore, by constitutional amendment, an equal and permanent balance of sectional power. Otherwise, self-preservation would require the South to separate, and to fight if the North refused to accept secession in peace.

Daniel Webster, in his famous reply on March 7, insisted: "There can be no such thing as a peaceable secession." Recoiling in horror from the prospects of disunion and fratricidal war, he pleaded for compromise and for a charitable spirit toward the South. He concurred with southern complaints against the abolitionists, and supported Clay's demand for an effective fugitive slave law. The territorial issue, he claimed, should be no cause for further discord. Convinced that slave labor could never be profitable in the western territories, Webster saw no need for a further legal exclusion that could only antagonize the South.

On March 11 the growing antislavery audience in the Senate found a spokesman in William H. Seward, the New York Whig leader who had helped engineer Taylor's candidacy but who now failed to support the president's plan. Seward, whom Webster described as "subtle and unscrupulous" and bent "to the one idea of making himself president," gave political force to the traditional abolitionist doctrine concerning the territories: "There is a higher law than the Constitution, which regulates our authority over the domain . . . the common heritage of mankind."

The Compromise of 1850. These and other great speeches raised momentous issues; but it is likely that they changed few votes. The second level of struggle involved political infighting that ranged from bribes and lobbying by speculators in Texas bonds to patient and tireless work by committees of experts committed to American political procedures and to the technicalities of constitutional law. Apart from the moderating influence of powerful banking and business interests, which stood to gain by national unity, four circumstances contributed to the final congressional approval of the compromise of 1850.

First, despite signs of an ominous sectional division of parties, Stephen Douglas rallied a core of Democrats, particularly from the Old Northwest and border states, who could counteract the combined pressures of southern and northern extremists. Second, Douglas's drive to win southern support for a railroad connecting Chicago with the Gulf of Mexico (the Illinois Central) demonstrated the rewards that could be gained through sectional cooperation. Third, under Douglas's leadership the Senate wisely abandoned an "Omnibus Bill" that combined most of the compromise in one package. This move allowed both houses of Congress to form sectional alliances that were just barely strong enough to carry each measure —the North overcoming southern resistance to the admission of California and the abolition of the slave trade in the District of Columbia; the South, thanks to many northern abstentions, having its way in enacting the new Fugitive Slave Law. Finally, President Taylor, who had shown no sympathy for the compromise, suddenly died in July. Millard Fillmore, his successor, was close to Webster and Clay and threw the full weight of his administration behind the compromise. Fillmore also skillfully defused the explosive crisis over the Texas–New Mexico boundary. In September much of the nation sank back in relief, assuming that the adoption of Clay's and Douglas's proposals marked the end of serious sectional conflict.

Thus the Compromise of 1850 was made up of the following points: (1) the admission of California as a free state; (2) the organization of the rest of the Mexican cession into two territories, New Mexico and Utah, without federal restriction on slavery; (3) adjustment of the Texas–New Mexico boundary; (4) the award of $10 million to Texas as compensation for the land yielded to New Mexico; (5) prohibition of the slave trade but not of slavery itself in the District of Columbia; and (6) a stringent fugitive slave law. This complex congressional agreement created the illusion of peace; but there was no real consensus on any of the critical issues. In the District of Columbia, trading and selling of slaves continued, though not as openly as before. Blacks, and particularly Indians, continued to be held as slaves on the supposedly free soil of California. The Fugitive Slave Law, which deprived accused blacks of a jury trial and of the right to testify in their own defense, dramatized the agonizing consequences of enforcing a national compromise for which the North had little taste.*

*For the northern reaction to the Fugitive Slave Law, see Chapter 15, page 407.

One of the northern responses to this law was the serial publication in 1851 of Harriet Beecher Stowe's *Uncle Tom's Cabin,* a novel that soon reached millions in book form and in stage presentations. Mrs. Stowe's popular classic, today often underrated as a work of literary persuasion, interpreted the moral and psychological evils of slavery in terms perfectly attuned to the culture of northern evangelical Protestantism. It encouraged every reader who sympathized with the fictional fugitives, in their harrowing ordeal of escape, to share the guilt of a compromise that gave national sanction to slave catchers.

Popular Sovereignty.   It was on the territorial issue that the Compromise of 1850 seeded the worst storm clouds of the future. The compromise was deliberately ambiguous concerning the territories. Congress appeared to reaffirm its authority to prohibit slavery in the territories, for it delegated this authority to the legislatures of Utah and New Mexico, subject to the possible veto by a federally appointed governor or by Congress itself. To appease the South, however, Congress publicly registered doubts about the constitutionality of this authority, which could be determined

The Compromise of 1850

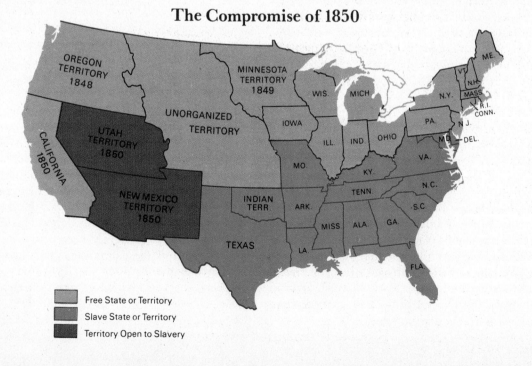

Free State or Territory

Slave State or Territory

Territory Open to Slavery

only by the Supreme Court. In effect, Congress invited slaveholders to challenge the constitutionality of any restrictions territorial governments might make on their property rights before the state governments had been established. Most Southerners reluctantly accepted "popular sovereignty" because it at least left the doors open to slavery. Northern moderates—"doughfaces" to their antislavery enemies—were convinced that popular sovereignty would ultimately guarantee free states while avoiding a congressional showdown that would lead to the South's secession.

To pragmatists like Daniel Webster and Stephen Douglas it seemed inconceivable that national policy of any kind could reverse the dominant western pattern of free-labor settlement. Cultivating cotton was too profitable and the value of slaves too great to encourage risky experiments in the semiarid West. It is true that in 1852 Utah legally recognized slavery and that in 1857 New Mexico adopted a slave code. Yet neither territory acquired more than a handful of Negro slaves. Southerners, long accustomed to the security of slave patrols and local law-enforcement agencies, were fearful of taking valuable human property into a region where courts might invoke the old Mexican law prohibiting slavery and where legislatures might at any time be swayed by the convictions of a free soil and anti-Negro majority. Moderates like Douglas advertised the Compromise of 1850 as a "final settlement," but in fact it narrowed the area of further acceptable compromise. The belief grew in the South that disunion would be the inevitable, and the only honorable, response to any further northern threats.

The Know-Nothing Upsurge and Collapse of the Whigs

Between 1853 and 1856 the two-party system rapidly disintegrated as the Whigs literally disappeared and as the Democrats suffered disastrous losses in the North while acquiring unassailable dominance in the South. The reasons for this dramatic political transformation are still a matter of controversy. Even in 1852 the Whigs were seriously divided as a result of the Compromise of 1850. In deference to southern demands, the party's platform of 1852 endorsed this essentially Democratic "final settlement" of the slavery issue. Southern Whigs, however, were infuriated by the party's refusal to renominate Fillmore, who was viewed by many Northerners as a puppet of the Slave Power. Winfield Scott, the military hero who was finally nominated, showed signs of becoming a Seward protégé like Zachary Taylor.

The Election of 1852. Because Southerners no longer trusted northern Whigs as reliable allies in the defense of slavery, the party suffered a devastating defection of southern voters in the election of 1852. In the North, simultaneously, a distinctive Whig identity was blurred. The Whig platform was very similar to the Democratic platform, and Whigs made clumsy and unsuccessful attempts to compete with the Democrats for the votes of immigrant Catholics. This strategy alienated the growing number of Whig nativists—as well as many native-born Democrats of Protestant background—who believed that the professional politicians' hunger for votes had betrayed America's heritage of republicanism, Protestantism, and independence from foreign influence, including that of the Catholic pope.

The remarkable upsurge of political nativism, expressed in 1854 by the Know-Nothing party, was symptomatic of a widespread popular hostility toward the traditional parties. On the one hand, the decisive victory in 1852 of Franklin Pierce, a bland northern Democrat from New Hampshire, could be interpreted as confirmation of a national desire for compromise and mediocrity. On the other hand, the results of state and local elections showed that voters felt that the existing parties were unresponsive to the people's needs. Anti-Catholic nativism suddenly became the vehicle for asserting previously vague grievances.

Know-Nothing Victories. Though anti-Catholicism had been deeply embedded in the American colonial experience, until 1854 this prejudice had lacked national political focus. The Order of the Star-Spangled Banner, the nucleus of the Know-Nothing party, remained an obscure secret society until the local spring elections of 1854 when entire tickets of secret Know-Nothing candidates were swept into office by write-in votes. Local dignitaries of the traditional parties, often confident that they were uncontested, found themselves thrown out of office by men they had never heard of. In Massachusetts the Know-Nothings won 63 percent of the popular vote. By 1855 the Know-Nothings, officially called the American party, had captured control of most of New England. They had become the dominant party opposing the Democrats in New York, Pennsylvania, California, and the border states. They had made striking inroads in Virginia, North Carolina, Georgia, and other southern states, and for a time held the balance of power in Congress. In much of the Northeast the Know-Nothings had defeated or prevented the spread of the new Republican party, which had been founded in 1854 to prevent the extension of slavery into the western territories. In effect, in two years the Know-Nothings had replaced the Whigs as a national political force.

The causes of this revolutionary realignment are difficult to assess. The religious revivals of the 1820s and 1830s had cultivated the belief that the survival of republican government depended on the liberating and unifying force of Protestantism. Protestant revivalists had repeatedly attacked any cohesive corporate group, such as the Freemasonic order or the Mormon or Catholic churches, which supposedly put institutional loyalty above individual moral choice. Prominent northern clergymen, mostly Whigs, had saturated the country with lurid and often hysterical anti-Catholic propaganda. This had contributed to mob violence and church burning, which culminated in a bloody Philadelphia riot in 1844.

Between 1845 and 1854 this traditional prejudice was greatly intensified by the arrival of nearly 3 million immigrants, the majority of whom were Catholics. These newcomers, with their divergent values and life-styles, threatened the Whig dream of an ordered, morally progressive, and homogeneous society—or what one Know-Nothing congressman referred to as a "unity of character and custom." For their part, such Catholic leaders as Archbishop John Hughes of New York made no apologies for their own mobilization of political power or for their own vision of a Catholic America. As Hughes launched a counteroffensive against Protestant indoctrination in the public schools, nativists warned that immigrant voters slavishly obeyed the orders of their priests who, as the agents of European despotism, sought to undermine America's republican institutions. The fact that the Catholic church had opposed the European revolutionary movements of 1848 reinforced many people's fear of antirepublican subversion.

Disintegration of National Party System. The Know-Nothing movement also reflected more immediate ethnic and economic conflicts, especially as native-born workers began blaming immigrants for low wages and unemployment. Though there was little foundation for this belief, nativism had special appeal for artisans and manual workers who associated immigrants with a new and threatening America —an America of increasing urban poverty, of factories and railroads, of rising prices and abruptly changing markets. In the South and in the border states, people also hoped that the Know-Nothing movement would finally end the "needless" sectional disputes over slavery.

In 1856 Millard Fillmore ran as the candidate of the combined American and Whig parties and received nearly 44 percent of the popular vote in the slaveholding states. Nativism was weaker in the Old Northwest, where there was a greater tolerance for immigrants. Yet there the Republicans capitalized on a similar disenchantment with the old parties, often at the expense of the Democrats. In 1854 the Democrats suffered irretrievable losses throughout the North—their representatives in Congress fell from ninety-one to twenty-five. These sudden defections to the Know-Nothing and Republican parties meant that, henceforth, northern Democrats would have little leverage within the restructured national party.

The Know-Nothing movement is significant because it helped to destroy the existing party system. Once in power, the Know-Nothings failed to restrict immigration or to lengthen the traditional five years' residence required for naturalized citizenship. Like other parties, the short-lived American party proved

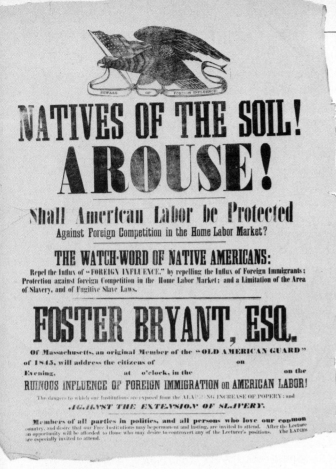

BROADSIDE FOR A KNOW-NOTHING LECTURE
(American Antiquarian Society)

to be vulnerable to political ambition and compromise. But before being absorbed by the Republicans, the Know-Nothings brought about a massive shift in voter alignments, undermined national party discipline, and hastened the total disappearance of the Whigs. The importance of this ominous development cannot be exaggerated. When the discipline of the party system was swept away, sectional conflict could no longer be suppressed or safely contained.

The Confrontation over Kansas

Stephen Douglas had long been interested in the organization and settlement of the Nebraska Territory—the vaguely defined region west and northwest of Missouri and Iowa, an immense portion of the Louisiana Purchase that had been reserved for Indians and was legally exempt from white settlement. As a senator from Illinois, Douglas had a frank interest in transcontinental railway routes, which, he expected, would make Chicago the hub of mid-America. He was also an ardent patriot and expansionist, convinced that America had been commissioned to free the world from despotism. He thought that the only serious obstacle to this mission was England, which had instigated the subversive activities of American abolitionists, who in turn had provoked the militancy of southern extremists. These Southerners had then blocked the organization of territories north of the Missouri Compromise line of 36°30'.

By 1854, when Douglas was chairman of the Senate Committee on Territories, he had concluded that the Missouri Compromise must be modified to overcome southern fears if the Nebraska country was to be opened to settlement, if the nation was to be bound together by transcontinental railroads and telegraph, if Americans were to fulfill their mission of driving Great Britain from the continent, and if Douglas himself was to reunite and lead the fractured Democratic party. He therefore drafted a bill that applied to Nebraska the popular sovereignty provision that Congress had already applied to Utah and New Mexico under the terms of the Compromise of 1850. This unexpected move destroyed nearly four years of relative sectional peace.

The Kansas-Nebraska Act. Douglas tried at first to play down the contradiction between popular sovereignty and the slavery prohibition of 1820, which applied to all the Louisiana Purchase territory north of the present state of Oklahoma. In 1850 Congress had left it to the courts to resolve any conflicts between popular sovereignty and the unrepealed Mexican law prohibiting slavery in Utah and New Mexico, and Douglas hoped to bypass the Missouri Compromise in the same way. But William Seward and other antislavery Whigs plotted to make the Nebraska bill as objectionable as possible. At the same time, a powerful group of southern senators, the disciples of Calhoun, conspired to make repeal of the Missouri Compromise a test of Democratic party loyalty.

After a series of caucuses Douglas recognized that the Nebraska bill could not pass unless Southerners were assured that all territories would be legally open to slaveholders. Aided by his southern allies, he helped to persuade President Pierce to throw administration support behind a new proposal that would declare the Missouri Compromise "inoperative and void" because it was "inconsistent with the principles of nonintervention by Congress with slavery in the States and Territories, as recognized by the legislation of 1850." This new bill would also provide for the organization of two separate territories, Kansas and Nebraska. By simply affirming that the rights of territorial governments were "subject only to the Constitution of the United States," Douglas's new bill evaded the critical question whether popular sovereignty included the right to exclude slavery. In this form the Kansas-Nebraska bill of 1854 won almost unanimous support from southern Whigs and Democrats and from enough northern Democrats to pass both houses of Congress.

Southern leaders, no less than Stephen Douglas, were astonished by the outrage that exploded across the North. Opponents interpreted the bill as the violation of a "sacred compact," the Missouri Compromise, and as a shameless capitulation to the Slave Power. The legislatures of five northern states passed resolutions condemning the Kansas-Nebraska Act. When Douglas was traveling by rail, he saw so many figures of himself hanging from trees and burned in effigy that he joked, "I could travel from Boston to Chicago by the light of my own effigy." According to the law's defenders, the cries of betrayal were sheer hypocrisy, for antislavery Northerners themselves had repudiated the principle of the Missouri Compromise by refusing to extend the compromise line to the Pacific coast. Yet the breach of faith, however interpreted, led to a rapid dissolution of other shared understandings and political restraints. For the first time, antislavery and proslavery moderates began to perceive each other as more dangerous than the extremists.

Rise of the Republican Party. What most alarmed proslavery moderates was the sudden appearance of a new and wholly sectional party, scornfully termed the "Black Republicans." This party, in the eyes of its enemies, professed moderation but tried to use the goal of excluding slavery from the territories as a means of capturing control of the federal government. Instead of being satisfied that California was free and that the number of free states was certain to increase, the self-styled Republicans (who had resurrected Jefferson's party label) seemed even to moderate Southerners to be intent on humiliating the South and on reducing the slave-holding states to the status of a colony.

By the mid-1850s Southerners were keenly aware of the growing discrepancy in wealth between their own rural economy and the economy of the urbanizing North. The great cotton boom of the 1850s had proved that even unparalleled southern prosperity could not narrow the gap. Picturing themselves as the nation's true producers of wealth, slaveholders blamed northern middlemen, epitomized by Wall Street bankers and merchants, for siphoning off their just rewards. The new Republican party represented the final and fatal spearhead of the conspiracy as it allied Free-Soilers, antislavery Democrats, and remnants of powerful Whig combines such as the Seward and Weed machine of New York. Whereas the earlier Liberty and Free Soil parties had never had a chance of success, the Republicans in 1856, hardly two years after their appearance, carried eleven of the sixteen free states. General John C. Frémont, the Republican presidential candidate, amassed an astonishing popular vote and would have won over Buchanan, the Democrats' candidate, if he had carried Pennsylvania and Illinois.

The Crisis over Kansas. Even for antislavery moderates, however, the events in Kansas following passage of the Kansas-Nebraska Act showed that compromise had only encouraged proslavery conspirators to begin to take over the western territories. The Republicans believed that unless drastic countermeasures were taken, America's free white workers would be deprived of the land and opportunity that was their birthright. Congress, by failing to provide definite legal measures for excluding slavery from the territories, had guaranteed that the issue would be decided by numerical and physical force.

The crisis over Kansas was actually the result of complex rivalries and aspirations. The government opened the territory to settlement before Indian treaties had been ratified and before Indian tribes, many of them recently removed to Kansas from the East, had been dispossessed and pushed onto reservations. In 1854 thousands of white settlers began the scramble for Kansas land, searching for the best town sites and the likely railroad routes of the future. Kansas, even without the slavery issue, would have been the scene of a speculative mania and a shameless defrauding of the Indians.

But the passions generated by slavery swept aside the last fragile restraints, such as the frontier's customary rules against "jumping," or disregarding,

prior land claims. According to Missouri's fiery Senator David R. Atchison, a free Kansas would inevitably lead to the demise of slavery in Missouri: "We are playing for a mighty stake, if we win we carry slavery to the Pacific Ocean; if we fail we lose Missouri, Arkansas, and Texas and all the territories; the game must be played boldly." Atchison thus helped to organize bands of "Border Ruffians" to harass settlers from the free states. On the opposite side, New Englanders organized an emigrant aid crusade with the purpose of colonizing Kansas with free-state settlers. Although Stephen Douglas referred to the Emigrant Aid Society as "that vast moneyed corporation," the movement was in fact poorly financed, and it succeeded in transporting barely one thousand settlers to Kansas. But the movement's sensational promotion fed the fantasies of Missourians and Southerners that eastern capitalists were recruiting armies of abolitionists and equipping them with Sharps rifles.

The Kansas-Nebraska Act, 1854

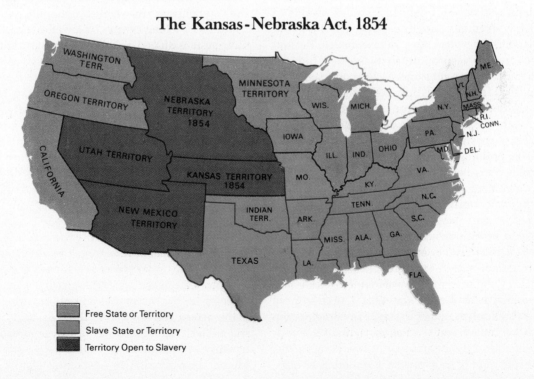

The acts of terrorism reached a climax in 1856 and became, in effect, a civil war. Antislavery newspapers declared that war had actually begun when a large proslavery force, supposedly acting under the authority of law enforcement officials, sacked the free-state town of Lawrence. The revenge for such proslavery outrages was even more savage. Even fervid southern alarmists had not imagined anything as brutal as John Brown's retaliatory massacre at Pottawatomie Creek. Brown, a wild and messianic ne'er-do-well with an abolitionist background and abolitionist connections, who thought of himself as an agent of God's vengeance, led four of his sons and two followers in a night attack on an unprotected settlement. They brutally executed five men and boys who were vaguely associated with the proslavery party.

In Congress all pretense of civility collapsed. In 1856 speakers became inflamed, personal, malicious. Senator Charles Sumner of Massachusetts, after denouncing "the crime against Kansas" and "the rape of a virgin territory, compelling it to the hateful embrace of slavery," delivered studied insults to the elderly Andrew Butler, a senator from South Carolina. On the Senate floor Butler's cousin, Preston Brooks, later savagely attacked the seated Sumner with a cane, leaving him unconscious and seriously injured. This triumph of "Bully" Brooks, a congressman from South Carolina, won applause from much of the South. For many Northerners, Sumner's Senate seat, which remained empty for over three years during his prolonged recovery, was a silent warning that Southerners could not be trusted to respect any codes, agreements, or sets of rules.

The same warning on a larger scale seemed to come out of the chaos of Kansas politics. By 1857 there could be no doubt that the overwhelming majority of Kansas settlers opposed admitting the territory as a slave state. Like the white settlers in California and Oregon, they also wanted to exclude free blacks along with slaves. For most Kansans these were in themselves minor issues compared to the disposal of Indian lands, squatter rights, rival railroad routes, and the desirability of free homesteads. What made slavery an explosive question in Kansas, and what made Kansas a detonating fuse for the na-

tion, was the federal government's effort to bypass the people's will.

The Pierce and Buchanan administrations made a series of miscalculations. In the first tumultuous stage of settlement, the Pierce administration had legally recognized a proslavery territorial legislature established by wholesale fraud; some seventeen hundred Missourians had crossed the border to cast illegal votes. Many moderates hoped that the flagrant acts of this provisional legislature—such as making it a felony to question the right to hold slaves in Kansas —would soon be repealed by a more representative body. But the free-state settlers chose to boycott the elections that the "legal" proslavery government authorized and to establish their own extralegal government and constitution.

The Lecompton Constitution.   In 1857 the Buchanan administration was thus committed to support the outcome of an official election of delegates to a constitutional convention, in Lecompton, Kansas, in preparation for statehood, even though only one in twelve eligible voters went to the polls. By then, the South had become convinced that the security of the slave system hinged on making Kansas a slave state. Buchanan had become equally convinced that the survival of the Democratic party hinged on appeasing the South (in 1856, 119 of his 174 electoral votes had come from slave states). In Kansas, there were no moderating pressures on the proslavery convention that drafted the convention's "Lecompton constitution." In Washington, the declining power of the northern Democrats gave a similarly unrestrained hand to the southern Democrats who dominated Buchanan's administration.

For Stephen Douglas the vote in Kansas on the proslavery Lecompton constitution was a total subversion of popular sovereignty. The voters, instead of being allowed to accept or reject the constitution as a whole, were asked only to approve the article guaranteeing for the future the right of property in slaves. If the article were rejected, the Constitution would still protect the legal status of slaves already in the territory. Although the free-state majority again registered their protest by abstaining from this vote, Buchanan exerted the powers of his office to pressure

Congress into admitting Kansas as a slave state. This policy brought a bitter break with Douglas, who denounced Buchanan's attempt to "force this constitution down the throats of the people of Kansas, in opposition to their wishes." In 1858, as in 1854, Congress became the scene of a violent sectional struggle. But this time Douglas led the antiadministration forces. Buchanan stood firm, sacrificing much of his remaining Democratic support in the North. In the end, in 1858, the Buchanan administration suffered a crushing defeat when the free state party forced a popular vote in Kansas on the whole of the Lecompton constitution. The territory's electorate rejected the constitution by a vote of nearly 10 to 1, though at the cost of indefinitely postponing statehood. (As it turned out, Kansas became a free state in 1861.)

Dred Scott and the Lincoln-Douglas Debates

The Lecompton struggle contributed to a fatal split in the Democratic party. The Democratic party had survived a stormy period which had led to the sectional division of the largest Protestant churches and benevolent societies, to say nothing of the collapse of the Whigs. The party had given the South a disproportionate access to national power, but an access dependent on winning the support of northern allies. As the number of such allies began to dwindle, they were partly replaced by southern Whigs. Thus as the Democratic party became more southern in character, there were fewer restraints on attempts to test the party loyalty of northern Democrats and to adopt an avowedly proslavery program. The Lecompton constitution was actually the second critical test imposed on northern Democrats. The first test was the *Dred Scott* decision.

The Dred Scott Decision. The Southerners who dominated the Supreme Court decided to use the *Dred Scott* case as a way to resolve critical issues that Congress had long evaded. From the time that the Court received the case, late in 1854, to its long-de-

layed decision in 1857, the paramount issue was whether Congress had the constitutional right to prohibit slavery in any territory or to delegate such a right to territorial governments, as implied by Stephen Douglas's formula of "popular sovereignty." In the recently disputed territories of New Mexico, Utah, and Kansas, no judicial cases involving the exclusion of slavery had yet arisen.

There had been many previous suits for freedom by slaves who had lived with their masters as temporary residents of free states. Even southern courts had sometimes granted freedom to such slaves, but the decisions had depended on complex technical issues that mostly involved state law. What distinguished Dred Scott, a Missouri slave who sued the state for his freedom, was that he and his master, an army surgeon, had lived together for several years not only in the free state of Illinois but in a part of Wisconsin Territory where slavery had been *federally* prohibited by the Missouri Compromise. Despite this clear violation of federal law, Scott's initial trials in Missouri courts were confined to narrower issues.

In 1854 technical complications allowed Scott's lawyers to transfer his suit for freedom to the United States Circuit Court for the District of Missouri. This first federal trial raised a preliminary question that courts had never resolved and that affected the enforcement of the Fugitive Slave Law of 1850. Were any blacks citizens to the extent of being qualified by the Constitution to bring suit in a federal court? After years of debate and postponement in the United States Supreme Court, this jurisdictional question enabled Chief Justice Roger Taney to link Scott's individual claim with momentous constitutional issues. For if blacks were not citizens entitled to constitutional rights and privileges, Dred Scott would be subject only to the laws of Missouri, and blacks seized under the provisions of the Fugitive Slave Law of 1850 would have no recourse to federal courts. The *Dred Scott* case also involved a second question of enormous significance. The court also had to decide if Congress had exceeded its powers in 1820 when it had outlawed slavery in the Louisiana Purchase north of 36'30°. If so, Dred Scott was still a slave and therefore could not bring suit in federal court.

By the end of 1856 the *Dred Scott* case had received widespread national publicity, with newspapers summarizing the opposing arguments delivered before the Court. Although informed observers anxiously awaited a verdict that might have explosive political consequences, they generally expected the Court to deny its jurisdiction on narrow technical grounds, thus confirming the judgment of lower courts that Scott was still a slave. When the decision was finally announced, in 1857, seven of the justices rejected Scott's claim to freedom but all nine wrote separate opinions. There is still controversy over what parts of the "Opinion of the Court," written by Chief Justice Taney, represented the opinion of a majority of the justices.

Taney's opinion arrived at three sweeping conclusions: first, Taney held that at the time the Constitution of the United States had been adopted, blacks had "for more than a century been regarded as beings of an inferior order . . . so far inferior that they had no rights which the white man was bound to respect; and that the negro might justly and lawfully be reduced to slavery for his benefit." Taney further contended that neither the Declaration of Independence nor the privileges and immunities of the Constitution had been intended to apply to blacks, whether slave or free. Even if later free blacks in certain states had been granted citizenship, Taney said, they were not citizens "within the meaning of the Constitution of the United States." They were not entitled to the rights and privileges of a citizen in any other state, nor could they sue in a federal court.

Second, after denying the Court's jurisdiction over Dred Scott, Taney reinforced his argument by moving on to the substantive issues. As for Scott's residence in Illinois, the Court had already recognized the principle that the status of a slave taken to a free state should be determined by the laws of the slave state to which he had returned. On Scott's residence in the federal territory north of 36°30', Taney ruled that the Missouri Compromise had been unconstitutional, since Congress had no more power in a federal territory than in a state to deprive a citizen of his property. Finally, having argued that slaves could not be differentiated from other forms of property

protected by the Fifth Amendment, Taney concluded that Congress could not give a territorial government powers that exceeded those of the federal government: "It could confer no power on any local Government, established by its authority, to violate the provisions of the Constitution." This judgment struck directly at Douglas's interpretation of popular sovereignty, and affirmed the extreme southern view that the people of a territory could not legally discriminate against slave property until they acquired the sovereignty of statehood.

Reaction to the Decision.   Both the South and President Buchanan were jubilant. Despite vigorous dissenting opinions from Justices John McLean and Benjamin R. Curtis, the highest court in the land had ruled that excluding slavery from the territories, the goal that had brought the Republican party into existence, was unconstitutional. Republican newspapers like the New York *Tribune* scornfully replied that the decision was "entitled to just as much moral weight as would be the judgment of a majority of those congregated in any Washington bar-room." Stephen Douglas, the leading contender for the Democratic presidential nomination in 1860, remained silent for many weeks. He wholly agreed with the denial of black citizenship and took credit for the congressional repeal of the Missouri Compromise. Yet his relations with Buchanan and the South were already strained, and he knew that his future career hinged on finding a way to reconcile the southern version of limited popular sovereignty, embodied in the *Dred Scott* decision, with his own constituents' demand for genuine self-determination.

In an important speech at the Illinois statehouse, in May 1857, Douglas presented his response to the *Dred Scott* decision. He argued that the constitutional right to take slaves into a territory was a worthless right unless sustained, protected, and enforced by "police regulations and local legislation." By contrasting an empty legal right with the necessary public support to enforce such a right, Douglas denied any meaningful contradiction between the *Dred Scott* decision and his own principle of popular sovereignty. Two weeks later Abraham Lincoln gave his reply to

Douglas before the same forum. Terming the *Dred Scott* decision erroneous, Lincoln reminded his audience that the Supreme Court had frequently overruled its own decisions, and promised: "We shall do what we can to have it to over-rule this."

Since 1854, when he had attacked the Kansas-Nebraska Act, Lincoln had begun making a new career by pursuing Stephen Douglas. Elected to Congress as a Whig in 1846, he had suffered politically from his opposition to the Mexican War. Lincoln was a self-educated Kentuckian, shaped by the Indiana and Illinois frontier. In moral and cultural outlook, however, he was not far from the stereotyped New Englander. He abstained from alcohol, revered the idea of self-improvement, dreamed of America's technological and moral progress, and condemned slavery as a moral and political evil. "I have always hated slavery," he told a Chicago audience in 1858, "I think as much as any Abolitionist. . . . I have always hated it, but I have always been quiet about it until this new era of the introduction of the Nebraska Bill began. I always believed that everybody was against it, and that it was in course of ultimate extinction."

The Kansas-Nebraska Act taught Lincoln that men like Douglas did not care whether slavery was "voted *down* or voted *up*." It also allowed him to exercise his magnificent talents as a debator and stumpspeaker, talents which had already distinguished him as a frontier lawyer, a state legislator, and an attorney and lobbyist for such corporations as the Illinois Central Railroad. Lincoln's humor, his homespun epigrams, his unaffected self-assurance, all diverted attention from his extraordinary ability to grasp the central point of a controversy and to compress an argument into its most lucid and striking form. In 1856, after a period of watchful waiting, Lincoln played an important part in the belated organization of the Illinois Republican party. Two years later the Republican state convention unanimously nominated him to succeed Douglas as United States senator.

The Lincoln-Douglas contest was unprecedented both in form and in substance. At this time senators were still elected by state legislatures, and no party convention had ever nominated a candidate. In an acceptance speech on June 16, 1858, Lincoln concisely and eloquently stated the arguments he would present directly to the people, appealing for a Republican legislature that would then be committed to elect him to the Senate. Since Douglas had unexpectedly repudiated the Lecompton constitution and had joined the Republicans in fighting it, Lincoln needed to persuade the electorate that Douglas's own crusade for popular sovereignty had rekindled the slavery agitation and had led directly to the *Dred Scott* decision and the Lecompton constitution. According to Lincoln, Douglas's moral indifference to slavery disqualified him as a leader who could stand firm against the future aggressions of the Slave Power. For Lincoln was wholly convinced that the conflict over slavery would continue until a crisis had been reached and passed. As he said in his famous "House Divided" speech:

"A house divided against itself cannot stand.

I believe this government cannot endure, permanently half *slave* and half *free*.

I do not expect the Union to be *dissolved*—I do not expect the house to *fall*—but I *do* expect it will cease to be divided.

It will become *all* one thing, or *all* the other.

Either the *opponents* of slavery, will arrest the further spread of it, and place it where the public mind shall rest in the belief that it is in course of ultimate extinction; or its *advocates* will push it forward, till it shall become alike lawful in *all* the States, *old* as well *as new*—*North* as well as *South*.

Have we no *tendency* to the latter condition?"

The "House Divided" speech signified a turning point in American political history. Lincoln stated that expediency and a moral neutrality toward slavery had undermined the Founders' expectation that slavery was "in the course of ultimate extinction." If the North continued to make compromises and failed to defend a boundary of clear principle, the South was certain to dictate "a second Dred Scott decision," depriving every state of the power to discriminate against slave property. In Lincoln's view, Douglas's Kansas-Nebraska Act had been part of a master plan or conspiracy, which Lincoln compared to "a piece of *machinery*" that had been designed to legalize slavery, step by step, throughout the United States. In asserting that "the people were to be left 'perfectly free' 'subject only to the Constitution,'" Douglas had provided "an exactly fitted *niche,* for the Dred Scott decision to afterwards come in, and declare the perfect freedom of the people, to be just no freedom at all."

Lincoln was not an abolitionist. He was convinced that prohibiting the further spread of slavery would be sufficient to condemn it to "ultimate extinction," a belief shared by many southern leaders. Yet he insisted on a public policy aimed at that goal—a public policy similar to that of England in the 1820s or, in Lincoln's eyes, to that of the Founders. For Lincoln, repudiating popular sovereignty was the same as repudiating the moral indifference exemplified by Douglas; and this was the first step toward national redemption.

The Lincoln-Douglas Debates. Because Douglas seemed to be the nation's most likely choice for president in 1860, his struggle with Lincoln for reelection to the Senate commanded national attention. Making full use of newly constructed railroads, the two candidates traveled nearly ten thousand miles in four months. They crisscrossed Illinois, their tireless voices intermingling with the sound of bands, parades, fireworks, cannon, and cheering crowds. Each community tried to outdo its rivals in pageantry and in winning the greatest turnout from the countryside. Lincoln and Douglas agreed to participate in seven face-to-face debates, which are rightly regarded as classics in the history of campaign oratory. Douglas tried to make the most of his experience as a seasoned national leader (at forty-five he was four years younger than Lincoln), and to portray his opponent as a dangerous radical. According to Douglas, Lincoln's "House Divided" speech showed a determination to impose the moral judgments of one section on the other. Lincoln's doctrines threatened to destroy the Union and to extinguish the world's last hope for freedom. Douglas also exploited the racial prejudice of his listeners, drawing laughter from his sarcastic refusal to question "Mr. Lincoln's conscientious belief that the negro was made his equal, and hence his brother."

Lincoln searched for ways to counteract the image of a revolutionary. Always insisting on the moral and political wrong of slavery, he repeatedly acknowledged that the federal government could not interfere with slavery in the existing states. He opposed repeal of the Fugitive Slave Law. He wholly rejected the idea of "perfect social and political equality with the negro." He did maintain, however, that blacks were as much entitled as whites to "all the natural rights enumerated in the Declaration of Independence, the right to life, liberty and the pursuit of happiness." If the black was "perhaps" not equal in moral or intellectual endowment, "in the right to eat the bread, without leave of anybody else, which his own hand earns, *he is my equal and the equal of judge Douglas, and the equal of every living man.* [Great applause.]"

The election in Illinois was extremely close. The Republicans did not win enough seats in the legislature to send Lincoln to the Senate, but the campaign immediately elevated him to national prominence. Lincoln had succeeded in articulating and defending a Republican antislavery ideology that combined a fixity of purpose with a respect for constitutional restraints. Lincoln had also magnified the gap that separated the Republicans from Douglas and other anti-Lecompton Democrats. He had further isolated Douglas from proslavery Democrats in the South who were already embittered by Douglas's "treachery" with regard to the Lecompton constitution. They were then outraged by Douglas's response to Lincoln in the debate at Freeport, Illinois, where he had maintained that regardless of what the Supreme Court might decide about the constitutionality of slavery in a territory, the people had the "lawful means to introduce it or exclude it" as they pleased. Repeating his familiar point that slavery could not exist "a day or an hour anywhere" unless it was supported by local police regulations, Douglas emphasized that the "unfriendly legislation" of a territorial government could effectually prevent slavery from being introduced. As Lincoln quipped, this was to say, "A thing may be lawfully driven from a place where it has a lawful right to stay."

In 1859 the breach between Douglas and the South could no longer be contained. The people of

STEPHEN A. DOUGLAS, 1813–1861
Wooden folk sculpture of Stephen Douglas, who opposed Abraham Lincoln in the epic senatorial election of 1858 as well as in the presidential election of 1860. At left, the "Little Giant" in his prime. *(Below: Courtesy, National Portrait Gallery, Smithsonian Institution, Washington, D.C.; left: Brady Collection, National Archives)*

Kansas ratified a new constitution prohibiting slavery, thereby giving bite to Douglas's "Freeport Doctrine." In the Senate, where Douglas had been ousted from his chairmanship of the Committee on Territories, he led the fight against the demand for a federal slave code protecting slave property in all the territories. During a tour of the South, Douglas became alarmed by the growing movement, led by young proslavery "fire-eaters," to revive and legalize the African slave trade. Looking ahead to the Democratic convention of 1860, Douglas issued what amounted to an ultimatum about the party platform. Northern Democrats, he insisted, would not allow the party to be used as a vehicle for reviving the African slave trade, securing a federal slave code, or pursuing any of the other new objectives of southern extremists. Douglas warned that Northerners would not retreat from defending genuine popular sovereignty, even though popular sovereignty was clearly running against the interests of the South.

The Ultimate Failure of Compromise

By 1860 a multitude of hitherto separate fears, aspirations, and factional interests had become polarized into opposing visions of America's heritage and destiny. Traditional systems of trust and reciprocity had collapsed.

John Brown's Raid. John Brown, who had warred against slavery in Kansas, was a key symbol of this polarization. Since 1857 Brown had been lionized by the most eminent New England reformers and literary figures. Backed financially by a secret group of abolitionists, Brown also cultivated intimate ties with free black communities in the North. On the night of October 16, 1859, he and some twenty heavily armed white and black followers seized part of the federal arsenal at Harpers Ferry, Virginia. Brown hoped to begin the destruction of slavery by igniting a slave insurrection and creating in the South a free-soil asylum for fugitives. After resisting federal troops for two days, Brown surrendered; he was tried for conspiracy, treason, and murder, and was hanged.

During his trial Brown claimed to have acted under the "higher law" of the New Testament, and insisted, "If I had done what I have for the white men, or the rich, no man would have blamed me." For Brown the higher law was not a philosophical abstraction but a moral command to shed blood and die in the cause of freedom. In the eyes of sedentary reformers and intellectuals, Brown's courage to act on his principles made him not only a revered martyr but a symbol of all that America lacked. Democratic editors and politicians, however, saw Brown's criminal violence as the direct result of the irresponsible preaching of William H. Seward and other "Black Republicans." The New York *Herald* reprinted Seward's speech on the "irrepressible conflict" alongside news accounts from Harpers Ferry. Many Southerners came to the stunned realization that Brown's raid could not be dismissed as the folly of a madman, since it had revealed the secret will of much of the North. A Virginia senator concluded that Brown's "invasion" had been condemned in the North "only because it failed." In the words of Jefferson Davis, a Mississippi senator who had been Pierce's secretary of war, the Republican party had been "organized on the basis of making war" against the South.

Paradoxically both the Republicans and southern extremists agreed that slavery must expand under national sanction if it were to survive. They also agreed that if the *Dred Scott* decision was valid, the government had an obligation to protect slave property in all the territories. This denial of any middle ground made it logical for southern fire-eaters to argue that a revived African slave trade would allow more whites to own slaves and would thus help to "democratize" the institution. Above all, both the Republicans and southern extremists rejected popular sovereignty as Douglas had defined it. For Southerners, the Constitution prohibited either Congress or a territorial legislature from depriving a settler of his slave property. For Republicans, the Constitution gave Congress both the duty and power to prevent the spread of an institution that deprived human beings of their inalienable right to freedom.

Because these positions were irreconcilable, the northern Democrats held the only keys to possible compromise in the presidential election of 1860. But like the Republicans, the Douglas Democrats had drawn their own firm limits against further concessions to southern extremists. Early in 1860 Jefferson Davis challenged those limits by persuading the Senate Democratic caucus to adopt a set of resolutions committing the federal government to protect slavery in the territories. For Davis and other southern leaders, a federal slave code was the logical extension of the *Dred Scott* decision, and the principle of federal protection of slave property an essential plank in the forthcoming Democratic platform. The Douglas Democrats knew that such a principle of guaranteed protection would completely undercut their reliance on legislation "unfriendly" to slavery in a territory, and that such a plank would guarantee their defeat in the North.

Division of Democratic Party. In April 1860 the fateful Democratic national convention met at

THE ELECTION OF 1860
A cartoonist's view of the presidential race between Lincoln, the tall railsplitter, and Douglas, who is carrying a jug of liquor and whose record on slavery in the territories constitutes an insuperable obstacle (black man waiting in fence to stop Douglas). *(Library of Congress)*

Charleston. When a majority of the convention refused to adopt a platform similar in principle to Davis's Senate resolutions, the delegates from eight southern states withdrew, many of them assuming that this disunionist gesture would force the Douglas faction to compromise. Douglas held firm to his principle of popular sovereignty and as a result could not muster the two-thirds majority required for nomination. In a surprise move the northern Democrats then agreed to adjourn the convention and to reconvene six weeks later in Baltimore.

There the Democratic party finally destroyed itself as a national force. Delegates from the Lower South again seceded, and this time adopted an extreme proslavery platform and nominated John C. Breckinridge of Kentucky for president. The northern remnants of the party remained loyal to popular sovereignty, however it might be modified in practice

by the *Dred Scott* decision, and nominated Douglas.

Meanwhile, the division of the Democrats at Charleston had given the Republicans greater flexibility in nominating a candidate. In 1858 Douglas had portrayed Lincoln as a flaming abolitionist, and the South had accepted the image. To the North, however, Lincoln appeared more moderate and less controversial than the better-known Senator Seward of New York. Unlike Seward, Lincoln was not popularly associated with the higher-law doctrines that had led to Harpers Ferry. Although Lincoln disapproved of Know-Nothing nativism, he was more discreet than Seward and thus stood less chance of losing the nativist vote in critical states like Pennsylvania. If some Northerners regarded him as a crude buffoon from the prairies, he appealed to many Northerners as the tall rail-splitter of humble origins, a man of the people, an egalitarian. Except for his general endorsement

CAMPAIGN POSTER
The Republican candidates for president and vice president in 1860. *(Library of Congress)*

of the Homestead Act, protective tariffs, and a trans-continental railroad—all programs that were popular in the North and West and that had been blocked in Congress by the South—Lincoln was associated with few issues and had made few enemies. In May, at the Republicans' boisterous convention in Chicago, Lincoln finally overcame Seward's early lead and received the nomination.

The presidential campaign of 1860 was filled with the noisy hucksterism and carnival atmosphere that had been standard since 1840. The Republicans tended to discount the warnings of serious crisis, and contemptuously dismissed southern threats of secession as empty bluff. The Breckinridge Democrats tried to play down such threats and to profess their loyalty to the Constitution and Union. Yet various groups of moderates realized that both the Constitution and Union were in jeopardy. This was the message of the new Constitutional Union party, which was led largely by former Whigs and which won many supporters in the Upper South. And this was the message that Stephen Douglas repeated bravely and incessantly—in the South as well as in the North—in the first nationwide speaking campaign by a presidential candidate.

The Election of 1860. In November the national popular vote was divided among four candidates, and Lincoln received only 40 percent of the national total. Yet he received 180 electoral votes, 57 more than the combined total of his three opponents. He carried every free state except for New Jersey, and won 4 of New Jersey's 7 electoral votes. In ten of the slave states, however, he failed to register a single popular vote. Breckinridge, the southern Democrat, captured all the states of the Lower South as well as Delaware, Maryland, Arkansas, and North Carolina. John Bell, the leader of the once powerful Whig party in Tennessee and the candidate of the Constitutional Union party, carried Tennessee, Kentucky, and Virginia. Though Douglas received approximately 525,000 more popular votes than Breckinridge, and trailed Lincoln by only 491,000, he won 12 electoral votes (9 from Missouri and 3 from New Jersey). In many respects it was not really a national election. In the North it was essentially a contest between Lincoln and Douglas; in the South between Breckinridge and Bell.

For the South the worst fears and predictions of forty years had come true. The United States had never had an administration avowedly hostile to black slavery. Lincoln's reassurances regarding the constitutional protection of slavery in the existing states could not mitigate the crucial facts. The election had proved that the North was populous enough to bestow national power on a minority party that had no support in the South. The Republican party was committed to free-labor ideology and to the proposition that slavery was a moral wrong. Slaveholders would have to take Lincoln's professions of restraint on good faith. If he or his successors should become more militant, they could not be checked by a balance of political power. A dominant sectional party would control federal patronage, the postal service and mili-

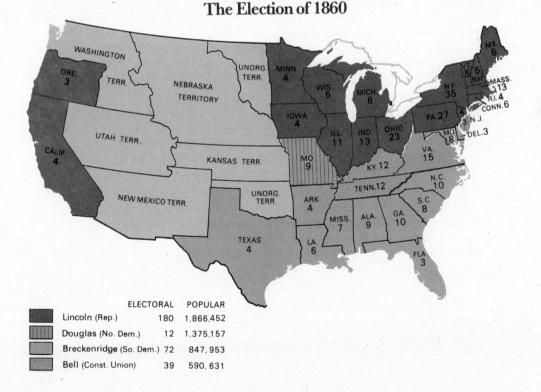

The Election of 1860

	ELECTORAL	POPULAR
Lincoln (Rep.)	180	1,866,452
Douglas (No. Dem.)	12	1,375,157
Breckenridge (So. Dem.)	72	847,953
Bell (Const. Union)	39	590,631

tary posts, the appointment of federal judges and other officeholders. Such considerations strengthened the hand of secessionists. On December 20, 1860, South Carolina crossed the threshold that had been so closely approached during the nullification crisis. A special convention repealed the state's ratification of the Constitution and withdrew South Carolina from the Union. Unlike Jackson when faced with similar defiance, President Buchanan maintained that the federal government could do nothing to prevent the move.

Unionists mounted stiffer resistance to secession in the other states of the Lower South. The chief controversies, however, involved timing—whether to follow the stampede of the fire-eating militants or to wait until Lincoln had shown his true colors. By February 1, 1861, the militants had triumphed in Mississippi, Florida, Alabama, Georgia, Louisiana, and Texas. Inevitably the shock produced reflex actions toward the traditional saving compromise. Senator John Crittenden of Kentucky initiated the first of such moves two days before South Carolina officially seceded. Though Crittenden's proposed amendments to the Constitution were defined as moderate, they matched the most extravagant southern demands of a few years before. Even so, the leaders of the Lower South knew that no "compromise" would be secure unless the Republican party miraculously repudiated its antislavery principles. Most Republicans could not publicly approve Crittenden's "unamendable" amendment guaranteeing the permanent security of slavery. Nor could they return to the old Democratic proposal for extending the Missouri Compromise line to the Pacific. The 1850s had shown that federal commitment to establishing and protecting slavery south of that line would only encourage southern ambitions in the Caribbean and Latin America. As Lincoln confidentially warned William Kellogg, his mouthpiece in Congress: "Entertain no proposition for a compromise in regard to the *extension* of slavery. The instant you do, they have us under again; all our labor is lost, and sooner or later must be done over. . . . The tug has to come and better now than later."

By 1860 the North and South had moved beyond the reach of compromise. The United States had originally emerged from an act of secession, from a final rejection of compromise with England. Even after independence had been won, Americans continued to perceive Britain as a conspiratorial power threatening to hold back the nation's expansive energies. But despite this threat, America continued to prosper and expand. The period from 1820 to 1860 witnessed a progressive extension of limits, an overleaping of boundaries of every kind. History seemed to confirm the people's wish for total self-determination. The American people, like the American individual, seemed to be free from the burdens of the past and free to shape their own character. The one problem their ingenuity could not resolve was Negro slavery, which the Founding Fathers had seen as an unwanted legacy of British greed. Paradoxically the South increasingly came to regard Negro slavery as the necessary base on which freedom must rest. For the North a commitment to slavery's ultimate extinction was the test of freedom. Each section detected a fatal change in the other, a betrayal of the principles and mission of the Founding Fathers. Each section feared that the other had become transformed into a despotic and conspiratorial power very similar to the original British enemy. And both sections shared a heritage of standing firm against despotism.

It was not accidental that the greatest novel of the period, Herman Melville's *Moby Dick* (1851), tells of the destruction that inevitably flows from denying all limits, rules, and boundaries. The novel concerns Captain Ahab's relentless and stubborn pursuit of a great white whale, a "nameless, inscrutable, unearthly thing" that becomes a symbol for all the opposing, unknown forces of life. Ahab, who commands a crew containing most of the races and types of mankind, thinks that he can become the master of his own fate. Ignoring a series of warnings and portents, he is incapable of admitting that he might be wrong or that there might be forces beyond his control.

Melville's novel is full of rich and universal meaning concerning the heroic yet impossible quest to know the unknowable. Since Americans of the

1850s believed that men were born free and that God would ensure the triumph of democracy in the world, they could not accept Melville's brooding skepticism. Nevertheless, there was a lesson for pre–Civil War America in this tale of a highly rational but half-crazed captain—a captain who becomes so obsessed with his mission that he finally throws his navigation instruments overboard, so that he can steer only toward the visible spout of the whale. Captain Ahab seeks liberation in an unswerving pursuit and conquest of limits. In the end he dooms himself and his ship to destruction.

CHRONOLOGY

1846   Wilmot Proviso fuses question of slavery's expansion with consequences of Mexican War.
Walker tariff, adopted for revenue only, eliminates principle of protection.

1848   Gold discovered on American River in California.
Van Buren, running for president on Free-Soil ticket, receives 10 percent of popular vote.
Zachary Taylor elected president.

1850   In Congress, violent sectional debate culminates in Compromise of 1850.
Fugitive Slave Law requires federal agents to recover escaped slaves from sanctuaries in the North.
Taylor's death makes Millard Fillmore president.

1851   Herman Melville's *Moby Dick.*

1852   Franklin Pierce elected president.
Harriet Beecher Stowe's *Uncle Tom's Cabin.*

1853   Upsurge of political nativism, the Know-Nothings.

1854   Spectacular Know-Nothing election victories.
Collapse of Whigs.

1854   New Republican party emerges.
Commodore Perry opens Japan to American trade.
Kansas-Nebraska Act rekindles sectional controversy over slavery.

1856   John Brown's murderous raid at Pottawatomie Creek.
James Buchanan elected president.

1857   Dred Scott decision.
In Kansas, proslavery Lecompton constitution ratified as free-state men refuse to vote.

1858   Lincoln-Douglas debates.

1859   John Brown's raid on Harpers Ferry.

1860   Democratic party deadlocked at Charleston convention finally divides along sectional lines at Baltimore.
Abraham Lincoln elected president.
South Carolina secedes from the Union.

1861   Mississippi, Florida, Alabama, Georgia, Louisiana, and Texas secede.

SUGGESTED READINGS

David M. Potter, *The Impending Crisis, 1848–1861* (1976), continues to be the best guide to the topics discussed in the present chapter. See also William J. Cooper, *The South and the Politics of Slavery 1828–1865* (1978). The titles on the causes of the Civil War, listed at the end of Chapter 18 in Part Four are also highly relevant.

On California, the best general guide is Andrew F. Rolle, *California: A History* (1969). For the California gold rush and western mining in general, see Rodman W. Paul, *California Gold: The Beginning of Mining in the Far West* (1947); and Paul, *Mining Frontiers of the Far West, 1848–1880* (1963). Kevin Starr, *Americans and the California Dream, 1850–1915* (1973), presents brilliant vignettes of early California history. For the experiences of blacks in California, see Rudolph M. Lapp, *Blacks in Gold Rush California* (1977). Chinese immigration and anti-Chinese sentiment is admirably treated in Alexander Saxton, *The Indispensable Enemy: Labor and the Anti-Chinese Movement in California* (1975).

Holman Hamilton, *Prologue to Conflict* (1964), is the most detailed and accurate account of the Compromise of 1850. For the preceding presidential election, see Joseph G. Rayback, *Free Soil: The Election of 1848* (1970). Stanley W. Campbell, *The Slave Catchers: Enforcement of the Fugitive Slave Law, 1840–1860* (1968), traces the consequences of the most unpopular provision of the Compromise of 1850. Stephen Douglas's motives for introducing the Kansas-Nebraska Act are judiciously weighed in Robert W. Johannsen, *Stephen A. Douglas* (1973). This definitive biography is also an excellent source on the later Kansas controversy and the Lincoln-Douglas debates. Roy F. Nichols, "The Kansas-Nebraska Act: A Century of Historiography," *Mississippi Valley Historical Review*, 43 (September 1956), 187–212, is an invaluable guide to the controversial issues. The tangled local conflicts over land and railroad sites are illuminated in Paul W. Gates, *Fifty Million Acres: Conflicts over Kansas Land Policy, 1854–1890* (1954); and James C. Malin, *The Nebraska Question, 1852–1854* (1953). For Harriet Beecher Stowe's world-famous response to the Kansas controversy, see Philip van Doren Stern, *Uncle Tom's Cabin, an Annotated Edition* (1964); and Charles H. Foster, *The Rungless Ladder: Harriet Beecher Stowe and New England Puritanism* (1956).

The political realignment of the 1850s has been reinterpreted in Michael F. Holt, *The Political Crisis of the 1850s* (1978). Ray Billington, *The Protestant Crusade, 1800–1860* (1938), provides an outstanding overview of anti-Catholic nativism. For the intellectual ties between nativism and other movements, see David B. Davis, "Some Themes of Counter-Subversion," *Mississippi Valley Historical Review*, 47 (September 1960), 205–24. The best studies of political nativism are Michael F. Holt, "The Politics of Impatience: The Origins of Know-Nothingism," *Journal of American History*, 60 (September 1973), and Holt, *Forging a Majority: The Formation of the Republican Party in Pittsburgh* (1969).

The best brief account of the origins and early history of the Republican party is Hans L. Trefousse, "The Republican Party, 1854–1864," in *History of U.S. Political Parties*, ed. Arthur M. Schlesinger, Jr., Vol. 2, 1141–72 (4 vols., 1973). See also Trefousse, *The Radical Republicans* (1969). Eric Foner, *Free Soil, Free Labor, Free Men: The Ideology of the Republican Party before the Civil War* (1970), is a penetrating study of the Republicans' thought and values. The definitive study of the *Dred Scott* decision is Don E. Fehrenbacher, *The Dred Scott Case: Its Significance in American Law and Politics* (1978).

John Brown, a man of violence, has been the subject of violently conflicting interpretations. For traditional and hostile views, see James C. Malin, *John Brown and the Legend of Fifty-Six* (1942); and the brilliant essay by C. Vann Woodward in *The Burden of Southern History* (1960). More sympathetic evaluations can be found in Stephen B. Oates, *To Purge the Land with Blood: A Biography of John Brown* (1970); Benjamin Quarles, *Allies for Freedom: Blacks and John Brown* (1974); and Louis Ruchames, ed., *John Brown: The Making of a Revolutionary* (1969).

Johannsen's biography of Douglas, listed above, treats the Lincoln-Douglas debates and a penetrating analysis can be found in Don E. Fehrenbacher, *Prelude to Greatness: Lincoln in the 1850s* (1962). The debates themselves are presented in an authoritative edition by Paul M. Angle, ed., *Created Equal? The Complete Lincoln-Douglas Debates of 1858* (1958). Harry V. Jaffa, *Crisis of the House Divided: An Interpretation of the Issues in the Lincoln-Douglas Debates* (1959), gives the brilliant, far-reaching, and somewhat eccentric interpretation of a conservative political philosopher.

Most of the biographical studies of Lincoln listed in Part Four, at the end of Chapter 18, are relevant to this chapter. Fehrenbacher's *Prelude to Greatness* is an important source, and mention should be made of James G. Randall, *Lincoln, the Liberal Statesman* (1947); Benjamin Quarles, *Lincoln and the Negro* (1962); and above all, Allan Nevins, *The Emergence of Lincoln* (2 vols., 1950).

The climactic impasse between North and South is imaginatively presented in two major studies: Roy F. Nichols, *The Disruption of American Democracy* (1948); and David M. Potter, *Lincoln and His Party in the Secession Crisis* (1942). Avery O. Craven, *The Coming of the Civil War* (1942), stresses the importance of propaganda and irrationality. For the hopes and fears of contemporaries, see J. Jeffrey Auer, ed., *Antislavery and Disunion, 1858–1861: Studies in the Rhetoric of Compromise and Conflict* (1963). No one has yet written a wholly satisfactory account of the secessionist movements in the South. For conflicting interpretations, see William L. Barney, *The Secessionist Impulse: Alabama and Mississippi* (1974); Steven A. Channing, *Crisis in Fear: Secession in South Carolina* (1970); Charles B. Dew, "Who Won the Secession Election in Louisiana?" *Journal of Southern History*, 36 (February 1970), 18–32; Dwight L. Dumond, *The Secession Movement, 1860–1861* (1931); William J. Evitts,

A Matter of Allegiances: Maryland from 1850 to 1861 (1974); and R. A. Wooster, *The Secession Conventions of the South* (1962).

Two works that give a fascinating picture of the northern response to secession are Kenneth M. Stampp, *And the War Came: The North and the Secession Crisis, 1860–61* (1950); and Howard C. Perkins, ed., *Northern Editorials on Secession* (2 vols., 1942). For the election of 1860, see Elting Morison,

"Election of 1860," in *History of American Presidential Elections, 1789–1968,* ed. Arthur M. Schlesinger, Jr., Vol. 2, 1097–1122 (4 vols., 1971). On the futile gestures for compromise, see Albert J. Kirwan, *John J. Crittenden: The Struggle for the Union* (1962); and Robert G. Gunderson, *Old Gentlemen's Convention: The Washington Peach Conference of 1861* (1961).

PART FOUR

David Herbert Donald

Uniting the Republic

1860–1877

*T*hese [Northern] people hate us, annoy us, and would have us assassinated by our slaves if they dared," a Southern leader wrote when he learned that a "Black Republican," Abraham Lincoln, would certainly be elected president in 1860. "They are a *different* people from us, whether better or worse and *there is no love* between us. Why then continue together?" The sectional contests of the previous decades suggested that Americans had become members of two distinct, and conflicting, nationalities. By 1860, Northerners and Southerners appeared not to speak the same language, to share the same moral code, or to obey the same law. Compromise could no longer patch together a union between two such fundamentally different peoples. "I do not see how a barbarous and a civilized community can constitute one state," Ralph Waldo Emerson gravely concluded for many Northerners. "The North and the South are heterogeneous and are better apart," agreed the New Orleans *Bee.* "We [Southerners] are doomed if we proclaim not our political independence."

On first thought, the four-year civil war that broke out in 1861 seems powerfully to confirm this idea that the Union and the Confederacy were two distinct nations. Yet the conduct of the war suggested that Northerners and Southerners were not so different as their political and intellectual leaders had maintained. At the beginning of the conflict both governments tried in much

Overleaf: Mathew Brady's photograph of the ruins of Richmond, Virginia, April, 1865. *(Library of Congress)*

the same ways to mobilize for battle their invertebrate, unorganized societies. As the war progressed, both Union and Confederacy adopted much the same diplomatic, military, and economic policies. By the end of the war both governments were committed to abolishing slavery, the one institution that had most clearly divided the sections in 1860.

In the backward glance of history, then, the Civil War takes on a significance different from its meaning to contemporaries and participants. In retrospect it is clear that there was less a struggle between two separate nations than a struggle within the American nation to define a boundary between the centralizing, nationalizing tendencies in American life and the opposing tendencies toward localism, parochialism, and fragmentation. The issue, then, was the familiar one of majority rule and minority rights: How could a society follow the dictates of the majority of its members without infringing on the essential interests of those who were in the minority? For Americans of the Civil War era, this was no new question; it had been a central concern of American political philosophers from James Madison to John C. Calhoun. Even today, when the balance of power has shifted so markedly toward a national, centralized society, the rights of regional and ethnic minorities remain a topic for hot dispute.

CHAPTER 18

Stalemate
1861–1862

During the first two years of the Civil War, as the Union and the Confederacy grappled with each other inconclusively, it seemed that two distinct and incompatible nations had emerged from the American soil. Certainly the aims announced by their leaders were totally inconsistent. President Abraham Lincoln announced that the United States would "constitutionally defend, and maintain itself"; the territorial integrity of the nation must remain inviolate. For the Confederate States, President Jefferson Davis proclaimed that his country's "career of independence" must be "inflexibly pursued." As the rival governments raised and equipped armies, attempted to finance a huge war, and sought diplomatic recognition and economic assistance abroad, the people of the two nations increasingly thought of each other as enemies: "Yankees" and "Rebels." It is easy to understand why Lord John Russell, the British foreign minister, concluded: "I do not see how the United States can be cobbled together again by any compromise. . . . I suppose the break-up of the Union is now inevitable."

A shrewder observer might have reached the opposite conclusion. Perhaps the most striking thing about the war in America was the fact that both sides carried it on through virtually identical methods. The Union and the Confederate governments faced the same wartime problems and arrived at the same wartime solutions. Northerners and Southerners on the battlefields found each other not two alien peoples but mirror images. That identity made the conflict truly a brother's war.

The Rival Governments

The government of the Confederate States was in most respects a duplicate of that of the United States, from which the Southern states had just withdrawn. Framed by delegates from six states of the Lower South (delegates from Texas, which seceded on February 1, 1861, arrived late), the Constitution largely followed the wording of the one drawn up in Philadelphia in 1787. To be sure, the new charter recognized the "sovereign and independent character" of

INAUGURATION OF JEFFERSON DAVIS

On February 18, 1861, Jefferson Davis, standing in front of the state capitol at Montgomery, Alabama, took the oath of office as the first—and, as it proved, only—President of the Confederate States of America. Davis is the thin, tall figure behind the lectern. To his right is William L. Yancey, a leading secessionist; to his right, Howell Cobb, president of the Confederate Senate, who administered the oath. *(Library of Congress)*

the constituent states, but it also announced that they were forming "a permanent federal government," and it listed most of the same restrictions on state action included in the United States Constitution. Unlike

that document, it used no euphemism about persons "held to Service or Labour" but recognized explicitly "the right of property in negro slaves." Otherwise, the two documents were substantially and intentionally identical. As secessionist Benjamin H. Hill of Georgia explained, "We hugged that [United States] Constitution to our bosom and carried it with us."

Inaugurating the Presidents. For president of the new republic, the Montgomery convention chose Jefferson Davis, of Mississippi, who had ardently defended Southern rights in the United States Senate but who had only reluctantly come to advocate secession.* If the crowds that thronged the streets of Montgomery on February 18, 1861, hoped to hear a stirring inaugural from the new Southern head of state, they were disappointed. Stepping forward on the portico of the Alabama statehouse, Davis gave a long, legalistic review of the acts of Northern aggression that had led to the formation of the new state. While Davis pledged he would, if necessary, "maintain, by the final arbitrament of the sword, the position which we have assumed among the nations of the earth," he spoke in a tone more melancholy than martial. He saw himself as the leader of a conservative movement. "We have labored to preserve the Government of our fathers in its spirit," he insisted.

Just two weeks later, from the portico of the yet unfinished Capitol in Washington, another conservative took his inaugural oath. The capital was thronged, as Nathaniel Hawthorne wrote, with "office-seekers, wire-pullers, inventors, artists, poets, prosers (including editors, army correspondents, attachés of foreign journals, and long-winded talkers), clerks, diplomatists, mail contractors, [and] railway directors." On public buildings along the route of the

---

*The Montgomery convention drew up a provisional constitution of the Confederacy, constituted itself the provisional legislature of the new republic, and named Jefferson Davis the provisional president. It also drew up a permanent constitution, which was submitted to the states for ratification. After that, regular elections were held in the fall of 1861 both for members of the Confederate Congress and for president. Reelected without opposition, Davis was formally inaugurated as the first and only regular president of the Confederate States on February 22, 1862.

inaugural procession, sharpshooters were strategically placed, to prevent any pro-Southern interruption of the proceedings. Abraham Lincoln's inaugural address was similar in tone to Davis's. Vowing that the Union would be preserved, Lincoln gave a low-keyed version of the previous sectional quarrels, explained his personal views on slavery, and pledged that he contemplated "no invasion—no using of force" against the seceded states. In a warning softened by sadness, he reminded his listeners of the oath he had just taken to preserve, protect, and defend the government of the United States and entreated his Southern fellow citizens to pause before they assailed it. "In *your* hands, my dissatisfied fellow-countrymen," he concluded, "and not in *mine*, is the momentous issue of civil war."

Organizing the Two Administrations.   In the weeks immediately following the two inaugurations, the central problem confronting both Davis and Lincoln was not so much whether either should start a civil war but whether they could form viable governments. In Davis's Confederacy, everything had to be started afresh. Even the most routine legal and governmental matters could not be taken for granted. For instance, it was not certain, until the Confederate Congress passed an act, whether the laws of the United States passed before 1861 and the decisions of the United States courts were binding in the seceded states. The new nation had to choose a flag—over the opposition of some purists who claimed that the Confederacy, representing the true American spirit, ought to retain the Stars and Stripes and let the Union look for a new banner.

In selecting his cabinet advisers, President Davis theoretically had a free hand, but in fact his range of choice was severely limited. No man of doubtful loyalty to the new government could be permitted a place in his cabinet; no Southern Unionist in the tradition of Henry Clay, John J. Crittenden, and John Bell was invited. On the other hand, because Davis wanted the world to see that the Confederacy was governed by sober, responsible men, he excluded from his council all the most conspicuous Southern fire-eaters. Then, too, he had to achieve some balance

between former Whigs and former Democrats, and he felt obliged to secure a wide geographical spread by appointing one member of his original cabinet from each of the seven Confederate states, except Mississippi, which he himself represented. As a result of these elaborate calculations, Davis's cabinet consisted neither of his personal friends nor of the outstanding political leaders of the South, except for Secretary of State Robert Toombs, of Georgia, who served only briefly.

Such a cabinet might have sufficed in a country where administrative procedures and routines were firmly rooted. Instead in the Confederacy there was everywhere a lack of preparation, a lack of resources for running a government. Typical was the Confederate Treasury Department, which initially consisted of one unswept room in a Montgomery bank, "without furniture of any kind; empty . . . of desks, tables, chairs or other appliances for the conduct of business." The secretary of the treasury had to pay for the first rickety furniture out of his own pocket.

Disorganization and improvisation also characterized Lincoln's government in Washington. The Union had the advantage of owning the Capitol, the White House, and the permanent records of the United States government, and it had a recognized flag and a postal system. But in other respects it was thoroughly demoralized. Lincoln's government had no clear mandate from the people, for the president had received less than 40 percent of the popular vote in the 1860 election. It had an army of only 14,657 men, and every day army and navy officers announced that they were defecting to the South. Its treasury was empty. Some of the most experienced clerks in the Washington offices were leaving to join the Confederacy, and others who remained were of suspect loyalty. Adding to the confusion was the fact that Lincoln's was the first Republican administration and under the prevailing spoils system, party workers who had helped elect the Republican candidate now flocked to Washington, expecting to oust Democratic officeholders. Accompanied by their representatives or senators and bearing huge rolls of recommending letters, the office seekers besieged Lincoln in the White House. Wryly the president compared himself to an innkeeper whose clients demanded that he rent rooms in one wing of his hotel while he was trying to put out a fire in the other.

To add to the confusion, not one member of the Lincoln administration had previously held a responsible position in the executive branch of the national government, and many, including the president himself, had no administrative experience of any sort. Like Davis, Lincoln made no attempt to form a coalition government; for his cabinet he did not choose leaders of the Douglas Democracy or the Constitutional Union party. Nor after a few unsuccessful efforts did he name Unionists from the South. Instead, all members of his cabinet were Republicans. That fact, however, scarcely gave his government unity, for several of Lincoln's cabinet appointees had themselves been candidates for the Republican nomination in 1860 and hence were rivals of Lincoln and of each other. The most conspicuous member was Secretary of State William H. Seward, wily and devious, extravagant in utterance but cautious in action, who felt that he had a duty to save the country through compromise and conciliation despite its bumbling, inexperienced president. Seward's principal rival in the cabinet was Secretary of the Treasury Salmon P. Chase, pompous and self-righteous, who had an equally condescending view of Lincoln's talents and who lusted to become the next president of the United States. The other members, with whom Lincoln had had only the slightest personal acquaintance, were appointed because they were supposed to have political influence or to represent key states.

Winning the Border States

Desperately needing time to get organized, these two shaky rival administrations immediately confronted a problem and a crisis, which were intimately interrelated. The problem concerned the future of the eight remaining slave states, which had not yet seceded. Though tied to the Deep South by blood and sentiment and fearful of abolitionist attacks upon their "peculiar institution" of slavery, these states had refused to rush out of the Union. In January 1861,

ABRAHAM LINCOLN
"Probably," wrote Walt Whitman, "the reader has seen physiognomies . . . that, behind their homeliness or even ugliness, held superior points so subtle, yet so palpable, making the real life of their faces almost as impossible to depict as a wild perfume or fruit taste . . . such was Lincoln's face—the peculiar color, the lines of it, the eyes, mouth, expression. Of technical beauty it had nothing—but to the eye of a great artist it furnished a rare study, a feast, and fascination." *(Library of Congress)*

Virginia had elected a convention to consider secession, but it dillydallied and did nothing. In February, North Carolinians and Tennesseans voted against holding secession conventions. When the Arkansas and Missouri conventions did meet in March, they voted not to secede. Up to April 1861, Kentucky, Maryland, and Delaware held no elections or conventions. But the loyalty of all these states to the Union was clearly conditional upon the policy Lincoln's government adopted toward the Confederacy.

Crisis Over Fort Sumter.   The crisis was the first test of that policy. It concerned the fate of the United States installations in the seceded states that still remained under Federal control. At Fort Pickens in Pensacola Bay, an uneasy truce held between the Union troops in the garrison and the Confederate force on the mainland. The real trouble spot was Fort Sumter, in the harbor of Charleston, South Carolina. Its garrison, which consisted of about seventy Union soldiers and nine officers under the command of Major Robert Anderson, was no serious military threat to the Confederacy, but its presence at Charleston, the very center of secession, was an intolerable affront to Southern pride. Confederates insisted that President Davis demonstrate his devotion to the Southern cause by forcing Anderson and his men out immediately. Many Northerners, who had despairingly watched during the final months of the Buchanan administration as fort after fort was turned over to the Confederates, also saw Sumter as a test of the strength and will of the Lincoln administration.

Despite these pressures, there were in both governments powerful voices that urged compromise or at least delay. All but two members of Lincoln's cabinet initially thought that Sumter should be evacuated. Davis's secretary of state was equally adverse to hasty action. When the Confederate cabinet discussed attacking Fort Sumter, Toombs solemnly warned: "The firing upon that fort will inaugurate a civil war greater than any the world has yet seen."

But Anderson's situation made some action necessary. After Charleston authorities prohibited further sale of food to the troops in the fort, his men faced starvation. The day after Lincoln was inaugurated he learned that the garrison, unless supplied, could hold out no longer than April 15. Since Lincoln had just pledged that he would "hold, occupy, and possess" all places and property belonging to the government, he promptly directed his secretary of the navy to begin outfitting an expedition to provision Fort Sumter. At the same time, recognizing how dangerously explosive the Charleston situation was, he explored alternatives. One possibility was to reinforce Fort Pickens, in the relatively calm area of Florida; that would allow Lincoln to demonstrate his firmness of purpose, even if he was obliged to withdraw Anderson from the Charleston harbor. But the naval expedition sent to Florida miscarried, the Union commander at Pickens misunderstood his orders, and the planned reinforcement could not be completed in time for Washington to know about it before Anderson's deadline for surrender. Another possibility was to consent to a peaceable withdrawal from Fort Sumter in return for assurances that the still vacillating border states would remain in the Union. "If you will guarantee to me the State of Virginia, I shall remove the troops," Lincoln confidentially promised a prominent Virginia Unionist. "A State for a fort is no bad business." But the Virginians delayed, a rainstorm kept a delegation of Unionists from reaching Washington, and they could give no firm promises. Seeing no other possible course, Lincoln let the expedition bearing food and supplies sail for Sumter.

President Davis understood that in merely supplying Fort Sumter Lincoln was not committing an act of aggression. Indeed, he predicted that for political reasons the United States government would avoid making an attack so long as the hope of retaining the border states remained. But the Confederate president's hand was forced too. Hot-headed Governor Francis Pickens and other South Carolina extremists, impatient with Davis's caution, prepared to attack the fort. Rather than let Confederate policy be set by a state governor, Davis ordered General P. G. T. Beauregard, in command of the Confederate forces at Charleston, to demand the surrender of Fort Sumter. Anderson responded that he would soon be starved out, but he failed to promise to withdraw by a definite date. Beauregard's officers felt they had no alternative but to reduce the fort. At 4:30 A.M. on April 12 firing began. Outside the harbor the relief expedition Lincoln had sent watched impotently while Confederates bombarded the fort. After thirty-four hours, with ammunition nearly exhausted, Anderson was obliged to surrender.

Promptly Lincoln called for 75,000 volunteer soldiers to put down the "insurrection" in the South. On

May 6 the Confederate Congress countered by formally declaring that a state of war existed. The American Civil War had begun.

Both at that time and later there was controversy about the responsibility for precipitating the conflict. Critics claimed that Lincoln by sending the expedition to provision Fort Sumter deliberately tricked the Confederates into firing the first shot. Indeed, some months after the event Lincoln himself told a friend that his plan for sending supplies to Major Anderson had "succeeded." "They attacked Sumter," he explained; "it fell, and thus, did more service than it otherwise could." That statement clearly reveals Lincoln's wish that if hostilities began, the Confederacy should bear the blame for initiating them, but it does little to prove that Lincoln wanted war. It is well to remember that throughout the agonizing crisis the Confederates took the initiative at Sumter. It was Charleston authorities who cut off Anderson's food supply; it was Confederate authorities who decided that, though the fort offered no military threat, Anderson must surrender; and it was the Southerners who fired the first shot. Writing privately to the Confederate commander at Fort Pickens, President Davis acknowledged that there would be a psychological advantage if the Southerners waited for the Federal government to make the initial attack; but, he added, "When we are ready to relieve our territory and jurisdiction of the presence of a foreign garrison that advantage is overbalanced by other considerations." These other considerations impelled Davis to demand the surrender of Fort Sumter.

Decisions in the Border States. If intent can be tested by consequences, it is evident that, initially at least, it was the Confederacy, not the Union, that benefited from the attack upon Fort Sumter. The slave states still in the Union had now to make a choice of allegiances, and for a time it seemed that all would join the Confederacy. Virginia Governor John Letcher spurned Lincoln's call for troops as a bid "to inaugurate civil war," and on April 17 the state convention hastily passed a secession ordinance. Technically it was subject to popular ratification, but in actuality it immediately linked to the Confederacy the most

populous and influential state of the Upper South, with its long tradition of leadership, its vast natural resources, and its large Tredegar Iron Works.

Other border slave states acted only a little less precipitously. On May 6 the Arkansas convention voted, with only five dissenters, to withdraw from the Union. When Lincoln's call for troops reached Governor Isham Harris of Tennessee, he replied haughtily: "In such an unholy crusade no gallant son of Tennessee will ever draw his sword," and began private negotiations with Confederate officials. On May 7 the Tennessee state legislature ratified the arrangements Harris had already made and voted to secede. On May 20 the North Carolina convention, under pressure from pro-Confederate newspapers to withdraw forever from the "vile, rotten, infidelic, puritanic, negro-worshipping, negro-stealing, negro-equality . . . Yankee-Union," unanimously adopted a secession ordinance.

Far to the west, the Confederacy scored another victory in the Indian Territory (later to become the state of Oklahoma). Confederate Commissioner Albert Pike had little success with the Plains Indians there, but he won over most of the so-called civilized tribes, many of whom were slaveholders. The Confederacy agreed to pay all annuities that the United States government had previously provided, and it allowed the Choctaws, Chickasaws, Creeks, Seminoles, and Cherokees to send delegates to the Confederate Congress. In return these tribes promised to supply troops for the Confederate army. Most of them loyally supported the Southern effort throughout the war, and the Cherokee chief, Brigadier General Stand Watie, did not formally surrender until a month after the war was over. A rival faction among the Cherokees, headed by Chief John Ross, and most of the Plains Indians favored the Union cause.

Elsewhere along the border, the Confederacy fared less well. Though it was a slave state with sentimental ties to the South, Delaware never really contemplated secession. Much more painful was the decision of Maryland, a state bitterly divided. On April 19 a pro-Confederate mob in Baltimore fired upon a Massachusetts regiment en route to Washington, and communications were then cut between

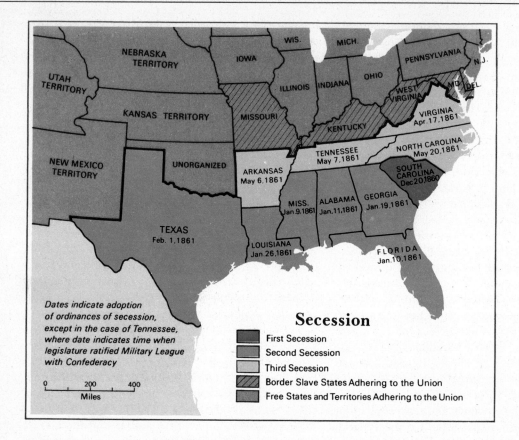

Dates indicate adoption
of ordinances of secession,
except in the case of Tennessee,
where date indicates time when
legislature ratified Military League
with Confederacy

0   200   400
Miles

Secession

First Secession
Second Secession
Third Secession
Border Slave States Adhering to the Union
Free States and Territories Adhering to the Union

the Union capital and the rest of the country. For a time it seemed highly probable that Maryland would secede. But Lincoln arranged for further shipments of Union troops to bypass Baltimore until passions could cool. By May, Baltimore was back under Federal control, and the mayor, along with nineteen members of the state legislature, was unceremoniously arrested and jailed without trial. In the 1861 fall elections, Maryland chose an uncompromising Unionist as governor, and thereafter there was no further question of secession.

In Missouri the Union cause was managed with less skill. Though the pro-Southern governor denounced Lincoln's call for troops as "illegal, unconstitutional, revolutionary, inhuman, [and] diabolical," public opinion was so evenly divided that no steps toward secession probably would have occurred had not Union Commander Nathaniel Lyon precipitated

hostilities by overrunning an encampment of pro-secessionist militia near St. Louis. Confederate sympathizers rallied to protect them, and for two days there was bloody street fighting in the city. Open warfare followed. Union forces controlled the area around St. Louis; secessionists commanded by Sterling Price, most of the rest of the state. After General John C. Frémont became commander of the department of the West, with his headquarters in St. Louis, the territory under Union control was gradually extended. During the next three years, guerrilla warfare devastated the Missouri countryside, as neighbor fought neighbor. The bitterness was further aggravated when free-soil men from Kansas, remembering how Missouri "border ruffians" had once tried to extend slavery into their state, crossed the border to take revenge upon secessionist sympathizers. In turn, Confederate gangs, the most notorious led by the horse thief and murderer William C. Quantrill, preyed upon Missouri Unionists.

Far more skillful was Lincoln's handling of Kentucky, which was his native state as well as that of Jefferson Davis. As in Missouri, the governor was an outright secessionist, but strong Unionist sentiment prevented the calling of a state convention. Out of this statemate rose the anomalous situation of Kentucky declaring itself neutral in any conflict between the United States and the Confederacy. Between May and September of 1861 both the Lincoln and the Davis governments ostensibly acquiesced in this policy of neutrality; at the same time, each tried quietly to strengthen the hands of its partisans in Kentucky. Finally, suspecting that Federal forces were about to seize a position in Kentucky, the Confederates moved first and took Columbus. Union troops then entered Paducah, and neutrality was dead. These months of indeterminate status gave Kentucky Unionists a chance to plan and organize, so that the state did not, like Tennessee, join the Confederacy nor, like Missouri, become a fierce battleground. In bringing about this outcome, Lincoln himself played a large role, for he gave Kentucky affairs close attention and took pains to assure prominent Kentuckians in private interviews that he "intended to make no attack, direct or indirect, upon the institution or property [meaning slavery] of any State."

Although most Virginians favored the Confederacy, the Union had loyal supporters in the western counties of that state, long disaffected from the planter oligarchy of the tidewater region and little interested in slavery. When the Virginia convention voted for secession, a sizable minority of the delegates, mostly from these western counties, were opposed, and they went home vowing to keep their state in the Union. A series of exceedingly complex maneuvers followed, including the summoning of several more or less extralegal conventions and the creating of a new government for what was termed "reorganized" Virginia, rivaling that at Richmond. This "reorganized" government then gave permission—as required by the United States Constitution—for the counties west of the mountains to form a new and overwhelmingly Unionist state of West Virginia. Not until 1863, when

all these steps were completed, was the new state admitted to the Union. Thus by that date there were no fewer than three state governments on Virginia soil: the pro-Confederate government at Richmond; the "reorganized" pro-Union government, which had only a small constituency and huddled under the protection of Federal guns at Alexandria; and the new Union government of West Virginia.

In summary then, after the firing of Fort Sumter, the border slave states divided. Virginia, Arkansas, Tennessee, and North Carolina went with the Confederacy; Delaware, Maryland, Missouri, and Kentucky remained in the Union, where they were presently joined by West Virginia.

Importance of the Border States. It is impossible to exaggerate the importance that these decisions, made early in the conflict, had upon the conduct of the Civil War. For the Confederacy, the accession of states from the Upper South was essential. For all the brave talk at Montgomery, the Confederacy was not a viable nation so long as it consisted only of the seven states of the Deep South. So limited, its population was only one-sixth of that of the remaining states of the Union. In all the Gulf states in 1861 there was not a foundry to roll heavy iron plate or to cast cannon, nor a large powder works, nor indeed a single factory of importance. But when Virginia, North Carolina, Arkansas, and Tennessee joined the Confederacy, they almost doubled its population. What is more, they brought to the new nation the natural resources, the foundries and factories, and the skilled artisans that made it possible to rival the Union. To recognize the economic and psychological strength added by these states of the Upper South—and also to escape the sweltering summer heats of Montgomery—the Confederacy in May 1861 removed its capital from Montgomery to Richmond.

If the states of the Upper South brought the Confederacy strength they also limited its freedom of action. So important were Richmond and Virginia that defending this area became the passion of the Confederate government, so absorbing that it neglected the vital western theaters of military operations.

For Lincoln's government, too, the border states were vital. If Maryland had seceded, the capital at Washington would have been surrounded by enemy territory, cut off from the Union states of the North and the West. Confederate control of Kentucky would have imperiled river transportation along the Ohio, and the secession of Missouri would have endangered Mississippi river traffic and cut off communication with Kansas and the Pacific coast. While Lincoln grieved over the secession of the states that joined the Confederacy, he could take comfort in the fact that by keeping four slave states in the Union he was preventing the Southern armies from recruiting from a population that was three-fifths as large as that of the original Confederacy.

So important were the border states for the Union government that special pains had to be taken not to disturb their loyalty. In particular, Lincoln saw that there must be no premature action against slavery. European nations might fail to understand the nature of the American Civil War and Northern abolitionists might denounce their president as "the slave-hound from Illinois," but Lincoln knew that to tamper with slavery would result in the loss of the border states, particularly Kentucky. "I think to lose Kentucky is nearly the same as to lose the whole game," he wrote to a friend. "Kentucky gone, we cannot hold Missouri, nor, as I think, Maryland. These all against us, and the job on our hands is too large for us. We would as well consent to separation at once, including the surrender of this capitol."

Raising the Armies

While Lincoln and Davis were moving in parallel fashion to win the support of the border states, ordinary folk, North and South, were rallying around their flags. On both sides the firing on Fort Sumter triggered a rush to enlist. "War! and volunteers are the only topics of conversation or thought," an Oberlin College student reported when the news reached Ohio. "The lessons today have been a mere form. I cannot study. I cannot sleep, I cannot work, and I don't know as I can write." An Arkansas youth recorded identical emotions: "So impatient did I become

for starting that I felt like a thousand pins were pricking me in every part of the body and [I] started off a week in advance of my brothers."

The Rush to Volunteer.   Ordinarily a volunteer offered to enlist in one of the regiments that was being raised in his community. Wealthy citizens and prominent politicians usually took the lead in recruiting

UNITED STATES VOLUNTEERS
In both the Union and the Confederacy the first step in raising a regiment was often the publication of a broadside like this one *(shown right)* calling for volunteers. *(Library of Congress)*

PRIVATE JOHN WERTH, RICHMOND HOWITZER BATTALION, C.S.A. *(below)* AND AN ILLINOIS VOLUNTEER OF 1861 *(lower right)*
As soon as volunteers were sworn in and received their uniforms and equipment, most rushed to photographers' studios to have pictures made for their loved ones. *(Below, The Museum of the Confederacy, Richmond; right, Library of Congress)*

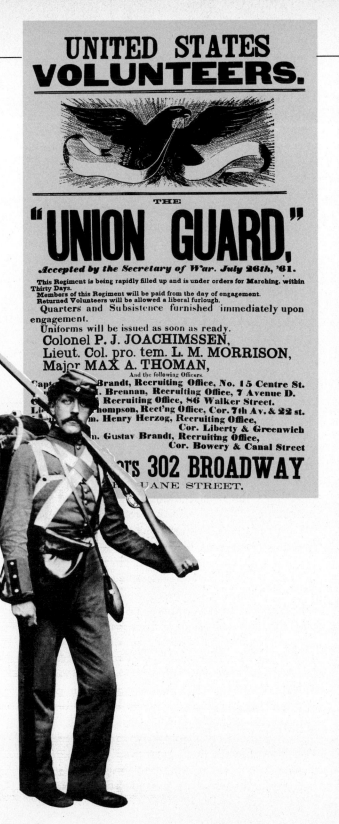

these companies. Inevitably these regiments displayed a wide variety of arms, ranging from rusty flintlocks to the latest sharpshooting rifles. Often their uniforms bore distinctive insignia; for instance, a Louisiana battalion recruited from the daredevil New Orleans roustabouts called themselves the Tigers, and their scarlet skullcaps bore mottoes like "Tiger on the Leap" and "Tiger in Search of a Black Republican." Perhaps the most colorful, and impractical, uniforms were those of the Northern Zouave regiments, dressed in imitation of the French troops in North Africa. These soldiers, wearing their red fezzes, scarlet baggy trousers, and blue sashes, were magnificent in a military review, but when they had to wade across a stream, their baggy garments ballooned around them and they floated down the current like so many exotic waterlilies. When a regiment's ranks were filled, there was invariably a farewell ceremony, featuring hortatory addresses, lengthy prayers, and the presentation of the regimental flag, often hand-sewn by patriotic wives and sweethearts of the enlisted men. Then, loaded with hams, cakes, and sweetmeats provided by fond mothers and wives, the men went off to war.

Wartime Maladministration. Neither Union nor Confederate War Departments knew what to do with this flood of volunteers. Leroy P. Walker, the first Confederate secretary of war, had had no military training and no administrative experience. An amiable Southern gentleman, fond of prolonged conversation with visitors, of writing discursive three-page business letters, and of filing his correspondence by piling it in a chair after he had read it, Walker was wholly unable to cope with the situation. Complaining that he lacked equipment and arms, he refused the services of regiment after regiment. Perhaps 200,000 Confederate volunteers were thus rejected during the first year of the war.

The Northern war office was equally chaotic. Simon Cameron, the secretary of war, had been forced upon Lincoln as part of a political bargain. Cameron's main objective was to become the undisputed boss of Pennsylvania politics. There is no evidence that he used his cabinet position to line his own pockets, but he did employ his huge patronage to strengthen his faction of Pennsylvania Republicans. Lacking administrative talents, Cameron like Walker, simply could not deal with the flood of volunteers, nor could he supervise the hundreds of contracts his office had to make for arms, ammunition, uniforms, horses, and dozens of other articles for the army. Inevitably there was haste, inefficiency, and corruption. For instance, in October 1861, General Frémont, desperately needing mounts for his cavalry in Missouri, contracted to purchase 411 horses. Subsequent investigation proved that 350 of the beasts supplied him were undersized, under or overaged, ringboned, blind, spavined, and incurably unfit for service; 5 were dead. Unable to equip the Union volunteers as they rushed to defend the flag, Cameron thought it was his principal duty "to avoid receiving troops faster than the government can provide for them."

As the war wore on, the initial enthusiasm for volunteering abated, and many of the men rejected by Walker and Cameron in the early months of the conflict were never available again. Soon even those whose services had been accepted began to exhibit less enthusiasm for the war. Most had expected the army to be like the peacetime militia, to which all able-bodied white men belonged; the monthly militia rallies had been the occasion for fun and frolic, punctuated by a little, uneven military drill, a considerable amount of political oratory, and a great deal of drinking. Now they discovered that war was not a lark. Belonging to the army meant discipline, spit-and-polish cleaning of equipment, and hours of close-order drill. A soldier's life was one of endless monotony, punctuated occasionally by danger from enemy bullets and more frequently by disease resulting from inadequate food and clothing, lack of vaccination, filthy drinking water, and open latrines. By the end of 1861, many Union volunteers were beginning to count the weeks until the end of their three-year term of enlistment. Confederate regiments, which had been enrolled for twelve months, were about ready to disband in the spring of 1862.

Reorganization and Conscription. Of necessity, then, Lincoln and Davis moved, almost simultaneously, to strengthen their War Departments in order to give more central direction to their armies. In January 1862, having persuaded Cameron to become American minister to Russia, Lincoln named a former Democrat, Edwin M. Stanton, to the War Department. Brusque and imperious, Stanton quickly reorganized the War Department, regularized procedures for letting war contracts, and investigated frauds. Standing behind an old-fashioned writing desk, looking like an irritable schoolmaster before a willful class, Stanton heard all War Department business in public. Patronage seekers, even when accompanied by congressmen, he brusquely dismissed; contractors had to state their prices in clear, loud voices; and even a petitioner bearing a letter of introduction from the president might be abruptly shown the door. Working incessantly, Stanton saw to it that the Union army became the best supplied military force the world had ever seen.

It took a bit longer for Davis to find a war secretary to his liking. When Walker, to everyone's relief, resigned in September 1861, Davis replaced him briefly with Judah P. Benjamin, who subsequently became Confederate secretary of state, and then with George Wythe Randolph, who did much to see that Robert E. Lee and Thomas J. ("Stonewall") Jackson had the necessary arms and supplies for their 1862 campaigns. But when Randolph and Davis disagreed over strategy, the secretary had to go, and in November 1862 James A. Seddon succeeded Randolph. Sallow and cadaverous, looking, as one of his clerks remarked, like "an exhumed corpse after a month's interment," Seddon was nevertheless diligent and efficient. Moreover, he had the good sense to give solid support to subordinates of great ability. Perhaps the most competent of these was General Josiah Gorgas, head of the Confederate ordnance bureau. Thanks to Gorgas's exertions, the Confederacy, which in May 1861 had only about 20 cartridges for each musket or rifle, by 1862 built powder plants capable of producing 20 million cartridges—enough to supply an army of 400,000 men for twelve months.

While both presidents were strengthening their War Departments, they also moved, in 1862, to take a more active role in recruiting troops. Because the twelve-month period of enlistment of Confederate troops expired in the spring, Davis warned that the Southern army would be decimated just as Federal forces were approaching Richmond. Uncomfortably ignoring the principle of state sovereignty proclaimed in the Confederate Constitution, the Southern Congress on April 16, 1862, passed a national conscription act, which made every able-bodied white male between the ages of eighteen and thirty-five subject to military service. This first conscription law in American history, however, allowed for numerous exemptions, ranging from druggists to Confederate government officials; and a subsequent law excused from military service planters or overseers supervising twenty or more slaves. The purpose of the Con-

federate conscription act was less to raise new troops than to encourage veterans to reenlist. If the men stayed in the army, the law provided, they could remain in their present regiments and elect new officers; if they left, it threatened, they could be drafted and assigned to any unit that needed them.

Lincoln's government moved toward conscription a little more slowly. After the bloody campaigns in the summer of 1862, volunteering all but stopped, and the army needed 300,000 new men. Union governors suggested to the president that a draft would stimulate volunteering, and on July 17 the Federal Congress passed a loosely worded measure authorizing the president to set quotas of troops to be raised

PRESENTATION OF COLORS, 1ST MICHIGAN INFANTRY, MAY, 1861

Regiments were raised under state, not national, auspices. Before a regiment left home to join the Union or Confederate army, there was usually a formal ceremony, where the governor or some other high-ranking state official made a patriotic speech and presented the fighting men with their regimental flag. *(Courtesy of the Burton Historical Collection of the Detroit Public Library)* by each state and empowering him to use Federal force to draft them if state officials failed to meet their quotas. Intentionally a bogeyman, which the governors used to encourage enlistments, this first Union conscription law brought in only a handful of men.

Financing the War

If it became hard for both the Union and the Confederate governments to raise troops, it was even harder to supply and pay them. Though the United States in 1860 was potentially one of the great industrial nations of the world, it was still primarily an agricultural country, with five out of six of its inhabitants living on farms. The factories that would be called upon to supply vast armies were mostly small in scale. Some 239 companies manufactured firearms in 1860; their average invested capital was less than $11,000. Textile mills, especially for the manufacture of woolens, were larger, but ready-made clothing was still sewn in small shops. The country produced an abundance of foodstuffs, but there was no effective wholesale marketing system for meat and grain. Maps showed that by 1860 the country was crisscrossed by 30,000 miles of railroads, but most of these were in fact short spans, each under its own corporate management, often not connected to other lines at common terminals and even having different rail gauges. The sending of a boxcar from, say, Baltimore to St. Louis was an undertaking that required diplomacy, improvisation, frequent transshipment, long delays, and a great deal of luck. Commercial transactions were impeded by the fact that the United States in 1860 had no national bank; indeed, it did not even have a national currency, for the bills issued by the numerous state banks, depreciating at various rates, formed the principal circulating medium.

Problems of the Treasury Departments.   Yet Union and Confederate leaders had somehow to mobilize this invertebrate economy so that it could support an enormous war effort. Both governments relied primarily upon privately owned factories to supply their armies, rather than upon government-operated ones. Necessity more than a theoretical preference

for free enterprise lay behind this choice. If individual businessmen and corporations had little experience in the large-scale production of goods, the civil servants at Washington and Richmond had even less. Where it seemed useful, both governments supplemented the output of private undustry with production from government-owned plants. While the Lincoln administration was purchasing firearms from Colt, Remington, and dozens of other manufacturers, it continued to rely upon its own armories, especially the one at Springfield, Massachusetts, for some of its best weapons. Because the South was even more largely rural and agricultural than the North, it had to be more active in establishing government-owned plants, the most successful of which was the huge powder factory at Augusta, Georgia. But both governments contracted with private individuals and corporations for most of the arms, clothing, and other equipment needed for the armies.

It was easier to contract for supplies than it was to pay for them. Both Union and Confederacy began the war with empty treasuries. When Secretary of the Treasury Chase took up his duties in Washington, he was horrified to discover that between April and June 1861 the expenses of the Union government would exceed its income by $17 million. Inexperienced in financial matters, Chase, whose reputation had been built on his work as an antislavery lawyer and politician, desperately cast about for solutions.

Chase's difficulties were nothing compared to those of his Confederate counterpart, Christopher G. Memminger, who had to make bricks without clay as well as without straw. Like Chase, Memminger had no extensive experience in financial matters, and his neat, systematic mind was troubled by the free and easy ways of government finance during wartime. He did what he could to bring about order—by requiring Confederate Treasury employees to keep regular 9-to-5 hours, by outlawing drinking on the job and by insisting that his visitors curb their customary garrulity and state their business. Such measures, however, did little to solve Confederate financial difficulties.

Sources of Revenue.   Neither secretary seriously thought of financing the war through levying taxes.

26TH NEW YORK INFANTRY AT FORT LYON, VIRGINIA
Once accepted into the Union or Confederate army, volunteers found they had a great deal still to learn before they were soldiers. These New York volunteers, manning the fortifications surrounding Washington, were receiving lessons in close-order drill. *(Library of Congress)*

For either the Union or the Confederacy to impose heavy taxation in 1861 might well have killed the citizens' ardor for war. Americans simply were not used to paying taxes to their national government; there had been no federal excise duties during the thirty-five years before the war. In 1860 the United States Treasury had no internal revenue division, no assessors, no inspectors, and no agents. Since tariffs were a more familiar method of raising revenues, both secretaries hoped for large customs receipts. But when Republicans in the Union Congress passed the highly protective Morrill Tariff in 1861 and raised rates even higher in 1862, they effectively killed that source of revenue. Similarly, the Union blockade of the South reduced the amount and value of goods brought into Confederate ports and cut the Southern income from tariffs. In desperation the Union government resorted to a direct tax (levied upon each state in proportion to population) of $20 million in August 1861; much of it was never collected. The same month the Confederates imposed a "war tax" of 0.5 percent on taxable wealth. Davis's government, like Lincoln's, had to rely upon the states to collect this tax, and most of them preferred issuing bonds or notes rather than levying duties upon their people.

In neither country was borrowing a realistic possibility for financing the war. Products of the Jacksonian era with its suspicion of paper certificates of indebtedness, Americans of the 1860s were a people who preferred to hoard rather than invest their surplus funds. The rival Union and Confederate governments themselves shared this same suspicion of paper and this trust in specie. In the North, Secretary Chase insisted that the banks of New York, Philadelphia, and Boston subscribe to a $150 million federal bond issue, but he was unwilling to take anything but gold or silver in payment. The drain on the banks' reserves, coupled with uncertainty over the course of the war, forced Northern banks to suspend specie payment for their notes in December 1861. Nor was Chase more successful in his early attempts to sell Union bonds directly to small investors. The Confederacy followed much the same course in its borrowing. An initial loan of $15 million was quickly subscribed to, with the result that Southern banks, including the strong institutions of New Orleans, were obliged to give up virtually all their specie to the new government; consequently they could no longer redeem their notes in gold or silver. Memminger's attempt to sell subsequent Confederate bonds directly to the Southern people ran into the difficulty that nobody had any specie. Urged by Vice-President Alexander H. Stephens and other Confederate orators, planters in the fall of 1861 subscribed tobacco, rice, cotton, and other commodities to purchase bonds. Since the Union blockade cut off the market for these products, the Confederate government realized little from the loan.

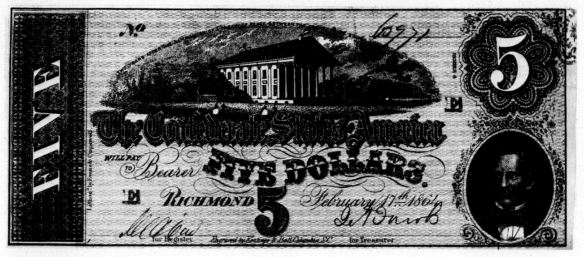

CONFEDERATE PAPER MONEY
Both the Confederacy and the Union were obliged to resort to paper money in order to finance the war. In the South engravers were few and incompetent. As a result the likenesses they produced of President Davis and other Confederate officials were so unprepossessing as to raise doubts about the artists' loyalty to the Southern cause.

Recourse to Paper Money. In consequence, by early 1862 both governments moved to the issue of paper money, backed only by the promise that it would some day be redeemed in specie. Both Treasury secretaries came reluctantly to this policy. Memminger, a prominent hard-money advocate before the war, was obliged to resort to the printing presses in 1861. The Confederacy issued $100 million in paper money in August 1861, and the next year it printed millions of dollars more. Having denounced "an irredeemable paper currency, than which no more certainly fatal expedient for impoverishing the masses and discrediting the government of any country, can well be devised," Chase found it even more embarrassing than Memminger to resort to treasury notes. But by January 1862 he had no alternative. Declaring that an issue of paper money was now "indispensably necessary," he persuaded Congress to authorize the printing of $150 million in non-interest–bearing United States treasury notes (which were promptly dubbed "greenbacks," because of their color). Rarely does history provide such a tidy illustration of how huge impersonal forces overrule the preference and will of individual statesmen.

Wartime Diplomacy

In diplomacy as in economic policy the Union and the Confederacy moved along parallel paths during the first two years of the war. Neither Lincoln nor Davis had much knowledge of diplomacy or took an active role in the conduct of foreign policy. Both, however, had difficulties with their secretaries of state. Seward, Lincoln's principal adviser, would ultimately rank as one of the greatest secretaries of state, but in the early stages of the Civil War he gave evidence of wild eccentricity, coupled with personal ambition. At the height of the Sumter crisis, he submitted to Lincoln a private memorandum complaining that the government as yet had no policy for dealing with secession, announcing his readiness to take over the president's function and shape a suitable policy, and suggesting that the proper course for the administration was to "change the question before the public from one upon slavery . . . for a question upon union or disunion" by precipitating a confrontation with foreign powers. If allowed, Seward would "seek explanations from Great Britain and Russia"— for what offenses he did not specify; he "would demand explanations from Spain and France, categorically, at once," presumably over their threatened intervention in the affairs of Santo Domingo and Mexico; and if Spain and France did not respond forthwith, he would urge a declaration of war against these powers. Lincoln, to his enduring credit, quietly filed away this memorandum, refrained from dismissing a secretary who planned to bring on a world war, and allowed Seward time to return to his senses.

Despite Lincoln's reticence, word of Seward's bellicosity leaked out in conversation at Washington dinner tables, and diplomats at the capital soon had a pretty good idea of what was in the secretary's mind. From the diplomatic dispatches, European governments during the first two years of the war learned to view all Seward's policies with skepticism, even after the secretary had returned to sobriety and moderation. Perhaps, however, the awareness of Seward's hair-trigger temper did something to make those governments more cautious in their relations with the United States and less willing to recognize the Confederacy.

Davis, too, had trouble with his state department. Robert Toombs, the first Confederate secretary of state, was as ambitious and overbearing as he was able. It was a relief when he decided that the path to glory lay on the battlefield rather than in the cabinet and resigned to take a commission in the Southern army. His successor, R. M. T. Hunter, was equally ambitious, and—perhaps with an eye on the 1868 Confederate presidential election—he too promptly resigned, to become senator from Virginia. In March 1862, Davis finally found his man in Judah P. Benjamin, who had already been Confederate attorney general and secretary of war. Serving until the end of the war, Benjamin cleverly reflected the changing moods of his chief, but he was not an innovator in foreign policy. In the words of a critical Northerner who visited Richmond during the war, Benjamin had a "keen, shrewd, ready intellect, but not the stamina to originate, or even to execute, any great good, or great wickedness."

Union and Confederate diplomatic appointments abroad were rather a mixed lot. If Lincoln lacked tact in appointing Carl Schurz, considered a "red republican" for his participation in the German revolution of 1848, as minister to conservative, monarchical Spain, Davis showed a total failure to understand British antislavery sentiment by sending William L. Yancey, the most notorious Southern fire-eater, as first Confederate commissioner to London. On the positive side, the Union minister to Great Britain, Charles Francis Adams, exhibited the patience and restraint required in his difficult assignment; and the pride, the chilly demeanor, and the punctiliousness of this son and grandson of American presidents made him a match even for the aristocratic British foreign minister, Lord John Russell. Of the Confederate emissaries abroad, probably John Slidell of Louisiana proved ablest; wily, adroit, and unscrupulous, he was perfectly at home in the court of Napoleon III.

European Neutrality. Much to the disappointment of Americans on both sides, the attitudes of European powers toward the Civil War were not primarily shaped by the actions of American ministers, secretaries of state, or even presidents. Nor, during 1861 and 1862, were they shaped by appeals to economic self-interest. Southerners, firmly believing that cotton was king, expected that pressure from British and French textile manufacturers would compel their governments to recognize the Confederacy and to break the blockade. But as it happened, European manufacturers had an ample stockpile of cotton, purchased before the outbreak of hostilities, and were therefore not much affected when Southern cotton was cut off in 1861. By 1862 cotton mills in both Britain and France were suffering, but Union and Confederate orders for arms, ammunition, and other equipment counterbalanced these losses. There was great hardship among the workers in the cotton mills, especially in the Lancashire district of England, where unemployment was high, but their complaints were relatively ineffectual since Britain still did not allow these men to vote.

Northerners were equally disappointed by the attitude of European governments. Knowing the strength of the antislavery movement abroad, particularly in Great Britain and France, they expected the European powers to condemn the slaveholding Con-

COTTON IN THE STOCKS.

M. Mercier :—"HOW MUCH LONGER IS THIS TO LAST? OR ARE YOU WAITING
UNTIL WE INTERFERE?"

"COTTON IN THE STOCKS"

The Union blockade sealed off Southern exports of cotton and helped produce severe hardships in the textile-producing regions of Great Britain and France. This 1862 cartoon shows the French minister to Washington, Henri Mercier, threatening Uncle Sam with European intervention if the blockade is not lifted. *(Library of Congress)*

federacy. Their hope was unrealistic because, during the early years of the war, the Union government took no decisive steps toward emancipation. Indeed, Lincoln pledged that he would not interfere with slavery where it existed, Seward branded the abolitionists and "the most extreme advocates of African slavery" as equally dangerous to the Union, and Union generals helped Southern masters reclaim their runaway slaves. It was scarcely surprising that European opponents of slavery were confused and could do little to influence the attitudes of their governments toward the war in America.

What Northerners and Confederates alike failed to understand was that the policy of European states toward the Civil War would be determined largely by considerations of national self-interest. Since the Crimean War, an uneasy balance of power had prevailed in Europe, and no nation was eager to upset it by unilateral intervention in the American conflict. But concerted action by the European powers was always difficult because of mutual suspicion, and in the 1860s it was virtually impossible because of the nature of the British government. The British prime minister, Lord Palmerston, who was nearly eighty years old, headed a shaky coalition government, which was certain to fall if it undertook any decisive action. With the British government immobilized, the Russians favorable to the Union cause, and the Prussians and the Austrians mostly indifferent to the conflict, the inclination of the ambitious Napoleon III to meddle in favor of the Confederacy was effectively curbed.

As a result, European nations announced their neutrality early in the war. Queen Victoria's proclamation of May 13, 1861, was typical in recognizing that a state of war existed between the United States and "the states styling themselves the Confederate States of America" and in declaring British neutrality in that war. None of these proclamations recognized the Confederacy as a nation—that is, no one declared that it was a legitimate, independent power, entitled to send ambassadors and ministers abroad and to receive those from other nations, to enter into treaties with other powers, or, in general, to be treated just like any other sovereign state. But the proclamations did recognize the Confederates as belligerents. That meant that the Southerners were not to be considered simply as a group of riotous or insurrectionary individuals but as participants in a systematic, organized effort to set up their own independent government. Recognition as a belligerent, under international law, entitled the Confederacy to send out privateers without their being considered pirate ships. Recognition that a state of war existed in America also meant that the Union government could not simply declare Southern ports closed to foreign ships; to exclude foreign shipping it would have to maintain an effec-

tive blockade of the Confederacy. Initially these proclamations seemed a great Confederate sucess. In fact,
however, they were both necessary and warranted by
international law and, despite Seward's rantings,
were truly impartial.

The Trent Affair. In November 1861, the rash action
of a Union naval officer threatened to upset this neutrality. Learning that Davis was replacing the temporary commissioners he had sent to France and Britain
by permanent envoys, John Slidell and James M.
Mason, Union Captain Charles Wilkes decided to
capture these diplomats en route. Off the shore of
Cuba on November 8, 1861, his warship stopped the
British merchant ship, the *Trent*, Union officers
boarded and searched the vessel, and Mason and
Slidell were unceremoniously removed, to be transported to Boston for imprisonment. When news of
Wilkes's action, in clear violation of international
law, reached Europe, hostility toward the Union government flared up. "You may stand for this," Prime
Minister Palmerston told his cabinet, "but damned
if I will!" The foreign minister, Russell, drafted a
stiff letter demanding the immediate release of the
envoys. It was clear that the Lincoln government
faced a major crisis if it held its prisoners. After con-
ferring with cabinet members and senators, Lincoln
decided on Christmas day to release the Southern
envoys. He would fight only one war at a time.

Even with the firm intention of remaining neutral,
European powers found their patience tested as the
American war stretched on without apparent chance
of ending. International relations were disturbed,
commerce was disrupted, textile manufacturing was
suffering, and neither North nor South seemed able
to achieve its goal. Increasingly, support built up in
both France and Britain for offering mediation to the
combatants, and such an offer inevitably involved
recognition of the Confederacy as an independent
nation. In September 1862, Palmerston and Russell
agreed to explore a mediation plan involving France
and Russia as well as Great Britain, but pro-Union
members of the British cabinet, like the Duke of
Argyll and George Cornewall Lewis, replied with
strong arguments against mediation. Faced with dis-

"CAVALRY OFFICER" BY WINSLOW HOMER
Even after a year of combat, Americans, North and
South, could not reconcile themselves to the fact that
modern war requires regimentation. They continued to
think of themselves as individualists, like this dashing
union cavalry officer, sketched by Winslow Homer.
*(Courtesy Cooper-Hewitt Museum, The Smithsonian Institu-
tion's National Museum of Design)*

sension within his unstable coalition and given no
encouragement by Russia, Palmerston by October
1862 changed his mind and concluded that the Euro-

pean states must continue to be lookers-on till the war took a more decided turn.

Battles and Leaders

But on the battlefields in 1861 and 1862 there were no decided turns. Engagement followed engagement, campaign followed campaign, and neither side could achieve a decisive victory. The stalemate was baffling to armchair strategists, in both the South and the North, who had been sure that the war would be short and decisive, ending in an overwhelming victory for their own side.

Confederate war planners counted among their assets the fact that some of the best graduates of West Point led their armies and that President Davis himself had military training and experience. They believed that Southern men had more of a fighting spirit than Northerners, and they were probably correct in thinking that Southerners had more experience in handling firearms and were better horsemen. They knew that the Confederacy would generally act on the defensive and assumed that the offensive Union army would have to be at least three times as large as that of the South. Since Southern forces could operate on interior lines, they could move more quickly and easily than Union forces, which would have to travel longer distances. While recognizing the superiority of the Union navy, Southerners knew that the Confederacy had 3,500 miles of coastline, with innumerable hidden harbors and waterways through which shipping could escape. When Confederate strategists added to all these assets the fact that Southern soldiers were fighting on their home ground, where they knew every road and byway, they saw no reason to doubt ultimate victory.

But an equally good case could be made for the inevitability of a Union victory. The population of the Union in 1860 was about 20.7 million; that of the Confederacy, only 9.1 million. Moreover, 3.5 million of the inhabitants of the South were blacks, mostly slaves, who, it was presumed, would not be used in the Confederate armies. Along with this superiority in manpower, the North had vastly more economic strength than the Confederacy. The total value of all manufactured products in all eleven Confederate states was less than one-fourth of that of New York alone. The iron furnaces, forges, and rolling mills in the United States were heavily concentrated in the North. The North in 1860 built fourteen out of every fifteen railroad locomotives manufactured in the United States. Northern superiority in transportation would more than compensate for Southern interior lines, as only 30 percent of the total rail mileage of the United States ran through the Confederacy. The Union navy, which experienced few defections to the South, was incomparably superior, and the blockade President Lincoln announced at the outbreak of hostilities would cut off, or at least drastically reduce, Southern imports from Europe. When Northern planners added to the advantages of their side the possession of the established government, the recognition of foreign powers, and the enormous enthusiasm of the people for maintaining the Union, they could not doubt that victory would be sure and swift.

Jomini's Game Plan.   In fact, these assets substantially canceled each other during the first two years of the war and produced not victory but deadlock. As the armies engaged in complex maneuvers and in indecisive battles, Union and Confederate commanders largely employed the same strategic plans, for most had learned the art of war from the same teachers. In fifty-five of the sixty biggest battles of the war, the generals on both sides had been educated at West Point, and in the remaining five, a West Pointer led one of the opposing armies. At the military academy they had studied the theories of the French historian and strategist Baron Henri Jomini. Some read Jomini's works in the original French or in translation; more, doubtless, absorbed his ideas from the abridgement and interpretation of his work *Elementary Treatise on Advance-Guard, Outpost, and Detachment of Service of Troops* (1847), written by Dennis Hart Mahan, who for a generation taught at the academy and greatly influenced his students.

Although in fact a complex body of doctrine, subject to many differing interpretations, Jomini's

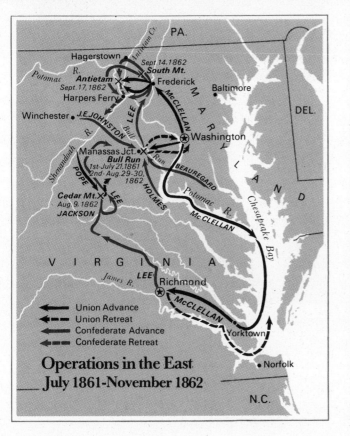

Hagerstown
PA.
Antietam Cr.
Sept. 14, 1862
South Mt.
Potomac R.
Antietam X
Sept. 17, 1862
Frederick
Baltimore
Harpers Ferry
DEL.
Winchester
J.E. JOHNSTON
LEE
McCLELLAN
M A R Y L A N D
Shenandoah R.
Bull Run
Manassas Jct. X
Bull Run
1st-July 21, 1861
2nd- Aug. 29-30, 1862
Washington
BEAUREGARD
Bull Run
POPE
LEE
HOLMES
Potomac R.
McCLELLAN
Chesapeake Bay
Cedar Mt. X
Aug. 9, 1862
JACKSON
V I R G I N I A
James R.
LEE
Richmond
McCLELLAN

→ Union Advance
⇢ Union Retreat
← Confederate Advance
⇠ Confederate Retreat

Operations in the East
July 1861-November 1862

Yorktown

• Norfolk

N.C.

military theories as understood by American commanders stressed the importance of the conquest of territory and emphasized that the seizure of the enemy's capital was "ordinarily, the objective point" of an invading army. Jomini envisaged a battle situation in which two armies were drawn up in opposing lines, one offensive, and the other defensive, and he even prepared a set of twelve diagrams showing the possible orders of battle. In all twelve, a major determinant of victory was the concentration of force—the bringing to bear of a powerful, united force upon the enemy's weakest point. Warfare was thus something like an elaborate game of chess, an art that only professional soldiers could fully master.

Most of the military operations during the first two years of the Civil War can best be understood as a kind of elaborate illustration of Jomini's theories,

slightly modified to fit the American terrain. The first big battle of the war occurred on July 21, 1861, when Union General Irwin McDowell, under much pressure from Northern newspapers and much badgered by exuberant politicians in the Congress, reluctantly pushed his poorly organized army into Virginia. He expected to encounter the Confederates, under General Beauregard, near Centreville. In the ensuing battle of Bull Run (or Manassas), both armies tried to apply the same battle plan from Jomini's treatise; each attempted a main attack upon the enemy's left flank, to be followed by a secondary thrust at his center and right wings. If completely executed, the two plans would have had the amusing result of leaving each army in its opponent's original place. But the Confederates also followed another of Jomini's principles, that of concentration of force and, using the railroad, rushed General Joseph E. Johnston's troops from the Shenandoah Valley to join Beauregard's main force. The Union troops fought bravely and initially seemed to be carrying the day, but after Johnston's men were in position, the Union army was thrown back and then routed. Weary and disorganized, Federal troops limped back to the Potomac and to safety. The Confederates were almost equally demoralized by their victory and were unable to pursue. The South's easiest opportunity to follow Jomini's maxim and seize the enemy's capital had to be given up.

After this initial engagement, it was clear that both armies needed reorganization and training before either could attempt further campaigns. As a result, despite growing impatience for action, there was little significant military action during the rest of 1861, except for minor engagements in Kentucky and Missouri. During this period General George Brinton McClellan, who was credited with some overrated small successes in western Virginia, was summoned to Washington to bring order to the Union army. With enormous dash and enthusiasm, the young commander began to whip the Federal regiments into fighting shape. He insisted on careful drill and inspection; he demanded the best of food and equipment for his men; and he refused to move forward until his army was thoroughly prepared.

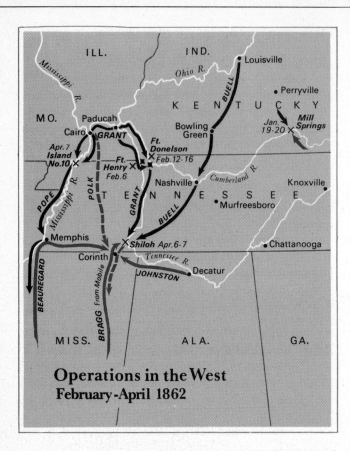

Operations in the West
February-April 1862

GENERAL GEORGE BRINTON McCLELLAN
Union General McClellan, the "Little Napoleon" of the Civil War, seemed to have everything it took to make a great general. He was handsome and brave; he was a superb organizer and administrator; and he knew all that the books taught about the art of war. But, as Lincoln painfully found out, McClellan had one great fault: he had "the slows." *(National Archives)*

The War in the West, 1862. By early 1862, Union armies, not merely those in the East but in all the theaters of war, were ready to advance, and, taking advantage of numerical superiority, Union commanders concentrated their forces on a series of weak spots in the Confederate defenses, just as Jomini had directed. In January, General George H. Thomas defeated a Confederate force at Mill Springs, Kentucky, and made a significant break in the Southern defense line west of the mountains. The next month General Ulysses S. Grant made an even more important breach in that line, when in collaboration with the Union gunboats on the Tennessee and Cumberland rivers, he captured Fort Henry and Fort Donelson, requiring the Confederate army in the latter fort to accept his terms of unconditional surrender.

The Southerners now had to abandon Tennessee.

Union armies under Grant and Don Carlos Buell pushed rapidly after them until checked at the battle of Shiloh (April 6–7). Dissatisfied with Grant's generalship, General Henry Wager Halleck, who was the Union commander for the entire western theater, took personal charge of the army after Shiloh. A dedicated disciple of Jomini, whose works he had translated, Halleck concentrated his force for a push on Corinth, Mississippi, in order to break the important rail connection that linked Memphis and the western portion of the Confederacy with the East.

The Peninsula Campaign. A Union advance in the eastern theater promised to be equally successful. After long delays, McClellan began his offensive against Richmond, not by going directly overland, but by transporting his troops to Fort Monroe, on the peninsula between the York and James rivers. Bitterly complaining because Lincoln violated the principle of concentration and held back 40,000 troops to defend Washington, McClellan nevertheless prepared to follow Jomini's maxims and seize the Confederate capital.

At this point in the gigantic, synchronized Union offensive, designed to crush the Confederacy, everything began to go wrong. The difficulties stemmed partly from human inadequacies. Although good theoreticians and able administrators, Halleck and McClellan were indecisive fighters. Halleck took nearly two months to creep from Shiloh to Corinth, stopping to fortify his position each night. By the time he reached his destination, the Southern army had moved south with all its provisions. Equally cautious was McClellan's advance on the Peninsula, where he allowed 16,000 Confederate soldiers under General John B. Magruder to hold up his magnificent army of 112,000 until the Confederates could bring reinforcements to Richmond. The trouble was partly that these Union campaigns required the coordinated movement of forces larger than anything seen before on the American continent, though few of the commanding officers had ever led anything larger than a regiment. But chiefly the Union failure was due to the fact that able Confederate generals had read the same books on strategy as the Union commanders and knew how to fight the same kinds of battles.

While McClellan slowly edged his way up the Peninsula, Confederate Commander Joseph E. Johnston, who had rushed in with reinforcements, kept close watch until the Union general injudiciously allowed his forces to be divided by the flooded Chickahominy River. Applying Jomini's principle of concentration on the enemy's weakest spot, Johnston on May 31–June 1 fell upon the exposed Union wing in battles at Fair Oaks (or Seven Pines), which narrowly failed of being a Confederate triumph. When Johnston was wounded in this engagement, President Davis chose Robert E. Lee to replace him.

Lee quickly revealed his military genius by showing that he knew when to follow Jomini's principles and when to flout them. Remembering from his days

at West Point how slow McClellan was, Lee allowed "Stonewall" Jackson to take 18,000 men from the main army for a daring campaign through the Shenandoah Valley. Jackson defeated and demoralized the Union forces in the Shenandoah and so threatened Washington that Lincoln withheld reinforce-

UNION ORDNANCE READY FOR TRANSPORTATION FROM YORKTOWN
For McClellan's push up the Peninsula in the hope of capturing Richmond, the Union war department assembled the largest collection of men and materiel ever collected on the American continent. But, as events proved, Union generalship did not equal Union resources. *(National Archives)*

ments that he had promised McClellan. When Jackson had accomplished this objective, Lee reverted to the principle of concentration and ordered Jackson promptly to rejoin the main army before Richmond. The combined Confederate force fell upon McClellan's exposed right flank at Mechanicsville. Lee failed to crush McClellan; but in a series of engagements known as the Seven Days (June 25–July 1), he forced the Union army to beat a slow, hard-fought retreat to the banks of the James River, where it lay under the protection of Federal gunboats. Lee had saved Richmond.

The Confederate Counter-Offensive.   As the Union advances ground to a halt by midsummer, 1862, the Confederates planned a grand offensive of their own. In the West, two Southern armies under Generals Braxton Bragg and Edmund Kirby-Smith in August swept through eastern Tennessee; by September,

they were operating in Kentucky, where they were in a position to cut the supply line for Buell's army in Tennessee. The early phases of their offensive were brilliantly successful, but the campaign as a whole was fruitless because of a lack of coordination between the two Southern armies and because of Bragg's indecisiveness. After a bloody battle at Perryville (October 8), the Confederate forces withdrew toward Chattanooga, followed, at a respectful distance, by the Union army.

The more daring part of the Confederate offensive was in the East. While McClellan's army was slowly being withdrawn from the Peninsula, Lee turned quickly upon Union forces in central Virginia under the braggart General John Pope, and concentrating his entire strength upon this segment of the Federal army, scored a brilliant Confederate victory in the second battle of Bull Run (August 29–30). Free then to push into the North, Lee crossed the Potomac

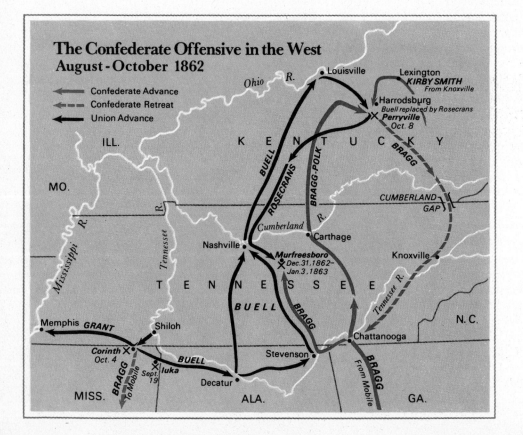

into Maryland, where he hoped to supply his ragged army and to rally the inhabitants of that state to the Confederate cause.

Lee's invasion of Maryland ended with the battle of Antietam (September 17), an indecisive engagement whose very inconclusiveness clearly demonstrated the impossibility of ever ending the war so long as it was fought by the conventional rules. Union General McClellan, again in command, moved slowly to catch up with Lee's army, because he wished to concentrate all his forces for an attack. Lee in turn waited in a defensive position behind Antietam Creek at Sharpsburg, Maryland, because he too needed to concentrate his troops, a portion of whom had been sent on a successful expedition to capture Harpers Ferry. When McClellan was finally ready to take the offensive, he followed one of Jomini's battle plans precisely, and Lee defended his position by the same rules. The result was the bloodiest day of the Civil War. In areas of the battlefield like the cornfield, the Dunker church, the Bloody Lane, and Burnside's bridge, men fell as in a slaughterhouse. By the end of the day, there were more than 25,000 casualties, with at least 5,000 dead. The next day an eyewitness noted "the most appalling sights upon the battle-field . . . the ground strewn with the bodies of the dead and the dying . . . the cries and the groans of the wounded . . . the piles of dead men, in attitudes which show the writhing agony in which they died—faces distorted . . . begrimed and covered with clotted blood, arms and legs torn from the body or the body itself torn asunder."

Quietly Lee slipped back into Virginia, and McClellan did not pursue him. The Confederate offensive was over, and with it ended an era. If Jomini's strategy could only lead to stalemate, it was time for both Union and Confederacy to experiment with new ways of waging war.

CHRONOLOGY

1861 Secession of remaining states of Deep South (Texas, Louisiana, Mississippi, Alabama, Georgia, and Florida).

Jefferson Davis begins serving as president of the Confederate States of America.

Abraham Lincoln inaugurated as president of the United States of America.

Firing on Fort Sumter precipitates war.

Secession of border slave states (Virginia, North Carolina, Tennessee, and Arkansas).

Union army routed at first battle of Bull Run (Manassas).

McClellan heads Union Forces.

Trent affair threatens to change European neutrality.

1862 Both Union and Confederacy adopt paper money.

Union general, U. S. Grant, captures Fort Henry and Fort Donelson.

Grant defeated at Shiloh.

Battle of the ironclads: *Virginia (Merrimack)* vs. *Monitor.*

McClellan's Peninsula campaign brings Union army to outskirts of Richmond, the Confederate capital.

Robert E. Lee becomes commander of Army of Northern Virginia.

Confederate victory at second battle of Bull Run.

Stalemate between Lee and McClellan at Antietam.

Confederate invasion of Kentucky.

Lincoln issues preliminary Emancipation Proclamation.

Confederate victory at Fredericksburg.

SUGGESTED READINGS

There are two excellent guides to the vast literature on the causes of the Civil War: Howard K. Beale, "What Historians Have Said about the Causes of the Civil War," in *Theory and Practice in Historical Study* (Social Science Research Council *Bulletin*, No. 54 [1946], 55–102), and Thomas J. Pressly, *Americans Interpret Their Civil War* (1954). Kenneth M. Stampp, *The Imperiled Union* (1980), offers an insightful analysis of these conflicting interpretations. Edwin C. Rozwenc, ed., *The Causes of the American Civil War* (1972), and Kenneth M. Stampp, ed., *The Causes of the*

Civil War (1974), contain extensive extracts from writings by contemporaries and subsequent historians.

Peter J. Parish, *The American Civil War* (1975), is the best one-volume history. *The Civil War and Reconstruction* (1969), by J. G. Randall and David Donald, is more comprehensive and has a fuller bibliography. Of the older large-scale studies, James Ford Rhodes, *History of the United States from the Compromise of 1850...*, Vols. 3–5 (1895–1904), remains valuable. The fullest modern account is Allan Nevins, *The War for the Union* (4 vols., 1959–71), a work of enormous scholarship, which, however, concentrates on the North. Bruce Catton, *The Centennial History of the Civil War* (3 vols., 1961–65), is eloquent and imaginative.

Mark M. Boatner, III, *The Civil War Dictionary* (1959), is a useful, accurate reference work. For maps, see Vincent J. Esposito, ed., *The West Point Atlas of American Wars* (2 vols., 1959).

The best Civil War anthologies are Henry S. Commager, ed., *The Blue and the Gray* (2 vols., 1950), and William B. Hesseltine, ed., *The Tragic Conflict* (1962). Francis T. Miller, *The Photographic History of the Civil War* (10 vols., 1911), offers the most complete pictorial coverage, but the photographs are poorly reproduced. Better pictorial histories, using modern photographic techniques, are David Donald, ed., *Divided We Fought* (1952), and Richard M. Ketchum, ed., *The American Heritage Picture History of the Civil War* (1960).

On the Sumter crisis, see David M. Potter, *Lincoln and His Party in the Secession Crisis* (1942), Kenneth M. Stampp, *And the War Came* (1950), and Richard N. Current, *Lincoln and the First Shot* (1963).

The best history of the Confederacy is Emory M. Thomas, *The Confederate Nation, 1861–1865* (1979). The fullest life of the Confederate president is Hudson Strode, *Jefferson Davis* (3 vols., 1955–64); the most recent is Clement Eaton, *Jefferson Davis* (1977). Students will learn much from Rembert W. Patrick, *Jefferson Davis and His Cabinet* (1944). Three Confederate diaries are invaluable: May B. Chesnut, *A Diary from Dixie*, ed. by Ben A. Williams (1949); John B. Jones, *A Rebel War Clerk's Diary* (2 vols., 1866); and Robert G. H. Kean, *Inside the Confederate Government*, ed. by Edward Younger (1955).

Abraham Lincoln has been the subject of many distinguished biographies. The best one-volume life is Stephen B. Oates, *With Malice Toward None* (1977); Benjamin P. Thomas's *Abraham Lincoln* (1952) is also valuable. The fullest and most flavorful of the biographies is Carl Sandburg, *Abraham Lincoln: The War Years* (4 vols., 1939). The most scholarly and critical is *Lincoln the President* (4 vols., 1945–55), by J. G. Randall and Richard N. Current. Several volumes of essays deal with important and controversial aspects of Lincoln's career: Richard N. Current, *The Lincoln Nobody Knows* (1958); David Donald, *Lincoln Reconsidered* (1956); Norman A. Graebner, ed., *The Enduring Lincoln* (1959); and J. G. Randall, *Lincoln the Liberal Statesman* (1947). See also Edmund Wilson's thoughtful essay on Lincoln in his *Patriotic Gore* (1962). The diaries of three of Lincoln's cabinet officers are indispensable: Howard K. Beale, ed., *The Diary of Edward Bates* (1933); David Donald, ed., *Inside Lincoln's Cabinet* (Salmon P. Chase) (1954); and Howard K. Beale and Alan W. Brownsword, ed., *Diary of Gideon Welles* (3 vols., 1960).

The standard work on Anglo-American relations remains Ephraim D. Adams, *Great Britain and the American Civil War* (2 vols., 1925). Frank L. Owsley, *King Cotton Diplomacy* (1959), David P. Crook, *The North, the South, and the Powers* (1974), and Brian Jenkins, *Britain and the War for the Union* (1974), are also valuable. Lincoln's role in foreign policy is overdramatized in Jay Monaghan, *Diplomat in Carpetslippers* (1945). For correctives, see Glyndon G. Van Deusen, *William Henry Seward* (1967), Martin B. Duberman, *Charles Francis Adams* (1961), and David Donald, *Charles Sumner and the Rights of Man* (1970). Franco-American relations are admirably covered in Lynn M. Case and Warren F. Spencer, *The United States and France: Civil War Diplomacy* (1970), and Daniel B. Carroll, *Henri Mercier and the American Civil War* (1971).

On social and economic conditions, see Paul W. Gates, *Agriculture and the Civil War* (1965), and Mary E. Massey, *Bonnet Brigades: American Women and the Civil War* (1966). Developments on the Southern home front are sketched in Charles W. Ramsdell, *Behind the Lines in the Southern Confederacy* (1944), and Bell I. Wiley, *The Plain People of the Confederacy* (1943). Emerson D. Fite, *Social and Industrial Conditions in the North during the Civil War* (1910), remains the best survey. For the continuing debate on the effect of the war on Northern economic growth, see Ralph Andreano, ed., *The Economic Impact of the American Civil War* (1962), and David T. Gilchrist and W. David Lewis, eds., *Economic Change in the Civil War Era* (1965).

Studies dealing with other aspects of the Civil War are listed at the end of the following chapter.

CHAPTER 19

Experimentation
1862–1865

At the outset of the Civil War both President Lincoln and President Davis assumed that the conflict would be a limited and relatively brief one, waged in a conventional fashion by armies in the field and having little impact on the economic, social, and intellectual life of their sections. The events of 1861–62 proved these expectations utterly wrong. It slowly became clear that to carry on the war Americans, in both North and South, had to break with tradition and engage in broad experimentation. They had to try new forms of government action, new modes of social and economic cooperation, and new patterns of thought.

Since the Union was ultimately victorious, it would be easy to conclude that Northerners were more willing to experiment, better able to mobilize all their resources, for what has been called the first modern war. But such a judgment makes the historian the camp follower of the victorious army. The record shows, instead, that both the Confederacy and the Union attempted innovations that for the time were daringly original. It also shows that both sides during the final years of the war resorted to much the same kinds of experimentation.

Evolution of a Command System

The bloody and indecisive campaigns of 1861 and 1862 made innovators out of both Union and Confederate soldiers. Experience under fire convinced them not to follow Jomini's tactics. The French writer had conceived of a tactical situation where infantrymen, drawn up in close, parallel lines, blazed away at each other with muskets capable of being loaded perhaps twice a minute and having an effective range of one hundred yards. But Civil War soldiers were equipped with rifles which not only were more quickly loaded but had an effective range of about eight hundred yards. In Jomini's day the offensive force had the great advantage; rushing forward with bayonets fixed, charging troops could break the defenders' line before they had time to reload. In the Civil War, on the other hand, the advancing force was exposed to accurate fire during the last half-mile of its approach. In consequence, nine out of ten infantry assaults failed, and the Civil War soldier had little use for his bayonet—except perhaps as a spit on which to cook meat.

Soldiers on both sides rapidly learned how to make defensive positions even stronger. At the beginning of the war, most military men were scornful of breastworks and entrenchments, arguing that they simply pinned down a defending force and made it more vulnerable to a charge. When Lee, upon assuming command of the Army of Northern Virginia in 1862, ordered his men to construct earthworks facing McClellan's advancing troops, Confederate soldiers bitterly complained and called their new general the King of Spades. But when they saw how entrenchments saved lives, they changed their tune, and Lee became to the Confederate common soldier "Marse Robert," the general who looked after his men's welfare. What Confederate generals started, Union commanders imitated. By the end of 1862, both armies dug in wherever they halted. Using spades and canteens, forks and sticks, soldiers pushed up improvised earthworks and strengthened them with fence rails and fallen logs.

Experience also quietly killed off Jomini's view that warfare was restricted to professionals. In the early days of the conflict, commanders believed warfare should not injure civilians. When McClellan's army pushed up the Peninsula, the general posted guards to keep his soldiers from raiding Confederate farmers' cornfields. Similarly Halleck permitted slaveowners to search his camp in order to reclaim their runaway slaves. By the end of 1862, such practices vanished. Soldiers joyfully foraged through civilians' watermelon patches, cornfields, and chicken roosts, while their officers ostentatiously turned their backs. Northern generals exhibited a growing reluctance to permit the recapture of fugitive slaves who had fled to the Union lines. As early as May 1861, General Butler at Fort Monroe, Virginia, refused to return three such fugitives on the ground that they were contraband of war. "Contrabands" became a code name for escaped slaves, and in 1862 the Federal Congress showed what it thought of Jomini's notion of limited warfare by prohibiting any Federal military officer from returning runaways.

Lincoln Takes Command.   The deadlock of 1861–62 also brought about a transformation of the command systems of both Union and Confederate armies. Because the Union lost so many battles during the first two years of the conflict, Lincoln was forced to experiment first. His initial venture came in mid-1862. Since he distrusted McClellan's capacity to keep an eye on the general progress of the war while also leading a campaign to capture Richmond, he brought in Halleck from the West to serve as his military adviser and gave him the grand title of general in chief. The position was not a viable one, for it placed Halleck in conflict with the other generals, especially McClellan; it also often put him at odds with Secretary of War Stanton, and exposed him to what he called the "political Hell" of pressure from congressmen. In addition, Halleck's slowness, his indecisiveness, and his rigid adherence to Jomini's principles made him hostile to all innovation, and Lincoln soon concluded that he was of little more use than a clerk.

Seeing no alternative, Lincoln again tried to direct military operations himself. In the eastern theater he replaced McClellan, after his failure to follow up his partial success at Antietam, with that bumbling incompetent, Ambrose E. Burnside. Burnside led the Army of the Potomac into the battle of Fredericksburg on December 13, 1862, one of the most disastrous, and surely the least necessary, Federal defeats of the war. Replacing Burnside with "Fighting Joe" Hooker, a boastful egotist fond of the bottle, brought no better luck to the Union cause. The battle of Chancellorsville (May 1–4, 1863) was still another Confederate victory—but one won at a great price, for "Stonewall" Jackson was accidentally fired upon by his own Southern soldiers and mortally wounded.

Still trying to direct military operations himself, Lincoln watched anxiously as Lee in midsummer of 1863 began his second invasion of the North, this time pushing into Pennsylvania. When Hooker appeared unable or unwilling to pursue the Confederates, Lincoln replaced him with the shy, scholarly George Gordon Meade, who assumed command of the army only three days before the climactic battle of Gettysburg (July 1–3, 1863). Rushing all available forces to that Pennsylvania town, Meade succeeded in turning back the invaders. At last the Army of the

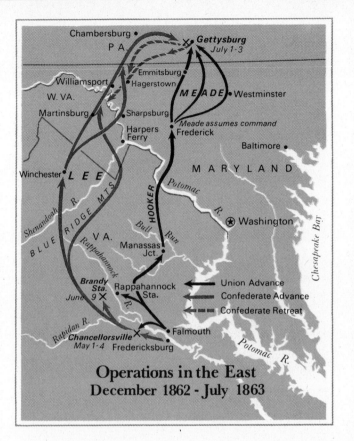

Potomac had won a victory—but Meade failed to pursue, and Lee's army recrossed the Potomac to safety. "We had them within our grasp," Lincoln lamented. "We had only to stretch forth our hands and they were ours. And nothing I could say or do could make the Army move."

When Lincoln tried personally to plan strategy for the trans-Appalachian theater of war, he was no more successful. After the battle of Perryville, it was clear that Buell must be replaced, and Lincoln chose W. S. Rosecrans. Lincoln urged him to push on to Chattanooga, the rail hub of the Confederacy, but en route Rosecrans encountered Bragg's army in the bloody and indecisive battle of Murfreesboro (December 30, 1862–January 2, 1863). Though Rosecrans claimed victory, his army was so badly mauled that he could not advance for another six months. Finally, in June 1863 he maneuvered the Confederates out of

Chattanooga, but in pursuing Bragg's army he received a smashing defeat at Chickamauga (September 19–20). Only the rocklike determination of General George H. Thomas prevented the reverse from becoming a rout, and Rosecrans's army limped back into Chattanooga. Disoriented by defeat, Rosecrans, as Lincoln said, behaved "like a duck hit on the head," and allowed Bragg to besiege the city.

Farther west, Lincoln's personal direction of the Union armies proved equally ineffectual. Here the main objective was Vicksburg, the last major city on the Mississippi River still in Confederate hands; when it fell, the eastern part of the Confederacy would be severed from the trans-Mississippi region.

Grant's Success at Vicksburg. Grant commanded the Union forces in this area after Halleck went to Washington, and William Tecumseh Sherman was his ablest lieutenant. After a frontal assault on the almost impregnable bluffs of Vicksburg failed to drive out the Confederates, commanded by General John C. Pemberton, Grant, without aid from Washington, devised a bold new strategy. Using the navy's gunboats and transports to run his ammunition and supplies past the Vicksburg batteries, he marched his army to a point on the west bank below the city, staged a rapid amphibious crossing, and before the Confederates could recover from their surprise, pushed inland. To the dismay of Washington, he thus abandoned his base of supplies, announcing that he planned to live on the countryside. First he struck at Jackson, the capital of Mississippi, to drive back the small Confederate force General Joseph E. Johnston had collected there, and then he turned on Pemberton's army and forced it into Vicksburg. After two ill-advised assaults, the Union army settled down to besiege the city, while from the river the Union gunboats kept up a constant bombardment. As civilians in the city took to caves for safety and as starvation made mule meat a delicacy, Pemberton fought back as well as he could, but on July 4, 1863—the day after Gettysburg—he had to surrender his army and the city.

When the news reached Washington, Lincoln, who had distrusted Grant's strategy, wrote the general a handsome apology: "I now wish to make the

MAJOR GENERAL ULYSSES SIMPSON GRANT, U.S.A., IN THE FALL OF 1863

Grant lacked the polish of McClellan, the brilliance of Sherman, and the flamboyance of Sheridan. But he had one quality more important than any of these. As Lincoln concisely put it: "I can't spare this man—he fights." (Library of Congress)

Operations in the West, 1863
The Vicksburg Campaign

personal acknowledgment that you were right, and I was wrong." The president was happy to be proved wrong, for Grant's success meant that he finally had a general who knew how to plan a campaign and fight it. Putting Grant in command of all the troops in the West, Lincoln directed him to relieve the army cooped up in Chattanooga. Quickly Grant and Sherman came to the rescue, opened up a line of communication to the starving Union troops in Chattanooga, now commanded by Thomas instead of the inept Rosecrans, and brought in reinforcements. On November 23–25 the combined forces routed Bragg's encircling army and forced it back into Georgia.

Two New Systems of Command. This further victory gave Lincoln a solution to the problem of command, which had so long vexed him. Early the next year he brought Grant to Washington, where he received the rank of lieutenant general, and assigned him to command all the armies of the United States. Initially Washington observers thought the burden might be too much for this "short, round-shouldered man," of whom they now received their first glimpse. One observer reported that the new lieutenant general "had no gait, no *station*, no manner, rough, light-brown whiskers, a blue eye, and rather a scrubby look withal . . . rather the look of a man who did, or once did, take a little too much to drink." But appearances were deceiving, for in the next few days Grant set forth a broad strategy for winning the war. Taking advantage of Northern superiority in manpower, he planned a simultaneous advance of all Union armies, so that the Confederates must divide their forces or else leave their territory open to invasion. The idea of involving all the Federal forces at once made sense to Lincoln. "Oh, yes! I can see that," he exclaimed. "As we say out West, if a man can't skin he must hold a leg while somebody else does." Accepting Grant's plan, Lincoln created a modern command system for the United States army, with the president as commander in chief, Grant as general in chief, and Halleck as essentially a chief of staff, while Stanton as secretary of war ably supported all the others.

Meanwhile the Confederate command system was also evolving through experimentation. The tremendous victories won by Lee and the Army of Northern Virginia obviated the need for constant changing of command in the East, but by 1863 it was evident that there must be a reorganization of Confederate commanders in the West. Davis instituted what was, in effect, a theater command system, with Lee in control of the forces in Virginia, Joseph E. Johnston, now recovered from his wound, in command of the troops between the mountains and the Mississippi River, and Edmund Kirby-Smith in charge of all troops in the vast trans-Mississippi region.

The new system was only partially successful. Made a kind of super-commander of the trans-Mississippi theater, which was becoming increasingly isolated as Union forces captured point after point along the Mississippi, Kirby-Smith did an effective job of recruiting and reorganizing the troops in his region. He stepped up trade with Mexico, so that impressive amounts of European munitions and supplies were brought in by way of Matamoros. So strengthened, "Kirby-Smithdom," as it was popularly called, fared better than most of the rest of the South, but Kirby-Smith did little to make the vast resources of his command available to the government at Richmond.

In the central theater a strong Confederate command system failed to emerge. Johnston claimed he did not know the extent and nature of his duties. Repeatedly he asked whether he was supposed to take field command of the widely separated armies of Bragg, near Chattanooga, and of Pemberton, at Vicksburg, or was merely to serve as adviser to those generals. Knowing that both were protégés of the president, he did not dare give a positive order to either. In consequence, he made only a feeble effort to replace the unpopular Bragg and diverted a few

of his troops to support Pemberton. Unable to persuade Pemberton to leave Vicksburg while there was still time, Johnston watched in impotent impatience as the Confederate army was cornered and starved into surrender.

The brilliant successes of Lee and his lieutenants in the eastern theater allowed the Army of Northern Virginia to operate pretty much as it wished, without much regard for the needs of the Confederacy elsewhere. Lee, who had direct access to President Davis, resisted any attempt to weaken his force. In mid-1863, rather than attempt to relieve Vicksburg, Lee deliberately chose to stage a new invasion of the North, in the vain hope that it would relieve pressure on Confederate armies elsewhere. The result was the defeat at Gettysburg and the capture of Vicksburg.

Even so, Lee was by 1864 the only Confederate commander who retained the confidence of the country and of his troops. As Southern defeats became more numerous than victories, a strong demand swelled up in the Confederate Congress for coordinated direction of all the Southern armies, and men naturally looked to Lee. The general was, however, averse to these broader responsibilities and did all that he could to discourage the plan. When the Congress in January 1865 passed an act requiring the appointment of a commander in chief of all the armies, it had Lee in mind, and Davis named him. In accepting the new position, Lee made it clear that he would continue to be essentially a theater commander, responsible only to Davis. The Confederacy thus reached Appomattox without ever developing a truly unified command system, comparable to that of the Union.

The Naval War

In naval warfare necessity compelled the Confederates to take the lead in experimentation. Southerners were not a seagoing people, with a tradition of shipbuilding. Secretary of the Navy Stephen R. Mallory had initially not a single ship at his command. He had to improvise, and he did so with imagination and remarkable success.

In the early months of the war the long Southern

coastline seemed to be at the mercy of the Union fleet, which could pick the most vulnerable points for attack. In November 1861, a Union flotilla commanded by Flag Officer Samuel F. DuPont routed the weak Confederate defenders of Port Royal Sound, and Federal troops occupied Beaufort and the adjacent South Carolina Sea Islands. The victory gave the vessels in the Atlantic blockading fleet a much needed fueling station, and it also brought freedom to the numerous slaves of the area. In February and March 1862, another Union expedition easily reduced Confederate positions on Roanoke Island and at New Bern, North Carolina, and enabled the Federal blockaders to keep a closer watch on Hatteras Sound. David G. Farragut's fleet in April 1862 helped capture New Orleans, the Confederacy's largest city.

By this time the Confederacy had greatly strengthened its coastal defenses, and further Union successes came slowly and at great cost. In April 1863 the Confederates repelled a vast Union armada, commanded by DuPont, which tried to capture Charleston. That citadel of secession remained in Confederate hands until nearly the end of the war, when Sherman's advance compelled Southern troops to abandon it. Equally effective were the Confederate defenses of Wilmington, North Carolina, which became the main Southern port on the Atlantic through which supplies from Europe were imported. Not until January 1865 could Federal troops capture Fort Fisher, the principal defense of Wilmington. The powerfully protected harbor of Mobile remained in Southern hands until August 1864, when the sixty-three-year-old Admiral Farragut, lashed in the rigging of his flagship so that he would not fall to his death if wounded, led his fleet past the defending Confederate forts to stop the last remaining major Southern port on the Gulf.

Innovations in Naval Warfare.   To supplement the coastal batteries that protected these and other harbors, the Confederate navy experimented with new weapons. They used torpedoes extensively for the first time in warfare. These "infernal machines," constructed of kegs, barrels, and cans filled with explosives, were sometimes anchored at the entrance of Southern harbors, at other times were turned loose to float with the tide toward attacking Union vessels, and on still other occasions were propelled at the end of a long pole by a small boat, whose crew was willing to undertake the suicidal risk. Even more risky were the several Confederate experiments with submarine warfare. The most successful of these novel vessels was the *H. L. Hunley,* propelled under water by a crank turned by its eight-man crew. After four unsuccessful trials, in which all members of the crews were lost, the *Hunley* in February 1864 sank the Union warship *Housatonic* in Charleston harbor, but the submarine itself was lost in the resulting explosion.

Quickly comprehending that the Confederacy could never build as large a fleet as the Union, Secretary Mallory early in the war urged the construction of iron-armored ships, against which the wooden vessels of the North would stand no chance. Despite shortages of iron and lack of rolling mills, the Confederacy developed a surprising number of these vessels. The most famous of the Confederate ironclads was the *Virginia,* originally the United States warship *Merrimack,* which the Federals sank when they abandoned Norfolk navy yard at the beginning of the war. Raised and repaired, the *Virginia* had her superstructure covered with four-inch iron plate, and she carried a cast-iron ram on her prow. On March 8, 1862, just as McClellan began his campaign on the Peninsula, the *Virginia* emerged and began attacking the wooden vessels of the Union fleet at Hampton Roads. In the first day's action she destroyed two of the largest ships in the squadron and ran a third aground. Reappearing the second day, she found her way barred by a curious Union vessel, the *Monitor,* which looked like a tin can on a raft. Belatedly contracted for by the slow-moving Union navy department, the *Monitor,* designed by John Ericsson, was a low-lying ironclad with a revolving gun turret. The battle between the *Virginia* and the *Monitor* proved a draw, but the Confederate ship had to return to Norfolk to repair her defective engines. Two days later, when forced to abandon Norfolk, the Southerners ran the *Virginia* ashore and burned the vessel to prevent its capture. The South's most promising hope for breaking the blockade was lost.

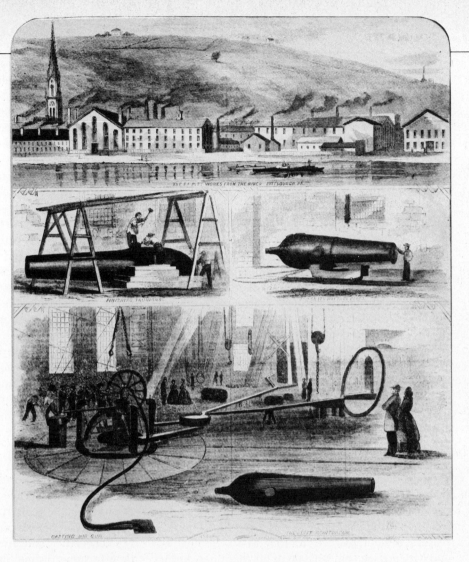

MAKING GUNS FOR THE NEW MONITORS AT PITTSBURGH, PENNSYLVANIA

The success of the North was due in considerable measure to its economic superiority over the South. The Fort Pitt ironworks at Pittsburgh, which manufactured guns for the fleet of monitors, had their counterparts in a dozen other Northern cities. Confederate ordnance depended almost entirely upon imports from Europe and the output of the Tredegar ironworks in Richmond. *(Courtesy, Carnegie Library of Pittsburgh)*

Mallory was equally prompt in purchasing or commissioning conventional vessels for the Confederate navy, ships designed not to combat Union warships but to harass the United States merchant marine. The most successful of these vessels was the C.S.S. *Alabama*, built to Southern specifications at the Laird shipyards in Liverpool and commanded by Raphael Semmes. Ranging over the Atlantic, Indian, and Pacific oceans, the *Alabama* between 1862 and 1864 hunted down and destroyed sixty-nine Union merchantmen, valued at more than $6 million. Not until nearly the end of the war could the Union navy corner and sink the raider. By this time, however, the *Alabama*, along with other Confederate cruisers, had virtually exterminated the United States carrying trade.

However imaginative and innovative, Confederate navy officials could not keep pace with the growth of the Union navy, under the slow but honest direction of Gideon Welles. Drawing upon the vast industrial resources of the North and upon the experience of its seagoing population, Welles was able to build up the United States navy from its 42 active vessels in 1861, only 26 of which had steam power, to 671 ships in December 1864, of which 71 were ironclad. Navy personnel rose from 7,400 at the start of the war to 68,000 at its end. Superbly equipped and managed, the Union fleet maintained an ever-tightening blockade of the Southern coast. According to the best, but not wholly reliable, statistics, the Union fleet captured not more than 1 in 10 blockade runners in 1861, and not more than 1 in 8 in 1862. But by 1864 they caught 1 in 3, and by 1865 every other one.

The Wartime Economy

Inevitably these huge military and naval operations put a heavy strain upon the economic resources of the combatants. In the Confederacy one result was a sharp shift in the nature of Southern agriculture. When the outbreak of war cut off Northern markets and the blockade increasingly sealed off European outlets for cotton and tobacco, farmers, at the urging of the Confederate and state governments, turned to producing grain and other foodstuffs. Cotton production in the South dropped from 4 million bales in 1861 to 300,000 in 1864.

In the North, too, farmers began producing more grain. Partly because of inflation, the price of wheat rose from 65¢ a bushel in December 1860 to $2.26 in July 1864, and farmers, especially in the Middle West, saw a chance to make money. At first the labor shortage kept them from expanding their acreage, for many farmhands enlisted in the Union army at the outbreak of the war, but machines soon made up for the absent men. One of Cyrus Hall McCormick's reapers could replace from four to six farmhands, and McCormick sold 165,000 of his machines during the war.

Industry in both the Union and the Confederacy also grew. As the Union blockade cut off imports, Southern factories had a virtual monopoly in that region, and the demands of the army and the needs of the civilians provided an insatiable market. It is hard to measure Southern industrial growth, both because there was no Confederate census and because inflation affected all prices, yet there are some clues to show that manufacturing could be very profitable. For instance, the 1862 conscription acts exempted the owners of certain basic industries provided that their annual profits were no more than 75 percent. Under the astute management of Joseph Anderson, the Tredegar Iron Works at Richmond, the largest privately owned factory in the South and the primary source for Confederate cannon, made profits of 100 percent in 1861 and of 70 percent in 1862.

Northern manufacturing was equally profitable, especially when it produced items needed for the army. With the demand for uniforms, woolen mills, which had averaged dividends of only 9 percent for the years before the war, by 1865 were able to pay 25 percent dividends, and the number of woolen mills more than doubled. Investors were willing to pour money into such industries more confidently because Congress raised tariffs to levels that virtually excluded competing European products. War demands made the mass production of ready-made clothing profitable, and the army's need for shoes speeded the introduction of Gordon McKay's machine for sewing soles to uppers. Simultaneously, in an unrelated development, the discovery of oil at Titusville, Pennsylvania, in 1859, led to a wartime boom in the new petroleum industry.

Structural Changes in the Two Economies.   These changes had an important impact on the structure of the American economy. The increase in the number of factories, particularly in the Confederacy, encouraged entrepreneurship. In the North, men like John D. Rockefeller and Andrew Carnegie, who started their fortunes during the war, continued to dominate the industrial scene after 1865. When the South began rebuilding its industry in the 1870s and 1880s, it looked for leadership to its wartime entrepreneurs and to the Confederate commanders who likewise had experience in directing the labor of large numbers of men. The war also encouraged the growth of large, rather than small, factories. Obliged to contract for huge shipments, both Union and Confederate governments naturally turned to the manufacturing companies financially and physically able to handle them. The selective process was accelerated because larger firms could pay an agent in Washington or Richmond who understood the requirements of the army and navy—as well as those of influential congressmen and bureaucrats.

Most important of all, the wartime experience changed attitudes toward the role of the national government in the economy. Since the destruction of the Second Bank of the United States in the Jackson era, the national government had done little to regulate or control the economy, but during the war both the Union and the Confederate governments took steps that affected every branch of economic life. In passing the Homestead Act of May 20, 1862, which offered any citizen 160 acres of the public domain after five years of continuous residence, the Union Congress signaled its intention henceforth to give more attention to the nation's farmers, as it did in creating a federal Department of Agriculture that same year. The Morrill Act of 1862, giving vast tracts of the public domain to endow agricultural (land-grant) colleges, was further evidence of the same purpose. Both governments found it necessary to regulate transportation, especially railroads, during the war. Davis, despite his strict interpretation of the Confederate Constitution, urged his Congress to finance the construction of some missing links in the Southern rail system. Lincoln in July 1862 signed the Pacific Railroad Act, giving enormous tracts of the public land to support the construction of a transcontinental rail route.

In both the United States and the Confederacy, private citizens became aware, often for the first time, of the economic impact of their national governments. In the Confederacy, the Impressment Act of March 1863 authorized government agents to seize civilians' food, horses, wagons, or other supplies if required for the army and to set an arbitrary price for the confiscated goods. In the Union the creation of a new national banking system in 1863 (amended and strengthened in 1864) meant, among other things, that a uniform national currency began to replace the dozens of issues by local banks. Citizens, paying national taxes in national currency, grew accustomed to the idea that their national government would henceforth play a positive role in the economic life of the country.

Inflation and Its Consequences

During the desperate final years of the Civil War, both Union and Confederate Treasury Departments had to experiment with new ways to finance the war. Both imposed broad excise duties. The Union internal revenue act of July 1, 1862, has been fairly characterized as an attempt to tax everything. Duties were imposed upon all sorts of manufactures, with a fresh duty levied each time the raw material underwent a new process. In a carriage, for instance, the leather, the cloth, the wood, and the metal would each be taxed; then the manufacturer was taxed for the process of putting them together; the dealer was taxed for selling the carriage; and the purchaser, having paid a sufficient price to cover all these duties, was taxed in addition for ownership. Heavy duties fell upon luxuries, like billiard tables and yachts, and taxes upon professions and occupations covered, as Representative James G. Blaine said, "bankers and pawn brokers, lawyers and horse-dealers, physicians and confectioners, commercial brokers and peddlers." Ultimately these taxes brought in about 21 percent of the total wartime expenditures of the Union government.

The Confederacy moved more slowly, but on April 24, 1863, it too adopted a comprehensive tax measure, which included an income tax, occupational and license taxes ranging from $40 for bowling alleys to $500 for bankers, and what a later generation would call an excess profits tax. A unique feature of the Confederate legislation was the tax-in-kind, which compelled producers of wheat, corn, oats, potatoes, sugar, cotton, tobacco, and other farm products to pay one-tenth of their crop each year to the government. A last, desperate attempt in March 1865 to tax all coin, bullion, and foreign exchange was made too late to have any effect. All told, the Confederacy raised only about 1 percent of its income from taxes.

The sale of bonds contributed little more to the Confederate treasury. Values were so uncertain in the wartime South that investors were afraid to tie up their money in such fixed investments, and doubts spread as to when and whether the Confederate government would even pay the interest on its obligations. In the Union, on the other hand, bonds became a major source of revenue. Unable initially to sell bonds even at a discount, Secretary Chase appointed his friend, Jay Cooke, the Philadelphia banker who also had an office in Washington, special agent of the Treasury Department. Using high-pressure advertising, Cooke launched an extensive propaganda campaign, extolling the merits of the "five-twenties" (bonds bearing 6 percent interest, which could be paid off at the expiration of five, and must be redeemed in twenty, years). He was so successful that between 600,000 and a million citizens were persuaded to invest in the public debt, and the entire loan of half a billion dollars was oversubscribed. But in 1864, as the war stretched on endlessly and victory appeared nowhere in sight, the market for bonds collapsed. Resigning for political reasons, Chase left office at an opportune moment to preserve his reputation as a financier, and Cooke went with him. Chase's successor, William Pitt Fessenden, could only raise money through short-term loans at an exorbitant rate of interest. Not until the very end of the war, when victory was obviously near, did the sale of Union bonds pick up, and Cooke, reappointed special agent, attracted large additional numbers of investors.

The Resort to Paper Money. Necessarily, therefore, both governments continued to depend upon paper money. The Union treasury, which had cautiously issued its first greenbacks in 1862, continued to print more and more during the rest of that year and during 1863 as well, until most of the $450 million authorized by Congress was in circulation. The value of the greenbacks gradually declined. A Union treasury note with a face value of one dollar was worth 99.86¢ in gold in 1862, but by 1864 it was worth only 62.66¢ and by early 1865, 50.3¢. In the Confederacy, where the printing presses never stopped, paper money had even less value. Perhaps $2 billion in unredeemable paper was issued in all. A Confederate treasury note for one dollar, worth 82.7¢ in gold in 1862, dropped to 29¢ in 1863 and to 1.7¢ in early 1865. In a desperate attempt to check the slide, the Confederate Congress in February 1864 undertook a partial repudiation of these notes, but the confusing and complex legislation was badly administered and served further to undermine trust in the government and its money. Having lost the confidence of the country, Memminger resigned in the summer of 1864—at about the same time that Chase left the Union Treasury Department. His successor, the South Carolina banker and businessman George A. Trenholm, could devise no better solution for the Confederacy's financial woes than to urge citizens to donate to the government their money, jewels, gold and silver plate, and public securities.

The excessive amount of paper money was only one of many factors that produced runaway inflation in both the North and the South. With importations

UNION PAPER MONEY: A "GREENBACK"
Secretary Chase decided to print Union legal-tender notes with a patented green ink. Consequently they became known as "greenbacks."

largely cut off, in the North by the highly protective tariff and in the South by the Union blockade, with the productive labor force sharply reduced because of the number of men in military service, and with a huge portion of all goods required to supply the armies and navies, civilians had to expect shortages and high prices.

Profits and Deprivation. In both sections there were some who profited from the wartime economy. War contracts helped pull the Union economy out of a sharp depression, and higher prices spurred on manufacturers, who could now look for higher profits. The demand for grain, along with the Homestead Act, encouraged new settlers to begin farming, and the development of new industries, like petroleum, made for quick fortunes. The wartime boom in the North had a hectic quality about it, and men spent their easily earned money quickly lest it be worth less in the future. Many of the new rich were extravagant and hedonistic. Censoriously the New York *Independent* asked in June 1864:

Who at the North would ever think of war, if he had not a friend in the army, or did not read the newspapers? Go into Broadway, and we will show you what is meant by the word "extravagance." Ask [A. T.] Stewart [the department-store owner] about the demand for camel's-hair shawls, and he will say "monstrous." Ask Tiffany what kinds of diamonds and pearls are called for. He will answer "the prodigious," "as near hen's-egg size as possible," "price no object." What kinds of carpetings are now wanted? None but "extra." . . . And as for horses the medium-priced five-hundred-dollar kind are all out of the market. A good pair of "fast ones" . . . will go for a thousand dollars sooner than a basket of strawberries will sell for four cents.

But not all elements in the North shared in this wartime prosperity. Wages lagged sadly behind prices, so that in real income a worker between 1861 and 1865 lost 35 percent of his wages. Women, who composed one-fourth of the nation's manufacturing force in 1860, were especially hard hit. As more and more wives and mothers found it necessary to work, since soldiers could only send them a pittance for support, employers actually cut their wages. Even the United States government participated in this practice. At the Philadelphia armory, the government

in 1861 paid a seamstress 17¢ for making a shirt; three years later, when prices were at their highest, it cut the wage to 15¢. Meanwhile private contractors paid only 8¢.

Suffering in the North was, however, relatively minor when compared to that in the South. To be sure, residents of some parts of the agricultural South who were never disturbed by Union troops had only minor shortages to complain of. As imported goods disappeared from the grocers' shelves, they resorted to sassafras tea and to "coffee" made of parched rye, okra seeds, corn, and even sweet potatoes, the grounds of which were said to form a remarkable cleaning agent for curtains and carpets. Since salt was in short supply, meat could not be preserved, and Southerners ate more chicken and fish. As clothing wore out, they increasingly turned to homespun, and velvet draperies and brocaded rugs found new use as gowns and overcoats.

The thousands of Southerners in the path of the armies had to think not just of shortages but of survival. Hundreds of families fled before the invading Union armies, often attempting to take their slaves with them, but nowhere could these refugees find assurance of safety. Their lives took on a desperate, nightmarish quality, and merely existing from one day to the next was a struggle. There was never enough of anything, including food. Recalling these unhappy days, one writer declared that "the Confederacy was always hungry."

The greatest destitution appeared in towns and cities, where supplies had to be brought in over the rickety Southern railroad system. White-collar workers, especially those on fixed salaries from the government, were particularly hard hit. The celebrated diary of J. B. Jones, a clerk in the Confederate War Department at Richmond, is a melancholy record of shortages and high prices. In May 1864 he reported that beans in Richmond were selling for $3 a quart, meal for $125 a bushel, and flour $400 a barrel. Richmond, he observed, was an astonishingly clean city, since "no garbage or filth can accumulate." The citizens of the Confederate capital were obliged to be "such good scavengers" that there was "no need of buzzards."

Deprivation was the more painful because, as in

the North, some made enormous profits from the war. The blockade runner, who preferred to bring in compact, expensive items like silks and jewels rather than bulky supplies for the army, often reaped fantastic profits. Speculators flourished. As early as the winter of 1862, the governor of Mississippi learned that the families of volunteers in his state were seriously suffering for want of corn and salt, while rich planters held back their ample supply of both commodities, waiting for the inevitable rise in prices. Even more remunerative was trading with the enemy, a practice completely illegal but tacitly condoned by both Confederate and Union officials. Southern women and men who were initiated into the mysteries of the trade bought up as much cotton as they could find in their neighborhoods and took it to convenient exchange points like Memphis and Natchez to sell to the Yankees for coffee, clothing, and luxuries. Late in the war they accepted payment in United States greenbacks, which Southerners valued more than their own depreciated money.

Conscription and Conflict

Along with economic inequity, the unfairness of conscription was the subject of bitter complaints on the part of both Northerners and Southerners during the Civil War. The Confederate conscription act of 1862 ostensibly made all able-bodied white males between the ages of eighteen and thirty-five equally eligible for military service, but the Southern Congress promptly began exempting large categories of men.

As men rushed to enter "bombproof" occupations and claim exemptions, the outcry against the Confederate conscription system grew louder. One of the most vociferous critics was Governor Joseph E. Brown of Georgia, who protested, "The conscription Act, at one fell swoop, strikes down the sovereignty of the States, tramples upon the constitutional rights and personal liberty of the citizens, and arms the President with imperial power." After attempting unsuccessfully to induce the Georgia supreme court to declare conscription unconstitutional, Brown pro-

ceeded to undermine the policy by naming his supporters to state jobs exempt from military service. According to some estimates he put 15,000 able-bodied Georgians into this exempt category; certainly he created 2,000 justices of the peace and 1,000 constables, none of whom had to serve in the army. Less prominent than Brown but equally potent were the critics who complained that conscription was class legislation that benefited the educated and the wealthy. They raised especial objection to the so-called "twenty-nigger" provision, which clearly favored planters at the expense of farmers. "Never did a law meet with more universal odium than the exemption of slave owners," wrote Senator James Phelan of Mississippi to President Davis. "It has aroused a spirit of rebellion . . . and bodies of men have banded together to desert."

Despite intense criticism and dubious results, the Davis administration continued conscription, for it saw no other way to raise the needed number of men. Indeed, as the war progressed, it was obliged to experiment with even more stringent legislation. In a new conscription act of February 17, 1864, the Confederate Congress declared that all white males between the ages of seventeen and fifty were subject to the draft, with the seventeen-year-old boys and the men above forty-five to serve as a reserve for local defense. As a concession to small planters, the act exempted one farmer or overseer for every plantation with fifteen slaves, but it abolished most other exemptions, on the theory that once skilled laborers were in the army the government could detail them to the forges and factories where they were most needed. Total mobilization of manpower was, however, far beyond the competence of the shaky Confederate government, and in practice the industrial-detail system never worked. As the Confederacy scraped the bottom of the barrel, more and more white Southerners began thinking about the one group of able-bodied males who did not serve in the armies, the Negroes.

In the North, too, conscription evoked bitter criticism. The first effective Northern draft act, passed by the Union Congress on March 3, 1863, was patently unfair. Declaring that all able-bodied males between the ages of twenty and forty-five (except for certain high governmental officials and the only sons of widows and infirm parents) were liable to military service, the act promptly contradicted itself by permitting those who could afford to do so to hire substitutes. In an effort to keep the price of substitutes down, it also permitted a man to purchase outright exemption from military service for $300.

As in the South, there was immediate and widespread hostility toward conscription. The system favored the wealthiest citizens and the most prosperous sections of the country. A well-to-do man like George Templeton Strong of New York, for example, did not dream of serving in the army; he paid $1,100 for a substitute, "a big 'Dutch' boy of twenty or thereabouts," who, as Strong remarked complacently, "looked as if he could do good service." Rich towns and counties raised bounty funds to encourage volunteering, so that none of their citizens would have to be drafted, and as the war progressed, they offered higher and higher bounties. The volunteers they sought were by no means all local residents who needed a little financial inducement; many of them were professional bounty hunters, who went from place to place, enlisting, receiving bounties, and promptly deserting. Perhaps the record for bounty jumping was held by one John O'Connor, who when

arrested in March 1865 confessed to thirty-two such desertions.

Part of the outcry against conscription in the North stemmed from the inequity of the quotas the president was authorized to announce for each state, presumably giving credit for the number of volunteers it had previously supplied. The Democratic governor of New York, Horatio Seymour, engaged in acrimonious correspondence with Lincoln and finally forced the president to admit that the quota assigned to the Empire State was excessive. Such concessions, however, came too late to placate those threatened by the draft. In Wisconsin, Kentucky, and Pennsylvania, in Troy, Newark, and Albany, there was outright resistance to the enrolling officers, and in several instances Federal troops had to be brought in to quell the insurgents. None of these outbreaks compared in extent or ferocity to that in New York City, where the drawing of the first draftees' names triggered a three-day riot (July 13–15, 1863) by a mob of predominantly Irish workingmen. Turning first against the enrollment officers and the police, the rioters then exhibited their hostility toward the rich by plundering fine houses and rifling jewelry stores. Toward Negroes, whom the rioters feared as economic competitors and blamed for the war and hence for conscription, the mob acted with hideous brutal-

THE NEW YORK DRAFT RIOTS: BATTLE IN SECOND AVENUE AND 22ND STREET AT THE UNION STEAM WORKS, JULY 14, 1863
Conscription triggered resistance in the North. The largest riot was in New York City, where Federal troops, fresh from the Gettysburg campaign, had to be called in to restore order. *(The New York Public Library)*

ity. After sacking and looting a Negro orphan asylum they chased down any blacks unwary enough to appear on the streets and left those they could capture hanging from lampposts. The Union government had to rush in troops from the Gettysburg campaign to stop the rioting and disperse the mob.

Despite all resistance, Lincoln's government continued conscription because, as in the Confederacy, there seemed to be no other source for soldiers. Even so, the draft remained cumbersome and often ineffectual. In 1864, for instance, 800,000 names were drawn, but so many were exempted because of health or occupation and so many others hired substitutes or paid the commutation fee that only 33,000 were actually inducted into the army. As conscription proved both unfair and ineffective, citizens in the North, like those in the South, began to think of the value of black soldiers.

Steps Toward Emancipation

Just as the Negro played a central part in causing the Civil War, so was he to play a major role in determining its outcome. At the outset there was a tacit agreement that the Civil War was to be a white man's fight, and both Union and Confederate governments in 1861 refused to accept black regiments. In the Confederacy during the first two years of the war, virtually nobody questioned the correctness of this decision. After all, as Vice-President Alexander H. Stephens announced, slavery was "the real 'cornerstone'" upon which the Confederate States had been erected, and few Southern whites could even contemplate the possibility of putting arms into the hands of slaves or of freeing blacks who became soldiers.

In the Union, on the other hand, there were from the beginning powerful voices urging the emancipation of slaves and the enlistment of black men in the army. Frederick Douglass, the leading spokesman of blacks in the North, constantly insisted: "Teach the rebels and traitors that the price they are to pay for the attempt to abolish this Government must be the abolition of slavery." Abolitionists, white

and black, repeatedly instructed Lincoln that he could win the war only if he emancipated the slaves. Senator Charles Sumner of Massachusetts visited the White House almost daily in his efforts to persuade Lincoln that emancipation was the *"one way to safety*, clear as sunlight—pleasant as the paths of Peace."

So influential was this antislavery sentiment that several of the president's subordinates who fell into disfavor with the administration tried to appeal to it. But President Lincoln, aware of the dangerous complexity of the issue, patiently overruled each of these subordinates, declaring that emancipation was a question "which, under my responsibility, I reserve to myself."

Nonmilitary Employment of Blacks. Unwillingness to arm or emancipate the slaves did not signify any reluctance to employ blacks in nonmilitary service. Slaves were the backbone of the Confederate labor force. Had blacks not continued to till and harvest the grain, the Confederacy could never have fielded so large an army. Equally important was the role played by blacks, slave and free, in the industrial production of the Confederacy. In the Tredegar Iron Works, for example, half the 2,400 employees were blacks; they included not merely unskilled workers but puddlers, rollers, and machinists. Blacks also performed indispensable service for the quartermaster and commissary departments of the Confederacy, serving as teamsters, butchers, drovers, boatmen, bakers, shoemakers, and blacksmiths, and they were nurses in many Confederate hospitals.

So essential was Negro labor to the existence of the Confederacy that President Davis had to ensure that enough blacks were available for this service. From the beginning of the war, Confederate authorities from time to time compelled slaves to work on fortifications, and some states, notably Virginia, moved promptly to require owners to lease their slaves to the government when needed. But the Confederate government itself did not act until March 1863, when the Confederate Congress, despite much opposition from planters, authorized the impressment of slaves, whose owners were to receive

A BLACK FAMILY ON THE J. J. SMITH PLANTATION, BEAUFORT, SOUTH CAROLINA, 1862.
(Library of Congress)

$30 a month. In February 1864 it permitted military authorities to impress more slaves, with or without the consent of the owners.

Meanwhile the Union was also making full use of the labor of blacks. As slaves fled from their masters to the camps of the Union army, they were put to use as teamsters, cooks, nurses, carpenters, scouts, and day laborers. Perhaps half a million blacks crossed over to the Union lines, and nearly 200,000 of these performed labor for the army. Many of these "contrabands" brought with them valuable information about the disposition of Confederate troops and supplies. Occasionally some brought even more

valuable assets. Robert Smalls and his brother, who were slaves in Charleston, South Carolina, in May 1862 daringly seized the Confederate sidewheel steamer *Planter,* navigated it out of the harbor ringed with Confederate guns, and delivered it to the blockading Union fleet.

Debate Over Emancipation in the North. When the war appeared to have reached a stalemate, Northern sentiment in favor of freeing and arming the slaves grew. Republican congressmen were ahead of the president on these questions. As early as August 1861, they had passed an act declaring that slaves used to support the Confederate military were free. In March 1862 Congress forbade the return of fugitive slaves by the military. And on July 17, 1862, in a far-reaching confiscation act, it declared that slaves of all persons supporting the rebellion should be "forever free of their servitude, and not again [to be] held as slaves." These measures were, however, poorly drafted and not readily enforced, so that they had little practical consequence. More effective was the act of April 16, 1862, abolishing slavery in the District of Columbia.

But powerful forces in the North were opposed to emancipation. The border states, where slavery still prevailed, were of such uncertain loyalty that they might try to break away from the Union if emancipation became a Northern war aim. In the free states, anti-Negro prejudice was rampant, and many feared that emancipation would produce a massive migration of blacks to the North, where they would compete with white laborers for jobs. Belief in the inferiority of the Negro race was general, and the experience of Union soldiers in the South often strengthened this stereotype, for the fugitives who fled to their camps were mostly illiterate, ragged, and dirty.

During the initial stages of the war Lincoln, who hated slavery, could move toward emancipation only in a circuitous fashion. In early 1862 he made an earnest, though ultimately unsuccessful, plea to the border states to devise plans of gradual, compensated emancipation, for which he promised federal financial assistance. At the same time, he took anti-Negro sen-

FERROTYPE OF SERGEANT J. L. BALLDWIN OF COMPANY G, 56TH U.S. COLORED INFANTRY

Early in the war even President Lincoln thought "that the organization, equipment and arming of negroes, like other soldiers, would be productive of more evil than good." But after the Emancipation Proclamation the Union government began systematically to recruit for colored military units. By the end of the war 178,895 black soldiers were serving in the Union armies, and they saw action in Virginia, South Carolina, Florida, Mississippi and elsewhere. "The emancipation policy and the use of colored troops," Lincoln declared, were "the heaviest blow yet dealt to the rebellion." *(Chicago Historical Society)*

came to think it was time to enroll blacks in the army. But most influential in changing Lincoln's mind was his grim recognition after eighteen months of combat that the war could not be ended by traditional means. "We . . . must change our tactics or lose the war," he concluded.

Waiting only for McClellan to check Lee's invasion at Antietam, Lincoln issued, on September 22, 1862, a preliminary emancipation proclamation announcing that unless the rebellious states returned to their allegiance he would on January 1, 1863, declare that "all persons held as slaves" in the territory controlled by the Confederates were "then, thenceforward, and forever free." Since the president justified his action on the ground of military necessity, it was appropriate that the definitive Emancipation Proclamation at the beginning of the new year officially authorized the enrollment of black troops in the Union army.

Promptly the War Department began to accept Negro regiments. These were not, to be sure, the first black soldiers to serve in the war, for a few Negroes had been enrolled without permission from Washington in the Federal forces on the Sea Islands of South Carolina, in Louisiana, and in Kansas, but now large numbers of blacks joined the army. They were enrolled in segregated regiments, in nearly all cases with white officers, and they received less pay than did white soldiers. By the end of the war, the number of Negroes in the Union army totaled 178,895—more than twice the number of soldiers in the Confederate army at Gettysburg.

At first most Union officials thought black regiments would be useful only for garrison duty, but in bitterly contested engagements such as Fort Wagner and Port Hudson, Miliken's Bend and Nashville, they demonstrated how well they could and would fight. The battle record of these black troops did much to change popular Northern stereotypes of the Negro. In the early stages of the war, cartoonists and caricaturists portrayed blacks as invisible men; their faces were vague and featureless blobs of black, hardly human. But with emancipation and the enrollment of Negroes in the army, war artists began to take a closer look, to depict blacks with distinctive, recognizably human features, and finally, in a kind of per-

timent into account by favoring plans to colonize freedman in Central America and in Haiti.

By the fall of 1862, however, Lincoln felt able to act decisively against slavery. By failing to adopt his program of gradual emancipation, the border states had lost their chance. Blacks showed little interest in his plans for colonization, which in any case were poorly thought out and could only lead to disaster. As casualties mounted, Northern soldiers, without necessarily shedding their prejudices against Negroes,

CHANGING NORTHERN IMAGES
OF THE BLACK MAN
The Dis-United States: A Black Business

Teaching the Negro Recruits the Use of the Minié Rifle

The Escaped Slave in the Union Army

verse tribute to their merit, to sketch them with Nordic profiles.

The South Moves Toward Emancipation. Meanwhile, and much more slowly, sentiment was growing in the Confederacy for the military employment of blacks. Support for arming the slaves emerged first in those areas scourged by Northern armies. After Grant's successful Vicksburg campaign, the Jackson *Mississippian* boldly called for enrolling slaves as soldiers in the Confederate army. Though other Mississippi and Alabama newspapers echoed the call for black recruits, the most powerful voice for arming the slaves was that of General Patrick R. Cleburne, who witnessed how easily the powerful Union army broke the thin Confederate line at Chattanooga. Seeing no other source of manpower, Cleburne, together with his aides, addressed a long letter to General Joseph E. Johnston, who had succeeded Bragg as commander of the army of Tennessee, urging "that we immediately commence training a large reserve of the most courageous of our slaves, and further that we guarantee freedom within a reasonable time to every slave in the South who shall remain true to the Confederacy in this war."

So drastic a proposal was bound to rouse strong opposition, and President Davis, upon learning of Cleburne's letter, ordered it suppressed. But the subject would not die. As Union armies moved closer to the Confederate heartland, Virginia editors also began to urge arming the blacks, and at an October 1864 meeting Southern governors proposed "a change of policy on our part" as to the slaves. Finally, on November 7, 1864, President Davis, in a deliberately obscure message to Congress, put himself at the head of the movement. Urging further impressment of blacks for service with the army, Davis argued that the Confederate government should purchase the impressed slaves.

However obscurely phrased, Davis's proposal clearly looked toward the end of slavery, and it at once encountered powerful resistance. Davis, said his enemies, proposed the confiscation of private property; he was subverting the Constitution. His plan would be a confession to the world of the South's weakness. It would deplete the labor force needed to feed the army. And most frightening of all, it would arm black men, who at best might desert to the Union armies and at worst might use those arms against their masters.

Despite all opposition, the Confederate government pushed ahead with the plan, for it had no other reservoir of manpower. In February 1865 the scheme received the backing of General Lee, who wrote that employing blacks as soldiers was "not only expedient but necessary" and announced plainly that "it would be neither just nor wise . . . to require them to serve as slaves." The next month the Confederate Congress passed, by a very close vote, an act calling for 300,000 more soldiers, irrespective of color. No provision was made in the act to free blacks who enrolled, but the Confederate War Department in effect smuggled emancipation into the measure through the orders it issued for its enforcement. Promptly the recruiting of black troops began, and some black companies were raised in Richmond and other towns. By this time, however, it was too late, even for such a revolutionary experiment, and none of the black Confederate soldiers ever saw service.

Europe and the War

Though the Union and Confederate governments moved toward emancipating and arming the blacks because of military necessity, both recognized how profoundly their actions affected the continuing struggle for European recognition and support. Well-informed Americans were aware of the intensity of European antislavery sentiment. But so long as neither government took a bold stand against the South's peculiar institution, European antislavery leaders were puzzled and divided by the war. Lincoln's Emancipation Proclamation ended the confusion. European antislavery spokesmen soon recognized that the proclamation marked a new era. Within three months after the final Emancipation Proclamation was issued, fifty-six large public meetings were held in Great Britain to uphold the Northern cause.

Union diplomacy had need of such popular support, for there still lurked the possibility of European intervention in the war. Though the gravest threat had passed in the fall of 1862, before the full effect of the Emancipation Proclamation could be sensed abroad, the French emperor continued to contemplate the advantages that might come of meddling in American affairs. Hoping that a divided United States would assist enterprise of establishing a puppet empire under the Emperor Maximilian in Mexico, Napoleon in February 1863, when Northern military fortunes were at their nadir after Fredericksburg, offered to mediate between the two belligerents. Shrewdly judging that Great Britain and Russia were not behind the French move, Secretary of State Seward spurned the offer.

More dangerous to the Union cause than Napoleon's clumsy diplomacy were the warships being built for the Confederacy in British shipyards. Supplying either belligerent in a war with armed ships was contrary both to international law and to British statutes, but through a loophole in the law it was legal to sell separately unarmed vessels and the armaments that would convert them into men of war. In March 1862 the ship that became the C.S.S. *Florida* sailed from a British shipyard, and in July of that year the more powerful *Alabama* set forth to begin her depredations. Even as these raiders swept the Union merchant marine from the high seas, a more formidable Confederate naval threat, this time to the blockade itself, was being forged in the form of two enormous ironclad steam rams under construction at the Laird yards in Liverpool.

The British government wished to observe its neutrality laws, but the legal machinery was slow and cumbersome. When Union minister Charles Francis Adams called the attention of the foreign office to the rams, Lord Russell replied that he could not act to detain them unless there was convincing evidence of Confederate ownership. Adams and his aides rushed to secure affidavits to prove that the vessels were intended for the Confederacy, but British law officers were unconvinced. Finally, in utter exasperation, Adams on September 5, 1863, sent Russell a final warning against permitting the ships to sail, adding: "It would be superfluous in me to point out to your

Lordship that this is war." Fortunately, two days before receiving Adams's ultimatum, Russell had already decided to detain the rams, and the Confederates' final hope of breaking the blockade was lost.

With that crisis, the last serious threat of European involvement in the American war disappeared. So indifferent, or even hostile, to the Southern cause was the British cabinet that late in 1863 Confederate Secretary of State Benjamin ordered Mason, his envoy, to leave London on the grounds that "the Government of Her Majesty [Queen Victoria] . . . entertains no intention of receiving you as the accredited minister of this government."

Keenly aware of the influence that emancipation had exerted in uniting European opinion against the South, President Davis sought similarly to capitalize on the actions that the Confederate States took against slavery during the final months of the war. In January 1865 he sent Duncan F. Kenner, one of the largest slaveholders in Louisiana, on a secret mission to Europe, authorizing him to promise the emancipation of the slaves in return for European recognition and aid to the Confederacy. The experiment came too late, for now it was evident that Northern victory was inevitable. Neither the French nor the British government expressed interest in Kenner's proposal.

Wartime Politics in the Confederacy

The military and diplomatic advantages resulting from emancipation were to a considerable extent counterbalanced by its political disadvantages. In the Confederacy there had been from the beginning of the war a sizable disloyal element. Unionism was strong in the Upper South, in the mountain regions, and in some of the poorer hill counties. As the war progressed, some of these disaffected Southerners joined secret peace societies, such as the Order of the Heroes, which had its following in the Carolinas and Virginia. Disloyalty extended into the ranks of the Confederate army, especially after conscription was initiated, and desertion was widespread. About one out of every nine soldiers who enlisted in the Confederate army deserted. Sometimes they formed guerrilla bands that preyed equally upon Confederate and Union sympathizers. When halted by an enrolling officer and asked to show his pass to leave the army, a deserter would pat his gun defiantly and say, "This is my furlough."

Probably no action of the Davis administration could have won over these actively disloyal citizens, but the policies of the Confederate government alienated also a large number of entirely loyal Southerners. Some of these critics complained that President Davis was timid and tardy. He was sickly, neurasthenic, and indecisive, they said; he could not tolerate strong men around him and relied for advice upon sycophants; he did not know how to rouse the loyalty and the passions of the Southern people; he lacked courage to put himself at the head of the Southern armies and lead the Confederacy to victory.

A much larger group of Confederates censured their president for exactly opposite reasons. Davis's plan to arm and free the slaves reinforced their conviction that he intended to undermine the principles upon which the Confederacy had been founded. Conscription, they argued, had begun the subversion of state sovereignty, guaranteed by the Constitution. They found evidence of Davis's dictatorial ambitions in his requests that Congress suspend the writ of habeas corpus, so that the disloyal could be arrested and imprisoned without trial. Grudgingly Congress agreed to the suspension for three limited periods, but late in 1864 it rejected Davis's appeals for a further extension on the ground that it would be a dangerous assault upon the Constitution. Although infringements of civil liberties were infrequent in the Confederacy and no Southern newspaper was suppressed for publishing subversive editorials, the critics warned that Davis was reaching after imperial powers. Leading this group of Davis's critics was none other than the vice-president of the Confederate states, Alexander H. Stephens, who spent most of the final years of the war not in Richmond but in Georgia, stirring up agitation against the president's allegedly unconstitutional usurpation of power and simultaneously complaining of Davis's "weakness and imbecility."

The congressional elections of 1863, held after Southerners had begun to realize the gravity of their defeats at Gettysburg and at Vicksburg, greatly strengthened the anti-Davis bloc. During the following year, the president was often able to muster a majority in Congress only because of the consistent support of representatives from districts overrun or threatened by advancing Federal armies. In some instances these districts were unable to hold regular elections in 1863 and their incumbent congressmen, chosen in the early days of complete commitment to the Confederate cause, remained in office; in any case, representatives from these occupied regions had little to lose from measures that taxed and bled the rest of the Confederacy. But by the desperate winter of 1864–65, not even this support could give Davis control of Congress. Now in a majority, his critics refused his request for control over the state militias and rejected his plea to end all exemptions from conscription. Even as Sherman's army advanced through the Carolinas, Congress endlessly debated his plan for arming the slaves. It passed, over Davis's opposition, an act creating the post of general in chief, advising the president to name Lee. Fearful of attacking the president directly, congressional critics began investigations of several of his cabinet officers, and they introduced resolutions declaring that the resignation of Secretary of State Judah P. Benjamin, Davis's closest friend and most trusted adviser, would be "subservient of the public interest." Secretary of War Seddon also came under fire, and when the Virginia delegation in Congress called for his resignation, he felt obliged to leave the cabinet. In January 1865, for the first and only time, the Confederate Congress overrode a presidential veto.

Wartime Politics in the North

Meanwhile in the North, Abraham Lincoln and his government were subjected to the same kinds of criticism. Pro-Confederate sympathy was strongest in the states of the Upper South that remained in the Union, in those parts of the Old Northwest originally settled by Southerners, and in cities like New

slaves, and the confiscation of rebel property. The Radicals, on the other hand, represented by Chase in the cabinet and by Sumner and Thaddeus Stevens in the Congress, were eager to try more drastic experiments; they demanded that the entire Southern social system be revolutionized, that Southern slaveholders be punished, and, increasingly, that blacks should have not merely freedom but civil and political equality.

Lincoln refused to align himself with either faction and tried to be even-handed in distributing federal patronage to both. He shared the desire of the Conservatives for a speedy peace and a prompt reconciliation between the sections, but he recognized that in casting about for votes to carry through their plans, they would be "tempted to affiliate with those whose record is not clear," even persons infected "by the virus of secession." As for the Radicals, he conceded that "after all their faces are set Zionwards," but he objected to their "petulant and vicious fretfulness" and thought they were sometimes "almost *fiendish*" in attacking Republicans who disagreed with them. For his neutrality, the president gained the distrust and abuse of both factions.

The Election of 1864.   The schism within the Republican party was the more serious because the presidential election of 1864 was approaching. In General George B. McClellan the Democrats had a handsome, glamorous candidate, and they had a powerful set of issues. They could capitalize upon war weariness. They made much of Lincoln's arbitrary use of executive power and the infringement of civil liberties. They objected to the unfairness of the draft. They showed how the Republican Congress had benefited the Northeast by enacting protective tariffs, handing out railroad subsidies, and creating a national banking system. Endlessly the Democrats rang the changes on the anti-Negro theme, charging that the Lincoln administration had changed a war for Union into a war for emancipation. If Lincoln was reelected, they charged, Republicans were planning to amalgamate the black and white races; the word "miscegenation" made its first appearance in an 1864 campaign document.

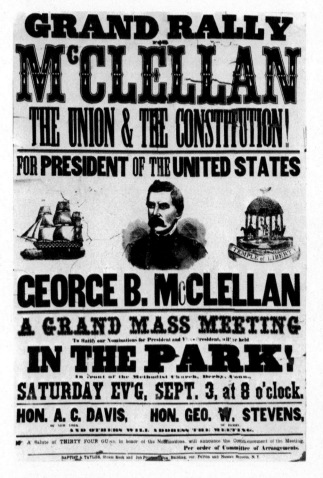

MCCLELLAN POSTER
Both war Democrats and peace Democrats attended the national party convention that assembled in Chicago on August 29, 1864. To please the former the convention chose as the Democratic presidential candidate General George B. McClellan, who favored vigorous prosecution of the war and claimed that he could be more effective than Abraham Lincoln. To placate the peace Democrats the convention adopted a platform calling for a cessation of hostilities and condemning "four years of failure to restore the Union by the experiment of war." With the nominee facing one direction and the platform slanting in another, the Democratic drive for the presidency was probably doomed from the start, but the victories of Union armies in the South cinched the reelection of Abraham Lincoln. *(Smithsonian Institution, Division of Political History)*

Even in the face of such powerful opposition, the Republicans in the winter of 1863–64 divided sharply when Lincoln in December 1863 announced a plan for reconstructing the Southern states. Promising amnesty to all Confederates except a few high government officials, the president proposed to reestablish civilian government in the conquered areas of the South when as few as 10 percent of the number of voters in 1860 took an oath swearing future loyalty to the United States Constitution and pledging acceptance of emancipation. Fearing that this program would replace the antebellum leadership in control of the South and would leave freedmen in peonage, the Radicals pushed through Congress the Wade-Davis bill, requiring that over half the number of 1860 voters in each Southern state swear allegiance and participate in drafting a new constitution before it would be readmitted to the Union. When Lincoln killed this measure, passed at the very end of the 1864 congressional session, by a pocket veto, Radicals were furious. Senator Benjamin F. Wade and Representative Henry Winter Davis, the sponsors of the vetoed bill, issued a manifesto, accusing the president of "usurpations" and claiming that he had committed a "studied outrage upon the legislative authority of the people."

Because Lincoln had control of the federal patronage and of the party machinery, he was readily renominated in June 1864 by the Republican national convention, which selected Andrew Johnson of Tennessee as his running mate, but the unanimity of the vote was only a façade. After an unsuccessful attempt to run Chase as a rival to Lincoln, some ultra-Radicals had already thrown their support to a third-party ticket headed by General Frémont, who had been hostile to the president since his removal from command in Missouri. Other Radicals tried, even after Lincoln had been renominated, to persuade the party to pick a new candidate. As late as September 1864 a questionnaire sent to Republican governors, leading editors, and prominent congressmen elicited a virtually unanimous response that if Lincoln could be persuaded to withdraw from the race, Republicans should name another standardbearer. As Massachusetts Governor John A. Andrew

JEFF DAVIS'S NOVEMBER NIGHTMARE
A Northern cartoon shows Lincoln's reelection in 1864 as evidence that there would be no letting up in pressure upon the Confederacy. *(Library of Congress)*

expressed the general sentiment, Lincoln was "essentially lacking in the quality of leadership." So bleak was the outlook that the president himself a few weeks before the elections conceded that McClellan was likely to win.

Northern Victory

Until the fall of 1864, then, the wartime history of the United States and of the Confederate States moved in parallel lines as each government improvised experiments that might lead to victory. But in the finals months of the struggle the course of the two rivals markedly diverged. Increasing dissension and disaffection marked Jefferson Davis's last winter in office, while Abraham Lincoln won triumphant reelection in November 1864. By April 1865 the Confederacy was dead, and a month later Davis was in irons, like a common criminal, at Fort Monroe. The Union was victorious, and Lincoln, killed by the bullet of the mad assassin John Wilkes Booth, lived in memory as the nation's martyred president who freed the slaves and saved the Union.

Campaigns in the East, 1864–1865. The very different fates of the Lincoln and Davis administrations were decided, in large part, on the battlefield. When Grant became general in chief of the Union armies in 1864, he determined to make his headquarters not in Washington but with the often-defeated Army of the Potomac. Working closely with Meade, the actual commander of that army, he developed a plan for pushing Lee back upon the defenses of Richmond. Checked in the bloody battle of the Wilderness (May 5–7), Grant did not retreat, as previous Union generals had done, but pushed around Lee's right flank, attempting to get between him and the Confederate capital. Checked again at Spotsylvania (May 8–12), Grant again did not retreat but sent word to Washington: "I propose to fight it out along this line if it takes all summer."

After a disastrous direct assault on the Confederate lines at Cold Harbor (June 3), Grant again skill-

fully maneuvered around Lee's right flank, crossed the James River, and joined the Union troops already there under General Butler. He then instituted what became known as the "siege" of Petersburg and Richmond—incorrectly so, since the two cities were not fully surrounded and since supplies continued to come in from the South and West. But as Grant's lines constantly lengthened, he cut these access routes one by one. Pinned down before Richmond, Lee remembered "Stonewall" Jackson's brilliant diversionary campaign of 1862 and sent what men he could spare under Jubal A. Early into the Shenandoah Valley. Though Early achieved initial success and even pushed on to the outskirts of Washington, Grant did not loosen his grip on Richmond. Instead he sent brash, aggressive Philip H. Sheridan to the Shenandoah Valley, ordering him not merely to drive out the Confederates but to devastate the countryside so that thereafter a crow flying over it would have to carry its own rations. Sheridan followed his orders explicitly, and Early's army was smashed. More than ever before, the fate of the Confederacy was tied to Richmond and to Lee's army.

Campaigns in the West, 1864–1865. Meanwhile, on May 7, 1864, Sherman began his slow progress through northwestern Georgia, opposed by the wily Joseph E. Johnston, who made the Union troops pay for every foot they advanced. But as Sherman neared the railroad hub of Atlanta, President Davis, who had never trusted Johnston, removed the general and put John B. Hood in command. In a series of attacks upon overwhelmingly superior Union forces—exactly the sort of engagement Johnston had so skillfully avoided —Hood was defeated; and on September 2 Sherman occupied Atlanta. News of the victory reached the North just before the presidential election and made a farce of the Democratic platform's assertion that the war was a "failure."

Next, casually dispatching Thomas to fend off

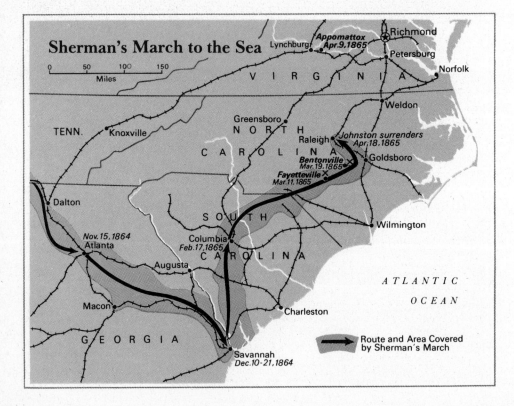

A DEAD CONFEDERATE SOLDIER AT FORT MAHONE, NEAR PETERSBURG, VIRGINIA, APRIL 2, 1865

In the final bloody battles of the war the Confederacy lost men who could not be replaced. "Where is this to end?" asked General Josiah Gorgas. "No money in the Treasury—no food to feed Gen. Lee's army—no troops to oppose Gen. Sherman—what does it all mean . . . ? Is the cause really hopeless?" *(Library of Congress)*

Hood and to hold Tennessee, Sherman turned his back on the smoking ruins of Atlanta and set out on a march toward Savannah and the sea, where he knew that a Union fleet was waiting with supplies.* Meeting only desultory resistance, Sherman's men cut a swath through central Georgia, destroying railroads, military supplies, and even many private houses. Sherman's objective was as much psychological as military. "I can make the march," he had promised Grant, "and make Georgia howl!"

Offering captured Savannah to Lincoln as a Christmas present, Sherman turned his army north, pushing aside the depleted Confederate forces, again under the command of Johnston. His men took Co-

lumbia, South Carolina, which was burned either by intention or by accident, and drove on into North Carolina. Grant, meanwhile, clamped down ever tighter on Richmond. At last, on April 2, 1865, Lee found his position untenable, and warning President Davis and his government to flee, he tried to lead his ragged troops to join Johnston's dwindling force. Cut off by Grant, he had no alternative but to surrender, and on April 9 at Appomattox Court House he told his weary, hungry men to lay down their arms. On April 18 Johnston followed by surrendering to Sherman (although the final terms were not agreed on until April 26). When the news reached the trans-Mississippi region, Kirby-Smith capitulated in June. The war had lasted almost precisely four years.

The Union cause, and the Lincoln administration, were the beneficiaries of these victories. The critics of the government had been most vocal, their opposi-

---

* Attempting to force Sherman to turn back, Hood invaded Tennessee but was checked in the battle of Franklin (November 30, 1864) and routed in the battle of Nashville (December 15–16).

tion most powerful, in the heartbreaking summer months of 1864, when Grant seemed to be getting nowhere in Virginia and Sherman appeared unable to bag his enemy in Georgia. Northern morale and support for the president mounted perceptibly at the news of Sherman's success at Atlanta and of Farragut's victory at Mobile Bay. Conversely, support for Davis's administration dwindled and critical voices became louder as Confederate reverse followed reverse. In a certain sense, then, victory begot victory, and defeat defeat.

Why the North Won the War.   Yet this is circular reasoning and does not explain the final Union triumph after so many earlier Confederate successes. For a fuller understanding one must turn to the slow but steady mobilization of the North's infinitely superior economic resources and to the gradual erosion of those in the South. The effect of Northern economic and industrial superiority was not fully felt until after more than two years of war; it took time to award contracts, to expand factories, to recruit skilled laborers, and to deliver the products. But by 1863, observers noted that Lee's veterans invading Pennsylvania looked like a gaggle of "barefooted, ragged, lousy, [but] disciplined, desperate ruffians," so badly supplied and so poorly fed that their line of march was "traceable by the deposit of dysenteric stool the army leaves behind it." By 1863 the Union armies, on the other hand, were so completely equipped that their paraphernalia became a hindrance. When Northern soldiers advanced, they shucked off layers of greatcoats, blankets, and other unnecessary supplies. Nowhere was Northern economic superiority more evident by the end of the war than in its transportation system. By that time Southern railroads simply had worn out. In the Union, on the other hand, some 5,000 more miles of railroad were in operation in 1865 than at the start of the war—a figure that does not include the numerous military railroads operated in the South—and, under the necessity of linking up with the newly authorized Union Pacific Railroad, Northern lines all converted to a standard rail gauge.

But supplies do not fight wars, nor do trains; men do. From the start the overwhelming numerical preponderance of the Northern population counted heavily against the Confederacy, and during the conflict that advantage increased. During the four years of war more than 180,000 male immigrants of military age settled in the North, while there was virtually no immigration to the Confederacy. In addition, the black population of the country became another vast source of Union manpower. Confederates dared not tap this source until their cause was already lost.

But men, no matter how numerous, fight well only if ably led by their military commanders and inspired by their political leaders. It would be hard to argue that Northern generalship was superior to that of the South. While Grant has his admirers, to most students Robert E. Lee is the greatest Civil War commander. Nor is it easy to maintain that the political leadership of the North was markedly superior. Later generations, recalling the eloquence of the Gettysburg Address and the mystical beauty of the second inaugural address, have found it difficult to remember that for most of his administration Lincoln was considered uninspiring and ineffectual. Had Lincoln been defeated for reelection in 1864, he would doubtless be rated as an honest but unsuccessful president. On the other hand, had the Southern states been able to win their independence, Jefferson Davis would undoubtedly rank as the George Washington of the Confederacy.

There were, of course, important differences between the two wartime presidents, but these were of less significance than the differences in the political systems in which they had to work. Like many more recent emerging nations, the Confederacy tried to present a façade of unity to the world. It was a one-party, or more properly, a no-party state. Southerners feared that party divisions would suggest they were less than unanimous in seeking independence. The most careful analysis of the voting records of Confederate congressmen has been able to show, at most, only incipient party lines. Small temporary factions rather than permanent political parties dominated Congress. President Davis's enemies were many, and they were constantly attacking him from all directions, like a swarm of bees; his friends were divided, and he could never rally them into a unified cohort.

"GENERAL ROBERT E. LEE LEAVING THE MCLEAN HOUSE AFTER THE SURRENDER AT APPOMATTOX, 1865" BY A. W. WAUD

After accepting Grant's terms of surrender, Lee stepped out to the porch of the McLean House and signaled his orderly to bring up his horse. While the animal was being bridled, one of Grant's aides remembered, Lee "gazed sadly in the direction . . . where his army lay—now an army of prisoners. He thrice smote the palm of his left hand slowly with his right fist in an absent sort of way." Then he mounted, and Grant saluted him by raising his hat. "Lee raised his hat respectfully, and rode off at a slow trot to break the sad news to the brave fellows whom he had so long commanded." *(Library of Congress)*

As with the Congress, so with the people. It is safe to guess that if at any point the voters of the Confederacy had been asked to endorse their president or to topple him, Davis would have received overwhelming support. But lacking political parties, Southerners had no way of making this sentiment felt.

In the Union, on the other hand, the two-party system remained active. The Democrats remained a formidable, if not always united, force throughout the war. They came close to winning a majority in Congress in the 1862 elections; even in 1864 McClellan received 45 percent of the popular vote—at a time when the strongest opponents of the Republican party were still out of the Union and, of course, not

voting. Such a powerful opposition party compelled the Republican factions, however bitterly at odds with each other, to work together. Conservatives and Radicals might disagree over slavery, emancipation, and reconstruction, but they all agreed that any Republican administration was better than a Democratic one. It was, then, the absence of political machinery in the South that weakened Davis's regime and rendered him unable fully to mobilize the material and spiritual resources of the Confederacy. And it was the much maligned two-party system that allowed Lincoln, despite quarrelsome and impassioned attacks from fellow Republicans, to experiment boldly and to grow into an effective wartime leader.

CHRONOLOGY

1863   Lincoln issues final Emancipation Proclamation.
Confederates defeat Union army under Hooker at Chancellorsville.
Lee's invasion of the North checked by Union army under Meade at Gettysburg.
Grant captures Vicksburg.
Draft riots in the North.
Confederate army under Bragg defeats Union forces at Chickamauga.
Union victory at Chattanooga (Lookout Mountain and Missionary Ridge).
Lincoln offers lenient reconstruction program.

1864   Grant named Union general in chief.
Grant's direct advance on Richmond checked at the Wilderness, Spotsylvania, and Cold Harbor.
Grant moves south of James River to begin "siege" of Petersburg.

Sherman pushes back Confederates under Joseph E. Johnston and captures Atlanta.
Farragut captures Mobile.
Lincoln reelected president over Democrat McClellan.
Sherman marches from Atlanta to the sea.

1865   Sherman pushes northward through South Carolina and North Carolina.
Lee gives up Petersburg and Richmond, and Confederate government flees.
Lee surrenders at Appomattox. Johnston surrenders to Sherman. Kirby-Smith surrenders Confederate forces west of the Mississippi.
Lincoln assassinated; Andrew Johnson becomes president.

SUGGESTED READINGS

The studies listed at the end of the previous chapter continue, for the most part, to be pertinent to the topics discussed in the present chapter.

Of the enormous literature on the military operations during the Civil War, only a few of the most important titles can be listed here. On the Northern armies, the most comprehensive works are Kenneth P. Williams's five-volume study, *Lincoln Finds a General* (1949–59), and Bruce Catton's absorbing trilogy: *Mr. Lincoln's Army* (1951); *Glory Road* (1952); and *A Stillness at Appomattox* (1953). Among the best biographies of Union generals are Warren W. Hassler, Jr., *General George B. McClellan* (1957); Bruce Catton, *Grant Moves South* (1960), and *Grant Takes Command* (1969); and Lloyd Lewis, *Sherman* (1932).

The most elaborate account of military operations from a Southern point of view is Shelby Foote, *The Civil War* (3 vols., 1958–74). Douglas S. Freeman, *Lee's Lieutenants* (3 vols., 1942–44), is an important examination of Confederate commanders in the eastern theater, while western operations receive excellent treatment in Thomas Connelly, *Army of the Heartland* (2 vols., 1967–71). Among the most significant biographies of Confederate generals are Douglas S. Freeman, *R. E. Lee* (4 vols., 1934–35),

Frank E. Vandiver, *Mighty Stonewall* (1957), and Grady McWhiney, *Braxton Bragg and Confederate Defeat* (1969).

On the recruitment of the Northern armies, see Fred A. Shannon, *The Organization and Administration of the Union Army* (2 vols., 1928), and Eugene C. Murdoch, *One Million Men: The Civil War Draft in the North* (1971). Adrian Cook, *Armies of the Street* (1974), is the definitive treatment of New York City draft riots. A. B. Moore, *Conscription and Conflict in the Confederacy* (1924), is still the best study of its subject.

Two books by Bell I. Wiley provide a fascinating social history of the common soldier of the Civil War: *The Life of Johnny Reb* (1943), and *The Life of Billy Yank* (1952).

The best accounts of Civil War naval operations are Virgil C. Jones, *The Civil War at Sea* (3 vols., 1960–62), and Bern Anderson, *By Sea and by River* (1962). See also John Niven's fine biography, *Gideon Welles: Lincoln's Secretary of the Navy* (1973).

On the function played by political parties in the Union and the Confederacy, see Eric L. McKitrick's brilliant essay, "Party Politics and the Union and Confederate War Efforts," in William N. Chambers and Walter D. Burnham, eds., *The American Party Systems* (1967), pp. 152–81. The story of Confederate politics has to be pieced together from Wilfred B. Yearns, *The Confederate Congress* (1960); Thomas B. Alexander and Richard E. Beringer, *The Anatomy of the Confederate Congress* (1972); Frank L. Owsley, *State Rights in the Confederacy* (1925); Georgia L. Tatum, *Disloyalty in the Confederacy* (1934); and James Z. Rabun, "Alexander H. Stephens and Jefferson Davis," *American Historical Review,* 58 (1953), 290–321. On Union politics, see William B. Hesseltine, *Lincoln and the War Governors* (1948); T. Harry Williams, *Lincoln and the Radicals* (1941); Grady McWhiney, ed., *Grant, Lee, Lincoln and the Radicals* (1964); Hans L. Trefousse, *The Radical Republicans* (1969); James A. Rawley, *The Politics of Union* (1974); and William F. Zornow, *Lincoln and the Party Divided* (1954). For conflicting interpretations of the amount of disaffection and disloyalty in the North, see Wood Gray, *The Hidden Civil War* (1942), George F. Milton, *Abraham Lincoln and the Fifth Column* (1942), and Frank L. Klement, *The Copperheads in the Middle West* (1960).

Benjamin Quarles, *The Negro in the Civil War* (1953), is a comprehensive study. James M. McPherson, ed., *The Negro's Civil War* (1965), is a valuable set of documents, skillfully interwoven. Bell I. Wiley, *Southern Negroes, 1861–1865* (1938), is the standard account; on Confederate moves toward emancipation it can be supplemented by Robert F. Durden's excellent study, *The Gray and the Blacks* (1972). The early chapters of Leon F. Litwack, *Been in the Storm So Long* (1979), superbly recapture the activities and attitudes of slaves during the war. Benjamin Quarles, *Lincoln and the Negro* (1962), and John H. Franklin, *The Emancipation Proclamation* (1963), are both valuable. James M. McPherson, *The Struggle for Equality* (1964), is a fine account of abolitionists' efforts during the war and afterward. The authoritative account of Negro troops in the Union army is Dudley T. Cornish, *The Sable Arm* (1956).

For varying explanations of the collapse of the Confederacy, see Henry S. Commager, ed., *The Defeat of the Confederacy* (1964); David Donald, ed., *Why the North Won the Civil War* (1960); Charles H. Wesley, *The Collapse of the Confederacy* (1922); and Bell I. Wiley, *The Road to Appomattox* (1956).

CHAPTER 20

Reconstruction

1865–1877

A house divided against itself cannot stand," Abraham Lincoln prophesied in 1858. The Civil War proved that the United States would stand, not as a loose confederation of sovereign states but as one nation, indivisible. Never again would there be talk of secession. The war also ended slavery, the most divisive institution in antebellum America. Weakened by the advances of the Union armies and undermined by Lincoln's Emancipation Proclamation, slavery received its death blow in February 1865, when the Congress adopted the Thirteenth Amendment, outlawing slavery and involuntary servitude. Ratified by three-fourths of the states, the amendment became a part of the Constitution in December 1865.

But the Civil War did not settle the terms and conditions on which the several states, sections, races, and classes would live in the firmly united "house." Those problems formed the agenda of the Reconstruction era, one of the most complex and controversial periods in American history. During these postwar years some basic questions had to be answered: What, if any, punishment should be imposed on Southern whites who had supported the Confederate attempt to disrupt the Union? How were the recently emancipated slaves to be guaranteed their freedom, and what civil and political rights did freedmen have? When and on what conditions were the Southern states so recently in rebellion to be readmitted to the Union—that is, entitled to vote in national elections, to have senators and representatives seated in the United States Congress, and, in general, to become once more full-fledged, equal members in the national body politic?

The initial moves to answer these questions came from the president, whose powers had been greatly expanded during the war years. President Lincoln in December 1863 announced a generous program of amnesty to repentant rebels and inaugurated a plan for reorganizing loyal governments in the South when as few as 10 percent of the voters in 1860 were willing to support them. After the assassination of Lincoln in April 1865, President Andrew Johnson, his successor, continued the process of Reconstruction under a

"Westward the Course of Empire Takes Its Way" by Emanuel Leutze. Courtesy of National Collection of Fine Arts, Smithsonian Institution

From Eden to Babylon

Just as the Civil War required Americans to reconsider the meaning of national loyalty, so it compelled them to rethink the bases of a good society. Before the war their vision of America was primarily agrarian. Most of the inhabitants of the United States lived on farms, planatations, and ranches. Of course there were bustling cities, but most city dwellers had been born in the countryside, whether in the United States, Ireland, Germany, or England. It was natural, then, that when mid-century Americans portrayed themselves, it was as farmers, herdsmen, trappers, and explorers —not as businessmen, factory laborers, or clerks.

Just before the outbreak of the war Emanuel Leutze accurately recaptured the Americans' definition of themselves in Westward the Course of Em-

pire Takes Its Way, which filled a six-hundred-square-foot panel in the rotunda of the national Capitol. It was not a great painting, not even a good painting; in it, as one contemporary remarked, "confusion reigns paramount." But it did serve to perpetuate the myth that Americans were a people close to the land, who drew their strength from nature.

Nature had a special place in the thought of antebellum Americans. The most influential American philosophical work published in the first half of the nineteenth century was Ralph Waldo Emerson's essay on that topic. "Nature," to Emerson and the thousands who read his essays and heard him lecture, included those "essences unchanged by man: space, the air, the river, the leaf." It was to be distinguished from "art," the imposition of man's will upon nature that resulted in "a house, a canal, a statue, a picture." "Nature," then, had emotional and moral primacy over "art," and most Americans believed, with Emerson himself, that by shedding all artifice man could again become part and parcel of nature itself.

A self-taught Massachusetts painter, Erastus Salisbury Field, perfectly recaptured the spirit behind Emerson's ideas. With only three months of informal training as an artist, Field personified the spirit of spontaneity and improvisation that Emerson extolled. More important, his early paintings showed an attachment to, and a meticulous interest in, nature. The land he portrayed was a tidied-up, New England version of Leutze's sprawling continent. Field's *The Garden of Eden* did not have a specifically American setting, though his neatly paired animals of peculiar anatomy and his trees with their improbable fruit might have flourished in America, if anywhere. There is, however, a distinctively American note in Field's treatment of nudity in the Garden of Eden: a clump of strategically placed lilies preserves Adam's modesty, and Eve lurks behind some unlikely blossoms. Clearly for Field, as for Emerson, man is at his best when most closely linked to nature, in a scene unmarred by human artifice or ingenuity.

"The Garden of Eden" by Erastus Salisbury Field. M. and M. Karolik Collection, Museum of Fine Arts, Boston

"Proposed Arcade Railroad Under Broadway" by Samuel B. B. Nowlan. Yale University Art Gallery, Mabel Brady Garvan Collection

Magnum

During the Civil War years Americans' perception of the good society dramatically changed. The war may not have stimulated economic growth, but it did promote mechanization. Steam power largely replaced horse power and water power. Machines of ever increasing complexity, with fascinating gears and gauges, replaced men. The vast foundries and rolling mills that had turned out cannons during the war were diverted to the production of structural iron girders, and later steel beams, which made possible a new American architecture. No longer was it necessary to erect buildings out of huge piles of masonry, and no longer was it dangerous to build them too high. Using steel beams, innovative architects like Louis Sullivan invented the skyscraper, a triumphant fusing of form and function. Imaginative engineers, like Samuel B. B. Nowlan of New York, foresaw the day when whole cities would be made of steel, and Nowlan's sketch, *Proposed Arcade Railroad under Broadway,* looked ahead to a new era in urban design.

Robert C. Lautman, Washington, D. C.

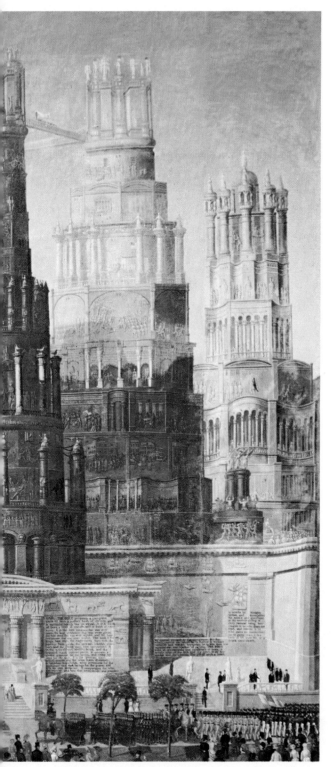

Postwar Americans found the new technology exhilarating to the point of intoxication. Gone now was the day when Erastus Field portrayed man in the bosom of nature. Instead, looking forward to the Centennial Exposition in Philadelphia, the aging Field painted his *Historical Monument of the American Republic.* Field's picture showed America as wholly urban, entirely built over with huge towers, with round or octagonal sides, rising in diminishing stages. The central and tallest tower commemorated Abraham Lincoln and the Constitution. Near the top, several of these towers were joined together with vaulting steel bridges, along which steam railroad trains puffed. As a significant reminder of Civil War days, soldiers paraded the avenue in front of Field's monumental vision of America as Babylon.

By 1876, then, Field's ideas, like those of most Americans, had completely shifted. Rural peace paled beside the attractions of mechanized urban life. The machine was now the magnet of the American mind. When the novelist William Dean Howells visited the Centennial Exposition, he, like thousands of other Americans, was most impressed by the gigantic Corliss engine, which gave power to the 8000 other machines, large and small, that sewed cloth, printed newspapers, made shoes, and pumped water on the thirteen-acre Exposition grounds. After comparing the displays of painting and sculpture with the Corliss engine, Howells concluded: "It is in these things of iron and steel that the national genius most freely speaks."

"Historical Monument of the American Republic" by Erastus Salisbury Field. Museum of Fine Arts, Springfield, Massachusetts, The Morgan Wesson Memorial Collection

"Max Schmitt in a Single Skull" by Thomas Eakins. Metropolitan Museum of Art, Alfred N. Punnett Fund and Gift of George D. Pratt, 1934

The greatest painter of the postwar period, Thomas Eakins of Philadelphia, shared Howells's admiration of the machine and his respect for the scientific knowledge that it represented. Just as the Corliss engine was "an athlete of steel and iron, without a superfluous ounce of metal on it," so a painting, thought Eakins, should be lean and objective. In order to portray the human figure scientifically, he studied anatomy at Jefferson Medical College. Eakins also linked painting with mathematics, because both were disciplines in which "the complicated things are reduced to simple things."

Eakins's portrait, *Max Schmitt in a Single Skull*, shows how perfectly he fused art, anatomy, and the mathematics of perspective. More subtly it also speaks of the changed values of postwar American society. In decisive contrast to the absence of all man-made artifacts in Leutze's painting and in Field's *The Garden of Eden*, a superb steel bridge is a vital part of Eakins's portrait. More emphatically than any number of words, the presence of that bridge shows that, by the end of the Civil War era, Americans had come to think of nature as something to be spanned, conquered, and controlled.

similar plan. Johnson, like Lincoln, expected Southern whites to take the lead in establishing new state governments loyal to the Union. To initiate the process he appointed a provisional governor for each of the former Confederate states (except those where Lincoln had already initiated Reconstruction) and directed them to convene constitutional conventions. These were expected to adopt the Thirteenth Amendment ending slavery, nullify or repeal the ordinances of secession, and repudiate state debts incurred for the prosecution of the war. By early 1866 each of the states that had once formed the Confederacy completed most of these required steps, and the president viewed the process of Reconstruction as concluded. He recommended that the senators and representatives chosen by these reorganized governments be promptly given their rightful seats in Congress.

From the outset presidential Reconstruction had its critics. Congress, which had jealously watched the executive branch augment its power during the war, was ready to reassert its equality, if not its hegemony. Unlike President Lincoln, Andrew Johnson, a Tennessee Democrat and former slaveholder, had no popular mandate, and the taciturn, inflexible, and pugnacious new occupant of the White House did not understand that politics is the art of compromise.

After an initial attempt to cooperate with the new president, Republican leaders in 1866 began to devise their own plans for Reconstruction. The first congressional plan was embodied in the Fourteenth Amendment to the Constitution, which made it clear that blacks were citizens of the United States and tried to define the rights and privileges of American citizens. When the Southern states refused to ratify this amendment, congressional Republicans moved in 1867 to a more stringent program of reorganizing the South by requiring Negro suffrage. Under this second plan of congressional Reconstruction, every Southern state (except for Tennessee, which had been readmitted to the Union in 1866) received a new constitution that guaranteed to men of all races equal protection of the laws, and between 1868 and 1871 all were readmitted to the Union. Republican governments, which depended heavily on Negro votes, con-trolled these states for a period ranging from a few months in the case of Virginia to nine years in the case of Louisiana.

Paths Not Taken

Contemporaries called this the period of Radical Reconstruction or, very often, Black Reconstruction, and it is easy to understand why many Americans of the 1860s and '70s viewed these changes as little short of revolutionary. To their Constitution, which had not been altered since 1804, were added during the five years after the Civil War the Thirteenth Amendment, ending slavery, the Fourteenth Amendment, defining the rights of citizens, and the Fifteenth Amendment (1870), prohibiting discrimination in voting on account of race or color. The national government, so recently tottering on the edge of defeat, was now more powerful than in any prevous point in American history. The Southern ruling class of whites, lately in charge of their own independent government, were petitioners for pardon. More than 3 million blacks, slaves only a few months earlier, were now free, entitled to the same privileges as all other citizens. Americans fairly gasped at the extent and the speed of the transformation wrought in their society, and it is hardly surprising that most subsequent historians accepted this contemporary view of the Reconstruction era as one of turbulent disorder.

Without denying that real and important changes did occur during the Reconstruction period, it might help to put these into perspective by inventing a little conterfactual history, a recital of conceivable historical scenarios that were never acted out. For instance, it would be easy to imagine how the victorious North might have turned angrily on the prostrate South. In 1865 Northerners had just finished four years of war that cost the Union army more than 360,000 casualties. To destroy the Confederacy required Americans of that and subsequent generations to pay in taxes at least $10 billion. Northerners had reason to believe, moreover, that their Confederate opponents had prosecuted the war with fiendish barbarity. Sober

RUINS OF RICHMOND
When the Confederate government evacuated Richmond on April 3, 1865, orders were given to burn supplies that might fall into the enemy's hands. There were heavy explosions as ironclads, armories, and arsenals were blown up. The next morning, as the fires spread, a mob of men and women, whites and blacks, began to plunder the city. *(Library of Congress)*

Union congressmen informed their constituents that the Confederates employed "Indian savages" to scalp and mutilate the Union dead. Reliable Northern newspapers told how in April 1864 General Nathan Bedford Forrest and his Confederates overran the defenses of Fort Pillow, Tennessee, manned by a Negro regiment, and, refusing to accept surrender, deliberately beat, shot, and burned their prisoners. The influential *Harper's Weekly Magazine* carried apparently authentic drawings of a goblet that a Southerner had made from a Yankee soldier's skull and of necklaces made of Yankee teeth that Southern ladies wore. When Union armies liberated Northern prisoners from such hell-holes as Andersonville, Georgia,

pictures of these half-starved skeletons of men, clad in grimy tatters of their Union uniforms, convinced Northerners that Jefferson Davis's policy had been "to starve and freeze and kill off by inches the prisoners he dares not butcher outright."

After the murder of Abraham Lincoln by the Southern sympathizer John Wilkes Booth, an outraged North could easily have turned on the conquered Confederacy in vengeance. The victorious Northerners might have executed Jefferson Davis, Alexander H. Stephens, and a score of other leading Confederates and might have sent thousands more into permanent exile. The triumphant Union might have erased the boundaries of the Southern states and divided the whole region into new, conquered territories. They might have enforced the confiscation acts already on the statute books and have seized the plantations of rebels, for distribution to the freedmen.

No such drastic course was followed. With the exception of Major Henry Wirtz, commandant of the infamous Andersonville prison, who was hanged, no Confederate was executed for "war crimes." A few Southern political leaders were imprisoned for their part in the "rebellion," but in most cases their release was prompt. To be sure, Jefferson Davis was kept in prison for two years at Fort Monroe, and he was under indictment for treason until 1869, when all charges were dropped. His case was, however, as unusual as it was extreme, and one reason for the long delay in bringing him to trial was the certainty that no jury, Northern or Southern, would render an impartial verdict. There was no general confiscation of the property of Confederates, no dividing up of plantations.

Equally conceivable is another scenario—another version of history that did not happen—this time featuring the Southern whites. For four years Confederate citizens had been subjected to a barrage of propaganda designed to prove that the enemy was little less than infernal in his purposes. Many believed the Southern editor who claimed that Lincoln's program was "Emancipation, Confiscation, Conflagration, and Extermination." According to the North Carolina educator Calvin H. Wiley, the North had "summoned to its aid every fierce and cruel and licentious passion of the human heart"; to defeat the Confederacy it was ready to use "the assassin's dagger, the midnight torch, . . . poison, famine and pestilence." Such charges were easy to credit in the many Southern families that had relatives in Northern prison camps, such as the one at Elmira, New York, where 775 of 8,347 Confederate prisoners died within three months for want of proper food, water, and medicine. The behavior of Union troops in the South, especially of Sherman's "bummers" in Georgia and the Carolinas, gave Southerners every reason to fear the worst if the Confederate government failed.

It would therefore have been reasonable for Confederate armies in 1865, overwhelmed by Union numbers, to disband quietly, disappear into the countryside, and carry on guerrilla operations against the Northern invaders. Indeed, on the morning of the day when Lee surrendered at Appomattox, Confederate General E. P. Alexander advocated just such a plan. He argued that if Lee's soldiers took to the woods with their rifles, perhaps two-thirds of the Army of Northern Virginia could escape capture. "We would be like rabbits and partridges in the bushes," he claimed, "and they could not scatter to follow us." The history of more recent wars of national liberation suggests that Alexander's judgment was correct. At the least his strategy would have given time for thousands of leading Southern politicians and planters, together with their families, to go safely into exile, as the Tories did during the American Revolution.

But, once again, no such events occurred. Some few Confederate leaders did go into exile. For instance, General Jubal A. Early fled to Mexico and thence to Canada, where he tried to organize a Southern exodus to New Zealand; but finding that nobody wanted to follow him, he returned to his home and his law practice in Virginia. A few hundred Confederates did migrate to Mexico and to Brazil. But most followed the advice of General Lee and General Wade Hampton of South Carolina, who urged their fellow Southerners to "devote their whole energies to the restoration of law and order, the reestablishment of agriculture and commerce, the promotion of education and the rebuilding of our cities and dwellings which have been laid in ashes."

Still a third counterfactual historical scenario comes readily to mind. Southern blacks, who had been for generations oppressed in slavery, now for the first time had disciplined leaders in the thousands of Negro soldiers who had served in the Union army. They also had arms. Very easily they could have turned in revenge on their former masters. Seizing the plantations and other property of the whites, the freedmen might have made of the former Confederacy a black nation. If the whites had dared to resist, the South might have been the scene of massacres as bloody as those in Haiti at the beginning of the nineteenth century, when Toussaint L'Ouverture and Dessalines drove the French out of that island.

Many Southern whites feared, or even expected, that the Confederacy would become another Santo Domingo. They were much troubled by reports that blacks were joining the Union League, an organization that had originated in the North during the war to stimulate patriotism but during the Reconstruction era became the bulwark of the Republican party in the South. The secrecy imposed by the League on its members and its frequent nocturnal meetings alarmed whites, and they readily believed reports that the blacks were collecting arms and ammunition for a general uprising. Fearfully, Southern whites read newspaper accounts of minor racial clashes. Indeed, whites were told, racial tension was so great that blacks "might break into open insurrection at any time."

But no such insurrection occurred. Though the freedmen unquestionably coveted the lands of their former masters, they did not seize them. Indeed, black leaders consistently discouraged talk of extralegal confiscation of plantations. Nor did freedmen threaten the lives or the rights of whites. One of the earliest black political conventions held in Alabama urged a policy of "peace, friendship, and good will toward all men—especially toward our white fellow-citizens among whom our lot is cast." That tone was the dominant one throughout the Reconstruction period, and in many states blacks took the lead in repealing laws that disfranchised former Confederates or disqualified them from holding office.

The point of these three exercises in counterfactual history is, of course, not to argue that the Civil War brought about no changes in American life. The preservation of the Union and the emancipation of the slaves were two consequences of incalculable importance. It is, instead, to suggest the inadequacy of conventional accounts of the Reconstruction period as a second American Revolution. During these postwar years there were swift and significant alterations in the society of the South, but the shared beliefs and institutions of the American people, North and South, black and white, set limits to these changes.

Constitutionalism as a Limit to Change

One set of ideas that sharply curbed experimentation and political innovation during the Reconstruction period can be labeled constitutionalism. It is hard for twentieth-century Americans to understand the reverence with which their nineteenth-century ancestors viewed the Constitution. That document, next to the flag, was the most powerful symbol of American nationhood. Tested in the trial of civil war, the Constitution continued to command respect approaching veneration during the Reconstruction era.

State Rights. Among the most sacrosanct provisions of the Constitution were those that separated the powers of the state and the national governments. Although the national government greatly expanded its role during the war years, Americans still tended to think of it as performing only the specific functions enumerated in the Constitution, which granted it virtually no authority to act directly on any individual citizen. The national government could not, for instance, prevent or punish crime; it had no control over public education; it could not outlaw discrimination against racial minorities; and it could not even intervene to maintain public order unless requested to do so by the state government. Virtually everybody agreed, therefore, that if any laws regulating social and economic life were required, they must be the work of state and local, not of national, government.

Nobody, consequently, even contemplated the possibility that some federal agency might be needed to supervise the demobilization after Appomattox. Everybody simply assumed that after some 200,000 of the Union army volunteers bravely paraded down Pennsylvania Avenue on May 23–24, 1865, and received applause from President Johnson, the cabinet, the generals, and the members of the diplomatic corps, the soldiers would disband and go back to their peaceful homes. This is precisely what they did. Of the more than one million volunteers in the Union army on May 1, 1865, two-thirds were mustered out by August, four-fifths by November. To the demobilized soldiers, the United States government offered no assistance in finding jobs, in purchasing housing, or in securing further education. It paid pensions to those injured in the war and to the families of those who had been killed, but beyond that it assumed no responsibility. Nor did anybody think of asking the national government to oversee the transition from a wartime economy to an era of peace. Without notice the various bureaus of the army and navy departments by the end of April 1865 simply suspended requisitions and purchases, government arsenals slowed down their production, and surplus supplies were sold off.

Hardly anybody had the thought that the national government might play a role in rebuilding the wartorn South. The devastation in the South was immense and ominous. The Confederate dead totaled more than a quarter of a million. In Mississippi, for instance, one-third of the white men of military age had been killed or disabled for life. Most Southern cities were in ruins. Two-thirds of the Southern railroads were totally destroyed; the rest barely creaked along on worn-out rails with broken-down engines. But none of this was thought to be the concern of the United States government.

The failure of the national government to come to the rescue was not caused by vindictiveness. To the contrary, Union officials often behaved with marked generosity toward Confederates. After Lee's hungry battalions surrendered at Appomattox, Grant's soldiers freely shared with them their rations. All over the South, Federal military officials drew on the full Union army storehouses to feed the hungry. But beyond these attempts to avert starvation the Federal government did not go, and very few thought that it should. Not until the twentieth century did the United States make it a policy to pour vast sums of money into the rehabilitation of enemies it had defeated in war.

Rebuilding had, therefore, to be the work of the Southern state and local authorities, and this task imposed a heavy tax on their meager resources. In Mississippi, one-fifth of the entire state revenue in 1866 was needed to provide artificial limbs for soldiers maimed in the war. For the larger tasks of physical restoration, the resources of the South were obviously inadequate. Borrowing a leaf from antebellum experience, Southern governments did the only thing they knew how to do—namely, they lent the credit of the state to back up the bonds of private companies that promised to rebuild railroads and other necessary facilities. Since these companies were underfinanced and since the credit of the Southern state governments after Appomattox was, to say the least, questionable, these bonds had to be sold at disadvantageous prices and at exorbitant rates of interest. In later years, when many of these companies defaulted on their obligations and Southern state governments had to make good on their guarantees, these expenditures would be condemned as excessive and extravagant, and Democrats blamed them on the Republican regimes established in the South after 1868. In fact, however, the need for physical restoration immediately after the war was so obvious and so pressing that nearly every government, whether controlled by Democrats or Republicans, underwrote corporations that promised to rebuild the region.

The Freedmen's Bureau. Even in dealing with the freedmen—the some 3 million slaves emancipated as a result of the war—the United States government tried to pursue a hands-off policy. Few influential leaders, either in the North or in the South, thought that it was the function of the national government to supervise the blacks' transition from slavery to freedom. Even abolitionists, genuinely devoted to the welfare of blacks, were so accustomed to thinking of the Negro as "God's image in ebony"—in other words, a white man in a black skin—that they had no plans for assisting him after emancipation. In 1865 William Lloyd Garrison urged the American Anti-Slavery Society to disband, since it had fulfilled its function, and he suspended the publication of *The Liberator.* Sharing the same point of view, the American Freedmen's Inquiry Commission, set up by the Union War Department in 1863, unanimously opposed further governmental actions to protect the blacks. "The negro does best when let alone," argued one member of the commission, Samuel Gridley

Howe, noted alike for his work with the deaf, dumb, and blind and for his hostility to slavery; "We must beware of all attempts to prolong his servitude, under pretext of taking care of him. The white man has tried taking care of the negro, by slavery, by apprenticeship, by colonization, and has failed disastrously in all; now let the negro try to take care of himself."

But the problem of the care of the freedmen could not be dismissed so easily. Wherever Union armies advanced into the South, they were "greeted by an irruption of negroes of all ages, complexions and sizes, men, women, boys and girls . . . waving hats and bonnets with the most ludicrous caperings and ejaculations of joy." "The poor delighted creatures thronged upon us," a Yankee soldier reported, and they insisted: "We'se gwin wid you all." "What shall be done with them?" commanders in the field plaintively wired Washington.

The administration in Washington had no comprehensive answer. Initially it looked to private philanthropic organizations to rush food, clothing, and medicine to the thousands of blacks that thronged in unsanitary camps around the headquarters of each Union army. The New England Freedmen's Aid Society, the American Missionary Association, and the Philadelphia Society of Friends promptly reponded, but it was soon clear that the problem was too great for private charity.

Gradually sentiment grew in the North for the creation of a general "Emancipation Bureau" in the federal government—only to conflict directly with the even stronger sentiment that the national government had limited powers. Out of this conflict emerged the Freedmen's Bureau Act of March 3, 1865. Congress established, under the jurisdiction of the War Department, the Bureau of Refugees, Freedmen, and Abandoned Lands and entrusted to the new agency, for one year after the end of the war, "control of all subjects relating to refugees and freedmen." To head the new organization, Lincoln named Oliver O. Howard, a Union general with paternalistic views toward blacks.

At first glance, the Freedmen's Bureau seems to have been a notable exception to the rule that the national government should take only a minor, passive role in the restoration of the South. Howard had a vision of a compassionate network of "teachers, ministers, farmers, superintendents" working together to aid and elevate the freedmen, and, under his enthusiastic impetus, the bureau appointed agents in each of the former Confederate states. The most urgent task of the bureau was issuing food and clothing, mostly from surplus army stores, to destitute freedmen and other Southern refugees. This action unquestionably prevented mass starvation in the South. The bureau also took the initiative in getting work for freedmen. Fearful on the one hand that Southern planters would attempt to exploit and underpay the freedmen, troubled on the other by the widespread belief that blacks, once emancipated, were not willing to work, the bureau agents brought laborers and landlords together and insisted that workers sign labor contracts.

No part of the bureau's work was more successful than its efforts in the field of education. The slow work of educating the illiterate Southern blacks had already begun under the auspices of army chaplains and Northern benevolent societies before the creation of the bureau. Howard's bureau continued to cooperate with these agencies, providing housing for black schools, paying teachers, and helping to establish normal schools and colleges for the training of black teachers. All these educational efforts received an enthusiastic welcome from the freedmen. During the day classrooms were thronged with black children learning the rudiments of language and arithmetic; in the evenings they were filled with adults who were "fighting with their letters," learning to read so that they would not be "made ashamed" by their children. "The progress of the scholars is in all cases creditable and in some remarkable," reported one of the teachers. "How richly God has endowed them, and how beautifully their natures would have expanded under a tender and gentle culture."

Even more innovative was the work of the bureau in allocating lands to the freedmen. During the war many plantations in the path of Union armies had been deserted by their owners, and army commanders like Grant arranged to have these tilled

PRIMARY SCHOOL IN CHARGE OF MRS. GREEN, VICKSBURG, MISSISSIPPI
Freedmen were avid for learning. In schools sponsored by the Freedmen's Bureau, grandparents sat alongside toddlers, as all sought knowledge.

by the blacks who flocked to his camp. The largest tract of such abandoned land was in the Sea Islands of South Carolina, which were overrun by Federal troops in the fall of 1861. Though speculators bought up large amounts of this land during the war, sizable numbers of black residents were able to secure small holdings. When General W. T. Sherman marched through South Carolina he ordered that the Sea Islands and the abandoned plantations along the river banks for thirty miles from the coast be reserved for Negro settlement and directed that black settlers be given "possessory titles" to tracts of this land not larger than forty acres. The act creating the Freedmen's Bureau clearly contemplated the continuation of these policies, for it authorized the new bureau to lease confiscated lands to freedmen and to "loyal refugees." The bureau could also sell the land

to these tenants and give them "such title thereto as the United States can convey."

But if the Freedmen's Bureau was an exception to the policy of limited federal involvement in the reconstruction process, it was at best a partial exception. Though the agency did invaluable work, it was a feeble protector of the freedmen. Authorized to recruit only a minimal staff, Howard was obliged to rely heavily on Union army officers stationed in the South—at just the time when the Union army was being demobilized. Consequently the bureau never had enough manpower to look after the rights of the freedmen; toward the end of its first year of operation it employed only 799 men, 424 of whom were soldiers on temporary assigned duty. Important as the work of the bureau was in Negro education, its chief function was to stimulate private philanthropy in this field. In providing land for the freedmen, the bureau was handicapped because it controlled only about 800,000 acres of arable land in the entire South, enough at best for perhaps one black family in forty. Moreover, its efforts to distribute lands to the Negroes were repeatedly undercut both by the Congress and the president. The very wording of the act creating the bureau suggested congressional uncertainty about who actually owned deserted and confiscated lands in the South. President Johnson issued pardons to Southerners that explicitly included "restoration of all rights of property." In October 1865 the president directed Howard to go in person to the Sea Islands to notify blacks there that they did not hold legal title to the land and to advise them "to make the best terms they could" with the white owners. When blacks bitterly resisted what they considered the bureau's betrayal, Union soldiers descended on the islands and forced blacks who would not sign labor contracts with the restored white owners to leave. Elsewhere in the South the record of the bureau was equally dismal.

In short, belief in the limited role to be played by the national government affected the rehabilitation of the freedmen, just as it did the physical restoration of the South and the demobilization in the North. The United States government was supposed to play the smallest possible part in all these matters,

A GROUP OF FREEDMEN IN RICH-
MOND, VIRGINIA, 1865

A central problem of Reconstruction years was the future
of the freedmen. Nobody had
made any plans for a smooth
transition from slavery to
freedom. Consequently, when
emancipation came, as one
former slave recalled, "We
didn't know where to go.
Momma and them didn't
know where to go, you see,
after freedom broke. Just like
you turned something out,
you know. They didn't know
where to go." *(Library of
Congress)*

and its minimal activities were to be of the briefest
duration.

It is certain that most whites in the North and
in the South fully approved these stringent limitations on the activities of the national government.
What the masses of freedmen thought is harder to
determine. On the one hand stands the protest of
Sea Island blacks when they learned they were about
to be dispossessed: "Why, General Howard, why do
you take away our lands? You take them from us who
have always been true, always true to the Government! You give them to our all-time enemies! That is
not right!" On the other is Frederick Douglass's reply
to the question, "What shall we do with the Negroes?" The greatest black spokesman of the era
answered: "Do nothing with them; mind your business, and let them mind theirs. Your *doing* with them
is their greatest misfortune. They have been undone
by your doings, and all they now ask and really have
need of at your hands, is just to let them alone."

Laissez-Faire as a Limit to Change

Along with the idea of limited government went the
doctrine of laissez-faire ("let things alone"), which
sharply limited what the government could do to
solve economic problems that arose after the Civil
War. Except for a handful of Radical Republicans,
such as Charles Sumner and Thaddeus Stevens, most
congressmen, like most academic economists, were
unquestioning believers in an American version
of laissez-faire. Though they were willing to promote economic growth through protective tariffs
and land grants to railroads, they abhorred governmental inspection, regulation, and control of economic activities. These matters were ruled by the
inexorable laws of economics. "You need not think
it necessary to have Washington exercise a political
providence over the country," William Graham Sumner, the brilliant professor of political and social
science, told his students at Yale. "God has done

that a great deal better by the laws of political economy."

Reverence for Private Property. No violation of economic laws was deemed more heinous than interference with the right of private property—the right of an individual or group to purchase, own, use, and dispose of property without any interference from governmental authorities. There was consequently never a chance that congressmen would support Thaddeus Stevens's radical program to confiscate all Southern farms larger than 200 acres and to divide the seized land into 40-acre tracts among the freedmen. "An attempt to justify the confiscation of Southern land under the pretense of doing justice to the freedmen," declared the New York *Times,* which spoke for educated Republicans, "strikes at the root of all property rights in both sections. It concerns Massachusetts quite as much as Mississippi."

Informed opinion in the North held that the best program of Reconstruction was to allow the laws of economics to rule in the South with the least possible interference by the government. Obsessed by laissez-faire, Northern theorists left out of their calculations the physical devastation wrought in the South by the war, and they did not recognize how feeble were the section's resources to rebuild its economy. Even excluding the loss of property in slaves, the total assessed property evaluation of the Southern states shrank by 43 percent between 1860 and 1865.

Southern Economic Adjustments. Northern pundits also failed to take into account the psychological dimensions of economic readjustment in the South. For generations Southern whites had persuaded themselves that slavery was the natural condition of the black race, and they truly believed that their slaves were devoted to them. But as Union armies approached and slaves defected, they were compelled to recognize that they had been living in a world of misconceptions and deceits. So shattering was the idea that slaves were free that some Southern whites simply refused to accept it. Even after the Confederate surrender, some owners would

not inform their slaves of their new status. A few planters angrily announced they were so disillusioned that they would never again have anything to do with blacks, and they sought, vainly, to persuade European immigrants and Chinese coolies to work their fields.

Even those whites who overtly accepted the reality of emancipation betrayed the fact that, on a deeper emotional level, they still could only think of blacks as performing forced labor. "The general interest both of the white man and of the negroes requires that he should be kept as near to the condition of slavery as possible, and as far from the condition of the white man as is practicable," explained Edmund Rhett of South Carolina. "Negroes must be made to work, or else cotton and rice must cease to be raised for export." The contracts that planters in 1865, under pressure from the Freedmen's Bureau, entered into with their former slaves were further indications of the same attitude. Even the most generous of these contracts provided that blacks were "not to leave the premises during work hours without the consent of the Proprietor," that they would conduct "themselves faithfully, honestly and civilly," and that they would behave with "perfect obedience" toward the landowner.

Blacks, too, had difficulties in adjusting to their new status that were never anticipated by the devotees of laissez-faire. *Freedom*—that word so often whispered in the slave quarters—went to the heads of some blacks. A few took the coming of "Jubilee," with the promise to put the bottom rail on top, quite literally. Nearly all blacks had an initial impulse to test their freedom, to make sure it was real. During the first months after the war there was, then, much movement among Southern blacks. "They are just like a swarm of bees," one observer noted, "all buzzing about and not knowing where to settle."

Much of this black mobility was, however, purposeful. Thousands of former slaves flocked to Southern towns and cities where the Freedmen's Bureau was issuing rations, for they knew that food was unavailable on the plantations. Many blacks set out to find husbands, wives, or children, from whom they had been forcibly separated during the

CELEBRATION FOR NEWLY MAR-
RIED BLACK COUPLES
Legally slaves could not
marry. When blacks became
free, they sought to regularize
their marital arrangements
and to legitimatize their children. Many Southern states
passed blanket laws for this
purpose, but thousands of
Negroes desired formal wed-
ding ceremonies. *(The New
York Public Library)*

slave days. A good many freedmen joined the general movement of Southern population away from
the seaboard states, devastated by war, and migrated
to the Southwestern frontier in Texas. Most blacks,
however, did not move so far but remained in the
immediate vicinity of the plantations where they
had labored as slaves.

The reluctance of freedmen in 1865 to enter
into labor contracts, either with their former masters
or with other white landowners, was also generally
misunderstood. Most blacks wanted to work—but
they wanted to work on their own land. Freedmen
knew that the United States government had divided
up some abandoned plantations among former slaves,
and many believed that on January 1, 1866—the anni-
versary of their freedom under Lincoln's Emancipation Proclamation—all would receive forty acres and
a mule. With this prospect of having their own farms,
they were unwilling to sign contracts to work on
somebody else's plantation.

Even when the hope of free land disappeared,
freedmen were averse to signing labor contracts
because, as has been noted, so many white landowners expected to continue to treat them like slaves.
Especially repugnant was the idea of being again

herded together in the plantation slave quarters,
with their communal facilities for cooking and wash-
ing and infant care, and their lack of privacy. Emancipation did much to strengthen the black family.
Families divided by slave sales could now be reunited. Marital arrangements between blacks, which
had had no legal validity during slavery, could be
regularized. Freedmen's Bureau officials performed
thousands of marriage ceremonies, and some states
passed general ordinances declaring that blacks who
had been living together were legally man and wife
and that their children were legitimate. This precious
new security of family life was not something blacks
were willing to jeopardize by returning to slave quarters. Before contracting to work on the plantations,
they insisted on having separate cabins, scattered
across the farm, each usually having its own patch for
vegetables and perhaps a pen for hogs or a cow.

When these conditions were met, freedmen in
the early months of 1866 entered into labor contracts,
most of which followed the same general pattern.
Rarely did these arrangements call for the payment
of wages, for landowners were desperately short of
cash and freedmen felt that a wage system gave
planters too much control over their labor. The most

common system was sharecropping. Although there were many regional and individual variations, the system usually called for the dividing of the crop into three equal shares. One of these went to the landowner; another went to the laborer—usually black, though there were also many white sharecroppers in the South; and the third went to whichever party provided the seeds, fertilizer, mules, and other farming equipment.

For the planter this system had several advantages. At a time when money was scarce, he was not obliged to pay out cash to his employees until the crop was harvested. He retained general supervision over what was planted and how the crop was cultivated, and he felt he was more likely to secure a good harvest because the freedmen themselves stood to gain by a large yield. Blacks, too, found the sharecropping system suited to their needs. They had control over how their crops were planted and when

they were cultivated and harvested. They could earn more money by working harder in the fields.

The Breakup of the Plantation System. To some observers the disappearance of the slave quarters and the resettling of families in individual, scattered cabins seemed to mark a revolution in the character of Southern agriculture. According to the United States census, the number of Southern landholdings doubled between 1860 and 1880 and their average size dropped from 365 acres to 157 acres. In fact, the census figures were misleading, because the census takers failed to ask farmers whether they owned their land or were sharecroppers. An examination of tax records, which show land ownership, in the representative state of Louisiana helps correct the distortion of the census. Between 1860 and 1880 in Louisiana the number of independently owned farms of less than 100 acres actually dropped by 14

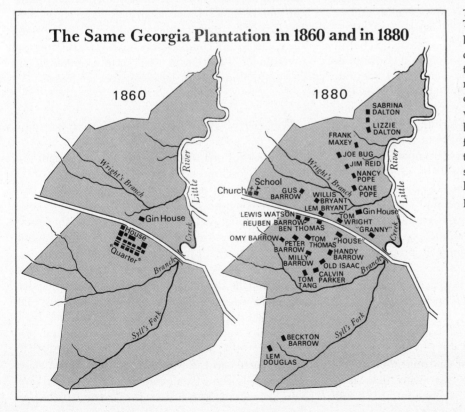

The Same Georgia Plantation in 1860 and in 1880

THE SAME GEORGIA PLANTATION IN 1860 AND 1880

Before the Civil War slave quarters were located close together, all near the white master's house, so that he could impose order and prevent secret meetings of the blacks. After emancipation freedmen insisted upon scattering out over the plantation, so that each family could have its own house and some privacy.

percent, while during the same period the number of plantations increased by 287 percent. By 1900 plantations of 100 acres or more encompassed half the cultivated land in the state, and more than half the farmers were not proprietors.

If the postwar period did not see the breakup of large plantations, it did bring some significant changes in ownership and control of the land. Hard hit by debt, by rising taxes, and by increasing labor costs, many Southern planters had to sell their holdings, and there was an infusion of Northern capital into the region after the war. More tried to cling to their acres by going heavily into debt. Since the banking system of the postwar South was inadequate, the principal source of credit was the local merchant, who could supply both the landowner and his sharecroppers with clothing, shoes, some food, and other necessities to tide them over the lean months between the planting of the tobacco or cotton crop and its harvest. On each sale the merchant charged interest, to be paid when the crop was sold, and he also charged prices ranging from 40 percent to 110 percent higher for all goods sold on credit. It is hardly surprising that those planters who could afford to do so set up their own stores and extended credit to their own sharecroppers, and quite soon they discovered they were making more profits on their mercantile enterprises than from farming. Planters who could not make such arrangements frequently had to sell their lands to the neighborhood merchant. It is not accidental that in William Faulkner's fictional saga of Southern history the power of planter families like the Compsons and the Sutpens diminished during the postwar years, while the Snopes family of storekeepers, hard-trading, penny-pinching, and utterly unscrupulous, emerged properous and successful.

It would be a mistake, however, to accept the novelist's hostile characterization of the Southern merchant without reservation. If the storekeeper insisted on a crop-lien system, which required the farmer legally to pledge that the proceeds from his crop must go first to pay off his obligation to the merchant, it was because he was aware that, as in both 1866 and 1867, crops throughout the South could fail. And if the merchant urged farmers to forget about soil conservation, diversification, and experimentation with new crops, it was because he knew that the only way to pay his own debts was to insist that his debtors must raise cotton and tobacco, for which there was a ready cash market.

Thus merchants, landowners, and sharecroppers, thus white Southerners and black Southerners, became locked into an economic system that, at best, promised them little more than survival. At worst, it offered bankruptcy, sale of lands, and hurried nocturnal migrations in an attempt to escape from a set of debts in one state with but little more than the hope of starting a new set in another.

By the 1880s, then, the South had become what it remained for the next half-century, the economic backwater of the nation. In 1880 the per capita wealth of the South was $376, that in the states outside the South $1,086. Yet it was this impoverished region that had to deal with some of the most difficult political and racial problems that ever have confronted Americans. In attacking these problems, Southerners, black and white, could expect no assistance from the government, since such intervention would violate the immutable laws of laissez-faire economics.

Political Parties as a Limit to Change

Of the institutions that checked radical change during Reconstruction, none were more influential than the national political parties. The fact that both parties were conglomerates of disparate and often competing sectional and class interests meant that party policy had to be arrived at through compromise and concession. In that process extreme and drastic measures were nearly always screened out.

Nationally the Democratic party during the postwar years was torn by two conflicting interests. On the one hand, Democrats sought the immediate readmission of the Southern states under the governments President Johnson had set up. Controlled by whites hostile to the Republican party, these states would surely send Democrats to Congress and support Democratic candidates in a national election.

Even during the 1850s, the South had increasingly become a one-party region; now the goal of a solidly Democratic South appeared within reach. On the other hand, too enthusiastic advocacy of the Southern cause could hurt Democrats in the North by reviving talk of disloyalty and the Copperhead movement during the war. To minimize the effectiveness of such attacks, Democrats had no choice but to urge restraint on their colleagues in the former Confederacy.

Among Republicans, similar constraints operated to dampen any ideas of taking vengeance on the South or of encouraging blacks to seize control of that region. From its inception the Republican party had been an uneasy admixture of antislavery men, former Whigs, disgruntled Democrats, and Know-Nothings. How tenuous were the ties that bound these groups together became evident in the factional disputes that racked Lincoln's administration, and for the party it was a bad omen that the sharpest disagreements among Republicans concerned Lincoln's plan to reorganize the Southern state governments.

Presidential Reconstruction. During the first year after Lincoln's death, quarrels among Republicans were somewhat muted because practically all members of the party joined in opposing President Johnson's program of Reconstruction. Followed by only a handful of Conservative Republicans, including Secretary of State Seward and Navy Secretary Gideon Welles, Johnson began to work closely with the Democrats of the North and South. He announced that the Southern states had never been out of the Union, and he insisted that, under the provisional governments he had set up, they were entitled to be represented in Congress.

It is easy to understand why almost all Republicans whether they belonged to the Radical or the Moderate factions, rejected the president's argument. Members of both wings of the party were outraged when the Southern elections in 1865, held at the direction of the president, resulted in the choice of a Confederate brigadier-general as governor of Mississippi, and they were furious when the new Georgia

legislature named Alexander H. Stephens, the vice-president of the Confederacy, to represent that state in the United States Senate.

What made these newly elected Southern officials more threatening to Republicans was the fact that (though many had been Whigs before the war) they clearly contemplated allying themselves with the Democratic party. However much Republicans disagreed among themselves, they all agreed that their party had saved the Union. They believed, with Thaddeus Stevens, "that upon the continued ascendancy of that party depends the safety of this great nation." Now that ascendancy was threatened. What made the threat so grave, and so ironic, was the fact that when the Southern states were readmitted to the Union they would receive increased representation in Congress. Prior to the ratification of the Thirteenth Amendment, only three-fifths of the slave population of the South had been counted in apportioning representation in the House of Representatives; but now that the slaves were free men, all would be counted. In short, the Southern states, after having been defeated in the most costly war in the nation's history, would have about fifteen more representatives in Congress than they had had before the war. And under the president's plan, all of the Southern Congress unquestionably would be Democrats.

Equally troubling to Republicans of all factions was the fear of what white Southerners, once restored to authority, would do to the freedmen. The laws that the Southern provisional legislatures adopted during the winter of 1865–66 gave reason for anxiety on this score. Not one of these governments considered treating black citizens just as they treated white citizens. Instead, the legislatures adopted special laws, known as the Black Codes, to regulate the conduct of freedmen. On the positive side, these laws recognized the right of freedmen to make civil contracts, to sue and be sued, and to acquire and hold most kinds of property. But with these rights went restrictions. The laws varied from state to state, but in general they specified that blacks might not purchase or carry firearms, that they might not assemble after sunset, and that those who were idle or unemployed should "be liable to imprisonment, and to hard labor, one or both, ... not exceeding twelve months." The Mississippi code prohibited blacks from renting or leasing "any lands or tenements except in incorporated cities or towns." That of South Carolina forbade blacks from practicing "the art, trade or business of an artisan, mechanic or shopkeeper, or any other trade, employment or business (besides that of husbandry, or that of a servant)." So clearly did these measures seem designed to keep the freedmen in quasi-slavery that the Chicago *Tribune* spoke for a united, outraged Republican party in denouncing the first of these Black Codes, that adopted by the Mississippi legislature: "We tell the white men of Mississippi that the men of the North will convert the state of Mississippi into a frog-pond before they will allow any such laws to disgrace one foot of soil over which the flag of freedom waves."

The Fourteenth Amendment. Unwilling, for all these reasons, to recognize the regimes Johnson had set up in the South, all Republicans easily rallied in December 1865, when Congress reassembled, to block seating of their senators and representatives. All agreed to the creation of a special joint committee on Reconstruction to handle questions concerning the readmission of the Southern states and their further reorganization. In setting up this committee, congressional Republicans carefully balanced its membership with Radicals and Moderates. If its most conspicuous member was the Radical Stevens, its powerful chairman was Senator William Pitt Fessenden, a Moderate.

Congressional Republicans found it easier to unite in opposing Johnson's plan of Reconstruction than to unite in devising one of their own. Recognizing that it would take time to draft and adopt a constitutional amendment and then to have it ratified by the requisite number of states, congressional leaders early in 1866 agreed on interim legislation that would protect the freedmen. One bill extended and expanded the functions of the Freedmen's Bureau, and a second guaranteed minimal civil rights to all citizens. Contrary to expectations, Johnson

vetoed both these measures. Refusing to recognize that these measures represented the wishes of both Moderate and Radical Republicans, the president claimed that they were the work of the Radicals, who wanted "to destroy our institutions and change the character of the Government." He vowed to fight these Northern enemies of the Union just as he had once fought Southern secessionists and traitors. The Republican majority in Congress was not able to override Johnson's veto of the Freedmen's Bureau bill (a later, less sweeping measure extended the life of that agency for two years), but it passed the Civil Rights Act of 1866 over his disapproval.

While relations between the president and the Republicans in Congress were deteriorating, the joint committee on Reconstruction continued to meet and consider various plans for reorganizing the South. With its evenly balanced membership, the committee dismissed, on the one side, the president's theory that the Southern states were, in reality, already reconstructed and back in the Union. On the other side, it discarded the theory of Thaddeus Stevens that the Confederacy was conquered territory over which Congress could rule at its own discretion, and it rejected Charles Sumner's more elaborate argument that the Southern state governments had committed suicide when they seceded, so that their land and inhabitants now fell "under the exclusive jurisdiction of Congress." More acceptable to the majority of Republicans was the "grasp of war" theory advanced by Richard Henry Dana, Jr., the noted Massachusetts constitutional lawyer, who was also the author of *Two Years before the Mast.* Dana argued that the federal government held the defeated Confederacy in the grasp of war for a brief and limited time, during which it must act swiftly to revive state governments in the region and to restore promptly the constitutional balance between national and state authority. Dana's theory was an essentially conservative one, in that it called for only a short period of federal hegemony and looked toward the speedy restoration of the Southern states on terms of absolute equality with the loyal states.

Finding in Dana's theory a constitutional source of power, the joint committee after much travail pro-

RECONSTRUCTION: UNCLE SAM VISITS THE SHOP OF
A. JOHNSON, TAILOR

Taking off from Andrew Johnson's frequent bragging
about his humble origins as a tailor, this cartoon shows
the president and Secretary of State Seward busily
mending Uncle Sam's coat, badly torn by the recently
ended Civil War.   *(American Antiquarian Society)*

was also no disagreement about the provision declaring the Confederate debt invalid.

All the other provisions, however, represented a compromise between Radical and Moderate Republicans. For instance, Radicals wanted to keep all Southerners who had voluntarily supported the Confederacy from voting until 1870, and the arch-Radical Stevens urged: "Not only to 1870 but 18,070, every rebel who shed the blood of loyal men should be prevented from exercising any power in this Government." Moderates favored a speedy restoration of all political rights to former Confederates. As a compromise the Fourteenth Amendment included a provision to exclude high-ranking Confederates from office but one that did not deny them the vote.

Similarly, the Fourteenth Amendment's provisions to protect the freedmen represented a compromise. Radicals like Sumner (who was considered too radical to be given a seat on the joint committee) wanted an unequivocal declaration of the right and duty of the national government to protect the civil liberties of the former slaves. But Moderates drew back in alarm from entrusting additional authority to Washington. The joint committee came up with a provision that granted no power to the national government but restricted that of the states: "No State shall make or enforce any law which shall abridge the privileges and immunities of citizens of the United States; nor shall any State deprive any person of life, liberty, or property, without due process of law; nor deny to any person within its jurisdiction the equal protection of the laws."

Finally, another compromise between Radicals and Moderates resulted in the provision of the amendment concerning voting. Though Sumner and other Radicals called Negro suffrage "the essence, the great essential," of a proper Reconstruction policy, Conservatives refused to give to the national government power to interfere with the state requirements for suffrage. The joint committee thereupon devised a complex and, as it proved, unworkable plan to persuade the Southern states voluntarily to enfranchise blacks, under threat of having reduced representation in Congress if they refused.

The efficacy of the Fourteenth Amendment as a

duced the first comprehensive congressional plan of Reconstruction in a proposed Fourteenth Amendment to the Constitution, which was endorsed by Congress in June 1866 and submitted to the states for ratification. Some parts of the amendment were noncontroversial. All Republicans accepted the opening statement of the amendment; "All persons born or naturalized in the United States, and subject to the jurisdiction thereof, are citizens of the United States and of the State wherein they reside." There

"RETURN OF THE PRODIGAL SON
—NEW VERSION"
In this Republican view of
Reconstruction, the Northern
Democrat urges Mrs. United
States to welcome the return
of the South as the prodigal
son. But the South is unre-
generate and tells their
mother: "Yes, by the thunder,
I've come back, and d'ye hear?
Hurry up them cakes and hot
whiskey, and don't let us see
any darn'd niggers around."
(American Antiquarian Society)

program of Reconstruction was never tested because of the outbreak of political warfare between President Johnson and the Republican party, which had elected him vice-president in 1864. During the summer of 1866, Johnson and his friends tried to create a new political party, which would rally behind the president's policies the few Conservative Republicans, the Northern Democrats, and the Southern whites. With the president's hearty approval, a National Union Convention held in Philadelphia in August stressed the theme of harmony among the sections. The entry into the convention hall of delegates from Massachusetts and South Carolina, arm in arm, seemed to symbolize the end of sectional strife. The president himself went on a "swing around the circle" of leading Northern cities, ostensibly on his way to dedicate a monument to the memory of another Democrat, Stephen A. Douglas. In his frequent public speeches he defended the constitutionality of his own Reconstruction pro-

gram and berated the Congress, and particularly the Radical Republicans, for attempting to subvert the Constitution. In a final effort to consolidate sentiment against the Congress, he urged the Southern states not to ratify the proposed Fourteenth Amendment. With the exception of Tennessee, which was controlled by one of Johnson's bitterest personal and political enemies, all the former Confederate states rejected the congressional plan.

The Second Congressional Program of Reconstruction. When Congress reassembled in December 1866, the Republican majority had therefore to devise a second program of Reconstruction. Cheered by overwhelming victories in the fall congressional elections, Republicans were even less inclined than previously to cooperate with the president, who had gone into political opposition, or to encourage the provisional regimes in the South, which had rejected their first program. Republican suspicion that Southern whites were fundamentally hostile toward the freedmen was strengthened by reports of a race riot in Memphis during May 1866, when a mob of whites joined in a two-day indiscriminate attack on blacks in that city, and of a more serious affair in New Orleans four months later, when a white mob, aided by the local police, attacked a black political gathering with what was described as "a cowardly ferocity unsurpassed in the annals of crime." In New Orleans 45 or 50 blacks were killed, and 150 more were wounded.

Once again, however, the Republican majority in Congress found it easier to agree on what to oppose than what to favor in the way of Reconstruction legislation. Stevens urged that the South be placed under military rule for a generation and that Southern plantations be sold to pay the national debt. Sumner wanted to disfranchise large numbers of Southern whites, to require Negro suffrage, and to create racially integrated schools in the South. Mod-

erate Republicans, on the other hand, were willing to retain the Fourteenth Amendment as the basic framework of congressional Reconstruction and to insist on little else but ratification by Southern states.

The second congressional program of Reconstruction, embodied in the Military Reconstruction Act of March 2, 1867, represented a comprise between the demands of Radical and Moderate Republican factions. It divided the ten former Confederate states that had not ratified the Fourteenth Amendment into five military districts. In each of these states, there were to be new constitutional conventions, for which black men were allowed to vote. These conventions must draft new constitutions that had to provide for Negro suffrage, and they were required to ratify the Fourteenth Amendment. When thus reorganized, the Southern states could apply to Congress for readmission to the Union.

The radical aspects of this measure, which were pointed out by Democrats during the congressional

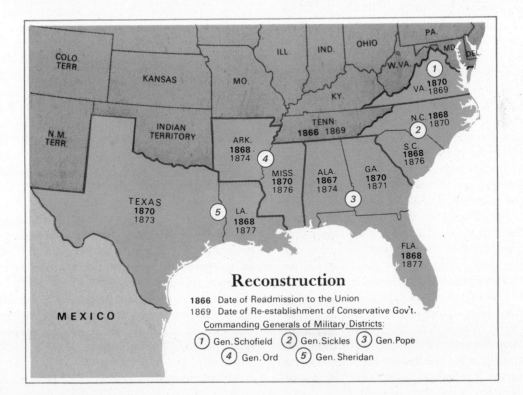

Reconstruction

1866 Date of Readmission to the Union
1869 Date of Re-establishment of Conservative Gov't.
Commanding Generals of Military Districts:
① Gen. Schofield ② Gen. Sickles ③ Gen. Pope
④ Gen. Ord ⑤ Gen. Sheridan

debates and were denounced by President Johnson in his unsuccessful veto of the act, were easy to recognize. In particular, the requirement of Negro suffrage, which Sumner sponsored, seemed to Radicals "a prodigious triumph."

In fact, however, most provisions of the Military Reconstruction Act were more acceptable to Moderate than to Radical Republicans. The measure did nothing to give land to the freedmen, to provide education at national expense, or to end racial segregation in the South. It did not erase the boundaries of the Southern states, and it did not even sweep away the provisional governments Johnson had established there, though it did make them responsible to the commanders of the new military districts. So conservative was the act in all these respects that Sumner branded it as "horribly defective."

Intent on striking some kind of balance between the Radical and Conservative wings of the Republican party, the framers of the Military Reconstruction Act drafted the measure carelessly, and it promptly proved, as Sumner had predicted, "Reconstruction without machinery or motive power." Facing the acceptance of military rule or Negro suffrage, the provisional governments in the South chose the former, correctly believing that army officers were generally in sympathy with white supremacy. To get the Reconstruction process under way, Congress had therefore to enact a supplementary law (March 23, 1867), requiring the federal commanders in the South to take the initiative, when the local governments did not, in announcing elections, registering voters, and convening constitutional conventions. During the summer of 1867, as the president, the attorney general, and Southern state officials tried by legalistic interpretations to delay the Reconstruction program, Congress had to pass two further supplementary acts, explaining the "true intent and meaning" of the previous legislation.

With these measures, the fabric of congressional Reconstruction legislation as it affected the South was substantially completed. Both the first and the second congressional plans of Reconstruction were compromises between the Radical and the Moderate factions in the Republican party. The Radicals' insistence on change was essential in securing the adoption of this legislation, but the Moderates blocked all measures that would have revolutionary social or economic consequences in the South.

Impeachment. The same need to compromise between the factions of the Republican party dictated the policy of Congress toward the president during the Reconstruction years. Almost all Republicans were suspicious of the president and were fearful that he intended turning the South over to Confederate rule. Most were angered by Johnson's repeated veto messages, assailing carefully balanced compromise legislation as the work of Radicals and attacking the Congress itself as an unconstitutional body, since it refused to seat congressmen from all the states. Republicans of both factions were, therefore, desirous of keeping a close eye on the president and were willing to curb executive powers that had grown during the war. In 1867, fearing that Johnson would use his power as commander in chief to subvert their Reconstruction legislation, Republican factions joined to pass an army appropriations bill that required all military orders to the army, including those of the president himself, to go through the hands of General Grant. Suspecting that Johnson wanted to use the federal patronage to build up a political machine of his own, they adopted at the same time the Tenure of Office Act, which required the president to secure the consent of the Senate not merely when he appointed officials but when he removed them.

Up to this point the Republicans in Congress were prepared to go in striking unanimity—but no further. When Radical Republican James M. Ashley in January 1867 moved to impeach the president, he was permitted to conduct a seriocomic investigation of Johnson's alleged involvement in Lincoln's assassination, his purported sale of pardons, and other trumped-up charges; but when Ashley's motion reached the floor of the House of Representatives Moderate Republicans saw that it was soundly defeated.

A subsequent attempt at impeachment fared

better, but it also revealed how the Radical and Moderate factions checked each other. In August 1867 President Johnson suspended from office Secretary of War Edwin M. Stanton, whom he correctly suspected of having collaborated closely with the Radicals in Congress, and, as required by the Tenure of Office Act, he asked the Senate to consent to the removal. When the Senate refused, the president removed Stanton and ordered him to surrender his office. News of this seemingly open defiance of the law caused Republicans in the House of Representatives to rush through a resolution impeaching the president, without waiting for specific charges against him to be drawn up.

The trial of President Johnson (who was not present in court but was represented by his lawyers) was not merely a test of strength between Congress and the chief executive, but between the Radical and the Moderate Republicans. Impeachment managers from the House of Representatives presented eleven charges against the president, mostly accusing him of violating the Tenure of Office Act but also censuring his repeated attacks upon the Congress. With fierce joy Radical Thaddeus Stevens, who was one of the managers, denounced the president: "Unfortunate man! thus surrounded, hampered, tangled in the meshes of his own wickedness—unfortunate, unhappy man, behold your doom!"

But Radical oratory could not persuade Moderate Republicans and Democrats in the Senate to vote for conviction. They listened as Johnson's lawyers challenged the constitutionality of the Tenure of Office Act, showed that it had not been intended to apply to cabinet members, and proved that, in any case, it did not cover Stanton, who had been appointed by Lincoln, not Johnson. When the critical vote came, Moderate Republicans like Fessenden voted to acquit the president, and Johnson's Radical foes lacked one vote of the two-thirds majority required to convict him. Several other Republican Senators who for political expediency voted against the president were prepared to change their votes and favor acquittal if their ballots were needed.

Nothing more clearly shows how the institutional needs of a political party prevented drastic

"AWKWARD COLLISION ON THE GRAND TRUNK COLUMBIA RAILROAD"
This cartoon depicts presidential and congressional Reconstruction as two engines going in opposite directions on the same rails. Andrew Johnson, driver of the locomotive "President," says: "Look here! One of us has got to back." But Thaddeus Stevens, driver of the locomotive "Congress," replies: "Well, it ain't going to be me that's going to do it, you bet!" *(Library of Congress)*

change than did this decision not to remove a president whom a majority in Congress despised, hated and feared. The desire to maintain the unity of the national Republican party, despite frequent quarrels and incessant bickering, overrode the wishes of individual congressmen. Moderate Republicans felt that throughout the Reconstruction period they were constantly being rushed from one advanced position to another in order to placate the insatiable Radicals. With more accuracy, Radical Republicans perceived that the need of retaining Moderate support prevented the adoption of any really revolutionary Reconstruction program.

Racism as a Limit to Change

A final set of beliefs that limited the nature of the changes imposed upon, and accepted by, the South during the Reconstruction period can be labeled racism. In all parts of the country, white Americans looked with suspicion and fear on those whose skin was of a different color. For example, in California white hatred built up against the Chinese, who had begun coming to that state in great numbers after the discovery of gold and who were later imported by the thousands to help construct the Central Pacific Railroad. White workers resented the willingness of the Chinese to work long hours for "coolies'" wages; they distrusted the unfamiliar attire, diet, and habits of the Chinese; and they disliked all these things more because the Chinese were a yellow-skinned people. Under the leadership of a newly arrived Irish immigrant, Dennis Kearney, white laborers organized a workingman's party, with the slogan, "The Chinese must go."

The depression of 1873 gave impetus to the movement, for day after day thousands of the unemployed gathered in the sand lots of San Francisco to hear Kearney's slashing attacks on the Chinese and on the wealthy corporations that employed them. In the summer of 1877 San Francisco hoodlums, inspired by Kearney, burned 25 Chinese laundries and destroyed dozens of Chinese houses. Politically the movement was strong enough to force both major parties in California to adopt anti-Chinese platforms, and California congressmen succeeded in persuading their colleagues to pass a bill limiting the number of Chinese who could be brought into the United States each year. Since the measure clearly conflicted with treaty arrangements with China, President Rutherford B. Hayes vetoed it, but he had his secretary of state initiate negotiations leading to a new treaty that permitted the restriction of immigration. Congress in 1882 passed the Chinese Exclusion Act, which suspended all Chinese immigration for ten years and forbade the naturalization of Chinese already in the country.

Northern Views of the Black Race. If white Americans became so agitated over a small number of

"THE MARTYRDOM OF ST. CRISPIN"
Racism in postwar America took many forms. Here the artist Thomas Nast shows the obviously 100 percent American "St. Crispin," the patron saint of shoemakers, threatened by the cheap labor of Chinese immigrants. *(American Antiquarian Society)*

Chinese, who were unquestionably hard-working and thrifty and who belonged to one of the most ancient of civilizations, it is easy to see how they could consider blacks an even greater danger. There were more than 3 million Negroes, most of them recently emancipated from slavery. The exploits of black soldiers during the war—their very discipline and courage—proved that Negroes could be formidable opponents. The fact that blacks were no longer portrayed as invisible men but now, in photographs and caricatures, had sharply etched identities exacerbated, rather than allayed, white apprehensions. More clearly than ever before Negroes seemed distinctive, alien, and menacing.

Most American intellectuals of the Civil War generation accepted unquestioningly the dogma that blacks belonged to an inferior race. Though a few reformers like Charles Sumner vigorously attacked this notion, a majority of even philanthropic Northerners accepted the judgment of the distinguished Harvard scientist Louis Agassiz that while whites during antiquity were developing high civilizations "the negro race groped in barbarism and never originated a regular organization among themselves." Many credited Agassiz's conjecture that Negroes, once free, would inevitably die out in the United States. Others reached the same conclusion by studying the recently published work of Charles Darwin, *Origin of Species* (1859), and they accepted the Darwinian argument that in the inevitable struggle for survival "higher civilized races" must inevitably eliminate "an endless number of lower races." Consequently the influential and tenderhearted Congregational minister Horace Bushnell could prophesy the approaching end of the black race in the United States with something approaching equanimity. "Since we must all die," he asked rhetorically, "why should it grieve us, that a stock thousands of years behind, in the scale of culture, should die with few and still fewer children to succeed, till finally the whole succession remains in the more cultivated race?"

When even the leaders of Northern society held such views, it is hardly surprising that most whites in the region were overtly anti-Negro. In state after state whites fiercely resisted efforts to extend the political and civil rights of blacks, partly because they feared that any improvement of the condition of Negroes in the North would lead to a huge influx of blacks from the South. At the end of the Civil War only Maine, New Hampshire, Vermont, Massachusetts, and Rhode Island allowed Negroes to have full voting rights, and in New York blacks who met certain property-holding qualifications could have the ballot. During the next three years in referenda held in Connecticut, Wisconsin, Kansas, Ohio, Michigan, and Missouri, constitutional amendments authorizing Negro suffrage were defeated, and New York voters rejected a proposal to eliminate the property-holding qualifications for black voters. Only in Iowa, a state where there were very few blacks, did a Negro suffrage amendment carry in 1868, and that same year Minnesota adopted an ambiguously worded amendment. Thus at the end of the 1860s most Northern states refused to give black men the ballot.

In words as well as in votes, the majority of Northerners made their deeply racist feelings evident. The Democratic press constantly cultivated the racial fears of its readers, and they regularly portrayed the Republicans as planning a "new era of miscegenation, amalgamation, and promiscuous intercourse between the races." From the White House, denouncing Republican attempts "to Africanize the [Southern] half of our country," President Andrew Johnson announced: "In the progress of nations negroes have shown less capacity for self-government than any other race of people.... Whenever they have been left to their own devices they have shown an instant tendency to relapse into barbarism." Even Northern Republicans opposed to Johnson shared many of his racist views. Radical Senator Timothy O. Howe of Wisconsin declared that he regarded "the freedmen, in the main ... as so much animal life," and Senator Benjamin F. Wade of Ohio, whom the Radical Republicans would have elevated to the presidency had they removed Johnson, had, along with a genuine devotion to the principle of equal rights, an incurable aversion to blacks. Representative George W. Julian of Indiana, one of the few Northern congressmen who had no racial prejudice, bluntly told his colleagues in 1866: "The real trouble is that *we hate the negro*. It is not his ignorance that offends us, but his color.... Of this fact I entertain no doubt whatsoever."

Both personal preferences and the wishes of constituents inhibited Northern Republicans from supporting measures that might alter race relations. When Sumner sought to expunge federal laws that recognized slavery or to prohibit racial discrimination on the public transportation in the District of Columbia, his colleagues replied: "God has made the negro inferior, and ... laws cannot make him equal." Such congressmen were hardly in a position to scold the

South for racial discrimination or to insist on drastic social change in that region.

Southern Views of the Black Race. If racism limited the innovation that Northerners were willing to propose during the Reconstruction period, it even more drastically reduced the amount of change that white Southerners were prepared to accept. The note of racial bigotry runs through both the private correspondence and the public pronouncements of Southern whites during the postwar era. "Equality does not exist between blacks and whites," announced Alexander H. Stephens. "The one race is by nature inferior in many respects, physically and mentally, to the other. This should be received as a fixed invincible fact in all dealings with the subject." A North Carolina diarist agreed: "The Anglo-Saxon and the African can never be equal . . . one or the other must fall." Or, as the Democratic party of Louisiana resolved in its 1865 platform: "We hold this to be a Government of white people, made and to be perpetuated for the exclusive benefit of the white race; and . . . that people of African descent cannot be considered as citizens of the United States, and that there can, in no event, nor under any circumstances, be any equality between the white and other races." The Black Codes were the legal embodiment of these attitudes.

These racist views shaped the attitudes of most Southern whites toward the whole process of Reconstruction. They approved of President Johnson's plan of Reconstruction because it placed government in the Southern states entirely in the hands of whites. They rejected the Fourteenth Amendment primarily because it made blacks legally equal to whites. They watched with incredulity bordering on stupefaction

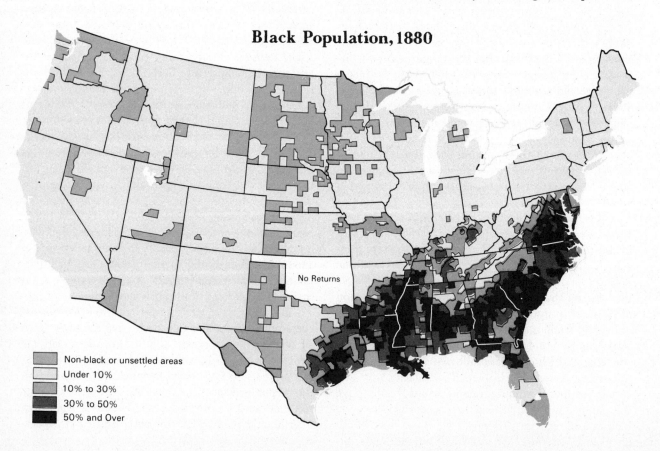

Black Population, 1880

No Returns

Non-black or unsettled areas
Under 10%
10% to 30%
30% to 50%
50% and Over

as Congress passed the 1867 Military Reconstruction Act, for they simply could not believe that the freedmen were to vote. Stunned, they saw army officers supervise the process of voter registration, a process that excluded many prominent whites who had participated in the Confederate government but included more than 700,000 blacks, who formed a majority of eligible voters in South Carolina, Florida, Alabama, Mississippi, and Louisiana. Knowing that these Negro voters were well organized by the Union League, often with the assistance of agents of the Freedmen's Bureau, whites were more apathetic than surprised when the fall elections showed heavy majorities in favor of convening new constitutional conventions.*

With hostile and unbelieving eyes, most Southern whites observed the work of these conventions, which between November 1867 and May 1868 drafted new constitutions for the former Confederate states. To Southern whites unaccustomed to seeing blacks in any positions of public prominence, the presence of freedmen in these conventions meant that they were Negro-dominated. In fact, except in the South Carolina convention, in which blacks did form a majority, only between one-fourth and one-ninth of the delegates were Negroes. Whites ridiculed the Negro members' ignorance of parliamentary procedures, and they laughed sardonically when they read how the "coal black" temporary chairman of the Louisiana convention put a question by asking those who favored a motion "to rise an stan on der feet" and then directing "all you contrairy men to rise."

The reactions of Southern whites to the constitutions these conventions produced were also determined by their racial prejudice. Generally they denounced these new charters as "totally incompatible with the prosperity and liberty of the people." In fact the constitutions, often copied from Northern models, were generally improvements over the ones they superseded. In addition to requiring Negro suffrage (as Congress had directed), they promised all citizens of the state equality before the law. They reformed

financial and revenue systems, reorganized the judiciary, improved the organization of local government, and, most important of all, instituted a state-supported system of public education, hitherto notably lacking in most Southern states.

The Reconstruction Governments in the South.
Because these constitutions guaranteed racial equality, Southern whites tried, without great success, to block their ratification. In Alabama, whites boycotted the ratification election; in Mississippi, they cast a majority of votes against the new constitution. In Virginia, ratification was delayed because the conservative army commander of that district discovered that there was no money to hold an election, and in Texas all moves toward the creation of a new government lagged several months behind those in the Eastern states. Despite all the foot-dragging, new governments were set up, and in June 1868 Congress readmitted representatives and senators from Alabama, Arkansas, Florida, Georgia, Louisiana, North Carolina, and South Carolina. Two years later the reconstruction of Virginia, Mississippi, and Texas was completed, and in early 1870 these states were also readmitted. Meanwhile Georgia experienced one further reorganization after the legislature of that state attempted to exclude Negroes who had been elected to that body. But by 1871, when Georgia senators and representatives again took their seats in Congress, all the states of the former Confederacy had undergone the process of Reconstruction and had been readmitted to the Union.

With bitter hostility, most Southern whites witnessed this reorganization of their state governments, and the name "Black Reconstruction," which they gave to the ensuing period of Republican ascendancy in the South, reveals the racial bias behind their opposition. In fact, these Southern state governments were not dominated by Negroes, and the proportion of offices held by blacks was smaller than the percentage of blacks in the population. Only in South Carolina did blacks dominate the state legislature. No Negro was elected governor, though there were black lieutenant governors in South Carolina, Louisiana, and Mississippi. Only in South Carolina was

---

*The Texas election was not held until February 1868. Tennessee had no election, because it had already been readmitted to the Union.

LET US HAVE PEACE.

COLORED RULE IN A RECON-
STRUCTED (?) STATE

As postwar racism mounted,
cartoonists no longer depicted
Negroes as handsome, intelligent fighters for freedom but
painted them as grotesque
and animal-like. In addition
to perpetuating racial stereotypes, this drawing of
Thomas Nast's exaggerates
the number and influence of
blacks in the Southern legislatures. (*American Antiquarian Society*)

there a black state supreme court justice. During the
entire Reconstruction period only two blacks, Hiram
R. Revels and Blanche K. Bruce, both from Mississippi and both men of exceptional ability and integrity, served in the United States Senate, and only
fifteen blacks were elected to the House of Representatives.

Even to the most racist Southern whites it was
obvious that most of the leaders of the Republican
party in the South, and a large part of the Republican
following as well, were white. To those white Republicans born in the North, racists gave the label Car-
petbaggers, because they allegedly came South with
no more worldly possessions than could be packed
into a carpetbag, or small suitcase, ready to live on
and to exploit the prostrate region. The term, with
its implication of corruption, was applied indiscriminately to men of Northern birth who had lived in the

South long before the war as well as to newly arrived
fortune hunters, many of them recently discharged
Union army officers.

Southern-born white Republicans were called
Scalawags, a term that cattle drovers applied to "the
mean, lousy and filthy kine that are not fit for butchers or dogs." Again the term was used indiscriminately. Southern racists applied it to poor hill-country
whites, who had long been at odds with the planters
in states like North Carolina and Alabama and now
joined the Republican party as a way of getting back
at their old enemies. But other Scalawags were members of the planter, mercantile, and industrial classes
of the South; many of these were former Whigs who
distrusted the Democrats, and they felt at home in a
Republican party that favored protective tariffs, subsidies for railroads, and appropriations for rebuilding
the levees along the Mississippi River. A surprising

number of Southern-born white Republicans were former high-ranking officers in the Confederate army, like General P. G. T. Beauregard and General James Longstreet, who knew at first hand the extent of the damage wrought by the war and were willing to accept the victor's terms without procrastination.

Bitterly as they attacked these white Republicans, Southern Democrats reserved their worst abuse for Negroes, and they saw in every measure adopted by the new reconstructed state governments evidence of black incompetence, extravagance, or even barbarism. In truth, much that these state governments did supplied the Democrats with ammunition. The postwar period was one of low political morality, and there was no reason to expect that newly enfranchised blacks would prove any less attracted by the profits of politics than anybody else. Petty corruption prevailed in all the Southern state governments. Louisiana legislators voted themselves an allowance for stationery—which covered purchases of hams and bottles of champagne. The South Carolina legislature ran up a bill of more than $50,000 in refurbishing the statehouse with such costly items as a $750 mirror, $480 clocks, and 200 porcelain spittoons at $8 apiece. The same legislature voted $1,000 to the Speaker of the House of Representatives to repay his losses on a horse race.

Bad as these excesses were, Southern Democrats were angered less by them than by the legitimate work performed by the new state governments. Unwilling to recognize that Negroes were now equal members of the body politic, they objected to expenditures for hospitals, jails, orphanages, and asylums to care for blacks. Most of all they objected to the creation of a public school system. Throughout the South there was considerable hostility to the idea of educating any children at the cost of the taxpayer, and the thought of paying taxes in order to teach black children seemed wild and foolish extravagance. The fact that black schools were mostly conducted by Northern whites, usually women, who came South with a reforming mission, did nothing to increase popular support; too many of the teachers stated plainly and publicly their intention to use "every endeavor to throw a ray of light here and there,

among this benighted race of ruffians, rebels by nature." Adding to all these hostilities was a fear that a system of public education might some day lead to a racially integrated system of education. These apprehensions had little basis in fact, for during the entire period of Reconstruction in the whole South there were significant numbers of children in racially mixed schools only in New Orleans between 1870 and 1874.

The Ku Klux Klan. Not content with criticizing Republican rule, Southern Democrats organized to put an end to it. Theirs was a two-pronged attack. On the one hand, they sought to intimidate or to drive from the South whites who cooperated politically with the Republican regimes; on the other, they tried to terrorize and silence blacks, especially those active in politics. Much of this pressure was informal and sporadic, but much was the work of racist organizations that sprang up all over the South during these years. The most famous of these was the Ku Klux Klan, which originated in 1866 as a social club for young white men in Pulaski, Tennessee. As the Military Reconstruction Act went into effect and the possibility of black participation in Southern political life became increasingly real, racists saw new potential in this secret organization with its cabalistic name and its mysterious uniforms of long flowing robes, high conical hats that made the wearers seem preternaturally tall, and white face masks.

In 1867 the Klan was reorganized under a new constitution that provided for local dens, each headed by a Grand Cyclops, linked together into provinces (counties), each under a Grand Titan, and in turn into realms (states), each under a Grand Dragon. At the head of the whole organization was the Grand Wizard, who, according to most reports, was former Confederate General Nathan Bedford Forrest. Probably this elaborate table of organization was never completely filled out, and certainly there was an almost total lack of central control of the Klan's activities. Indeed, at some point in early 1869 the Klan was officially disbanded. But even without central direction its members, like those of the Order of the White Camellia and other racist vigilante groups, continued in their plan of disrupting the new Republican regimes in the South and terrorizing their black supporters.

Along with other vigilante organizations, the Klan was an expression of the traditional racism of Southern whites. They were willing to accept the defeat of the Confederacy, and they were prepared to admit that slavery was dead; but they could not bring themselves to contemplate a society that would treat blacks and whites as equals. As a group of South Carolina whites protested to Congress in 1868: "The white people of our State will never quietly submit to negro rule. . . . We will keep up this contest until we have regained the heritage of political control handed down to us by honored ancestry. That is a duty we owe to the land that is ours, to the graves that it contains, and to the race of which you and we alike are members—the proud Caucasian race, whose sovereignty on earth God has ordained."

The appeal was shrewdly pitched, for the Southern racist knew how to reach his Northern counterpart. Joined together, their fears of men with darker skins helped to undercut the Reconstruction regimes in the South and to halt any congressional efforts at further innovative Reconstruction legislation.

The Restoration of "Home Rule"

The effectiveness of these limitations on social and political experimentation in the South became evident as early as the fall congressional elections in 1867, which the Democrats won by a landslide. Responding to the popular mood of conservatism, the Republican party in 1868 passed over Radical candidates for the presidency, like Benjamin F. Wade, and nominated Ulysses S. Grant, whose affiliation with Republicans was of recent date but whose broad popular appeal as a military hero was unrivaled. Elected by a surprisingly narrow margin over former Governor Horatio Seymour of New York, the Democratic candidate, Grant shrewdly sized up the attitude of the country toward Reconstruction and in his inaugural address announced his policy: "Let us have peace."

Just what he meant was not immediately clear.

Some thought the new president was addressing the white Ku Kluxers who were trying to overthrow the Reconstruction governments in the South; others believed that he was speaking to Northern Radicals who wanted to bring about further changes in Southern society. As it proved, Grant had both extremes in mind. On the one hand, the president warmly supported the immediate and unconditional readmission of Virginia to the Union, even though Radicals like Sumner warned that the Virginia legislature was "composed of recent Rebels still filled and seething with that old Rebel fire." On the other, Grant was outraged by the terrorism rampant in the South, and he insisted that Congress pass a series of Enforcement Acts (1870–71) enabling him to crush the Ku Klux Klan. Under this legislation, the president proclaimed martial law in nine South Carolina counties where white terrorists were most active, and federal marshals arrested large numbers of suspected Klansmen in North Carolina, Mississippi, and other Southern states. In brief, then, Grant's policy was to warn Southern whites that the national government would not tolerate overt violence and organized military activity—but to let them understand that at the same time they would not be harassed if they regained control of their state governments through less revolutionary tactics.

The "Redemption" of the South. Quickly accepting the hint, Southern whites promptly undertook the restoration of what they euphemistically called "home rule"—which meant the rule of native white Democrats. Aware of Northern sensitivities, they now downplayed, when possible, the more brutal forms of terrorism and outright violence. White Republicans were subjected to social pressure and economic boycott; many fled the South, and others joined the Redeemers (as the advocates of home rule and white supremacy liked to call themselves). Redeemers exerted economic pressure on blacks by threatening not to hire or extend credit to those who were politically active.

In several states whites organized rifle clubs, which practiced marksmanship on the outskirts of Republican political rallies. Usually blacks were cowed by these tactics. In a few cases, however, when they organized and tried to defend themselves, there occurred what Southern newspapers called "race riots"—a better term would have been "massacres," for the more numerous and better armed whites overpowered the blacks and slaughtered their leaders. In state after state Republican governors appealed to Washington for additional federal troops, but Grant, convinced that the public was tired of "these annual autumnal outbreaks" in the South, refused.

In consequence of Grant's policy, the Redeemers quickly gained power in Virginia, North Carolina, Tennessee, and Georgia. In 1875 they won control of Alabama, Mississippi, Arkansas, and Texas, and early in 1877 they ended Republican rule in Florida. By the end of Grant's second administration, South Carolina and Louisiana were the only Southern states with Republican governments.

The Election of 1876. The fate of these two remaining Republican regimes in the South became intricately connected with the outcome of the 1876 presidential election. The Democratic nominee, Sam-

uel J. Tilden, undoubtedly received a majority of the popular votes cast—though, equally undoubtedly, thousands of blacks who would have voted for his Republican rival, Rutherford B. Hayes, were kept from the polls. But Tilden lacked one vote of having a majority in the electoral college unless he received some of the votes from South Carolina, Florida, and Louisiana, all of which submitted to Congress competing sets of Democratic and Republican ballots. (There was also a technical question of the eligibility of one Republican elector from Oregon.)

Consequently when Congress assembled in December 1876 it confronted a crisis. If it decided to accept the disputed Democratic electoral votes, Republican control of the White House would be broken for the first time in a quarter of a century and the Reconstruction of the South would be ended. If Congress accepted the Republican electoral votes, that decision would run counter to the will of a majority of the voters in the country.

To resolve the impasse required a compromise— not a single compromise, but a complicated, interlocking set of bargains. After intricate and secret

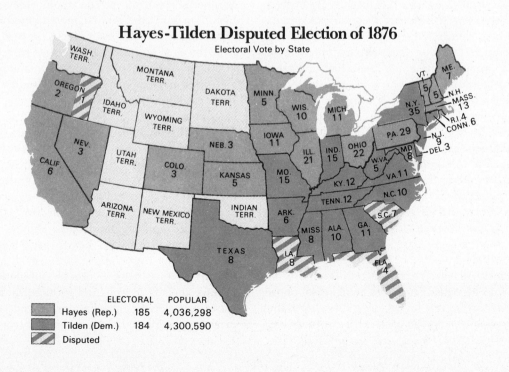

Hayes-Tilden Disputed Election of 1876
Electoral Vote by State

	ELECTORAL	POPULAR
Hayes (Rep.)	185	4,036,298
Tilden (Dem.)	184	4,300,590
Disputed		

negotiations, several agreements were reached. First, Congress decided that the disputed electoral votes should be referred to a special electoral commission, which should consist of five members from the House of Representatives, five members from the Senate, and five associate justices from the Supreme Court. This body was composed of eight Republicans and seven Democrats, and on every disputed ballot the commission ruled in favor of Hayes by that same vote. In consequence of these decisions, Tilden's electoral vote remained at 184, while Hayes's slowly mounted to 185. In March 1877, for the fifth time in succession, a Republican president was inaugurated.

Democrats reluctantly accepted the election of Hayes because of some other bargaining that took place while the electoral votes were being counted. One set of compromises came to be known as the Wormley agreement, because it was negotiated in the luxurious Washington hotel owned by the Negro restaurateur James Wormley. Representing Hayes at these sessions were Senator Sherman, Representative Garfield, and other prominent Republicans. Across the table sat Southern Democratic leaders, including Senator John B. Gordon, the former Confederate General who now represented Georgia in Congress, and L. Q. C. Lamar, once Confederate minister to Russia, who was senator from Mississippi. The Republicans promised the Southerners that, if allowed to be inaugurated, Hayes "would deal justly and generously with the south." Translated, that meant that Hayes would withdraw the remaining federal troops from the South and acquiesce in the overthrow of the Republican regimes in South Carolina and Louisiana. The Southerners found the terms acceptable, and they promptly leaked the news of the agreement, so as to protect themselves from charges that they had betrayed their section.

Behind the Wormley agreement lay other, less formal, compromises. Hayes's backers promised that the new president would not use federal patronage in the South to defeat the Democrats. They further pledged that he would support congressional appropriations for rebuilding levees along the flood-ridden Mississippi River and for constructing a transconti-

nental railroad along a Southern route. In return, Southerners agreed to allow the Republicans to elect Garfield Speaker of the new House of Representatives, with the power to determine the membership of congressional committees. More important, they promised to protect the basic rights of blacks, as guaranteed in the Thirteenth, Fourteenth, and Fifteenth Amendments to the Constitution.

Once Hayes was inaugurated, virtually all these informal agreements were flouted by both sides. Hayes, for his part, ordered the removal of federal troops from the South and did appoint a Southerner, former Confederate David M. Key, to his cabinet as postmaster general. But two-thirds of the federal officeholders in the South remained Republicans. Hayes changed his mind about supporting a Southern transcontinental railroad alleging that federal funding would lead to corruption.

Southern Democrats for their part reneged on their promise to support Garfield for Speaker, and, once the House was organized under Democratic leadership, they eagerly joined in an investigation of alleged fraud in Hayes's election. Only a very few Southern Democratic politicians, like Governor Wade Hampton of South Carolina, remembered their promises to respect the rights of blacks. Instead, almost all took the final withdrawal of federal troops from the South as a signal that the Negro, already relegated to a position of economic inferiority, could be excluded from Southern political life.

Disfranchisement of Blacks. Southern whites had to act cautiously, so as not to offend public opinion in the North or to invite renewed federal intervention, but they moved steadily and successfully to reduce Negro voting. One of the simplest devices was the poll tax, adopted by Georgia in 1877 and quickly copied by other Southern states. To Northerners the requirement that a voter had to pay $1 or $2 a year did not seem unreasonable, yet in fact, since three-fourths of the entire Southern population had an average income of only $55.16 in 1880, the poll tax was a considerable financial drain, especially to poverty-stricken blacks. More imaginative was the "eight

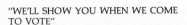

"WE'LL SHOW YOU WHEN WE COME
TO VOTE"
The attitude of Northern women
contributed to the declining interest in the problems of the South.
Many women who had loyally
supported the war and emancipation felt that they, as well as the
freedmen, should have been enfranchised under the Reconstruction amendments to the Constitution. In 1869 Elizabeth Cady
Stanton, Susan B. Anthony, and
others organized the National
Woman Suffrage Association to
promote a sixteenth amendment to
the Constitution, enfranchising
women. *(American Antiquarian
Society)*

box" law, adopted by South Carolina in 1882 and
imitated by North Carolina and Florida. Under this
system ballots for each contested race had to be de-
posited in separate boxes. Thus a voter must cast in
one box his ballot for governor, in another box his
ballot for sheriff, and so forth. The system frustrated
the illiterate Negro voter, who could no longer bring
to the polls a single ballot, marked for him in advance
by a Republican friend. To make the task of semiliterate voters more difficult, election officials period-

ically rearranged the order of the boxes. Still another
device, which did not become popular until the late
1880s, was the secret, or Australian, ballot. Ostensibly
introduced in the South, as in the North, in order to
prevent fraud, the secret ballot actually discriminated
heavily against blacks, for as late as 1900 the number
of illiterate adult Negro males ranged from 39 percent
in Florida to 61 percent in Louisiana.

Despite all these devices, Southern blacks continued to vote in surprising numbers. In the 1880

presidential election, for example, more than 70 percent of the eligible Negroes voted in Arkansas, Florida, North Carolina, Tennessee, and Virginia, and between 50 percent and 70 percent voted in Alabama, Louisiana, South Carolina, and Texas. To the Redeemers these black voters posed a double threat. They were numerous enough that ambitious Northern Republicans might be tempted again to try federal intervention in state elections, with the hope of breaking the now solidly Democratic South. Even more dangerous was the possibility that poor whites in the South, whose needs for public education and welfare the business-oriented Redeemers consistently neglected, might find common cause with their black peers.

The Redeemers saw both these dangers materialize after 1890. Shortly after the Republicans gained control of the House of Representatives in 1889, Representative Henry Cabot Lodge of Massachusetts introduced a strong bill for federal control of elections, which was promptly christened the Force Bill. Though Democrats in the Senate defeated Lodge's bill in January 1891, Redeemers saw in it a threat to renew "all the horrors of reconstruction days." Their fear was doubtless the greater because the almost simultaneous rise of the Populist movement threatened, as never before, to split the white voters of the region. Appealing to farmers and small planters, the Populist party was the enemy of lawyers and bankers and of the rising commercial and industrial spokesmen of the "New South." Some of the Populist leaders, like Thomas Watson of Georgia, were openly critical of the Redeemers' policy of repressing the blacks and seemed to be flirting with the Negro voters.

Faced with this double threat, Southern states moved swiftly to exclude the Negro completely and permanently from politics. Mississippi led the way with a constitutional convention in 1890 that required voters to be able to read and interpret the Constitution to the satisfaction of the white registration officials. It is not hard to imagine how difficult even a graduate of Howard University Law School would have found the task of satisfactory constitutional exegesis. In 1898 a Louisiana constitutional convention improved on the Mississippi example by requiring a literacy test of all voters except the sons and grandsons of persons who voted in state elections before 1867. Since no Louisiana Negroes had been permitted to vote before that date, this provision allowed illiterate whites to vote, while the literacy test excluded most Negro voters.

State after state across the South followed, or elaborated on, these requirements. South Carolina held a disfranchising convention in 1895. North Carolina amended its constitution to limit suffrage in 1900. Alabama and Virginia acted in 1901–2, and Georgia adopted a restrictive constitutional amendment in 1908. The remaining Southern states continued to rely on the poll tax and other varieties of legislative disfranchisement. When opponents of these measures accused their advocates of discriminating against the Negroes, Carter Glass of Virginia replied for his entire generation: "Discrimination! Why that is precisely what we propose; that exactly is what this convention was elected for."

It took time, then, for the complete working out of the political compromises of the Reconstruction era. Not until the end of the nineteenth century did white Southerners receive the full price they had exacted in permitting the election of Rutherford B. Hayes. But by 1900 that payment had been made in full. The Negro was no longer a political force in the South, and the Republican party was no longer the defender of Negro rights.

CHRONOLOGY

1865 Lincoln assassinated; Andrew Johnson becomes president.

Johnson moves for speedy, lenient restoration of Southern states to Union.

Congress creates Joint Committee of Fifteen to supervise reconstruction process.

Thirteenth Amendment ratified.

1866 Johnson breaks with Republican majority in Congress by vetoing Freedmen's Bureau bill and Civil Rights bill. Latter is passed over his veto.

Congress approves Fourteenth Amendment and submits it to states for ratification.

Johnson and Republicans quarrel. Republicans win fall congressional elections.

Ku Klux Klan formed.

1867 Congress passes Military Reconstruction Act over Johnson's veto. (Two supplementary acts in 1867 and a third in 1868 passed to put this measure into effect.)

Congress passes Tenure of Office Act and Command of Army Act to reduce Johnson's power.

1868 Former Confederate states hold constitutional conventions, for which former slaves are allowed to vote, and adopt new constitutions guaranteeing universal suffrage.

Arkansas, Alabama, Florida, Georgia, Louisiana,

North Carolina, and South Carolina readmitted to representation in Congress. Because of discrimination against Negro officeholders, Georgia representatives are expelled. (State is again admitted in 1870.)

President Johnson impeached. Escapes conviction by one vote.

Republicans nominate Ulysses S. Grant for president; Democrats select Governor Horatio Seymour of New York. Grant elected president.

1869 Congress passes Fifteenth Amendment and submits it to states for ratification.

1870 First Ku Klux Klan (or Enforcement) Act gives Grant power to move against white terrorists in South. A second act in 1871 further strengthens president's hand.

1872 Grant reelected president.

1876 Republicans nominate Rutherford B. Hayes for president; Democrats nominate Samuel J. Tilden. Tilden secures majority of popular vote but electoral vote is in doubt because of disputed returns from three Southern states.

1877 After elaborate political and economic bargaining, Congress creates an electoral commission, which rules that all disputed ballots belong to Hayes, who is inaugurated president.

SUGGESTED READINGS

The Civil War and Reconstruction (1969), by J. G. Randall and David Donald, continues to be useful, especially for its full bibliography. Three modern treatments of the postwar period are John H. Franklin, *Reconstruction after the Civil War* (1961), Kenneth M. Stampp, *The Era of Reconstruction* (1965), and Rembert W. Patrick, *The Reconstruction of the Nation* (1967).

The best account of steps taken during the Civil War to reorganize the Southern states is Herman Belz, *Reconstructing the Union* (1969). William B. Hesseltine, *Lincoln's Plan of Reconstruction* (1960), argues that Lincoln had not

one but many approaches to Reconstruction, all of them unsuccessful. Peyton McCrary, *Abraham Lincoln and Reconstruction* (1978), is the authoritative account of developments in Louisiana, where Lincoln's experiment in Reconstruction was most fully tested.

Robert W. Winston, *Andrew Johnson, Plebeian and Patriot* (1928), is the best of several unsatisfactory biographies of that president. More valuable are the markedly favorable estimates of Johnson's program in George F. Milton, *The Age of Hate* (1930), and Howard K. Beale, *The Critical Year* (1930), and the strongly critical analyses in

Eric L. McKitrick, *Andrew Johnson and Reconstruction* (1960), LaWanda Cox and John H. Cox, *Politics, Principle, and Prejudice* (1963), and W. R. Brock, *An American Crisis* (1963).

Four major studies of postwar constitutional changes are Harold M. Hyman, *A More Perfect Union* (1973), Stanley I. Kutler, *Judicial Power and Reconstruction Politics* (1968), William Gillette, *The Right to Vote* (1965), and Charles Fairman, *Reconstruction and Reunion* (1971).

George R. Bentley, *A History of the Freedmen's Bureau* (1955), is a standard work, but it should be supplemented by William S. McFeely, *Yankee Stepfather: General O. O. Howard and the Freedmen* (1968), and Louis S. Gerteis, *From Contraband to Freedman* (1973).

Leon Litwack, *Been in the Storm So Long* (1979), is a masterful account of the transition from slavery to freedom. Four state studies of black responses to emancipation are especially valuable: on South Carolina, Willie Lee Rose, *Rehearsal for Reconstruction* (1964), and Joel Williamson, *After Slavery* (1965); on Alabama, Peter Kolchin, *First Freedom* (1972); and on Mississippi, Vernon L. Wharton, *The Negro in Mississippi* (1947).

Fred A. Shannon, *The Farmer's Last Frontier* (1945), and E. Merton Coulter, *The South during Reconstruction* (1947), give good general accounts of economic changes in the postwar South. Recently these changes have been reappraised by historians and economists using sophisticated quantitative methods: Stephen J. DeCanio, *Agriculture in the Postbellum South* (1974); Robert Higgs, *Competition and Coercion: Blacks in the American Economy* (1977); and Roger Ransom and Richard L. Sutch, *One Kind of Freedom: The Economic Consequences of Emancipation* (1977). For a thoughtful evaluation of this new literature, see Harold D. Woodman, "Sequel to Slavery: The New History Views the Postbellum South," *Journal of Southern History*, 43 (1977), 525–54. On the alleged breakup of the plantation system, see Roger W. Shugg, *Origins of Class Struggle in Louisiana* (1939), and on the continuing dominance of the planter class, see Jonathan M. Wiener, *Social Origins of the New South* (1978).

Two articles provide the best brief introduction to the modern interpretation of Reconstruction politics: Larry G. Kincaid, "Victims of Circumstance: An Interpretation of Changing Attitudes toward Republican Policy Makers and Reconstruction," *Journal of American History*, 57 (1970), 48–66, and Michael L. Benedict, "Preserving the Constitution: The Conservative Basis of Radical Reconstruction," *ibid.*, 61 (1974), 65–90. See also Hans L. Trefousse, *The Radical Republicans* (1969), David Donald, *The Politics of Reconstruction* (1965), and Michael L. Benedict, *A Compromise of*

Principle (1974). Among the fullest biographies of Radical leaders are Fawn M. Brodie, *Thaddeus Stevens* (1959), David Donald, *Charles Sumner and the Rights of Man* (1970), and Benjamin P. Thomas and Harold M. Hyman, *Stanton* (1962).

David M. DeWitt, *Impeachment and Trial of Andrew Johnson* (1903), is the standard account, strongly pro-Johnson in tone. Michael L. Benedict's book of the same title (1973) is a useful, anti-Johnson corrective. The best explanation of why impeachment occurred when it did is to be found in Hans L. Trefousse, *Impeachment of a President* (1975).

On American racial attitudes, George M. Fredrickson, *The Black Image in the White Mind* (1971), is excellent. On Northern racism, see V. Jacque Voegeli, *Free but Not Equal* (1967), and Forrest G. Wood, *Black Scare* (1968). A thoughtful and provocative essay is C. Vann Woodward, "Seeds of Failure in Radical Race Policy," *American Philosophical Society Proceedings*, 110 (1966), 1–9.

On the work of the Reconstruction governments in the South, see W. E. B. DuBois, "Reconstruction and Its Benefits," *American Historical Review* (1910), 781–99, and DuBois, *Black Reconstruction* (1935). The best accounts of Reconstruction in individual states are Francis B. Simkins and Robert H. Woody, *South Carolina during Reconstruction* (1932), Jerrell H. Shofner, *Nor Is It Over Yet: Florida in the Era of Reconstruction* (1974), Thomas B. Alexander, *Political Reconstruction in Tennessee* (1950), James W. Garner, *Reconstruction in Mississippi* (1901), and Joe G. Taylor, *Louisiana Reconstructed* (1974).

On the education of blacks after the war, see Henry A. Bullock, *A History of Negro Education in the South* (1967), William P. Vaughn, *Schools for All* (1974), and Roger A. Fischer, *The Segregation Struggle in Louisiana* (1974).

Southern white resistance to the Reconstruction process is the theme of Michael Perman, *Reunion without Compromise* (1973). Allen W. Trelease, *White Terror* (1971), is a harrowing account of white vigilantism, as carried on by the Ku Klux Klan and less formally organized groups.

On Grant's presidency the best, but not entirely satisfactory, account is William B. Hesseltine, *Ulysses S. Grant, Politician* (1935). William Gillette, *Retreat from Reconstruction* (1980), is the best account of Grant's Southern policy.

C. Vann Woodward, *Reunion and Reaction* (1951), is a highly original reexamination of the compromises of 1876–77. On the Redeemer regimes, see Woodward's authoritative *Origins of the New South* (1951). The best study of the disfranchisement of blacks is J. Morgan Kousser, *The Shaping of Southern Politics* (1974).

Appendix

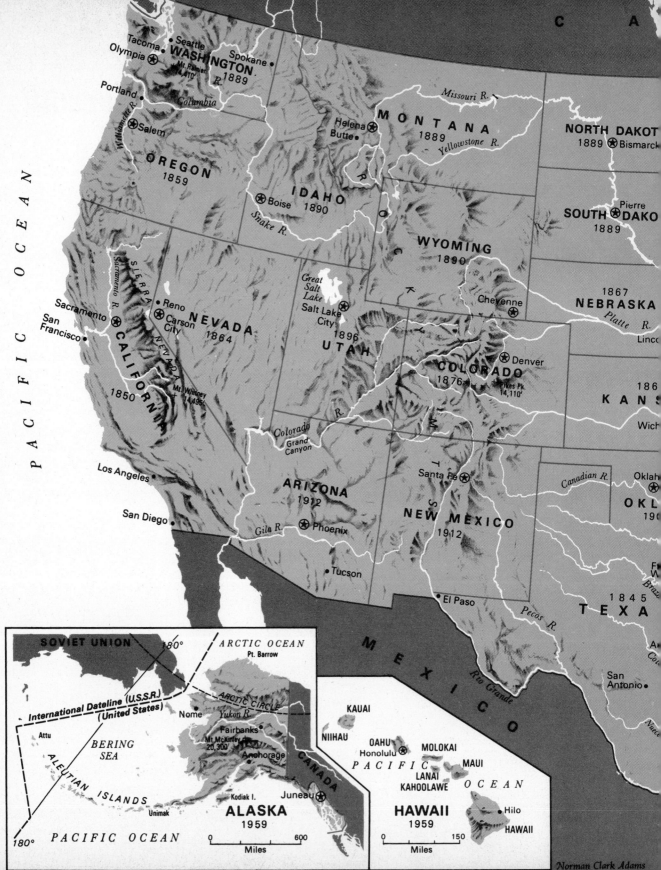

PACIFIC OCEAN

CANADA

WASHINGTON 1889
Tacoma · Seattle · Spokane
Olympia ⊛
Mt. Rainier 14,410'
Portland
Columbia R.
Willamette R.
Salem ⊛

OREGON 1859

MONTANA 1889
Helena ⊛
Butte ·
Missouri R.
Yellowstone R.

NORTH DAKOTA 1889 ⊛ Bismarck

IDAHO 1890
Boise ⊛
Snake R.

SOUTH DAKOTA 1889
Pierre ·

WYOMING 1890
Cheyenne ·

NEBRASKA 1867
Platte R.
Lincoln

NEVADA 1864
Reno ·
Carson City ⊛

SIERRA NEVADA
Sacramento R.
Sacramento ⊛
San Francisco

Great Salt Lake
Salt Lake City ⊛
UTAH 1896

COLORADO 1876
Denver ⊛
Pikes Pk. 14,110'

KANSAS 1861
Wichita

CALIFORNIA 1850
Mt. Whitney 14,495'
Los Angeles ·
San Diego ·

Colorado R.
Grand Canyon

ARIZONA 1912
Phoenix ⊛
Gila R.

Santa Fe ⊛

NEW MEXICO 1912

OKLAHOMA 1907

Tucson ·

El Paso ·

Canadian R.

TEXAS 1845

MEXICO

Rio Grande
Pecos R.

San Antonio ·

SOVIET UNION
180°
ARCTIC OCEAN
Pt. Barrow
International Dateline (U.S.S.R.)
(United States)
ARCTIC CIRCLE
Nome ·
Yukon R.
Attu
BERING SEA
Fairbanks ·
Mt. McKinley 20,300'
Anchorage
ALEUTIAN ISLANDS
Kodiak I.
Unimak
Juneau ⊛
ALASKA 1959
CANADA
180°
PACIFIC OCEAN
0   600
Miles

KAUAI
NIIHAU
OAHU
Honolulu ⊛
MOLOKAI
MAUI
PACIFIC
LANAI
KAHOOLAWE
OCEAN
HAWAII 1959
Hilo ·
HAWAII
0   150
Miles

ii

Norman Clark Adams

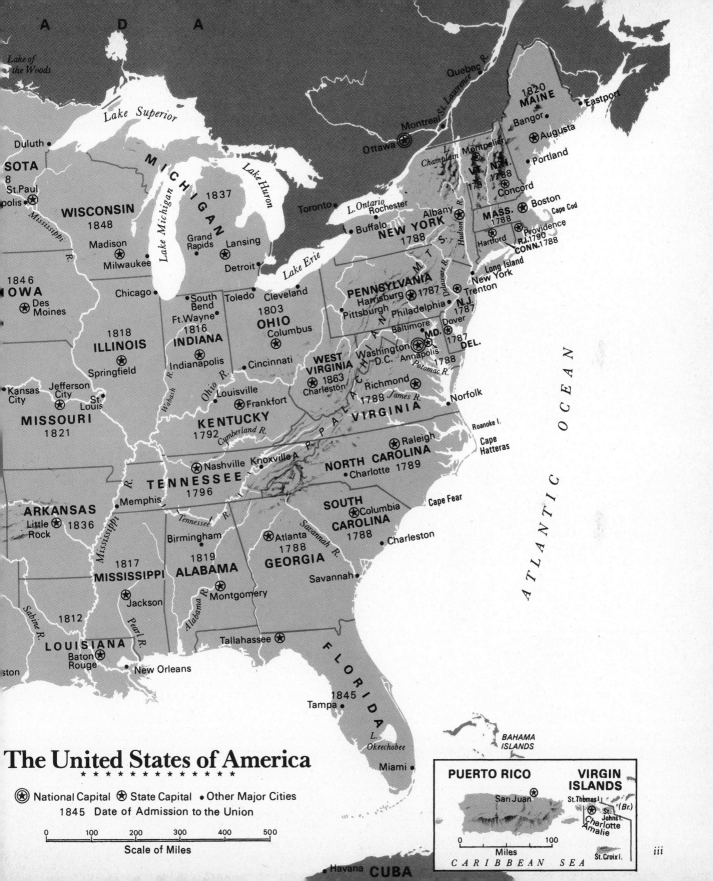

The United States of America
★ ★ ★ ★ ★ ★ ★ ★ ★ ★ ★ ★ ★ ★

⊛ National Capital ✪ State Capital • Other Major Cities
1845 Date of Admission to the Union

0   100   200   300   400   500
Scale of Miles

PUERTO RICO   **VIRGIN ISLANDS**

BAHAMA ISLANDS

San Juan   St. Thomas I.
                          (Br.)
                St. John I.
              Charlotte Amalie
0   100
Miles   St. Croix I.

CARIBBEAN SEA

iii

Declaration of Independence

IN CONGRESS, JULY 4, 1776

THE UNANIMOUS DECLARATION OF THE THIRTEEN UNITED STATES OF AMERICA

When, in the course of human events, it becomes necessary for one people to dissolve the political bands which have connected them with another, and to assume, among the powers of the earth, the separate and equal station to which the laws of nature and of nature's God entitle them, a decent respect to the opinions of mankind requires that they should declare the causes which impel them to the separation.

We hold these truths to be self-evident: That all men are created equal; that they are endowed by their Creator with certain unalienable rights; that among these are life, liberty, and the pursuit of happiness; that, to secure these rights, governments are instituted among men, deriving their just powers from the consent of the governed; that whenever any form of government becomes destructive of these ends, it is the right of the people to alter or to abolish it, and to institute new government, laying its foundation on such principles, and organizing its powers in such form, as to them shall seem most likely to effect their safety and happiness. Prudence, indeed, will dictate that governments long established should not be changed for light and transient causes; and accordingly all experience hath shown that mankind are more disposed to suffer, while evils are sufferable, than to right themselves by abolishing the forms to which they are accustomed. But when a long train of abuses and usurpations, pursuing invariably the same object, evinces a design to reduce them under absolute despotism, it is their right, it is their duty, to throw off such government, and to provide new guards for their future security. Such has been the patient sufferance of these colonies; and such is now the necessity which constrains them to alter their former systems of government. The history of the present King of Great Britain is a history of repeated injuries and usurpations, all having in direct object the establishment of an absolute tyranny over these states. To prove this, let facts be submitted to a candid world.

He has refused his assent to laws, the most wholesome and necessary for the public good.

He has forbidden his governors to pass laws of immediate and pressing importance, unless suspended in their operation till his assent should be obtained; and, when so suspended, he has utterly neglected to attend to them.

He has refused to pass other laws for the accommodation of large districts of people, unless those people would relinquish the right of representation in the legislature, a right inestimable to them, and formidable to tyrants only.

He has called together legislative bodies at places unusual, uncomfortable, and distant from the depository of their public records, for the sole purpose of fatiguing them into compliance with his measures.

He has dissolved representative houses repeatedly, for opposing, with manly firmness, his invasions on the rights of the people.

He has refused for a long time, after such dissolutions, to cause others to be elected; whereby the legislative powers, incapable of annihilation, have returned to the people at large for their exercise; the state remaining, in the mean time, exposed to all the dangers of invasions from without and convulsions within.

He has endeavored to prevent the population of these states; for that purpose obstructing the laws for naturalization of foreigners; refusing to pass others to encourage their migration hither, and raising the conditions of new appropriations of lands.

He has obstructed the administration of justice, by refusing his assent to laws for establishing judiciary powers.

He has made judges dependent on his will alone, for the tenure of their offices, and the amount and payment of their salaries.

He has erected a multiude of new offices, and sent hither swarms of officers to harass our people and eat out their substance.

He has kept among us, in times of peace, standing armies, without the consent of our legislatures.

He has affected to render the military independent of, and superior to, the civil power.

He has combined with others to subject us to a jurisdiction foreign to our constitution, and unacknowledged by our laws, giving his assent to their acts of pretended legislation:

For quartering large bodies of armed troops among us;

For protecting them, by a mock trial, from punishment for any murders which they should commit on the inhabitants of these states;

For cutting off our trade with all parts of the world;

For imposing taxes on us without our consent;

For depriving us, in many cases, of the benefits of trial by jury;

For transporting us beyond seas, to be tried for pretended offenses;

For abolishing the free system of English laws in a neighboring province, establishing therein an arbitrary government, and enlarging its boundaries, so as to render it at once an example and fit instrument for introducing the same absolute rule into these colonies;

For taking away our charters, abolishing our most valuable laws, and altering fundamentally the forms of our governments;

For suspending our own legislatures, and declaring themselves invested with power to legislate for us in all cases whatsoever.

He has abdicated government here, by declaring us out of his protection and waging war against us.

He has plundered our seas, ravaged our coasts, burned our towns, and destroyed the lives of our people.

He is at this time transporting large armies of foreign mercenaries to complete the works of death, desolation, and tyranny already begun with circumstances of cruelty and perfidy scarcely paralleled in the most barbarous ages, and totally unworthy the head of a civilized nation.

He has constrained our fellow-citizens, taken captive on the high seas, to bear arms against their country, to become the executioners of their friends and brethren, or to fall themselves by their hands.

He has excited domestic insurrection among us, and has endeavored to bring on the inhabitants of our frontiers the merciless Indian savages, whose known rule of warfare is an undistinguished destruction of all ages, sexes, and conditions.

In every stage of these oppressions we have petitioned for redress in the most humble terms; our repeated petitions have been answered only by repeated injury. A prince, whose character is thus marked by every act which may define a tyrant, is unfit to be the ruler of a free people.

Nor have we been wanting in our attentions to our British brethren. We have warned them, from time to time, of attempts by their legislature to extend an unwarrantable jurisdiction over us. We have reminded them of the circumstances of our emigration and settlement here. We have appealed to their native justice and magnanimity; and we have conjured them, by the ties of our common kindred, to disavow these usurpations, which would inevitably interrupt our connections and correspondence. They, too, have been deaf to the voice of justice and of consanguinity. We must, therefore, acquiesce in the necessity which denounces our separation, and hold them, as we hold the rest of mankind, enemies in war, in peace friends.

We, therefore, the representatives of the United States of America, in General Congress assembled, appealing to the Supreme Judge of the world for the rectitude of our intentions, do, in the name and by the authority of the good people of these colonies, solemnly publish and declare, that these United Colonies are, and of right ought to be, FREE AND INDEPENDENT STATES; that they are absolved from all allegiance to the British crown, and that all political connection between them and the state of Great Britain is, and ought to be, totally dissolved; and that, as free and independent states, they have full power to levy war, conclude peace, contract alliances, establish commerce, and do all other acts and things which independent states may of right do. And for the support of this declaration, with a firm reliance on the protection of Divine Providence, we mutually pledge to each other our lives, our fortunes, and our sacred honor.

JOHN HANCOCK [*President*]
[*and fifty-five others*]

The Articles of Confederation and Perpetual Union

BETWEEN THE STATES OF NEW HAMPSHIRE, MASSACHUSETTS BAY, RHODE ISLAND
AND PROVIDENCE PLANTATIONS, CONNECTICUT, NEW YORK, NEW JERSEY,
PENNSYLVANIA, DELAWARE, MARYLAND, VIRGINIA,
NORTH CAROLINA, SOUTH CAROLINA, GEORGIA.*

ARTICLE 1.

The stile of this confederacy shall be "The United States of America."

ARTICLE 2.

Each State retains its sovereignty, freedom and independence, and every power, jurisdiction, and right, which is not by this confederation expressly delegated to the United States, in Congress assembled.

ARTICLE 3.

The said states hereby severally enter into a firm league of friendship with each other for their common defence, the security of their liberties and their mutual and general welfare; binding themselves to assist each other against all force offered to, or attacks made upon them, or any of them, on account of religion, sovereignty, trade, or any other pretence whatever.

ARTICLE 4.

The better to secure and perpetuate mutual friendship and intercourse among the people of the different states in this union, the free inhabitants of each of these states, paupers, vagabonds, and fugitives from justice excepted, shall be entitled to all privileges and immunities of free citizens in the several states; and the people of each State shall have free ingress and regress to and from any other State, and shall enjoy therein all the privileges of trade and commerce, subject to the same duties, impositions, and restrictions, as the inhabitants thereof respectively; provided, that such restrictions shall not extend so far as to prevent the removal of property, imported into any State, to any other State of which the owner is an inhabitant; provided also, that no imposition, duties, or restriction, shall be laid by any State on the property of the United States, or either of them.

If any person guilty of, or charged with treason, felony, or other high misdemeanor in any State, shall flee from justice and be found in any of the United States, he shall, upon demand of the governor or executive power of the State from which he fled, be delivered up and removed to the State having jurisdiction of his offence.

Full faith and credit shall be given in each of these states to the records, acts, and judicial proceedings of the courts and magistrates of every other State.

ARTICLE 5.

For the more convenient management of the general interests of the United States, delegates shall be annually appointed, in such manner as the legislature of each State shall direct, to meet in Congress, on the 1st Monday in November in every year, with a power reserved to each

*This copy of the final draft of the Articles of Confederation is taken from the *Journals*, 9:907–925, November 15, 1777.

State to recal its delegates, or any of them, at any time within the year, and to send others in their stead for the remainder of the year.

No State shall be represented in Congress by less than two, nor by more than seven members; and no person shall be capable of being a delegate for more than three years in any term of six years; nor shall any person, being a delegate, be capable of holding any office under the United States, for which he, or any other for his benefit, receives any salary, fees, or emolument of any kind.

Each State shall maintain its own delegates in a meeting of the states, and while they act as members of the committee of the states.

In determining questions in the United States, in Congress assembled, each State shall have one vote.

Freedom of speech and debate in Congress shall not be impeached or questioned in any court or place out of Congress: and the members of Congress shall be protected in their persons from arrests and imprisonments, during the time of their going to and from, and attendance on Congress, *except for treason*, felony, or breach of the peace.

ARTICLE 6.

No State, without the consent of the United States, in Congress assembled, shall send any embassy to, or receive any embassy from, or enter into any conference, agreement, alliance, or treaty with any king, prince, or state; nor shall any person, holding any office of profit or trust under the United States, or any of them, accept of any present, emolument, office or title, of any kind whatever, from any king, prince, or foreign state; nor shall the United States, in Congress assembled, or any of them, grant any title of nobility.

No two or more states shall enter into any treaty, confederation, or alliance, whatever, between them, without the consent of the United States, in Congress assembled, specifying accurately the purposes for which the same is to be entered into, and how long it shall continue.

No state shall lay any imposts or duties which may interfere with any stipulations in treaties entered into by the United States, in Congress assembled, with any king, prince, or state, in pursuance of any treaties already proposed by Congress to the courts of France and Spain.

No vessels of war shall be kept up in time of peace by any State, except such number only as shall be deemed necessary by the United States, in Congress assembled, for the defence of such State or its trade; nor shall any body of forces be kept up by any State, in time of peace,

except such number only as, in the judgment of the United States, in Congress assembled, shall be deemed requisite to garrison the forts necessary for the defence of such State; but every State shall always keep up a well regulated and disciplined militia, sufficiently armed and accoutred, and shall provide, and constantly have ready for use, in public stores, a due number of field pieces and tents, and a proper quantity of arms, ammunition and camp equipage.

No State shall engage in any war without the consent of the United States, in Congress assembled, unless such State be actually invaded by enemies, or shall have received certain advice of a resolution being formed by some nation of Indians to invade such State, and the danger is so imminent as not to admit of a delay till the United States, in Congress assembled, can be consulted; nor shall any State grant commissions to any ships or vessels of war, nor letters of marque or reprisal, except it be after a declaration of war by the United States, in Congress assembled, and then only against the kingdom or state, and the subjects thereof, against which war has been so declared, and under such regulations as shall be established by the United States, in Congress assembled, unless such State be infested by pirates, in which case vessels of war may be fitted out for that occasion, and kept so long as the danger shall continue, or until the United States, in Congress assembled, shall determine otherwise.

ARTICLE 7.

When land forces are raised by any State for the common defence, all officers of or under the rank of colonel, shall be appointed by the legislature of each State respectively, by whom such forces shall be raised, or in such manner as such State shall direct; and all vacancies shall be filled up by the State which first made the appointment.

ARTICLE 8.

All charges of war and all other expences, that shall be incurred for the common defence or general welfare, and allowed by the United States, in Congress assembled, shall be defrayed out of a common treasury, which shall be supplied by the several states, in proportion to the value of all land within each State, granted to or surveyed for any person, as such land and the buildings and improvements thereon shall be estimated according to such mode as the United States, in Congress assembled, shall, from time to time, direct and appoint.

The taxes for paying that proportion shall be laid and levied by the authority and direction of the legislatures of the several states, within the time agreed upon by the United States, in Congress assembled.

ARTICLE 9.

The United States, in Congress assembled, shall have the sole and exclusive right and power of determining on peace and war, except in the cases mentioned in the 6th article; of sending and receiving ambassadors; entering into treaties and alliances, provided that no treaty of commerce shall be made, whereby the legislative power of the repective states shall be restrained from imposing such imposts and duties on foreigners as their own people are subjected to, or from prohibiting the exportation or importation of any species of goods or commodities whatsoever; of establishing rules for deciding, in all cases, what captures on land or water shall be legal, and in what manner prizes, taken by land or naval forces in the service of the United States, shall be divided or appropriated; of granting letters of marque and reprisal in times of peace; appointing courts for the trial of piracies and felonies committed on the high seas, and establishing courts for receiving and determining, finally, appeals in all cases of captures; provided, that no member of Congress shall be appointed a judge of any of the said courts.

The United States, in Congress assembled, shall also be the last resort on appeal in all disputes and differences now subsisting, or that hereafter may arise between two or more states concerning boundary, jurisdiction or any other cause whatever; which authority shall always be exercised in the manner following: whenever the legislative or executive authority, or lawful agent of any State, in controversy with another, shall present a petition to Congress, stating the matter in question, and praying for a hearing, notice thereof shall be given, by order of Congress, to the legislative or executive authority of the other State in controversy, and a day assigned for the appearance of the parties by their lawful agents, who shall then be directed to appoint, by joint consent, commissioners or judges to constitute a court for hearing and determining the matter in question; but, if they cannot agree, Congress shall name three persons out of each of the United States, and from the list of such persons each party shall alternately strike out one, in the petitioners beginning, until the number shall be reduced to thirteen; and from that number not less than seven, nor more than nine names, as Congress shall direct, shall, in the presence of Congress, be drawn out by lot; and the persons whose names shall be so drawn, or any five of them, shall be commissioners or judges to hear and finally determine the controversy, so always as a major part of the judges who shall hear the cause shall agree in the determination; and if either party shall neglect to attend at the day appointed, without shewing reasons which Congress shall judge sufficient, or, being present, shall refuse to strike, the Congress shall proceed to nominate three persons out of each State, and the secretary of Congress shall strike in behalf of such party absent or refusing; and the judgment and sentence of the court to be appointed, in the manner before prescribed, shall be final and conclusive; and if any of the parties shall refuse to submit to the authority of such court, or to appear or defend their claim or cause, the court shall nevertheless proceed to pronounce sentence or judgment, which shall, in like manner, be final and decisive, the judgment or sentence and other proceedings being, in either case, transmitted to Congress, and lodged among the acts of Congress for the security of the parties concerned: provided, that every commissioner, before he sits in judgment, shall take an oath, to be administered by one of the judges of the supreme or superior court of the State where the cause shall be tried, "well and truly to hear and determine the matter in question, according to the best of his judgment, without favour, affection, or hope of reward": provided, also, that no State shall be deprived of territory for the benefit of the United States.

All controversies concerning the private right of soil, claimed under different grants of two or more states, whose jurisdictions, as they may respect such lands and the states which passed such grants, are adjusted, the said grants, or either of them, being at the same time claimed to have originated antecedent to such settlement of jurisdiction, shall, on the petition of either party to the Congress of the United States, be finally determined, as near as may be, in the same manner as is before prescribed for deciding disputes respecting territorial jurisdiction between different states.

The United States, in Congress assembled, shall also have the sole and exclusive right and power of regulating the alloy and value of coin struck by their own authority, or by that of the respective states; fixing the standard of weights and measures throughout the United States; regulating the trade and managing all affairs with the Indians not members of any of the states; provided that the legislative right of any State within its own limits be not infringed or violated; establishing and regulating post offices from one State to another throughout all the United

States, and exacting such postage on the papers passing through the same as may be requisite to defray the expences of the said office; appointing all officers of the land forces in the service of the United States, excepting regimental officers; appointing all the officers of the naval forces, and commissioning all officers whatever in the service of the United States; making rules for the government and regulation of the said land and naval forces, and directing their operations.

The United States, in Congress assembled, shall have authority to appoint a committee to sit in the recess of Congress, to be denominated "a Committee of the States," and to consist of one delegate from each State, and to appoint such other committees and civil officers as may be necessary for managing the general affairs of the United States, under their direction; to appoint one of their number to preside; provided that no person be allowed to serve in the office of president more than one year in any term of three years; to ascertain the necessary sums of money to be raised for the service of the United States, and to appropriate and apply the same for defraying the public expences; to borrow money or emit bills on the credit of the United States, transmitting, every half year, to the respective states, an account of the sums of money so borrowed or emitted; to build and equip a navy; to agree upon the number of land forces, and to make requisitions from each State for its quota, in proportion to the number of white inhabitants in such State; which requisitions shall be binding; and, thereupon, the legislature of each State shall appoint the regimental officers, raise the men, and cloathe, arm, and equip them in a soldier-like manner, at the expence of the United States; and the officers and men so cloathed, armed, and equipped, shall march to the place appointed and within the time agreed on by the United States, in Congress assembled; but if the United States, in Congress assembled, shall, on consideration of circumstances, judge proper that any State should not raise men, or should raise a smaller number than its quota, and that any other State should raise a greater number of men than the quota thereof, such extra number shall be raised, officered, cloathed, armed, and equipped in the same manner as the quota of such State, unless the legislature of such State shall judge that such extra number cannot be safely spared out of the same, in which case they shall raise, officer, cloathe, arm, and equip as many of such extra number as they judge can be safely spared. And the officers and men so cloathed, armed, and equipped, shall march to the place appointed and within the time agreed on by the United States, in Congress assembled.

The United States, in Congress assembled, shall never engage in a war, nor grant letters of marque and reprisal in time of peace, nor enter into any treaties or alliances, nor coin money, nor regulate the value thereof, nor ascertain the sums and expences necessary for the defence and welfare of the United States, or any of them: nor emit bills, nor borrow money on the credit of the United States, nor appropriate money, nor agree upon the number of vessels of war to be built or purchased, or the number of land or sea forces to be raised, nor appoint a commander in chief of the army or navy, unless nine states assent to the same; nor shall a question on any other point, except for adjourning from day to day, be determined, unless by the votes of a majority of the United States, in Congress assembled.

The Congress of the United States shall have power to adjourn to any time within the year, and to any place within the United States, so that no period of adjournment be for a longer duration than the space of six months, and shall publish the journal of their proceedings monthly, except such parts thereof, relating to treaties, alliances or military operations, as, in their judgment, require secrecy; and the yeas and nays of the delegates of each State on any question shall be entered on the journal, when it is desired by any delegate; and the delegates of a State, or any of them, at his, or their request, shall be furnished with a transcript of the said journal, except such parts as are above excepted, to lay before the legislatures of the several states.

ARTICLE 10.

The committee of the states, or any nine of them, shall be authorized to execute, in the recess of Congress, such of the powers of Congress as the United States, in Congress assembled, by the consent of nine states, shall, from time to time, think expedient to vest them with; provided, that no power be delegated to the said committee, for the exercise of which, by the articles of confederation, the voice of nine states, in the Congress of the United States assembled, is requisite.

ARTICLE 11.

Canada acceding to this confederation, and joining in the measures of the United States, shall be admitted into and entitled to all the advantages of this union; but no other colony shall be admitted into the same, unless such admission be agreed to by nine states.

ARTICLE 12.

All bills of credit emitted, monies borrowed and debts contracted by, or under the authority of Congress before the assembling of the United States, in pursuance of the present confederation, shall be deemed and considered as a charge against the United States, for payment and satisfaction whereof the said United States and the public faith are hereby solemnly pledged.

ARTICLE 13.

Every State shall abide by the determinations of the United States, in Congress assembled, on all questions which, by this confederation, are submitted to them. And the articles of this confederation shall be inviolably observed by every State, and the union shall be perpetual; nor shall any alteration at any time hereafter be made in any of them, unless such alteration be agreed to in a Congress of the United States, and be afterwards confirmed by the legislatures of every State.

These articles shall be proposed to the legislatures of all the United States, to be considered, and if approved of by them, they are advised to authorize their delegates to ratify the same in the Congress of the United States; which being done, the same shall become conclusive.

Constitution of
the United States of America

PREAMBLE

We the people of the United States, in order to form a more perfect union, establish justice,
insure domestic tranquillity, provide for the common defense, promote the
general welfare, and secure the blessings of liberty to ourselves and
our posterity, do ordain and establish this Constitution
for the United States of America.

ARTICLE I

Section 1. All legislative powers herein granted shall be vested in a Congress of the United States, which shall consist of a Senate and a House of Representatives.

Section 2. The House of Representatives shall be composed of members chosen every second year by the people of the several States, and the electors in each State shall have the qualifications requisite for electors of the most numerous branch of the State Legislature.

No person shall be a Representative who shall not have attained to the age of twenty-five years, and been seven years a citizen of the United States, and who shall not, when elected, be an inhabitant of that State in which he shall be chosen.

Representatives and direct taxes shall be apportioned among the several States which may be included within this Union, according to their respective numbers, *which shall be determined by adding to the whole number of free persons, including those bound to service for a term of years and excluding Indians not taxed, three-fifths of all other persons.* The actual enumeration shall be made within three years after the first meeting of the Congress of the United States, and within every subsequent term of ten years, in such manner as they shall by law direct. The number of Representatives shall

NOTE: Passages that are no longer in effect are printed in italic type.

not exceed one for every thirty thousand, but each State shall have at least one Representative; *and until such enumeration shall be made, the State of New Hampshire shall be entitled to choose three, Massachusetts eight, Rhode Island and Providence Plantations one, Connecticut five, New York six, New Jersey four, Pennsylvania eight, Delaware one, Maryland six, Virginia ten, North Carolina five, South Carolina five, and Georgia three.*

When vacancies happen in the representation from any State, the Executive authority thereof shall issue writs of election to fill such vacancies.

The house of Representatives shall choose their Speaker and other officers; and shall have the sole power of impeachment.

Section 3. The Senate of the United States shall be composed of two Senators from each State, *chosen by the legislature thereof,* for six years; and each Senator shall have one vote.

Immediately after they shall be assembled in consequence of the first election, they shall be divided as equally as may be into three classes. The seats of the Senators of the first class shall be vacated at the expiration of the second year, of the second class at the expiration of the fourth year, and of the third class at the expiration of the sixth year, so that one-third may be chosen every second year; *and if vacancies happen by resignation or otherwise, during the recess of the legislature of any State, the Executive thereof may make temporary appointments until the next meeting of the legislature, which shall then fill such vacancies.*

No person shall be a Senator who shall not have attained to the age of thirty years, and been nine years a citizen of the United States, and who shall not, when elected, be an inhabitant of that State for which he shall be chosen.

The Vice-President of the United States shall be President of the Senate, but shall have no vote, unless they be equally divided.

The Senate shall choose their other officers, and also a President *pro tempore*, in the absence of the Vice-President, or when he shall exercise the office of President of the United States.

The Senate shall have the sole power to try all impeachments. When sitting for that purpose, they shall be on oath or affirmation. When the President of the United States is tried, the Chief Justice shall preside: and no person shall be convicted without the concurrence of two-thirds of the members present.

Judgment in cases of impeachment shall not extend further than to removal from the office, and disqualification to hold and enjoy any office of honor, trust or profit under the United States: but the party convicted shall nevertheless be liable and subject to indictment, trial, judgment and punishment, according to law.

Section 4.   The times, places and manner of holding elections for Senators and Representatives shall be prescribed in each State by the legislature thereof; but the Congress may at any time by law make or alter such regulations, except as to the places of choosing Senators.

The Congress shall assemble at least once in every year, and such meeting *shall be on the first Monday in December, unless they shall by law appoint a different day.*

Section 5.   Each house shall be the judge of the elections, returns and qualifications of its own members, and a majority of each shall constitute a quorum to do business; but a smaller number may adjourn from day to day, and may be authorized to compel the attendance of absent members, in such manner, and under such penalties, as each house may provide.

Each house may determine the rules of its proceedings, punish its members for disorderly behavior, and with the concurrence of two-thirds, expel a member.

Each house shall keep a journal of its proceedings, and from time to time publish the same, excepting such parts as may in their judgment require secrecy; and the yeas and nays of the members of either house on any question

shall, at the desire of one-fifth of those present, be entered on the journal.

Neither house, during the session of Congress, shall, without the consent of the other, adjourn for more than three days, nor to any other place than that in which the two houses shall be sitting.

Section 6.   The Senators and Representatives shall receive a compensation for their services, to be ascertained by law and paid out of the treasury of the United States. They shall in all cases except treason, felony and breach of the peace, be privileged from arrest during their attendance at the session of their respective houses, and in going to and returning from the same; and for any speech or debate in either house, they shall not be questioned in any other place.

No Senator or Representative shall, during the time for which he was elected, be appointed to any civil office under the authority of the United States, which shall have been created, or the emoluments whereof shall have been increased, during such time; and no person holding any office under the United States shall be a member of either house during his continuance in office.

Section 7.   All bills for raising revenue shall originate in the House of Representatives; but the Senate may propose or concur with amendments as on other bills.

Every bill which shall have passed the House of Representatives and the Senate, shall, before it become a law, be presented to the President of the United States; if he approve he shall sign it, but if not he shall return it with objections to that house in which it originated, who shall enter the objections at large on their journal, and proceed to reconsider it. If after such reconsideration two-thirds of that house shall agree to pass the bill, it shall be sent, together with the objections, to the other house, by which it shall likewise be reconsidered, and, if approved by two-thirds of that house, it shall become a law. But in all such cases the votes of both houses shall be determined by yeas and nays, and the names of the persons voting for and against the bill shall be entered on the journal of each house respectively. If any bill shall not be returned by the President within ten days (Sundays excepted) after it shall have been presented to him, the same shall be a law, in like manner as if he had signed it, unless the Congress by their adjournment prevent its return, in which case it shall not be a law.

Every order, resolution, or vote to which the concurrence of the Senate and House of Representatives may be necessary (except on a question of adjournment) shall be presented to the President of the United States; and before the same shall take effect, shall be approved by him, or being disapproved by him, shall be repassed by two-thirds of the Senate and House of Representatives, according to the rules and limitations prescribed in the case of a bill.

Section 8.   The Congress shall have power

To lay and collect taxes, duties, imposts, and excises, to pay the debts and provide for the common defense and general welfare of the United States; but all duties, imposts and excises shall be uniform throughout the United States;

To borrow money on the credit of the United States;

To regulate commerce with foreign nations, and among the several States, and with the Indian tribes;

To establish an uniform rule of naturalization, and uniform laws on the subject of bankruptcies throughout the United States;

To coin money, regulate the value thereof, and of foreign coin, and fix the standard of weights and measures;

To provide for the punishment of counterfeiting the securities and current coin of the United States;

To establish post offices and post roads;

To promote the progress of science and useful arts by securing for limited times to authors and inventors the exclusive right to their respective writings and discoveries;

To constitute tribunals inferior to the Supreme Court;

To define and punish piracies and felonies committed on the high seas and offenses against the law of nations;

To declare war, grant letters of marque and reprisal, and make rules concerning captures on land and water;

To raise and support armies, but no appropriation of money to that use shall be for a longer term than two years;

To provide and maintain a navy;

To make rules for the government and regulation of the land and naval forces;

To provide for calling forth the militia to execute the laws of the Union, suppress insurrections, and repel invasions;

To provide for organizing, arming, and disciplining the militia, and for governing such part of them as may be employed in the service of the United States, reserving to the States respectively the appointment of the officers, and the authority of training the militia according to the discipline prescribed by Congress;

To exercise exclusive legislation in all cases whatsoever, over such district (not exceeding ten miles square) as may, by cession of particular States, and the acceptance of Congress, become the seat of government of the United States, and to exercise like authority over all places purchased by the consent of the legislature of the State, in which the same shall be, for erection of forts, magazines, arsenals, dock-yards, and other needful buildings;—and

To make all laws which shall be necessary and proper for carrying into execution the foregoing powers, and all other powers vested by this Constitution in the government of the United States, or in any department or officer thereof.

Section 9.   The migration or importation of such persons as any of the States now existing shall think proper to admit shall not be prohibited by the Congress prior to the year 1808; but a tax or duty may be imposed on such importation, not exceeding $10 for each person.

The privelege of the writ of habeas corpus shall not be suspended, unless when in cases of rebellion or invasion the public safety may require it.

No bill of attainder or ex post facto law shall be passed.

No capitation, or other direct, tax shall be laid, unless in proportion to the census or enumeration herein before directed to be taken.

No tax or duty shall be laid on articles exported from any State.

No preference shall be given by any regulation of commerce or revenue to the ports of one State over those of another; nor shall vessels bound to, or from, one State, be obliged to enter, clear, or pay duties in another.

No money shall be drawn from the treasury, but in consequence of appropriations made by law; and a regular statement and account of the receipts and expenditures of all public money shall be published from time to time.

No title of nobility shall be granted by the United States: and no person holding any office of profit or trust under them, shall, without the consent of the Congress, accept of any present, emolument, office, or title, of any kind whatever, from any king, prince, or foreign state.

Section 10.   No State shall enter into any treaty, alliance, or confederation; grant letters of marque and reprisal; coin money; emit bills of credit; make anything but gold and silver coin a tender in payment of debts; pass any bill of attainder, ex post facto law, or law impairing the obligation of contracts, or grant any title of nobility.

No State shall, without the consent of Congress, lay any imposts or duties on imports or exports, except what may be absolutely necessary for executing its inspection laws: and the net produce of all duties and imposts, laid by any

State on imports or exports, shall be for the use of the treasury of the United States; and all such laws shall be subject to the revision and control of the Congress.

No State shall, without the consent of Congress, lay any duty of tonnage, keep troops or ships of war in time of peace, enter into any agreement or compact with another State, or with a foreign power, or engage in war, unless actually invaded, or in such imminent danger as will not admit of delay.

ARTICLE II

Section 1. The executive power shall be vested in a President of the United States of America. He shall hold his office during the term of four years, and, together with the Vice-President, chosen for the same term, be elected as follows:

Each State shall appoint, in such manner as the legislature thereof may direct, a number of electors, equal to the whole number of Senators and Representatives to which the State may be entitled in the Congress; but no Senator or Representative, or person holding an office of trust or profit under the United States, shall be appointed an elector.

The electors shall meet in their respective States, and vote by ballot for two persons, of whom one at least shall not be an inhabitant of the same State with themselves. And they shall make a list of all the persons voted for, and of the number of votes for each; which list they shall sign and certify, and transmit sealed to the seat of government of the United States, directed to the President of the Senate. The President of the Senate shall, in the presence of the Senate and House of Representatives, open all the certificates, and the votes shall then be counted. The person having the greatest number of votes shall be the President, if such number be a majority of the whole number of electors appointed; and if there be more than one who have such majority, and have an equal number of votes, then the House of Representatives shall immediately choose by ballot one of them for President; and if no person have a majority, then from the five highest on the list said house shall in like manner choose the President. But in choosing the President the votes shall be taken by States, the representation from each State having one vote; a quorum for this purpose shall consist of a member or members from two-thirds of the States, and a majority of all the States shall be necessary to a choice. In every case, after the choice of the President, the person having the greatest number of votes of the electors shall be the Vice-President. But if there should remain two or more who have equal votes, the Senate shall choose from them by ballot the Vice-President.

The Congress may determine the time of choosing the electors and the day on which they shall give their votes; which day shall be the same throughout the United States.

No person except a natural-born citizen, *or a citizen of the United States at the time of the adoption of this Constitution,* shall be eligible to the office of President; neither shall any person be eligible to that office who shall not have attained to the age of thirty-five years, and been fourteen years a resident within the United States.

In case of the removal of the President from office or of his death, resignation, or inability to discharge the powers and duties of the said office, the same shall devolve on the Vice-President, and the Congress may by law provide for the case of removal, death, resignation, or inability, both of the President and Vice-President, declaring what officer shall then act as President, and such officer shall act accordingly, until the disability be removed, or a President shall be elected.

The President shall, at stated times, receive for his services a compensation, which shall neither be increased nor diminished during the period for which he shall have been elected, and he shall not receive within that period any other emolument from the United States, or any of them.

Before he enter on the execution of his office, he shall take the following oath or affirmation:—"I do solemnly swear (or affirm) that I will faithfully execute the office of the President of the United States, and will to the best of my ability preserve, protect and defend the Constitution of the United States."

Section 2. The President shall be commander in chief of the army and navy of the United States, and of the militia of the several States, when called into the actual service of the United States; he may require the opinion, in writing, of the principal officer in each of the executive departments, upon any subject relating to the duties of their respective offices, and he shall have power to grant reprieves and pardons for offenses against the United States, except in cases of impeachment.

He shall have power, by and with the advice and consent of the Senate, to make treaties, provided two-thirds of the Senators present concur; and he shall nominate, and by and with the advice and consent of the Senate, shall appoint ambassadors, other public ministers and consuls, judges of the Supreme Court, and all other officers of the United States, whose appointments are not herein otherwise provided for, and which shall be established by law: but Congress may by law vest the appointment of such inferior officers, as they think proper, in the President alone, in the courts of law, or in the heads of departments.

The President shall have power to fill up all vacancies that may happen during the recess of the Senate, by granting commissions which shall expire at the end of their next session.

Section 3.   He shall from time to time give to the Congress information of the state of the Union, and recommend to their consideration such measures as he shall judge necessary and expedient; he may, on extraordinary occasions, convene both houses, or either of them, and in case of disagreement between them, with respect to the time of adjournment, he may adjourn them to such time as he shall think proper; he shall receive ambassadors and other public ministers; he shall take care that the laws be faithfully executed, and shall commission all the officers of the United States.

Section 4.   The President, Vice-President and all civil officers of the United States shall be removed from office on impeachment for, and on conviction of, treason, bribery, or other high crimes and misdemeanors.

ARTICLE III

Section 1.   The judicial power of the United States shall be vested in one Supreme Court, and in such inferior courts as the Congress may from time to time ordain and establish. The judges, both of the Supreme and inferior courts, shall hold their offices during good behavior, and shall, at stated times, receive for their services a compensation which shall not be diminished during their continuance in office.

Section 2.   The judicial power shall extend to all cases, in law and equity, arising under this Constitution, the laws of the United States, and treaties made, or which shall be made, under their authority;—to all cases affecting ambassadors, other public ministers and consuls;—to all cases of admiralty and maritime jurisdiction;—to controversies to which the United States shall be a party;—to controversies between two or more States;—*between a State and citizens of another State;*—between citizens of different States;—between citizens of the same State claiming lands under grants of different States, and between a State, or the citizens thereof, and foreign states, citizens or subjects.

In all case affecting ambassadors, other public ministers and consuls, and those in which a State shall be party, the Supreme Court shall have original jurisdiction. In all the other cases before mentioned, the Supreme Court shall have appellate jurisdiction, both as to law and fact, with such exceptions, and under such regulations, as the Congress shall make.

The trial of all crimes, except in cases of impeachment, shall be by jury; and such trial shall be held in the State where said crimes shall have been committed; but when not committed within any State, the trial shall be at such place or places as the Congress may by law have directed.

Section 3.   Treason against the United States shall consist only in levying war against them, or in adhering to their enemies, giving them aid and comfort. No person shall be convicted of treason unless on the testimony of two witnesses to the same overt act, or on confession in open court.

The Congress shall have power to declare the punishment of treason, but no attainder of treason shall work corruption of blood, or forfeiture except during the life of the person attainted.

ARTICLE IV

Section 1.   Full faith and credit shall be given in each State to the public acts, records, and judicial proceedings of every other State. And the Congress may by general laws prescribe the manner in which such acts, records, and proceedings shall be proved, and the effect thereof.

Section 2.   The citizens of each State shall be entitled to all privileges and immunities of citizens in the several States.

A person charged in any State with treason, felony, or other crime, who shall flee from justice, and be found in another State, shall on demand of the executive authority of the State from which he fled, be delivered up, to be removed to the State having jurisdiction of the crime.

No person held to service or labor in one State, under the laws thereof, escaping into another, shall, in consequence of any law or regulation therein, be discharged from such service or labor, but shall be delivered up on claim of the party to whom such service or labor may be due.

Section 3.   New States may be admitted by the Congress into this Union; but no new State shall be formed or erected within the jurisdiction of any other State; nor any State be formed by the junction of two or more States, or parts of States, without the consent of the legislatures of the States concerned as well as of the Congress.

The Congress shall have power to dispose of and make all needful rules and regulations respecting the territory or other property belonging to the United States; and nothing in this Constitution shall be so construed as to prejudice any claims of the United States, or of any particular State.

Section 4. The United States shall guarantee to every State in this Union a republican form of government, and shall protect each of them against invasion; and on application of the legislature, or of the executive (when the legislature cannot be convened), against domestic violence.

ARTICLE V

The Congress, whenever two-thirds of both houses shall deem it necessary, shall propose amendments to this Constitution, or, on the application of the legislatures of two-thirds of the several States, shall call a convention for proposing amendments, which, in either case, shall be valid to all intents and purposes, as part of this Constitution, when ratified by the legislatures of three-fourths of the several States, or by conventions in three-fourths thereof, as the one or the other mode of ratification may be proposed by the Congress; provided *that no amendments which may be made prior to the year one thousand eight hundred and eight shall in any manner affect the first and fourth clauses in the ninth section of the first article;* and that no State, without its consent, shall be deprived of its equal suffrage in the Senate.

ARTICLE VI

All debts contracted and engagements entered into, before the adoption of this Constitution, shall be as valid against the United States under this Constitution, as under the Confederation.

This Constitution, and the laws of the United States which shall be made in pursuance thereof; and all treaties made, or which shall be made, under the authority of the United States, shall be the supreme law of the land; and the judges in every State shall be bound thereby, anything in the Constitution or laws of any State to the contrary notwithstanding.

The Senators and Representatives before mentioned, and the members of the several State legislatures, and all executive and judicial officers, both of the United States and of the several States, shall be bound by oath or affirmation to support this Constitution; but no religious test shall ever be required as a qualification to any office or public trust under the United States.

ARTICLE VII

The ratification of the conventions of nine States shall be sufficient for the establishment of this Constitution between the States so ratifying the same.

Done in Convention by the unanimous consent of the States present, the seventeenth day of September in the year of our Lord one thousand seven hundred and eighty-seven and of the Independence of the United States of America the twelfth. In witness whereof we have hereunto subscribed our names.

[Signed by]
G° WASHINGTON
Presidt and Deputy from Virginia
[and thirty-eight others]

Amendments to the Constitution

ARTICLE I*

Congress shall make no law respecting an establishment of religion, or prohibiting the free exercise thereof; or abridging the freedom of speech, or of the press; or the right of the people peaceably to assemble, and to petition the government for a redress of grievances.

*The first ten Amendments (Bill of Rights) were adopted in 1791.

ARTICLE II

A well-regulated militia being necessary to the security of a free State, the right of the people to keep and bear arms shall not be infringed.

ARTICLE III

No soldier shall, in time of peace, be quartered in any house without the consent of the owner, nor in time of war, but in a manner to be prescribed by law.

ARTICLE IV

The right of the people to be secure in their persons, houses, papers, and effects, against unreasonable searches and seizures, shall not be violated, and no warrants shall issue but upon probable cause, supported by oath or affirmation, and particularly describing the place to be searched, and the persons or things to be seized.

ARTICLE V

No person shall be held to answer for a capital, or otherwise infamous crime, unless on a presentment or indictment of a grand jury, except in cases arising in the land or naval forces, or in the militia, when in actual service in time of war or public danger; nor shall any person be subject for the same offense to be twice put in jeopardy of life or limb; nor shall be compelled in any criminal case to be a witness against himself, nor be deprived of life, liberty, or property, without due process of law; nor shall private property be taken for public use without just compensation.

ARTICLE VI

In all criminal prosecutions, the accused shall enjoy the right to a speedy and public trial, by an impartial jury of the State and district wherein the crime shall have been committed, which district shall have been previously ascertained by law, and to be informed of the nature and cause of the accusation; to be confronted with the witnesses against him; to have compulsory process for obtaining witnesses in his favor, and to have the assistance of counsel for his defense.

ARTICLE VII

In suits at common law, where the value in controversy shall exceed twenty dollars, the right of trial by jury shall be preserved, and no fact tried by a jury shall be otherwise reexamined in any court of the United States, than according to the rules of the common law.

ARTICLE VIII

Excessive bail shall not be required, nor excessive fines imposed, nor cruel and unusual punishments inflicted.

ARTICLE IX

The enumeration in the Constitution, of certain rights, shall not be construed to deny or disparage others retained by the people.

ARTICLE X

The powers not delegated to the United States by the Constitution, nor prohibited by it to the States, are reserved to the States respectively, or to the people.

ARTICLE XI
[*Adopted 1798*]

The judicial power of the United States shall not be construed to extend to any suit in law or equity, commenced or prosecuted against one of the United States by citizens of another State, or by citizens or subjects of any foreign state.

ARTICLE XII
[*Adopted 1804*]

The electors shall meet in their respective States, and vote by ballot for President and Vice-President, one of whom, at least, shall not be an inhabitant of the same State with themselves; they shall name in their ballots the person voted for as President, and in distinct ballots the person voted for as Vice-President, and they shall make distinct lists of all persons voted for as President, and of all persons voted for as Vice-President, and of the number of votes for each, which lists they shall sign and certify, and transmit sealed to the seat of government of the United States, directed to the President of the Senate;—the President of the Senate shall, in the presence of the Senate and House of Representatives, open all the certificates and the votes shall then be counted;—the person having the greatest number of votes for President shall be the President, if such number be a majority of the whole number of electors appointed; and if no person have such majority, then from the persons having the highest numbers not exceeding three on the list of those voted for as President, the House of Representatives shall choose immediately, by ballot, the President. But in choosing the President, the votes shall be taken by States, the representation from each State having one vote; a quorum for this purpose shall consist of a member or members from two-thirds of the States, and a majority of all the States shall be necessary to a choice. And if the House of Representatives shall not choose a President whenever the right of choice shall devolve upon them, before *the fourth day of March* next following, then the Vice-President shall act as President, as in the case of the death or other constitutional disability of the President.

The person having the greatest number of votes as Vice-President shall be the Vice-President, if such number be a majority of the whole number of electors appointed; and if no person have a majority, then from the two highest numbers on the list the Senate shall choose the Vice-President; a quorum for the purpose shall consist of two-thirds of the whole number of Senators, and a majority of the whole number shall be necessary to a choice. But no person constitutionally ineligible to the office of President shall be eligible to that of Vice-President of the United States.

ARTICLE XIII
[*Adopted 1865*]

Section 1. Neither slavery nor involuntary servitude, except as a punishment for crime whereof the party shall have been duly convicted, shall exist within the United States, or any place subject to their jurisdiction.

Section 2. Congress shall have power to enforce this article by appropriate legislation.

ARTICLE XIV
[*Adopted 1868*]

Section 1. All persons born or naturalized in the United States, and subject to the jurisdiction thereof, are citizens of the United States and of the State wherein they reside. No State shall make or enforce any law which shall abridge the privileges or immunities of citizens of the United States; nor shall any State deprive any person of life, liberty, or property, without due process of law; nor deny to any person within its jurisdiction the equal protection of the laws.

Section 2. Representatives shall be apportioned among the several States according to their respective numbers, counting the whole number of persons in each State, excluding Indians not taxed. But when the right to vote at any election for the choice of Electors for President and Vice-President of the United States, Representatives in Congress, the executive and judicial officers of a State, or the members of the legislature thereof, is denied to any of the male inhabitants of such State, being twenty-one years of age and citizens of the United States, or in any way abridged, except for participation in rebellion, or other crime, the basis of representation therein shall be reduced in the proportion which the number of such male citizens shall bear to the whole number of male citizens twenty-one years of age in such State.

Section 3. No person shall be a Senator or Representative in Congress, or Elector of President and Vice-President, or hold any office, civil or military, under the United States, or under any State, who, having previously taken an oath, as a member of Congress, or as an officer of the United States, or as a member of any State legislature, or as an executive or judicial officer of any State, to support the Constitution of the United States, shall have engaged in insurrection or rebellion against the same, or given aid or comfort to the enemies thereof. Congress may, by a vote of two-thirds of each house, remove such disability.

Section 4. The validity of the public debt of the United States, authorized by law, including debts incurred for payment of pensions and bounties for services in suppressing insurrection or rebellion, shall not be questioned. But neither the United States nor any State shall assume or pay any debt or obligation incurred in aid of insurrection or rebellion against the United States, or any claim for the loss of emancipation of any slave; but all such debts, obligations, and claims shall be held illegal and void.

Section 5. The Congress shall have power to enforce, by appropriate legislation, the provisions of this article.

ARTICLE XV
[*Adopted 1870*]

Section 1. The right of citizens of the United States to vote shall not be denied or abridged by the United States or by any State on account of race, color, or previous condition of servitude.

Section 2. The Congress shall have power to enforce this article by appropriate legislation.

ARTICLE XVI
[Adopted 1913]

The Congress shall have power to lay and collect taxes on incomes, from whatever source derived, without apportionment among the several States, and without regard to any census or enumeration.

ARTICLE XVII
[Adopted 1913]

Section 1. The Senate of the United States shall be composed of two Senators from each State, elected by the people thereof, for six years; and each Senator shall have one vote. The electors in each State shall have the qualifications requisite for electors of [voters for] the most numerous branch of the State legislatures.

Section 2. When vacancies happen in the representation of any State in the Senate, the executive authority of such State shall issue writs of election to fill such vacancies: Provided, that the Legislature of any State may empower the executive thereof to make temporary appointments until the people fill the vacancies by election as the Legislature may direct.

Section 3. This amendment shall not be so construed as to affect the election or term of any Senator chosen before it becomes valid as part of the Constitution.

ARTICLE XVIII
[Adopted 1919; Repealed 1933]

Section 1. *After one year from the ratification of this article the manufacture, sale, or transportation of intoxicating liquors within, the importation thereof into, or the exportation thereof from the United States and all territory subject to the jurisdiction thereof, for beverage purposes, is hereby prohibited.*

Section 2. *The Congress and the several States shall have concurrent power to enforce this article by appropriate legislation.*

Section 3. *This article shall be inoperative unless it shall have been ratified as an amendment to the Constitution by the legislatures of the several States, as provided by the Constitution, within*

seven years from the date of the submission thereof to the States by the Congress.

ARTICLE XIX
[Adopted 1920]

Section 1. The right of citizens of the United States to vote shall not be denied or abridged by the United States or by any State on account of sex.

Section 2. The Congress shall have power to enforce this article by appropriate legislation.

ARTICLE XX
[Adopted 1933]

Section 1. The terms of the President and Vice-President shall end at noon on the 20th day of January, and the terms of Senators and Representatives at noon on the 3d day of January, of the years in which such terms would have ended if this article had not been ratified; and the terms of their successors shall then begin.

Section 2. The Congress shall assemble at least once in every year, and such meeting shall begin at noon on the 3d day of January, unless they shall by law appoint a different day.

Section 3. If, at the time fixed for the beginning of the term of the President, the President-elect shall have died, the Vice-President-elect shall become President. If a President shall not have been chosen before the time fixed for the beginning of his term, or if the President-elect shall have failed to qualify, then the Vice-President-elect shall act as President until a President shall have qualified; and the Congress may by law provide for the case wherein neither a President-elect nor a Vice-President-elect shall have qualified, declaring who shall then act as President, or the manner in which one who is to act shall be selected, and such persons shall act accordingly until a President or Vice-President shall have qualified.

Section 4. The Congress may by law provide for the case of the death of any of the persons from whom the House of Representatives may choose a President whenever the right of choice shall have devolved upon them, and for the case of the death of any of the persons from whom the

Senate may choose a Vice-President whenever the right of choice shall have devolved upon them.

Section 5.   Sections 1 and 2 shall take effect on the 15th day of October following the ratification of this article.

Section 6.   This article shall be inoperative unless it shall have been ratified as an amendment to the Constitution by the Legislatures of three-fourths of the several States within seven years from the date of its submission.

ARTICLE XXI
[Adopted 1933]

Section 1.   The eighteenth article of amendment to the Constitution of the United States is hereby repealed.

Section 2.   The transportation or importation into any State, Territory, or Possession of the United States for delivery or use therein of intoxicating liquors, in violation of the laws thereof, is hereby prohibited.

Section 3.   This article shall be inoperative unless it shall have been ratified as an amendment to the Constitution by conventions in the several States, as provided in the Constitution, within seven years from the date of submission thereof to the States by the Congress.

ARTICLE XXII
[Adopted 1951]

Section 1.   No person shall be elected to the office of President more than twice, and no person who has held the office of President, or acted as President, for more than two years of a term to which some other person was elected President shall be elected to the office of President more than once. But this article shall not apply to any person holding the office of President when this article was proposed by the Congress, and shall not prevent any person who may be holding the office of President, or acting as President, during the term within which this article becomes operative from holding the office of President or acting as President during the remainder of such term.

Section 2.   This article shall be inoperative unless it shall have been ratified as an amendment to the Constitution by the legislatures of three-fourths of the several States within seven years from the date of its submission to the States by the Congress.

ARTICLE XXIII
[Adopted 1961]

Section 1.   The District constituting the seat of Government of the United States shall appoint in such manner as the Congress may direct:

A number of electors of President and Vice-President equal to the whole number of Senators and Representatives in Congress to which the District would be entitled if it were a State, but in no event more than the least populous State; they shall be in addition to those appointed by the States, but they shall be considered for the purposes of the election of President and Vice-President, to be electors appointed by a State; and they shall meet in the District and perform such duties as provided by the twelfth article of amendment.

Section 2.   The Congress shall have the power to enforce this article by appropriate legislation.

ARTICLE XXIV
[Adopted 1964]

Section 1.   The right of citizens of the United States to vote in any primary or other election for President or Vice-President, for electors for President or Vice-President, or for Senator or Representative in Congress, shall not be denied or abridged by the United States or any State by reason of failure to pay any poll tax or other tax.

Section 2.   The Congress shall have the power to enforce this article by appropriate legislation.

ARTICLE XXV
[Adopted 1967]

Section 1.   In case of the removal of the President from office or of his death or resignation, the Vice President shall become President.

Section 2.   Whenever there is a vacancy in the office of the Vice President, the President shall nominate a Vice President who shall take office upon confirmation by a majority vote of both Houses of Congress.

Section 3.   Whenever the President transmits to the President pro tempore of the Senate and the Speaker of the House of Representatives his written declaration that he is unable to discharge the powers and duties of his office, and until he transmits to them a written declaration to the contrary, such powers and duties shall be discharged by the Vice President as Acting President.

Section 4.   Whenever the Vice President and a majority of either the principal officers of the executive departments or of such other body as Congress may by law provide, transmit to the President pro tempore of the Senate and the Speaker of the House of Representatives their written declaration that the President is unable to discharge the powers and duties of his office, the Vice President shall immediately assume the powers and duties of the office as Acting President.

Thereafter, when the President transmits to the President pro tempore of the Senate and the Speaker of the House of Representatives his written declaration that no inability exists, he shall resume the powers and duties of his office unless the Vice President and a majority of either the principal officers of the executive department[s] or of such other body as Congress may by law provide, transmit within four days to the President pro tempore of the Senate and the Speaker of the House of Representatives their written declaration that the President is unable to discharge the powers and duties of his office. Thereupon Congress shall decide the issue, assembling within forty-eight hours for that purpose if not in session. If the Congress, within twenty-one days after receipt of the latter written declaration, or, if Congress is not in session, within twenty-one days after Congress is required to assemble, deter-

mines by two-thirds vote of both Houses that the President is unable to discharge the powers and duties of his office, the Vice President shall continue to discharge the same as Acting President; otherwise, the President shall resume the powers and duties of his office.

ARTICLE XXVI
[*Adopted 1971*]

Section 1.   The right of citizens of the United States, who are eighteen years of age or older, to vote shall not be denied or abridged by the United States or by any State on account of age.

Section 2.   The Congress shall have power to enforce this article by appropriate legislation.

ARTICLE XXVII
[*Sent to States, 1972*]

Section 1.   Equality of rights under the law shall not be denied or abridged by the United States or by any State on account of sex.

Section 2.   The Congress shall have the power to enforce, by appropriate legislation, the provisions of this article.

Section 3.   This amendment shall take effect two years after the date of ratification.

Presidential Elections*

Election	Candidates	Parties	Popular Vote	Electoral Vote
1789	**George Washington**	No party designations		69
	John Adams			34
	Minor Candidates			35
1792	**George Washington**	No party designations		132
	John Adams			77
	George Clinton			50
	Minor Candidates			5
1796	**John Adams**	Federalist		71
	Thomas Jefferson	Democratic-Republican		68
	Thomas Pinckney	Federalist		59
	Aaron Burr	Democratic-Republican		30
	Minor Candidates			48
1800	**Thomas Jefferson**	Democratic-Republican		73
	Aaron Burr	Democratic-Republican		73
	John Adams	Federalist		65
	Charles C. Pinckney	Federalist		64
	John Jay	Federalist		1
1804	**Thomas Jefferson**	Democratic-Republican		162
	Charles C. Pinckney	Federalist		14
1808	**James Madison**	Democratic-Republican		122
	Charles C. Pinckney	Federalist		47
	George Clinton	Democratic-Republican		6
1812	**James Madison**	Democratic-Republican		128
	DeWitt Clinton	Federalist		89
1816	**James Monroe**	Democratic-Republican		183
	Rufus King	Federalist		34

*Candidates receiving less than 1% of the popular vote are omitted. Before the Twelfth Amendment (1804) the Electoral College voted for two presidential candidates, and the runner-up became vice-president. Basic figures are taken primarily from *Historical Statistics of the United States, 1789–1945* (1949), pp. 288–90; *Historical Statistics of the United States, Colonial Times to 1957* (1960), pp. 682–83; and *Statistical Abstract of the United States, 1969* (1969), pp. 355–57.

†"Min." indicates minority president—one receiving less than 50% of all popular votes.

Election	Candidates	Parties	Popular Vote	Electoral Vote
1820	**James Monroe**	Democratic-Republican		231
	John Q. Adams	Independent Republican		1
1824	**John Q. Adams** (Min.)†	Democratic-Republican	108,740	84
	Andrew Jackson	Democratic-Republican	153,544	99
	William H. Crawford	Democratic-Republican	46,618	41
	Henry Clay	Democratic-Republican	47,136	37
1828	**Andrew Jackson**	Democratic	647,286	178
	John Q. Adams	National Republican	508,064	83
1832	**Andrew Jackson**	Democratic	687,502	219
	Henry Clay	National Republican	530,189	49
	William Wirt	Anti-Masonic ⎫		7
	John Floyd	National Republican ⎬ 33,108		11
1836	**Martin Van Buren**	Democratic	762,678	170
	William H. Harrison	Whig ⎫		73
	Hugh L. White	Whig ⎪		26
	Daniel Webster	Whig ⎬ 736,656		14
	W. P. Mangum	Whig ⎭		11
1840	**William H. Harrison**	Whig	1,275,016	234
	Martin Van Buren	Democratic	1,129,102	60
1844	**James K. Polk** (Min.)*	Democratic	1,337,243	170
	Henry Clay	Whig	1,299,062	105
	James G. Birney	Liberty	62,300	
1848	**Zachary Taylor** (Min.)*	Whig	1,360,099	163
	Lewis Cass	Democratic	1,220,544	127
	Martin Van Buren	Free Soil	291,263	
1852	**Franklin Pierce**	Democratic	1,601,274	254
	Winfield Scott	Whig	1,386,580	42
	John P. Hale	Free Soil	155,825	
1856	**James Buchanan** (Min.)*	Democratic	1,838,169	174
	John C. Frémont	Republican	1,341,264	114
	Millard Fillmore	American	874,534	8
1860	**Abraham Lincoln** (Min.)*	Republican	1,866,452	180
	Stephen A. Douglas	Democratic	1,375,157	12
	John C. Breckinridge	Democratic	847,953	72
	John Bell	Constitutional Union	590,631	39
1864	**Abraham Lincoln**	Union	2,213,665	212
	George B. McClellan	Democratic	1,802,237	21
1868	**Ulysses S. Grant**	Republican	3,012,833	214
	Horatio Seymour	Democratic	2,703,249	80
1872	**Ulysses S. Grant**	Republican	3,597,132	286
	Horace Greeley	Democratic and Liberal Republican	2,834,125	66

*"Min." indicates minority president—one receiving less than 50% of all popular votes.

Election	Candidates	Parties	Popular Vote	Electoral Vote
1876	**Rutherford B. Hayes** (Min.)*	Republican	4,036,298	185
	Samuel J. Tilden	Democratic	4,300,590	184
1880	**James A. Garfield** (Min.)*	Republican	4,454,416	214
	Winfield S. Hancock	Democratic	4,444,952	155
	James B. Weaver	Greenback-Labor	308,578	
1884	**Grover Cleveland** (Min.)*	Democratic	4,874,986	219
	James G. Blaine	Republican	4,851,981	182
	Benjamin F. Butler	Greenback-Labor	175,370	
	John P. St. John	Prohibition	150,369	
1888	**Benjamin Harrison** (Min.)*	Republican	5,439,853	233
	Grover Cleveland	Democratic	5,540,309	168
	Clinton B. Fisk	Prohibition	249,506	
	Anson J. Streeter	Union Labor	146,935	
1892	**Grover Cleveland** (Min.)*	Democratic	5,556,918	277
	Benjamin Harrison	Republican	5,176,108	145
	James B. Weaver	People's	1,041,028	22
	John Bidwell	Prohibition	264,133	
1896	**William McKinley**	Republican	7,104,779	271
	William J. Bryan	Democratic	6,502,925	176
1900	**William McKinley**	Republican	7,207,923	292
	William J. Bryan	Democratic; Populist	6,358,133	155
	John C. Woolley	Prohibition	208,914	
1904	**Theodore Roosevelt**	Republican	7,623,486	336
	Alton B. Parker	Democratic	5,077,911	140
	Eugene V. Debs	Socialist	402,283	
	Silas C. Swallow	Prohibition	258,536	
1908	**William H. Taft**	Republican	7,678,908	321
	William J. Bryan	Democratic	6,409,104	162
	Eugene V. Debs	Socialist	420,793	
	Eugene W. Chafin	Prohibition	253,840	
1912	**Woodrow Wilson** (Min.)*	Democratic	6,293,454	435
	Theodore Roosevelt	Progressive	4,119,538	88
	William H. Taft	Republican	3,484,980	8
	Eugene V. Debs	Socialist	900,672	
	Eugene W. Chafin	Prohibition	206,275	
1916	**Woodrow Wilson** (Min.)*	Democratic	9,129,606	277
	Charles E. Hughes	Republican	8,538,221	254
	A. L. Benson	Socialist	585,113	
	J. F. Hanly	Prohibition	220,506	
1920	**Warren G. Harding**	Republican	16,152,200	404
	James M. Cox	Democratic	9,147,353	127
	Eugene V. Debs	Socialist	919,799	
	P. P. Christensen	Farmer-Labor	265,411	

*"Min." indicates minority president—one receiving less than 50% of all popular votes.

Election	Candidates	Parties	Popular Vote	Electoral Vote
1924	**Calvin Coolidge**	Republican	15,725,016	382
	John W. Davis	Democratic	8,386,503	136
	Robert M. La Follette	Progressive	4,822,856	13
1928	**Herbert C. Hoover**	Republican	21,391,381	444
	Alfred E. Smith	Democratic	15,016,443	87
1932	**Franklin D. Roosevelt**	Democratic	22,821,857	472
	Herbert C. Hoover	Republican	15,761,841	59
	Norman Thomas	Socialist	881,951	
1936	**Franklin D. Roosevelt**	Democratic	27,751,597	523
	Alfred M. Landon	Republican	16,679,583	8
	William Lemke	Union, etc.	882,479	
1940	**Franklin D. Roosevelt**	Democratic	27,244,160	449
	Wendell L. Wilkie	Republican	22,305,198	82
1944	**Franklin D. Roosevelt**	Democratic	25,602,504	432
	Thomas E. Dewey	Republican	22,006,285	99
1948	**Harry S Truman** (Min.)*	Democratic	24,105,812	303
	Thomas E. Dewey	Republican	21,970,065	189
	J. Strom Thurmond	States' Rights Democratic	1,169,063	39
	Henry A. Wallace	Progressive	1,157,172	
1952	**Dwight D. Eisenhower**	Republican	33,936,234	442
	Adlai E. Stevenson	Democratic	27,314,992	89
1956	**Dwight D. Eisenhower**	Republican	35,590,472	457
	Adlai E. Stevenson	Democratic	26,022,752	73
1960	**John F. Kennedy** (Min.)*	Democratic	34,226,731	303
	Richard M. Nixon	Republican	34,108,157	219
1964	**Lyndon B. Johnson**	Democratic	43,129,484	486
	Barry M. Goldwater	Republican	27,178,188	52
1968	**Richard M. Nixon** (Min.)*	Republican	31,785,480	301
	Hubert H. Humphrey, Jr.	Democratic	31,275,166	191
	George C. Wallace	American Independent	9,906,473	46
1972	**Richard M. Nixon**	Republican	45,767,218	520
	George S. McGovern	Democratic	28,357,668	17
1976	**Jimmy Carter**	Democratic	40,276,040	297
	Gerald R. Ford	Republican	38,532,630	241
1980	**Ronald W. Reagan**	Republican		
	Jimmy Carter	Democratic		

*"Min." indicates minority president—one receiving less than 50% of all popular votes.

Presidents and Vice-Presidents

Term	President	Vice-President
1789–1793	George Washington	John Adams
1793–1797	George Washington	John Adams
1797–1801	John Adams	Thomas Jefferson
1801–1805	Thomas Jefferson	Aaron Burr
1805–1809	Thomas Jefferson	George Clinton
1809–1813	James Madison	George Clinton (d. 1812)
1813–1817	James Madison	Elbridge Gerry (d. 1814)
1817–1821	James Monroe	Daniel D. Tompkins
1821–1825	James Monroe	Daniel D. Tompkins
1825–1829	John Quincy Adams	John C. Calhoun
1829–1833	Andrew Jackson	John C. Calhoun (resigned 1832)
1833–1837	Andrew Jackson	Martin Van Buren
1837–1841	Martin Van Buren	Richard M. Johnson
1841–1845	William H. Harrison (d. 1841) John Tyler	John Tyler
1845–1849	James K. Polk	George M. Dallas
1849–1853	Zachary Taylor (d. 1850) Millard Fillmore	Millard Fillmore
1853–1857	Franklin Pierce	William R. D. King (d. 1853)
1857–1861	James Buchanan	John C. Breckinridge
1861–1865	Abraham Lincoln	Hannibal Hamlin
1865–1869	Abraham Lincoln (d. 1865) Andrew Johnson	Andrew Johnson
1869–1873	Ulysses S. Grant	Schuyler Colfax
1873–1877	Ulysses S. Grant	Henry Wilson (d. 1875)
1877–1881	Rutherford B. Hayes	William A. Wheeler
1881–1885	James A. Garfield (d. 1881) Chester A. Arthur	Chester A. Arthur
1885–1889	Grover Cleveland	Thomas A. Hendricks (d. 1885)
1889–1893	Benjamin Harrison	Levi P. Morton
1893–1897	Grover Cleveland	Adlai E. Stevenson
1897–1901	William McKinley	Garret A. Hobart (d. 1899)
1901–1905	William McKinley (d. 1901) Theodore Roosevelt	Theodore Roosevelt
1905–1909	Theodore Roosevelt	Charles W. Fairbanks
1909–1913	William H. Taft	James S. Sherman (d. 1912)
1913–1917	Woodrow Wilson	Thomas R. Marshall
1917–1921	Woodrow Wilson	Thomas R. Marshall
1921–1925	Warren G. Harding (d. 1923) Calvin Coolidge	Calvin Coolidge
1925–1929	Calvin Coolidge	Charles G. Dawes
1929–1933	Herbert C. Hoover	Charles Curtis
1933–1937	Franklin D. Roosevelt	John N. Garner

Term	President	Vice-President
1937–1941	Franklin D. Roosevelt	John N. Garner
1941–1945	Franklin D. Roosevelt	Henry A. Wallace
1945–1949	Franklin D. Roosevelt (d. 1945) Harry S Truman	Harry S Truman
1949–1953	Harry S Truman	Alben W. Barkley
1953–1957	Dwight D. Eisenhower	Richard M. Nixon
1957–1961	Dwight D. Eisenhower	Richard M. Nixon
1961–1965	John F. Kennedy (d. 1963) Lyndon B. Johnson	Lyndon B. Johnson
1965–1969	Lyndon B. Johnson	Hubert H. Humphrey, Jr.
1969–1974	Richard M. Nixon (resigned 1974)	Spiro T. Agnew (resigned 1973); Gerald R. Ford
1974–1976	Gerald R. Ford	Nelson A. Rockefeller
1976–**1980**	Jimmy Carter	Walter F. Mondale
1980–	Ronald W. Reagan	George Bush

Growth of U.S. Population and Area

Census	Population of Contiguous U.S.	Percent of Increase Over Preceding Census	Land Area, Square Miles	Population Per Square Mile
1790	3,929,214		867,980	4.5
1800	5,308,483	35.1	867,980	6.1
1810	7,239,881	36.4	1,685,865	4.3
1820	9,638,453	33.1	1,753,588	5.5
1830	12,866,020	33.5	1,753,588	7.3
1840	17,069,453	32.7	1,753,588	9.7
1850	23,191,876	35.9	2,944,337	7.9
1860	31,443,321	35.6	2,973,965	10.6
1870	39,818,449	26.6	2,973,965	13.4
1880	50,155,783	26.0	2,973,965	16.9
1890	62,947,714	25.5	2,973,965	21.2
1900	75,994,575	20.7	2,974,159	25.6
1910	91,972,266	21.0	2,973,890	30.9
1920	105,710,620	14.9	2,973,776	35.5
1930	122,775,046	16.1	2,977,128	41.2
1940	131,669,275	7.2	2,977,128	44.2
1950	150,697,361	14.5	2,974,726*	50.7
†1960	178,464,236	18.4	2,974,726	59.9
1970	204,765,770 (including Alaska and Hawaii)			

*As remeasured in 1940.
†Not including Alaska (pop. 226,167) and Hawaii (632,772).

Index